A Note on the Author

BEN MACINTYRE is a columnist and Associate Editor on *The Times*. He has worked as the newspaper's correspondent in New York, Paris and Washington. He is the author of ten previous books including *Agent Zigzag*, shortlisted for the Costa Biography Award and the Galaxy British Book Award for Biography of the Year 2008, and the *Sunday Times* bestseller *Operation Mincemeat*. His most recent book is *SAS: Rogue Heroes*, the first authorised biography of the SAS.

benmacintyre.com

DOUBLE CROSS

&

A SPY AMONG FRIENDS

Two True Tales of Wartime Deceit and Duplicity

Ben Macintyre

BLOOMSBURY PUBLISHING

LONDON · OXFORD · NEW YORK · NEW DELHI · SYDNEY

BLOOMSBURY PUBLISHING
Bloomsbury Publishing Plc
50 Bedford Square, London, WC1B 3DP, UK

BLOOMSBURY, BLOOMSBURY PUBLISHING and the Diana logo are
trademarks of Bloomsbury Publishing Plc

Double Cross was first published in Great Britain 2012
A Spy Among Friends was first published in Great Britain 2014
This edition published 2018

Copyright © Ben Macintyre, 2012, 2014
Map in *Double Cross* by John Gilkes
Afterword in *A Spy Among Friends* © David Cornwell 2014

Ben Macintyre has asserted his right under the Copyright, Designs and
Patents Act, 1988, to be identified as Author of this work

For legal purposes the Acknowledgements on p. 405 of *Double Cross* and
p. 339 of *A Spy Among Friends* constitute an extension of this copyright page

A catalogue record for this book is available from the British Library

ISBN: 978-1-5266-0478-1

2 4 6 8 10 9 7 5 3 1

Typeset by Newgen Knowledge Works (P) Ltd., Chennai, India and
Hewer Text UK Ltd, Edinburgh
Printed and bound in Great Britain by CPI Group (UK) Ltd, Croydon CR0 4YY

To find out more about our authors and books visit
www.bloomsbury.com and sign up for our newsletters

DOUBLE
CROSS

For Callum, Pablo, Minnie and Wilf

'Tangle within tangle, plot and counter-plot, ruse and treachery, cross and double-cross, true agent, false agent, double agent, gold and steel, the bomb, the dagger and the firing party, were interwoven in many a texture so intricate as to be incredible and yet true.'

– Winston Churchill

'The enemy must not know where I intend to give battle. For if he does not know where I intend to give battle he must prepare in a great many places. And when he prepares in a great many places, those I have to fight in any one place will be few. And when he prepares everywhere he will be weak everywhere.'

– Sun Tzu

CONTENTS

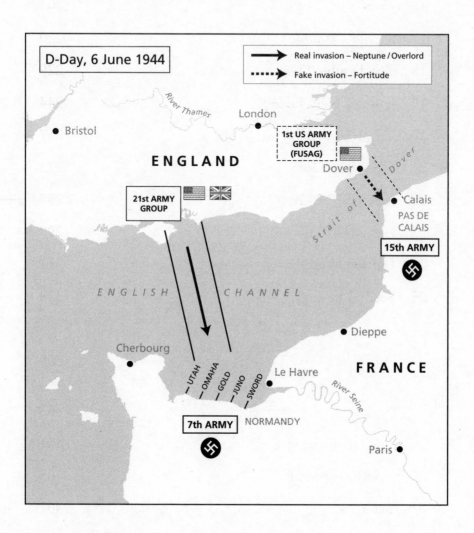

D-Day, 6 June 1944

Real invasion – Neptune / Overlord
Fake invasion – Fortitude

River Thames
London
Bristol
ENGLAND

1st US ARMY
GROUP
(FUSAG)

Dover
Dover

21st ARMY
GROUP

Calais
PAS DE
CALAIS

Strait of

15th ARMY

ENGLISH   CHANNEL

Cherbourg

Dieppe

FRANCE

UTAH
OMAHA
GOLD
JUNO
SWORD

Le Havre

River Seine

7th ARMY

NORMANDY

Paris

THE AGENTS AND THEIR HANDLERS

Dusan 'Dusko' Popov
MI5 codename: Tricycle, Skoot
MI5 case officer: Billy Luke, Ian Wilson
Abwehr codename: Ivan
Abwehr case officer: Ludovico von Karsthoff, Johnny Jebsen

Roman Czerniawski
MI5 codename: Brutus, Armand, Walenty
MI5 case officer: Christopher Harmer, Hugh Astor
Abwehr codename: Hubert
Abwehr case officer: Oscar Reile

Lily Sergeyev
MI5 codename: Treasure
MI5 case officer: Mary Sherer
Abwehr codename: Solange, Tramp
Abwehr case officer: Emile Kliemann

Juan Pujol García
MI5 codename: Garbo, Bovril
MI5 case officer: Tomás Harris
Abwehr codename: Arabel
Abwehr case officer: Karl-Erich Kühlenthal

Elvira de la Fuente Chaudoir
MI5 codename: Bronx, Cyril
MI5 case officer: Christopher Harmer, Hugh Astor
Abwehr codename: Dorette
Abwehr case officer: Helmut 'Bibi' Bleil, Berndt Schluetter

Preface

In the summer of 1943, a genteel and soft-spoken intelligence officer, wearing tartan trousers and smoking a pipe, put the finishing touches to a secret weapon he had been working on for more than three years. This weapon – unique in its power and unlimited in its range – was quite different from any built before or since. It was so shrouded in secrecy that its inventors were, for some time, unaware that they possessed it, and unsure how to use it. This weapon did not kill or maim. It did not rely on science, engineering or force. It did not destroy cities, sink U-boats or pierce the armour of Panzers. It did something far more subtle. Instead of killing the enemy, it could get inside his head. It could make the Nazis think what the British wanted them to think, and therefore do what the British wanted them to do.

Tar Robertson of MI5 had built a weapon that could lie to Hitler, and at the most critical juncture of the Second World War, he urged Winston Churchill to use it.

Allied military planners were already working on plans for the great assault on Nazi-occupied Europe. The D-Day invasion, so long awaited, would decide the outcome of the war, and both sides knew it. If the Allies could sweep across the English Channel and break through the massive German coastal defences known as the 'Atlantic Wall', then the Nazis might be rolled back out of Paris, Brussels, and then across the Rhine all the way to Berlin. Hitler, however, was convinced that if the invaders could be successfully resisted in the early stages of an assault, even for one day, then the attack would fail; Allied morale would slump, and it would take many months before another invasion could be attempted. In that time, Hitler could concentrate on destroying the Red Army on the Eastern Front. The first twenty-four hours would be, in Erwin Rommel's famous words, the 'longest day': how that day would end was far from certain.

D-Day stands today as a monumental victory and, with hindsight, historically inevitable. It did not look that way in prospect. Amphibious assaults are among the most difficult operations in warfare. The Germans had constructed a 'zone of death' along the French coast more than five miles deep, a lethal obstacle course of barbed wire, concrete and over 6 million mines, behind which lay heavy gun emplacements, machine-gun posts and bunkers. As Field Marshal Sir Alan Brooke, Chief of the Imperial General Staff, observed in a gloomy diary entry just before D-Day: 'It may well be the most ghastly disaster of the whole war.'

In war, no variable is more important, and less easy to control, than the element of surprise. If the Germans could be confused or, even better, actively misled as to where and when the landings would take place, then the odds on success improved dramatically. German forces in occupied France greatly outnumbered the invaders, but if they could be kept in the wrong place, at the right time, then the numerical equation appeared less daunting. By 1944, the war was claiming the lives of 10 million people a year. The stakes could not have been higher, or the margin for error smaller.

At the Tehran Conference in November of 1943, the first of the 'Big Three' meetings bringing together Churchill, Roosevelt and Stalin, the Allies laid plans for the invasion of Europe, codenamed 'Operation Overlord', that would take place in May 1944 (later delayed by a month), with

General Dwight Eisenhower as Supreme Allied Commander, and General Bernard Montgomery as Allied ground forces commander, for the assault across the Channel. During the conference, Winston Churchill turned to Josef Stalin and uttered a typically Churchillian remark that has since become a sort of myth: 'In wartime, the truth is so precious that she should always be attended by a bodyguard of lies.' Stalin, who had little time for literary metaphor, replied: 'This is what we call military cunning.' The D-Day invasion would be protected and supported by a comprehensive, worldwide deception campaign, a body of lies to shield the truth: in a tip of the hat to Churchill's remark, it was codenamed 'Bodyguard'.

The central aim of Operation Bodyguard was to fool the Germans into believing the invasion was coming at a point where it was not, and that it was not coming in the place where it was. More than that, to ensure that those troops preparing to fight off the bogus invasion were not redeployed to repel the real one, the deception must be maintained *after* D-Day. Goliath could be cut down to size only if he didn't know which direction David's sling-shot was coming from, and was kept guessing. The target range for a cross-Channel invasion, however, was extremely narrow. The Germans were sure to spot the build-up of troops in Britain, and since the assault had to take place within fighter range, there were only a handful of suitable spots for a massed landing. In the words of one planner, it was 'utterly impossible to disguise the fact that the major attack would come somewhere between the Cherbourg Peninsula and Dunkirk'.

The most obvious target was the Pas de Calais in the northeast, the region nearest the British coast. Deep-water ports at Calais and Boulogne could easily be resupplied and reinforced once they were in Allied hands, and a bridgehead in Calais would offer the most direct route for a march on Paris and the German industrial heartland in the Ruhr. The logic of attacking Calais was not lost on German tacticians. Hitler himself identified Calais as the likeliest target: 'It is here that the enemy must and will attack, and it is here – unless all the indications are misleading – that the decisive battle against the landing forces will be fought.' Hitler was fully alert to the possibility of being misled: he had been wrong-footed over the invasions of North Africa and Sicily. He would be far harder to dupe this time.

By July 1943, Allied military planners had concluded that, 'in spite of the obvious advantages of the Pas de Calais provided by its proximity to our coasts', the coast of Normandy north of Caen represented a better target. The Normandy beaches were long, wide and gently sloping, with suitable gaps in the dunes through which an invading force could spread quickly inland. The lack of a deep-water anchorage would be ingeniously solved by constructing vast artificial ports, codenamed 'Mulberry harbours'.

The successful deception surrounding the Sicilian landings in 1943 had persuaded the Germans that the most likely target was *not* the real target. Now, the aim was reversed: Hitler must be made to think that the most plausible target really *was* the target. Along the mighty Atlantic Wall the brickwork was thinnest in Normandy. That was where the wrecking ball would hit. But in order to strike with maximum effect, the truth would need to be protected by a bodyguard of liars, which is precisely what Tar Robertson had created.

Robertson and the small team of intelligence officers under his command specialised in turning German spies into double agents. This was the 'Double Cross System', coordinated by the intensely secret Twenty Committee, so named because the number twenty in Roman numerals, XX, forms a double cross. Hitherto these double agents – several dozen in number – had been used defensively: to catch more spies, obtain information about German military intelligence, and lull the enemy into believing he was running a large and efficient espionage network in Britain, when he was running nothing of the sort. In June 1943, Robertson reached the startling conclusion that every single German agent in Britain was actually under his control. Not some, not most, but *all* of them – which meant that

Robertson's team of double agents could now begin feeding the Germans not just snippets of falsehood, but a gigantic, war-changing lie.

The D-Day deception plot involved every branch of the secret war machine: scientists laid false trails, engineers built dummy tanks, radio operators put up a barrage of fake signals, and counterfeit generals led non-existent armies towards targets that were never in danger. While the overall, global deception campaign was codenamed Bodyguard, the plan specifically covering the cross-Channel invasion, the pivotal element in the deception, was named 'Fortitude', the quality most essential to its success. Operation Fortitude, the ruse to bottle up German troops in the Pas de Calais and keep them there, was an extraordinary collective effort, but at its core it depended on Robertson's spies, and a web of deception so intricate and strong that it would snare Hitler's armies, and help to carry thousands of soldiers across the Channel in safety.

The military saga of D-Day has been described many times, and the role of Operation Fortitude in that victory, though long shrouded in secrecy, has slowly emerged since the war. But the story of the five spies who formed the nucleus of the Double Cross system, Robertson's secret weapons, has never been fully told before. The spies themselves expected their story to remain hidden, as it would have done had the Security Service (better known as MI5) not chosen, in recent years, to declassify its wartime intelligence files. Indeed, if their stories had been told at the time, no one would have believed them.

For the D-Day spies were, without question, one of the oddest military units ever assembled. They included a bisexual Peruvian playgirl, a tiny Polish fighter pilot, a mercurial Frenchwoman, a Serbian seducer and a deeply eccentric Spaniard with a diploma in chicken farming. Together, under Robertson's guidance, they delivered all the little lies that together made up the big lie. Their success depended on the delicate, dubious relationship between spy and spymaster, both German and British.

This is a story of war, but it is also about the nuanced qualities of psychology, character and personality, the thin line between fidelity and treachery, truth and falsehood, and the strange impulsion of the spy. The Double Cross spies were, variously, courageous, treacherous, capricious, greedy and inspired. They were not obvious heroes, and their organisation was betrayed from within by a Soviet spy. One was so obsessed with her pet dog that she came close to derailing the entire invasion. All were, to some extent, fantasists, for that is the very essence of espionage. Two were of dubious moral character. One was a triple, and possibly a quadruple, agent. For another, the game ended in torture, imprisonment and death.

All weapons, including secret ones, are liable to backfire. Robertson and his spies knew only too keenly that if their deception was rumbled, then rather than diverting attention from Normandy and tying up German forces in the Pas de Calais, they would lead the Germans to the truth, with catastrophic consequences.

The D-Day spies were not traditional warriors. None carried weapons, yet the soldiers who did owed the spies a huge and unconscious debt as they stormed the beaches of Normandy in June 1944. These secret agents fought exclusively with words and make-believe. Their tales begin before the outbreak of war, but then overlap, interconnect, and finally interlock on D-Day, in the greatest deception operation ever attempted. Their real names are a mouthful, a sort of European mélange that might have sprung from a period novel: Elvira Concepcion Josefina de la Fuente Chaudoir, Roman Czerniawski, Lily Sergeyev, Dusko Popov and Juan Pujol García. Their codenames are blunter and, in each case, deliberately chosen: Bronx, Brutus, Treasure, Tricycle and Garbo.

This is their story.

1

Raw Recruits

Dusko and Johnny were friends. Their friendship was founded on a shared appreciation of money, cars, parties and women, in no particular order, and preferably all at the same time. Their relationship, based almost entirely on frivolity, would have a profound impact on world history.

Dusan 'Dusko' Popov and Johann 'Johnny' Jebsen met in 1936, at the University of Freiburg in southern Germany. Popov, the son of a wealthy industrialist from Dubrovnik, was twenty-five. Jebsen, the heir to a large shipping company, was two years older. Both were spoilt, charming and feckless. Popov drove a BMW; Jebsen, a supercharged Mercedes 540K convertible. This inseparable pair of international playboys roistered around Freiburg, behaving badly. Popov was a law student, while Jebsen was taking an economics degree, the better to manage the family firm. Neither did any studying at all. 'We both had some intellectual pretensions,' wrote Popov, but we were 'addicted to sports cars and sporting girls and had enough money to keep them both running'.

Popov had a round, open face, with hair brushed back from a high forehead. Opinion was divided on his looks: 'He smiles freely showing all his teeth and in repose his face is not unpleasant, though certainly not handsome,' wrote one male contemporary. 'A well-flattened, typically Slav nose, complexion sallow, broad shoulders, athletic carriage, but rather podgy, white and

Dusko Popov

well-kept hands,' which he waved in wild gesticulation. Women frequently found him irresistible, with his easy manners, 'loose, sensual mouth' and green eyes behind heavy lids. He had what were then known as 'bedroom eyes'; indeed, the bedroom was his main focus of interest. Popov was an unstoppable woman-iser. Jebsen cut a rather different figure. He was slight and thin, with dark blond hair, high cheekbones and a turned-up nose. Where Popov was noisily gregarious, Jebsen was watchful. 'His coldness, aloof-ness, could be forbidding, yet everyone was under his spell,' Popov wrote. 'He had much warmth too, and his intelligence was reflected in his face, in the alertness of his steel-blue eyes. He spoke abruptly, in short phrases, hardly ever used an adjec-tive and was, above all, ironic.' Jebsen walked with a limp, and hinted that this was an injury sustained in some wild escapade: in truth it was caused by the pain of varicose veins, to which he was a secret martyr. He loved to spin a story, to 'deliberately stir up situations to see what would happen'. But he also liked to broker deals. When Popov was challenged to a sword duel over a girl, it was Jebsen, as his second, who quietly arranged a peace-ful solution, to Popov's relief, 'not thinking my looks would be improved by a bright red cicatrix'.

Jebsen's parents, both dead by the time he arrived in Freiburg, had been born in Denmark, but adopted German citizenship when the shipping firm of Jebsen & Jebsen moved to Hamburg. Jebsen was born in that city in 1917, but liked to joke that he was really Danish, his German citizenship being a 'flag of convenience' for

business purposes: 'Some of
my love of my country has to
do with so much of it actually
belonging to me.' A rich,
rootless orphan, Jebsen had
visited Britain as a teenager,
and returned a committed
Anglophile: he affected English
manners, spoke English in
preference to German, and
dressed, he thought, 'like a
young Anthony Eden, con-
servatively elegant'. Popov
remarked: 'He would no
more go without an umbrella
than without his trousers.'

Johnny Jebsen

Preoccupied as they were with having fun, the two student
friends could not entirely ignore the menacing political changes
taking place around them in the Germany of the 1930s. They
made a point of teasing the 'pro-Nazi student intelligentsia'.
The mockery, however, had a metal strand to it. 'Under that
mask of a snob and cynic and under his playboy manners',
Jebsen was developing a deep distaste for Nazism. Popov found
the posturing Nazi Brownshirts ridiculous, and repulsive.

After graduation, Popov returned to Yugoslavia, and set
himself up in the import–export business, travelling widely.
Jebsen headed to England, announcing that he intended to
study at Oxford University and write books on philosophy. He
did neither (though he would later claim to have done both).
They would not meet again for three years, by which time the
world was at war.

In early 1940, Popov was living in Dubrovnik, where he had
opened his own law firm, and conducting affairs with at least
four women, when he received a telegram from his old friend,
summoning him to Belgrade: 'Need to meet you urgently'.

Their reunion was joyful, and spectacularly bibulous. They went on a bender through Belgrade's nightspots, having enlisted 'two girls from the chorus of one of the clubs'. At dawn, all four sat down to a breakfast of steak and champagne. Jebsen told Popov that in the intervening years, he had become acquainted with the great English writer, P. G. Wodehouse. With his monocle and silk cravat, Jebsen now looked like an oddly Germanic version of Bertie Wooster. Popov studied his old friend. Jebsen wore the same expression of 'sharp intelligence, cynicism and dark humour', but he also seemed tense, as if there was something weighing on his mind. He chain-smoked, and 'ordered his whiskies double, neat, and frequently. In style, his clothes still rivalled Eden's, but his blond hair was no longer so closely trimmed and he had a neglected moustache, reddened by tobacco.'

A few days later, the friends were alone, at the bar of a Belgrade hotel, when Jebsen lowered his voice, looked around in a ludicrously conspiratorial manner, and confided that he had joined the Abwehr, the German military intelligence service, 'because it saved him from soldiering, of which he was very much afraid as he is a heavy sufferer from varicose veins'. Jebsen's recruiter was a family friend, Colonel Hans Oster, deputy to Admiral Wilhelm Canaris, the chief of the Abwehr. He now had the formal but vague Abwehr title of *Forscher*, meaning researcher, or talent scout, with the technical rank of private, attached to a 400-strong special detachment of the Brandenburg Regiment. This unit was in reality 'a wangle by Canaris to keep a number of young men out of the clutches of compulsory service'. Jebsen was a freelance spy, on permanent leave from the army, with a personal assurance from Canaris that he would never wear uniform, never undergo military training, and never be sent to war. He was free to spend his 'time travelling throughout Europe on his private business and financial affairs, so long as he held himself available to help the Abwehr when called upon to do so'.

'Hitler is the undisputed master of Europe,' Jebsen declared. 'In a few months' time, he'll probably finish off England, and then America and Russia will be glad to come to terms with him.' This was pure Nazi propaganda, but Jebsen's expression, as usual, was glintingly ironic. 'Would you dine with a friend of mine,' Jebsen asked suddenly, 'a member of the German Embassy?' The friend turned out to be one Major Müntzinger, a corpulent Bavarian and the most senior Abwehr officer in the Balkans. Over brandy and cigars, Müntzinger made his pitch to Popov, as subtle as a sledgehammer. 'No country can resist the German army. In a couple of months, England will be invaded. To facilitate the German task and to make an eventual invasion less bloody, you could help.' Müntzinger shifted to flattery. Popov was well connected. His business was the ideal cover for travelling to Britain, where he must know many important and influential people. Why, did he not know the Duke of Kent himself? Popov nodded. (He did not admit that he had visited Britain only once in his life, and had met the Duke for a matter of minutes at Dubrovnik's Argosy Yacht Club.) Müntzinger continued: 'We have many agents in England, quite a number of them excellent. But your connections would open many doors. You could render us great service. And we could do the same for you. The Reich knows how to show its appreciation.' Jebsen drank his whisky and said nothing. Müntzinger was somewhat vague about the kind of information Popov might gather: 'General. Political.' And then, after a pause: 'Military. Johnny will introduce you to the proper people when and if you accept.' Popov asked for time to think the offer over, and in the morning, he accepted. Jebsen had recruited his first spy for German intelligence. He would never recruit another.

Popov, meanwhile, had begun to develop what he called 'a little idea of my own'.

In 1941, the Interallié was the most important spy network in Nazi-occupied France. Indeed, as one British intelligence officer remarked, it was virtually the only one, 'our sole source of information from France' in the early part of the war. The network consisted of scores of informers, agents and sub-agents, but ultimately the Interallié was the creation of one spy, a man to whom conspiracy and subterfuge were second nature, who regarded espionage as a vocation. His French collaborators knew him as Armand Borni; he also used the codename 'Walenty', or 'Valentine'. His real name was Roman Czerniawski, and in a very short time, through sheer energy, conviction and a soaring sense of his own worth, he had become the most valuable British spy in France.

Czerniawski was a Polish patriot, but that phrase cannot do justice to his essential Polishness, and the depths of his attachment to his motherland. He lived for Poland, and was perfectly prepared (at times, almost anxious) to die for it. 'His loyalty is entirely to his own country, and every problem he sees is bound up with the destiny of the Polish people,' wrote one of his fellow spies. He loathed the Germans and Russians with equal intensity for carving up his country, and dreamed only of restoring the Polish nation. Every other loyalty, every other consideration, was secondary. He stood just five foot six inches tall, with a thin face and intense, close-set eyes. He smiled readily, and spoke at machine-gun speed.

The son of a well-to-do Warsaw financier, Czerniawski had trained as a fighter pilot before the war, but a serious crash had left him partially sighted and deskbound. The German invasion of Poland in September 1939 found Captain Czerniawski at air force headquarters in Warsaw, a specialist in military intelligence and the author of a well-received treatise on counter-intelligence. Czerniawski was a professional, 'a man who lives and thinks spying', as one colleague put it. He regarded the spy trade as an honourable calling 'based on the highest ideals of human endeavour'. As the Polish army crumbled beneath the German onslaught, Czerniawski escaped to Romania, and then, using forged documents, made his way to France, where Polish forces were regrouping. When France fell in 1940, his division was disbanded, but rather than join his compatriots in

Britain to continue the fight from there, Czerniawski went underground. He persuaded a young French widow, Renée Borni, to lend him her late husband's identity. As the Germans began their occupation, a peasant whose papers identified him as Armand Borni wobbled along beside them on a borrowed bicycle, taking mental notes, and already congratulating himself. 'Every signpost, every sign on a truck, every distinguishing mark of any sort, meant far more to me than to anybody

Roman Czerniawski

else.' Here were the seeds of what he would grandly refer to as his 'vision'. While the Polish government-in-exile in London fought one kind of war, he would mount another. He imagined 'small cells of resistance, multiplying with great speed, joining together and forming one screen of eyes'.

Czerniawski made his way to the unoccupied South of France, where he made contact with the Polish secret service and obtained formal approval for his plan to establish a network in the occupied zone. A few nights later, he was dining alone at La Frégate, a restaurant in Toulouse, when a young woman asked if she might occupy the empty seat at his table. 'She was small, in her thirties. Her pale, thin face, with thin lips, was animated by very vivid eyes.' Mathilde Carré simultaneously sized up her diminutive and accidental dining companion: 'Thin and muscular, with a long narrow face, rather large nose and green eyes which must originally have been clear and attractive but were now flecked with contusions as the result of a flying accident.' Czerniawski introduced himself 'in an appalling French accent'. They fell into conversation. After dinner he walked her home.

Mathilde Carré was highly intelligent, overwrought and, at the moment she met Czerniawski, teetering on the edge of a nervous breakdown. The child of bourgeois Parisian parents, she had studied at the Sorbonne, worked briefly in an insurance company, trained as a teacher, and then married a childhood friend, before swiftly discovering she could not stand him. The war was the excuse she needed to leave her husband. With the French army in retreat, she found work in a dressing station, treating the wounded. There she met a lieutenant in the French Foreign Legion, and made love to him 'under the eyes of an enormous crucifix' in the bishop's cell of a seminary at Cazères sur Garonne. He was gone in the morning, and she was pregnant. She decided to keep the baby, and then miscarried. One night, she stood on a high bridge, about to kill herself, but then changed her mind: 'Instead of throwing myself into the Garonne, I would fling myself into the war. If I really intended to commit suicide, it would be more intelligent to commit a useful suicide.' To celebrate this decision, she had taken herself out to dinner at La Frégate.

Czerniawski's abundant self-assurance made Mathilde feel instantly secure. 'Every time he spoke of the war his eyes flashed. He would not accept that Poland had been defeated. He radiated a kind of confidence and the enthusiasm of youth, an intelligence and willpower which would alternately give place to the airs of a spoilt, affectionate child.' They met again the next night, and the next. 'A great bond of friendship was swiftly forged.' Both would later deny they had ever been lovers with such vehemence that the denials were almost certainly untrue.

Three weeks after their first meeting, Czerniawski confessed that he was a spy, and asked Mathilde to help him realise his 'vision' of a multi-celled intelligence network. She said he could count on her; together they would 'do great things'. The theatricality of the moment was compounded by Czerniawski's announcement that he had already selected a codename for his new accomplice: she would be 'La Chatte', the She-Cat, because 'you walk so quietly, in your soft shoes, like a cat'. She raised the slim fingers of one hand in a claw: 'And I can scratch as well if I wish.' Perhaps it was a warning.

Roman Czerniawski and Mathilde Carré formed a most effective spy partnership. In Paris, they rented a room in Montmartre, and set about constructing an entire espionage network. 'It will be inter-Allied,' Czerniawski announced. 'The boss will be a Pole, the agents mostly French, and all working for the Allies.' The Interallié network was born.

Mathilde acted as chief recruiter (since some Frenchmen declined to work for a Pole), while Roman gathered, collated, typed and dispatched intelligence material to London. The first recruits were Monique Deschamps, codenamed 'Moustique' (Mosquito), a tiny, chain-smoking firebrand of a woman, and René Aubertin, a former French army tank commander. Gradually the network expanded to include railway workers, police, fishermen, criminals and housewives. They sent whatever intelligence they had gathered to one of numerous 'post boxes' across Paris: the lavatory attendant at La Palette, the Berlitz language school by the Opéra, and a concierge on Rue Lamarck 'who had received a bayonet thrust in the buttocks when the Germans entered Paris, so it was only natural that he should hate them'. Mathilde gathered up their intelligence. 'In her black fur coat, red hat and small, flat, red shoes she moved swiftly from one appointment to another,' wrote Czerniawski, 'bringing new contacts, new possibilities, leaving me free to concentrate on studying the news from our agents and condensing it into our reports.'

Czerniawski's aim was to build up a complete picture of German forces in occupied France, the Order of Battle: troop positions and movements, ammunition dumps, aerodromes, naval and radar installations. 'To defeat the enemy you have to know where he is; the more exactly you know where he is, the easier it can be,' he wrote. He typed up the condensed reports on tissue paper. Every few weeks, a courier codenamed 'Rapide', 'a tall, thin Pole of indeterminate age with a muddy complexion and a small black moustache', boarded the 11 a.m. Marseille train for Bordeaux at the Gare de Lyon. Ten minutes before departure, he locked himself in the first-class toilet. Over the toilet bowl was a metal sign reading: '*Remplacez le couvercle après l'usage*'. Inserting a handkerchief between screwdriver and screw to avoid tell-tale scratching, Rapide carefully loosened the sign-plate, inserted the tissue-paper report behind, and then screwed it back on. After the train had crossed the border into unoccupied France, an agent of Polish intelligence would perform the procedure in reverse, retrieving the report and inserting a reply to be picked up when the train arrived back in Paris. From unoccupied France, Polish intelligence relayed the message via courier through the neutral Iberian Peninsula to the Polish government in exile in London, which passed it on to the British Secret Services. Every one of Czerniawski's reports ended up with MI6, Britain's foreign intelligence organisation, more formally known as the Secret Intelligence Service, or SIS.

The network, or La Famille as they called it, expanded swiftly. A radio the size of a portable typewriter was smuggled across the border from Vichy France, installed in a top-floor flat near the Trocadero and used to send coded information. Renée Borni, the widow who had furnished Czerniawski's false identity, moved to Paris to work on coding and decoding the wireless messages. Czerniawski gave her the codename 'Violette'. She became his lover. By the middle of 1941, Czerniawski could boast that his 'Big Network composed of French patriots, directed by a Pole and working for England, was now the last stronghold of Allied resistance against Germany'. Three more underground wireless stations were established. Some reports were 400 pages long, including maps and diagrams. Impossible to send by radio, these were photographed, and the undeveloped film smuggled across the Spanish border, 'packed in such a way that, opened by an unauthorised person, it would be exposed to the light and so made useless'.

Interallié intelligence poured into London in a swelling torrent, ever more detailed and precise, and sometimes so fast that its recipients could not keep up. When a spy discovered the route intended for the personal train of Hermann Goering, the Luftwaffe chief, Czerniawski immediately radioed the information to London, and was dismayed when the train was not attacked. A message arrived the next day. 'RE: GOERING TRAIN SORRY WE GOT THE NEWS TOO LATE TO USE IT FOR THE RAF STOP.'

Inevitably, there were tensions within the group. Mathilde loathed Renée, considering her 'a typical little provincial woman, and badly dressed'. Czerniawski insisted there was 'no question of any jealousy', but he reflected that Mathilde was a 'strange woman, idealistic but ruthless, ambitious, very nervous and highly strung'.

In the autumn of 1941, Czerniawski was told to report to an airfield near Compiègne, where a plane would pick him up to bring him to London for a debriefing. On 1 October, an RAF Lysander glided out of the sky, piloted by a man with a moustache, Squadron Leader J. 'Whippy' Nesbitt-Dufort, whose only French, by way of greeting, was 'C'est la vie'. On arrival in England, Czerniawski was met by Colonel Stanislaw Gano, the head of Polish intelligence. 'You've kept us all busy on this side,' said Gano, who looked, Czerniawski thought, like 'the head of some business firm'. For twenty-four hours he was quizzed on every aspect of his network. Gano seemed particularly interested in Mathilde Carré. 'We are perfect partners,' Czerniawski assured him. Finally, to his amazement, he was ushered into the presence of General Wladislaw Sikorski, the Polish Prime Minister. Sikorski gravely declared that Czerniawski had been awarded the *Virtuti Militari*, the highest Polish military decoration. 'I was petrified by the suddenness, unexpectedness

and solemnity of the moment,' Czerniawski later wrote. He
would soon be dropped by parachute back into France to
continue his work. The little Polish spy was proud, but with
gratification came a niggling doubt, a small premonitory stab of
anxiety: 'Subconsciously I felt a disturbing uneasiness.'

Elvira de la Fuente Chaudoir spent night after night at the
gaming tables in Hamilton's Club or Crockford's Casino in
Mayfair, and though she sometimes won, she always lost in the
end. It was most frustrating. But when Elvira wasn't gambling,
she was bored to death; which was why she had agreed to have
lunch with a man who, she had been told, might offer her a
most interesting and well-paid job.

  Boredom stalked Elvira Chaudoir like a curse. Her father,
a Peruvian diplomat, had made a fortune from guano, the
excrement of seabirds, bats and seals, collected off the coast of
Peru and exported as fertiliser. Elvira grew up in Paris, where
she was expensively educated, and tremendously spoilt. In
1934, at the age of twenty-three, to escape the tedium, she had
fled into the arms of Jean Chaudoir, a Belgian stock exchange
representative for a gold-mining firm. Jean turned out to be a
crashing bore, and life in Brussels was 'exceedingly dull'. After
four years of marriage, and a number of unsatisfactory love
affairs with both men and women, she came to the conclusion
that 'she had nothing in common with her husband' and ran
away to Cannes with her best friend, Romy Gilbey, who was
married to a scion of the Gilbey gin dynasty, and very rich.
Elvira and Mrs Gilbey were happily losing money made from
gin in a casino in Cannes when the Germans invaded France;
they fled, in an open-top Renault, to St Malo, before taking a
boat for England.

  In London, Elvira moved into a flat on Sloane Street, but the
tedium of life swiftly descended once more. She spent her evenings
shuttling between the bar at the Ritz and the bridge tables, losing
money she did not have. She would have borrowed from her parents,

but they were stuck in France. She tried to join the Free French forces gathering around the exiled Charles de Gaulle, but was told she was unsuitable. She did a little translating for the BBC, and found it dreary. She complained, to anyone who would listen, that she could not get an interesting job because she was Peruvian. One

Elvira de la Fuente Chaudoir

of those who happened to be listening, one night at Hamilton's, was an RAF officer, who told a friend in military intelligence, who passed her name on to someone in MI6. And so it was that Elvira Chaudoir now found herself, at the age of twenty-nine, in the grill room of the Connaught Hotel, sitting across the table from a middle-aged man in a rumpled suit with a bristling white moustache and the eyes of a hyperactive ferret. He had introduced himself as 'Mr Masefield'. His real name was Lieutenant Colonel Claude Edward Marjoribanks Dansey, also known as 'Haywood', 'Uncle Claude' and 'Colonel Z'. He was assistant chief of MI6.

Claude Dansey was witty, spiteful and widely disliked by his fellow spies. Hugh Trevor-Roper, the waspish historian who worked in wartime intelligence, considered him to be 'an utter shit, corrupt, incompetent, but with a certain low cunning'. Dansey was a most unpleasant man, and a most experienced spy. They made an odd couple: Elvira, tall and over-dressed, with a sweet, rather innocent face, her auburn hair arranged into a question mark over her forehead; Dansey, small, bald, bespectacled and intense. Elvira rather liked this fizzing little man, and as the conversation unfolded it became clear that he knew a great deal about her. He knew about Mrs Gilbey and the unsuccessful evenings at the bridge table; he knew her father had been appointed Peruvian chargé d'affaires to the collaborationist Vichy government in France; he knew what was, or rather what was not, in her bank account. 'I realised he must have been tapping my telephone. There was no other way he could have learned so much about me and my friends,' she later reflected.

Dansey offered her a job. Her Peruvian passport, he explained, meant that she could travel with comparative ease in occupied Europe, and her father's diplomatic status would provide cover for an extended visit to Vichy France. She could report on political matters, but more importantly she might get herself recruited as an agent by the Germans. This is the intelligence technique known as 'coat-trailing', dangling a potential recruit before the opposition in the hope that, if recruited, they can then be put to work as a double agent. She would be well paid for her efforts. Elvira did not hesitate.

The MI6 assessment of their new recruit was blunt: 'Attractive in appearance. She speaks fluent French, English and Spanish. She is intelligent and has a quick brain but is probably rather lazy about using it. A member of the international smart gambling set, her friends are to be found in any of the smart bridge clubs in London.' Surveillance revealed that her 'tastes appear to be in the direction of the "high spots"'. Police reported 'hilarious parties' at the Sloane Street flat, with 'rowdy behaviour, singing and shouting late at night, and the arrival of drunken men and women in the small hours'. Deputy Chief Constable Joseph Goulder noted, with disapproval and some understatement, that Mrs Chaudoir 'favours the companionship of women who may not be careful of their virginity'. Though Elvira might have come across as some dizzy-headed socialite, in reality she was bright and resourceful, and with a cast-iron cover: a good-time girl with no interests beyond the next cocktail, the next bed partner and the next bet. She was also attractive to both sexes and hungry for cash, qualities which might come in useful. As Dansey knew from a lifetime of espionage, even the most intelligent and discreet of people will tend to indiscretion if they think they are talking to a foolish and beddable woman.

In a flat in Knightsbridge, Elvira was taught how to use secret ink using a match head impregnated with a chemical powder. Once in France, she would write 'apparently innocuous letters' to a cover address in Lisbon. 'Between the lines of those letters I was to insert my intelligence reports penned in an undetectable fluid that could be developed by Dansey's technicians.' Elvira was a swift learner. 'She is very intelligent and quick to grasp essentials,' her instructor reported.

Her budding spy career very nearly came to an early end when a certain Sub-Lieutenant Burnett of the Royal Naval Volunteer Reserve reported that, one night at Crockford's, he had overheard Elvira Chaudoir boasting 'she was being taught a secret service code in the neighbourhood of St James's and that shortly she was to be sent to Vichy'. Elvira was given a severe scolding, and told 'she must abstain from divulging information which may have come to her knowledge'. Chastened, she promised to be more discreet, but the incident had demonstrated one of her more aggravating (and endearing) traits: like many spies, she found it hard to keep a secret.

Elvira was given the oddly masculine codename 'Cyril', and told to stand ready to go to France. Her war was about to become very interesting indeed.

Juan Pujol García had been many things in his short life: cinema proprietor, businessman, cavalry officer (though he feared horses) and reluctant soldier. He had spent most of the Spanish Civil War in hiding from Francoist forces. A graduate of the Royal Poultry School at Arenys de Mar, Spain's most prestigious college for chicken farmers, he ran a poultry farm outside Barcelona, though he hated chickens. Pujol had no head for figures and the business went bust. Stocky and spry, with a high forehead and 'warm brown eyes with a slightly mischievous tint', he looked like a fighting bantam. When the Second World War broke out, Pujol decided he wanted to spy for the British. 'I must do something,' he told himself. 'Something practical; I must make my contribution towards the good of humanity.' Hitler was 'a psychopath', Pujol concluded, and so he must support the Allies. 'I wanted to work for them, to supply them with confidential information which would be of interest to the Allied cause, politically or militarily.'

Quite where and how he would obtain such information, he had yet to work out. 'My plans were fairly confused,' he later admitted. His memoirs, written many years later, suggest that his quixotic, deeply held determination to fight Hitler sprang from an aggressive form of pacifism, and an abiding distrust of political extremism in any form. He was a supremely gentle soul, proud never to have fired a gun; he planned to fight Nazism in a different way. 'I was fascinated by the origin of words,' he wrote many years later. 'The pen is mightier than the sword. I believe this sincerely and absolutely. I have devoted the greater part of my life to this ideal, using all my talents, all my convictions, all possible schemes, machinations and stratagems.' Pujol would fight a unique sort of war, with words as his only weapons.

In January 1941, the twenty-nine-year-old Catalan approached the British Embassy in Madrid, with an offer to spy against the Germans. He was politely but firmly told to go away. In a variant of Groucho Marx's dictum, the British did not want anyone in the club who wanted to be a member. Pujol next tried the Germans, pretending to be a keen fascist willing to spy against the British – in the hope that, once recruited, he could then betray them. The Germans told him they were 'extremely busy'. But the little Catalan with the oddly intense eyes continued to badger the Germans in Spain, schooling himself in National Socialism until he could 'rant away as befitted a staunch Nazi'. Finally (mostly to get him to shut up), the Germans said that if he could get to Britain, via Lisbon, he would be considered for intelligence work. This was enough for Pujol. From that point on, he began to worm his way into German confidences, and in particular those of Major Karl-Erich Kühlenthal of the Madrid Abwehr station.

Kühlenthal would be comprehensively duped in the course of Operation Mincemeat, the deception in which a dead body was floated ashore in Spain, carrying forged documents indicating an Allied landing in Greece rather than Sicily. The German officer was efficient, paranoid and stupendously gullible. From Pujol's point of view, he was the ideal case officer. Kühlenthal duly equipped Pujol with secret ink, cash, the codename 'Agent Arabel', and some advice: 'He should be careful not to underestimate the British, as they were a formidable enemy.' On his arrival in Lisbon, Pujol once more contacted the British, and once more was rejected. This left him in something of a quandary, since he needed to start feeding information to the Germans as soon as possible. On 19 July 1941, he sent a telegram to Kühlenthal announcing his safe arrival in Britain.

But he was not in Britain. Pujol was still in Portugal. Denied the opportunity to gather real intelligence, for either side, he decided to invent it, with the help of the Lisbon public library, second-hand books and whatever he could glean from newsreels. He dug out the names and addresses of real British

Juan Pujol

munitions companies, consulted a *Blue Guide to England* for relevant place names, and a Portuguese publication entitled *The British Fleet* as a primer on naval matters. Pujol had never been to Britain. He simply imagined it, sending back detailed, long-winded reports about things he thought he might have seen had he been there. Pujol's style was exhaustingly verbose, a thicket of clauses and sub-clauses, adjectival swamps and overwrought sentences that stretched to a distant grammatical horizon. He would later claim that this extraordinary writing style was a way of filling up the page without saying very much. Though he loved to play with words, his reports were full of glaring errors. He could never get to grips with British military nomenclature or culture. He imagined that Glaswegian drinking habits must be similar to those in Spain; he wrote: 'There are men here who would do anything for a litre of wine.' His German controllers not only failed to spot his mistakes, but heaped praise on Agent Arabel, particularly when he claimed to have recruited two sub-agents in Britain who were, of course, entirely fictional. For nine months, Pujol remained in Lisbon, doing what spies, when stuck for real information, have always done: he invented what he thought his spymasters wanted to hear. He would continue to make it up, magnificently, for the rest of the war.

Major Emile Kliemann of the German Abwehr was having a most agreeable war. Occupied Paris was an exceptionally pleasant place to be, if you happened to be one of the occupiers. He had an office on the Champs-Elysées, a comfortable apartment near the Bois de Boulogne, plenty of disposable cash and very little to do. Most importantly, he had a new mistress, named Yvonne Delidaise. A French woman with a German mother, Yvonne was demanding, expensive, and twenty years his junior. His dumpy Austrian wife was still in Vienna, and certain to remain there. This was also a source of satisfaction. Kliemann's job was recruiting informers and ferreting out French spies, but his indefatigable colleague Hugo Bleicher seemed happy to do the hard work, which was just fine with Kliemann. A Viennese businessman, posted to Paris in June 1940, Kliemann had little time for Nazism. Indeed, he 'did not particularly like Germans', and rather hoped that Germany would not win the war too quickly as he wanted nothing more than to continue his newfound Parisian life, making love to Yvonne and meeting the odd dodgy character in his favourite café, Chez Valerie. Portly and broad-shouldered, Kliemann wore a neatly clipped moustache, and a gold signet ring on the third finger of his left hand with the initials 'EK'. He dressed with what he considered understated elegance, dyed his sideburns, and wore his hair carefully parted and greased down. He played the violin and collected antique porcelain. At forty-three, Major Emile Kliemann was vain, romantic, clever, staggeringly lazy and consistently unpunctual. As befits a spy chief, he had assembled an impressive number of aliases – 'Killberg', 'von Carstaedt', 'Polo', 'Octave' and 'Monsieur Jean' – though not a single workable spy.

On 13 October 1941, Kliemann reluctantly arranged to meet a potential recruit, a twenty-nine-year-old Frenchwoman of Russian origin, recommended by one of his colleagues. Her name was Lily Sergeyev.

Kliemann was two hours late for their rendezvous at the Café du Rond-Point. The young woman waiting at the corner table was handsome, without being beautiful. She had curly brown hair, bright blue eyes and a square chin. In fluent German, Lily Sergeyev explained that she was a journalist and painter. Her father had been a Tsarist government official but after the Revolution, when Lily was five, the family had emigrated to Paris. Her grandfather, she announced with pride, had been the last Imperial Russian Ambassador to Serbia. Her uncle, General Yevgeni Miller, had commanded the Fifth Russian Army in the First World War and then vanished in 1937, and was executed in Moscow two years later. Her father now sold cars. Her mother was a dressmaker. She considered herself French. She wanted to spy for Germany.

THE NATIONAL ARCHIVES

Lily Sergeyev

Kliemann was intrigued. Lily seemed vivacious, intelligent and, most importantly, interested in Kliemann. He invited her to dinner at the Cascade restaurant, near the Bois de Boulogne, explaining that Yvonne, his 'secretary', would meet them there. The young woman insisted on bringing her dog, a small, white, male terrier-poodle cross named Babs, to which she was obviously devoted.

Once they were seated in the restaurant, Lily told her story. A restless spirit, she had made a number of epic journeys across Europe by bicycle and on foot, including one that had taken her through Hitler's Germany. There she had been impressed by the efficiency of the Nazi regime, and had written a series of admiring articles for the French press. She had even interviewed Goering, who had 'promised to obtain for her a personal interview with Hitler'. This had not materialised. In 1937, a German journalist named Felix Dassel, whom she had met on her travels, told her he was working for German intelligence, and asked Lily if she wanted a job. She had declined, but when the Germans marched into Paris, Dassel had reappeared. Over dinner at Maxim's, she told him that the British had 'let the French down badly and that she had no love for them'. Dassel asked her again if she was prepared to work for the Germans; this time, she accepted. It was Dassel who had recommended that Kliemann arrange this meeting.

Yvonne was yawning by this point in Lily's story, but Kliemann was curious. She seemed genuine enough, and enthusiastic, though nervous. 'It might be quite easy for me to get to Portugal, to

Australia, or to England,' she said. 'I have relatives in all those places and nobody would be surprised if I wanted to get out of France.'

Kliemann pondered. 'I am interested in your project,' he said finally. 'I think we will send you to Portugal. I very much doubt that you will be allowed to go to England.'

Then, suddenly, Kliemann caught Lily's wrist, and fixed her with what he plainly believed was a penetrating, spy-masterly stare: '*Why* do you want to work for us?'

There was a long and uncomfortable pause. Her reply, when it came, was an odd one.

'Major, you are an intelligent man: how much can my answer be worth to you? I can tell you that it is from conviction, a matter of principle, or because I love Germany, or else I hate the British. But if you were the enemy, if I were here to spy on you, to betray you, do you think that my answer would be any different? So will you allow me not to answer?'

He smiled and replied that 'of course, she was right'.

Kliemann dropped off Lily and her little dog at her parents' flat near the Trocadero. 'I will make contact again soon,' said the Major. Then, as usual, he did nothing at all.

In her diary, Lily wrote: 'Babs lifts up his shaggy, truffle-like nose and looks at me inquiringly.' (The diary is written entirely in the present tense, and much of it is devoted to her dog.) 'I take Babs on my knees, on the drawing-room sofa, and say in his pink ear: "It's a fine game, it's a grand game, but, you know, if we lose it, we'll lose our lives . . . or mine, at any rate."' Babs would be the first to perish in the game.

2

A Bit of an Enigma

Dusko Popov, the Serbian playboy, was not as feckless and apolitical as he seemed. The invitation from his old friend Johnny Jebsen to work for German intelligence was an attractive one. The year of 1940 was a time of deep anxiety as the German army rampaged across Europe. Poland had been under German occupation since September the previous year; Denmark had been invaded in April, followed by Norway; Belgium and the Netherlands surrendered in May; France had fallen in June. Yugoslavia might be next. A Serbian businessman with interests across Europe would need German friends and, as Popov told Jebsen, he was keen 'to get an easy living'.

But within days of accepting Major Müntzinger's offer, Popov began to work on his own plan. A small seed of courage had taken root in this hitherto callow and shallow soul. A few days after the dinner with Müntzinger, he contrived to bump into John Dew, First Secretary at the British Embassy in Belgrade, at a legation party. In a quiet moment on the terrace, he told Dew that an old university chum, now an Abwehr officer, had made moves to recruit him. 'Interesting,' said Dew (who privately suspected Popov was 'an awful crook'). 'Be a good thing for you to keep in touch with that chap.' Dew put Popov in contact with the MI6 station chief in the Yugoslav capital. 'Continue your conversation with the Germans,' Popov was advised. 'Be friendly but don't overdo it. Ask for time to prepare your trip.'

Johnny Jebsen laid out Popov's mission on behalf of German intelligence: he would travel to London, via neutral Portugal, under the guise of a businessman exporting raw materials from Yugoslavia to Britain. Once there, he should begin sending back information by writing letters in secret ink. This was the principal method of covert communication between spies, a way of passing information that was becoming something of an espionage art in 1940. Jebsen showed Popov how to make the ink using a tablet of Pyramidon, a common treatment for headache, dissolved in white gin. When Popov had something to report, he should write an 'insignificant letter in type' on one side of a piece of paper, and use the ink and a sharpened matchstick to write invisibly on the other. The letter should then be sent to 'Maria Elera', at an address in Lisbon, where it would be picked up by the Abwehr. When a developer chemical was applied to the paper, the secret writing would appear.

Maria Elera was described by Jebsen as 'a young girl, about twenty-two, a journalist, Mulatto, who would pass as his girlfriend'. She would soon become exactly that. Popov would report to the Abwehr station in Lisbon. 'Your spymaster will be Major Ludovico von Karsthoff,' Johnny explained. 'You may find yourself liking him.' Finally, Popov was handed a list of questions, covering subjects as diverse as Britain's coastal defences, deployment of troops, civilian morale and politics: 'Who were Churchill's enemies? Who was in favour of starting to negotiate peace with Germany?' Popov immediately handed the questionnaire over to MI6. By November, Popov, codenamed 'Ivan' by his German handlers, was ready to go.

Popov and Jebsen met for a farewell drink at the Serbian King Hotel in Belgrade. 'We are now both in the same service,' Jebsen remarked. There was something about his smile that gave Popov pause. Here was a German spy who was a devotee of P. G. Wodehouse; a mouthpiece for Nazi propaganda who said he was terrified of fighting, but who obviously relished the risky world of espionage, knew how to make secret ink and professed himself 'strongly pro-British'. Jebsen even employed a British secretary, Mabel Harbottle, a starchy English spinster who might have stepped from the pages of a Wodehouse novel. Miss Harbottle had formerly worked for Joachim von Ribbentrop, Hitler's Foreign Minister, and though a German citizen, Mabel remained 'British at heart'. She flatly refused to type his letters unless reassured that whatever Jebsen was doing for the Germans 'could not hurt British interests'. Jebsen gave her that assurance – an odd commitment from a man specifically employed by the German Reich to do as much damage as possible to British interests. As Popov put it, Johnny was 'a bit of an enigma'.

The same was true of Jebsen's new boss, Admiral Canaris, one of the most puzzling figures of the Second World War. Supple and sinuous, and a master of the espionage game, Canaris was held in some awe by the other leaders of the Third Reich, including Hitler. Himmler loathed and distrusted him. So did Ribbentrop. Canaris was determined to win the espionage battle for Germany, yet his loyalties were shifting, his personal convictions opaque. He was openly friendly to Jews, and would help save many from the gas chambers. He made little secret of his disdain for the hysterical violence of the Nazis. And he ran the Abwehr, the great sprawling German intelligence machine, as a personal fiefdom, with little reference to the High Command. But then, the Abwehr was itself an anomaly within the Nazi military structure. Its officers tended to be drawn from the German upper classes, old-fashioned military types with little sympathy for the boorish ideology of Nazism: some were professionals, but many were lazy and corrupt, and a number of senior officers were actively opposed to the Hitler regime.

'What is Canaris like?' Popov asked his old friend. 'A sensitive man, unobtrusive,' came the considered reply, 'with much curiosity, vast intelligence, and a great sense of humour. He gives the impression of preferring to listen rather than to speak.' Johnny Jebsen might have been describing himself.

Popov would later insist that Jebsen knew, from the outset, that he would make contact with the British, and wanted him to do so. Secretly anti-Nazi, a devoted Anglophile, Jebsen was already playing a subtle and dangerous double game. Popov was only pretending to work for the Germans and Jebsen, it seemed, was only pretending to believe that he was. Each was lying, both knew it, and neither admitted it. 'There was a curious ambiguity about friendship for people in our positions,' wrote Popov. 'You tried to convince yourself that a friend would be on the right side, yet you couldn't dare trust that friendship far enough to reveal yourself.'

Popov arrived in Lisbon a week later, where he was met by a chauffeur and driven in an Opel sedan to a large stucco villa in the Moorish style in the seaside resort of Estoril. At the door of Villa Toki-Ana he was greeted by a gentlemanly figure with a warm smile and a mass of 'blackish hair on his hands'. Popov was training himself to spot distinguishing features.

'I have been instructed to help you to the utmost,' said his host. 'You have inspired a lot of faith at the Tirpitzufer [Abwehr headquarters in Berlin], and they are making ambitious plans for you.' Johnny had been right: Popov felt immediately drawn to Ludovico von Karsthoff: 'He was tall and dark and his movements were those of a big cat.' Von Karsthoff gave Popov the name of another German agent in London, a Czechoslovak named Georges Graf, who could be contacted in case of emergencies. In the evening they drank champagne and dined sumptuously. Though Popov would never know it, von Karsthoff's real name was Kremer von Auenrode, an educated and worldly aristocrat from Trieste whose main objective was to get through the war with maximum pleasure and minimum danger.

At dawn on 20 December 1940, Dusko Popov, Yugoslavian businessman, alighted at Whitchurch airport near Bristol. There he was met by Jock Horsfall, a pre-war racing driver who was MI5's most trusted chauffeur. As they neared the capital,

Popov's registration card

Popov could see the menacing roseate glow over London: the Luftwaffe's bombers had departed, but the fires were still burning.

In the lobby of the Savoy Hotel, a tall officer in the striking tartan trousers of an officer in the Seaforth Highlanders strode forward, hand outstretched. 'Popov, hello. I'm Robertson.' He looked, thought Popov, 'like Hollywood's concept of a dashing British military type'. Popov felt an instinctive liking for another spymaster, this one on the other side. 'Let's get acquainted,' said the Englishman, ushering him towards the bar. 'We'll get down to business tomorrow.'

This urbane, upper-class Englishman with distinctive trousers might have been welcoming a new member into one of London's more exclusive clubs – which, in a way, he was.

Major Müntzinger's boast that Germany had 'many agents in England' was entirely correct. But so far from being 'excellent', most of them were hopeless, many were actively disloyal, and a number were already working against Germany as double agents.

The counter-espionage section of MI5, known as B Section, was presided over by Guy Liddell, a shy, cello-playing spy-hunter, whose voluminous diaries offer an extraordinary insight into the wartime work of this remarkable secret organisation. In combating German espionage, Liddell faced two overriding and interconnected problems: a huge host of spies that did not exist, and a second, much smaller body of secret agents that most certainly did.

With the outbreak of war, Britain was gripped by what Liddell called a 'Fifth Column Neurosis', the unshakable and all but universal belief that the country was riddled with enemy spies, preparing to rise up if Hitler launched an invasion. This fear was stoked by spy novels, an excitable press and a peculiarly British urge to play amateur sleuth. 'There is a well-defined class of people prone to spy-mania,' wrote Winston Churchill, who had the mania himself. These imagined spies came disguised as nuns, butcher's boys, churchwardens and travelling salesmen. They appeared perfectly respectable. The head of Home Forces insisted that 'the gentlemen who are the best behaved and the most sleek are the stinkers who are doing the work and we cannot be too sure of anybody'. A spy might look like your bank manager. Indeed, he might *be* your bank manager. Robert Baden-Powell, the original Scout master, insisted he could identify a German spy from the way he walked, but only from behind. Reports flooded in to MI5 detailing the nefarious activities of this hidden spy army: they were poisoning the ice cream, leaving marks on telegraph poles to guide the invading forces, drugging cigarettes and training the inmates of lunatic asylums as suicide squads. When six cows stampeded on the tiny island of Eilean Mor in the Scottish Hebrides, this was immediately adduced to secret enemy activity. That the spies were invisible was merely proof of how fiendishly clever they were at disguising themselves. Even pigeons were suspect, since it was widely believed that enemy agents had secret caches of homing pigeons around the country which they used to send messages back to Germany. Britain's fear of spy-pigeons would eventually come home to roost in a most unlikely fashion.

These spy sightings were, as Liddell put it, 'junk', but the suspicion that Germany had launched an espionage campaign against Britain was entirely accurate. In July 1940, the Abwehr held a conference in Kiel, attended by Germany's most senior intelligence officers, at which a plan was drawn up (codenamed 'Operation Lena', after the wife of a senior Abwehr officer) to recruit and train dozens of spies, and dispatch them to Britain to conduct sabotage operations, infiltrate British society, and collect information on troops, airfields, civilian morale and anything else that might aid a German invasion. German spies began slipping into the country: they came by boat, submarine and parachute; some, like Popov, came legally, or disguised as refugees. Of the two dozen spies or so deployed to Britain between September and November 1940, five were German, while the others were variously Dutch, Scandinavian, Cuban, Swiss, Belgian, Spanish and Czechoslovak. These were far removed from the super spies imagined by a nervous British public. Most were poorly trained and petrified; some spoke no English at all, and had only a sketchy notion of the country they were supposed to blend into. They did not look like your next-door neighbour – they looked like spies. Only a few were genuine Nazis. The rest were variously motivated by greed, adventure, fear, stupidity and blackmail. Their number included several criminals, degenerates and alcoholics. According to one MI5 report, 'a high proportion suffered from venereal disease'. Some had opportunistically volunteered to spy against Britain, with the intention of defecting. Some were anti-Nazi from the outset. This motley collection of invasion spies had only this in common: not a single one escaped detection.

The task of intercepting enemy spies was made immeasurably simpler after cryptanalysts at Bletchley Park, the British code-breaking centre in Buckinghamshire, cracked the Abwehr wireless code, and began reading Germany's most closely held secrets. The breaking of the 'Enigma', the German cipher machine, was the most important intelligence triumph of this, or any other war: here was an information gold mine, referred to variously as 'Ultra' or the 'Most Secret Sources' (or 'MSS'), and guarded more jealously than any other wartime secret. With access to the wireless traffic passing between Berlin and its Abwehr stations, from the end of 1940 the British could track German intelligence operations from start to finish, and plan accordingly. With advance warning from the Bletchley Park codebreakers, these incompetent and highly visible spies were 'easy prey'. Once in custody, they were taken to the secret wartime interrogation centre at Latchmere House in Richmond, Camp 020, under the command of Captain (later Colonel) Robin Stephens.

Known as 'Tin-eye', on account of the monocle permanently screwed into his right eye, Stephens was xenophobic, rude, manipulative, ruthless and brilliant. Spies were subjected to intense interrogation using every method to extract the truth short of physical violence. Those deemed unsuitable as double agents were either imprisoned, or tried and executed. The others, a small minority, were offered a choice: work for Britain against Germany, or face the hangman's noose. 'You have forfeited your life, but there is a way of saving your life,' was how Tin-eye framed the issue. Unsurprisingly, this argument proved persuasive. Of the twenty-five German spies sent to Britain between 3 September and 12 November 1940, all but one was caught (the lone evader shot himself); five were executed; fifteen were imprisoned; and four became double agents, the first recruits of what would grow into a substantial army of deceivers.

The officer in command of this fledgling force was Thomas Argyll Robertson, known as Tommy, but more usually Tar, on account of his initials. Spymasters are expected to be intense types, ferociously clever and faintly sinister. On the surface, Tar Robertson appeared to be none of these. The son of a Scottish banker, he was cheery, amiable, funny and self-mocking. If he ever opened a book, there is no record of it. As a young man he had, according to one relative, 'an almost suicidal appetite for dusk to dawn partying, pretty women, and fast cars', expensive tastes that put paid to his army career in the Seaforth Highlanders when he ran out of funds. After an undistinguished stint in the City, in 1933 he was recruited into MI5 through the old boy network. He retained a military air, and the tartan

Tar Robertson

army trousers which earned him the nickname 'Passion Pants'. In demeanour, he was 'a perfect officer type, who could have been played by Ronald Colman', the English actor, with 'friendly eyes and an assertive way about him'. His family considered him 'less than promising'. But once installed in MI5, Tar revealed a natural talent for hanging around in pubs and picking up gossip. He was 'immensely personable and monstrously good looking', according to one colleague, 'with a charm that could melt an iceberg' and an 'unmistakable twinkle' that encouraged the spilling of confidences. Beneath the affability and 'delightful chuckle' was a personality of granite determination, and a ruthless streak. Hugh Trevor-Roper considered his Secret Service colleagues 'by and large pretty stupid – some of them very stupid'. But Tar he regarded as a 'real genius', with an uncanny knack for reading character and knowing, instinctively, when he was being misled. Robertson knew better than anyone else in British intelligence how to spot a lie, and therefore how to tell one.

The British Secret Services traditionally took a fastidious approach to double agents, regarding the practice of 'turning' intercepted spies and using them to mislead the enemy as faintly disreputable. Such creatures were classed as *agents doubles* – in French, as if to underline that this was typically duplicitous Continental behaviour. But before the war, MI5 recruited only one truly important double agent, an experiment that had almost ended in disaster. Arthur Owens was a Welsh-born electrical engineer with a 'shifty look', who began his spying career by providing information to MI6 after his visit to German shipyards. Owens also made contact with the Abwehr, which gave him the task of recruiting radical Welsh nationalists for sabotage operations. (This was an early hint of the Abwehr's bizarre but firmly held belief that the Welsh valleys were filled with violent secessionists awaiting the opportunity, with Nazi encouragement, to rise up against their English oppressors.) He then turned double agent, and agreed to work against the Germans. Tar was made case officer to Owens (codenamed 'Snow', a partial anagram of his surname) and eventually concluded that this 'stupid little man given to doing silly things at odd times' was playing each side against the other, but inefficiently. The case was eventually wound up, largely because Owens was a fantasist, whose mind did not 'work on logical lines'. Yet the Snow case had helped Bletchley Park to break the Abwehr code, provided useful leads on tracking down other German spies, and 'saved us from absolute darkness on the subject of German espionage', according to Dick White, Liddell's deputy. It also gave Robertson an early taste of just how fickle, troublesome and yet valuable a double agent could be.

It was Tar who had pointed out that simply capturing, executing or interning enemy spies, however satisfying as an act of war, offered no long-term benefit. There was nothing tender-hearted in Tar's desire to preserve German spies from the gallows: this was hard-eyed calculation. The questions asked of spies by their German spymasters offered useful clues to what the Abwehr did not know; if the Germans believed they had a functioning network of spies in Britain, they might feel it unnecessary to send more; if the Abwehr thought its spies were alive, at liberty and functioning well, it would open up possibilities for dialogue and deception. A live spy was more useful than a dead one, though a lot more trouble. Section B1A was launched, a new subsection of Liddell's B Section, with Tar Robertson at the helm.

The first spies selected as double agents proved to be duds. Georges Graf (codenamed, punningly, 'Giraffe') was a Czechoslovak citizen who had served in the French army before being dispatched to Britain by the Abwehr. Popov had been given his name by von Karsthoff, so the Germans obviously trusted him, and Popov's willingness to pass his name on to the British, unaware that Graf had already been turned, was proof that he was playing straight. Kurt Goose (codenamed 'Gander', naturally), landed by parachute in October with only a transmitting wireless; unable to receive messages from his handlers, he was of limited use, and the Gander case was swiftly wound up, as was Giraffe. Of greater interest were two Scandinavians, who had trained together in the Hamburg Abwehr station: Gøsta Caroli, a Swedish journalist who had lost a fortune in an Uppsala silver fox farm, and Wulf Schmidt, a Danish fascist. Caroli parachuted into the Northamptonshire countryside on the night of 6 September 1940, landed badly, and staggered into a ditch to try to sleep off his concussion, where a farmhand spotted his feet sticking out of a hedge. He was carrying a radio transmitter, £200 and a loaded pistol. Schmidt landed two weeks later, sprained an ankle, limped into the Cambridgeshire village of Willingham in a natty blue suit but with an unmistakable foreign accent, and was promptly arrested.

Though a 'fanatical Nazi', in the view of Tin-eye Stephens, Caroli agreed to work as a double agent if Schmidt's life was spared. With cruel but effective psychological manipulation, Schmidt was told that his friend had betrayed him; enraged, he spilled the beans and agreed to change sides. Caroli was given the codename 'Summer', but the Swede seems to have had second thoughts. One evening, in his safe house in Hinxton, near Cambridge, Caroli crept up behind his minder while he was playing patience and tried to throttle him with a piece of rope. When this failed, he apologised, tied the man to a chair and ran off with a tin of pilchards, a pineapple and a large canvas canoe. He then stole a motorcycle and motored, very slowly, towards the coast, with the canoe balanced on his head. He intended to paddle to Holland. A roadman reported to police that a man with a canoe had fallen off his motorcycle on the Pampisford Road, and 'he had helped the man throw the canoe over a hedge'. Caroli was arrested outside Ely. Clearly unreliable, the Swede was declared unfit for double-agent work, and imprisoned for the rest of the war. After initial resistance, Schmidt proved much more cooperative, and was given the codename 'Tate' because Robertson thought he looked like the music-hall comedian Harry Tate. He would prove to be the longest-serving double agent of them all.

The handling of double agents, Tar concluded, was going to require considerable subtlety: 'The double agent is a tricky customer and needs the most careful supervision. His every mood has to be watched.' These erratic characters showed an alarming propensity to swap sides. If any of them managed to break away and make contact with the Germans, Robertson reflected, this could 'blow our whole show'. If the Germans invaded, and there was a danger the double agents might fall into enemy hands, 'they will be liquidated forcibly'. Robertson was becoming fond of his brood of double agents. But he would not hesitate to kill them if he had to.

This, then, was the newly formed club into which Dusko Popov was welcomed by a smiling Tar Robertson in the lobby of the Savoy Hotel. The new double agent had already been given the codename 'Skoot', a play on his name, carrying the hint that Popov might 'pop off', or scoot, at any moment. (Under wartime rules, a spy's codename, or *nom de guerre*, should contain no hint of his or her identity. Robertson joyously and consistently ignored this directive, and established his own rule: every spy name must contain a joke, a pun, a hint or a nudge.) Tar had already learned enough about his new recruit's mode of life to know that a cell at Camp 020 and a grilling from Tin-eye Stephens were neither necessary nor advisable. Instead, Popov was lodged in a comfortable room at the Savoy, where Robertson and his colleagues interrogated him on his story: his recruitment by Johnny Jebsen, the meeting with Müntzinger, his encounter with the suave, hairy-handed von Karsthoff in Lisbon; his questionnaire and his instructions for making secret ink.

Popov struck his interrogators as open and honest, and his story was corroborated by information from Most Secret Sources. He made no monetary demands, and seemed to want to work as a double agent for the British out of a combination of anti-Nazi conviction and a thirst for adventure. Tar was impressed. 'I have a strong feeling we are on to something good.' As a businessman from a neutral country, Popov could travel freely between London and Lisbon, and maintain direct, personal contact with his German handler. The Germans seemed 'absolutely obsessed with the idea that he has a wide circle of friends and business connections in England', even though he knew virtually nobody in the country. 'It will be necessary to supply him with the names of a number of supposed friends.'

After four days in his company, Tar was convinced that the young Serb with the carefree attitude was playing straight, and prepared to risk his life. 'Skoot left an exceedingly favourable first impression upon all of us. His manner was absolutely frank and we all considered without question that he was telling the truth.' A token of appreciation was in order, and Tar knew exactly what sort of reward Skoot would enjoy: on Christmas Eve 1940, MI5 laid on the most extravagant party that bomb-battered London could provide.

Courtnay Young, a junior officer in B Section, was appointed Popov's carousing partner. They began by consuming a substantial lunch with Robertson at Quaglino's restaurant. The remainder of the afternoon was spent playing billiards at the Lansdowne Club, with plenty of beer. In the early evening they drank sherry at the Universities' Club, before heading back to the Savoy for dinner. Young then suggested that they go dancing at the Suivi Club, where they met two attractive young women who danced with them all night. These, too, had been furnished by MI5. Skoot 'was obviously pleased by the interest shown by the two girls', reported Young, who had some difficulty keeping up with the pace of Popov's revelry. 'He enjoyed himself thoroughly [and] took part in the usual Christmas bonhomous rioting, well lubricated with champagne.' In the early hours, Popov and his minder staggered back to the Savoy, 'both viewing things through slightly rose-tinted spectacles'.

To retain German confidence, Agent Skoot would need to feed his handlers some true, but harmless information – known in spy jargon as 'chicken-feed', filling and substantial, but lacking in real nourishment. He would also need a convincing cover story. For this, Tar turned to Ewen Montagu, an officer in naval intelligence who would later devise Operation Mincemeat. Montagu was rich, well-connected, and a keen yachtsman – just the sort of person that the Germans would expect Dusko Popov to befriend. They met in the bar of the Savoy, where Montagu handed over a batch of true, low-level information on naval matters that could be passed to the Germans without danger, and some minor untruths, including the suggestion that British merchant convoys would be accompanied by at least one submarine in the future. In a small way, that might give the U-boat wolfpacks pause for thought. Before they parted, Montagu handed Popov a handwritten note, to show to the Germans as proof that he had indeed met this friendly and indiscreet naval officer. 'I much enjoyed meeting you,' wrote

Montagu. 'It is so nice at these troubled times to meet another who is as mad as I am about sailing.' In response to the question of which British figures were opposed to Churchill, he was told to cite Lords Brocket, Lymington and Londonderry as 'definitely members of the party that would be prepared to accept peace terms with Germany'. The three peers were widely suspected of pro-German sympathies, and there could be no harm in confirming what the Germans must already know.

Montagu was captivated by Popov: 'I found him a most charming person and would be most surprised if he is not playing straight with us,' he told Tar. 'I hope that his having met me and having laid the foundation for further information will satisfy his employers. I should have thought it ought to be enough to show for a first visit to this country.'

On 2 January 1941, the Twenty or XX Committee was formed to oversee the Double Cross system, the first and only government body named with a Roman numerical pun. The committee was formed to coordinate the work of double agents and supply these agents with a stream of chicken-feed to build up the credibility of the spies. John Masterman, an Oxford history don, part-time detective novelist and sportsman, was appointed Chairman of the Twenty Committee, which included directors of intelligence for the Army, Navy and RAF, and representatives of MI5, MI6, Home Forces and Home Defence. While Robertson and the case officers of B1A would be responsible for the day-to-day running of the double agents, the Twenty Committee would manage overall strategy and cook up a diet of harmless truths, half-truths and uncheckable untruths to feed to the enemy. The committee met, at MI5 headquarters in 58 St James's Street, every Thursday afternoon for the rest of the war. 'Giraffe's case died chiefly through lack of nourishment,' in Masterman's opinion. No double agent would ever go hungry again.

The Twenty Committee was referred to by its members as

'The Club', and Masterman organised it with a particular sort of club in mind: a cricket club. 'Running a team of double agents is very like running a club cricket side,' he wrote, and as a first-class cricketer himself, he approached the task exactly as if he was assembling 'a thoroughly well-trained and trustworthy team' of cricketers. Masterman was a cold fish, apparently without romantic feelings for either sex. But cricket was different. 'Cricket was my first and most enduring passion,' he wrote. He thought of espionage in terms of stumpings, no balls, innings and over rates, and of spies as 'players', some of whom 'required a good deal of net practice before they were really fit to play in a match'. The relationship between cricket (that most English of sports) and spying (at which the British have always excelled) is deep-rooted and unique. Something about the game attracts the sort of mind also drawn to the secret worlds of intelligence and counter-intelligence – a complex test of brain and brawn, a game of honour interwoven with trickery, played with ruthless good manners and dependent on minute gradations of physics and psychology, with tea breaks. Some of the most notable British spies have been cricketers, or cricket enthusiasts. Hitler played cricket, but only once. In 1930, it was claimed that, having seen British POWs playing in southern Germany during the First World War, the Nazi party leader asked to be 'initiated into the mysteries of our national game'. A match was played against Hitler's XI, after which he declared that the rules should be altered by the 'withdrawal of the use of pads' and using a 'bigger and harder ball'. Hitler could not understand the subtlety of a game like cricket; he thought only in terms of speed, spectacle, violence. Cricket was the ideal sport on which to model an organisation bent on stumping the Führer.

Tar Robertson was no mean cricketer himself – a left-arm spinner, whose speciality was a 'cunningly spun, deceptively slow ball'. As Tar assembled his team, Masterman was already imagining a time when they would be 'ready to take the field for what might be a decisive match' against German intelligence.

'The prime difficulty was that we never knew the date when this decisive match would take place.' It would be many months before the Double Cross players were ready to compete, but Masterman knew that in Dusko Popov, he had already found a singularly talented opening batsman.

On the day the Twenty Committee was born, Tar took his new protégé to lunch, and rehearsed, in detail, the story he was to tell the Germans. Twenty-four hours later, Skoot was on a plane back to Lisbon. 'We have in him a new agent of high quality,' Tar reported, confident that the sheer force of Popov's personality would protect him. If Tar was right, then Agent Skoot might help win the war; if not, then Dusko Popov was already as good as dead.

Roman and the Cat

Roman Czerniawski, the diminutive Polish spy, parachuted back into occupied France at dawn on 8 November 1941. He landed in a melon field, in the rain, not far from Tours. As he headed back to Paris on an overcrowded bus, wearing a beret and mackintosh, he reflected: 'I wonder if anybody here could imagine that I had my dinner in England.'

Safely back among his family of spies, Czerniawski announced that a celebration was in order. The 16th of November would mark the first anniversary of the Interallié network, and there was much to be proud of: some fifty agents, each with two or three sub-agents, had so far produced no less than ninety-seven reports, furnishing the British with 'a complete picture of the German Order of Battle'.

The leaders of the network assembled at the Montmartre flat – Roman, Mathilde Carré, Renée Borni and Maurice Wlodarczyk, a former Polish naval radio operator who worked the transmitter. They ate sandwiches and sipped the black-market champagne Czerniawski had managed to scrounge. At 8 p.m., they gathered around the wireless to listen to the BBC. Each section head of the Interallié had instructions to tune in. At 8.15, the BBC announcer played a snatch of patriotic French music, and then intoned: 'Many Happy Returns to our Family in France on the occasion of their anniversary.' They clinked glasses. Maurice sent a wireless message to London: 'AGAINST

THE GERMANS ALWAYS AND IN EVERY WAY. *VIVE LA LIBERTÉ!*'

The team drifted away. Czerniawski, a little tipsy, reflected that their underground work was taking its toll: Mathilde, in particular, was 'overworked and was obviously tired'. As co-founder of the network she seemed irked that Czerniawski had received a medal, the *Virtuti Militari*, while her work was barely acknowledged. The next night Roman and Renée Borni dined in their favourite restaurant. He asked the band to play 'Gloomy Sunday', also known as 'The Hungarian Suicide Song', a hit that year for Billie Holiday. 'Why did you ask for that?' asked Renée. 'It's so sad.' In the rainy street, as they were walking home, Roman noticed a man in a raincoat, his face obscured by an umbrella. He tried to recall the half-remembered face. 'I must be tired,' he thought.

Czerniawski was in deep sleep when a gunshot went off, and the Gestapo burst into his bedroom. Renée screamed. 'The light was switched on and in front of me I saw the man in the mackintosh and beret with a revolver in his hand.' Now he recognised him: Hugo Bleicher, the most feared German counter-intelligence officer in Paris. It was an 'intelligent face', Roman reflected, with eyes that were 'sharp, but not violent'. He was bundled into a waiting car, and driven directly to the Hôtel Edward VII, headquarters of the secret military police. 'If only someone could warn Mathilde,' Roman thought.

When Mathilde Carré got home from her early morning walk she saw, without immediately comprehending, that her door was splintered, hanging off its hinges. At the same moment, a burly Gestapo officer appeared at her elbow. She felt oddly calm as he led her away. 'It was a great gamble and today I have lost. But I'm a good gambler,' Mathilde reflected.

The Interallié network, so painstakingly assembled, had been torn apart in days, destroyed from within because of 'an ordinary denunciation dictated by personal spite'.

Hugo Keiffer, a former airman with a reputation as a 'wide boy', had been responsible for smuggling messages into France from Britain on the Normandy fishing boats. One of his own informants ratted on him, a certain Madame Denbié, because, it was said, he had refused to sleep with her. Under torture, Keiffer revealed the name of his contact in the network, a Pole named Krotki, who in turn directed the Gestapo to the flat in Montmartre. When Bleicher burst into Roman Czerniawski's bedroom, he did not even know the name of the man he was arresting.

Mathilde Carré was also brought to the Hôtel Edward VII, and cracked at once. 'I was like an animal caught in the headlights,' she recalled. Hugo Bleicher offered her a deal. Other senior members of the network had already confessed, he lied, and implicated her. 'You have committed enough crimes to be shot several times over.' He offered her the choice between collaboration and death, warning: 'If you double-cross me you will be shot immediately without trial.' He pushed a cup of ersatz coffee towards her across the desk. If she cooperated, he would pay her 6,000 francs a month. 'Great Britain makes other people work hard for her, and doesn't even pay them decently,' he added sourly. In the First World War, Bleicher had been sent on an espionage mission across the lines, dressed in British uniform, and was captured. A prisoner for two years, he claimed he had been treated 'inhumanely' by his British captors, 'not only with handcuffs on his wrists but manacles on his ankles'. Bleicher 'loathed Britain'.

It took Mathilde just ten minutes to accept Hugo Bleicher as her new master. She would look back on this decision as 'the greatest act of cowardice of my life'. Yet it had been a 'purely animal' reaction, prompted by survival instinct: 'winning Bleicher's confidence seemed the surest means of one day being able to escape'. That morning, Mathilde had a pre-arranged meeting with an agent at the Pam Pam restaurant. Bleicher told her to keep the rendezvous: 'You must behave normally.

Your life and liberty depend on it.' The agent was arrested as he entered the café.

Afterwards Bleicher took Mathilde to lunch. 'You see how easy it is,' he said. Unable to eat, she caught sight of herself in the mirror, with 'a strangely haunted look in my eyes'. She began passing names to Bleicher, and 'one by one' all her former comrades were picked up and interrogated: Madame Gaby at la Palette, Maurice the radio operator, 'Rapide' the courier. Some broke down and implicated others. 'A few men proved their mettle, but in comparison women showed better spirit,' Czerniawski later wrote. A week after the first arrests, more than sixty Interallié agents and sub-agents had been rounded up. Mathilde revealed every aspect of the network she had helped to build, enough evidence to ensure Roman Czerniawski's death many times over.

Bleicher was delighted. Another man might simply have smashed the network and killed everyone in it, but Bleicher was cleverer than that. Ostensibly for her own safety, Mathilde was moved into Bleicher's home, a large mansion in the elegant Paris suburb of Saint Germain en Laye. 'We have decided to continue the messages from Interallié,' Bleicher told her. 'We're going to play some fine tricks on the British. We shall inform them that Armand [Roman Czerniawski] and Violette [Renée Borni] have been arrested, but you are going to stress in a message to London that you managed to save the third [wireless] set and that you will continue with your principal agents. No one in the network knows you are in our hands.' This was the German version of Double Cross.

Mathilde claimed that Bleicher treated her with perfect courtesy during these weeks. Refined and teetotal, in the evenings he would play the piano for her. Soon, they became lovers. Later, in overwrought prose, Mathilde struggled to explain why: 'I had felt the icy breath of death and suddenly found warmth once more in a pair of arms. I hated myself for my weakness, and as a result of my abasement I hated the Germans even more.'

At the Hôtel Edward VII, Roman Czerniawski was subjected to an exhausting interrogation, but no violence. He told Hugo Bleicher nothing. What annoyed him most was the small, fat Gestapo officer who had rubbed his hands with glee as Roman was marched in, and 'started to laugh contentedly'. The Pole had expected to be tortured, and then killed. Instead, he was transferred to Fresnes prison, south of Paris, and left in a dank cell.

Czerniawski had been in prison for six weeks, and was rather surprised to still be alive, when he learned of Mathilde Carré's treachery. He had been 'treated severely but without brutality', questioned repeatedly, denied exercise and fed scraps, yet no one had laid a finger on him. German and Vichy newspapers, predicting imminent Nazi victory, were left in his cell. Bleicher appeared from time to time, but instead of issuing threats he was full of flattery, remarking that he was most impressed by the Interallié organisation, and 'the completeness of the records which they found at his HQ'.

Roman did not know what to make of this red-faced man with the thick glasses, who, though 'intelligent and quick-witted', was 'always boasting'. He was nettled to see the German was wearing *his* pullover, stolen from his flat, but he conceded that there was something impressive about the Abwehr counter-espionage officer. 'He is a man of great ability and ingenuity and a specialist in running double agents,' he noted. 'Also a man of great personal ambition.'

One morning, Renée Borni appeared in Roman Czerniawski's cell, ushered in by a warder. The last Roman remembered of his lover was her 'terrified eyes' as she was frog-marched away from the Montmartre flat. Renée quickly explained what her jailers had told her: that Mathilde had 'given everything away'; the Interallié network was destroyed. Even so, 'the Germans felt an extraordinary admiration for our methods', she said, suggesting that Roman 'might exploit this favourable circumstance'.

Renée was certainly a plant, whether willing or otherwise – sent to weaken his resolve. Roman's first response was to try to make sense of Mathilde's betrayal. 'It is possible she acted under German blackmail,' he reasoned. 'When working in this terrain one cannot apply any rules concerning the trust one may place in individuals. The only value is a man's character and his resistance in moments of crisis and his loyalty to ideals.' Many years later, he was still pondering her behaviour, and his own.

Roman's morale improved after Renée's visit. He had been contemplating suicide, fearing interrogations 'by force', but now Czerniawski was once again plot-hatching, his favourite activity. As one of his spymasters observed, 'a firing squad did not fit in with his grandiose and dramatic ideas of his own destiny'. Renée's visit had suggested a way out of this predicament. Which was, of course, precisely what Bleicher had intended.

On 29 November, Roman Czerniawski handed his jailers a letter addressed to General Otto von Stülpnagel, Germany's military commander in France. For sheer gall, it was remarkable even by Czerniawski's standard: 'No collaboration which might be proposed to me could come about unless I was convinced that I was working for the good of the Polish nation,' he told Stülpnagel. 'If the German nation has amongst its plans the reconstruction of the rights of the Polish nation, in this case alone discussions about my collaboration could take place. Any such discussion must take place with an officer of the General Staff who knows these problems and is authorised to discuss them with me.'

No one had actually *asked* Czerniawski to collaborate. He was making an offer, but in such a way that it sounded as if he was accepting one.

The next day a man in the uniform of a colonel entered the cell, and saluted. Czerniawski bowed. The fellow was middle-aged and 'lantern-jawed', with 'thick grey hair and an intelligent look'. He introduced himself as Oscar Reile, chief of counter-intelligence for the Paris Abwehr office. Roman noted his 'manicured' fingernails. This man was a negotiator, a fixer, not a fighter.

Without preamble, Reile launched into a lecture on Nazi history. The National Socialists were the New Romans, he explained. The Führer did not wish to oppress Poland, and asked only for Polish support to counter the Bolshevik threat from the East: 'We do not deny the rights of the Polish nation, but we ask its cooperation.' In defying Germany, Poles like Czerniawski were opposing the tide of history. 'You have tied yourself on one hand with capitalist-Jewish England and, on the other, with Communist-Bolshevik Russia,' the Colonel continued. 'By joining us you will contribute to our programme to advance Europe by several centuries in one leap.' General Sikorski, he said, was backing the wrong horse: 'Whatever collaboration Poland might have with Great Britain would be merely to help the selfish aims of Great Britain. All things considered, the best solution would be to come under the cultural protection of Germany, since German culture is preferable to barbarian culture.'

It was an extraordinary performance, revealing an 'excellent knowledge of Polish history' and perfectly pitched to appeal to a patriotic anti-communist Pole, weakened by hunger but fattened up on a diet of Nazi propaganda, and fearful that his country might fall under Soviet rule. Above all, it played on Roman Czerniawski's abundant vanity, suggesting that he alone could 'raise the Polish nation on the side of Germany'.

Thus began what Czerniawski described as the 'war of nerves'. He would later claim that he had merely played a part, pretending to discuss collaboration, 'as though I had really swallowed their propaganda', when it is unlikely he ever had any such intention. He was determined, however, to keep fighting for Poland, and in order to do that, he needed to get out of prison. As the German officer rose to leave, Czerniawski dropped an unsubtle hint: 'In my opinion England is leading us Poles, up the garden path . . .'

When Oscar Reile returned a few days later, he was in civilian clothes. The propaganda lecture continued. 'The Germans were at the doors of Moscow . . . The war against England would certainly be won.' If Roman Czerniawski sided with Germany, and persuaded his compatriots to do likewise, he would 'be working for the good of the Polish nation'. The Pole responded hotly that 'he would never under any circumstances work against my countrymen'. Colonel Reile smiled broadly.

Czerniawski composed another letter. 'The future of Poland lies in German hands, the British will do nothing for us, and deliver us to the Russian barbarism,' he wrote. 'I am prepared to discuss placing myself at the disposal of Germany while at the same time being of use to my own country, Poland.' If the Germans could smuggle him into Britain, he said, he would spy for Germany. Once in place, he could gather information on British aircraft and tank production, troop deployments and above all 'preparations for, and the possibilities of, a second front'. In short, he would 'do for Germany what he had been doing in France against them'. He promised great things: 'I will group around me persons dissatisfied with the British alliance and thus create a powerful fifth column' ready to rise up 'the moment that Germany attacks England'. He made just two demands: 'That the agents of Interallié captured with him were not to be put to death and were to be set free at the conclusion of the war [and that] Germany would, after winning the war, assist his country and people in a manner commensurate with the valuable work he would no doubt have achieved.'

Much of this was posturing nonsense, but some was undoubtedly genuine. With his re-ignited self-confidence, Czerniawski truly believed that he could negotiate on behalf of Poland, and change the course of the war. It was, Reile admitted, 'an extremely odd situation: a captured spy was laying down conditions'.

The effect of the letter was instantaneous. Two new German officers appeared in his cell and 'in unusually polite and friendly terms, expressed their pleasure at the fact that, after all, I had come to realise the good brought by National Socialism to the "New Europe".' If Roman Czerniawski could deliver all he promised, then he would find Germany 'highly appreciative'. But how, they asked, could they be sure he would not betray them? The Pole's response was indignant: 'I told them I could carry out my mission successfully only on condition that I enjoyed their absolute trust.' But Reile knew better than to rely on the word of a man who had already amply demonstrated his talent for subterfuge. Czerniawski's mother was in occupied Poland, he pointed out; his brother was in a German POW camp; his lover sat in a nearby cell, and dozens of members of his network had been rounded up. 'Your companions are in prison,' Reile remarked pointedly. 'You know yourself what the sentence will be, if the courts have to impose a punishment for spying in wartime.'

Czerniawski responded hotly: 'If I work for you, it will be for ideological reasons. There will be no need for reprisals.' But the German did not need to spell out the threat: if he should double-cross them, his friends, colleagues and family would be killed.

The Pole had long considered himself as a prime candidate for martyrdom, but more than his own life was now at stake. 'Should I fail, the fury of the Germans would know no bounds,' he reflected. 'I knew that the fate of my former colleagues was practically a foregone conclusion, but now I was involving my mother and my brother. This time I had no right to commit any mistakes.'

On the afternoon of 14 July 1942, two Gestapo NCOs entered Czerniawski's cell and ordered him to put on his shoes. One was small and pudgy. The other looked tough and cunning, 'like an intelligent boxer'. Czerniawski wondered, for a moment, if he was about to be killed. He was led out of the prison gates, and driven to a flat on the Rue Dufrenoy where Colonel Oscar Reile was waiting. Reile handed over a set of civilian clothes, false papers taken from him at the time of his arrest, 10,000 francs in ration coupons and some money, to 'enable him to go to the barber and have a shave'. Reile laid out his instructions: Czerniawski should make his way to unoccupied France, re-establish contact with the Polish underground, and get himself smuggled to Britain. Bleicher would shadow him in the Vichy zone, in case of difficulties. Czerniawski should tell Polish intelligence that he had given the Germans the slip while being transferred between prisons. 'The prison would be notified that I had escaped en route to the car.' His new German codename would be 'Hubert'.

Canaris himself had approved the plan to woo Czerniawski, play on his patriotism, recruit him and then send him to Britain, but Reile was fully aware of the dangers. 'The English knew that Armand had fallen into our hands,' he later wrote. 'Our English opposite numbers would quite obviously assume that he had been released from prison by us, and sent over with secret orders. There was the risk that the enemy Intelligence Service would then attempt to transmit misleading information to us.' But Reile was confident that if Czerniawski began feeding him falsehoods, he would spot the deception and be able to pick up important clues as to the real intentions of the British by reading Roman's messages 'in reverse'. 'If the enemy attempted to mislead us we could, under certain circumstances, gather important information.' Czerniawski could hardly believe his 'fantastic' luck. He went to a barber on the Rue Pigalle to have his prison beard removed, and then ate in a Russian restaurant. Walking back to the flat, he stopped from time to time to check if he was being tailed. No one seemed to be following him. He was free, after a fashion.

Coat Trailing

Elvira de la Fuente Chaudoir, boredom-prone good-time girl and aspiring spy, was perched at the roulette table in a Cannes casino when she was approached by a Frenchman named Henri Chauvel, a wealthy Nazi collaborator, who asked her out to dinner. She had no hesitation in accepting.

Elvira had spent several weeks 'coat trailing' through the South of France, spending time in casinos and expensive restaurants while maintaining her 'cosmopolitan cover as a society girl mixing in the very top circles', without so much as a sniff from German intelligence. Cannes was an oasis of self-indulgence. In her diary, Elvira described the 'small class of unscrupulous millionaires', living it up in southern France while war raged. 'People who get all the food they want, who wear lovely clothes, and who, though dancing is forbidden even to them, spend their nights gambling in the casinos.' There was nothing she liked better than dancing and gambling. But having spent the funds provided by MI6, she was almost broke again. Her existence was 'altogether more agreeable than enduring the Blitz in London', but Elvira was beginning to feel guilty. 'I felt I was doing little to justify Dansey's investment in me.' She needed someone to pick up her coat. Henri Chauvel seemed like a good start.

Of the millionaires enjoying life in the South of France in the spring of 1941, few were more unscrupulous than Chauvel, a property owner and entrepreneur who had discovered that currying favour with the Germans was a most effective way of making money. He took Elvira to dinner at the Carlton Hotel, which he owned, and ordered champagne. Chauvel was 'obviously rolling in money'. At the bar, a group of men was getting noisily drunk. One stood out from the others, 'very tall, with pitch-black hair'. He spoke French, but even from a distance Elvira could hear his strong German accent. 'The German seemed very interested in me and looked at me all the time,' she wrote. 'He was young and good-looking.' She asked Chauvel if he knew him.

'I'll introduce you to him, but in the end he's just a pig like the others,' said the Frenchman, piqued at Elvira's interest in another man. She pressed him for a name. Chauvel shrugged: 'He is a secret agent of Goering's and changes his name every day.'

A few days later, Elvira was at the bar of the Miramar Hotel, drinking a whisky, when the German appeared at her shoulder, bowed, and introduced himself as 'Bibi'. His real name was Helmut Bleil. He had arrived in unoccupied France in 1940 as part of the commission enforcing the terms of the Franco-German armistice, but his role as an economic expert was a cover. Like Johnny Jebsen, he was a freelance spy. But unlike Jebsen, he had no formal role in the Abwehr, having 'been recruited personally by Goering'. Bibi bought Elvira another drink, and then invited her to dinner at 'one of the most expensive black-market restaurants'. He seemed an odd, but intriguing fellow. His hands shook and he drank heavily, but he had the most 'graceful walk' and was 'obviously a gentleman'. He appeared deeply anxious. Elvira wondered if he might have an 'inferiority complex'. Later he confessed that he feared he might be 'spotted as a German', and shot in the street by the Resistance.

At first, Bibi 'seemed to want to keep the conversation to ordinary things'. When she asked him what he did, 'he laughed and said he was supposed to be attached to the Madrid Embassy as an "economic specialist"'. He didn't elaborate. Elvira explained that she was separated from her husband, and visiting her parents in Vichy. Casually, she remarked that she had run out of money, and would soon be returning to England. After dinner, he said he would like to take her to the casino. Despite his peculiar combination of swagger and paranoia, Elvira found him a 'pleasant fellow'.

Elvira and Bibi met again the next evening, and the next. One moment he was full of laughter, and 'enjoyed everything like a child', the next he would be saturated in alcoholic gloom, telling her: 'The war was very silly and such a pity and the Russians were awful and it would have been much more sensible for England and Germany to unite against Russia.'

'Why are you going back to England?' he asked. 'You could have a much better time in Paris, and London is going to be bombed worse than ever.'

Finally, Bibi made his move, but tentatively. Apropos of nothing at all, he observed that 'his Portuguese banker had told him there were packets of money to be made in England at the moment'. There was a pause. 'We might do some little business together.' Elvira sensed that here, at last, was 'an opportunity to start justifying my SIS salary. I pricked up my ears.'

'How much does a woman like you need to live really well in London?' asked the German.

Elvira told him she would be quite happy with 'anything over a hundred a month'.

'That is very little,' said Bibi, looking relieved. 'And very easy to make.'

'How?' asked Elvira.

They sat talking on the deserted Cannes seafront until three in the morning. Bibi explained that he had 'friends' who would pay generously for political, financial and industrial information about Britain. 'After the war, everyone will be very poor so it is up to each one of us to try to make some money now. After all, that is the only thing that counts.' He was 'rather vague' about exactly how she should obtain this information. As Bleil stared out over the dark Mediterranean, he said soberly: 'You will have to be terribly careful and never tell a soul about it. Because, if you do, you will be the first to pay.' The words hovered somewhere between a warning and a threat.

Within forty-eight hours, Bibi reported that his 'friends' had agreed to pay her £100 a month 'to start with, and extra sums for good information'. The money would be paid through Swiss and Portuguese accounts, disguised as alimony payments from her ex-husband. Her codename would be 'Dorette'. She would communicate using secret ink, he said, a 'marvellous trick' by which she could write to them without ever being discovered. Letters should be sent either to Chauvel at the Hôtel de Paris, Monte Carlo, or to a cover address in Lisbon. 'We just want facts, not opinions or reactions . . .'

Elvira interrupted him.

'This is already quite different to the "little business" we were originally meant to do together.'

'This is infinitely more interesting, and if you are successful, it represents a life job.'

Ten days later, an excited Bleil, already quite drunk, met Elvira in a Cannes park shortly before noon. 'He looked around nervously and asked me if I was sure I wasn't being followed.' Then he reached into his pocket and handed her a small bottle of colourless liquid. 'The Germans are the greatest chemists in the world and this is their newest and best invention.' Elvira did not say that she already had a bottle of British secret ink in her handbag. They repaired to the empty lounge of the Hôtel Majestic, where Bleil ordered champagne.

'I always act on intuition,' Bleil said. 'And I feel I can just trust you. If I am wrong, it will ruin my whole career.'

Elvira felt a stab of remorse. Bibi might be a sozzled Nazi spy, but in character he was a child, and seemed hopelessly out of his depth. 'I felt rather sorry for him, and frankly almost wished I had kept out of all this, but bucked myself up by thinking that since you start doing a job you must do it fully and shut all softness away.'

Bleil's hands were trembling. He reached for his hip flask. 'You must never breathe a word of this to any living soul,' he said, and swigged.

Elvira merely remarked: 'I have no desire to spend the rest of the war in prison.'

Lily Sergeyev was being driven mad by the waiting. She had volunteered to spy for Germany, but Germany was in no hurry whatever to take up the offer. Even her terrier-poodle Babs seemed to be feeling the strain. For almost a year she had kicked her heels in Paris, while Major Emile Kliemann, nominally her Abwehr case officer, arranged meetings which he failed to turn up for on time. When he did appear, he enthusiastically discussed the missions Lily might perform for the Third Reich, and then did nothing at all. Plans to send her as a spy to Syria, Australia and Dakar all came to nothing. Kliemann was far more interested in exploring the pleasures of Paris and discussing his love life. He remained besotted with Yvonne Delidaise, 'a nice girl but without much principle' in Lily's opinion. Yvonne had long fair hair, blue eyes, a turned-up nose, and dressed in frills, which Kliemann liked to buy her. In her diary, Lily described Yvonne as 'pretty but rather fat in build and has very broad hips'. She was, however, twenty-six years old, and Kliemann, nearing fifty, was infatuated. He played her the violin until he wept. One night he told Lily that he had decided to divorce his wife and marry Yvonne, but had not yet got around to telling his wife, or Yvonne.

Kliemann paid Lily a retainer of 3,000 francs a month. She was taught Morse code by Richard Delidaise, Yvonne's brother, a barman at Le Bourget airport and a keen Nazi collaborator who had qualified as a wireless instructor before the war. Once she had mastered the rudiments of Morse, he revealed to her the mysteries of coding. Next, in an apartment near the Opéra, she was introduced to two bald men who 'looked a little like birds of prey'. They taught her how to make secret ink by melting a special, unidentified substance, dipping a toothpick in it, and then writing on 'ordinary writing paper that has been rubbed all over with dry cotton wool in order to raise the fibres very slightly'.

Lily, however, felt no closer to being sent on a spying mission than she had been when she first met Kliemann, and her patience was fraying fast. Unpredictable and ambitious, her motives were complicated. She would later claim to have been driven by the purest patriotism, and always intended to switch sides as soon as possible. But she was also motivated by adventure, and the belief that she was destined to play the leading lady in her own drama. She had become fond of genial, romantic, inefficient Kliemann, but found him infuriating. Lily was not a patient woman. To make matters worse, she was suffering from painful kidney stones. 'This has been dragging on so long, the war will be over before I have had time to do anything,' she complained to her diary.

Finally, after Kliemann failed to turn up for yet another meeting, Lily Sergeyev threw an almighty tantrum. Yvonne Delidaise found herself on the receiving end. 'I am sick of it,' Lily ranted. 'I don't like to be made a fool of. It is always the same: he is not there, or he's just left, or he's in a conference. Nothing has been done for over a year. So let's call it a day . . .' Then she slammed down the telephone.

When Kliemann turned up the next day and tried to pacify her, she tore a strip off him. 'You shall not continue to treat me as if I was an old boot. I am not going to listen to you. I'm fed up, and you can look for someone else.'

Perhaps it was this histrionic performance that jolted Kliemann into action. More likely the Major realised that unless he actually demonstrated some sort of activity to his bosses, his lotus life in Paris might be in jeopardy. But whatever the reason, the sluggish German espionage machine cranked into life.

Kliemann arranged for them to rendezvous and then, to Lily's astonishment, kept to it. 'It is the first time the Major has ever arrived on time for an appointment,' she wrote. He was suddenly a paragon of crisp efficiency. He had orders from Berlin: Lily was to make her way to Britain, via Madrid, posing as a refugee keen to 'serve the Allied cause by any means in your power'. She would use the codename 'Solange', while Kliemann would sign his messages 'Octave'. She would be met in Madrid by one of the local Abwehr agents: 'He could recognise you by your little dog, as you insist on taking Babs with you.' Kliemann would join her in Madrid in a few weeks' time and bring her a wireless transmitter hidden inside a gramophone player. He ended with a pompous exhortation: 'I have confidence in your success. You must not doubt. You MUST succeed.'

As the train pulled out from Gare d'Austerlitz, Lily – Agent Solange – wrote in her diary: 'I wave a handkerchief at Mummy standing on the platform. Babs sniffs with satisfaction. I pull up the window, make a place for Babs. I'm leaving France, to try to help those who want to set her free.'

The Club

In the MI5 offices on St James's Street, John Masterman was thinking, as usual, about spies and cricket. The Double Cross team was shaping up into a decent squad, he reflected, with new contenders for the First XI appearing all the time. Some of the new arrivals were naturals, eager to play, and signed up almost immediately; others were untalented or uncooperative, and dealt with accordingly.

Josef Jakobs, a forty-three-year-old German dentist, was found in a Cambridgeshire field in early February with a broken ankle. Unable to move, he had fired his revolver to attract attention. After interrogation at Camp 020, Tin-eye Stephens briskly concluded that Jakobs was a 'scrofulous Nazi' and 'manifestly unemployable as a double agent', since he showed no inclination to collaborate. He was tried and sentenced to death by firing squad. 'He died at the Tower of London,' wrote Tin-eye, 'a brave man. His last words directed the firing squad to shoot straight.'

Much more promising were two young Norwegians, John Moe and Tör Glad, who had been dropped off the Scottish coast by German seaplane, and then rowed ashore to the rocky shoreline of Banffshire in a rubber dinghy loaded down with sabotage equipment, a wireless and two bicycles. They immediately turned themselves in to the astonished Scottish police. Their story was corroborated by Bletchley's Most Secret

Sources, and they were duly enrolled into the Double Cross system with the codenames 'Mutt' and 'Jeff', after the popular American comic strip about two mismatched and somewhat dim-witted gamblers. The names were unfair, as Mutt and Jeff would develop into unflashy but solid middle-order all-rounders.

Danish fascist Wulf Schmidt, alias Agent Tate, was also proving a useful player, though he was not allowed to operate his own transmitter, owing to lingering doubts that his 'newfound loyalty to this country would survive any real strain'. But the chicken-feed Tate sent to Germany appeared to be going down well, and in time he would become, in Masterman's words, 'a pearl among agents', setting the record for the longest continuous radio contact with Germany.

By far the most talented of the early recruits was Dusko Popov – Agent Skoot – the libidinous Serb playboy, who was not only proving good at the game, but slightly too good to be true. First one side, and then the other, trusted him, and then began to wonder whether they should. The first to raise serious doubts was William (Billy) Luke, the MI5 case officer assigned to handle him. An industrialist from Glasgow who owned a linen thread company, Luke was not unlike Popov in character, with a roving eye and a taste for the high life – which was exactly why Tar Robertson had chosen him for the job. He could match Popov drink for drink, and almost girl for girl. But Billy

PRIVATE COLLECTION

Billy Luke

Luke was worried: 'I cannot help regarding him with a good deal of suspicion. I just have the general feeling that he may be a most accomplished liar.' Had Popov lied to MI5? Might he be a plant?

After a month in Lisbon, Popov flew back to London, where he was subjected to a second interrogation even more penetrating than the first. Popov told Robertson and Luke that he had been warmly welcomed at Lisbon's Portela airport by von Karsthoff himself. Back at the Villa Toki-Ana, he had recited his rehearsed story in detail, describing the meeting with Ewen Montagu and the snippets of information he had supposedly gleaned. Von Karsthoff had then flown to Paris to report to his Abwehr superiors, and returned with the verdict that although they were 'not very impressed and thought the answers too general', they felt Popov would make an excellent agent. There was no hint of suspicion. Indeed, they seemed to have 'blind confidence' in 'Agent Ivan', and wanted him dispatched back to England to gather more intelligence as soon as possible. Von Karsthoff had issued Popov with fresh secret ink, and a lengthy new questionnaire, covering a vast array of subjects, including morale, military matters and politics. 'You'll soon want to know what Churchill had for dinner,' Popov remarked.

The Abwehr 'expected much from his second visit', von Karsthoff observed. Great rewards would be his if Popov worked hard and improved the quality of his information. He hinted at a possible mission to the United States. Popov had happily spent the remaining weeks in Lisbon, wining and dining at von Karsthoff's expense, establishing business contacts, and conducting an affair with a divorced French marquise. Popov was certain: the trip to Lisbon had been a resounding success.

The amusements laid on for Popov the previous Christmas had given him a taste of London's wartime highlife, and he was a little disappointed to find he was now expected to make his own entertainment. 'London is rather a dull place,' he wrote to Johnny Jebsen, in secret ink. 'Most of the nice girls have gone to the country and whisky is 16 shillings a bottle. That would make you very unhappy.' Popov did not demand to be paid – the Germans were already rewarding him handsomely – but as MI5 would soon discover, he did expect to be provided with what he considered the necessities of life: namely, wine, women and song. Especially women. Tar Robertson was a man of the world, but even he was mildly taken aback when Popov 'hinted that a little high-class feminine society would be most acceptable'. Robertson had never been asked to act as a procurer before, but he knew where to find an expert. Sergeant Lewis of the Metropolitan Police Vice Squad was asked for 'suggestions as to possible female acquaintances who might be used as agents'. MI5 was not looking for a prostitute, Tar insisted, but 'a woman purely and simply to entertain Skoot and keep him out of mischief, at the same time to keep us informed of the various curious associations which he is making in this country'. Lewis said he had a candidate in mind.

Popov's MI5 file contains a number of amorous notes sent to Popov from 'Gwennie', who was married to 'Charles' and worked, during daylight hours, for the Red Cross. (A typical example reads: 'I won't be able to see you tomorrow after all as Charles is unexpectedly coming to London!! He won't be here for long so I'll ring you as soon as I can. I'm so sorry as I was ready for you! Love Gwennie.') She was almost certainly an MI5 plant; Popov almost certainly knew it, and he certainly did not mind. Gwennie's full name has been carefully expunged from the record. She remains one more unsung heroine, performing sterling, though unconventional, wartime service for her country.

Von Karsthoff's new questionnaire indicated significant German interest in Scotland's coastal defences, and so it was decided that Billy Luke would take Popov on a tour of his homeland: that way Popov could accurately describe to von Karsthoff what he had seen, while being steered away from things he should not see. It would also be an opportunity for

Luke to test Popov's honesty, and show him a good time. Just how a good a time Popov was having could be measured by the colour of his face. 'Complexion depends on previous night's activity,' Tar Robertson noted dryly. 'If the night has been a good one, from his point of view, the complexion is rather white and blotchy.'

Their tour of the north turned into an extended pub crawl, the days spent among 'typical Scottish scenery' and the nights 'filled with jovial entertainment in congenial company'. They visited Loch Lomond and Gareloch, stopping for regular refreshments, and then headed to Edinburgh. Popov later recalled: 'There was a law that existed at that time that you couldn't have a drink unless you had travelled five miles and so my case officer, being a true Scotsman, interpreted this as meaning that you *had* to stop and have a drink every five miles.' In Edinburgh they stayed at the Central Hotel, drank at the American Bar and the Piccadilly Club, and dined at the Malmaison and the Mirabel. Popov was plainly not spying for Germany, Luke reported, since 'he made no effort to obtain information of any kind, nor did he ask any questions which could be connected with espionage'. But in the course of their evening pleasures, Popov did drop one particularly interesting hint, about his friend Johnny Jebsen: 'He did not think it would be difficult to persuade Jebsen that he is fighting on the wrong side. Jebsen is at heart pro-British.' Popov even suggested he might be able to recruit for MI5 the man who had recruited him to German intelligence, 'especially if he could meet him in Madrid, provide him with vivacious and beautiful feminine society and lose money to him at poker'. Here was a tempting prize: a member of the Abwehr who might be lured into the Double Cross pack. 'It may be desirable to enlarge on this theme,' wrote Luke.

After three days of carousing and sightseeing, Luke returned to London, white and blotchy, impressed by Popov's stamina, and fully reassured that he was not, after all, playing a triple game. 'He is quite definitely working for us and not the

Germans,' wrote Luke. 'Clever, versatile and firm of purpose, he has personality and charm and would feel at home in society circles in any European or American capital, being much the usual type of international playboy. He misses no opportunity of disparaging the Germans and the Nazi leaders and has a great hatred of Goebbels, a whole-hearted admiration and respect for the English and is convinced that Great Britain will win the war.' His prodigious womanising might eventually be a problem, Luke predicted: 'He is fond of the society of attractive women, who are apparently plentiful in Dubrovnik, where it seems that virtue is at a discount. His amorous exploits would provide material for Maurice de Kobra' – the French erotic novelist. But Luke was now certain that Popov was dependable, and ready to risk his life again by returning to Lisbon: 'Skoot is an ingenious, cheerful and amusing companion of whose sincerity and loyalty I, personally, am satisfied.' Unknown to Popov, his older brother Ivo, a doctor in Belgrade, had also approached MI6 with an offer to spy against the Germans: the Popov family was firmly on side.

Reassured, Tar set about 'building up' Popov with some first-class chicken-feed, verifiable but harmless answers to his questionnaire that would convince his Abwehr handler that he was, indeed, the efficient and energetic spy he seemed to be. Von Karsthoff had suggested that Popov should recruit some sub-agents, should he find anyone suitable. MI5 obliged: the first was Dickie Metcalfe, a former army intelligence officer. To von Karsthoff, Metcalfe would be portrayed as a disgruntled, broken-down gambler working for an arms dealer, who had been cashiered for passing fake cheques and was prepared to spy on his former colleagues because 'he hates them all'. The real Metcalfe was portly (he was given the codename 'Balloon'). A second sub-agent was lined up in the more svelte form of Friedl Gaertner, a thirty-four-year-old Austrian cabaret singer, well connected in London society, who had already done work for MI5. Her father had been a member of the Nazi party so it was hoped that, when the Germans came to check up on her, she would be considered reliable. Gaertner was a 'link with people of a high state of society in this country' and therefore 'in a position to get good information from indiscretions of well-placed friends in government and diplomatic circles'. She was given the codename 'Gelatine' because the B1A men thought she was a 'jolly-little-thing'. Popov also saw her that way. Inevitably, they became lovers.

Now that he was no longer considered likely to 'scoot', Popov was also awarded a new codename, more fitting to his status as the most promising of double agents. He was rechristened 'Tricycle'. This may have been, in part, a reference to Popov's insatiable appetites and his reputed but probably apocryphal taste for three-in-a-bed sex. It also recognised that the Tricycle network now consisted of one big wheel – Popov – supported by two smaller ones, Agents Balloon and Gelatine.

While Robertson was playing word games with his agent's *nom de guerre*, Popov had some fun with Tar's nickname. He had asked MI5 for help in setting up his own import-export business, which would provide good cover as well as a genuine income. 'They propose to buy and sell anything in any market,' wrote Tar, who arranged for Popov to occupy a lair of offices in Imperial House, 80 Regent Street. MI5 even produced an attractive part-time secretary to handle Popov's correspondence and mind the business. In a tip of the hat to his spymaster, Popov named the new company 'Tarlair Ltd'.

As he prepared to head back to Portugal once again, Popov was a little anxious that 'the answers we had given him to his questionnaire were lacking in detail and would jeopardise his supposed position as a good spy'. He was also suffering 'slight moral scruples about the part he was playing', simultaneously befriending and betraying von Karsthoff. Masterman offered a typically donnish and convoluted reassurance: 'The strictest moral censor, having regard to his motives, would not cavil his conduct.' Popov, whose English was not quite Oxbridge standard, surely had not a clue what he was saying. Luke spoke a simpler language, telling him 'that the work he had undertaken was extremely valuable to this country'. That conversation seemed to reassure Popov, for he penned a farewell letter to his case officer that revealed an unexpected depth of purpose in this apparently pleasure-seeking young man. 'It would be difficult for me to define the feeling I experience on leaving your brave country. I am leaving with a heart filled with hope. You, my dear Luke, are the classical example of English calm, [a] manifestation of the most powerful English weapon, "to remain human". It is this that will demolish Hitler's machine.'

On the day of Popov's departure, Luke took him to lunch at the Savoy and found him cheery, but 'somewhat tired', pale and blotchy. He had spent what he called 'an expensive evening' the night before, after an exhausting week featuring Friedl, Gwennie, the 400 Club, Coconut Grove and dinners at the Hungaria. Popov requested 'a small automatic revolver in case of need', and seemed entirely unfazed when Luke explained that this might be tricky, and possibly unwise. Popov was stepping back into extreme danger, and they both knew it: 'We could do nothing to help him if things went wrong.' Agent Tricycle sauntered off with 'a slightly rolling gait, the very reverse of military', to catch the Lisbon plane, leaving MI5 to pay his stupendous hotel bill.

Luke and Popov were birds of a feather, and Tar observed the bond growing between them with satisfaction. In the shifting, shadowy world of Double Cross, the relationship between agent and handler was fundamental: 'A case officer should be personally responsible for each agent, with his hands, as it were, on the pulse of the patient from morning until night, and with an eye on every twist and turn of the patient's mind.' David Petrie, the chief of MI5, had ordered that B Section should 'command the best talent and experience that the service possesses', but it was not easy to find people equipped to act as friend, psychologist and patient nursemaid to a group of individuals who were, almost by definition, erratic, frequently infuriating and quite possibly disloyal.

Section B1A was expanding, and what had started as an experiment was fast becoming a major enterprise. 'The running and control of double agents', wrote Masterman, 'is a very long, laborious and infinitely complicated task. A truly formidable work of coordination, preparation and crucial analysis.' Each double agent required 'the whole-time service of a case officer to control and organise him, a wireless officer to monitor and perhaps submit his messages, at least two guards, possibly an officer with a car to collect his information and probably a housekeeper to look after and feed the whole party.' The MI5 offices in St James's Street were becoming distinctly crowded. Tar Robertson sat in the first office, while the adjoining room was shared by Masterman and John Marriott, Tar's chief assistant and deputy. A solicitor in civilian life, Marriott was 'the collector of facts', a stickler for rules and economies; the dry, nit-picking counterpoint to Tar's extravagance and ebullience, who peered at the world suspiciously through bottle-top spectacles. The case officers, already five in number, sat together in the largest office, along with two filing clerks and another officer responsible for disseminating intelligence arising from the cases.

The officers, each handpicked by Robertson, were a distinctly unorthodox crew: in addition to Billy Luke, their number included Cyril Mills, a part-time circus impresario, Hugh Astor, the son of *The Times* owner Lord Astor, and two very different lawyers, Ian Wilson, methodical and withdrawn, and Christopher Harmer, witty, intuitive and glintingly clever. As shown by the effort that went into choosing codenames, the agent-runners delighted in word play, and the atmosphere at Number 58 was relaxed, and frequently hilarious. They were an extraordinarily youthful team: Tar was just thirty when war began, and Hugh Astor was just twenty-three when he joined the team. Harmer, a year younger than Tar, described B1A as a group of 'overgrown schoolboys playing games of derring-do absorbed from reading schoolboy books and adventure stories'. There was also one 'schoolgirl', although it would have taken a brave man to describe her as such.

Gisela Ashley, who went by the spy name of Susan Barton, was at this time the only woman in the section, and a most formidable intelligence operative. German-born and vigorously anti-Nazi, Gisela had left Germany in the 1920s, appalled by the rise of German fascism. She married a British man and then divorced him when he turned out to be homosexual, retained her British citizenship, joined MI5, and established a lifelong partnership with another intelligence officer, Gilbert Lennox, with whom she wrote a number of successful stage plays. 'Mrs Barton' had been a 'casual agent' for some years before the war, reporting on the German community in Britain. Her play *Third Party Risk* opened at St Martin's Theatre in 1939, shortly after she moved to The Hague under diplomatic cover to spy on the Germans. There the secretary of the German naval attaché took a shine to her, and Gisela appeared to be on the point of penetrating the German legation when disaster struck. In November 1939, two MI6 agents were lured to a rendezvous at Venlo on the Dutch border, in the belief that they were meeting an anti-Nazi officer, and were kidnapped. One of them, astonishingly, was carrying a list of British agents' names in his pocket, including, it was feared, that of Gisela Ashley. She was hurriedly recalled, and assigned to Robertson's section. Gisela's brother was by now a U-boat captain, but Mrs Barton's loyalty was never in doubt. With her 'real understanding of German and Nazi mentality', she played a vital role in B1A, and as the lone woman in a unit composed of men, she offered an important corrective to some of the more extreme chauvinism around her. Masterman barely noticed women; Marriott found the opposite sex tiresome and unpredictable; Wilson refused to allow women solicitors in his law firm. But they could not ignore Gisela Ashley. The vivacious Mrs Barton, the secretary who opened his mail and ran the Tarlair office, was Gisela Ashley, special agent, carefully placed at Popov's elbow to keep an eye on him.

Christopher Harmer would later remark: 'Thank God for Tar, I say, he gave us all our heads and encouraged us and, if we were doing something stupid, he pulled us up by tact and persuasion rather than by direction.' Tar Robertson was a 'born leader', according to Masterman, 'gifted with independent judgement', but he was also a firm believer in mixing business with pleasure. Indeed, he saw no distinction between the two, and was a devotee of the three-hour lunch. Rank counted for little: Robertson was a major, and would end the war as a lieutenant colonel, but most of the staff of B1A had no military rank at all. But beneath the public-school banter, the puns and badinage, ran deep veins of anxiety, in a community cauterised by secrecy and suffused with uncertainty. Every case officer was acutely aware that a single slip could bring the entire project crashing down, with catastrophic consequences. Most Secret Sources showed that the Germans were constantly assessing and reassessing their agents, trusting them and doubting them, and those judgements, in turn, had to be evaluated and re-evaluated by Section B1A, prompting Tar to remark: 'In this game one never knew quite how things would appear to the opposition, although one did one's best to guess.'

The Germans, he reasoned, must assume that some of their agents had been intercepted, and would surely suspect that at least some of these were working as double agents. Perhaps that suspicion could be used to advantage: if a double agent was run 'in an obviously bogus fashion', the Germans might assume general incompetence on the part of the British and therefore overlook the real double agents. Alphonse Timmerman, a Belgian ship's steward, was arrested as a spy in early 1941, but declined to cooperate. While Timmerman (codenamed 'Scruffy') languished in prison, B1A began sending secret ink letters in his name to his German handler. These contained a number of glaring errors, to indicate that Timmerman was being controlled. It was a brilliant plan, typical of the lateral thinking beloved of the Double Cross team, and it failed utterly. The Germans never spotted the deliberate mistakes, and 'seemed unable to realise that Scruffy was obviously controlled'. This unshakeable faith in their spy was confirmed by Most Secret Sources. The Scruffy case was terminated. This was a disappointment for B1A, but far more so for Alphonse Timmerman, who was executed. The Abwehr even failed to spot his death notice in *The Times*. Slowly, it began to dawn on Tar Robertson that the Abwehr really might be as gullible as they seemed. Yet Tar remained convinced that other spies must be at large in Britain, perhaps even working within MI5. And he was right.

In February 1941, Guy Liddell, the head of B Section, took on a new personal assistant. He was tall, thin, good looking and homosexual; a brilliant art historian and a linguist with all the right social connections. His name was Anthony Blunt, and he was a Soviet spy. Four years earlier, Blunt, a secret and dedicated communist, had been recruited into the NKVD (later the KGB) by Dr Arnold Deutsch, alias Otto, the cultured espionage talent spotter responsible for forging the so-called Cambridge spy ring. At the urging of his Soviet handlers, Blunt had applied to join the intelligence services, and by 1941 he was at the very heart of Britain's secret war machinery. Liddell had little need of an assistant 'since he always does all the work again himself', and Blunt soon moved on to other work within the section. He had a finger in many of the most secret pies, working on German counter-espionage, running B Section's surveillance section, and intercepting the diplomatic bags of neutral countries. Languid, erudite and whimsical, he cut a distinctive figure in the corridors of the St James's building: he quoted *Winnie-the-Pooh*, while sipping on a bottle of cod-liver oil and malt and remarking 'that's what Tiggers like for breakfast', and liked to play leapfrog in the canteen.

Despite his charm, Blunt was not universally liked, although much of the animus was coloured by hindsight. 'He was a very nice and civilised man,' recalled Dick White, Liddell's deputy;

'and he betrayed us all.' Tar Robertson disliked Blunt intensely, but his attitude sprang not from any doubts about his loyalty but from a homophobia common to the time. 'I couldn't stick the man. One knew that he was queer and before the war one would not have countenanced letting him anywhere near the office.' Tar's distaste for Blunt's homosexuality did not stop him from discussing the most secret aspects of his work with him. In the public school parlance of the time, a gay man was said to be 'batting for the other side'; but Blunt was batting for the other side in a way that no one inside MI5 could possibly have imagined, and making a remarkable score.

Blunt first began passing secret information to his Soviet handler, Anatoli Gorsky, in January 1941, when the USSR and Germany were linked under the Molotov-Ribbentrop pact: passing military information to a power in alliance with Britain's enemy was an act of treason. Blunt would continue to feed secrets to Moscow, in vast volume, for the rest of the war. The Soviets gave him the codename 'Tony', the only example of a wartime codename that was actually an agent's real name – either a clever double bluff, or amazingly stupid. Blunt met his handler once a week to hand over documents, both originals and copies. He memorised vast amounts of material, consulted the MI5 archive to answer Moscow's special requests, and spent his lunch hour rummaging through the desks of colleagues. He passed on personal files, operational information, intelligence summaries, Bletchley Park intercepts, diplomatic wireless traffic, and details of MI5 tradecraft including surveillance and interrogation techniques. Seldom has an intelligence organisation been so comprehensively penetrated. 'Tony is a thorough, conscientious, efficient agent,' his Russian handler reported to Moscow. 'He tries to fulfil all of our tasks in time and as conscientiously as possible.' Britain and the Soviet Union would become allies against Hitler, but Blunt's torrential leakage of information to Moscow still represented the single gravest threat to the Double Cross operation. If Soviet intelligence was penetrated by the Germans, then the information he was passing to Moscow would end up in Berlin. Over the next four years, Blunt would hand the Soviets a staggering total of 1,771 documents.

But not for an instant did the Double Cross team suspect the double agent in their midst.

Garbo Takes the Stage

In the winter of 1941, the Bletchley Park team decoding Abwehr wireless traffic between Madrid and Berlin made a most alarming discovery. Tar Robertson's fears, it seemed, were justified: the Germans did indeed have an agent active in Britain, writing secret missives to a controller in Madrid. His codename was Agent Arabel. He seemed to be well-informed, energetic and resourceful, and had recruited at least two sub-agents. Most Secret Sources revealed that Berlin was delighted with his work.

The implications were potentially catastrophic. This mysterious Arabel was in a position to contradict information supplied by the Double Cross agents, in which case 'the duplicity of all MI5's double agents might be revealed'. An uncontrolled agent, particularly one as good as this, could not only unravel the network in Britain, but expose the agents, most notably Popov, to mortal danger. 'Who was this Arabel and how had he got into the country? Where had he sprung from? Where was he getting all this information from?'

The task of analysing intercepted traffic for counter-espionage purposes fell to B1B section of MI5, known as 'Special Research', headed by Herbert Lionel Adolphus Hart, a young Jewish lawyer who would go on to become Professor of Jurisprudence at Oxford. The more H. L. A. Hart and his team pored over the Arabel traffic, the stranger it appeared. His fabulously drawn-out messages appeared to be written by someone suffering from chronic verbal incontinence. But more than that, the information supplied by Arabel was frequently, and sometimes hilariously, wrong.

Arabel reported, for example, that the people of Liverpool indulged in 'drunken orgies and slack morals at amusement centres'. He appeared to believe that the summer heat was so intense in London that the diplomatic corps decamped *en masse* to Brighton for the summer months. He reported major naval manoeuvres on Lake Windermere (which is landlocked), involving an American-made amphibious tank (which had not been invented). He provided details of unreal army regiments, and even provoked the enemy into attempting to intercept a convoy, sailing from Malta, that did not exist. Arabel was submitting meticulous monthly expenses to Berlin, but in a most curious form. He claimed, for example, to have visited Glasgow by train, at a cost of '87 shillings and 10 pence' (this should have been rendered as £4 7s 10d). Britain's pre-decimal currency was confusing, but not so baffling that someone living in the country would not have grasped it after nine months. Such errors escaped the notice of the Abwehr, but the 'very wild messages' being relayed through Madrid presented MI5 with a peculiar riddle: this rogue spy was eccentric and innumerate, or a fraud, or mad.

In Lisbon, former chicken farmer Juan Pujol, invulnerable to rejection, had continued to pester the British to recruit him. Despite producing evidence to show he was now in the employ of the Germans, he was repeatedly turned down. His wife, Aracelli, his accomplice from the start, took up the cause and approached the American naval attaché in Lisbon, who contacted his opposite number in the British Embassy, who duly (but very slowly) sent a report to London. Finally, MI6 twigged that the German agent sending the bogus messages must be Juan Pujol García, the Spaniard who had repeatedly approached them in Lisbon. In the ancient British tradition of pointless inter-departmental rivalry, MI6 (responsible for intelligence overseas) still did not inform MI5 (responsible for counter-espionage in the UK) of Pujol's existence. Only a chance conversation between Tar Robertson and an MI6 officer from Lisbon alerted B1A to what was going on. Even then, MI6 was unwilling to allow Pujol to join the Double Cross team. 'I do not see why I should get agents and have them pinched by you,' was, according to Guy Liddell, the attitude taken by MI6's head of counter-intelligence. 'The whole thing is so narrow and petty that it really makes me quite furious,' wrote Liddell.

A 'walk-in', in spy jargon, is an informant or agent who, without prompting, contacts an intelligence organisation with an offer of information. Pujol had walked in to the British time after time, and then, when told he was not wanted, walked out again. Forced to rely on secondary sources and a first-rate imagination, he was in constant danger of exposure. His guide book, for example, compared Brighton to the Spanish town of San Sebastián. Since diplomats escaped the summer heat of Madrid by moving to San Sebastián, Pujol logically, and wrongly, assumed that the same must be true of Brighton. It was, MI5 observed, 'a miracle that he had survived so long'.

The squabble over control of Pujol was finally won by Tar Robertson, who was delighted by this inventive new addition to his team. The Catalan was smuggled out of Lisbon on a steamer to Gibraltar, and then flown by military aircraft to Plymouth, arriving on 24 April 1942. After two weeks of interrogation, MI5 declared that, despite his 'inexhaustibly fertile imagination', he was telling the truth. The Twenty Committee initially wondered whether he might be a plant, but evidence from Most Secret Sources (which MI6 now, reluctantly, agreed to share in full with the Double Cross team) proved the truth of his story beyond doubt. Pujol's wife and young son were brought out of Lisbon, and the family was reunited in a safe house at 35 Crespigny Road, Hendon, in the north London suburbs. Pujol was provided with a housekeeper, and a cover job translating for the BBC. Most importantly, he acquired a case officer.

Once again, Tar's choice was inspired. Tomás 'Tommy' Harris was a thirty-four-year-old half-Spanish artist, whose imagination was as vivid as Pujol's, but tempered by solid common sense. The son of a rich Mayfair art dealer, Harris moved in bohemian circles, and was friendly with the trio of Soviet moles, Kim Philby, Anthony Blunt and Guy Burgess, an association that would later lead to the (baseless) claim that he too had been a double agent. Of all those recruited to run double agents, Masterman considered Harris to be 'in some ways, the most remarkable'. One colleague described him thus: 'With fierce black eyes and a hawk-like nose, thick well-oiled hair slicked back from a low forehead, he looked like a casting director's ideal choice for a desert sheikh or a slinky tango lizard.' Harris and Pujol made an extraordinary double act. They spoke the same language, literally and metaphorically, and in time the combination of Harris's artistry and Pujol's flamboyant ingenuity would spin a web of deception that is as close to a thing of beauty as espionage can offer. Pujol's lexophilia had led him into spying: over the next three years, he and Harris would bombard the Germans with hundreds of thousands of words, 315 letters in secret ink, and more than 1,200 wireless messages. Pujol would clock up an innings like no other double agent. 'He played his game with masterly skill,' wrote Masterman, who dubbed him the 'Bradman' of the Double Cross team, after the Australian cricketer Donald Bradman, the greatest batsman of all time.

MI6 had given Pujol the codename 'Bovril', after the thick, salty meat extract which, like Marmite, appeals only to British palates, and only to some of those. It was possibly intended as a compliment, since Bovril was seen as a 'war food' that had sustained soldiers in the trenches during the previous war. MI5 changed his codename, partly to make a point to MI6, and partly because, after his dramatic work of subterfuge in Lisbon, he deserved something grander, more fitting to 'the best actor in the world' of spying. Juan Pujol García became Agent Garbo.

★

Where Garbo had been secretly smuggled to London from Lisbon, Tricycle openly shuttled back and forth between the two capitals, ostensibly as director of Tarlair Ltd, but in reality building up his credentials with both his German and British spymasters. The British authorities furnished the necessary paperwork for his 'mysterious business deals', while noting: 'We are going in very deep with Popov'. Seats on civilian flights between Lisbon and London were in hot demand, but space was always made for Popov, creating another source of concern. 'In time of war only diplomats, journalists and spies can travel about freely, and everyone knows Tricycle does not come into the first two categories.' Popov was confident von Karsthoff suspected nothing, but Luke was not so sure. 'The Germans may know he is doubling, but may consider that they get more information by letting him continue doing so than they would if he disappeared. I am not suggesting that Tricycle is aware that they know he is doubling.' Dusko Popov might be an unwitting pawn in a clever German bluff.

From Lisbon, Popov kept MI5 fully updated on his love life, which now incorporated Maria Elera, the twenty-two-year-old Brazilian journalist whose home in Lisbon had been supplied by von Karsthoff as the cover address for sending secret letters. Popov sent back photographs of Maria posing in sultry fashion on the steps of an aeroplane. In his file, these are labelled: 'His latest girlfriend'. But he did not neglect Gwennie: 'Missing you terribly darling, I adore you, hope to be back soon.' Was it possible, MI5 wondered, that someone so pathologically faithless in his romantic life could be loyal to one cause?

By the summer of 1941, Popov had passed over to the Germans vast swathes of information, some of it true, none of it harmful, and much merely confusing. He described various new military inventions: a new anti-gas battledress which the troops hated because of the smell; a silent aircraft engine; a high-velocity ammunition for machine guns; and an incendiary bomb made from a derivative of tar. His reports were garnished with snippets of political gossip, such as the news that Oswald Mosley, the interned British fascist, was 'degenerating in prison and has lost his personality'. Popov's sub-agent Dickie Metcalfe also began passing information, distinctly flavoured with the personality of a former soldier. The British infantry, Balloon reported, had been issued with a new seven-inch bayonet, 'which makes for much easier withdrawal from Huns'. MI6 was appalled by this joke: 'I wonder whether Balloon realises he is working for the Germans.'

The Double Cross 'traffic' sent to Germany was growing more sophisticated, as the Twenty Committee served up an increasingly potent cocktail of information and deception, mixing falsehood, half-truth and real, verifiable information approved by the relevant military authority. Gisela Ashley analysed incoming messages, and Tar began 'submitting to her all the traffic in its original German as a matter of routine'. It was she who first argued that the double agents should be used, not just to deceive individual spymasters, but to influence German thinking. 'We are the Double Cross section in that we send over to the Germans information which is either misleading or which we want them to have. It seems to me there is a much wider scope for such a section. Would it not be possible to push across propaganda or to give the Germans ideas that we want them to have?' The men of Double Cross tended to think exclusively in military terms, but Gisela suggested that they paint a misleading picture of Britain itself, by exaggerating anti-Jewish feeling, domestic fascism and industrial unrest: 'After all, any decent spy would naturally try to get over warnings and pointers with regard to domestic news in the country in which he is spying.'

Popov was supposed to be gathering his information from senior figures in the British establishment, so to fortify his cover story, he was introduced to some. Victor Cavendish-Bentinck, chairman of the Joint Intelligence Committee, met the young spy and wrote up his impressions. 'He is by temperament an adventurer who is very partial to the fleshpots of this world and he realises that a person of his type can enjoy the fleshpots better under democratic than totalitarian conditions.' There was some truth in this cynical assessment, but Popov was more than a mere sybarite. In lieu of payment, he hinted that he would like to be made British Consul in Dubrovnik after the war, and receive 'some sort of decoration' for his services. For all his insouciance, he was playing a deadly game, particularly after the German occupation of Yugoslavia from April 1941 left his family under direct Nazi threat. The Germans had reassured him that his relatives would be protected. 'I do not like this "protection" much,' he told Tar. 'My own life is much less important to me than that of my family.' Brave, self-indulgent, committed, venal and unfaithful, Popov was a man of the strangest honour: 'I am still satisfied that he is playing straight with us,' Luke reported to the Twenty Committee.

When in Lisbon, Popov stayed at the Palacio Hotel, gambled in the Estoril casinos, and squired one woman or another around town, often in the company of his spymaster and friend, whom he was comprehensively betraying. Ludovico von Karsthoff took his duties lightly and his pleasure seriously, and professed himself 'extremely pleased with the information provided'. Von Karsthoff rarely rose before midday, and spent much of his time in the gardens of Villa Toki-Ana, playing with his pet monkey, Simon, and his twin dachshunds, Ivan and Ivan. He had found in Popov, he believed, a man as self-indulgent as himself, who could improve his standing in the Abwehr, and perhaps make him some money on the side. One evening, over cognac, he announced that Berlin wanted Popov to go to America. German espionage operations in the US were a mess; the FBI was picking up German spies 'like whores on the Reeperbahn'. Popov should go to New York and build a spy network from scratch, just as he had done in London. That way, when the Americans finally entered the war, Germany would be ready. Popov would be paid a great deal of money.

When Popov returned to London and reported this approach, Tar Robertson was initially resistant, arguing that he was too valuable to be spared. Tricycle was running smoothly, highly respected in Berlin, and a means of direct personal contact with the enemy. But if he refused this mission, it might raise German suspicions. Popov himself was eager to go. He had never visited the United States, and New York sounded like his kind of town. If the FBI played its cards well, here was an opportunity to create an American version of Double Cross. Von Karsthoff seemed most accommodating and unsuspicious. And Johnny Jebsen, his best friend and patron, could be relied on to watch his back.

Whenever Popov returned to Lisbon, Johnny would come to meet him. Their friendship was as solid as ever, though neither could afford to be fully candid. To Popov's surprise, Jebsen revealed he had recently got married, to Eleonore Bothilde Petersen (known as Lore), an actress and the leading lady at the Frankfurt Theatre, though he still maintained a mistress in Paris, and another in Dublin. Jebsen seemed able to travel freely, but his activities, as both a businessman and a freelance spy, were deeply mysterious: he told Popov he had recently visited Finland, Sweden, Greece, Persia, and the coast of Italy to draw up a report on Italian defences for Japanese intelligence – Japan was not yet in the war, but Tokyo's secret interest in coastal defences would take on an ominous significance after Pearl Harbor.

Jebsen was supposed to be recruiting spies, but he happily admitted that the enrolment of Popov was his only success to date 'in this business'. He was clearly a figure of some importance within German intelligence. When the conversation shifted to one Professor Miller, a teacher and Nazi at Freiburg they had both disliked, Johnny remarked, half-casually: 'I am not cruel enough, but now I am in a position to get rid of anyone I hate. If I want to get rid of that man all I have to do is say that Professor Miller said this and that, and they will kill him at once, without question.' Then he added: 'If there is anyone you particularly want to have set free I might be able to arrange it.'

The situation in Germany was deteriorating, Jebsen reported. Aircraft production was down; food was becoming scarce and even clothing was in short supply. The dapper Jebsen, still styling himself as Anthony Eden, was having trouble maintaining his wardrobe: 'I would be willing to pay £600 for a suit of English clothes, but you cannot get them,' he complained. Even more intriguing was Jebsen's description of the in-fighting between factions within German intelligence, some of which were secretly opposed to Hitler. The turf war between the Abwehr and the SD (Sicherheitsdienst, the intelligence agency of the SS and the Nazi party) was particularly venomous, and getting worse. 'They are like cat and dog with each other,' Johnny observed.

This sort of information was intelligence gold dust, which made Jebsen's remarks either extraordinarily indiscreet, or entirely calculating. He made no secret of his disdain for Hitler, and dropped hints that he had fallen foul of some powerful people who disapproved of his louche lifestyle. 'Whenever I go to Germany, I can never be sure whether I will get out alive,' he said. Jebsen seemed thinner and more ravaged than before. His limp was worse, and his teeth stained brown from the cigarettes he smoked in a never-ending stream. Jebsen had good cause to fear returning to Germany, though he did not yet divulge the real reason to Popov. The Gestapo were after him. More than a year earlier he had been approached by one Heinz Jost, a high-ranking official in the SD, who said he had some forged British bank notes which he wished to exchange for dollars. Jebsen cautiously observed that the Reichsbank had 'advised it was contrary to international law to forge currency'. There the matter rested for a while. When Jost reappeared with bundles of £5 and £10 notes, Jebsen was told (or chose to believe) that this was genuine British currency, seized in Paris. Through a contact named Avramedes at the Bank of Greece in Switzerland, he began exchanging the notes for dollars, passing the bulk to Jost and keeping a substantial commission for himself. Some senior Gestapo officers also began passing him British cash to exchange. For nine months the arrangement had proved most satisfactory, as larger and larger amounts passed through Jebsen's hands.

Jebsen spent his profits on his wife, his mistresses, himself, and his favourite novelist – for some of the ill-gotten gains ended up in the hands of P. G. Wodehouse. The British writer had remained in France at the outbreak of war, and was duly interned, as an enemy alien, in Upper Silesia ('If this is Upper Silesia, one wonders what must Lower Silesia be like . . .?' he wrote). Released in June 1941, just before the age of sixty under the terms of the Geneva Convention (he was playing a game of cricket in camp when he heard he was to be freed), Wodehouse and his wife Ethel eventually took up residence in occupied Paris, but since the royalties from his books were blocked, they were extremely short of funds. Jebsen gave money to his old friend. After his release, Wodehouse had made a series of whimsical and deeply foolish radio broadcasts through the German propaganda service, in the naive belief that he would be admired for keeping a 'stiff upper lip' during his internment. Instead, he became a hate-figure in Britain, accused of collaborating with the Germans. It can only be imagined what Wodehouse's critics would have said had they known that this comic genius was being bankrolled by a German spy through an illegal currency scam involving the Gestapo, the Nazi security service and a fortune in forged British banknotes.

The forgery fiddle worked well for nine months, and then dramatically unravelled. A Swiss bank spotted the fakes, and Jebsen's Greek middleman refused to deal in them any more. Jebsen would later claim that he had honestly believed the notes were legal tender, and when he found out about the counterfeiting 'he did all he could to stop it', by reporting the matter to his superiors. More likely, he had known all along that he was dealing in duds, and cut his losses when he discovered the fiddle had been found out. In the ensuing row, Heinz Jost was dismissed from his comfortable post in the SD's foreign intelligence department and sent to the Eastern Front where he was placed in command of Einsatzgruppe A, the death squad responsible for killing thousands of Jews. Jost was now Jebsen's sworn enemy, whose friends in the Nazi hierarchy were determined 'to take revenge on his behalf'. Jebsen also had allies, most notably Canaris, the Abwehr chief. He confided to Popov that he had set up a crude form of insurance policy: 'I know too much about the dirty things that happen. I have got papers in a bank abroad, and if the bank does not receive a cable from me on this or that day, they will send the papers to a publisher.'

Jebsen's anti-Nazi remarks, and his willingness to discuss the most secret aspects of German intelligence, could only mean one thing: Jebsen knew Popov was working for British intelligence, and that the secret information he was supplying so casually would be passed straight back to London, as indeed it was. Popov was convinced his old friend knew what he was up to, a conviction that was strengthened when Jebsen observed: 'If you are caught by the British, you can tell them that I will come over to the British side and work in whatever way I can.' Jebsen was no more a loyal Abwehr officer than Popov was a genuine German agent. Each was lying to the other, and both knew they were being lied to. Theirs was a curious dance of deception, in which neither could afford to admit the truth.

Popov again urged MI5 to approach Johnny Jebsen in a neutral country, and recruit him. 'He is very pro-British and I think if he was sure he would be safe he would come over here. At heart he is anti-Nazi and he is always in difficulties with his superiors owing to his extravagant habits.' If Jebsen was smuggled to Britain, Popov urged, he would reveal everything he knew, and could then be 'placed in honourable retirement at some resort'.

Billy Luke was doubtful. 'I am not at all sure we could gain very much by having him here as he seems very much of the playboy type.' MI6 was also unconvinced by Popov's character reference for his friend, and 'not as confident as he is that Jebsen is anti-Nazi'. It would be better to keep an eye on Jebsen, and wait to see what else he might reveal.

Like all start-ups experiencing rapid expansion, a flood of new employees and increasing overheads, the Double Cross operation faced cash-flow problems. No double agent was cheap to run; those with extravagant tastes, like Dusko Popov, were fantastically expensive. But the Abwehr's money problems were even more acute. MI5 had to ensure that the Abwehr found a way to pay its spies, otherwise it would soon stop believing in them: if a spy continues to work without getting paid, then someone else must be paying him. The spies sent to Britain were always short of cash. The Abwehr attempted to get money to their agents in a variety of ways, including air drops, but with little success.

Knowing this, B1A had the double agents make ever more pressing demands for cash. Wulf Schmidt (Agent Tate) kept up a steady litany of complaint in what Masterman called his 'virile telegraphese': 'I am beginning to think you are full of shit,' he told his Hamburg controller, when the latter failed to supply funds. 'I shit on Germany and its whole fucking secret service.' Tate was finally told to wait in Victoria station, follow a Japanese man carrying a copy of *The Times* onto a double-decker bus, and then pick up the newspaper when he left it on the seat. The entire episode was covertly photographed by MI5. It yielded £200 in £1 notes, and the identity of a Japanese diplomat, assistant naval attaché Mitinori Yosii, who was working for German intelligence in violation of his country's neutrality. But leaving packets of cash on buses was no way to finance an entire spy ring. The Abwehr needed a better way to get money to its agents, and MI5 needed to find a way to help it.

Only a mind as supple as that of Dusko Popov could have come up with 'Plan Midas', a way to manufacture gold. His sub-agents, Gaertner and Metcalfe, needed payment but, as Popov explained to von Karsthoff, if he entered Britain carrying large quantities of cash this would certainly raise suspicions. Why not find a middleman in London who could plausibly pretend to be passing money to German agents, in return for reimbursement by the Germans in another country? The Germans would be reassured that their agents were being properly paid at last, and MI5 could simply pocket the cash. The enemy, believing it was financing its own agents, would end up paying for the double agents.

The chosen middleman was Eric Glass, a successful and wealthy Jewish theatrical agent. Glass would pretend to be fearful of German invasion, determined to save his skin and his fortune, and prepared to transfer funds to the US by unscrupulous means. The Germans would be told that Glass was willing to hand over money to Wulf Schmidt, who could then finance other agents in Britain by leaving cash in pre-arranged places. The Germans would then reimburse Glass by transferring money to his New York bank account, which MI5 could then appropriate.

Eric Glass was a flamboyant figure, half-Austrian and half-British: 'his delight in approaching a deal, and his inventive sagacity in clinching it, were a byword in theatre and film circles'. The part offered by MI5 appealed to him, and a deal was struck. Plan Midas was put into action. Glass, however, had developed doubts. The more he thought about what he was involved in, the more terrified he became. What if the Germans rumbled the plot? Would they try to kill him? In the best theatrical tradition, Glass grandly declared he could no longer play his part, and wanted to leave the stage.

In fact, he was no longer needed, as MI5 had direct access to the New York account set up in his name. The show could go on without him. But Glass knew enough about Plan Midas to jeopardise the project. Superintendent George Leanore of Special Branch, the police unit working with MI5, was deployed to put the frighteners on the theatrical agent, a job he seems to have carried out with ugly anti-semitic relish. 'He was in a complete flat spin and scared nearly out of his life,' Leanore reported, having told Glass 'to keep his mouth shut' or face the consequence. 'I said enough to let him feel that his life depended on that. He can be trusted not to tell anyone. This trust is based on the only thing that in this case really counts – sheer fright. Sorry to appear somewhat ruthless, but we are at war and I see no reason why the fears of a little Jew should in any way deflect us from our path.'

Midas would prove to be one of the most profitable and least-known operations of the war. On the German side, the plan was approved by the Abwehr's senior financial officer, who authorised an initial transfer of £20,000. Money which the Abwehr believed was being used to finance espionage operations in the UK poured into a New York bank account in the name of Eric Glass, and from there directly into MI5's coffers. Popov took a 10 per cent cut. Von Karsthoff also took a commission. The Germans were overjoyed. 'Heartiest congratulations,' read the message sent to Wulf Schmidt when he reported the first cash handover by Glass. 'On no account spend all the money at once on drink, for that you can wait until we come. We consider ourselves invited.' The Double Cross system was now not only self-financing but profitable, to Masterman's delight: 'The actual cash supplied by the Germans to maintain their and our system between 1940 and 1945 was something in the region of £85,000' – the equivalent of more than £4.5 million today.

Popov Goes Shopping

On a hot afternoon in August 1941, Dusko Popov boarded a plane at Portela field in Lisbon, bound for the United States. He was carrying $70,000 in cash and a telegram, on which were eleven microdots, barely visible to the naked eye, the latest in German espionage technology. Enlarged under a powerful microscope, these tiny specks would reveal themselves to be photographs of a new set of questionnaires drawn up by von Karsthoff. Recruited to spy on the British, Popov had spied on the Germans and now, in yet another twist, he was being sent by the Germans to spy on the Americans, with British approval.

Popov's mission for MI5 was to create an American counterpart to Double Cross by building up a network of fake double agents. MI5 had already sent the FBI a glowing character reference: 'Popov is a clever, attractive and courageous young man of whose sincerity and loyalty we are satisfied. He has an excellent brain, but dislikes work. He is fond of women, and yachting is his principal pastime. He has personality and charm and would be at home in society anywhere. He has refused payment from us of any kind, as he has received adequate payment from the German secret service and we are hoping that this happy state of affairs will continue.' Tar Robertson had been reluctant to see Popov go west. 'For the moment we can spare you,' he said, but 'we shall probably ask you to come back in the not-too-distant future.' Tar knew the opportunity to replicate the Double Cross system stateside was too good to pass up. Popov's American mission should have been a triumph. It was an unmitigated disaster.

The problem was partly cultural. The FBI, under the dictatorial and dynamic leadership of J. Edgar Hoover, took a very different approach to counter-espionage. The foreign spy, in Hoover's mind, was just another species of criminal, to be caught, tried and then executed with maximum publicity. The bureau had achieved a breakthrough success in 1941 with the capture of no fewer than thirty-three German spies, using one of their number as bait, in what Hoover proclaimed to be the 'greatest spy round-up in US history'. With time, the FBI would come to appreciate the value of double agents, but the immediate effect of that success was to convince Hoover that the only use for a captured spy was to capture more spies. As usual, MI5 reached for a cricket analogy: 'His first innings was too easy and he imagined apparently that the Huns would not learn the lesson.' The FBI was not equipped, psychologically or practically, to run double agents. 'It is a great pity,' wrote Masterman. Dusko Popov was exactly the sort of person Hoover loathed: dissolute, extravagant, sexually voracious and foreign. As Ewen Montagu observed: 'Hoover obviously only regarded Tricycle as potential fly-paper,' useful to trap more pests, but rather disgusting to handle. Relations between Popov and his new FBI handlers started badly, and grew steadily worse.

The questionnaires in the microdots Popov had brought to the US furnished an important insight into German thinking: Popov was instructed to set up a network to gather information on atomic research, military preparations, convoys, industrial production, politics and morale. With hindsight, the most crucial part of Popov's questionnaire asked for intelligence on Pearl Harbor, the Hawaiian naval base: its anchorages, submarine port, floating docks and mine defences. Popov later claimed that he (and, for that matter, Johnny Jebsen) had realised from the start that this questionnaire pointed to a looming Japanese attack on Pearl Harbor. This is unlikely. There is nothing in Popov's file to indicate that he understood, let alone warned anyone about, the significance of the questions. Four months after Popov's arrival, the Japanese attacked, catapulting America into war. Had the Allies missed a vital tip-off that might have changed history?

Certainly some in MI5 believed so, and blamed the FBI for failing to spot the clues. 'The mistake we made was not to take the Pearl Harbor information and send it separately to Roosevelt,' Tar Robertson said many years later. 'No one ever dreamed Hoover would be such a bloody fool.' Masterman was similarly critical: 'The questionnaire indicated very clearly that in the event of the United States being at war, Pearl Harbor would be the first point to be attacked, and that plans for this attack had reached an advanced stage by August 1941.' Actually, the questionnaire showed no such thing: it did not indicate that an air assault was planned, and still less that a Japanese attack was imminent. It merely demonstrated that the Germans were acutely interested in Pearl Harbor which, given that the US Pacific Fleet was based there, was hardly surprising. The simple truth is that no one – neither Popov, Jebsen, MI5 or the FBI – saw the questionnaire as the harbinger of the attack on Pearl Harbor, until after it happened.

Popov expected to be welcomed by the FBI, just as MI5 had embraced him, but in place of Tar's clubby congeniality he found only deep suspicion. From the moment he checked into the Waldorf Astoria, Popov was put under surveillance, which the FBI's 'G-men' made little effort to disguise. Under FBI control, he began sending secret letters back to von Karsthoff in Lisbon, but the US military authorities declined to provide any genuine information to put in these. He was told he could not visit Hawaii to investigate the defences there. Popov had been instructed to establish a radio link with Lisbon and Rio de Janeiro (home to an active Abwehr spy cell), but when the FBI did finally establish a radio transmitter, based on the North

Shore of Long Island, Popov was not permitted to know what information was being sent in his name. The FBI did not go in for jocular codenames: Popov was 'Confidential Informant ND 63', an austere title that aptly reflects the bureau's chilly attitude.

Held at arm's length by the FBI, and prevented from conducting any active espionage, Popov went on a spending binge of epic proportions. Hoover was already worried that the spy's playboy habits could 'embarrass the bureau', and the scale of his expenses seemed calculated to do just that. Within a short time he had acquired an apartment on Park Avenue, a summer house in fashionable Locust Valley on Long Island, a red Buick convertible and another girlfriend, the French film star Simone Simon, whom he had met before the war. When challenged over his wild expenditure, Popov blandly insisted that he needed to maintain his cover as a wealthy roué. Among the accoutrements he considered necessary for this purpose were a butler called Brooks, a half-deaf Chinese manservant called Chen-Yen, and a team of gardeners; he had his apartment refurbished by an interior designer, and spent $12,000 on furniture, antiques and several hundred gramophone records; he drank and danced at the Stork Club, skied in Sun Valley, Idaho, and motored south for a sunny vacation in Florida. He also began an affair with an expensive Englishwoman, soon to be divorced, named Terry Richardson, and set off a fresh spasm of disapproval within the FBI when he took her on holiday, since transporting a woman across state lines for 'immoral purposes' was illegal under the ludicrous Mann Act. The FBI suspected Mrs Richardson might be a German spy, but finally concluded she was merely a 'gold-digger'.

Popov's gold supplies, however, were dwindling. He kept half the money brought from Lisbon, and swiftly spent it. The Abwehr handed over another $10,000, and he spent that too. When the Germans failed to send more money, he demanded a loan from the FBI, in order to pay his tailor, shirt-maker, florist and staff. Popov treated the FBI as his private bank and although the bureau, with extreme reluctance, began to subsidise his high-living, relations deteriorated still further. Popov's Midas Plan was bringing in a steady stream of cash, but even MI5 expressed astonishment at Popov's spending. 'His financial behaviour in the US cannot be justified,' wrote John Marriott, noting that Popov was burning through more than $5,000 a month. 'I cannot distinguish his handling of this money from embezzlement.' The man with the tricky job of reining in Popov's profligacy was Colonel Walter 'Freckles' Wren of MI6. 'Tricycle should have a good talking-to,' he was told, 'so that he should adjust his expenditure to a more reasonable basis.' It was a vain hope.

Popov was living a Gatsbyesque life, but he was far from happy. Ewen Montagu, on a visit to the US to solidify intelligence relations between the Allies, 'found him depressed and worried, with all the gaiety which exudes from him completely gone'. Popov's family was in Yugoslavia, under Nazi rule, and by handling him so ineptly and undermining his credibility with the Germans, the FBI was placing them in extreme danger. 'Hoover's management of Tricycle could not have been more calculated to blow him if Hoover had sat down to devise and plan a method of doing so,' said Montagu, who tried to lift Popov's spirits by telling him 'that there were people who still believed in him, that we were ready to go to real trouble to keep him "alive" as a double agent [and] continue the work against the Nazis for which he had risked his life'.

Popov's fear that the Germans would lose faith in him was fully justified. In March 1942, Bletchley Park deciphered an Abwehr message revealing just how far Popov had fallen in German estimation. 'Berlin suspected Tricycle to be working for both sides and recommended extreme caution when dealing with him.' Popov was not told of the Germans' suspicions. Intriguingly, the intercepts also showed that 'a larger sum in dollars ought to have been paid to him' in the US, but his handlers in Lisbon had not passed it on: von Karsthoff and

Johnny Jebsen, it seemed, were skimming off funds intended
for Popov. His spymaster and friends were using him to rip off
their own bosses.

By the summer of 1942, Popov and the FBI had had enough
of each other. 'I cannot continue under this strain,' Popov
wrote. The bureau had even begun interfering in his love life –
the ultimate offence – by intercepting his telegrams to Simone
Simon. 'Tricycle suspects the evil hand of the FBI in everything,'
MI5 noted. He wanted out, and the FBI wanted him out. By
July he had racked up a debt to the FBI of $17,500, and the
bureau declared it was no longer prepared 'to maintain him
in his present state of living'. The Germans also failed to send
any more money, despite Popov's urgent appeals – yet another
indication of their waning confidence. An internal FBI report
stated: 'Popov has been totally unproductive so far as developing
any German espionage or other subversive activities in the
United States is concerned, and has been a continuous source
of annoyance in connection with his lavish expenditures . . . It
is therefore recommended that he be turned back to the British
for use by them in London.'

Tar Robertson was only too happy to bring Tricycle back
into the fold, but reintegrating him into the Double Cross
system would be tricky. The Germans were mistrustful, and
Popov would face an uphill task in regaining their trust. If he
failed to do so, then his sub-agents, and all the other connected
double agents being paid through Plan Midas, would fall under
suspicion: 'I need not repeat the importance to us of preserving
the Germans' faith in Tricycle because of his linkup with other
B1A agents,' wrote Tar. A choice was put to Popov: 'He could
end his double-agent work with our gratitude, or he could
come back via Lisbon and try to explain away his failure in
America and rehabilitate himself with his Abwehr masters.' He
chose to go back to Lisbon.

There was still the matter of Popov's debts. MI5 calculated he
had managed to spend $86,000 in just nine months, including

$26,000 on 'entertaining, social life, etc.'. Ian David Wilson, the thirty-eight-year-old London solicitor who had taken over from Billy Luke as Popov's case officer, was sent out to New York to try to extricate him from the mess, and prepare Popov for what was likely to be his toughest test so far. Wilson was an intriguing figure: with prominent ears, an awkward manner and a 'razor-keen mind', he was fiercely conventional and set in his ways: he worked in the same law firm all his life, never moved house, and avoided all forms of small talk. 'Quiet and introverted, he contributed very little to conversations.' Yet he had a truly remarkable capacity for concentration and absorbing detail. He completed *The Times* crossword, every morning, in a few minutes, never missing a clue. Happiest immersed in minutiae, he memorised every aspect of the case: he lived through Popov.

Wilson needed to find out what information Popov was supposed to have sent to the Germans, and explain where he got it; he would also need an explanation for his lack of productivity in the US, and some juicy new intelligence to convince von Karsthoff that he was still to be trusted. All of this required American cooperation, but the FBI, in Wilson's words, 'failed to produce any worthwhile information for Tricycle to take with him'. So Wilson and Popov simply invented a slew of American informants to explain 'how he had come into possession of certain information in the USA'. These fake informants were real people, including a Russian journalist named Igor Cassini, and Sol Bloom, 'a very pro-British Congressman and chairman of the House Foreign Affairs Committee', who had never exchanged a word with Popov. Hoover was outraged, and denounced the subterfuge as 'extremely objectionable'.

Wilson compiled a caustic report on the American handling of the case: 'The FBI have lost all interest in Tricycle. The FBI were either through incompetence, lack of power, lack of interest or lack of goodwill, of no assistance, and let us down badly.' Popov's debts to the bureau should be paid off, he recommended, 'to prevent any further deterioration in relations . . . in spite of the fact that the FBI have handled the case in such a way that they do not deserve to be repaid'. Tar Robertson read Ian Wilson's tirade with relish: 'It is a very outspoken document, but I do not see any object in mincing matters with such an organisation as the FBI.'

Now that he was back in the Double Cross team, Popov's old ebullience returned: after weeks of coaching by Wilson and Wren, he felt sure he could tell von Karsthoff a convincing tale. But Wilson was anxious. To repurchase German confidence, Popov would have to describe information he had never obtained from people he had never met. 'Tricycle himself showed great confidence in his ability to survive his meetings in Lisbon. His story is thin and cannot expect to survive searching interrogation, but he is satisfied that his personal relations with Johnny Jebsen and von Karsthoff will pull him through.'

Thrusting Popov back into suspicious German hands after the American debacle was Robertson's biggest gamble so far, and he knew it: 'His chances were nothing like even money. The odds must be at least two to one that he was blown. And, if he was, it was pretty certain that he would be tortured to squeeze him dry of information about our system, and there was an equally probable death sentence awaiting him at the end.'

Dusko Popov flew from New York on 12 October 1942, leaving behind 'an enormous number of gramophone records', a number of broken hearts and a stack of bills that would follow him, unpaid, for the rest of the war. Montagu thought Tricycle's decision to return to Lisbon was 'the greatest instance of cold-blooded courage that I have ever been in contact with'.

Before leaving New York, Popov had sent a telegram alerting von Karsthoff that he would be arriving in Lisbon on 14 October 1942. 'Will telephone office on arrival. Hope Johnny will be waiting for me.'

Instead he was welcomed back to Portugal by a smiling von Karsthoff, along with a clean-shaven, dark-haired man Popov had never met before, who gave his name as Kammler. Popov described this new officer, a lieutenant, as about twenty-eight years old, 'stiff in manner', and speaking English 'as if he learned it from a book'. His real name was Otto Kurrer: an officer in the Abwehr espionage division, he was there to take part in the debriefing of the prodigal agent. Their manner was friendly, but businesslike, and Popov could sense he was being regarded with 'some suspicion'.

Settled in the large salon of a comfortable apartment on the Avenida de Berna, von Karsthoff came straight to the point, and presented Popov with what sounded oddly like a school report. His work in England, before leaving for the US, had been 'very good'; in America it had initially been 'excellent'; then 'medium'; and then, for the last three months, 'terribly bad'. Von Karsthoff eyed him keenly: 'Now you know what Berlin thinks of you.'

Popov responded by telling von Karsthoff what he thought of Berlin. He delivered a furious broadside against the Abwehr for sending him to the US, under-supported and under-funded. He was now deeply in debt, he said, and it was all the fault of his German handlers. 'You send me there with no help whatsoever, no contacts, a few miserable dollars, and you expect me to produce results in no time . . .' It was a bravura performance, and put von Karsthoff on the defensive: 'We did all we could. It was Berlin's fault.' The Abwehr man seemed uninterested in the meagre haul of intelligence Popov had brought back from the US; he did not try to pick holes in his story; he did not even discuss the little intelligence he *had* sent. Von Karsthoff, it seemed, was not only willing to believe Popov's story, but unwilling to ask him anything that might make it harder for him to do so. The reasons for his eagerness were personal, professional and financial. Popov had long assumed that his German handlers were skimming off money that should have been passed to him. Kammler observed darkly that Popov had not received adequate funds in the US because Jebsen had 'embezzled' at least $10,000. They were all making money, illicitly, from Popov's spy salary: von Karsthoff, Jebsen, and even, it seemed, this man Kammler.

'Berlin are stupid fellows,' Kammler remarked. 'They are sitting at desks and don't realise the difficulties of being without money. Please work hard in the future or we shall all have trouble here. And you'll see we will be able to give you big bonuses.' Popov had become more than a spy in the eyes of his German handlers. He was a valuable business, and thus in a powerful bargaining position since von Karsthoff and Kammler were clearly terrified that he 'might make a scene with Berlin'. He now demanded full payment of all the money he claimed to be owed. The financial wrangling continued for days, but Popov had the upper hand. 'Kammler begged him not to make difficulties over money arrangements because such difficulties might cause Kammler to be removed from Lisbon and sent to the Russian front.' If Popov continued as before, they would all make money, and Berlin would be pleased. If he did not, then they were all in deep trouble. They could not afford for him to fail.

He had absolute faith in his own powers of persuasion and seduction, and rightly so, for three days later, London intercepted a message sent by von Karsthoff to Berlin, in which he reported that Popov had been subjected to 'severe' interrogation and no evidence had been found that he was engaging in 'double work': Popov was in the clear. 'Lisbon seem to have satisfied themselves that Tricycle was not double-crossing them,' Tar reported.

Popov spent a week in Lisbon arguing over money, until a deal was finally struck: the Germans would pay him $25,000, plus 6,000 Portuguese escudos, and a salary of $2,500 a month, depending on his performance. From Popov's standpoint, this was a remarkable bargain: a lump sum to repay debts he had not incurred, for services to the Third Reich he had not rendered, and a future stipend to continue betraying the Germans and supplying information that was either useless or false. The origin of the money, and Jebsen's role in the deal, were unclear, but Popov's old friend was somewhere in the background, pulling strings and lining his pockets.

Following the script laid out by Wilson, Popov declared that he intended to return to London and continue spying as before. 'Berlin wants information of direct use for military purposes,' von Karsthoff told Popov. Reports on public morale, industrial output and political gossip were all very well, but 'we are not so interested in people's feelings, not in production, but interested in purely military facts'. Specifically, Berlin wanted advance warning of Allied military plans. Now that America had entered the war, there would surely be a counter-attack to try to roll back the German occupation, in North Africa, France, Norway, or somewhere else. 'What about invasion?' von Karsthoff demanded. 'Where will it be? See what kind of training and instruction the army has. Are they learning any languages? What kind of beaches are they training on?' Popov should furnish as much information on military preparations as possible, and they would make their own deductions.

Popov landed back in Britain with this new mission, $25,000 in cash in his pocket, and five matches impregnated with a new type of secret ink sewn into the shoulder pads of his overcoat. A room was waiting for him in Claridge's Hotel, but Tar Robertson asked Jock Horsfall, the MI5 chauffeur, to drive Popov directly from the airport to his own house in west London, 'so that I can satisfy my curiosity and at the same time welcome him home'.

Popov seemed 'voluble and rather confused', expressing 'a great deal of vague feelings of grievance with regard to his American visit'. But there was no doubt whose side he was on. 'He is entirely friendly towards us and I have no doubt about his loyalty.' At a debriefing session the next morning, attended by Robertson, Masterman and Wilson, Popov searched through his pockets for the cash given to him by von Karsthoff, finally located the wads in his trenchcoat pocket, and dumped it all on the table. Masterman was stunned at his 'extraordinary casualness about money', and observed: 'It is quite probable that he would have lost or been robbed of this large sum of money without worrying very much about it.' Popov explained, without rancour, that his German handlers were on the fiddle, 'both by making profit on exchange and taking a considerable rake-off from money from Berlin'. He seemed to regard this as normal business practice. 'I was cheated by Johnny, I was cheated by von Karsthoff,' he said. 'I think Kammler earned a lot of money from the exchange.' Once again he urged MI5 to recruit Jebsen, whom he described as 'very anti-Nazi'. If properly handled, 'Johnny would give him a great deal of information'.

He was adamant that any German doubts about his loyalty had been dispelled: 'Any suspicion against me was cleared up on the first day.' Popov's best defence was the sheer force of his personality, Tar reflected, his uncanny 'ability to impose himself and his views on the Germans when personal contact could be made'. Von Karsthoff was 'not in any way suspicious', and had promised to send a letter to the Savoy Hotel with three microdots containing questionnaires for his new mission. The MI5 team was deeply relieved: 'Von Karsthoff has defended Tricycle as his agent and made a good deal out of the business.' Here were fine opportunities for blackmail and manipulation. But it was the German hunger for information about Allied invasion plans that set Tar thinking. Von Karsthoff wanted raw military intelligence, as much as possible, and urgently. 'We may be able to draw our own conclusions,' he had told Popov.

It was a revealing observation, for it suggested that with careful planning, the Germans might be guided into drawing, not their own conclusions, but the conclusions the Double Cross team wanted them to draw.

8

The Great Game

Roman Czerniawski met Hugo Bleicher, his German handler, in the lavatory of the Brasserie Georges in Lyon, on 15 August 1942. In the intervening weeks, the Polish spy had learned how to construct a wireless transmitter, memorised his code, and consumed food 'in enormous quantities' at a Chinese restaurant next door to the safe house on Rue Dufrenoy, rebuilding his strength after months in prison. Concealed in the heels of his shoes were two transmitting crystals. Czerniawski had slipped across the border into Vichy France, and made contact, as instructed by Colonel Oscar Reile, with Polish intelligence, explaining that he had escaped and now needed to get to Britain, quickly. He revealed nothing about his deal with the Colonel. The Polish secret service contacted MI6, and plans to evacuate the leader of the defunct Interallié network, who had miraculously evaded the clutches of the Germans, were set in motion: he would be smuggled into neutral Spain, using the underground route for escaping POWs, and then put on the next flight to Britain.

Bleicher had been shadowing him and thoroughly enjoying his 'free holiday' in southern France. He even brought along one of his French mistresses. The meeting in the Brasserie Georges was the first time they had met since Roman Czerniawski's 'escape'. Their conversation in the restaurant lavatory was brief, and quite odd.

With some embarrassment, Bleicher said that although he 'realised that any manifestation of mistrust on their part would jeopardise the affair', German bureaucratic rules required a 'written guarantee' of Czerniawski's loyalty. This was 'a mere formality'. Bleicher then handed over a piece of paper which stated, in German, that Czerniawski was 'starting to work for the National Socialist State in a military capacity, and undertaking his mission voluntarily, and if he failed in his duty the Germans would be entitled to take reprisals'. Here was a bold threat disguised as form-filling, a guarantee that if he reneged on his promises, then the people he loved would be killed. Only a state as murderous and bureaucratic as the Third Reich would require a man to sign his own family's death warrant, and consider it binding. Czerniawski signed.

The next day, Bleicher picked up a letter at the Hôtel d'Orléans. It read: 'Long Live Hitler, the Great Builder of a new Europe!' Czerniawski was on his way to Britain.

In London, Roman Czerniawski was greeted by the Polish community as a returning hero: a patriotic 'super-spy' who had defied the Germans in occupied Paris and then, astonishingly, managed to slip out of their grasp. During October 1942, he was interviewed by both British and Polish intelligence officers, and subjected to the 'most exhaustive and painstaking' interrogation. No one smelled a rat. The Polish pilot was praised for his 'great daring and initiative' in forging the Interallié network. 'He is a natural leader of men and has great organising ability,' MI5 noted. Colonel Stanislaw Gano of Polish intelligence, who had met Czerniawski in London the year before, welcomed him back with open arms. The story of his flight from German custody was 'amazing' and 'everyone was prepared to accept it as genuine'. Or almost everyone. Some found Czerniawski's account a little too heroic to be credible. A rumour began to circulate that 'there was something funny about his escape'.

Czerniawski was not the only member of the French network to reappear in Britain. Monique Deschamps ('Mosquito'), the 'tiny, vivacious and attractive' head of the Interallié's southern sector, had also escaped the Gestapo and made her way across the Channel. So, too, had Mathilde Carré. Like Czerniawski, she had agreed to work for the Germans as a double agent in Britain. Under Bleicher's instruction, she had used the captured Interallié wireless to maintain the fiction that she had escaped the round-up and was continuing her work as an Allied agent. In the spring of 1942, Bleicher had her send a message to London, asking to be evacuated as she feared she was about to be arrested. The British agreed to send a boat to collect her from the French coast. 'The plan was that in London I should get as many names as I could of agents working in France for the Allies . . . after that, the great roundup would take place. They promised me an enormous sum of money, a trip to Germany and the publication of my memoirs in the largest Nazi newspaper.' Mathilde was in thrall to her German lover. She promised to bring back for Bleicher 'a couple of pairs of shoes' from a London bootmaker. Bleicher may have hated the British, but he was partial to handmade English shoes.

Mathilde Carré was picked up by a fast British motor gun boat at Bihit point near Lannion, on the Brittany coast (Bleicher having ensured that no German patrol would be on hand to interrupt the rendezvous). In London she was interrogated by a uniformed British officer with impeccable manners and a steely look. 'Anglo-Saxon hypocrisy is so often preferable to Gallic excitability,' she later reflected. Once again, she broke almost immediately, confessing that she had been recruited as an Abwehr agent but insisting that she had always intended to betray the Germans as soon as she was on British soil. She did not, however, explain her relationship with Hugo Bleicher, or her role in the break-up of the Interallié network. The British did not quite know what to make of Mathilde Carré. She was lodged in a safe house, and kept under close surveillance.

Czerniawski's arrival in London sealed her fate. Mathilde had betrayed them all, he explained: 'Her guilt is the greater since, although she must have fully realised the extent of the catastrophe, she helped the Germans in their work.' Bleicher had doubtless put her under intense pressure, 'but there is no excuse whatever for treason and betrayal to the enemy of her colleagues, knowing that they will face the firing squad'. Czerniawski did not of course mention that he, too, had been recruited by German intelligence.

Mathilde was arrested and lodged in Aylesbury prison: she would spend the rest of the war behind bars.

Czerniawski, the decorated war hero, was given a desk job by the Polish government in exile. He moved into a flat in Brompton with Monique Deschamps, who became his lover. For the first time since the war began, Roman's life appeared to achieve a sort of calm. Then he dropped what MI5 called 'the bombshell'.

Six weeks after arriving in Britain, Czerniawski presented Colonel Stanislaw Gano of Polish intelligence with a sixty-four-page, typewritten document, written in English and entitled 'The Great Game'. It began: 'The Germans are entering the final stage of losing the game. It has become my ambition to conclude this affair in grand style . . .' Czerniawski then proceeded to describe, in detail, his recruitment by the German secret service: the conversations in his jail cell at Fresnes, the deal struck with Bleicher and Reile, the terms of his mission, and his faked escape from German custody. As proof he produced 'the wireless crystals which he had kept hidden in the heels of his shoes'. He had merely been playing a part, he said, 'carrying out a carefully worked out plan to fool the Germans'. He insisted: 'During the whole period of my "collaboration" with the Germans they did not receive from me the slightest hint which might have helped them in combating our or Allied organisations on the Continent.'

The double agent now offered to turn triple agent, pointing out that he was in a unique position to tell the German High

Command, via wireless, anything that Allied intelligence wanted to tell them. Czerniawski laid down the rules of his game: 'I shall discuss personally all data with the British, or rather with one Englishman, an officer who alone would hold the entirety of the affair in his hands and would be in charge of it . . . I would act as the expert.' No one else in Polish intelligence should know the truth about how he had really got out of France: 'The story of my escape, for the good of the cause, must continue to be regarded as true.'

This extraordinary document ended with a characteristically grandiose flourish: 'I am convinced that if an exact plan is laid down now and carried out logically and adhered to strictly, then the Great Game has all the chances of success and may yield great results. If I have acted wrong in organising the Great Game the news that I have perished in an air accident will save my family and my colleagues.'

When Colonel Gano had finished reading, he looked up, staggered, but before he could speak, in a final dramatic gesture, Czerniawski 'demanded a revolver to shoot himself, if his request were refused and he was found to have failed in his military duty'.

Gano's first reaction was shock, but his second was blind fury. Czerniawski had lied to his superior officers. He had deliberately concealed the true circumstances of his escape. He had struck a deal with the enemy, and had continued to hide the truth for weeks after arriving in Britain. He had made Gano look a fool. Czerniawski responded that he had not revealed the truth until now because he was not 'certain of the degree to which the Germans had penetrated Polish HQ in London'. The suggestion that the Polish government in exile might harbour enemy spies made Gano even angrier. He ordered Czerniawski to return to his flat and await further orders, and declared his belief (from which he never wavered) that Czerniawski was a 'sinister individual' who deserved to be shot.

Czerniawski's treatise (he called it 'his book') was passed to Tar Robertson at B1A. If Czerniawski was telling the truth, then he might be useful to the Double Cross team. If he was lying then, like Mathilde Carré, he should be locked up and, if necessary, tried and executed. The decision must be made quickly, since if Czerniawski was to demonstrate his worth to the Germans, he would need to make radio contact as soon as possible. Christopher Harmer was once again tasked with teasing out the motives of a potential double agent, and deciding his ultimate fate.

Harmer spent days interrogating Czerniawski. The resulting report is a masterpiece of psychology, a remarkable insight into the mind of a spy. Czerniawski was telling the truth, Harmer concluded, but not the whole truth, and only those parts of the truth that suited his purposes. He claimed the Abwehr had recruited him, whereas he had plainly volunteered to spy for them; he insisted he had been acting a part, but the Germans had successfully plied him with propaganda and stroked his vanity; he had come to Britain planning to see which way the winds of war were blowing, and only after assessing the situation had he decided to come clean.

'There are considerable doubts about his integrity,' wrote Harmer. 'It seems possible that he might be embarking on some form of triple cross.' But Czerniawski was reliable in one, important respect:

> His loyalty is entirely to his own country, and . . . every problem he sees is bound up with the destiny of the Polish people. He is of an intensely dramatic and egotistical nature. This may be due in some part to his size. It is necessary to avoid taking him at his own valuation. His character, sense of drama, and the feeling of self-importance which his intelligence work has given him – which makes him regard himself in some way as a sort of Joan of Arc of Poland – causes him to dramatise and overrate the part he has played.

Harmer tried to imagine what it must have been like for Czerniawski in Fresnes prison, 'a loyal and fervent Pole in a weak state, physically and mentally', and he reproduced the scene:

> As his condition gets lower, so his credibility of propaganda and ideas of grandeur become greater. Their confidence in him grows, and when he suggests that he might also act as a spy for them, they take this suggestion seriously. He himself really thinks that there may be a possibility of fixing up an arrangement between Poland and Germany.

But on reaching Britain, Harmer surmised, Czerniawski realised that his German jailers had misrepresented the political situation.

> He finds that so far from wanting collaboration, the Polish official circles here are determined to continue the fight against Germany. His health and strength and sense of judgment return, he realises that as a loyal and patriotic Pole, it is impossible for him to carry out his mission. With a dramatic gesture, therefore, he presents his book to his chief.

Czerniawski's loyalties depended entirely on what he perceived to be Poland's best interests. 'I do not think he is a spy using this story as his cover,' wrote Harmer. 'There is no evidence, nor any probability, that he has worked here to the detriment of Britain and for the benefit of her enemies.' He had already 'rendered very great service to this country', and properly handled, he could do so again:

> The Germans would have confidence in him given their hold on him. There is no reason why we should not open up his transmitter. With imagination, and with his very original mind, we might possibly confuse and deceive the Germans to a remarkable extent [but] a successful

exploitation of the opportunities is dependent on his willing cooperation.

Yet again, some senior members of B1A were unconvinced. Marriott, the stickler for rules, pointed out that it had been agreed 'we are never going to tolerate any person who has worked for our service agreeing in any circumstances to work for the Germans'. Masterman argued that 'the Germans have really lost nothing by letting him go: for they have cleaned up the whole of his organisation, and the only thing left would have been the doubtful satisfaction of executing him'. It seemed possible that the Germans had sent Czerniawski to Britain as a plant, 'knowing pretty well certainly that he would throw in his hand with us'. If so, they would know his messages were false from the outset. Were Bleicher and Oscar Reile simply using the Pole to try to find out what the British wanted the Germans to believe? 'We are not yet at all convinced as to his *bona fides*,' Guy Liddell wrote in his diary.

The dispute over Czerniawski provoked a blazing row between Masterman, representing the cautious old guard, and Christopher Harmer, the young enthusiast keen to run the Polish spy. Masterman seemed 'hell-bent on chopping him', thought Harmer, and even 'intrigued behind my back' to do so. The day before his wedding to his secretary Peggy, Harmer wrote Masterman 'one of the rudest letters I have ever sent'. They later made up. 'I loved the old boy,' wrote Harmer. 'I suppose he was only doing his job – of exercising a wise and mature restraint on the irresponsibilities of the hot-headed youngsters.' But the hothead stood his ground, insisting they should not 'throw the case away'. Tar Robertson agreed. The Abwehr radio station in Paris had been trying for weeks to make wireless contact. It was decided that Czerniawski should begin sending radio messages back to his German controllers, but only on a temporary basis 'under close supervision'. The Polish authorities, suspicious and resentful, convened a military court of inquiry, which issued a severe reprimand to Czerniawski and relegated him to a 'non-job'.

Czerniawski was delighted with the way matters had turned out. 'The NEW GAME is beginning,' he wrote to Harmer. 'The Germans lost the old one. They must lose the new one as well. In my opinion it is a difficult game, but it might yield enormous advantages, especially during the decisive moments which are drawing nigh.' More puffed up than ever, he now set out on the third lap of his extraordinary espionage career, with a new mission and a new name. As a spy in occupied France he had adopted the codename 'Walenty' (Valentine); as a spy for the Germans he had become 'Hubert'; and now, as a double agent for the Double Cross team, he was renamed once again. Henceforth he would be Agent Brutus.

The classically educated Harmer came up with this *nom de guerre*. 'Roman Czerniawski had been turned by the Germans, and then re-turned by us, so I thought "Et tu, Brute?" Of course he had carried out a very brave mission in Paris during the first year of occupation, so I thought of Brutus's final speech from *Julius Caesar* which begins "He was the noblest Roman of them all".' The words 'Et tu, Brute?' are also, of course, the most famous denunciation of treachery in literature; the words of a man who has been stabbed in the back by a friend he trusted. Harmer was convinced that Roman Czerniawski, unlike Shakespeare's famous Roman, would not betray him, but his playful choice of codename carried the unmistakable hint of anxiety.

The Flock

Agent Cyril, a potential new recruit to the Double Cross team, was not quite what MI5 had been expecting. Elvira de la Fuente Chaudoir was, Harmer later recalled, 'one of the most elegant women I had ever met'. She wore a cloche hat, and as she sat down she peeled off a pair of silk gloves, revealing 'beautifully varnished nails'. For a moment, Christopher Harmer was lost for words. 'She was really very striking.'

On her return from France, Elvira had been debriefed by MI6, which concluded her mission had been 'carried out to the best of her ability' and then handed her on to Tar Robertson with the recommendation that she be deployed as a double agent.

Harmer's task was to assess her usefulness. He introduced himself as 'Mr Palmer', while John Masterman, who sat in on the interview, called himself 'Masterson'. (Case officers used – and still use – pseudonyms as close as possible to their own names. That way, if someone happened to use their real name, the person who was not supposed to know it might assume he had misheard.) Over the next hour, Elvira told the story of her recruitment in Cannes by a German agent named 'Bibi', and the deal to furnish political and military information for £100 a month. She 'made a good impression', thought Harmer.

Tar Robertson was cautious. 'It is by no means clear that she has told us everything she knows.' Further investigation into her private life raised the possibility that she might be blackmailed over her 'Lesbian tendencies'. (For some reason, the word 'lesbian' is frequently capitalised in MI5 files: perhaps this was the result of a classical education, since the word is associated with the island of Lesbos, or perhaps the officers thought such an exotic species deserved special grammatical treatment.) She had been reprimanded before for indiscretion, and although 'she would appear to have learned wisdom, that point will have to be taken into account in considering her employment as a double agent'. Her German recruiter was also an unknown quantity. Britain's MI5 and M16 had, by now, amassed a great deal of information about German intelligence personnel. This data was entered onto punchcards and fed into a 'Hollerith Machine', an electrical tabulating apparatus originally invented to process data for the US census. Elvira's detailed description of Helmut Bleil was run through the device but 'disclosed no possible trace'. This anxious, amateur and alcoholic spy seemed to be operating semi-independently. 'We have not come across this man before.'

The most vigorous sceptic was Masterman, who did not want a woman on the team and pointed out that an indiscreet, cash-strapped 'Lesbian' with a gambling habit represented a serious security risk. 'We ought *not* to plunge into this case,' he wrote. 'I cannot help feeling that the Germans would not have given Cyril so much secret ink etc. unless they had fairly good evidence of her attachment to them. So I am driven back to the fear that she may in fact have deceived SIS.' Elvira had made no secret of her interest in money. 'She is a rather expensive woman,' noted Masterman. 'Has she cost SIS a packet?'

Harmer won the day. 'I think this woman is telling the truth,' he insisted. 'Bleil regards her as a bona fide agent and has so represented her to his masters.' Her social contacts, as a 'typical member of the cosmopolitan smart set', would enable her to report all sorts of misleading political and social gossip from the gaming tables and salons of London. Elvira was asked to explain why she wanted to become a double agent; her answer was revealing: 'She replied that she had no such desire at all, although she would do it if it was any use.' Whatever Masterman's suspicions, she was not motivated solely by money. On 28 October 1942, Elvira was officially brought into the Double Cross team. Harmer, now her case officer, 'impressed on her the absolute need for secrecy'. She, like Garbo, would be provided with a cover job at the BBC, and paid a monthly salary equal to the money she was receiving from the Germans. Under MI5 control, she should begin writing secret letters to Bleil at once. In case of difficulty she could contact 'Mr Palmer' on Grosvenor 3171. As a precaution, her letters would be intercepted, and her telephone bugged.

All she now needed was a suitable new codename; something sophisticated, racy and intoxicating, as befitted this beautifully manicured spy. 'I chose the name of a rum-based cocktail,' Harmer later recalled. (The Bronx Martini is usually made with gin, but the barman at the Hyde Park Hotel made a wartime version from rum, orange juice and sweet and dry Vermouth.) 'It was one of the very few cocktails you could buy during the war when gin was in short supply,' said Harmer. 'It was a very appropriate, short name for an exceptional woman.'

Elvira de la Fuente Chaudoir became 'Agent Bronx'.

The little Spanish gentleman who had moved into Number 35, Crespigny Road, Hendon, was a refugee from Franco's Spain, it was said, who did translation work at the BBC. Every morning Señor Pujol caught the Underground train into central London, and every evening he came back home to his family. He spoke little English, and seemed polite, shy and rather dull. Indeed, the only interesting thing about the new arrivals, from the neighbours' point of view, was the state of their marriage: their nightly rows in loud and incomprehensible Spanish were a source of considerable entertainment in Crespigny Road. The neighbours would have been surprised to discover that the Pujols were arguing over the finer points of espionage. They would have been even more astonished to learn that, instead of working at the BBC, the little Spanish man spent his days in a small office in Jermyn Street, making up an army of fake spies.

Juan Pujol possessed what his case officer, Tomás Harris, called a 'remarkable talent for duplicity'. Harris was no slouch in that department, but Agent Garbo was in a league of his own, a master of invention whose 'entire existence remained wrapped up in the successful continuation of the work'. Unlike other double agents, Pujol's 'absolute loyalty' was never questioned. He was, in the best way, an extremist and a fanatic. The pair spent all day at the Jermyn Street office, located conveniently close to the Double Cross headquarters, inventing a world of spies, devising stratagems, cooking up new chicken-feed and composing messages. They would break for lunch at Garibaldi's Italian restaurant, and then resume in the afternoon. Their make-believe sessions sometimes extended far into the evening.

By the end of 1942, the Garbo network included an airline employee, the courier who supposedly smuggled Garbo's letters to Lisbon, a wealthy Venezuelan student named Carlos living in Glasgow, his brother in Aberdeen, a Gibraltarian waiter in Chislehurst whose anti-British feelings were said to be exacerbated because 'he found the climate in Kent very disagreeable', a senior official in the Spanish section of the Ministry of Information, an anti-Soviet South African, and a Welsh ex-seaman living in Swansea described by Pujol as a 'thoroughly undesirable character'. The personality, activities and messages of each spy were carefully imagined, refined, and entered in a log book. Some of these sub-agents were supposedly conscious collaborators, while others were unwitting sources of secret information; some were given names, others remained anonymous. The information they theoretically supplied was written up in secret ink and dispatched inside innocuous letters that the Germans believed were either brought by courier or sent by air mail to various cover addresses in neutral Spain and

Portugal. In fact, they were transported in the diplomatic bag. Pujol's sub-agents were able to correspond with the Germans independently after he was authorised to supply them with secret ink; those agents then began recruiting their own sub-sub-agents. The network began to self-replicate and metastasise, until the work of Pujol and Harris came to resemble a limitless, multi-character, ever-expanding novel.

The early objective of the Garbo network, in the words of Harris, was 'to swamp the Germans with information, misinformation and problems'. The information, true and false, was vetted by the Twenty Committee; the problems were the fruit of pure creativity; all of it was written up in Pujol's bombastic style. 'I do not wish to end this letter without sending a *Viva Victorioso* for our brave troops who fight in Russia, annihilating the Bolshevik beast.' If the Germans could be inundated by this deluge of intelligence, 'in as much confusing bulk as possible', from myriad fake spies, it would at the very least dissuade them from trying to send over any more genuine ones. 'The greater the work we caused them to put into the Garbo case, the more they would become conscious of his importance to them.' By continually emphasising 'the fanatical loyalty, the quixotic temperament and the untiring energy' of Pujol himself, the Germans could be made increasingly dependent on this 'temperamental genius', who needed to be placated and flattered at all times. They sent money, encouragement and ever more extravagant 'expressions of high satisfaction'.

In response, Juan Pujol threw periodic hissy fits. His tone was that of a testy and demanding lover: 'Why have I been made to suffer?' His complaints were exhaustingly long-winded: 'I want you to know that if it were not for the esteem which I feel personally for you, which I feel you reciprocate, as well as the interest which I have in helping our cause for which I have fought for three years during our war, and continue to fight for, though in a more responsible position in order to terminate this plague of Reds, I must tell you that in all sincerity, and as

a friend, that I would have returned to Spain some time ago.'
The relationship between Pujol and his handler Karl-Erich
Kühlenthal began to resemble an abusive marriage, in which
one partner holds the other in abject submission. Pujol battered
Kühlenthal with verbiage. 'The more we dictated our terms, the
more they cooperated; the more arrogant and temperamental
Garbo became, the more considerate they were in return.'

The information provided by the Garbo network was
voluminous, but of strictly limited worth: low-grade military
information, political gossip, reflections on public opinion, the
occasional item of real deception, and physical evidence when
this was requested, such as gas mask crystals sent to Spain inside
a tin of Andrew's Liver Salts. When Garbo did send important,
real information, this was carefully timed to arrive too late to be
of use. It never occurred to Kühlenthal to wonder why items
of little importance, such as gas mask crystals, arrived promptly,
whereas the most significant nuggets were invariably delayed
in the postal system. It certainly occurred to John Marriott,
Robertson's silky deputy, who wondered how the Germans
could fail to see their agents as people 'who seldom or never
say anything untrue, but who equally never say anything which
is new'. The infatuated, dominated partner in any relationship
tends to overlook, sometimes wilfully, the small clues to
infidelity. In German eyes, Garbo's failure to supply high-grade
information in a timely way was not his fault, but theirs; and the
more often he tried and failed, the more they loved him.

One by one, as the flock of double agents fluttered into MI5's
coop, Tar Robertson began to imagine new ways of combating
German espionage, and using enemy spies to Allied advantage.
His thoughts, increasingly, turned to pigeons.

For some time, Robertson had been receiving long and
detailed reports on 'the possible uses, and actual uses, that Pigeons
can be put to from the point of view of espionage'. (Pigeons,
like Lesbians, frequently merited a capital letter.) The author

of these reports was one Flight Lieutenant Richard Melville Walker, who headed one of the most secret and peculiar units of MI5: 'The Pigeon Service Special Section, B3C,' charged with disrupting the enemy's use of pigeons, and deploying Allied pigeons for passing on secret intelligence.

To describe Flight Lieutenant Walker as a 'pigeon fancier' does not quite do justice to the depth of his passion. He adored pigeons. He lived for pigeons. His reports were long, cooing poems of love. 'Years of breeding have made the Carrier Pigeon into a thoroughbred,' he told Tar, with a 'magical' ability to find its way home over a range of up to 700 miles. Walker wrote about his homing pigeons in the same way that Robertson described his most valued agents: 'Out of a hundred birds of the same stock perhaps one will be that bird all breeders hope for – a bird of highly individual character, courageous and resourceful. Much depends on the individual bird and especially its character and intelligence.'

Britain had abandoned its military pigeon service after the First World War. But even before the outbreak of the Second World War, Walker realised that Britain was falling behind Germany in the pigeon race since these birds remained an important way of passing information across enemy lines: fast, reliable and virtually impossible to intercept. The Nazis incorporated pigeons into the very heart of the Reich: each of Germany's 57,000 pigeon fanciers had to have a certificate of political reliability from the Gestapo; Jews were banned from keeping pigeons, and the German Pigeon Federation was placed under the control of the SS. 'Himmler, who has been a pigeon fancier and enthusiast all his life, has brought his enthusiasm for pigeons into the Gestapo,' Walker reported. Eugenics theories were applied to pigeons, and 'any lofts where the pigeons did not come up to standard were wiped out'. In 1937, a pigeon race had been staged in which some 1,400 German pigeons were brought to Britain by plane and then released to fly home. Walker believed the race had been a cover 'to accustom as many

German pigeons as possible to the sea crossing from England to Germany'.

Walker was convinced that Nazi pigeons were now pouring into Britain, by parachute, high-speed motor launch and by U-boat, providing enemy spies in Britain with an undetectable method of sending information to occupied Europe. Walker was not alone in his pigeon paranoia: Basil Thomson, the veteran Scotland Yard spy-catcher, observed: 'It was positively dangerous to be seen in conversation with a pigeon.' Some experts claimed to be able to identify a pigeon with a German 'accent'.

With MI5's wholehearted backing, Flight Lieutenant Walker drew up maps of known pigeon lofts in occupied Europe, and logged suspicious pigeon sightings (homing pigeons tend to fly in a tell-tale straight line, particularly across water). He argued that agents should be sent into occupied territory with a knapsack of pigeons rather than a wireless, since 'they are easier to work and, once liberated, the agent has nothing incriminating to carry about'. Walker began to develop ever more elaborate ways for pigeons to carry secret messages: small holes burnt with a fine nail in the feathers; a tiny roll of rice paper inserted into the hollow part of the main wing feather; messages in Morse code written on the quills in waterproof ink. Evidence of enemy pigeon activity mounted: an exhausted bird dropped onto the Scilly Isles, off the Cornish coast, with an intelligence message in French; two German pigeons were blown across the Channel in bad weather, carrying routine training messages. 'Both birds are now prisoners of war, working hard breeding English pigeons,' Walker reported.

Flight Lieutenant Walker loved all pigeons, even enemy pigeons, but this was war. It was time to go on the attack. Walker brought in the falcons. In 1942, the falconry unit, comprising three peregrine falcons and a falconer, was established on the Isles of Scilly, with the task of intercepting enemy pigeons: it would eventually bring down a total of twenty-three pigeons, every one of which turned out to be British. These incidents of what might now be called 'friendly fire' did nothing to dampen Walker's enthusiasm: 'The falconry unit proved it could intercept pigeons,' he wrote triumphantly. Finally, the birds of prey went AWOL. But by this time Walker had come up with another ingenious plan. Homing pigeons are sociable creatures, and if a pigeon spots other pigeons flying about, it may join them and, particularly if tired, return with them to their home lofts. This gave Walker an idea: 'If all the fanciers living within ten miles of the coast from Cornwall to Norfolk could be organised to form a screen' by releasing their birds at staggered intervals, then 'any enemy pigeon on a homing flight would stand a good chance of coming across these pigeons exercising and would be tempted to join them.' Astonishingly, Walker was given permission to carry out the largest military deployment of pigeons ever attempted, a sort of aerial Home Guard. Walker boasted that the resulting screen 'covered an area roughly ten miles deep all along the coast from Land's End to Cromer'. It had no effect whatever, for the simple reason that the Germans had never attempted to use pigeons to send messages *from* Britain. Walker did not mind: 'Had they done so, it is fairly certain that the loft screen would have bagged a fair proportion of them.'

Walker's pigeon reports received an enthusiastic and supportive reception from Tar Robertson. The idea of using pigeons for deception lodged somewhere in his fertile mind, and would soon take flight.

True Agent, False Agent, Double Agent

As Brutus and Bronx joined the team, and Garbo and Tricycle spun their webs tighter, it dawned on Tar Robertson that he had built a form of weaponry that could inflict some major damage. Garbo (Pujol) had bewitched the Abwehr in Madrid. Brutus (Czerniawski) (assuming he was not playing some fiendish triple game) had established a brand new channel of communication to the Germans in occupied France. Bronx (Elvira Chaudoir) was up and running, writing letters to a mysterious branch of German intelligence, and Tricycle's (Popov) hold over the Lisbon branch of the Abwehr seemed even stronger, thanks to the corruption of his case officers. In each case, the German spy-handlers were being handled, unknowingly, by the spies: Garbo was running Kühlenthal; Brutus was in control of both Bleicher and Reile; Bronx had Bleil twisted around her elegantly manicured little finger; and Tricycle knew that the greed, ambition and paranoia of von Karsthoff and Kammler had turned his relationship with the Germans through 180 degrees. The double agents were now controlling their controllers.

The B1A team would later wonder why it had taken them so long to appreciate the full potential of the Double Cross system. Masterman put it down to an obsession with 'the idea there might be a large body of spies over and above those whom we controlled'. By the summer of 1942, Robertson felt 'reasonably certain' that no such body existed. Most Secret Sources gave no hint that the Abwehr was running any spies other than those already in the Double Cross team. By 1942, almost all the traffic of German intelligence services was being read, with over 200 messages decrypted every day. From this trove of information, MI5 constructed a detailed picture of the German intelligence, its personnel, methods, strengths and frailties; they knew who their enemies were, and what they were doing and thinking. Indeed, they probably knew more about the Abwehr than the Abwehr did.

In July 1942, emboldened and increasingly ambitious for his flock, Tar Robertson made an astonishing claim: he, and not Wilhelm Canaris, controlled the German espionage network in Britain and as a consequence, he could make Hitler and his generals think what he wanted them to think. The capabilities of this 'powerful weapon' were laid out in a formal memo to the Twenty Committee: 'The only network of agents possessed by the Germans in this country is that which is now under the control of the Security Service,' he wrote. 'The Combined General Staff in this country have, in MI5 double agents, a powerful means of exercising influence over the OKW' – the Oberkommando der Wehrmacht, the Supreme Command of the German Armed Forces.

The implications of Robertson's claim were extraordinary. Hitherto, the Double Cross organisation had been used to catch more spies, extract information on German intentions, seduce the enemy into believing he already had a functioning spy network, spread propaganda, and influence enemy thinking, but only at the margins. After months of passing over chicken-feed, true but harmless, there was now an opportunity to distribute information that was methodically misleading and potentially highly destructive. What had begun with the ad hoc interception and turning of enemy agents was developing into a genuine system in which the misleading information from one double agent could be bolstered by all the others, an intricate, self-reinforcing structure that could 'fill the German files with what we want'. From the summer of 1942, the Twenty Committee began trying to influence overall German strategy, to burrow into Hitler's thoughts in a way that could cause the Germans massive, and perhaps critical, damage.

'It was always in the back of our minds,' wrote Masterman. 'That at some time in the distant future a great day would come when our agents would be used for a grand and final deception of the enemy.' For the moment, caution ruled. Canaris was known to boast about his network of agents in Britain, but the Abwehr was becoming wary: 'The enemy is becoming increasingly ruthless and penetration of agent circles is not to be ruled out,' warned the Abwehr bosses in Berlin. The interconnected nature of the Double Cross system was a source of vulnerability as well as strength. As one German intelligence officer observed: 'if one pearl is false, the whole string is false'. It would take just one mistake or betrayal to reveal to the Germans that not one, not a few, not even most, but *all* their agents were false. In that case, so far from enabling Britain's High Command to shape German thinking, Hitler would know exactly what falsehoods the British were trying to feed him, and change his plans accordingly. For all his boldness, Robertson was haunted by the knowledge that if one of his double agents was really a triple agent, then so far from unveiling a war-changing new weapon, he could be leading the Allies towards disaster: 'It is always impossible to be certain in such cases whether the Germans are fooling us or we are fooling them,' he reflected. Gisela Ashley, B1A's expert on the German mentality, sought to reassure him, insisting that while 'the Nazis are very good double-crossers', they lacked the patience and guile to set up a 'carefully and cleverly worked out system of deception'.

'The very few really important agents', it was agreed, 'should be held in readiness for a large-scale deception which could at a crucial moment be of paramount operational importance.' This 'glittering possibility', as Masterman put it, was some way off, but it could be glimpsed in the distance, and it was brought an enormous step closer by the appointment, as Britain's chief deceiver, of a man with 'the most highly polished shoes in the British army'.

Colonel J. H. Bevan, the newest member of the Twenty Committee, was a strait-laced, cricket-playing, workaholic stockbroker of rare intelligence and impeccable attire. Johnny Bevan tended to judge others by appearances, taking particular exception to slovenly uniform, but there was probably no one in the British military establishment more acutely aware that appearances can be deceptive. From May 1942, he headed the London Controlling Section, known as LCS, with orders from Winston Churchill to 'prepare deception plans on a worldwide basis' and put in train 'any matter calculated to mystify or mislead the enemy'. As Controlling Officer, Bevan would become the mastermind of wartime deception, overseeing a worldwide web of deceit and mystification from the underground warren beneath Whitehall known as the Cabinet War Rooms.

In September 1942, Bevan was inducted into the arcane world of Double Cross. For the rest of the war, the double agents, no longer an exotic sideshow, would be fully integrated into military operations. 'We had an instrument which had been tried and tested and which we could offer to the Controlling Officer for his deception plans,' wrote Masterman. Bevan played this instrument like a virtuoso.

The initial test of Tar's claim came with Operation Torch, the invasion of North Africa in November 1942, the first great Allied amphibious offensive of the war. Bevan drew up a deception plan aimed at misleading the Germans into thinking the Allies intended to attack northern France and Norway, while simultaneously attempting to relieve Malta. Among the double agents used to put across the deception were the two Norwegians, Mutt and Jeff, Tricycle's sub-agents Balloon and

Gelatine, and Tate. But the main burden fell on Garbo and his fictional network. He and his agents reported troops massing in Scotland apparently poised to attack Norway, preparations for a fictional cross-Channel assault, and numerous other titbits which, when assembled, would encourage the Germans to tie down troops far from the real point of attack. At the very least it would sow confusion. Some of Garbo's fake agents, it transpired, were simply too well placed for their own good. 'William Gerbers' was a German-Swiss businessman living in Liverpool, who had been conjured into being by Garbo before he even arrived in Britain. Ships and troops were massing in the Mersey for the invasion of North Africa where Gerbers, had he existed, would surely have seen them. How to explain that this active agent had failed to report such an obvious prelude to invasion? The solution was simple and brutal: Gerbers was first rendered extremely ill with a 'lingering malady', and then put to death. MI5 even inserted a death notice in the *Liverpool Echo*, which Pujol clipped out and sent to his handlers. The Germans sent a letter of condolence.

To maintain his growing reputation, however, Garbo needed to demonstrate access to high-grade material. He therefore sent two letters, both containing correct information: the first accurately reported a convoy leaving the Clyde on 29 October ('I fulfil my duty by advising you of this danger'); the second relayed information, obtained through the Ministry of Information, indicating an imminent invasion of French North Africa. The B1A team contrived to ensure that these arrived in Spain on the eve of the invasion, too late to be of any use.

The Germans were wholly unprepared when Allied forces landed at Casablanca, Algiers and Oran in early November. Pujol's handlers were pleased, nonetheless, by the evidence of his loyalty and efficiency, even if the postal system had stymied his efforts. 'Your last reports are all magnificent but we are sorry they arrived late, especially those relating to the Anglo-Yankee embarkation in North Africa.' Bevan was promptly promoted. But Masterman was too hard-eyed a realist to claim credit for the Double Cross team: 'The success was not primarily a triumph for deception, and still less for the double-agent system.' The Germans seemed, in fact, to have fooled themselves into thinking that the Allies lacked sufficient shipping for such an invasion. The system might not yet be powerful enough to make the enemy believe a false plan, but it had helped disguise the real plan. Here was an exhilarating foretaste of what the spies might be able to achieve in the future.

With the eye of a successful coach, Masterman looked back on the season with satisfaction. By the end of 1942 'the team was distinctly stronger', he wrote. Some impressive new players were stepping up to the crease, in the shape of Bronx and Brutus. Garbo was piling on the runs. Tricycle was back in the squad. But cricket and espionage are games of patience as well as skill. 'If the agents were ever to have their big day in the future, they had to be built up and maintained so that at the right moment we could be sure that we had a team of trusted agents who would be ready when called upon.' The players, Masterman knew, are only the most visible parts of a successful team: winning also depends on the trainers, the specialist advisers, the backroom staff.

The double agents were a mixed, even a motley crew, but the men and women who ran the Double Cross system were, in some ways, even odder. Tar Robertson deliberately gathered around him people who were out of the ordinary. Their very strangeness set them apart from the herd, reinforcing secrecy but also a sense of exclusive camaraderie that a more conventional unit would never have achieved. There was John Masterman, dry and deliberate, 'an older, wiser statesman to stop the inexperienced young hotheads from doing something totally irresponsible'. Masterman could be 'guaranteed to argue each side of an issue with total logic and lucidity' and then 'come down with a dull thud on the side of the status quo'; John Marriott, the sharp-tongued Cambridge-educated solicitor, who did little to disguise his opinion that double agents were only one step removed from crooks, and that a short one; Tommy Harris, the extrovert art dealer; Billy Luke, the pleasure-loving industrialist; Cyril Mills from the world of the circus; and Hugh Astor, the scion of a newspaper dynasty. Each had been diverted from a more orthodox military path: Christopher Harmer was almost blind in one eye and therefore precluded from advancement in the service; childhood polio had left Astor with a permanent limp; Ian Wilson could handle humanity brilliantly on paper but found personal conversation almost impossible. Gisela Ashley would have made a fine military officer, had she not had the misfortune to be a woman. Ewen Montagu was too old for frontline action, and Masterman was troubled by guilt because he had been interned in Germany during the First World War, and had missed the action, and sacrifice, that claimed so many of his contemporaries. Unable to do battle physically, they compensated by devoting their talents to a form of intellectual warfare.

From behind their desks, these men and women fought a specialist conflict 'without any training whatsoever', using language, ideas and information as others fought with guns and bombs. It was the indefatigable Gisela Ashley who urged the team to come up with ever more extravagant forms of deception, and never to underestimate the literalness of the German mind. 'What may appeal to an Englishman, even an Englishman engaged in double-crossing, as absurd, unlikely or naïve, may be the very thing that a typical Nazi would swallow and do.'

Just as the double agents lived double lives, so each officer had to try to inhabit the life of his agent. 'The case officer had to identify himself with his case,' wrote Masterman. 'He had to see with the eyes and hear with the ears of his agent; he had to suffer himself the nervous prostrations which might follow an unusually dangerous piece of espionage; he had to rejoice with his whole heart at the praise bestowed by the Germans for a successful stroke.' More than that, the case officers had to imagine themselves into the lives of their German opposite numbers, after the 'most careful psychological study'. Through Elvira Chaudoir's letters, Hugh Astor sought to understand what made Helmut Bleil, her German handler, tick; Ian Wilson found himself trying to fathom the corrupt and charming Ludovico von Karsthoff; Tommy Harris began to feel something like kinship with Karl-Erich Kühlenthal, whose eager gullibility was the key to Garbo's fictional world. These were intimate enemies.

Handling such fissile human materiel, for such high stakes, was an emotionally demanding and highly stressful business. 'We were playing with dynamite,' said Masterman. Some, like Wilson, drank too much pink gin to alleviate the strain. Everyone smoked, all the time. Yet there was also a unique brand of merriment in the cramped and smoky rooms of St James's Street, a sense that their shared mission was not only important but was occasionally fun, and frequently absurd. Gisela Ashley found herself stumped, in a message to Popov, by a reference to the 'Gonorrhoea expert without hairs'. Who could the Germans be alluding to? Popov himself was miraculously free of VD. 'This might be a heavily jocular reference to Johnny Jebsen,' Wilson suggested, with convoluted delicacy. 'What we know of his habits makes the suggested description not entirely inapt. The hair on his head is described as thick, but the reference may not be to his head.' This was, truly, a strange war.

Much of the work was done on paper, with the careful gathering and sifting of material, the drafting and redrafting of messages. The Double Cross system was, in part, a triumph of filing. Masterman insisted that 'only a well-kept record can save the agent from blunders which may "blow" him or inconsistencies which may create suspicion'. The B1A files grew to 'a truly formidable size', each one indexed and cross-referenced, since 'the messages of any one agent had to be consistent with the messages sent by him at an earlier date and not inconsistent with the messages of other agents'. The evidence on enemy intelligence officers and agents grew to more than twenty volumes, a veritable *Who's Who* of German spying. The Garbo case alone would swell to twenty-one files, more than a million pieces of paper. The Germans continued to send over spies, though in dwindling number since the existing ones were doing such a good job: Josef Terradellas, a Catalan separatist who was turned to become 'Agent Lipstick'; Waldemar Janowsky, a German landed by U-boat in Canada, was run jointly with Royal Canadian Mounted Police and MI5. The most remarkable new arrival was Eddie Chapman, the British safecracker parachuted into East Anglia in December 1942 who would become 'Agent Zigzag'. Each fresh arrival, each intercepted spy, each potential new double agent, added to the strength of the system, and the mountain of paper.

With some trepidation, it was decided to introduce Winston Churchill to the Double Cross story. The hesitation did not spring from any sense that the Prime Minister was uninterested in spies. Quite the reverse; he was fascinated by deception, and would look back on wartime espionage with glee: 'Tangle within tangle, plot and counter-plot, ruse and treachery, cross and double-cross, true agent, false agent, double agent, gold and steel, the bomb, the dagger and the firing party, were interwoven in many a texture so intricate as to be incredible and yet true.' In fact, Churchill was far *too* interested in the delicate business of espionage, and there was a danger he might interfere. The Twenty Committee was unofficially approved by Churchill, but not subject to ministerial responsibility. That way, the committee 'could not claim to have been "authorised" to do' what they were doing, much of which was, strictly speaking, illegal. Today this would be called 'plausible deniability'. The arrangement gave the Double Cross team unusual freedom, and it kept Churchill at arm's length. When it was first proposed that the Prime Minister should be informed of what was actually going on, Guy Liddell, the head of B Section, feared that he might, 'on seeing some particular item, go off the deep end and want to take action, which will be disastrous to the work in hand'. But by the beginning of 1943, the system was running so well, its potential so great, and its substance so certain to appeal to Churchill's vivid imagination, that it was agreed to introduce him to the cast and the drama, a little at a time.

The first monthly report to Winston Churchill, in March 1943, offered an espionage inventory. 'In all, 126 spies have fallen into our hands. Of these, twenty-four have been found amenable and are now being used as Double Cross agents. In addition twelve real, and seven imaginary persons have been foisted upon the enemy as Double Cross spies. Thirteen spies have been executed.' The report described Garbo, Zigzag and Mutt and Jeff, who had just received a wireless, £200 in notes and sabotage equipment via parachute in a remote Scottish glen. Churchill was riveted. Across the report he scrawled: 'Deeply interesting'.

In time, he would be introduced to Tricycle, Brutus and Bronx. The reports were drafted by Anthony Blunt, who drew up a long version which was then boiled down for the Prime Minister; Agent Tony also passed the information to his Soviet handlers. Stalin was fully versed in the Double Cross system: indeed, as Christopher Andrew, the authorised historian of MI5, writes, the Soviet leader may well have 'seen more detailed reports than Churchill'.

The Prime Minister's marginalia showed why it had been wise not to get him too involved, too early. When informed that a clerk at the Portuguese Embassy was spying for both the Germans and Italians, he wrote: 'Why don't you shoot him?' But Churchill did not go off the deep end; instead he was gradually immersed in the story, the strange tale of cross and double cross, true agent, false agent, double agent.

Elvira Chaudoir was shaping up to be a 'very competent letter-writing agent', reported Masterman. The tap on her telephone had produced 'no evidence of any pro-German sentiments' and was maintained 'merely to keep an eye on her financial position'. This was, as usual, dire. Unpaid bills from various nightclubs showed that Elvira was enjoying her return to London's 'high spots'. 'She plays bridge or poker every night, principally at the Hamilton Club or Crockford's, obviously for high stakes,' her MI5 minder reported. 'She is not engaged in any sinister activity', although he added: 'It is not known whether she is continuing in her Lesbian tendencies.' (She was.)

Under the watchful eye of Hugh Astor, she began sending letters in secret ink to Helmut Bleil, care of the Banco Santo Espirito in Lisbon and the Hôtel de Paris in Monte Carlo. The cover letters consisted of 'completely meaningless feminine chat', according to Astor. 'This text is so much in her own style (which is very far removed from anything I could produce) that in my opinion any attempt to interfere with it would be liable to show that the text was written under control.' Between the lines, writing in capital letters with a matchstick dipped in secret ink, she began to record items that might be of interest to Bleil. Initially, her observations were banal: 'Last week I saw a man unloading a lorry full of foodstuffs into an old empty house next to the church at Roehampton.' But as she grew more confident, she and Astor began to insert half-truths, rumours, elements of propaganda and harmless military details. 'Her friends are to be found in any of the smart bridge clubs in London,' wrote Astor, and 'as a friend of several English "socialites" she has been in a position to pick up much indiscreet gossip from Government circles.' Among her acquaintance were aristocrats such as Lord Carnarvon, the Duke of Marlborough, Duff Cooper, Head of the Security Executive, and a number of senior military officers.

In addition to reporting items of interest she had really heard, with Astor's guidance Elvira made up additional snippets and attributed them to individuals she might plausibly claim to have met, including Churchill's son-in-law and the Chairman of a War Cabinet Committee, Duncan Sandys, and the press barons Lords Beaverbrook and Kelmsley. As ever, MI5 had no scruples about putting words in the mouths of real people. 'We took great care to make every detail as authentic as possible,' Astor later recalled. 'I'm afraid we took the names of a good many people in vain. We certainly suggested that the [former] War Minister, Oliver Stanley, and peers such as Lord Lovat and Lord Mountbatten were among her circle of friends. Of course, they had no idea Bronx was attributing some splendid indiscretions to them. If they'd known, they'd have been furious.' To supplement her income, Elvira wrote vigorously anti-Nazi articles for the British popular press, for which she apologised to Bleil in her secret letters: 'I hope you won't mind reading my article in *Sunday Graphic* as it was essential that I should get the reputation for hating Germany.'

The sum of £100 soon landed in her Swiss bank account, the first monthly payment from the Germans. It was a drop in the ocean of her debts. Harmer advised the MI5 accountants to be generous: 'As she is a woman with expensive tastes, we would come off better if we allowed her to keep what the Germans sent her.' The deposits to her account arrived with 'satisfactory regularity', but they were always 'minus several hundred pounds' suggesting that 'somebody on their side is taking a rake-off'. This fresh evidence of corruption planted the seed of an idea. Bronx sent a letter suggesting that Bleil or his associates should send her a large sum of money that she could invest, on their behalf, on the British stock exchange. 'It was hoped that an unscrupulous member of the Abwehr might see in this an opportunity of getting capital out of Germany' and creating 'a nest egg for after the war'. The money, of course, would be appropriated, enabling the case to become self-financing and solving her money problems. Elvira, needless to say, was enthusiastic about the plan, and extremely cross when her German handlers 'ignored this suggestion'. The Germans might be gullible, but they were not so foolish as to employ a woman with a gambling habit as a secret stockbroker.

Initially Elvira's reports consisted of economic morsels: as time went on, her range widened to include reports on political and military affairs. Her letters were a strange, almost surreal, mixture of the mundane, the personal and the important. 'Tank production retarded by lack of tracks,' she reported. 'Heavily in debt. Canadian invasion practices in Scotland. Increased number of American troops in London. Shortage of kitchen utensils.' She insisted on swift and regular payments: 'Money must be sent at beginning of month. Serious risk and no claims for expenses.' When the Germans asked for information on gas warfare defences, she gave 'a glowing account of the excellence of British preparations' and pointed out that 'the British had developed large stockpiles of chemical weapons to retaliate if the Germans resorted to a gas attack'. Masterman believed her report had helped to dissuade the Germans from mounting a gas attack, possibly saving many lives and proving that 'we can in some instances influence and perhaps change the operational intentions of the enemy'.

The only fly in the ointment sat in the secret intelligence service next door. Claude Dansey, deputy chief of MI6, took every opportunity to poison his protégée's mind against MI5, telling her that she was being grossly underpaid. 'He has apparently said that he did not think we were working along the right lines,' Astor reported through gritted teeth. 'It is interesting to note that the case is being supervised by Dansey in this indirect manner.' Interesting, and extremely annoying. A formal complaint was lodged, which only encouraged Dansey to redouble his interference.

MI5 began to wonder whether it was Bleil, or someone pretending to be him, who replied with letters in secret ink, praising her work. 'We have no knowledge of which section is running Bronx or who are the officers in control of her case,' wrote Astor. Even so, references to a female agent, 'a member of the international smart gambling set', began to appear in Most Secret Sources, indicating satisfaction at a high level with this new spy at the heart of the British social scene. 'Bronx is believed to be a reliable agent,' Astor recorded. 'It may be of course that Bleil or the officers running her know, or assume, that she is under control, but there is every reason to believe that the HQ at Berlin are led to believe that she is a reliable agent.' Six months after her return to Britain, Elvira was given a formal seal of approval: 'The evidence suggests that the Germans believe in Bronx.'

The clouds of doubt surrounding Agent Brutus took longer to disperse. The radio technicians of B1A constructed a wireless using the crystals he had brought from France, and under close supervision, Roman Czerniawski made his first radio contact with Paris shortly before Christmas 1942. The enthusiastic response from Oscar Reile, his German handler, suggested he had complete confidence in his agent. The same could not be said of the British, who still wondered whether the Germans had sent him to the UK knowing he would switch sides. 'They had studied him from the psychological standpoint,' Masterman observed. 'If they convinced themselves that he had thrown them over, his traffic from this country could be a source of great danger to us' since they would read his messages 'in reverse'. If, for example, he passed on evidence of an attack on Denmark, then the Germans, knowing he was controlled, would conclude that Denmark was safe. The Twenty Committee ruled that Brutus should be run 'sparingly' and not used for operational deception. He would be 'allowed to lead a free and normal life', but under close scrutiny, his telephone bugged and his mail opened. The Polish intelligence service also put him under surveillance. One false move, and he would be joining Mathilde Carré in prison.

Czerniawski was eagerly cooperative, and happily resumed a life of full-time espionage. Unlike so many of the spies sent to Britain, Brutus was a professional military observer. His first reports gave details of the Polish armed forces in Britain (which the Germans already knew) and political attitudes within the Polish community. After a month, he visited Scotland, and sent a description of military deployments in the north, which the Germans hailed as 'exceedingly good'. This was followed by a 'lengthy report on the south coast'. These field trips followed a pattern: Czerniawski, accompanied by his case officer (initially Harmer, and later Astor), would tour a given area, and then draw up his genuine observations and discoveries, complete with maps, insignia, and even the identities of individual commanding officers. Much of this information was far too important to be passed on to the Germans: the Twenty Committee would whittle it down, and add new touches, which Czerniawski would translate into his own distinctive 'telegraph French'. Sometimes he operated the wireless himself, at others he was mimicked by one of B1A's radio operators: 'Brutus is very easy to imitate because he is a very bad operator and commits very distinctive faults.' His messages to Colonel Reile were larded with self-praise: 'Several of my old agents who work in this country are very discontented on account of their treatment at the hands of the British. They are still bound to me by intense personal loyalty and will work for me without question.'

Czerniawski continued to behave as if the destiny of Poland lay in his hands, insisting he would continue to spy for Germany only 'if I have your government's undertaking, after the defeat of the Allies, to offer through me to the Polish government liberal peace terms'. There were moments of high anxiety. Whoever was operating the transmitter at the German end sometimes tried to trip him up, to test if Czerniawski was really the recipient: 'Every now and then they'd send us a trick question. "What is the name of your mother-in-law? When was she born?"' Astor noticed that when Czerniawski was operating the transmitter himself, he spelled London in the

French way, 'Londres', but left off the s. Could this be his control signal, the distinctive 'mistake' to alert his German masters that he was operating under British control? Astor casually asked him to address a handful of envelopes to London addresses: it soon became apparent that Czerniawski simply couldn't spell. Gradually, the fear that Czerniawski was working with the Germans ebbed: 'Almost certainly Brutus did not have a triple-cross mission,' wrote Harmer. 'His position as a German agent is clear. Namely, he is working for us.'

The secondary anxiety, that the Germans might suspect he was working for the British, lingered longer. Three months after the first radio transmission, Robertson was still feeling 'a little anxious about Brutus', keen to use him in active deception, but worried that in so doing they 'might warn the Germans instead of deceiving them'. He wanted 'evidence that he is fully trusted by the Germans, in which case he would be eligible for use in deception'. Most Secret Sources duly obliged, revealing that Abwehr reports on Agent Hubert contained 'no qualification to suggest that the source was not a genuine one'. Berlin described him as a 'very valuable wireless agent'. Brutus was becoming a trusted source of military intelligence. 'As confidence grew both in him, and in the Germans' belief in him, he was used more and more.'

While Czerniawski's stock rose with both his British and German spymasters, it plunged to new lows within the Polish government-in-exile. He 'threw his weight about and gave himself airs' and was 'at loggerheads with all the other officers'. Harmer had grown fond of this bull-headed Pole, but had to concede 'he is a vain and conceited man who spent a considerable period of the war in exciting activities and now found himself doing a largely academic job'. Colonel Gano, the head of Polish intelligence, wanted this 'infernal nuisance' sent on a mission to Persia to get him out of the way: 'He spends his whole time making very damaging criticisms of other people's work [and] is inordinately ambitious, prying into everything.'

Within weeks of arriving in Britain, he was 'embroiled in Polish politics' which, as in many small and unhappy expatriate communities, were deeply rancorous. Czerniawski espoused 'extreme anti-Bolshevism', lecturing anyone and everyone on the iniquities of the Soviet regime. He was a pathological plotter, reflected Harmer, and dreamed of setting up a new network, this time to mislead the Germans. He suggested that he recruit his lover Monique as a sub-agent. Harmer firmly told him to do nothing of the sort, and 'sensed that he was hurt'. Restless, troublesome and self-important, Czerniawski needed another outlet for his boundless capacity for intrigue. He soon found one, with calamitous results.

To mark the twenty-fifth anniversary of the founding of the Red Army, General Stanislas Ujejski, Inspector General of the Polish Air Force, attended a reception at the Soviet Embassy in London. Anti-Soviet feeling was running high among Polish expatriates after the Katyn massacre, in which thousands of Polish officers had been murdered on Stalin's orders. Czerniawski was outraged by what he saw as Ujejski's cosying up to a murderous regime. In early June, he wrote a blistering attack on the General entitled 'In Defence of our Colleagues', ran off hundreds of copies, and distributed them throughout London. His denunciation was written in pungent style, littered with exclamation marks, and calculated to cause maximum offence, which it did. 'The Soviets committed terrible crimes against the Poles. These Red soldiers ill-treated Polish women and bestially murdered thousands of our defenceless colleagues. It is unworthy for the head of the Polish Air Force to go to a tea party where they danced on the newly made graves of many Polish soldiers.' Ujejski was attacked as an overpaid, immoral, flattering coward, who should be sacked. 'The Polish Air Force deserves a better leader.' This was a resounding political polemic. It was also an act of mutiny.

Within hours of distributing his 'pamphlet', Czerniawski was arrested by the Metropolitan Police Special Branch at the request of the Polish government and charged with 'the gravest military indiscipline'. His flat was searched, and Czerniawski was imprisoned in Scotland to await court martial. His enemies in Polish intelligence rejoiced that the 'little tin-pot hero' was getting his comeuppance. Christopher Harmer and Tar Robertson were appalled. Just as Brutus was developing into a first-class double agent, he had brought matters to a screeching halt and now 'threatened the extinction of the case'.

Harmer rushed to his prison cell and found Czerniawski quite unrepentant, declaring pompously that 'any patriotic Pole would have done likewise'. When Harmer ticked him off for 'meddling in affairs which were not within his province', Czerniawski insisted 'it was the duty of someone to expose this, and he was the only person in a position to do so'. He seemed to be relishing the attention, and positively proud of stirring up a hornet's nest. From his cell he wrote letters to Monique 'which demonstrate a desire to dramatise himself and his life and a capacity for exhibitionism which almost shows the first signs of delusions of grandeur'.

If Czerniawski's radio suddenly fell silent, the Germans would assume he had been caught. A message, mimicking Brutus's wireless style, was immediately sent to Paris, reporting that he and other anti-Bolshevik Poles were suspected of distributing anti-Soviet propaganda. 'I foresee my arrest as very probable. I am hoping for the best but the situation is very dangerous.' Two weeks later, he sent another message: '20th June arrested in the clandestine anti-Russian affair. Detained in Scotland. Await trial. Foresee light punishment. Fear I am being watched at present. Until the end of the trial too dangerous to transmit. I regret difficulties. Morale good. Am hopeful.' This would explain his absence from the airwaves, and was sufficiently near the truth to be plausible if the Germans got wind of his arrest. Whether they would actually believe him was another matter entirely. Harmer was gloomy, and doubted 'whether the Germans will ever accept Brutus as one hundred per cent reliable'. Awaiting trial on charges of 'indiscipline and offensiveness to superior officers', Czerniawski suffered a (brief) moment of contrition, and apologised 'for the harm he had done to the great game'.

His career as a double agent was over, at least for now. Brutus had managed to stab himself in the back.

Cockade

Garbo's (Pujol) network grew more and more elaborate, as new fictitious spies were added to his roster. The widow of Wilhelm Gerbers, the spy killed off in Liverpool, stepped in to take his place; 'Agent Dagobert', the 'undesirable' Swansea seaman, began recruiting his own sub-agents, eventually assembling a team of seven. Most importantly, Garbo enrolled a radio operator. Letters in secret ink were slow and cumbersome; a wireless link would speed up communication with Madrid. Garbo told his German handlers that the Gibraltarian waiter, 'Fred', had found a friend, a Spanish Republican, with a wireless set he was prepared to operate on Pujol's behalf. In reality, the set was operated by Charles Haines, a former Lloyds Bank clerk and amateur radio ham now in the Intelligence Corps Field Security Section.

The Germans provided Pujol with a code, which Liddell described as 'perhaps the highest-grade cipher ever used by the Abwehr'. The volume and speed of the Garbo traffic increased exponentially. 'The one-man band of Lisbon developed an orchestra which played a more and more ambitious programme,' wrote Masterman. A report to Churchill sang the Spaniard's praises: 'Garbo himself works on average from six to eight hours a day – drafting secret letters, enciphering, composing cover texts, writing them and planning for the future. Fortunately, he has a facile and lurid style, great ingenuity and a passionate and quixotic zeal for his task.' Everyone, it seemed, was pleased with

Juan Pujol, except Mrs Pujol. For while his secret life flourished, his domestic life was floundering.

Aracelli Pujol was lonely, homesick and fractious. She was banned from contact with London's Spanish community lest she let something slip. She spoke no English, had no friends and seldom left the house in Crespigny Road. Tommy Harris disliked 'Mrs G', describing Aracelli as a 'hysterical, spoilt and selfish woman'. But her complaints were not unreasonable: her husband was up at dawn and worked late; when he finally came home to Hendon, he was exhausted and irritable; she was expected to cook, clean and look after their son. She threatened to leave him, but had nowhere to go. Number 35 Crespigny Road echoed to the sound of raised Spanish voices and breaking crockery. The Pujols' relationship was under the sort of strain familiar to many marriages, the only difference being that their domestic disharmony represented a direct threat to the Double Cross project. Juan Pujol was not the only man to use 'winning the war' as an excuse for neglecting his wife. But in his case, it happened to be true.

Aracelli first asked, then pleaded, and finally demanded to be allowed to return to Spain, if only 'for a week'. Harris was coldly unsympathetic, suggesting she was 'unbalanced'. Aracelli snapped. On 21 June 1942, she telephoned Harris and threatened to destroy the entire Garbo network by revealing his activities to the Spanish diplomatic authorities: 'I am telling you for the last time that if at this time tomorrow you haven't got me my papers ready for me to leave the country immediately – because I don't want to live another five minutes longer with my husband – I will go to the Spanish Embassy. I shall have the satisfaction that I have spoiled everything. Do you understand? I don't want to live another day in England.' Harris certainly did understand. Aracelli had to be stopped. He arranged for the Spanish Embassy to be put under surveillance, so she could be arrested if she appeared there. He also considered warning the Spanish Embassy that 'a woman of Mrs G's description is anxious to assassinate the Ambassador [which] would ensure her being flung out if she attempted to go to the Embassy'. Liddell thought it might be best to lock her up. Robertson wondered whether to go to Crespigny Road himself and 'read her the Riot Act'. Even Churchill was informed of the 'outburst of jealousy' from Mrs Garbo and her threat to 'ruin the whole undertaking'. But it was Pujol himself who came up with a drastic plan to subdue his wife by subterfuge.

The next day, a Special Branch officer arrived at Number 35 and told Aracelli that her husband was under arrest, and that he needed to collect his toothbrush and pyjamas. Juan Pujol had tried to quit as a double agent, the officer explained, because she had threatened to 'give the whole show away'. The belief that she had caused her husband's arrest produced a 'hysterical outburst' from Aracelli. She telephoned Harris in floods of tears and insisted that 'her husband had always been loyal to this country and would willingly sacrifice his life for our cause'. Later that day, she was found by Charles Haines in the kitchen filled with fumes from the gas oven, an apparent suicide bid which Harris coldly dismissed as 'ninety per cent play-acting'. Weeping and distraught, poor Aracelli's capitulation was complete. 'She pleaded that it was she who had been at fault and that if her husband could be pardoned she promised she would never again interfere with his work, or behave badly, or ask to return to Spain.' Pujol's plan had been brutal, effective and revealing: beneath his gentle manner, he was absolutely dedicated and quite ruthless, prepared to go to extreme lengths to preserve the network he had created, even if that meant double-crossing his own wife.

Dusko Popov, as ever, was living in 'considerable comfort'. He moved into Clock House, a charming cottage in Knightsbridge, which he rented for twelve guineas a week, and recommenced his affair with, among others, Gwennie, whose passionate missives were intercepted and copied by MI5: 'Please try to be ¼ way decent till I can pick up where I broke off. You are a sweetie and I love you (a little) Gwennie.' He was simultaneously conducting an affair with 'Mairi', who lived on Park Lane, and a young Yugoslavian woman from a wealthy family, Ljiljana Bailoni. (Popov would 'undoubtedly be an easier agent to run if he became a little more settled in his domestic habits', sighed Wilson.) He was heartily congratulated by von Karsthoff for the legibility and content of his secret letters: 'Your writing is wonderful . . . we can read every word.' His business, Tarlair, was booming, although even Gisela Ashley, monitoring Popov's activities, found it hard to keep track of exactly how the company worked. 'He gets particularly obscure when discussing matters of international finance,' John Marriott noted. Popov's debts, large and small, trailed after him: more than $10,000 still owing to the FBI, several thousand more to MI6 in New York, several hundred dollars to the Long Island Telephone Company and $215 to 'Trivett's Tested Seeds'. He paid none of them. He simply forwarded the bills to MI5, along with his tailor's invoice for eighteen silk shirts and a dozen monogrammed handkerchiefs.

The tide of war was turning. Popov could feel it in the 'humour and spirit of Londoners'. The great counter-attack against occupied Europe was in sight: 'Everyone, the Germans included, knew the invasion was coming.' Again, he lobbied his spymasters to recruit Johnny Jebsen, pointing out that once his friend 'realised that Germany was going to lose the war he would be only too willing to re-insure himself with the victors by telling them all he could'. Popov offered to make the approach himself, on his next visit to Lisbon: 'Johnny has never been pro-Nazi,' he insisted, and had access to high-grade information including 'full details of the personnel of the Abwehr and its agents in many countries'. Wilson had qualms about Jebsen's suspect financial activities – 'Johnny is always carrying out various more or less irregular deals as well as acting as an agent of the Abwehr' – but he was tempted by the prospect of recruiting an 'amoral,

opportunist and not particularly Nazi' informant within the
Abwehr at this critical juncture. Wilson toyed with getting Popov
to offer a promise 'to arrange for Johnny to receive favourable
treatment, providing that Johnny has something worthwhile to
sell to the British'. Jebsen had recruited Popov; now Popov might
recruit Jebsen. 'The Germans regard their personal friendship as
an essential part of the set-up,' Wilson observed, and if Jebsen
really was as anti-Nazi as Popov said, then he might make a
useful double agent himself: 'We must seek to take advantage of
Jebsen's outlook.'

As the winter of 1942 closed in, Popov described himself
as 'the shabbiest and coldest man in London', a statement that
was demonstrably untrue. He amused himself by demanding
additional luxuries, and wrote to Colonel 'Freckles' Wren of
MI6 in New York:

My heart is in very bad condition. My doctor who is my
biggest friend says it is too much alcohol, tobacco and sin.
The only remedy which I found efficient until now was
milk and chocolates. Please send $100 worth of any kind
of chocolate you can think of. I don't mind what they are.
I am taking them as medicine. Please send me at the same
time $100 of Nylons in 9, 9½ and 10 (Don't think I'm
promiscuous.)

Wren did not swallow Popov's claim of a medical chocolate
emergency. 'The chocolates are intended to delight the interiors
of those same exteriors which he wishes to decorate with
stockings.' But it was a measure of Popov's status that he could
instruct the British secret services to buy nylons for him, and
they grudgingly obliged.

We have done our best to carry out Tricycle's wishes with
regard to comforts for his lovelies, but I have a strong feeling
that this kind of business should now stop. It is legitimate for

an agent working abroad to supply douceurs if it is necessary to do so in the interests of the state at war: I cannot see how that principle can apply to Tricycle. Do you think it would be possible to bring home to Tricycle the fact that his country and we have a right to his unselfish duty?

Tar Robertson was indulgent, arguing that 'Tricycle has the Balkan outlook that all positions of influence can be turned to personal advantage'. To make matters worse, Popov's American creditors discovered that he worked for the British government in some capacity, and the Keystone Debt Collection Agency had begun demanding payment of his unpaid bills through diplomatic channels. 'The one thing that does strike me as urgent is that we should stop the debt collection agency trying to dun Tricycle further through the British Ministry of Information,' wrote Tar. Trivett's Tested Seeds finally got what it was owed, unaware that it had successfully extracted money from British intelligence.

At a meeting with Wilson in February, Popov announced 'his desire to do something more active in the way of outwitting the Germans', and was told there was 'certainly no intention of letting his case vegetate'. Popov asked to be parachuted into Yugoslavia to join the Chetnik partisans, insisting 'he was ready to take almost any risks to achieve anything that would be really useful'. The request was turned down. Popov was too valuable to be risked, but his demands and complaints, his restlessness and sexual shenanigans, his 'white silk shirts with soft collars and fancy ties' were starting to try even Wilson's vast reserves of tolerance: 'Tricycle is continuing to make an infernal nuisance of himself.' So it was agreed to send him back to Portugal.

'Every Double Cross agent is inclined to be vain, moody and introspective,' wrote Masterman, but these volatile personalities were proving ever harder to handle. One of the most important members of the team had got himself arrested, another was in the throes of a spectacular marital bust-up, and a third was

Tommy Argyll 'Tar' Robertson, the mastermind of Double Cross.

Camp 020: Latchmere House, the top secret interrogation centre in southwest London, where captured spies were imprisoned, grilled and 'turned'.

Gisela Ashley, alias 'Susan Barton', German-born expert on Nazism and the most senior woman in B1A.

J. C. Masterman, Oxford history don, cricketer, and the 'elder statesman' of the Double Cross system.

French film star Simone Simon, one of Popov's many lovers.

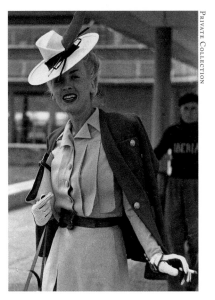

Dusko Popov, 'Agent Tricycle', Serbian playboy, international businessman and double agent.

Maria Elera, Brazilian model: photograph from the MI5 files labelled wearily, 'Popov's latest girlfriend'.

Popov with his first wife, Janine.

Roman Czerniawski, 'Agent Brutus': Polish patriot, trained intelligence officer and the most professional of the Double Cross spies.

Captain Czerniawski (*fourth from right*) with his Polish regiment shortly before the fall of France in 1940.

Pigeons were used to pass messages, gather intelligence from behind the lines and plant false information on the enemy.

D-Day troops at Weymouth heading into battle: 'It may well be the most ghastly disaster of the whole war.'

Lily Sergeyev, 'Agent Treasure', who brought 'a rich dowry: the confidence of the Germans'.

Babs, Lily's beloved dog, a critical, if unlikely, player in the D-Day story.

Mary Sherer, the only woman officer in the Double Cross team.

Lily Sergeyev's French identity card issued in November 1941, soon after her recruitment by German intelligence. In Paris, she was trained in the use of wireless, secret inks and coding.

Code-breakers at work at Bletchley Park, the secret code-breaking centre in the Buckinghamshire countryside codenamed Camp X. Deciphered German wireless messages were circulated as 'Most Secret Sources', or 'MSS'.

With information from the code-breakers, MI5 intercepted scores of enemy spies, such as John Moe and Tör Glad, double agents 'Mutt' and 'Jeff', pictured before their departure from Norway in 1941.

Anthony Blunt, MI5 officer, art expert and Soviet mole. 'He was a very nice and civilised man, and he betrayed us all.'

Guy Liddell, the shy, cello-playing head of MI5's counter-intelligence B Branch.

Admiral Wilhelm Canaris, the chief of the Abwehr, German military intelligence.

Hans Oster, Canaris's deputy and secret anti-Nazi plotter who recruited Jebsen to the Abwehr.

Paul Fidrmuc, 'Agent Ostro', prized Abwehr agent-runner and fraud.

Johnny Jebsen, 'Agent Artist'.

Johnny Jebsen in Turkey in
1942.

Johnny Jebsen on the
day of his marriage to
actress Lore Petersen,
to whom he was
serially unfaithful, but
deeply loyal.

Karl-Erich Kühlenthal of the Madrid Abwehr, Garbo's gullible German case officer.

Tomás Harris, the half-Spanish art dealer who helped Garbo to create a fictional network of twenty-seven sub-agents across Britain.

Juan Pujol Garcia, 'Agent Garbo', and his wife Aracelli, in Spain *c.* 1940, during a rare moment of domestic harmony.

Garbo in disguise, a man of 'great ingenuity, and a passionate and quixotic zeal for his task'.

Elvira Josefina Concepcion de la Fuente Chaudoir, 'Agent Bronx', seen here at the Hurlingham Club with MI5 case officer Billy Luke.

Major Christopher Harmer, a lawyer in peacetime, case officer for Brutus, Bronx, Mutt and Jeff.

Hugh Astor, case officer for Brutus and Bronx.

Helmut Bleil, the alcoholic German intelligence agent who recruited Elvira Chaudoir in the south of France.

Mathilde Carré outside the Montmartre restaurant where she betrayed the Interallié intelligence network.

Mathilde Carré, 'The Cat', the Resistance agent who helped to build, and then destroy, Czerniawski's network.

Colonel Oskar Reile, Czerniawski's German case officer.

Hugo Bleicher, the Abwehr's ruthless counter-espionage officer in Paris.

Monique Deschamps, 'Agent Moustique' (Mosquito), the French Resistance agent who would later marry Roman Czerniawski.

demanding women, chocolates and silk shirts while living the life of a pampered prince. Even Elvira Chaudoir was asking for more money, and flirting with MI6. The constant need to monitor, cajole, flatter and sustain these difficult people was taking a toll. However, the effort, expense and frustration would all be worthwhile if the Double Cross spies managed to deceive the Germans into making some large and disastrous mistake.

At the Casablanca Conference in January 1943, the Allies agreed that a cross-Channel invasion could not be undertaken before the spring of 1944. The main thrust for 1943 would be into Italy, via Sicily, while Stalin's Red Army continued the epic battle in the East. The Germans knew that an invasion of France was only a matter of time, and were already laying plans to reinforce the Atlantic Wall with millions of tonnes of cement and steel, using slave labour. They could not know that the Allies had decided to focus elsewhere in 1943, and therein lay an opportunity.

A deception plan, codenamed 'Cockade', was drawn up by the London Controlling Section to mount bogus threats to Norway and northern France, in the hope of drawing off German troops from the Mediterranean and the Eastern Front, or at least pinning down those in northern Europe. In early September, a mock invasion fleet would set sail from Kent and Hampshire apparently heading for Calais, to draw the Luftwaffe into battle over the Channel; another fake invasion force, this time American, would threaten Brittany, while a third fake force would threaten Norway. The central plank of the deception was to be nailed down by planting false information through the double agents. Cockade was not quite the grand roll of the dice envisaged by Masterman, but it was the most ambitious gamble so far.

The B1A team sprang into action. Von Karsthoff's messages to Popov indicated that 'invasion questions are no doubt what the enemy is chiefly interested in'. Therefore 'he ought to be supplied with a lot of items from which it is possible to draw all sorts of inferences about our future intentions'. Popov was again 'in his best mood', and looking forward to seeing Jebsen again. 'He should be back here in time to put over some really effective misinformation when invasion of the Continent becomes imminent,' wrote Wilson. In July, Popov flew to Lisbon once more (leaving MI5 to pay his overdue rent), carrying a briefcase full of hints indicating that an invasion of France was at hand: his tailor told him senior officers were ordering new battledress, hospitals were preparing beds, and electrically propelled canoes were being manufactured in large numbers. He told von Karsthoff he had 'taken his girlfriends to different south coast towns on various weekends', and in Southampton he spotted that shelters were being prepared for a retaliatory air attack, indicating the port would be 'active as a supply base for the invading army'.

Popov's sub-agents, Gelatine and Balloon, added corroborative details, while Mutt and Jeff, the two Norwegians, reported that Norway was under threat of attack from Scotland. Bronx relayed invasion gossip picked up from politicians, journalists and others, including a conversation with an invented Harley Street surgeon called Nielson, who told her of 'hospital arrangements for an invasion in autumn'. On 11 July, she wrote: 'France to be attacked in September. Increased production of invasion barges. Good harvest and increase in pig farming.' The reply congratulated her: 'Pleased with work. Exact details on invasion, will pay expenses of travel for this.'

The Garbo network reported concentrations of troops in Wales and Scotland, while Pujol himself claimed to have seen seven divisions near Brighton (though he was careful to point out this might be just an exercise); his sub-agents spotted assault craft gathering in the Channel ports, military camps near Southampton and torpedo boats massing in Dover.

On Robertson's orders, even Flight Lieutenant Walker's pigeons were enrolled into the deception. For some time, British intelligence had been dropping homing pigeons into occupied France carrying questionnaires about German defences, 'in the hope that at least some of them will fall into the hands of people who are supporters of the Allied cause', who were urged to fill out the forms and release the birds to fly back across the Channel. The pigeons were dropped by parachute, in cardboard containers, each with a small bag of corn. 'I gather some satisfactory results have been obtained from the answers to these questionnaires,' wrote Robertson. 'But some fall into the hands of the enemy.' Any method of seeking the truth can also be used to plant a lie. 'It occurs to me that this is a possible means of putting deception over to the enemy by the careful framing of the questionnaires, as presumably the Germans must, if they capture some of these birds, take notice of the kind of question being asked.'

Robertson gave orders that 'the questionnaire carried by pigeons dropped in the Pas de Calais and west coast areas should convey the impression that we are very keen on getting detailed intelligence about these areas in beach and coast defences, airfields, focal points on road and rail communications, detailed locations of formation headquarters and units, bridges, ports and installations for demolition etc.'. The Germans would read this, and assume an imminent invasion. Walker prepared his flock, and in August more than a thousand homing pigeons, each carrying a list of questions deliberately framed to suggest a looming attack, were dropped in a flapping deluge on Calais and Brittany. 'The mere fact of increasing the number of pigeons used has a certain deceptive value,' Robertson gleefully reported.

Finally, the day of the dummy invasion arrived. On 8 September, Agent Garbo reported that troops had been confined to barracks and assault craft were gathering. A mock invasion flotilla of some thirty ships headed for France, preceded by mine-sweepers. With information coming in from all sides, the Germans surely could not fail to think that a huge invasion was taking place.

But that is exactly what happened.

In response to the great charade the Germans did . . . nothing at all. The shore batteries did not open up, the Luftwaffe did not take to the air, and the High Command did not redeploy troops from places where they were needed. As one British officer wryly remarked: 'It was an inspiring sight to see everybody doing his stuff to perfection . . . except, unfortunately, the Germans.' The only indication that they even noticed the elaborate performance put on for their benefit came when 'a German coast-artillery subaltern on the far shore [was] overheard calling his captain on the radio to ask if anybody knew what all this fuss was about'. About ten miles off Boulogne, the bogus invasion force stopped, waited for the Germans to do something and, when they didn't, trailed home.

From the Allied point of view the attempted deception was 'disappointing in the extreme', not to say downright humiliating. It would later emerge that instead of reinforcing their defences in light of a perceived threat, the Germans had actually reduced their troop numbers in the run-up to the mock invasion, apparently convinced that there were still insufficient troops in Britain for a full-scale invasion. Garbo scrambled to cover his back with a message to his German handler: 'It appears the operation has been suspended. Troops surprised and disappointed.'

Cockade was a cock-up, but the Double Cross team could extract some crumbs of comfort. Popov seemed even more firmly in favour with his German bosses, and Garbo's credibility was actually reinforced by the farce. 'Your activity and that of your informants gave us a perfect idea of what is taking place over there,' enthused Kühlenthal, who was becoming infected by Garbo's rococo prose style. 'These reports, as you can imagine, have an incalculable value and for this reason I beg of you to proceed with the greatest care so as not to endanger in these momentous times either yourself or your organisation.' Messages marked 'urgent' were being relayed from the Garbo network to Berlin in under an hour. 'There can be no doubt of the high standing which Garbo enjoys with his masters,' Johnny Bevan told Tar Robertson. 'Garbo will have a very important role to play in the future.'

Some useful lessons were learned from the failed plan: any future deception would have to involve every branch of the military, to the fullest extent, on a far wider scale; no fake invasion would be believed unless a real one was taking place at the same time. The Double Cross players would have to up their game. Despite the disappointment, Masterman eagerly 'looked forward to the day when we should take part in the great final deception'. The episode also instilled fresh confidence in Tar Robertson, along with a profound, but not entirely helpful belief in 'the actual uses that Pigeons can be put to from the point of view of espionage'.

Discovered Treasure

Kenneth Benton was, formally speaking, His Majesty's Passport Control Officer in Madrid, in charge of visas, immigration and customs formalities. In reality he worked for MI6, recruiting agents and potential double agents and, with his wife Peggie, also an MI6 officer, organising a rich range of skulduggery to confound German espionage in the Iberian Peninsula. His opposite number in Madrid, Karl-Erich Kühlenthal, considered him a 'sly fox', a description that Benton had read in Most Secret Sources, and found rather flattering.

At 10.30 on the morning of 17 July 1943, Benton's secretary, Mollie Gillard, rang through to say that there was someone in the Embassy reception demanding an urgent interview to sort out a visa. Moments later, a 'rather attractive woman of about thirty' was ushered into his office, carrying a small white dog. The visitor perched on a chair with a creaking wicker back, the dog on her knee.

'My name is Benton,' said Benton. 'If what I understood is correct you wish to go to England to rejoin your family.'

'Not exactly,' said the young woman. 'I'm going there to spy.'

In good English, Lily Sergeyev described her recruitment in Paris by Major Emile Kliemann as 'Agent Solange', her training in the use of a wireless and secret ink, and her spying mission to Britain: she now wished to swap sides.

They sized one another up. Lily saw a 'classic example of "the Englishman": young, tall, and slim, with a long narrow head and a straight brow with thinning red hair'. Benton saw a typical Frenchwoman, 'made up and dressed to kill', with a self-dramatising manner, but clearly intelligent. He wondered whether she might be 'first and foremost a self-server'. During pauses in the conversation, she whispered remarks, in Russian, to her dog.

Lily explained that, as instructed by Kliemann, she had made contact with an Abwehr agent in Madrid, a man she knew only as 'Hans'. Kliemann himself had promised to bring a wireless to Madrid. He was late.

Benton told Lily to report back to Hans, and tell him that the British authorities had agreed to issue a visa, but the process might take several weeks. She should then wait for Kliemann to arrive. That afternoon, Benton sent a coded telegram to London, describing his meeting with Lily Sergeyev, and asking whether MI5 might have any use for her. He himself was 'doubtful'.

Benton's doubts were shared by John Masterman. 'I should be very cautious about agreeing that she should become a double agent working for us,' he wrote. 'She ought to be thoroughly interrogated and a full account obtained of her activities before we decide we can use her.' MI5 began a background check, interviewing people in Britain who knew Lily. 'She has respectable friends and relatives,' noted Tar, but these offered a contradictory picture of her loyalties. Virginia Hall, an American SOE agent who had known the Sergeyevs in Paris before the war, said she suspected that Lily was 'pro-German'. Anthony Blunt, who also knew her slightly, described Lily as 'a White Russian with slightly left views' (which was rich, coming from him). Her cousin, Dr Elizabeth Hill, who lived in Cambridge, was 'perfectly sure that Lily was pro-Allied in her sympathies', and thought her 'something of an adventuress, but an exceedingly clever girl'.

The person assigned to investigate Lily Sergeyev was Mary Sherer, the latest addition to Tar's team and the only woman case officer in B1A (though she was denied full officer status). Mary Corrie Sherer was twenty-nine, robust, ambitious, and with a sharp sense of humour 'often at other people's expense'. She joined MI5 as a secretary in 1938, and spent the first part of the war in the counter-sabotage section and working for British Security Coordination in New York, the clandestine arm of MI6, MI5 and SOE that sought to bring America into the war by means of propaganda, blackmail and espionage. A child of the Indian Raj and the daughter of a brigadier, Mary was military in bearing, and often wore a red jacket with epaulettes which she thought made her look like a general. She walked with a long, martial stride, swinging her arms, and humming little songs to herself when she thought no one could hear. In a male world, she assumed a carapace of toughness, smoking filterless Kent cigarettes and holding her gin as well as the next man. 'Mary was someone you did not want to cross, and was not quick to forgive any misdoings.' But there was also a gentleness to her, and a resolute sense of purpose.

After conducting the background check on Lily Sergeyev, Sherer concluded: 'She appears to be a character well-suited to becoming a double agent.' Mary Sherer 'had a great deal of character', according to Benton, and not for the last time she stood up to her sceptical male bosses, insisting that a woman double agent, equipped with her own wireless and a gullible German handler, would be highly valuable in the run-up to the Allied invasion of northwest Europe. Mary gave her the codename 'Treasure'.

After nearly two months in Madrid, Lily was becoming oppressed by a city 'full of menace and intrigue; a place where everyone is plotting, betraying, bribing or selling themselves'. She urged Hans, her Abwehr contact, to tell Kliemann to come quickly. Still he did not appear. 'I have got very good at lying,' she wrote in her diary. 'I am beginning to feel the nervous strain [of] this double game, this constant change of personality without any let-up when I can be myself again.' The only creature she could trust was her dog. Lily wrote to her sister: 'The heat in Madrid is torrid. Babs sleeps blissfully on his back with four feet in the air and his tongue hanging out. I have just been talking to him about you. He opened one eye and raised an ear; that means he remembers.'

She arranged another meeting with Benton, who told her she had done extremely well. 'We know a certain amount about Major Kliemann,' he explained. 'He's an important man in German intelligence – quite a formidable figure, in fact. I have the impression that you underestimate him. He has his weaknesses certainly – you think him a little absurd because he is always late for appointments. If he finds out that you've double-crossed him, he won't be late for the next rendezvous, I can promise you.'

Finally, word came from Hans that Kliemann was on his way, and would meet her at the Café Bakanik. When he eventually arrived, the dog jumped up to greet him. 'Babs licks his face while he continues to waggle his tail and whole body.' Lily felt moved by the sight of her dog and her German spymaster, so pleased to see one another: 'I look at them and think: at last, something genuine.' Kliemann was excited by the way Lily's mission was progressing. He preened himself, and ordered a steady stream of drinks. 'It will be quite something for me: to have set up an agent and actually get that same agent into England. It's incredible. It looks as if it's going to work.'

Kliemann, usually so lethargic, was all business. He planned to provide her with a radio set hidden inside a gramophone, with operating instructions written on a microdot concealed in the case. In order to read it, she would need to buy a small microscope. She should pretend to be interested in microbes. Indeed she should carry a book with her as cover: he recommended *The Microbe Hunters* by Paul de Kruif. Lily declined to say that she thought this was a ridiculously overcomplicated plan. By now quite drunk, Kliemann was enjoying his role, though Lily could sense he had something else on his mind. He suddenly grew pensive and gazed 'thoughtfully at the space in front of him, sighing deeply'.

'Anything wrong?' Lily asked, knowing that the conversation was about to turn to his favourite subject: Yvonne Delidaise, his mistress.

Kliemann buried his face in his hands. 'You must think me ridiculous. Maybe I am. She is young and pretty, gay and witty. And I? Look at me. A married man of forty-six.' The German spymaster ordered another bottle of wine, and poured his heart out. Yvonne had spent May in Madrid, at the Ritz, he said. After she returned to Paris, she was no longer the same towards him; something must have happened while she was here. And he wanted Lily's help to find out what.

With a fierce twinge of irritation, Lily understood that Kliemann had come to Spain with an ulterior motive that had nothing to do with her, and everything to do with his love life. Like most jealous lovers, he had already fixed on the rival he believed Yvonne to have been seeing in Madrid: Edgar Espirito Santo. 'He's Portuguese. A very wealthy banker. He used to see a lot of Yvonne. He's a lady-killer. Yvonne amused him. She is jolly and witty, but Yvonne doesn't mean a thing to him. I think she met him here. He always stops at the Ritz – and I want to know if he was there at the same time as Yvonne. I must know if she has been carrying on with that damned Espirito Santo. And if she has made a fool of me . . .'

'Then what?'

'Then I shall ask for a transfer to the Russian Front.'

'But what do you want me to do?'

She could make enquiries, suggested Kliemann, and see if the banker had been staying at the Ritz when Yvonne was in Madrid. Lily had come to Spain as a German spy, not as a freelance private detective for a middle-aged married man besotted with a younger woman. She was outraged.

'Major Kliemann, I don't care a hang about your ridiculous affairs,' Lily railed. 'In a few days, I shall be in England and you will be in Paris. I shall probably never see you again. Why should I care whether Yvonne is deceiving you or not?'

Kliemann was pleading, and plastered. She left him in the café.

The next day, she related this bizarre conversation to Benton, who reported back to MI5: Kliemann 'appears to be extremely pleased with her progress' and 'pathologically jealous' of his mistress, he wrote, two discoveries which, in combination, rendered him uniquely vulnerable. Lily was Kliemann's only spy. If she now became a prop for his frail sexual ego, then he would be even more in her debt, and even easier to manipulate. Benton advised her to report back to the Major that 'the object of Kliemann's jealousy was not at the Ritz, or even in Madrid, in May'. The MI6 officer then made his own enquiries, which suggested that Yvonne probably *had* been carrying on with the Portuguese banker. There was no sense in telling Kliemann that. 'Whatever the truth may be, the report must prove that Yvonne is faithful to him. Now that we know all about Major Kliemann we want him to stay in the job. We must make quite sure he doesn't get sent to the Russian Front.'

Kliemann was delighted with Lily's 'purely fictitious but reassuring report' affirming Yvonne's fidelity. Predictably, he had failed to find her a wireless set, but insisted he would be able to get one passed to her in Britain, by a Spaniard 'who was under great obligation to Kliemann's friends'. (MI5 would later conclude that this must have been a reference to Angel Alcazar de Velasco, the press attaché at the Spanish Embassy and a known German agent.) He then handed over two pellets of ink for secret writing, and a long questionnaire, clearly aimed at discovering the Allies' invasion plans, which he told her to memorise, and then destroy. 'What view is taken in authoritative English circles of landing preparations? Where are the barracks placed in coastal towns?' Kliemann wanted information on uniforms and troop movements, stoppage of leave, armaments production, and much more. Lily, and British intelligence, seemed to have Kliemann exactly where they wanted him: she was 'the personification of his hopes, the evidence of his subtlety, his courage and his flair'.

Only once did the conversation take a more sinister turn when Kliemann, with studied nonchalance, observed that after her abrupt departure from Paris, the Gestapo had put her parents' flat under surveillance. Lily did not like the sense of threat in that remark, and told him that 'if any harm came to her parents while she was away he would find her working for the other side against him'. It was half a joke, but Kliemann's response was immediate, sharp and entirely without humour: 'Naturally, should she double-cross him, she must consider that the lives of her parents were at stake.'

Kliemann now reached into a pocket with an air of great munificence, and handed Agent Solange a small package wrapped in tissue: inside was a diamond solitaire ring and a two-inch brooch in the shape of a branch with five small diamonds representing blossoms. The ring had cost 95,000 francs in Paris, he said, and the brooch 39,000 Portuguese escudos. In England, she could sell the jewellery, and say it had belonged to her grandmother. To this he added a pile of 7,000 Spanish pesetas, with an additional 2,000 pesetas as a bonus for setting his mind at rest about Yvonne's visit to Spain, a token of thanks for her 'help and sympathy'. Dinner over, Kliemann climbed into a taxi in the Plaza del Callao, and drove off with 'a cheery wave'. He was a happy man: his mistress was faithful, his bosses were pleased, and his star agent was now about to help win the war for Germany. That night, Lily wrote in her diary: 'He has gone. He hasn't found out anything. And now: England.'

Kenneth Benton of MI6 had grown to like Lily. He liked her still more when she reappeared in his office, with Babs in tow, and handed over Kliemann's questionnaire, proof of mounting German anxiety over the coming invasion. She was dressed up to the nines, having spent all the Spanish cash from Kliemann on clothes. 'I was getting to know her and felt she had a good feeling for the job. Everything was in order for her onward travel to Lisbon. Then she exploded her landmine.'

'Mr Benton,' said Lily. 'I have one more request. I have worked for you; I will continue to work for you; I don't ask for any payment. But I have one favour to ask: I want to keep Babs with me.'

Benton was taken aback. It wasn't possible. It wouldn't be allowed. There were quarantine laws.

'That's exactly it. I want to skip quarantine,' Lily explained. 'Babs has been vaccinated. I've got his anti-rabies certificate, and there is no danger. It's the only thing I ask for, but I do insist on it.'

British laws preventing dogs from entering the country until declared disease-free were some of the oldest, and silliest, in the statute book, maintained long after science and technology had effectively removed the rabies threat. This strange animal-based xenophobia probably had something to do with Britain being an island. Benton was happy to break every law in the book to help win the war, but he was not about to break the sacrosanct quarantine laws. He prevaricated. 'I'll see what I can do . . .'

But Lily would not be fobbed off. She would not leave without Babs. 'If my work is important it is worth this exemption; if it isn't worth that, then it isn't worth my going to England . . . To you, it's just a dog; but to me, it's Babs, and worth more than a million pounds. Just tell your people in London that.' She was working herself up into one of her rages. 'Why can't I go by Gibraltar?'

'Even if you did you would have to leave the dog in quarantine for six months. In fact, I'm not even sure they would allow that.'

'You can persuade them. After all, I'm going to be an important double agent.'

'I cannot persuade them. This is wartime, Lily.'

'Then I will refuse to go. I will stay here in Spain. I won't leave my poor little Babs.'

Desperate for the interview to end, Benton offered to find a kind owner for Babs. It was wartime; she had to make sacrifices.

Lily whispered angrily in Russian to her dog, before turning back to Benton. 'You shall not have him . . . He knows nothing about your war; all he wants is to be with me.'

Benton (who rather liked dogs) told her he would do his best, though he knew 'it was going to be impossible to get that wretched dog into Britain without passing through quarantine'. He had resorted to a very English sort of temporising, a commitment to do what he could, when he planned to do very little and believed that nothing could be done. But Lily had heard something very different: she had heard an Englishman promise to get her dog into Britain. That misunderstanding would have the most profound ramifications.

Benton asked London what to do about Lily's dog. 'Get her to Gibraltar, then leave it to Gibraltar colleagues to sort out,' came the reply. Benton reported back to Lily: 'My Gibraltar colleagues might be able to find a way of smuggling Babs to Britain, perhaps by sea.' In reality, this had already been ruled out by the MI6 officer on the island.

On 7 October 1943, Lily Sergeyev, travelling under an alias, arrived in Gibraltar under escort, with her dog. Benton did not fail to notice the 'suspicious looks' she gave him as they said goodbye. Sure enough, when she reached Gibraltar, the customs officer insisted she surrender the dog. 'I picked up Babs and handed him over,' Lily wrote in her diary. 'The difficult moment had arrived.' But their separation, she assured herself, would be temporary. She had Benton's 'promise'.

The next day an MI6 officer in plain clothes, who introduced himself as O'Shagar, came to see Agent Treasure at the hotel.

'From now on, you have nothing to worry about. We will take charge of everything,' he told her.

Lily pressed him about Babs and 'Mr Benton's promise to arrange for his transport and to make sure that he wouldn't have to go into quarantine'. O'Shagar replied that they'd 'see to that too'.

That night, at the hotel bar, she met a friendly American pilot, Lieutenant Kenneth Larson, who liked dogs. 'Why don't you send him to London with one of our pilots? They don't have to go through customs or any controls at all,' he said. 'Would you like me to fix it up for you?' The next morning she reported the conversation to O'Shagar, pointing out that this arrangement would 'save an awful lot of bother and red tape'. But she wanted a promise that if the American failed to deliver Babs to Britain, then MI6 would find a way to do so.

'You have my word,' said O'Shagar. (That, at least, was how Lily remembered the conversation.)

By some immutable law of travel, luggage always lets you down when you are in the greatest haste. Lily was about to board the flight for England, when the clasp on her suitcase gave way, spilling its contents everywhere. O'Shagar gathered up her scattered belongings, stuffed them in the broken suitcase, and promised to get it repaired and sent over on the next flight. Lily ran for the plane.

A few hours later, 'Dorothy Tremayne' landed at Bristol airport. The policewoman detailed to collect her had been told to look out for a woman with a small white dog and a large record player. She had no gramophone and no dog; she also had no suitcase. But she was in no doubt that the Frenchwoman complaining loudly in the arrivals hall must be Lily Sergeyev. 'Treasure' had finally been smuggled into Britain, bringing with her, in Masterman's words, 'a rich dowry: the confidence of the Germans'.

Back in Madrid, Kenneth Benton of MI6 suffered a 'feeling of guilt' when he learned that Lily had flown to England, leaving her beloved dog behind in Gibraltar. But then he reflected: 'After all, it was wartime, and sacrifices, as I had told her, had to be made by people and consciences alike.' Besides, Benton had other things on his mind: he was about to reel in an even bigger fish, an officer within the Abwehr itself.

The Walk-in

On 14 September 1943, Dusko Popov flew back to Britain, and was immediately taken to Clock House, the cottage rented by MI5, for a debriefing by Tar Robertson and Ian Wilson. Both were in a state of high excitement to see what Tricycle had brought back from Lisbon. Solemnly, Popov opened the 'diplomatic bag' provided by von Karsthoff. 'First of all a very large number of silk stockings fell out,' wrote Wilson. These were followed by a radio transmitter, a Leica camera and six rolls of film, ingredients for making secret ink, $2,000 and £2,500 in cash and yet more questionnaires. This complete spy kit was proof enough of German faith in Popov, but additional reassurance came from Most Secret Sources which, as Wilson reported, 'make it clear that Tricycle's reports to us are accurate, that for the most part the Germans still believe him, and that those members of the Abwehr who have reason to doubt him are so corrupt or so afraid of losing their jobs by disclosing awkward facts that they are doing all they can to support him'.

Popov explained that he had met up once again with Johnny Jebsen, and was now 'absolutely sure' that his friend knew he was a double agent: 'The way he talks to me and his whole behaviour shows this very clearly.' Jebsen had been even more candid than before, talking of 'that idiot Hitler' and speaking with a 'funny smile in his eyes' that left Popov in no doubt that he knew every word he said would be relayed straight back to the Allies. Jebsen's enemies in Berlin were machinating against him, he said, and the Gestapo was circling. But the part of Popov's report that really made his listeners sit up was Jebsen's account of 'some new invention' causing great excitement in Berlin, a multiple rocket device 'with the same effect as a 2,000 kilo bomb'.

Robertson immediately sent a memo to the Twenty Committee, informing the board of this most alarming information from Jebsen who seemed to be, 'for the first time, acting as a conscious informant'. Popov did not say explicitly that he had advised his friend to go to the British and offer himself as a double agent, but he almost certainly had. A full report was sent to Churchill:

> Tricycle has just returned from a visit to Lisbon where he has been in contact with members of the German secret service. He gained the impression that they no longer hope to win the war and expect it to be over shortly. He learnt from his spymaster who is also a close personal friend that the latter believes in the existence of a rocket gun for shelling London. The spymaster added that the raids on Germany had delayed the production of the gun by about two months, but that it should be in action by December and Tricycle would be well advised to leave London before then. The Germans further told Tricycle that they are well informed about the British Order of Battle. The Germans said that they had practically no agents in the USA, but that they had ten or twelve in the UK (this corresponds to those under our control). They also told him the story of a Major in the German secret service in Berlin who had suggested that the agents in England were under British control but was sacked for this suggestion within 24 hours.

The 'rocket gun' was the V1, the flying bomb being developed in Germany in order to bombard Britain into submission.

Jebsen's information corroborated what was already known about the new weapon, while his description of the Germans' faith in their British spy network underlined Tar's claim to control the whole thing: any German intelligence officer who dared suggest the spies were false was regarded as a heretic, and liable to be fired.

The final element in Popov's Lisbon haul was a plan that had been stewing for some time – a way to smuggle additional double agents into Britain, with German help. With MI5's approval, Popov had spun von Karsthoff an ingenious tale: since numerous Yugoslavs were anxious to get to Britain, why not introduce some secret Nazi spies among the genuine refugees? Popov's older brother Ivo, living in Belgrade, could select potential candidates. Ivo was held in high regard by the Germans, who saw him as a keen and dedicated collaborator, so highly trusted that he had been issued with travel papers, a Wehrmacht uniform and the rank of *Sonderführer* (Specialist Leader). Ivo Popov would select recruits, who with German assistance would be smuggled into Britain, via Spain, as refugees. Once they arrived in Britain, the younger Popov brother would take them in hand and add them to his spy network. Von Karsthoff leaped at the idea, and on 23 July sent a message to Berlin describing Popov's wheeze for infiltrating spies into Britain: 'I consider this plan a good one,' he wrote. 'I still consider Ivan as reliable, if kept under supervision.'

What von Karsthoff did not know was that Ivo Popov, like his brother, was working for the other side and had already been recruited by British intelligence as Agent 'Dreadnought'. Instead of choosing Nazi sympathisers for the so-called 'slipping out' operation, he would select his own anti-Nazi collaborators, who had been briefed to play the part. At the other end, Popov, Robertson and the Double Cross Committee would be waiting to welcome them. Every link of the chain was false. Instead of introducing keen new spies into Britain, the Germans would be helping to recruit, train, finance and transport a stream of ready-made double agents, pre-cooked and ready to serve.

The first agent to be 'slipped out' in this way was the Marquis Frano de Bona, an aristocratic Yugoslavian naval officer, and a friend and former carousing partner of Dusko Popov. At Ivo's instigation, de Bona was recruited by the Abwehr and trained as a wireless operator, and slipped into Spain. While waiting for his transfer to London as a refugee, the Marquis took up residence in a Madrid brothel, where he spent four days and nights, finally emerging exhausted and happy, but with a nasty dose of venereal crabs. On arrival in Britain he moved into Clock House with Popov, and became a double agent, the wireless operator for the Tricycle network. No longer would Popov and his sub-agents have to rely on secret writing to communicate with Germany. Whether because of his long hair, licentiousness or lice, the Marquis de Bona was awarded a most unflattering codename: he became Agent Freak.

Intriguingly, Freak's briefing in Germany offered indications that elements within the Abwehr were ready to sue for peace. Churchill read of de Bona's arrival:

> His main mission, it appears, was to contact Englishmen in high places and to impress upon them very strongly the view that Germany is open to approaches from this country with a view to stemming the flow of Communism across the Continent of Europe, and for this purpose they required the assistance of the British. The core of his instructions was that Germany was not to be forced to capitulate, but should be granted terms by this country to enable her to maintain a barrier in Eastern Europe against the Communist peril. It was emphasised that Germany was willing in order to obtain these terms, to get rid of Hitler, to introduce a democratic form of government acceptable to the English and Americans, [and] withdraw from all occupied territory.

This was the essence of the anti-Nazi resistance: to oust Hitler, ally with the West, defeat the Bolsheviks and salvage some

German pride. Anthony Blunt certainly passed this report to
the Soviets, doubtless compounding Stalin's suspicions that the
British and Americans might make peace with Germany and
then turn on the Soviet Union. Churchill believed that the war
could only end with Germany's unconditional surrender, but
de Bona brought hard evidence that Abwehr officers were now
actively manoeuvring to oust the Führer. Riven with conspiracy,
double-crossed from within, under attack from its rivals, German
military intelligence was starting to implode.

Kenneth Benton made his way upstairs in the British Embassy
in Madrid to a small attic room usually 'used as a bedroom for
escaped POWs'. There he found a young man 'who was chain-
smoking and looking rather sweaty and apprehensive'. The man
rose, shook hands, and spoke in perfect, accentless English: 'I
am an officer in the Abwehr and I wish you to protect me from
the Gestapo.'

Benton offered his guest a whisky. The Abwehr man 'smiled
rather charmingly' revealing nicotine-stained teeth: 'Where I
come from we love whisky, and I could certainly do with a
drink right now.'

Sipping whisky and soda, in his well-cut suit and monocle, he
might have been an Englishman. He wore a 'very small blond
moustache', and fiddled restlessly, lighting one cigarette from
another. 'My name is Johnny Jebsen,' he said. 'I suppose you
are Mr Benton.' The MI6 man was taken aback. His real name
was supposed to be a closely guarded secret, even within the
Embassy. Jebsen smiled again.

'You're in trouble?' asked Benton.

'The Gestapo are on my tail because I made a report on their
dealings in forged banknotes.'

'Have they followed you here?'

'No, I shook them off.'

Jebsen had every reason to be agitated. Not only was the
Gestapo closing in, but he had learned that Kammler, the Abwehr

official in Lisbon skimming Popov's pay, had denounced him to
the bosses in Berlin. Jebsen feared that his hotel room in Lisbon
might have been bugged and his 'indiscreet' conversations
with Popov overheard. His supporters within the Abwehr had
advised him to stay away from Germany. He might need an
escape route.

They talked for two hours, and as Jebsen relaxed, he became
ever more informative and opinionated, revealing the identities
of senior Abwehr officers in Spain and 'their special fields of
interest', his role as a freelance agent-recruiter, and sinking
German morale: 'There is hardly a soul any more in Germany
who believes in victory. Probably the only man who really
does is Hitler.' He drank more whisky, and cracked dark jokes:
'During an air raid Hitler, Goering, Goebbels and Himmler
took refuge in the same air raid shelter. The shelter received a
direct hit. Who was saved? Germany.' He described again the
'secret weapon' being built in Germany, 'which would spread
terror throughout the whole of the south of England'. Jebsen
said he 'did not know any details about the mystery weapon',
but could find out more.

'I'm giving you a lot of information, aren't I?' he remarked,
with a grin. 'Well, it'll be up to you to help me in return.'
Jebsen was ready to cut a deal. If the Gestapo came after him,
he wanted the British to get him out, quickly. In return, he
would reveal everything he knew. Benton knew that smuggling
Jebsen back to Britain from Spain would be simple enough, but
the consequences of such a move were unpredictable: when
the Abwehr discovered Jebsen's defection, they would assume
he had revealed all, and anyone associated with him would
immediately become suspect. Jebsen had thought of a solution.
He would leave a fake 'suicide note' to cover his sudden
disappearance, in which he would write: 'I shall take poison
and swim far out into the sea. It may be days before my corpse
is washed up and it will then be no longer recognisable.' It is
hard to imagine even the most idiotic Abwehr officer falling for

such an obvious ruse. MI5 would later dismiss Jebsen's suicide plot as a 'piece of extreme foolishness brought on by excessive nervous strain'.

Benton felt drawn to Jebsen. The spy spoke warmly of his love for England, his wish to study at Oxford after the war, his friendship with P. G. Wodehouse, and his bossy English secretary, Mabel Harbottle, who refused to type letters that might undermine the Allied war effort. 'He was an interesting and well-educated man and very good company,' thought Benton, but also worldly, cynical and dissolute. 'He had a great liking for pornographic films and admitted that one of the reasons why he came so frequently to Madrid was the existence of two clandestine Madrid cinemas which specialised in this kind of film.' He made no secret of his fears, and no claims to courage. With a 'visible shudder' he described the Ablege Kommando, a 'trained hijack team, skilled in seizing a wanted man and smuggling him back across the frontiers without arousing suspicion'. Even in neutral Spain, he might be kidnapped at any time and taken back to Germany, a prospect that terrified him.

Benton advised Jebsen to spend that night at the Embassy. 'It is in your interest. By tomorrow I'll have a safe house.' Over a last nightcap, Benton asked his new recruit if there were other Abwehr officers who might be willing to defect. Jebsen replied: 'I'm sure some of them have been turned and I know one Abwehr agent, a man I recruited myself, who has either been turned already or would go over to your side at the drop of a hat.'

'Who is that?'

'Dusan Popov,' Jebsen answered. 'He's a prolific agent, run from both Berlin and Lisbon.'

Jebsen had recruited Popov into the Abwehr. Popov, once turned, had urged the British to recruit Jebsen. Now Jebsen, in the process of being turned, urged the British to recruit Popov. He was being deliberately disingenuous. Jebsen knew by now, and probably had known from the beginning, that Popov was working for the British. Henceforth, they would be working together.

Benton sat up late, drafting a long report to London about Jebsen, whom he codenamed 'Artist'. The reply read: 'Artist is telling you the truth. He is a *Forscher*, and well known to us. This contact has great potential value. Use utmost caution.'

Jebsen told him he would remain in Spain for the time being, see what developed, and keep in touch. 'I was very sorry to part with Artist,' Benton later wrote. Jebsen was plainly being honest about his espionage activities, if not his financial dealings: 'Artist told me that he suspected the Gestapo of lining their pockets with forged British banknotes, but I was never quite sure it was not the other way around.' With Jebsen, it was always tricky to work out which way round the truth lay.

Lily Sergeyev's first moments on British soil could not have been more inauspicious. She had been told not to answer questions until she was interrogated. 'You won't have to open your mouth from here to London,' O'Shagar had told her as she left Gibraltar. Mary Sherer had sent instructions that she 'should be dealt with at the airport in an absolutely normal manner', since Lily was 'particularly anxious that as few people as possible should know about her case, as she has a family still in Paris'.

The very first official she encountered was an immigration officer named Gold, 'fat, with big ears', and a stickler for the rules. Gold asked her name. She refused to answer. He asked where she was born. Lily said nothing. Finally, in what was later admitted to be a 'rather ill-advised attempt to make her feel at ease', Gold remarked: 'It's all right, you needn't worry. We know all about you, the Germans have sent you here.'

Lily exploded. She had been in Britain less than an hour, and already some lumpen official with outsize ears was telling her that everybody knew her secret. Lily was still shouting when a severe-looking policewoman appeared, saying she had been sent to escort 'Miss Tremayne' to London.

She was driven to a house in Balham, through the pouring rain, and put to bed by a motherly woman calling herself 'Mrs Maud'. The next morning, after a deep and exhausted night's sleep and breakfast of porridge, she was ushered into a second-floor room to find a woman in a red suit, sitting 'on the edge of a chair, her arms folded, chin resting on her hands'. Mary Sherer appraised Agent Treasure coolly 'through slightly slanted greenish eyes'. For a few moments, neither spoke. Lily then perched on the sofa, and reeled off her story. Mary took notes, saying little. After an hour, she stood up: 'You can be extremely useful to us, and the opening you provide may be of vital importance. We will be delighted to work with you, but you must realise the gravity of the situation. By helping the British you will be working for France, for her liberation.' She escorted Lily to a waiting car.

Lily was driven to Flat 19, Rugby Mansions, in Kensington, and introduced to a Yugoslavian woman named Maritza, who would be her housekeeper, Mary explained. She did not explain that the flat was an MI5 safe house under surveillance: the phone was bugged, the post monitored, and Maritza Mihailovic was herself a double agent, codenamed 'The Snark' (after the Lewis Carroll nonsense poem *The Hunting of the Snark*. Since Carroll himself could not explain what a Snark was, this may be one codename with no relevance whatever to its subject). A domestic servant, she had been recruited by the Abwehr in Yugoslavia and arrived in England as a refugee in 1941. B1A had run her as a double agent for a time, but for unknown reasons the Germans had lost interest in her, and since 1943 she had worked for MI5 as a cleaner, and as a spy. The Snark would be keeping a close eye on Treasure.

Tar Robertson soon arrived, exuding bonhomie: 'So you are here at last. Let me congratulate you on your work: it's a great success. Now you must relax, forget your fears and uncertainty; nothing more can happen to you. You are among friends.'

Lily made no reply. She was fairly impervious to English charm. Robertson ploughed on.

'We look on you as a trump card. There is no doubt the German intelligence people have complete confidence in you, so we are in a unique position to feed them false information. We can pull off what is known in the trade as an "intoxication".'

With Mary Sherer's help, Tar explained, Lily would write her own letters. 'I want you, yourself, to draft all the messages,' said Tar. 'If you think that any of the stuff we want to send will seem unlikely to the Germans, you mustn't hesitate to say so. The possibilities open to us are so precious that we must not take even the smallest risk.' For the next four hours, she went through her story yet again. She drew a map of Madrid showing where she had met her German contacts, and even sketched portraits of Emile Kliemann and Yvonne Delidaise.

Lily's sketches of Emile Kliemann and Yvonne Delidaise

'That only leaves the financial question,' said Tar, beaming. 'We'll take over the money and jewellery and give you £50 a month and 10 per cent of anything else they send. Is that all right?' Lily nodded, but reflected that the Germans had offered her £250 a month. 'I am not doing this for the money,' she told her diary, 'but I am a little surprised.' The brooch and diamond ring were locked in the B1A safe, but not before MI5 had valued them and found the jewellery was worth just £100, 'rather a far cry from the £400 that Kliemann thought she would get'. The arrival of this promising new double agent was relayed to Churchill:

> A French citizen of Russian origin, she has lived most of her life in Paris, where she occupied herself with journalism, and at one time gained a considerable reputation as an artist. Through a fellow journalist, a German whom she had known before the war, Treasure gained her first introduction to the German secret service. It was a long time before Treasure was able to persuade her German masters to send her to this country. She has had extensive training in wireless transmission and in secret ink writing. She did not bring a wireless set with her, but was assured that arrangements had been made for one to be sent.

Anthony Blunt had made a special request 'to be informed when Treasure arrives'; news of Lily's arrival was certainly relayed to the Kremlin.

Mary Sherer was far too English to show it, but she was pleased with Lily, and already had the 'very strong conviction that this, her first double agent, was going to be a success, come what might'. Kim Philby, her colleague in MI6, remarked darkly: 'Poor girl. She's in for a disappointment. Never trust a Tsarist émigré.'

Lily glumly appraised her new home, the flat with its large, ill-furnished rooms, 'clean and impersonal, like the rooms of a hotel'. She went for a walk, Maritza hovering in attendance. The street was 'bleak and gloomy', and Rugby Mansions a 'plain-fronted house with neither imagination nor ornament, as sour as an old spinster suffering from jaundice'. She had imagined a London ferociously at war. This place was grey, damp and foggy. Lily thought of herself as a bird of colour, an artist, a child of bright adventure. This was not her world. 'What strikes me is the shabby appearance of everyone in the street: worn-out overcoats, shiny sleeves, dowdy clothes. In the shop windows the dresses are straight, without facing, lapels, or belt – everything remotely frivolous has been pitilessly sacrificed.' Her new handlers seemed detached and distant. Mary Sherer was a puzzle: 'I still cannot quite place her: is she my jailer, or nursery governess, or what?' she wrote. 'I don't even know what she feels about me, though I suppose this really doesn't matter very much.' Lowering her spirits still further was the nagging, and growing, pain in her kidneys, a recurrence of her old malady.

Lily missed Paris, stylish even under Nazi occupation. She missed the excitement of playing one side off against the other. She even missed Kliemann. But most of all, she missed Babs.

A Time for Fortitude

The D-Day deception plan went through many versions and many names in the months leading up to June 1944: Operation Jael (named after the Old Testament heroine who nailed her sleeping enemy's head to the floor with a tent peg) aimed to persuade the Germans there would be no invasion in 1944; then came 'Torrent' or 'Appendix Y', intended to convince them that Calais was the sole target. The plan for Operation Bodyguard, combining elements of the earlier plans, was finally completed by Johnny Bevan, 'haggard with sleeplessness', just before Christmas, 1943.

Bodyguard was worldwide in scope, and vaulting in ambition. Its aims were multiple: to tie down German troops in the Mediterranean with the bogus threat of assaults on the Dalmatian and Greek coasts; to dissipate German strength by suggesting that additional attacks might be made in northwest Italy, Bulgaria, Denmark and, most importantly, Norway; to implant the idea that the bombing of Germany would take precedence over land-based assaults, and make the Germans believe, for as long as possible, that no cross-Channel attack could take place until late summer. Bodyguard's aim was to baffle and bemuse, to keep German troops away from where they would most be needed, hold them down where they could do least harm, and lure them away from France and the Eastern Front, and towards Italy, the Balkans, Greece and Scandinavia.

Bodyguard would be implemented in various theatres of war, but its most important element by far was the plan to mislead Hitler over the planned Normandy landings.

The choice of codename for this particular operation – the crux of Bodyguard – was much debated. Churchill had given instructions that no codename should be selected that might seem flippant in retrospect, or give a hint of the individual or action involved. But he also disliked codenames that meant nothing at all, which is why the original choice, 'Mespot', was rejected. Also vetoed were 'Bulldog', 'Swordhilt', 'Axehead', 'Tempest', and, obscurely, 'Lignite'. Finally a name was selected that seemed to evoke the resolution required to pull it off: Operation Fortitude.

A vast, secret army set to work on Operation Fortitude, fabricating physical deception, including dummy landing craft and rubber tanks at key points, and technical deception in the form of great waves of radio traffic, a blizzard of electric noise mimicking great armies training and assembling where none existed. British diplomats dropped misleading hints at cocktail parties to be overheard by eavesdroppers and channelled back to Germany. Conspicuously large orders were made for Michelin Map 51, a map of the Pas de Calais area. The French resistance, SOE agents, Jedburgh saboteur and guerrilla teams, MI6, the code-breakers at Bletchley, secret scientists and camouflage engineers would each play a part in this great, sprawling, multi-faceted deception campaign. But at its core was Tar Robertson's tiny team of double agents, telling lies to their spymasters, in secret writing, by radio, and to their faces, forging a shield of deceit that would guard the soldiers, if it worked, onto the beaches of Normandy.

Many played a part in planning Operation Fortitude, but three principal architects of the deception plan stand out. Colonel Johnny Bevan, the head of the London Controlling Section; Major Roger Fleetwood-Hesketh, the leading intelligence officer within the Supreme Headquarters Allied Expeditionary

Force (SHAEF), whose task it was to merge military planning and deception, and Colonel David Strangeways, the head of General Montgomery's deception section. Christopher Harmer of B1A would act as liaison between the headquarters of the Expeditionary Force and the Double Cross team. These were very different men. Fleetwood-Hesketh – a barrister with 'one of the best claret cellars in England' – was 'charming and witty', with a fine sense of the absurd. Harmer described him as a 'most tidy and meticulous worker' but 'essentially a scorer rather than a player'. Strangeways, a hard-driving infantryman, was 'impossible and insufferable' according to Harmer, but frequently right, and occasionally inspired. Bevan, overworked and under stress, was liable to volcanic eruptions of temper, always followed by heartfelt apology. Their roles were often ill-defined and overlapping. Tempers frayed and snapped. The rows were spectacular, but the extent of their collaboration was even more remarkable. Between them, these individuals would fashion and then implement the most ambitious deception campaign ever attempted.

Operation Fortitude was revised over time. At one point, the acerbic Strangeways, in his own words, 'rewrote the thing entirely', igniting another furious argument (though his changes were finally accepted). In its final form, the plan had several, interlinked aims: to convince the Germans that the attack on Normandy (eventually scheduled for June) was merely diversionary, a ploy to draw off German forces before the main thrust of the invasion in the Pas de Calais around the middle of July; at the same time it sought to lure the Germans into preparing for an attack on Norway, along with another landing in the area of Bordeaux. Crucially, the threat to the Pas de Calais would be maintained for as long as possible after the Normandy landings, to ensure that the Germans did not send a large body of troops south to repel the real invasion.

The deception plan was divided in two: Fortitude North was the fake threat to Norway; Fortitude South would pose, and maintain, the threat to the Pas de Calais. In order for the plan to work, the Germans must be made to expect three separate invasions – a feint in Normandy and two major landings in Norway and the Pas de Calais – and therein lay a major hurdle. There were simply not enough soldiers in Britain to do what the planners wanted the Germans to believe they were about to do, so they invented them. It was Strangeways who came up with the idea of creating an entire fictional army in southeast England, poised to invade the northeast coast of France. This ghost army, supposedly stationed directly across the Channel from the Pas de Calais, was dubbed the First United States Army Group, or FUSAG. Another fake force, the British Fourth Army, would be created in Scotland, to keep German minds focused on a threat to Norway. These counterfeit armies would threaten bogus targets, while living soldiers prepared to attack the real target, in Normandy.

Masterman was itching for the game to start. 'We had always expected', he wrote, 'that at some one moment all the agents would be recklessly and gladly "blown" sky-high in carrying out the grand deception, and that this one great coup would bring our work to an end.' There were voices of caution, and some of scepticism, including the British Army representative on the Twenty Committee who insisted that 'the German General Staff will not move a single German division on an agent's report alone'. Unless, of course, they discovered the agent was a double agent, and the division was then moved in precisely the wrong direction. 'An agent who turned out not to be believed by the enemy might wreck the whole enterprise, or, even worse, his messages might be read "in reverse" and the true target of the attack be exposed instead of revealed.' There was every possibility the plan could backfire disastrously.

Churchill and Roosevelt were kept fully apprised of the roles planned for the double agents in the deception, as was Stalin, both officially and secretly. The NKVD mole Anthony Blunt, now promoted to major, was still burrowing deep into British intelligence, digging up every scrap of secret information he could find, and shipping it all to Moscow. 'I have managed to get myself in touch with Robertson who runs the double agents,' he told his Soviet handlers. 'In this way I can usually get an idea of what is actually planned and what is being put across as cover.' If there was an equivalent German mole within Soviet intelligence, then the entire deception would be blown. Or it might have been, had it not been for the paranoia ingrained into Soviet officialdom. Moscow did not believe what Blunt was telling them, because it was too good to be true. Having discovered that Britain was practising an intricate double-cross operation on the Germans, the Soviets convinced themselves that they, too, must be victims of such a deception. According to the warped logic of the NKVD, the Cambridge Five (Blunt, Kim Philby, Guy Burgess, Donald Maclean and John Cairncross) were sending such high-grade information that they must be double agents, sending deliberate disinformation; and since the information from the five tallied perfectly, this was further proof that they were in league.

The chief exponent of this gymnastic exercise in double-think was Colonel Elena Modrzhinskaya, a blonde, rotund, zealously conspiratorial NKVD officer responsible for assessing British intelligence. Her suspicion of Blunt and his fellow spies was based on the assumption, firmly held and quite wrong, that the British could not be so foolish as to allow former communists to occupy senior positions in the intelligence services. Therefore Blunt and the others must have been working for the British from the beginning. A splendidly incompetent NKVD surveillance team was sent to gather evidence of the Cambridge spies making contact with their British handlers. Since Blunt worked *inside* MI5, this 'evidence' of contact with British intelligence was not hard to find. As the D-Day deception was being crafted, Moscow sent a letter to its London spy chief warning of a vast, organised deception by these British double agents. 'Our task is to understand what disinformation our rivals are planting on us,' since 'all the data' from Blunt and the others indicated a double-cross operation. (The irony that Moscow was only aware of the existence of the British Double Cross system because Blunt had revealed it to them, was entirely lost on Colonel Modrzhinskaya.)

But in the mirroring world of espionage, Blunt and Modrzhinskaya might actually end up *supporting* the deception. If Agent Tony was a double agent, then his false information should be read in reverse; if he indicated that Normandy was the real target and the Pas de Calais a decoy, then the Pas de Calais must be the real target, and Normandy a feint. And if a German mole had penetrated Soviet intelligence, then that is the information he would be passing back to Berlin. In a nutshell: if the Germans believed that the Soviets thought the British were trying to make them believe something that was untrue, then the deception would still be on track. At the very least, Soviet suspicions would muddy the waters to an opacity beyond human penetration.

By the end of 1943, wrote Masterman, the Double Cross team was 'far more powerful and better equipped than it had ever been before'. The double agents were reaching peak fitness. Tricycle (Popov) was beloved and admired by his German handlers, with Jebsen, the latest addition to the team, on hand to protect him; Garbo sat in Crespigny Road, Hendon, arguing with his wife and spinning ever more elaborate fantasies; Treasure was now in place, lonely and lovesick without her dog, but ready to start feeding misinformation back to Kliemann. Bronx, the socialite spy, was in regular contact with Germany. Even the excitable Brutus might soon be back in play, if the Pole could be extracted from prison.

The Double Cross idea had always been based on lateral thinking without boundaries, a willingness to contemplate plans that others would dismiss as unworkable or, frankly, barmy. Flights of fantasy were integral to the system, which perhaps explains why, just as the D-Day deception plans were falling into place, the Double Cross system suddenly took wing, and soared into the surreal.

Of all the strands in Operation Fortitude, none was quite so bizarre, so wholly unlikely, as the great pigeon double cross, the first and only avian deception scheme ever attempted. Animal-based espionage and sabotage was all the rage among Allied plotters: SOE agents stuffed dead rats with explosives, and military zoologists explored the use of trained marine mammals for naval sabotage. In December 1943, Guy Liddell reported an American scheme for attacking Japan using thousands of exploding Mexican bats: 'These bats should be put into crates shipped to Seattle. Attached to the feet and wings of the bats were to be small incendiaries. The bats were to be released from an aeroplane near Tokio [sic], the idea being that they would fly down chimneys and that Tokio would go up in flames.' The idea never took off, but was taken seriously. 'It sounds like a perfectly wild idea but is worth looking into,' said Roosevelt.

People like Robertson and Walker flourished in that grey area between ingenuity and insanity; early in 1944 'our pigeon expert', as Robertson called Walker, approached B1A with an audacious new plan. With D–Day approaching, and having failed to make much impact on enemy pigeons in Britain (because there weren't any), the unstoppable Flight Lieutenant Walker 'began to wonder if there were not some more offensive way of attacking the German pigeon service'. He came up with the 'double-cross pigeon racket', a plan that might wipe out the enemy pigeon population at a stroke.

Every German intelligence station in occupied France had a pigeon section. Moreover, collaborationist French pigeon fanciers were being recruited as stay-behind agents, to harbour German homing pigeons and then release them with intelligence from behind the lines in the event of a successful Allied invasion. Walker began to wonder whether Himmler's interest in pigeons, and his taste for final solutions, could be manipulated to Allied advantage. If the Germans could be fooled into believing that British spy-pigeons had infiltrated their lofts, then it would throw suspicion on the entire German pigeon service: if they could no longer trust their own pigeons, they might kill the lot. In the winter of 1943, he presented MI5 with a top secret memo laying out his 'Pigeon Contamination Plan'.

A stray or lost pigeon will almost always find its way into some loft. If a number of British pigeons could be disguised as German pigeons by putting German rings on them and then released on the Continent (deliberately choosing second-rate birds which would be unlikely to attempt the long flight back), they would find their way eventually into German-controlled lofts. Sooner or later, the Germans would discover they were being fooled. They would find two birds with the same ring number, or a grey pigeon wearing a ring which their records clearly showed as belonging to a red pigeon. They would begin, then, to wonder how many of their pigeons were 'phoney', and the only thing they could do would be to call all their birds in and check them. Until they had checked all their birds in all their lofts they would be unable to use any pigeon services and by the time they had gone through them all, I would have delivered more 'phonies'.

MI5 was enthusiastic. With the Germans braced for an invasion, the discovery that their lofts had been penetrated by double-agent pigeons would 'throw them off balance at a critical psychological moment', in the words of Guy Liddell. The pigeon deception scheme was approved by MI5. After consulting expert technicians, Walker discovered a new aluminium welding process that could attach a forged leg-ring to a pigeon with a 'perfectly invisible joint'; he created a rubber stamp to counterfeit German wing markings; he constructed an automatic pigeon release system out of a weighted Hessian bag,

Flight Lieutenant Walker's diagrams for counterfeit wing markings

large enough to carry eight birds, that could be thrown from a plane with a strap attached that would pull off an elastic band and release the birds beyond the slip stream; he consulted the Air Ministry to find out 'when aircraft were going on special dropping missions'. And he began recruiting sluggish British carrier pigeons to be sent on this secret mission to infiltrate the German pigeon service, and destroy it from within. Soon there was a force of 350 double agent pigeons at his disposal, disguised as German pigeons, ready to do their bit.

The Allies now had a series of double-cross operations running simultaneously: a human one in Britain, another composed of pigeons, and a third, fledgling team of double agents, in America.

The Popov debacle in America had revealed the very different American and British attitudes towards double agents, but as the Allied intelligence services grew closer in the course of war, the FBI first became interested in the Double Cross system, and then extremely good at it. The chief impetus for this change of heart was a man not unlike Popov in character: a rich, profligate wastrel with an eye for the ladies and the main chance. Jorge José Mosquera, an Argentinian by birth, was the owner of a leather export company based in Hamburg. In 1941, he decided to relocate to South America. At this point the Abwehr had moved in, insisting that his funds would only be released if he agreed to spy for them in the New World. Mosquera agreed, headed to Uruguay, and promptly handed himself in at the American consulate in Montevideo. Described as 'a tall, pleasant-looking businessman with some glamour effect', he was given a new identity as Max Rudloff by the FBI.

Mosquera's German instructions were to make his way to New York, build a wireless transmitter, and begin sending military information as soon as possible. The FBI duly established a transmitter in a farmhouse on a secluded section of the Long Island coast, manned by three agents disguised as local workers and protected by a pack of guard dogs. Soon he was sending several transmissions a week, and recruiting fake sub-agents, in the manner of Garbo: an engineer who worked in an aircraft factory, an official in the War Department, and a civilian in the Navy Department. Mosquera had not been long in New York when he conceived a grand passion for a much younger woman of Italian extraction who wanted to be an opera singer. Mosquera demanded that the FBI hand over $15,000 to enable her to pursue her operatic career. The bureau arranged for Mosquera's inamorata to 'audition at the Metropolitan Opera', the first and only time that institution has taken an active role in international espionage.

Mosquera was only the first of the FBI's double agents. Next came a Dutchman named Alfred Meiler, a former diamond dealer sent to the US to gather information on atomic research, who turned himself in and was set to work reporting titbits of misinformation from naval dockyards. Helmut Goldschmidt, a Dutch-born Orthodox Jew who had renounced Judaism, deserted from the Dutch army, and then signed up with the Abwehr, was described by the FBI as 'an extremely selfish individual, arrogant, extremely difficult to control, and of a very low-grade moral character'. Goldschmidt handed himself in and became agent 'Peasant'. The most glamorous of the American-based double agents was Dieudonner Costes, a French former flying ace. Recruited by the Abwehr and sent on an espionage mission to the US, he turned himself in and was duly installed in New York's Park Lane Hotel, where he began sending letters in secret ink. 'Although he might not deliberately try to assist the Germans,' the FBI reported of the flamboyant, arrogant and dubious Costes, 'he does not hesitate to resort to falsehoods in any situations.'

The FBI took a cautious approach, seldom permitting double agents to fashion their own messages, 'chicken-feed' with misinformation thrown in. They reported on military production, insignia and the units departing for the European theatre. Folded into Operation Bodyguard, American double agents were set to work promoting the idea that the invasion would be postponed owing to lack of landing craft, industrial unrest and the slow build-up of American troops. The US agents were not in a position to report on the immediate preparations for the D-Day assault, yet the slow but steady trickle of corroborative material provided a distinct minor melody in the major symphony now under way.

As Masterman's small orchestra of double agents tuned up, a small, discordant note became audible, growing louder as the day of the grand performance approached. There was, it seemed, another band of spies in Britain, playing their own song. Early in 1942, Most Secret Sources revealed the existence of a highly regarded German agent codenamed 'Ostro'. A Czech businessman named Paul Fidrmuc, Ostro was based in Lisbon but boasted a wide espionage network, including five spies on British soil, as well as other parts of the British Empire, the Middle East and America. Ostro was highly paid for his reports, which were passed directly from the Abwehr in Lisbon to Berlin. Indeed, he was sometimes sent the reports from other agents for evaluation, and 'regarded in Berlin as a sort of prima donna who must not be ruffled'.

Ostro was reticent about his sources of information, for good reason: he was making it all up. Like Garbo before him, Fidrmuc had worked out that German hunger for information was so acute that the Abwehr would pay handsomely for invented information, and the more secretively that information was passed on, the more likely they were to believe it. Wartime intelligence often throws up such 'freelancers', canny individuals who realise that in a situation where the buyer cannot check the quality of the goods, dealing in false commodities is both easier and safer than genuine trade. The Germans had no idea that Ostro was feeding them nonsense, but the British did.

The Bletchley decrypts clearly showed that Fidrmuc's reports were an amalgam of imagination, half-baked deduction and quarter-baked gossip, bearing little relation to reality. Yet Ostro was anything but harmless. His reports would inevitably contradict, at times, what was being reported by the controlled double agents, and dilute their effect. More worryingly, his guesswork might accidentally reveal the truth. Ostro was spinning his own deception, and there was not room enough in the game for two. MI5, MI6 and the London Controlling Section discussed the options. Like Garbo, Ostro could be approached and brought under British control; alternatively, he could be discredited in Abwehr eyes if he was exposed as a fraud. A more radical alternative would be to kill him, an option backed by the shark-eyed John Marriott: 'If liquidation means the literal abolition of Ostro by doing away with him altogether . . . then I naturally consider that the best solution to the whole affair.' Garbo was a fabulist, who had been welcomed into the MI5 embrace; Ostro was also making it up, and might have to be murdered. 'We should try to buy him up or bump him off,' thought Liddell. For reasons more practical than humanitarian, it was finally agreed that MI5 would 'try to discredit Ostro rather than eliminate him'. Any move against Fidrmuc risked revealing how he had been rumbled, and Most Secret Sources must be protected at all costs. Ostro's life was spared, a decision MI5 would come to regret.

Enriching the Chicken-feed

As 1944 dawned, Juan Pujol was in the highest spirits: he was beloved of both the British and German intelligence services, and he had a new girlfriend. Somewhat ungallantly he described her to his German handlers as 'less than beautiful and rather dowdy in her dress [and] unaccustomed to attentions of the opposite sex', but 'delightfully indiscreet' – which was ideal since she worked as a secretary in the War Office and had access to useful information on the forthcoming invasion. She was also imaginary. Garbo's acquisition of a fantasy lover was part of his job, but it was also surely a reflection on the state of Pujol's marriage.

Tommy Harris led Garbo into ever more extreme and colourful realms of make-believe. 'I would never have had the nerve to allow any of my agents to be as audacious as he was,' Christopher Harmer later said. In addition to his plain new lover, Garbo's fictitious web now included an American sergeant ('jocular and fairly talkative'), a Greek deserter, a commercial traveller and, strangest of all, a group of fiercely anti-semitic Welshmen dedicated to bringing National Socialism to the valleys and toppling the British government by a campaign of assassination. 'The Brothers in the Aryan World Order' had just twelve members, led by an Indian poet named Rags. Three of the 'Brothers' were brought into the network, and a 'Sister', Theresa Jardine, a Wren (in the Women's Royal Naval Service) and the Hindi-speaking girlfriend of Rags. None of these people existed.

It would be reasonable, at this point, to wonder if Garbo and Harris had gone wildly over the top. Rags and his posse of Welsh fascists seem like caricatures, the villains of cheap melodrama. Could the Germans really be expected to believe that a gang of murderous racists planned to destroy the government and seize power, killing Jews, communists and other 'undesirables'? They could; because, of course, that is exactly what had happened in Germany. Importantly, the new recruits offered an opportunity to establish the network in sensitive coastal areas, ahead of the travel ban that would precede Operation Overlord, the invasion of Europe.

The Garbo network now consisted of a staggering twenty-four agents, of whom only one, Pujol himself, was real. With a secure telephone link to both MI5 and the Expeditionary Force headquarters, Pujol and Harris fed directly into military planning and the overarching deception. Over the next six months, Garbo's network would send an average of four wireless messages a day. Pujol himself was privy to Operation Fortitude, the cover plan and the real plan; he knew which divisions were genuine, and which false, where the attack would take place, and where it would not. He was more trusted than ever, by both sides. The Germans began submitting wish lists of secrets: the dates and targets of the invasion, the troops involved, types of landing craft, warships and embarkation points. He was specifically asked to inspect the coast between Weymouth and Southampton, where troops were already massing for the Normandy invasion. 'There is no concentration at special points,' he reported. The Brothers in the Aryan World Order were deployed to Brighton, Exeter, Harwich and Southampton, where they would be ideally situated to relay misinformation about the forthcoming invasion.

The poultry farmer from Barcelona was getting all his ducks in a row.

★

Elvira Chaudoir, Agent Bronx, was also wheedling her way deeper into German affections, by rather different methods. Her early letters contained snippets of political and economic gossip supposedly gleaned from the military officers, politicians, society ladies, industrialists and journalists she encountered around the gaming tables of fashionable London. From late 1943, Hugh Astor began to make her letters 'more military in character to enable her to play a part in current deception policy'. The response from Germany was swift and gratifying. She was bombarded with questions about military installations, troop movements and even the possible use of radar to divert 'radio controlled rockets'. Bronx reported rumours that 'big magnetic deflecting fields' were to be deployed. The exchange, Tar observed, 'showed German faith in Bronx on a crucial matter'. She passed on harmless information about egg rationing, and small items she imagined might be true ('Great invasion problem is seasickness. Canadians studying new cure'), but also deceptive material to suggest that the vast, slowly assembling US Army was plagued by logistical problems that would delay any attack. In Liverpool docks, she reported seeing 'hundreds of American tanks, many Jeeps, cases, cranes etc.', but added that the newspaper baron Lord Kelmsley had told her there would be 'no invasion for months' owing to a 'shortage of barges'.

The Germans were pleased: 'Good work. Good reward. Information wanted. Movement of troops in Scotland and S. England. Details of preparations for European landing.' A gambling party girl picked up in a French casino was being transformed, in German eyes, into an important agent with access to top-grade military information: 'The principal thing is the invasion of Europe, above all in France,' Helmut Bleil told her.

For all Elvira's apparent capriciousness, Bronx was no Brutus, playing one side against the other: 'Of the cases I have had to deal with, Bronx is the only one who has told the entire truth about her recruitment and mission,' reported Harmer. The tap on her telephone had produced only 'a lot of perhaps interesting, but irrelevant details about her private life', including a close relationship with Monica Sheriffe, a racehorse owner. 'Bronx assures me that Miss Sheriffe knows nothing about her work with this Department and I think that this is true,' wrote Hugh Astor, who took over the case when Harmer was transferred to the Expeditionary Force HQ. Her loyalty was beyond question. 'She was a British agent before she was ever recruited by the Germans, and is probably one of our most reliable agents.'

The regular German payments into her Swiss and Portuguese bank accounts now included a substantial bonus, yet Elvira was flat broke, with ballooning debts. Dunning letters from her bookmakers, dressmaker and various casinos mounted up on the doormat of her Mayfair flat. She did not open them. MI5 already had. She owed the Hamilton Club alone more than £1,000. Elvira begged her mother for more money. 'It is absolutely impossible to pay for lodging, food, clothes, dentists, medicine, amusements etc., with the amount I receive.' She did not mention that her amusements included a gambling habit worthy of a shipping tycoon, and a whopping drinks bill. As ever, her most sympathetic listener was Claude Dansey of MI6, who clucked with disbelief when told what MI5 was paying her. He gave her £15, and seemed determined, Harmer reported, 'to twist our tails by telling Bronx to get as much out of us as she could'. MI5 was livid that an officer in the sister service was interfering in this way: 'She has no right to discuss the matter with Dansey at all.'

Bronx could communicate only by secret letters (of which she had now sent more than fifty), but the postal service was so slow that anything she sent in the immediate build-up to invasion would arrive too late to be of any use. This thought seems to have occurred to her German handlers, for in February 1944 a letter arrived at Elvira's flat, written in secret ink, suggesting that if she uncovered invasion information she should send a message to the bank in Lisbon to indicate where and when the attack would take place. The warning should be in a 'plain language code', a message that looks perfectly innocuous to the uninitiated. Here was a perfect opportunity to plug Bronx into the heart of the D–Day deception.

The code suggested by Bleil was very simple. If and when she discovered the target, she should send a telegram, in French, to Antonio Manuel de Almeida, Director and General Manager of the Banco Espirito Santo in Lisbon, asking him to make a money transfer. The sum requested would indicate the target area. If she asked for £80, that meant the attack was aimed at the Atlantic coast of France; £70 would indicate northern France and Belgium; £60, northern France; £50 for the Bay of Biscay; £40, the Mediterranean; £30, Denmark; £20, Norway and £10 for the Balkans. Elvira was told to send the message only when 'absolutely certain of what will happen and a week before the landings are to take place'. The Portuguese bank was known to have links to Deutsche Bank, and had been under British surveillance for some time. Its owner, Richard Espirito Santo, was a personal friend of the Portuguese dictator, Salazar, and had played host to the Duke and Duchess of Windsor in 1940. (He was also the brother of Edgar Espirito Santo, the sometime lover of Yvonne Delidaise, Emile Kliemann's French mistress.) The plan set out by Bleil proved that, although Portugal was neutral, 'the general manager of the bank had certainly lent his name and good offices to the Germans in an attempt to obtain from this country most vital information about forthcoming military operations'. There was enough evidence here to warrant a formal complaint to the Portuguese government, but this would instantly scupper Elvira's career as an agent, and 'in view of the part which Bronx should be able to play in current deception plans, it is clearly against our interests to blow Bronx'.

Harmer pointed out that the geographical areas indicated by the plain language code were broad, and did not fit precisely with the Bodyguard plan. 'If it is desired to send a telegram indicating that the landing will be in the Pas de Calais area, the difficulty is that the codeword covers the whole of northern France and Belgium.' But improving the code by subdividing the target areas 'would appear too professional for someone of the character of Bronx'. Elvira nonetheless sent back a letter suggesting some refinements: if she wrote that she needed the money '*pour mon dentiste*', that would mean the information was 'certain'; if she wrote '*pour mon docteur*' it was 'almost certain'; but if the words used were '*pour mon médécin*', it was only 'probable'. She also added a timescale: '*tout de suite*' meant the landing would be in one week's time; '*urgent*' indicated an attack in a fortnight; '*vite*' would indicate a month; and if she asked for the cash '*si possible*', then the date was still uncertain. Here was a simple, swift and effective way of sending the Germans barking up the wrong tree, neatly disguised as a medical bill.

In August 1943 a Polish court martial had found Roman Czerniawski guilty of gross insubordination. 'Anxious to hush the whole matter up', the Polish authorities sentenced him to just two months' imprisonment. Since he had already been inside for six weeks, the remainder of his sentence was postponed until after the war. He never served it.

Czerniawski was vigorously unrepentant. Indeed, his rebellion and punishment raised him yet higher in his own estimation. His handler Christopher Harmer reported wearily that Brutus 'declined to give any promise that he will not interfere in Polish internal affairs'. Monique Deschamps, once Czerniawski's sub-agent, now his lover, was waiting for him when he got back to the Brompton flat and he immediately asked her to marry him. She was somewhat taken aback by this 'most unorthodox proposal of marriage', but told MI5, with an irony that suggests she knew exactly what she was dealing with, 'Ah, but you must remember that he is a super-man, and super-men are always eccentric.' She accepted his proposal. An internal MI5 memo wondered how much she knew about Czerniawski's espionage, but concluded that if he had let her in on the secret 'her personal loyalty to him was sufficient to make her keep her mouth shut'.

Czerniawski saw no reason why he should not immediately resume his role in the Double Cross team. MI5 was less sanguine. The Germans were likely to be suspicious at the 'peculiar circumstances of his arrest and release'. Czerniawski was fickle, irritating and meddlesome. 'We can never guarantee that he will not intrigue,' wrote Harmer. 'He can be a great nuisance to us if he gets into trouble again.' Yet he had also shown how useful he could be. Until Czerniawski's arrest, the Germans had shown complete faith in him and as a professional intelligence officer, his information was taken seriously in Berlin: 'Of all the agents, Brutus appears to be the one who works most directly to the military authorities.' Harmer insisted that despite his vexatious personality, Czerniawski was 'dynamic and industrious' and 'an excellent agent who is very easy to run – of all the people I have run he is the only one who has never complained'.

It was agreed that Brutus would resume contact with the enemy, but cautiously, and under close supervision. He would be steered away from active deception since, if he was suspected, this could backfire. Left idle, Czerniawski would certainly start plotting again, but perhaps, wrote Harmer, the run-up to D-Day would 'become sufficiently exciting to occupy his thoughts'. Most Secret Sources would be combed for evidence of German mistrust, and he would no longer operate his own wireless. Instead, he would tell the Germans he had recruited a wireless operator, a disgruntled and cash-strapped Polish former air force officer living in Reading, whose family had been killed by the Soviets and who was therefore willing to aid the Germans against the Bolsheviks for ideological reasons. In intelligence jargon, radio operators were known as 'pianists'; this fictional sub-agent was therefore given the codename 'Chopin', in honour of Poland's great pianist and composer. Chopin's compositions would be performed by MI5, from a transmitter in Richmond.

In late summer 1943, Czerniawski resumed radio contact
with Paris. Colonel Oscar Reile's response was welcoming, but
reserved. Sure enough, Bletchley Park intercepts indicated that
'Agent Hubert' was no longer fully trusted. Reile had begun
to wonder whether the radio was really being operated by
Czerniawski, or 'an enemy radio-operator who transmitted only
what the Intelligence Service allowed'. In his memoirs, written
many years later, Reile claimed that he had made up his mind,
with 'a probability bordering on certainty', that Czerniawski was
a British double agent. 'Not the least of my reasons for arriving
at this conclusion was that none of the radio messages which
came from England contained any enquiry about the sixty-six
members of the *Résau Interallié* who were still in the hands of
the Germans.' Czerniawski had agreed to spy for Germany on
condition they were not ill-treated, yet he never inquired about
the wellbeing of these hostages. This was a serious mistake on
the part of Czerniawski and his handlers, but it seems unlikely
that Reile really spotted it at the time. If Reile was genuinely
suspicious, he kept his doubts to himself.

As the weeks passed, German concerns about Brutus seemed
to evaporate. Czerniawski kept up a stream of chatty, informal
banter with Reile. Indeed, their relations appeared so cordial
that Harmer 'suggested, half-jokingly', that Brutus should
'send a personal message to the Colonel saying that in his view
Germany had lost the war but might still save Europe from
Bolshevism if the High Command were prepared to let the
English and Americans land unopposed'. Czerniawski leapt
at the idea of interceding personally with Hitler to ensure
the success of D-Day, and pronounced it 'an excellent idea'.
More surprisingly, Tar agreed: 'I like the suggestion,' he wrote.
Czerniawski set to work drafting a message to Reile, in which
he assumed the role of spokesman for the Polish nation.

> Colonel! I conceive it my duty to speak frankly to you. I am
> now convinced that Germany has lost the war . . . I must

ask you to state precisely the terms on which Germany is prepared to collaborate with my country. What will be our status in Europe and how far is Germany prepared to grant concessions before the end of the war? You know that I have risked everything for the ideals we have in common. The greatest service Germany could now offer to European civilisation would be for your High Command to indicate to the Anglo-American armies that when they land they can do so unopposed. Your armies could then unite with those of un-Bolshevised countries to save Europe from Communism.

It is not clear whether this message was ever sent. If it was, it had no effect.

By December 1943, Most Secret Sources had proved that the Brutus case was firmly back on track: 'The Germans appear to have regained confidence in him. They regard him once more as being genuine [and] once they have accepted him and regard him as an important agent, they are unlikely to go back on their judgment.' A few days before Christmas, the decoders sent through an intercepted message in which 'the Germans expressed their great appreciation of Brutus's work'. Harmer began lobbying for Czerniawski to be used for active deception in Operation Fortitude. 'The Brutus case could be developed as an effective means of deceiving the enemy,' he wrote. If not, it should be shut down, since continuing to stuff Reile with chicken-feed was 'a complete waste of time'. If the case was closed, Harmer suggested that MI5 send Reile a personal message saying: 'We have caught your man. It was clever of you to recruit him, but we know everything now. We think he is a little mad, and so we are not going to shoot him. We will, however, communicate with you from time to time to discuss matters of mutual interest.'

If, on the other hand, it was decided to keep the case running, then Czerniawski should send over high-grade military misinformation. Reile was asking specific questions about the forthcoming invasion, and so 'the opportunities for using this case for deception are very great'. Indeed, with Chopin tapping out regular messages to Paris, he might eventually rival the star of the team. 'Brutus is getting questions on the same level as Garbo' and the Brutus channel was an 'even better wireless link than Garbo'. In a note on the Brutus file, John Marriott observed: 'The objectives to be gained by running double agents are numerous, but there is one overriding objective: to delude the enemy to his undoing.' Czerniawski was reintegrated into the great deception.

Brutus marked his return to the team with a message to Reile laying down his conditions: the secret of the D-Day landings in exchange for Poland's liberty.

> The risks involved in helping the Axis to resist the coming offensive are justified only if I have your government's undertaking, after the defeat of the Allies, to offer through me to the Polish government liberal peace terms. In setting up an organisation to give you full and up-to-date information about military preparations for an invasion, I am acting solely from ideological motives and with the object of securing for Poland an honourable place in the new Europe. This is the only reward I ask.

The London winter wrapped around Lily Sergeyev like a soggy cloak. Her kidneys ached. She spent long hours alone in the Rugby Mansions flat, although Maritza Mihailovic, double agent Snark, was seldom far away. Every few days, Mary Sherer would march in with her attaché case, a model of brisk efficiency. Together, they would draft and redraft letters for Kliemann, cover letters to the address in Lisbon containing idle chat with messages beneath, in secret ink. 'The information doesn't seem to make much sense,' Lily wrote in her diary. 'Bits of conversations mentioning ranks and badges; trains supposedly seen in stations; information obtained by chance by overhearing conversations in the train.' She visited her relatives near Bristol, with Mary in attendance. Forces for the Normandy landings were already assembling in the area, but in her letters Lily described 'lonely countryside and empty main roads which were in fact bustling from dawn to dusk and through the night, with troop movements'.

Tar Robertson explained the plan in broad terms: 'For the last few months the Germans have been desperately trying to find out where we plan to land our forces. With your help, we can make them think that we have made our preparations to invade an area which in fact we have no intention of going anywhere near. If we succeed, the Germans will concentrate their troops in the worst possible places to cope with the landing when it is finally launched.' Lily was not told that the real target was Normandy, nor that Calais was the cover target: 'I don't try to guess what all these scraps might add up to. Obviously the Germans will make certain deductions from them,' she wrote in her diary.

Lily had expected to find excitement as a double agent. Instead, she was miserable. Mary Sherer and Gisela Ashley (whom she knew as 'Louisa') took her to lunch at Chez Kampinski restaurant, and tried to cheer her up. Lily liked Louisa – they called each other 'Ducky' – but could not warm to Mary, so proper, so reserved and so entirely unsympathetic to Lily's moods. Theirs was a head-on collision of culture and personality: the emotional, temperamental Frenchwoman and the buttoned-down, aloof Englishwoman. 'I want to love and hate; to be alive,' wrote Lily. 'I find the English cold, uncommunicative, undemonstrative, impenetrable. I would like to see Mary laugh, or cry, or scream; I would like to see her face express something. To me she seems almost an automaton.' Lily sensed, rightly, that beneath the no-nonsense manner was a far more vulnerable and interesting person. 'There is something about Mary, in the way she twists her legs in a spiral, in the way her stockings come down like a corkscrew, in the way she walks with a long stride, swinging her arms and perhaps humming a little song, which doesn't fit in with the tough face she wants to show the world.'

Lily repeatedly demanded to be reunited with Babs, but the response was always non-committal and evasive. She fired off increasingly irate telegrams to O'Shagar, the MI6 officer in Gibraltar, asking for news of the dog. In a note to Tar, Mary warned that Treasure was becoming 'very unreasonable' and that a major explosion was brewing. 'Treasure is very upset about the absence of her dog, and has seriously threatened that if the dog does not arrive soon she will not work anymore. I think this can be dealt with but it will mean a scene.' Mary was not as unsympathetic as she seemed; she was a dog lover herself, and felt for Lily; but in Mary's world, rules were sacred. 'I do not quite know what we can do to help, because if we have the dog sent over here officially it will have to go into quarantine, which from Treasure's point of view would be as bad as having it in Gibraltar. I am afraid that Treasure's American boyfriend has let her down and has no intention of smuggling the dog over here for her, I am wondering whether we could get the Royal Navy to help via Commander Montagu.' Britain was preparing for battle on an epic scale, and MI5 was seriously considering whether to deploy a Navy submarine to fetch a small dog, illegally, in order to placate a volatile double agent.

Lily had long complained of what she called 'her *internal* troubles'. In December she was 'seized with a fit of shivering and trembling'. Mary told her to snap out of it. 'You cannot be ill. You haven't any right to!' It was a joke, but not the sort that Lily appreciated. Ailing, lonely and filled with self-pity, Lily was spoiling for a fight. The ensuing exchange is detailed in her diary:

'Mary, it's obvious now that my pilot isn't going to bring Babs over. Could you do something about it?'

'No: I have already told you so.'

'Do you mean to say that you refuse to keep the promise made to me by Benton?'

'We can't help it if you were promised something contrary to the regulations.'

'In that case I don't have to keep the promise I made to work with you. From now on you can get on alone.'

Mary Sherer was furious. Her ingrained sense of duty simply did not accept that, in the middle of a war, someone could down tools and withdraw cooperation: 'You refuse to work?'

'Certainly.'

'But it's stupid. You know we need you.'

'Nevertheless, my work is not worth a small dog.'

'You act like a spoilt child! You want something and you mean to have it. Well, you can't. You're ill. You'll change your mind when you have thought things over.'

Mary stormed out of the room, slamming the door behind her. The next day, Christmas Eve 1943, Lily made a rambling entry in her diary. 'My brain is empty of thoughts. I'm lighter than the air, I'm gliding across the ceiling. I'm going to die.' Maritza, the housekeeper-spy, alerted Mary, who sent an urgent message to MI5 headquarters: 'Treasure is behaving in an eccentric manner, despite her fever, wandering around in her pyjamas, and sitting on the floor in the drawing room. Snark found her dancing.'

Delirious, Lily was rushed to St Mary's Hospital. Dr Hanfield Jones examined her, and diagnosed chronic kidney stones. When she came round, Mary Sherer was at her bedside. Lily was unwell, but not nearly as ill as she believed. The combination of a high fever and a highly developed sense of drama had convinced her that she was on her deathbed.

'It seems I won't live,' she told her case officer, with a gust of Gallic melodrama.

'Nonsense,' said Mary Sherer.

('I love the way Mary says nonsense,' Lily later wrote. 'She says it with so much conviction.')

Tar Robertson arrived the next day, carrying a bunch of jonquils and daffodils. Lily was feeling better, but still convinced she was dying, with maximum melodrama: 'I don't want to die here. If I died now, my soul would get lost in the fog.'

Robertson, usually so affable and cheery, struck Lily as oddly ill at ease. But she was feeling too weak for another row. She drifted off to sleep.

Over the next three weeks, Lily regained her appetite and some of her spirit. In early January, Lily sent a message in secret ink to Kliemann explaining that her long silence had been down to illness. She had obtained a Hallicrafter 'Sky Rider' radio that could receive but not transmit messages, she told him, and would be listening in for his messages on the agreed frequency. B1A's technicians duly set up the radio. Treasure could now receive orders and questions directly from Kliemann. His first message was encouraging: 'Information very interesting – Letters arrive well – Continue', and signed off with flirty courtesy: 'You are very charming.'

A shadow fell across Lily's brightening mood with the arrival of a telegram from Gibraltar, sent by Kenneth Larson, the American pilot who had agreed to bring over her dog, explaining that he had been forced to leave Babs in Algiers. The tone of the message struck her as odd. She showed it to her cousin: 'Why should he have left Babs in Algiers? I wonder if it's the truth. Maybe he has become attached to Babs and just wants to keep him.'

When she raised the matter of her dog with Tar Robertson, he changed the subject. Mary Sherer also declined to discuss it. Lily's sister Bimbo was living in Algiers: she would write and ask her to find out what had happened to Babs.

Mary Sherer had ambitions for Treasure. It was all very well receiving messages from Kliemann, but in order to play a full part in Operation Bodyguard she needed her own wireless set. Then, like Garbo, Brutus and Tricycle, she would be able to relay important misinformation instantly. 'Treasure could be used by us for deception,' Mary told Tar. 'She could cover various districts and could quote several reliable sources, notional and actual. The first message from the Germans indicated their confidence in Treasure. But she cannot be used for Overlord or other deception unless she gets her W/T [wireless transmitter].'

They tried to prod the sluggish Kliemann into providing a radio by reporting increased military activity: 'There is something in preparation,' Lily told him. 'I must have the promised radio transmitter.' Kliemann did nothing at all. Mary grumbled: 'If we let him "arrange" matters, either he won't know how to do it, or else it will take him so long that we will miss our opportunities.' They would have to set the ball rolling.

Mary Sherer drew up a bold plan: Lily should go to Lisbon, meet up with Kliemann, and get him to hand over a radio. It was a gamble, given Lily's volatility, but Sherer told Tar she was sure it would pay off: 'I believe, and I think you will agree, that Treasure is very capable of carrying out such a mission very successfully.' Tar gave his approval. A cover story was drawn up to explain how Lily had managed to travel to Portugal. She would tell Kliemann that through her cousin Elizabeth Hill, a Cambridge academic, she had obtained a job in the Film Division of the Ministry of Information working on the scripts of propaganda films to be shown in countries liberated from the Nazis. She would explain that she had been sent to Portugal to interview refugees and gather 'first-hand information about conditions in those countries'. It was a rather thin story, but Mary was bullish: 'You've made Kliemann swallow bigger pills than that.'

One evening, after a long day spent rehearsing her cover story with Mary, Lily returned to the flat to find a letter waiting from her sister, postmarked Algiers. She read the first sentence over and over, in stunned disbelief. 'My poor Darling, I hate the pain I will give you, but it's better you should know, so as not to make plans for the future: you will not see your Babs again: he has been run over.' Her dog, probably the only thing she had ever truly loved, the only creature to have shown her unconditional love, was dead.

Lily was distraught. 'Everything is indifferent to me now. The circle of loneliness has closed around me; I am alone, absolutely alone.' The account of Babs's death made no sense to her. Why had the dog been taken to Algiers? If he was in the care of the authorities, how had he been run over? Why had her handlers seemed so shifty when the subject was raised? Why had they failed to honour the promise to bring Babs to Britain?

When Mary Sherer arrived later that day, she said nothing about Babs, though Lily was convinced she knew what had happened to her beloved dog, and had known for some time. After the grief came boiling anger; Lily was in no doubt: the British had killed her dog. And she may have been right.

Lily believed, fervently and furiously, that Babs had been sacrificed by MI5, his death arranged as a convenient solution to a tiresome problem. Perhaps Babs was 'bumped off', sacrificed to the demands of war, or perhaps his death really was accidental. The fate of Babs the dog is a mystery. MI5's archives have been routinely 'weeded' since the war, but when a file is declassified it is usually accompanied by a file index which lists, in chronological order, all the items in the original file. In other words, one can see what has been removed. Between 25 November and 29 December 1943, no less than nine separate items were entered in the Treasure file relating to Babs. The index entry headings are specific: 'Report from Mary Sherer on Treasure and the dog'; 'Notes of enquiry re: quarantine regulations with regard to Treasure's dog'; 'To SIS request for enquiries to Gibraltar re: Treasure's Dog'; 'Note re: Treasure's dog', and so on. Every single one has been taken from the file and destroyed.

Mary Sherer was surprised how well, after her initial distress, Lily took the news of Babs's death. She seemed 'in good spirits and much more enthusiastic about her case', and eager to get to Lisbon and see Kliemann. Had she read Lily's diaries, Mary would have formed a rather different impression. Lily was a born actress, a slave to her feelings, but also quite adept at hiding them when she wanted to. 'I can change my skin quite easily now,' she wrote. Agent Treasure was in deep mourning for Babs, and quietly plotting revenge.

Artist Paints a Picture

Johnny Jebsen was getting cold feet. His disgust with the Nazi regime was undimmed, but something in his mottled conscience rebelled against the idea of betraying his German colleagues. Moreover, the danger from the Gestapo seemed to have receded. Kammler, the corrupt Lisbon Abwehr officer, had sent in a report claiming that Dusko Popov must be a double agent since his reports had deteriorated 'both in quantity and quality', and pointing the finger of suspicion at Jebsen. On hearing this, Jebsen launched a personal appeal to Admiral Canaris, the Abwehr chief, protesting 'violently against machinations by Kammler to discredit him' and declaring his 'intention of throwing up his work and returning to Berlin to enlist in the army' unless he was allowed to go to Lisbon to handle the Popov case in person. The bluff worked. Canaris ruled that Kammler's denunciation had been 'malicious', and packed him off to the Eastern Front.

Spiteful or not, Kammler's suspicions were spot on, and Canaris's motives for dismissing them were, like everything the Admiral did, opaque. Canaris was almost certainly plotting against Hitler. Jebsen was sent to Lisbon with vague orders to improve 'the cover under which correspondence with agents is carried out'. Reassured that he was no longer in immediate peril, Jebsen hinted to Kenneth Benton of MI6 that perhaps it would be better if, after all, he remained independent. He was firmly told that it was too late to back out, but reassured that 'if, as he says, he wishes to do everything possible to damage the Nazi regime, then he need have no scruples in dealing with us'. Jebsen's wobble was over: 'He was convinced that he had taken an irrevocable step and that it was only consistent with his anti-Nazi principles that he should henceforth participate actively and not merely passively in the fight against the present regime in Germany.' Agent Artist was in the team, for better or worse, and for ever.

The British now had, for the first time, a spy deep within the Abwehr, working 'unconditionally' for the Allied cause. 'The fact that Johann Jebson [sic] is prepared to give us information through Tricycle offers enormous possibilities,' observed Guy Liddell. But Jebsen was also a potential liability. A report to Churchill laid out the danger.

A difficult situation has arisen since [Tricycle's] spymaster has recently been in touch with British authorities in Madrid and has told them he is under serious suspicion from the Germans and might have to ask for asylum in the UK. He said he saw no hope of German victory and that if he could get a British passport which would enable him to live in peace after the war, he might be prepared to consider any reasonable offer. While this spymaster has in his possession an enormous amount of knowledge which would be very valuable, his defection at the present time would compromise agents who are working under him, and in whom hitherto the Germans have had confidence, such as Tricycle himself.

Popov's Tricycle network was not the only asset at risk. Jebsen simply knew too much. He knew which spies the Germans were running (or believed they were running) in Britain. If he passed on this information to British intelligence, and those agents continued to function, then he would know they were under British control. For the first time, a major disagreement erupted within B1A, a fierce turf war between competing case officers anxious to protect their own agents. Hugh Astor, now running Bronx, fired the opening salvo.

If Artist is energetic in providing information, he should in due course provide us with sufficient information to effect the arrest of at least Garbo and Treasure, and it seems to me that however delicately the matter is handled, it will ultimately become obvious to Artist that all of these agents are operating under control. Thus the fortunes of some of our most valued agents will be entirely dependent on the whims of a German whom we know to be brilliantly clever, but unscrupulous and dishonest, and who may turn over his knowledge to the Germans, either by his own volition or through force of circumstances. Artist has never acted out of loyalty to the Nazi party. It has always been his sole desire to serve his own interests. In the past it has always been to his advantage to safeguard the Tricycle organisation – this has freed him from serving on the Eastern Front and provided him with considerable scope for financial gain.

The danger of his being discovered by the Abwehr increases with every day which passes. He may be arrested by the Gestapo and compromise our agents under the stress of interrogation or to turn his own knowledge to his advantage. The sudden loss of a large number of our B1A agents would in itself be a serious blow, but it would be far more serious if this loss occurred after the agents have embarked on the implementation of the Overlord deception plan [i.e. Fortitude], since it would enable the Abwehr to read their traffic in the opposite sense. The sole function of a B1A agent at the present time is to play a part in the implementation of the deception plan. Any agent who is unable to fulfil this role is unworthy of reservation. Clearly the Tricycle organisation can play no part in the deception plan, since the fact that Tricycle is operating under control is liable at any time to come to the knowledge of the Germans. Under no circumstances should Artist be allowed to remain in the Peninsula.

'I agree with his arguments on all points,' wrote Tommy Harris, Garbo's case officer. 'I am quite convinced that each day longer he remains there, the risk to the whole of the Garbo case is increased. Unless steps are immediately taken to cease contact with Artist completely or evacuate him forthwith from Spain, then grave risks of blowing the Garbo case are inevitable.' If Jebsen was whisked to Britain, MI5 could 'interrogate him at leisure', argued Harris. 'We would be able to glean a considerable amount of reliable information from Artist and the danger of a number of our most valued agents becoming compromised would be averted.' But if Jebsen disappeared, the Germans would immediately suspect Popov: to protect the deception plan, Agent Artist must be extracted immediately, and Agent Tricycle must be shut down.

It fell to Ian Wilson, Popov's case officer, to make the opposing argument. A solicitor by training, dry and precise, Wilson had made a study of Johnny Jebsen, and he leapt to his defence with lawyerly ferocity.

I find myself in complete disagreement with Mr Harris and Mr Astor. I think I can claim to have a more detailed knowledge of Artist's outlook and position than anyone else in the office. The risk of Artist disclosing information has been greatly exaggerated. I cannot imagine circumstances in which it would cease to be to Artist's own interest, as well as his inclination, to continue to act in a manner advantageous to ourselves. I entirely disagree that he is unscrupulous and dishonest. He may be unscrupulous and dishonest towards the present German government, but he has been taking every care to protect the double agents of whom he has knowledge [Tricycle, Balloon and Gelatine]. Jebsen has been endeavouring to tell the truth to Tricycle, and has been doing so in the knowledge that Tricycle will pass the information to the British. There is no evidence that any statement he has made to us was not true. Of his own accord he ran the personal risk of endeavouring to maintain his own position. I do not, therefore, agree that he has always acted out of the sole desire to serve his own interests. Artist himself fears that he is in jeopardy, but we have no independent evidence to that effect. If Artist is grilled by the Abwehr or Gestapo, he will obviously endeavour to conceal that he has directly been giving information. It seems to me the height of folly deliberately to throw away a large part of our organisation at this stage.

Like most official bodies, when faced with competing factions and equally unpalatable alternatives, MI5 opted to do nothing but wait, watch and worry. The fate of the Double Cross system now hinged on the character of Johnny Jebsen, a brave and loyal spy in Wilson's estimation, but a dodgy, self-serving opportunist in the eyes of his MI5 colleagues.

There was 'less danger of Gestapo surveillance' in Lisbon, said Wilson, and Most Secret Sources would be scanned for any hint that the authorities were closing in on Jebsen: 'Should Artist find himself in danger of being kidnapped, he will be evacuated forthwith.'

Jebsen arrived in Lisbon on 16 October 1943, where he was taken 'under the wing' of a local MI6 officer, Charles de Salis. A thirty-three-year-old linguist and poet recruited to MI6 by Kim Philby (the head of MI6's Iberian desk later exposed as a Soviet spy), de Salis had spent much of his early life in Spain, where he became a friend of the poet Federico García Lorca. He was 'a modest aesthete', according to one account, 'an amusing raconteur and a mimic'. He and Jebsen hit it off at once. De Salis was under strict instructions: 'Artist is determined to carry on to the last possible moment, but should it become clear that the game is up, we feel that to prevent his being grilled we should send him to Gibraltar. You have full authority to get Artist out if, in your judgment, the game is up, leaving his associates in complete doubt as to his fate and destination.'

The Abwehr station in Madrid was large and well-organised, with more than 200 officers and some 300 secretaries. It spied around the clock, in obedience to the strenuous work ethic of Karl-Erich Kühlenthal who, though gullible, was considered by MI5 to be 'a very efficient, ambitious and dangerous man, with an enormous capacity for hard work'. By contrast, the Abwehr in Lisbon, under Ludovico von Karsthoff, ran at a leisurely pace. The Abwehr headquarters, a comfortable flat near the Embassy, consisted of about thirty personnel, half of whom were secretaries, as well as a number of dubious hangers-on with indeterminate roles. The Abwehr officers did little other than collect letters sent to the various Lisbon cover addresses. Indeed, there was very little work to do since the Germans believed that 'the characteristics of the Portuguese – their love of the melodramatics, their rumour-mongering and their general undependability – made them poorly fitted for the work of agents'. The only local informant of note was Paul Fidrmuc, Agent Ostro, who was, of course, a charlatan.

While Kühlenthal and his colleagues sweated away in Madrid, the officers of the Lisbon Abwehr station devoted themselves to pleasure, led by von Karsthoff, who 'set the example for their gay existence'. With money skimmed from Popov's payments, von Karsthoff had purchased a new Cadillac, a house in the country near Sintra, and another pet monkey. An Abwehr officer who arrived in Lisbon shortly before Jebsen was shocked by the behaviour of his new colleagues, who 'were leading a rather loose and immoral life in Lisbon, with little concern for their duties'. Some were sleeping with their secretaries. Others were cocaine abusers. 'All had enormous amounts of money, most had their own cars, made frequent pleasure trips throughout Portugal and spent their evenings gambling in the casinos.' Jebsen felt entirely at home. Since von Karsthoff was as dependent on Popov as he was, the Abwehr station chief was unlikely to make trouble – particularly after Jebsen promised him a 'post-war job as manager in a Vienna firm'. Jebsen began to relax, confident that his friends in Berlin would tip him off if his enemies were closing in, and the British would whisk him to safety.

There was even a possibility, if a crisis occurred, that Jebsen could be extracted without wrecking the Tricycle set-up. For Jebsen had contrived a bizarre fall-back plan, by convincing his bosses that he might be able to smuggle himself into England as a spy, with the help of one of the richest men in Britain. The tale Jebsen spun for the Abwehr went like this: his father had once saved the life of Lord Rothschild, of the banking family, who therefore had 'a debt of gratitude which he is anxious to repay by doing everything possible to assist him'; Rothschild had agreed to ask his 'influential friends' to arrange for Jebsen to enter the country as a refugee and avoid internment; once in Britain, posing as 'a discontented German out of favour with the regime', he would spy for Germany.

This story was completely fabricated, but to lend it credibility, Jebsen had 'for some months been conducting a completely fictitious correspondence with the Lord Rothschild whom he has invented'. British intelligence had followed this peculiar plot through wireless intercepts, and knew that 'there is a whole file deposited with the Abwehr containing carbon copies of Artist's letters and Rothschild's replies'. In reality, it would have been quite impossible for any private citizen, no matter how rich, to bend the rules so that a German citizen could enter Britain and 'remain at large'. The Abwehr did not know this, and in accordance with the Nazi convictions about the power of Jewish bankers, it was assumed that with 'the powerful backing of Lord Rothschild', any string could be pulled. When told about the Rothschild ruse, one senior Abwehr official observed: '*was diese Juden sich alles leisten*' (these Jews can get away with anything).

If Jebsen discovered that he was about to be arrested by the Gestapo, he would tell his Abwehr colleagues that the visa promised by his friend Rothschild had come through, and then vanish. The British would spirit him to London; the Germans would believe he was a loyal agent working in the UK, and B1A would deploy him as yet another double agent. To bolster the deception, MI5 faked a letter from the Home Office stating that 'Lord Rothschild has made a request that the case be given special treatment', which Jebsen could show to his colleagues as proof of his story. Robertson gave cautious approval to this convoluted charade, pointing out that the plan was 'ingenious, but not without dangers'.

Victor Rothschild, MI5's sabotage expert, was a real Lord Rothschild, and somewhat put out to discover that his name was being manipulated in this way. He had no connection whatever with Jebsen, and worried that if the story leaked out, people might leap to the wrong conclusions. 'It might appear unnecessarily finicky on my part but it might be as well to have it permanently on record that the whole Lord Rothschild–Artist saga is imaginary.'

On 10 November 1943, the DC3 to Lisbon took off from Whitchurch airport with no fewer than three Double Cross aficionados on board. Ian Wilson of MI5 and Major Frank Foley of MI6 travelled together as Mr Watson and Mr Fairclough. In another seat, studiously ignoring his case officers and travelling under his own name, was Dusko Popov. It had been decided that sending Tricycle back to Portugal would further strengthen his hand in the run-up to D-Day: 'After he returns to England, any deceptive material which we can pass over through him will have greater prospect of being implicitly believed.' Because of the uncertainty surrounding Jebsen, Popov did not yet pass over any positively misleading material, in case he was rumbled. Instead he carried a Yugoslavian diplomatic bag stuffed with the highest-grade chicken-feed for von Karsthoff: notes, photographs and documents, information that was accurate and apparently useful to the enemy, but essentially worthless. If all went according to plan, he would be back in Britain soon after Christmas, 'in time to participate in any major deception'.

Wilson and Foley intended to meet Jebsen in Lisbon, assess his character, debrief him, and boost his resolve: 'To make him feel that we regard him as being of great value to us; to prevent him from feeling he is betraying his own country; to treat him as a far-sighted and internationally minded man, who realises that the war is going to be won by the Allies, and that the Nazi party and military power in Germany will be eliminated.' They would tell him that 'any action that helps towards bringing the war to a speedy end will be to the advantage of Germany as well as the rest of the world in saving unnecessary loss of life by continued warfare'. Then they would quiz him on every aspect of German intelligence, from spies, to secret inks, to pigeons.

Charles de Salis of MI6 had arranged a rendezvous at a safe house in Lisbon. They had been waiting an hour when Jebsen shuffled in, an unkempt figure in a dark Homburg, dirty raincoat and unpolished shoes. He smiled broadly, and stuck out a hand. Wilson noted his nicotine-stained fingers, and ostentatious ruby wedding ring. Wilson was a deeply conservative English lawyer, a stolid upholder of all that was traditional and established; Johnny Jebsen was an international chancer, louche and unconventional. They had almost nothing in common. Yet from first sight, they established an affinity that would deepen with time. Johnny was a deal-maker, and before getting down to business, he wanted some guarantees: immunity from prosecution for anything he might have done in connection with the forgery swindle; help to obtain Danish or British citizenship after the war; and a promise that 'should anything happen to him, we will take care of his wife'. The final clause was a characteristic touch: Jebsen had started an affair with a secretary in the Lisbon Abwehr office; he had one mistress in Paris and another, of more recent acquisition, in Madrid. Yet he remained, despite his chronically adulterous habits, profoundly loyal to his actress wife Lore. His final request was a humane one: 'If through information obtained through Artist we are successful in arresting German agents, such agents will not be executed.'

Wilson's response was carefully couched: 'I made it clear that any assurances which he might receive from us were conditional on our being satisfied, when we had full information after the war, that he had in fact assisted us to the best of his ability and had not at any time endeavoured to mislead us.' This was enough for Jebsen: for all his cynicism, he believed profoundly, as a devotee of P. G. Wodehouse, that an Englishman's word was his bond.

Reassured, Jebsen began spilling the beans. Over the next four days, smoking an endless succession of cigarettes and drinking champagne as if it was water, he painted a detailed picture of the interior workings of the Third Reich intelligence apparatus, and the battle for power within the Nazi High Command. 'The Abwehr generally is demoralised and cynical and in fact the OKW [Oberkommando der Wehrmacht] have known for at least a year past that Germany has lost the war,' he said. German intelligence was in disarray, riddled with corruption and beset by internal feuding. Canaris was under intense pressure, with Himmler actively plotting to take over the Abwehr with his own SD, the Nazi party intelligence service. 'Himmler is the most ambitious man in Germany but knows that the army would not tolerate him in Hitler's place, so remains loyal. Contrary to popular belief, Hitler does not believe in shooting his old friends unless they have become a danger to himself. The leaders of the SS will remain loyal to Hitler and the rank and file of the SS are entirely under the influence of their leaders.' Jebsen's powers of recall were extraordinary; this nervous little man was 'a living dictionary on the whole of the Gestapo'.

Earlier that year, in Madrid, Jebsen had told Benton the rumours about a 'rocket gun' being developed by Hitler's scientists. Now he had more solid information, picked up not on the grapevine, but in the bedroom. While in Spain, in between defecting to MI6 and visiting his favourite pornographic cinema, Jebsen had found time to start an affair with a married woman, one Baroness Gertzen. She was secretary to a German aircraft manufacturer named Henschel, whose factories supplied parts for the flying bomb project. 'The Baroness is very much in love with Artist [and] was easily induced to talk about the likelihood of severe bombardment of the UK.' Jebsen told her that he would soon be travelling to Britain, and slyly pretended to be fearful 'of going to a country which might be the object of an attack by Hitler's secret weapon'. Jebsen even 'spun a yarn to the effect that there had been a prophecy about him being struck by lightning in December!'

Baroness Gertzen was privy to all her boss's correspondence, and remarkably naive: 'She immediately promised to give him all details of the weapon [and] guarantees to send a cable to Artist wherever he is as soon as she gets information that the rocket will be used. If he is in England, this will give him time to escape to Scotland!' The rocket gun, Jebsen reported, was being built at an 'experimental station located at Peenemünde' on Germany's Baltic coast. The British already had an idea of what was happening in Peenemünde. Indeed, the RAF had attacked the site back in August. Jebsen's willingness to hand over such explosive information, gleaned from pillow talk, was a measure of his commitment, and his guile.

One by one, he listed the German spies operating on British soil, and how they were rated in Berlin: Popov, under suspicion during his American sojourn, was once again cherished by the Abwehr; Balloon was 'lazy'; Gelatine patchy, but occasionally useful. The much-feted Agent Ostro 'never disclosed to anyone who his agents are or where he gets his information'. He promised to find out more about the mysterious Ostro. Jebsen went on to recite chapter and verse on the Garbo network, with 'full details of most secret agents', including how and what they were paid.

This was exactly what British intelligence had hoped he would not do. Wilson was dismayed: 'He has given us certain information which ought to have assisted us to trace these agents if they really existed and we did not already control them, and he may have drawn correct inferences from our reactions.' Jebsen observed that he had long been suspicious of the ease with which Garbo (Agent Arabel, as he was to the Germans) transmitted reports from Britain, and speculated that Kühlenthal himself might be in the pay of MI6: 'He left us in no doubt that he was personally convinced that we control that organisation.' Wilson did his best to 'confuse Artist's state of mind about B1A agents' and put him off the scent. Rooting out spies in Britain was 'relatively unimportant work', he blustered. But Johnny Jebsen was no fool. 'Artist left me with the clear impression that he did not believe that any agents purporting to write letters or send messages from England were genuine', and suspected that these spies were all either 'controlled or non-existent (or partly one and partly the other)'. When MI5 failed to act on the information he had supplied, he would know for certain that the German espionage network was a sham.

Jebsen's own position, he said, had 'considerably improved' since his arrival in Lisbon. Both Canaris and Georg Hansen, the head of Abwehr foreign intelligence, were protecting him, and he was under specific orders not to return to Germany until the Gestapo business had been sorted out. He knew there was still a danger 'that the Gestapo will effect his return to Germany and he will be summarily disposed of', but a friend in the SD had told him that 'kidnapping in Portugal was now almost impossible'. Even so, Jebsen knew what would happen if he was uncovered as a British spy: the Ablege Kommandos hit squad would be sent to get him. 'They have a poison which can be dissolved in water or added to food which is quite tasteless,' said Jebsen grimly. 'Twenty minutes after death there is no trace in the body.' He was confident he would be alerted to any imminent threat in time to act, but as an extra precaution he had started an affair with Lily Grass, secretary to Aloys Schreiber, the newly appointed head of counter-intelligence in Lisbon. If the Gestapo made a move on Jebsen, they would tell Schreiber beforehand, in which case Lily Grass would hear of it, and tip him off.

'Jebsen has been giving Lily Grass considerable attention,' reported Wilson. 'She is in love with Artist and if the latter takes the trouble to hide the fact that he finds her tedious, he will able to count on her support.' Wilson was impressed by Jebsen's resolve and ingenuity: 'We have formed a favourable impression of his nerve and do not believe he will seek shelter unless it is necessary.'

Wilson ran through Jebsen's 'highly complex' motives: 'A genuine dislike of Nazism; a belief in the British political system; a conviction that Germany has lost the war; a fear of communism which can only be avoided by increased English influence in Western Europe; a contempt for the corruption and inefficiency of the Abwehr; the realisation that his own future as a big businessman depends on the restoration of normal trading activities; a desire to reinsure himself.' Jebsen seemed impelled by a combination of opportunism, idealism and above all personal loyalty to Popov. If he had a credo, it was P. G. Wodehouse's 'Code of the Woosters': 'Never let a pal down'. 'He at no time spoke of any financial reward and I am sure he does not expect any financial assistance.' He was even prepared to fake information for the Germans on Britain's behalf: 'Artist says that if we want foodstuff we should let him write it – he knows exactly what the Germans want and has been writing the stuff for years.'

Jebsen was an odd figure, Wilson reflected, raddled and raffish but oddly romantic. 'Looks ten years older than his thirty years; reddish, blond hair combed back; heavy moustache; very slender, body bent forward; grey blue eyes and very pronounced cheekbones; unhealthy pale complexion (lung disease?); smokes about 100 cigarettes over a day; very bad teeth from frequent smoking; eats little and drinks only champagne; unable to drive; rides horseback; writes philosophical books.' Yet as Jebsen's trail of seduction showed, there was something intensely attractive about him, and a core of strength that belied his twitchy manner. Wilson trusted him. 'No doubt Artist is acting mainly out of self-interest but of a clear-sighted and long-term character. A man of his undoubted intelligence is unlikely to try to deceive us on any matter where he is liable to be found out after the war.' Wilson was quite sure that Jebsen was prepared to risk his life for the Allied cause. 'I am convinced that Artist sincerely desires to continue to work wholeheartedly with us.' When they parted, Wilson told him: 'I hope our collaboration will endure a very long time.'

Wilson's report caused both delight and consternation in London. This was intelligence of the highest quality, with the promise of more to come. On the other hand, as Astor and Harris had feared, Jebsen was in a position to expose the falsity of the German networks in Britain, now supplying actively deceptive material in the run-up to D-Day. 'The extent of Artist's possible knowledge of Garbo is a matter of some concern,' wrote Tar, who wondered whether Jebsen knew, or merely suspected that the German agents in Britain were frauds. 'Obviously if Artist were approached directly on this matter it would immediately arouse his suspicion.' Wilson assured him: 'I do not think he has any positive proof.' But then, Jebsen did not need any. The continued flow of information from the D-Day spies would be proof enough of the massive hoax being perpetrated on the German High Command.

'Artist's zeal and ability,' Churchill was told, 'has verged upon the embarrassing. He has begun to provide us with information about the networks maintained by the Germans in this country. Of these the principal one is the Garbo organisation of which it is clearly undesirable that he should make us too fully aware. We are engaged at the moment in the delicate operation of diverting this valuable agent's attention elsewhere. There is good promise of success.'

While Jebsen was getting to know his new British spymasters, Dusko Popov settled back in with his German handlers. Von Karsthoff was genuinely glad to see him: Popov was not only his most valuable intelligence asset, but the guarantor of his profligate lifestyle. He examined Popov's haul of information, with something less than a critical eye, and pronounced it excellent. Canaris had recently questioned whether Popov was 'worth his pay', but the latest batch of intelligence, von Karsthoff predicted, would convince the Abwehr chief that he was 'really valuable'. He threw a dinner party in Popov's honour, and invited Jebsen, Aloys Schreiber, the new head of counter-intelligence, and their secretaries. It was a bizarre occasion. Two of the guests were German intelligence officers, and two others were secretly working for British intelligence; Jebsen was sleeping with Schreiber's secretary, who was spying on her boss; the married von Karsthoff was having an affair with his secretary Elizabeth Sahrbach, while ripping off the Abwehr. Popov was conducting at least six love affairs. Everyone was involved in the lying and cheating game . . . except Mabel Harbottle, who was not sleeping with, or deceiving, anyone, and probably never had. Von Karsthoff proposed a congratulatory toast, declaring that, in return for his latest intelligence haul, Popov could expect a payment of $15,000.

Aloys Schreiber agreed that Popov's report was 'good and had been sent by courier to Berlin'. His manner, however, was chilly.

After the dinner party, von Karsthoff flew to Baden Baden for an Abwehr conference and returned ecstatic: Popov was now considered 'the best man the Abwehr have'. The accolade was duly passed back to Wilson in London, who observed: 'This may well have been deliberate flattery, but there seems to be no doubt he is at the moment extremely highly regarded.' With greedy relish, von Karsthoff told Popov that 'if his work was really good he could get almost anything he asked for'. Plans were already being laid to send him back to Britain, with more money, a fresh batch of secret ink, and a new questionnaire demanding a range of information on just about everything, as Popov later put it, 'short of a detailed account of Churchill's digestive processes'. Popov was instructed to begin transmitting from outside London, as Hitler's flying bombs would soon be laying waste to the capital.

For Popov and Jebsen, these weeks in Lisbon offered the first opportunity, since war began, to speak to one another without dissembling, or inferring, what could not be spoken. They were now officially on the same side in the game, though utterly different in temperament. As P. G. Wodehouse once remarked of cricket: 'Some batsmen are nervous all through a long innings. With others the feeling disappears with the first boundary.' Popov was unflappable, where Jebsen was a jangle of jagged nerves, but they made an outstanding partnership. They spent many happy, dissolute hours together: a pair of British spies pretending to be German spies, spending Hitler's money on themselves. Jebsen took a house in Estoril, with four servants, while Popov lived at the Palacio Hotel. They celebrated Christmas together, and Popov sent a cheery seasonal message, in secret ink, to MI5: 'I shall spend my Christmas in Portugal buying National Lottery tickets and letting people shine my shoes,' he wrote. 'Wishing you and all our friends a happy Christmas.'

But as he boarded the plane for London a week later, Popov's spirit was troubled. He knew he was leaving his old friend in dire peril. If Jebsen had asked for asylum, he would have been safely alongside him on the plane to Britain. But he had not. The Tricycle files contain a handwritten letter Popov wrote to Jebsen soon after his return to London. It offers a glimpse into what he called the 'dilemma' of spying, balancing duty against friendship, risking the life of someone he loved to protect thousands he would never know.

Given the choice between 'helping a friend and ruining a much bigger cause, or making a friend take a chance and try to save the cause,' he wrote, 'I would opt for the second solution. What is more, I am sure you would do the same.' In his uncertain English, Popov tried to tell Jebsen how much their friendship meant to him, and to the cause they now shared: 'If this case would depend on anybody else but you, I would be desperate.'

Monty's Double

On the day Popov landed back in Britain, a brilliant British Army officer and part-time transvestite emerged from an army cinema south of Naples, after a screening of the Billy Wilder film *Five Graves to Cairo*, with one of the last (and oddest) elements of the deception swirling around in his mind. Lieutenant Colonel Dudley Clarke was the head of 'A Force', a highly successful deception unit based in Cairo, and one of the architects of Bodyguard. He was a film buff with a flair for the dramatic. Indeed, Clarke's taste for dressing up had landed him in hot water a year earlier, when he was arrested in Madrid wearing women's clothes. *Five Graves to Cairo* was set in the North African campaign and starred Erich von Stroheim as Rommel. But it was Miles Mander, the actor playing a remarkably plausible General Montgomery, that set Clarke's peculiar mind whirring.

Montgomery would be Allied ground troops commander for the D–Day invasion. If an actor playing Montgomery were to be spotted somewhere else in the world, immediately before the invasion, then the Germans might assume the cross-Channel attack was not imminent. It could buy precious time, and soften German defences at a vital moment.

Clarke's idea was adopted with enthusiasm by the deception planners at LCS, and Operation Copperhead was born. But casting the right actor for the part proved tricky. Mander was found to be several inches taller than the real general, 'a physical handicap it was impossible to disguise'. A substitute was found, who then 'fell victim to a road accident and broke his leg'. The search was about to be abandoned, when a Soho theatrical agency came up with Meyrick Clifton James, an Australian-born lieutenant in the Army Pay Corps and a former variety performer. James was not a good actor. He could neither sing nor dance, and he had lost a finger in the trenches. He had volunteered to entertain overseas troops, but instead wound up in Leicester, performing in the Pay Corps' Variety Troupe. But he had one act that never failed to get the audiences cheering: with his thin face and grey, drooping moustache, he could do a splendid Monty impersonation. The actor David Niven, then a colonel in the Army Film Unit, contacted James and asked him to come to London where he was assigned to Montgomery's staff, under cover as a journalist, to study the general's speech patterns and mannerisms.

In February 1944, it was publicly announced that the victor of El Alamein had arrived in Britain to take command of Allied land forces. 'From then onwards it was certain that German agents would do their best to watch his movements.' But where should the fake Monty be exhibited for German viewing? 'Supposing he were to be seen somewhere in the Mediterranean a day or two before the Normandy invasion, the Germans would take it as a certain indication that they had at least a week or more to wait before the landings.' Gibraltar was selected as the ideal stage for Monty's double. The airfield there was known to be kept under surveillance by the Germans. The Rock was also the stamping ground of a particularly efficient and unscrupulous spy, Major Ignacio Molina Pérez, who had been in MI5's sights for some time.

Molina was on the staff of the Algeciras military governor and liaison officer between the Spanish government and the British authorities in Gibraltar. Spanish officials were supposed to be neutral; in reality, MI5 knew that Molina was a fully paid-up German spy codenamed 'Cosmos' and 'bad from head to foot':

'Molina has been decorated by the German government on various occasions, and it has been proved, with a wealth of detail, that Molina is the prime mover in an extensive Nazi secret service organisation in Spain and Morocco. Molina himself is not aware we are out for his blood,' the Defence Security Officer in Gibraltar reported. 'One of the most irritating aspects of the case is that although we know him to be a German agent, he continues to enjoy every facility to enter and leave the fortress. We have not been able to catch him *in flagrante delicto*. Something more must be done since at any moment he may get hold of some really valuable information.' Molina was the ideal target for the hoax: if he spotted Montgomery in Gibraltar, he would immediately alert the Germans, and the British would have copper-bottomed proof of Molina's espionage. Operation Copperhead might have the satisfactory side-effect of stuffing Agent Cosmos.

The ground was prepared by spreading rumours that Montgomery was coming to North Africa, via Gibraltar, in order to discuss plans for the invasion of southern France before the launch of the main invasion in the north. James began rehearsing his part, which meant changing his habits: James was a heavy drinker and smoker, whereas Monty was teetotal and loathed smoking. A prosthetic finger was constructed to replace the missing one. The fake Monty trimmed his moustache, dyed his sideburns and was issued with khaki handkerchiefs monogrammed 'B.L.M.'. 'Monty is rather flattered by the whole plan which, of course, is based on the theory that the Second Front could not possibly start without him,' Guy Liddell reported. 'This is just the sort of plan that might conceivably come off, like [Operation] Mincemeat.' In obedience to bureaucratic niceties, James would be paid the equivalent of a general's pay for every day he impersonated Monty.

While a boozy actor was rehearsing the part of a fake general, a real general was preparing to take over a fake army. With the bogus First US Army Group (FUSAG) supposedly assembling in Kent, the deception team needed someone to take command. George Patton, the inspiring, swashbuckling and supremely unpleasant general who had led US troops into Sicily, was under a cloud for abusing and slapping soldiers traumatised by battle in the belief that they were malingering cowards. 'I ought to shoot you myself,' General Patton told one terrified man. 'There's no such thing as shell shock. It's an invention of the Jews.' Eisenhower forced him to apologise and, to Patton's fury, denied him overall command of ground forces for the coming invasion. Instead Patton was ordered to serve under Montgomery, as commander of the Third Army.

The Germans rated Patton highly – 'that's the best man they have', Hitler insisted – and so, at the suggestion of Christopher Harmer, he was appointed commander of the ghost army. By a judicious combination of leaks, newspaper reports and double agent messages, the belief that General Patton was in command of FUSAG took root in German thinking. Patton stomped around England acting the part. He called himself 'a goddam natural born ham', which he most certainly was, loudly hailing other officers with such remarks as 'see you in the Pas de Calais!' The scandal over the slapping incident even reinforced the deception, since the Germans assumed this was an invented story to disguise Patton's command of the most important D-Day army. The General's outspoken tactlessness enraged Eisenhower. 'I am thoroughly weary of your failure to control your tongue,' he told him. But the intelligence services were delighted. Whenever Patton said something like 'it is the evident destiny of the British and Americans to rule the world', this made headlines, and the headlines made their way to Germany, keeping Nazi eyes firmly focused on Patton, and his bogus army.

The components of the plan were slotting into place. To keep enemy forces pinned down in Norway, Allied intelligence imagined into being the British Fourth Army, poised to attack from Scotland, supported by American Rangers deployed from Iceland. Fortitude North was backed up by wireless traffic mimicking a real army preparing for an amphibious landing and mountain warfare – in reality wireless trucks driving around Scotland sending volleys of Morse code into the ether, some 350 people representing a force of 100,000 men.

The officer in command of this notional force was General Sir Andrew 'Bulgy' Thorne, a whiskery First World War veteran who had met Hitler when he was military attaché at the British Embassy in Berlin in the 1930s. Thorne and Hitler had fought on opposite sides of the trenches at Ypres, and discussed their shared experiences. Hitler, it was calculated, would be more likely to take seriously an army under the command of an old warhorse he knew personally. Thorne even inspected real American troops in Northern Ireland as if he were their commanding officer, in the hope that German spies in Ireland would feed the information back to Germany. As the northern deception gathered speed, the planners would add additional touches: declaring the Firth of Forth a 'protected area', as if a great and secret host was assembling there; Soviet forces would mass on the Norwegian border, suggesting a simultaneous assault from the East. At the same time, diplomatic approaches were made to neutral Sweden, requesting the use of its airfields and asking the Swedish air force commander to consider a peacekeeping role in Norway in the event of an Allied invasion. (The pro-Nazi Swedish police chief was bugging the room in which this conversation took place, and the lie flew back to Berlin.)

The officer responsible for implementing Fortitude North described the 'strange mental attitude' brought on by inventing, organising and then deploying a completely invisible army: 'As time went on we found it hard to separate the real from the imaginary. The feeling that the Fourth Army really existed and the fact that it was holding German troops immobilised made one almost believe in its reality.' This was precisely the mesmeric effect the planners hoped to induce in Hitler. The Führer had always considered Norway his 'zone of destiny'; the aim of

Fortitude North was to keep his attention – and hundreds of thousands of German troops – fixed there.

A similar and even more elaborate charade was under way along the Channel coast. German forces defending Normandy, the Seventh Army, were formidable enough, but if they were reinforced by General Hans von Salmuth's mighty Fifteenth Army, currently defending the Pas de Calais, then Normandy would be all but impregnable. The Calais troops must be kept where they were, not only before, but for as long as possible after the first attack on Normandy. The real Allied army massing in southwest England to attack Normandy should be as invisible as possible, while the fake army, supposedly gathering in the southeast, should be as loud and noticeable as Patton himself. Like stage managers on a massive scale, the planners began assembling props, scenery and backdrops all over the southeast coast to simulate the mighty FUSAG, a force of 150,000 men, forming up, training and preparing for battle: fake troop camps, bogus airfields, more than 250 dummy assault landing craft known as 'wetbobs', and dummy tank landing craft known as 'bigbobs' (a 'wetbob' being public school parlance for a rower, while a cricketer was a 'drybob'). The bigbobs, built from hollow steel tubes and canvas, were so light that in high winds they broke loose and flew through the air, like enormous misshapen kites. Stray cows tended to eat the fake aircraft made from wood and canvas.

From April, wireless operators drove around Kent simulating the wireless traffic of an entire corps preparing for battle. Plans were drawn up to establish a ten-mile exclusion zone around the coast. Robertson could never be fully certain he had intercepted every spy, so as a precaution misleading signs were erected in Kent, pointing to fake embarkation points. In Dover, all was commotion as engineers scurried to and fro pretending to build tunnels and wireless stations. Imitation docks and an oil storage complex were constructed by set builders from Shepperton Studios following plans drawn up by the architect Basil Spence. King George VI's tour of this impressive and entirely unusable installation was duly reported in the press for the Germans to read.

German intelligence, watching and listening, could not fail to realise that the *Schwerpunkt,* the focal point of the cross-Channel attack, must be the Pas de Calais. The only problem was the Germans were not able to see clearly, and were hardly listening at all. Indeed, it has since emerged that they barely bothered to pick up the vast scree of wireless traffic, and were unable to locate where it was coming from when they did. Allied air supremacy meant that German reconnaissance was strictly limited. Huge effort went into physical deception, camouflage and signals traffic, but the Germans were not really paying attention. And why would they? They had numerous spies, on the ground, providing copious evidence of exactly what was going on. Why go to the trouble of intercepting, deciphering and translating an avalanche of 13,358 coded wireless messages, when they had direct information from Garbo and Brutus?

On 21 January, Tar Robertson had announced to the 'W Board', which provided operational intelligence for Double Cross purposes, that the moment of truth had arrived. He was, he said, '98 per cent certain that the Germans trusted the majority of their agents', although 'there must always remain the additional 2 per cent of doubt'. The odds were good enough for the board, which authorised the Twenty Committee to deploy the Double Cross agents in the way that had always been envisaged: to blow the entire project in the most elaborate and dangerous deception yet. Only agents in whom the Germans had absolute faith, as reflected in Most Secret Sources, would be selected, and since the postal service would be cut off in the run-up to invasion, active deception would be restricted to agents with wireless transmitters: Garbo, Brutus and Agent Tate (Wulf Schmidt) all had well-established radio contact; Treasure, it was hoped, would soon get a radio set from Kliemann. Bronx would continue her letters as long as possible and then send a last-minute message by telegram using the agreed plain language code.

That left Popov. Lingering uncertainty over Jebsen's safety and reliability provoked another heated debate, with some arguing that the Tricycle channel should not be used, and possibly dismantled altogether. It fell once more to Ian Wilson, his case officer, to mount the defence:

> It has been suggested that Tricycle and his group are barred from conveying deceptive material because of the risk that Artist will, willingly or under duress, disclose the fact that this group is controlled. The risk is extremely slight. It seems unthinkable that Artist would voluntarily blow this case in view of the care he has taken in the past to protect double agents and of the very considerable body of information he has given us, which has proved true whenever we have been able to check it. His motives for working for us are extremely complex [but] he is absolutely sincere in his actions. He cannot blow Tricycle without imminent danger of death to himself, his family, and Tricycle's family. Artist will be protected by the Abwehr from any attack on him by the Gestapo. Whatever danger existed has now diminished. Even if the Gestapo could get hold of Artist's person and extort a confession that Artist's agents were double-crossing, then the Abwehr would have to believe the confession. All the Abwehr officers, from the highest to the lowest, have a vested interest in supporting the *bona fides* of Tricycle. I very much doubt any of them would have the moral courage to admit that for years they have been fooled.

The Twenty Committee agreed to lift the veto on using Tricycle for deception. 'No ban', Wilson scrawled triumphantly across his memo. Popov was 'passed fit' to play in the final championship match.

The Double Cross team had presented their case with supreme confidence, but there was apprehension in St James's Street. Knowledge of the double-agent network, 'once confined to a small esoteric group of persons', was now widely distributed among civilians and military personnel, with an increased danger of leakage. Paul Fidrmuc, the rogue freelancer in Lisbon, was still spraying conjecture and fantasy at the Germans, but 'it was not impossible that Ostro might by fluke give the exact area of attack on the Continent, and thus destroy the deception plan'. And the Abwehr, the familiar enemy, was falling apart. If the organisation collapsed, or was subsumed by Himmler's SD, the intelligence agency of the SS and Nazi party, then the corrupt, lazy and gullible officers B1A had got to know so well might be replaced by men of a different, more effective stamp. Rats would begin to desert the leaking ship. Already a number of disaffected Abwehr officers were extending feelers, hinting at possible desertion. Here was the Artist problem writ large. If an officer with knowledge of the German spy network in Britain defected, his colleagues would naturally assume he had betrayed those networks; and if the networks continued regardless, they would realise the spies were under Allied control. 'In short, the German turncoat, in trying to assist us, would in fact destroy our entire system.' Even stone-souled John Masterman confessed to a 'gnawing anxiety' as the pace of deception accelerated. 'The whole existence of the double cross system hung in the balance just before D-Day,' he wrote. 'Failure was dangerously close.'

When the final, definitive deception plan was approved by Churchill in late February 1944, with just over three months to go, Christopher Harmer, the link between the double agents and the military planners, turned to Roger Fleetwood-Hesketh, his opposite number, and uttered the thought that all wondered, but few dared voice: 'I can't believe we will ever get away with it.'

The Double Dash

The participants in the deception, great and small, set to work. Flight Lieutenant Walker gathered his flock of second-rate pigeons; an Australian actor worked on his Montgomery impersonation; General Patton stamped around England, drawing attention to himself; and the American double agents, led by Max Rudloff, the libertine Argentinian, fed shreds of falsehood, indicating the attack would be delayed. But the central, swelling chorus of lies would come from the Double Cross spies, Hitler's most trusted source of information on the military build-up in Britain, and Churchill's trump cards.

The deception was built from myriad tiny fragments of misinformation, a mosaic for the enemy to piece together. Directly pointing to the Pas de Calais as the target area would be far too obvious, and exceedingly dangerous if the plot was rumbled. 'You cannot baldly announce to the enemy that such and such an operation is in preparation,' insisted Masterman. 'You cannot just volunteer information.' Instead, the great lie would be made up of snippets, gleanings and hints, buried in a mass of other information, some of it true.

Roman Czerniawski began implementing the bogus threat to Norway. Chopin, his wireless operator, sent a message to Oscar Reile reporting that the Polish spy was heading north for a Polish military conference. 'He had a good reason for visiting Scotland inasmuch as the majority of Polish troops were stationed there and he was recognised by the Germans as a highly trained military observer.' Agent Brutus began relaying the fake Allied Order of Battle, just as he once reported on the real strength of German troops in occupied France. He provided the Germans with the insignia and location of the Fourth Army headquarters in Edinburgh, described large bodies of troops in Stirling and Dundee, and offered evidence that American and Norwegian forces were also gathering. Brutus followed up by describing the arrival of Soviet staff officers in Edinburgh, to back up the notion of a pincer movement. The Norwegian agents Mutt and Jeff made similar observations, and Garbo's Scotland-based sub-agents pitched in, with troop-sightings in Dundee and major naval exercises on the Clyde. Freak, Popov's radio operator, invented a talkative American naval officer who revealed he would shortly be joining General Thorne's staff. The Germans were pleased. 'Your latest wires very satisfactory. Congratulations. Please state exact number of Divisions etc. belonging to Fourth Army under General Thorne.'

Like a spoilt lover, Czerniawski badgered his German handlers for expressions of affection and support, demanding money 'to increase the efficiency of his espionage activities' and new equipment: 'Urgently require two new wireless sets and two new codes. As result of my visit to Scotland I have report of many pages to send you urgently, and without the necessary assistance from you it will be impossible to transmit the information which I am collecting at sufficient speed.' The Germans responded soothingly: 'Many thanks for your hard and valuable work. What place can we best send you the money and the piano? Can you suggest a place which would be suitable for a plane to come low enough to drop what you want?' Czerniawski advised the Germans to parachute a package to him at a remote spot near Beccles in Suffolk. When there was no response, he sent a peevish message demanding to know 'whether the lack of reply was due to a lack of confidence in him'. Reile was unctuous: 'I have complete confidence in you but there are still difficulties.' German plans for re-equipping him came to nothing, but their willingness to try confirmed the esteem in which Czerniawski was held. 'He is a man who succeeds in creating the impression of Herculean ability, and from their knowledge of him the Germans will expect him to achieve the impossible or bust. Brutus is a professional spy and an artist at producing the most detailed and illustrated reports.'

The D-Day spies all swung into action for Fortitude South. By mid-February, Garbo's doughty team of fictional Welsh fascists were deployed all along the south coast, and Pujol was commended by Kühlenthal for the 'amplification of your network'; the Welsh spies, in particular, were 'giving the best results'. The Gibraltarian waiter was also well placed after supposedly getting a job in a canteen at a Hampshire military base. The sub-agents sent information to Pujol, which he gathered, graded, put into his own, inimitably dense prose, and then sent on by radio to Madrid, where Karl-Erich Kühlenthal consumed it with insatiable appetite. Garbo sent himself on a notional tour of the south coast: he reported seeing American soldiers but predicted the invasion 'would not happen for a long time', and certainly not 'until an assault force immeasurably greater in number than that which exists has been assembled'. The Germans could relax. 'I am surprised to hear of the nervousness which exists in official circles with regard to the Allied offensive ... I recommend once again calm and confidence in our work.' That work was already monumental, and would grow steadily in the following weeks: between the beginning of January and D-Day 500 wireless messages passed between Garbo and his controllers. Harris worried that no single person could, in reality, have marshalled such an enormous quantity of information. This thought never struck the Germans.

Dusko Popov gathered intelligence of a quality, complexity and duplicity greater than anything he had supplied before. He made his own tour of the Kent coast, and reported that preparations for a great armada were plainly under way, but incomplete. 'An extensive programme for preparing and improving cook houses, wash houses, tented camps and landing grounds has been drawn up, but nearly all of it still has to be done. In spite of intensive preparations there are no signs that invasion is imminent.' Dover harbour was being overhauled to accommodate a huge task force, he reported, but again, 'a lot of work still had to be done'. From Dover, he travelled on to Portsmouth, Southampton and Exeter, describing intense military commotion in the east, and inactivity in the west.

Tar debated whether to send Tricycle into the enemy camp once again. Alone among the double agents, only he could place the deception, physically, in enemy hands. 'His stock is very high in German eyes and it is desired to take advantage of this fact, and of the opportunity of his being able to take documents to the Germans.' Popov would go back to Lisbon one last time, carrying a 'mass of detailed information' to support the deception: eyewitness reports from the Channel ports, doctored documents, and conversations with Norwegian government officials in London who said they expected to be home before summer.

Johnny Jebsen reported that von Karsthoff was swallowing Popov's reports unchewed, and proclaiming that 'the landing in Western Europe will not take place until next spring'. Berlin's response was equally positive. Colonel Georg Hansen declared Popov the Abwehr's top spy and his radio connection 'the best in the whole Abwehr'. Jebsen shone a light directly into the minds of his colleagues. 'Their chief hope is to receive reports about the date of the landing in France,' he told MI6. 'It is quite possible to deceive with regard to the date as Tricycle's reliability is no longer in doubt, but all reports must contain a saving clause so that when an event which has been announced does not occur, the blame can be attributed to wrong information received. Reports submitted with a reservation are more easily believed than categorical statements.' These reports should be sent 'containing a wealth of small detail'. Jebsen was now actively coaching the Allied team.

While Brutus focused on the north, and Garbo and Tricycle worked on the southern deception, Bronx looked west. Most Secret Sources showed that Elvira's reports were now graded 'very important' and distributed to both the operational sections of the Abwehr and army intelligence HQ in Berlin. She still addressed her letters, in secret ink, to Bleil, unaware that the man who had recruited her in France was no longer handling her case. Her new controller was one Hauptmann Dr Berndt Schluetter, a former officer in the Paris Abwehr, now operating out of Cologne and an altogether more formidable figure than the feckless, drunken Bleil. Incoming letters to Bronx took on a more urgent tone: 'Important. Invasion details: Eisenhower's and Montgomery's HQs? Parts of coast evacuated? Concentration of ships and barges? Admiralty circles talk of invasion? Arrivals of American troops? Expenses and bonus for invasion news.' Bronx bolstered both Fortitudes South and North, but her singular hold on the Germans, it was decided, should be employed elsewhere in the deception.

The Germans had substantial forces deployed in the Bordeaux area of southwest France, most notably the feared 17th SS Panzergrenadier division. Once the invasion was under way, its tanks would certainly be deployed north to try to repel the Allies. Every hour the Panzers could be detained in the southwest would help. Just as the Fifteenth Army might be tied down in Calais by Operation Fortitude, so a new and equally fictitious threat would be aimed at the Bordeaux area: this was Operation Ironside. The imaginary assault would begin with an attack in the Bay of Biscay from the west coast ports of the UK, opening the way for an American force sailing directly from the US. Several double agents would contribute: Rudloff in the US reported that a force trained in fording rivers was assembling to tackle the watery terrain of southwest France; Tate said his girlfriend Mary, who worked in the Admiralty, had returned from Washington after working on a plan for a US expeditionary force.

Bronx had already agreed a code to be sent by telegram to warn of an invasion. 'She is independent and aloof from all our other agents, so that reasonable risks can be taken in running her without compromising any other agent.' Elvira would implement Operation Ironside almost single-handed, no small feat for an agent once dismissed as 'a good-time girl with no allegiance to anyone except herself'.

Timing was critical. 'In order to achieve our object of containing the German Panzer division in the region of Bordeaux, it will be necessary to time the telegram to arrive on D-2 [two days before D-Day].' Telegrams to Lisbon took five days. To reach the Germans in time, the message would have to be sent on or before 29 May. The telegram would 'indicate to the Germans that an attack will definitely be made against the Bay of Biscay', to be followed by a letter in secret ink, once the invasion was under way and the postal service was restored, 'providing a get-out for Bronx' by explaining how she had made a mistake. The only objection, as usual, came from MI6, sniping from the sidelines. Claude Dansey told Elvira it was 'ludicrous' to expect the Germans to swallow such an 'implausible' ruse. Astor reported: 'I told her I consider his opinion to be completely fallacious and that we were best qualified to decide on running her case.' The secret services tended to get far angrier with each other than they ever did with the enemy.

Mary Sherer spent three weeks coaching Lily Sergeyev on her cover story. In the evenings she took her to the theatre, or a movie. 'Sometimes Louisa [Gisela Ashley] comes as well,' Lily wrote. 'I'm very fond of Louisa, but somehow I just can't bring myself to trust her, or Mary, or Robertson. I suppose if I lived a long time in England, I would become like the English: cold, reserved, impersonal.' Even when Mary laughed in the cinema, it struck Lily as forced, 'a polite little laugh, prim and restrained, sort of a miser's laugh'. Since the death of her dog, she had begun to refer to the B1A team as 'Robertson and his gang'.

When Tar came to say farewell, Lily asked him: 'If Kliemann questions me about the invasion, do I say yes or no?'

'What do you think yourself?' he replied cryptically.

'I think it'll be soon.'

'Then tell him so.' There was a pause. 'You know how much we are counting on you.'

Agent Treasure shook Tar's hand without enthusiasm. 'His words don't make much impression on me.' She had bought a gift for Kliemann at Dunhill's on Piccadilly, a pigskin wallet engraved with the words: 'For Octave. A souvenir from London. 29th February, 1944. Solange.' She told Mary: 'I am absolutely sure of being able to cope with him.' In truth, she was looking forward to seeing Kliemann again.

Treasure landed in Lisbon on 1 March 1944. She had sent a letter ahead, telling Kliemann when she would be arriving. Inevitably, he wasn't there. She checked into the Palacio Hotel, telephoned the German legation, and left a message for Kliemann. A few hours later, 'a slim, fair youngster with slicked back hair and an ingratiating smile' knocked on her hotel room door and introduced himself as 'Hoppe'. Kliemann, he said, would be arriving soon. Treasure waited.

After the damp gloom of London, Lisbon in early spring was enchanting. She wandered the bazaars and fruit stalls, admiring the black and white marble pavements and the trees in bloom: these were Judas trees. The irony of the name was not lost on her. She made contact with MI6 and was told to be patient. Privately, the British wondered if Kliemann was a busted flush. A message had recently appeared in Most Secret Sources, indicating that 'Berlin were very pleased with the work she was doing, but were not pleased with Kliemann who was considered slack and inefficient' and might 'get the sack'. After twelve days of waiting, Treasure's patience was exhausted: she summoned Hoppe to her hotel, and blew a gasket. 'Kliemann is a saboteur,' she shrieked.

'He has no order, no method. He ought to be shot. You are all hopelessly incompetent. I am fed up with it.' Still, it took three more days before Hoppe reappeared, 'very excited', to tell her: 'Our friend is here!'

On the morning of 14 March, Hoppe drove her to the Place Pombal, at the top of Avenida Liberdade. A familiar, square-shouldered figure appeared, melodramatically, from behind the fountains. Kliemann embraced her warmly. He was smartly dressed, as always, in a blue suit and felt hat, but thinner, his hair greyer than before. She noted, for the first time, that his upper teeth were false. 'He looks much older,' she wrote. 'Something akin to pity stirs in me.'

Kliemann was delighted to see her, and as self-centred as ever. 'My stock has gone up recently because of your success,' he declared. 'You are the first person to have achieved this: to have got yourself into England, to have come out again, and to be able to return. I am very proud of you, Lily! Your success has helped my position a good deal. I nearly lost my job. If you give up now it'll be the end of me.'

In the back of Hoppe's car, Kliemann talked non-stop, mostly about himself. His leg had recently been poisoned, which is why he had lost weight, he said. He had spent Christmas with Yvonne at Thonon-les-Bains on the Swiss-French frontier. He wanted Yvonne to fire her maid who was 'lazy and impertinent and always answering him back'. Like all truly selfish people, Kliemann believed the minutiae of his life must be fascinating to all.

The car stopped outside an apartment block, and Kliemann led her upstairs to an empty flat. On the table lay a parcel, wrapped in paper and string. He was beaming with pride. She unwrapped it to find what looked like an ordinary transistor radio in a 'shabby' wooden case; inside was a transmitter, almost certainly a wireless taken from a captured British SOE agent. 'Here are the two holes to which you connect your tapper. It's the only outward sign that could arouse suspicions,' said

Kliemann. A wireless expert would show Lily how to make a Morse code tapper from household items. But first, Kliemann declared brightly, some sightseeing, and then lunch.

A few hours later Lily stood on the ramparts of the Castelo dos Mouros, the great Moorish fort looking out over Sintra. On the fifteen-mile drive from Lisbon, Kliemann had happily prattled away about how satisfied the bosses were with Lily and, more importantly, with him. 'Berlin was very pleased with her for getting to Bristol. Her descriptions of divisional signs were very well given and very precise. She was to send more like that.' In the future she must also send bomb damage reports. 'It is a very worrying business running agents,' he remarked. 'Because with most of them, I am always worrying about whether they are double-crossing or not. With you, in whom I have complete confidence, it makes me feel bad to be sending you to do such unpleasant things and to run such risks.' Still, he reflected, the war might soon be over: 'The situation is quite hopeless and it is only a matter of time before Germany will have to give in.' He did not seem unduly concerned.

They drove through delightful scenery, with blossoming fruit trees along the roadsides. Lily remembered thinking that she didn't feel like going back to England.

Lily had brought with her a small Zeiss camera. As they toured the castle, she said: 'What about a picture? It would be a souvenir.'

'What a good idea. You did well to bring your camera,' said Kliemann, never suspecting that the camera had been supplied by MI5 for the express purpose of obtaining his picture for their files. Lily snapped Kliemann as he clambered up through one of the castle turrets. Then she set the automatic shutter and took another photograph of the two of them together, beside a fountain. She is smiling a little coquettishly. He strikes his best spymaster pose. They are both visibly happy.

Kliemann ordered lunch at a small restaurant. While they were waiting for the food to arrive, she presented him with the wallet. His face lit up. Then he reached in his pocket and handed Lily a packet. Inside was a pretty bracelet, forty-five diamonds set in platinum, £300 in notes and 20,000 escudos. He was gathering more money, he said, which he would give her 'at midday tomorrow'. After the meal was cleared away, Kliemann grew serious.

'Do you think there is going to be an Allied invasion?'

Lily recalled what Tar had said. 'Yes.'

'I too. When do you think it will take place?'

'I think the landing is imminent.'

Kliemann frowned, and then launched into a prepared speech. 'Now listen to me carefully, Lily. The next big move in the war will be the Allied landing. Our only chance of winning, at the moment, is to throw them back into the sea. To do that we must know in advance where they are planning to land, so that we can prepare a hot reception. It could be in Holland or Belgium, but we don't think so. We are fairly sure that it will be in France, and there are two possibilities: either the Pas de Calais or Normandy. If they choose the Pas de Calais, the Allied troops will be concentrated on the Channel coast; but if it is to be Normandy, they will move them into the area around Bristol. Do you understand? What you must tell us is whether there is a build-up of troops and other activities, so we can work out where the enemy is making for.'

She should spend as much time as possible visiting her relatives in the West Country, paying particular attention to any military activity on Salisbury Plain, and reporting 'everything seen in or around Bristol'. Where was Eisenhower's headquarters? What exercises were taking place? Were invasion barges arriving in Bristol from America, and if so in what numbers? 'Information obtained by observation is of interest, but high-level gossip is not of much interest as it rarely proves accurate.' When her radio was working, she should transmit on Mondays, Wednesdays and Fridays, at 11 p.m. 'I want the transmissions to be as short as possible. The shorter the better.' Kliemann reached into his wallet, and presented Lily with a single British stamp, explaining that on the top left-hand corner was a microdot: 'These are the instructions for the transmitting set in case you forget anything.' She put the stamp in her note case.

Only now did Kliemann ask how she had managed to travel to Lisbon. Lily launched into her cover story about her job at the Ministry of Information and the propaganda films for which she was gathering material. Kliemann nodded approvingly. She had memorised numerous corroborative details, including how Alfred Hitchcock was working for the ministry's Film Division and exactly where the canteen was located. But he asked not a single question.

After lunch they strolled along the waterfront, and watched the fishing boats pull away from the coast. Kliemann turned to her. 'What is our hold over you?'

'My parents are still in Paris, as you once reminded me . . . but it would be better for you to realise that I am acting freely, rather than under pressure. You'd feel much surer of me.'

The answer seemed to satisfy this most incurious of spies. It was dark when they climbed into Hoppe's car for the drive back to Lisbon. As they passed through Estoril, Kliemann remarked: 'I would like to have shown you the casino and take you to a chic restaurant for dinner, but it wouldn't be wise. The place is full of international gangsters, double agents and intelligence agents. It is better that we shouldn't be seen together in public.'

The next morning, Hoppe showed her how to make a Morse code tapper using a block of wood, a nail, a kitchen knife and a book. He then handed over two new transmitting crystals and a list of frequencies, and taught her a new code. Kliemann arrived, carrying a large paper bag. Inside were 1,500 £1 notes. He explained that he had 'planned to hide the money in a cigar box but could not find one large enough'. He would try to find banknotes of a larger denomination, he said, and a bigger box.

Lily now explained that, as part of her propaganda work, she had made contact with the press attaché at the British Embassy

and he had agreed to send the radio to London in the diplomatic
bag. This was a most implausible story. The diplomatic bag was
used to transfer sensitive information; it was not a free luggage
transportation service for civilians. But once again, Kliemann
evinced no suspicion, and happily agreed that 'this was a wise
move, to avoid any possible curiosity by security officials at the
airport'.

There was one more important piece of business. Now that
she had a wireless, Lily would need a 'control signal', a way to
indicate that she was now transmitting under British control,
should she be caught. 'We must take all possible precautions,'
said Kliemann. 'Suppose the British unmask you. They won't
arrest you. They'll watch you for a short time. They'll register
all your transmissions to make sure they know your methods.
Then they'll force you to work for them, under the threat
of a revolver. I want to give you some means of warning us,
some sign which they cannot detect, but for which we'll be
watching very carefully.' Kliemann's plan was simple: 'If she
was discovered by the British and told to go on transmitting,
she was to call PSE QSL SK' – Morse shorthand for 'Please
acknowledge reception'. Lily replied that this was 'silly' – which
it was, since if she added something new to a message 'the British
would know that this was some sort of sign'. She suggested a
more subtle danger code.

'At the beginning of the message, between KA and the call-sign,
there is a dash. Sometimes I do it, sometimes not. If I do it twice
– once in the message and once in the repetition of the message –
it'll mean I'm no longer a free agent. But only if the dash is there
both times. If it's only in once, it doesn't mean anything. Because
now and then I may send it just to make it less noticeable. If they
comb through a series of my messages, they will see that it varies
and won't pay any attention when I repeat it.'

Kliemann was impressed: 'That's excellent.' In his notebook
he wrote: '*Strich zwischen Anfang und Nummer*', dash between the
beginning and number.

Clifton James,
Australian actor,
playing the part of
General Bernard
Montgomery.

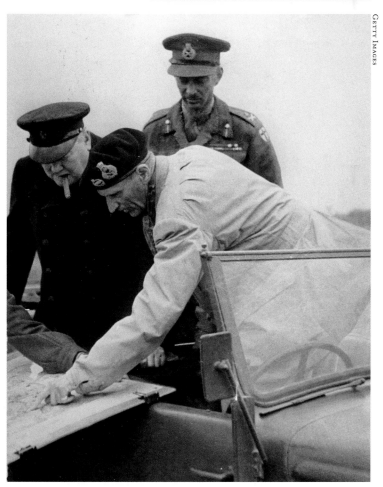

Winston Churchill and the real Monty, preparing for battle.

Dummy tanks ready for Operation Fortitude: hundreds of fakes would be deployed across southeast England, to give the impression of a vast army preparing to attack Calais.

The dummy tanks were easy to move, but tended to take off in high winds.

A dummy Hurricane fighter aircraft. It was hoped that no enemy spy would get close enough to spot the fake.

Dummy landing craft at anchor in the River Orwell, part of the fake flotilla ready to transport a bogus army in an invasion that would never take place.

Dusko Popov: a
dashing spy at war.

Roman Czerniawski's certificate for the award of the Virtuti Militari, Poland's
highest military decoration.

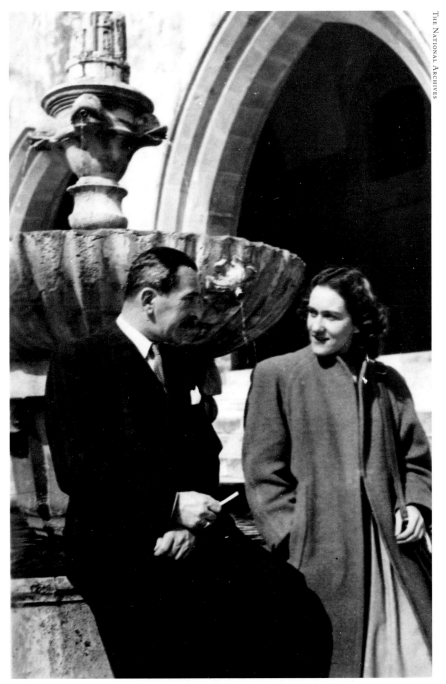

Emile Kliemann and Lily Sergeyev in the Castelo dos Mouros, Sintra, Portugal, March 1944. The photograph was taken with a Zeiss camera provided by MI5.

Claus von Stauffenberg,
ringleader of the July 1944
plot to assassinate Hitler.

Georg Hansen, anti-Nazi
plotter and head of German
counter-intelligence.

Baron Hiroshi
Oshima, Japanese
Ambassador to
Berlin, presents
his credentials
to Hitler, while
Foreign Minister
Von Ribbentrop
looks on.

Private Collection

Tar Robertson: 'immensely personable and monstrously good looking'.

The Times

Ian Wilson, the introverted but dedicated case officer for Dusko Popov and Johnny Jebsen.

Charles de Salis, MI6 officer in Lisbon and Jebsen's point of contact with British intelligence.

KEYSTONE / TopFoto

General Dwight
Eisenhower
and Winston
Churchill prepare
for the 'Great
Crusade'.

ULLSTEINBILD / TopFoto

General George
Patton: 'a goddam
natural born ham'.

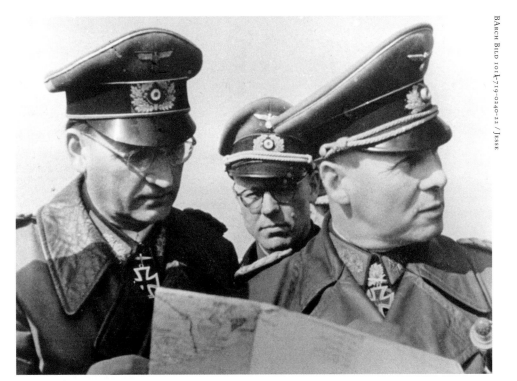

Erwin Rommel inspects German Channel defences, confident that the Atlantic Wall could not be breached.

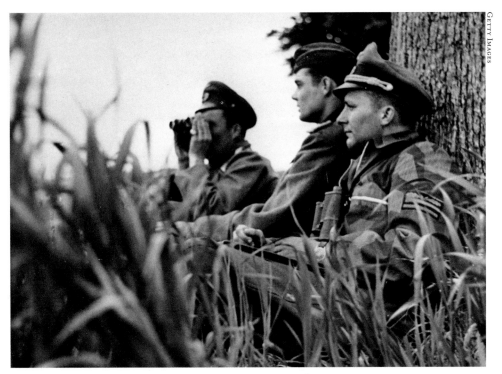

German officers on the coast of France, 1944, awaiting the invasion.

Hans Brandes, arms dealer, spy and Jebsen's 'friend'.

Major Wilhelm Kuebart: 'the most intelligent man in the Abwehr'.

Marie von Gronau, secretary at the Lisbon Abwehr station and Jebsen's lover.

Heinz Paul Moldenhauer, the Abwehr officer kidnapped with Jebsen.

Johnny Jebsen on the waterfront in Estoril, Lisbon, 1944.

Lieutenant Commander Mike Cumberlege, the piratical Royal Navy officer captured while attempting to blow up the Corinth canal.

One of the thirty-nine solitary cells in the basement of the Gestapo prison.

8 Prince Albrecht Strasse, Berlin: the Gestapo prison where Jebsen was held.

Invasion troops disembarking on D-Day. 'Just keep the Fifteenth Army out of my hair for two days,' said Eisenhower.

Troops reinforced the beachhead after the Normandy landings.

The vast artificial ports known as 'Mulberry Harbours', built in Britain and then floated across the Channel.

```
GROUP II/1A
MADRID 1 TO BERLIN
RSS 128, 130/9/6/44
TWC on 12996 kcs.          1050 GMT          9/6/44
AUT on 9288 kcs.           1107 GMT          8/6/44
256

267.  To HAROLD.  Please inform LUDWIG MARTIN at
your end.  Other Stellen not informed.  V ALARIC
ARABAL reports on 9th June from GOLFPLATZ via
FELIPE:  after personal discussion on 8th June in
LONDON with my agents DONNY DICK and DORICK, whose
reports were passed over today, I am of the opinion,
by reason of the large troop assemblage in South-
east and East ENGLAND which are not taking part in
the present operations, that these operations are
diversionary manoeuvres aiming to draw on themselves
enemy reserves in order subsequently to make a
decisive blow at another place.  Having regard to
the air-raids carried out there and the situation,
strategically favourable for this purpose, of the
above mentioned assembly area, this [blow] might well
be made in the PAS DE CALAIS area, especially as, if
there were such an attack, the nearer air-bases would
facilitate a continuous and very strong support by
the air force for such an undertaking.  According to
```

Abwehr message intercepted three days after D-Day, in which Garbo warns the Germans to expect a second 'decisive' invasion in the Pas de Calais.

Fortitude North: In Norway, German troops waited for an invasion that never came.

Fortitude South: a German tank of the Fifteenth Army defending the beaches of Calais.

The heavily fortified coast of the Pas de Calais, where the Germans expected a second, even larger Allied invasion.

Calais: 'It is here that the enemy must and will attack,' said Hitler.

Captured German map showing the invasion troops of FUSAG, the phantom army, clustered in southeast England: 'It was almost identical with Plan Fortitude'.

They arranged to meet the next day at 11.00 a.m. in the Praça di Commercio, a few hours before Lily's flight. Kliemann, astonishingly, was waiting, with a very large box of cigars under one arm. Inside, he whispered, under a layer of cigars and a false bottom, was £500 in £5 notes. They walked around the square, arm in arm. Kliemann paused by a fountain, lit a cigarette, and looked solemn.

'Even if it meant the end of my career, if you said you did not want to go back to England, I would not force you.'

'I would rather go on until the end,' said Lily.

Kliemann was a ridiculous spy, a vain and fragile egotist, but he was also capable of gentleness, and he was offering his spy a way out. Lily's British spymasters had never shown her such care.

Kliemann kissed her hand, and walked away.

In her diary Lily wrote: 'Five months ago I was so full of enthusiasm, so ready to love the British, so eager to help them. I admired them; I trusted them; I had faith in British fair play. I worked readily for them; I took risks on their behalf. In return, I only asked for one thing: to keep my dog. It wasn't asking much, but it was too much for them! Tomorrow I'll be in London, I'll hand them over the money, the code, the radio, everything . . . except for a dash! A dash that will enable me to destroy all my work, all *their* work, the minute I want to. I shall not use my power. I know that. But I will know that I have them at my mercy!'

Agent Treasure landed at Bristol airport at 5.30 the next morning, in thick fog, and was driven to a hotel. There she was given a cup of tea and some toast, along with a tiny square of margarine and half-teaspoonful of marmalade. A few minutes later, Mary Sherer strode in, bustling and businesslike. Lily handed over the box of cigars with the cash inside, the radio crystals, the stamp with the microdot, the diamond bracelet, and the photographs of Kliemann, smiling in the sun.

'He must be daft,' said Mary. 'The Colonel will be absolutely delighted.'

Robertson came to Rugby Mansions the next day to congratulate Lily in person. 'So here you are again!' he said jovially. 'We didn't really expect you.' And added: 'They are very fine cigars.'

The radio, money and bracelet were examined by MI5's experts. The transmitter was pronounced to be 'indistinguishable from an ordinary radio to the untrained eye'. Exactly thirty-nine of the £5 notes were forgeries. The bracelet was valued at £175.

Lily described her conversations with Kliemann, his hunger for information about military manoeuvres in the southwest, and his almost endearing naivety. 'I have nothing against Kliemann personally,' she told Mary. 'He has always treated me very well and it makes me feel very badly to have to lie to him and cheat him.'

'What would he do if he thought you were controlled?' Mary asked. 'Presumably he would not tell Berlin because this would make him look such a fool.'

'I am absolutely sure that if he thought I was double-crossing, he would report it.'

Mary sent a glowing report to Tar: 'Treasure gave a very good account of herself, particularly given the flimsy nature of her story. She did very well in Lisbon and has provided us with a new, very valuable channel of communication.'

Yet there was one aspect of Lily's story that troubled her. Mary had studied the files in B1A. So far, every wireless agent sent by the Germans had a 'control signal', a way to tip off the Abwehr that they had been caught and were sending messages under British direction. Sometimes this was merely a misspelling, or an added comma. Kliemann had briefed her intensively on how to operate her wireless, but 'no suggestion for indications of operation under duress was made'. Lily never mentioned a control signal: 'She states she was never given any security check or other means of informing the Germans if she was controlled by the British. In fact, they never spoke of the possibility of this happening.' Having made a note of this anomaly, Mary Sherer promptly forgot about it.

On 13 April, Mary took Lily to Hampstead Heath, to a house with a royal blue front door. The little radio transmitter had been set up in a top-floor bedroom. At twelve minutes past midnight, Lily sent a message to Kliemann: 'Arrived Safely'. She did not insert a dash, either in the message or its repetition. Over the next two months, whenever she tapped out a message, she thought about the dash. 'Every time I know that I can destroy the work of three years. Just a dash, and the Germans will know that I work under the control of the Intelligence Service . . . and the British will suspect nothing. This is my revenge – they made me a promise and they didn't keep it. Now I shall have them in my power.'

Jebsen's New Friend

Johnny Jebsen was a one-man production line of secrets. His reports, funnelled back to Britain via MI6 in Lisbon, contained an extraordinary wealth of detail about flying bombs, economic conditions in Germany, intelligence reports, and 'even an account of opinions expressed by Hitler and Himmler and Kaltenbrunner', the chief of the Reich Main Security Office (RSHA). Artist's information was gleaned from no less than thirty-nine sub-sources and informants, ranging from Abwehr secretaries to Canaris himself, and the quality was so good that MI6, territorial as ever, wondered whether it should be shared with other branches of intelligence, since there was 'no authority from C to act as a circulating section'. Jebsen grew bolder. The V2 rocket, the world's first long-range ballistic missile, was being manufactured at the Rax-Werke factory in Wiener-Neustadt, using slave labour from Mauthausen concentration camp. Passing on this information, he 'seriously and earnestly put the proposition that when his trouble with the Gestapo is cleared up he should return to Germany and organise the sabotage of the factory at Wiener-Neustadt'. Jebsen was now offering to sabotage the most potent secret weapon in the German arsenal. 'This proposal sounds fantastic, but I repeat that Artist takes it very seriously.' Even more extraordinary was Jebsen's suggestion that MI6 should recruit as a spy the wife of one of Britain's most famous novelists.

P. G. Wodehouse was now living with his wife Ethel in Paris, where the couple had regular contact with a number of high-ranking Germans. Jebsen saw an opportunity. Charles de Salis of MI6 reported:

P. G. Wodehouse and his wife were great friends of Artist, who helped them financially from time to time. They are at the moment in Paris. Mrs Wodehouse is very pro-British and is inclined to be rude to anyone who dares address her in German. She has on occasion said loudly in public places: 'If you cannot address me in English don't speak at all. You had better learn it as you will have to speak it after the war anyway.' Artist thinks she might be a useful source, as both she and her husband are in close touch with [Paul-Otto] Schmidt, Hitler's interpreter, who often talks to her of the conversations he has had to interpret between Hitler and the various foreigners who visit him. Wodehouse himself is entirely childlike and pacifist.

It is not known whether MI6 acted on this suggestion and recruited Ethel Wodehouse, but Jebsen's suggestion casts a new light on their time in Paris. Critics accused the novelist and his wife of living in queasy accommodation with the Nazis, after Wodehouse foolishly agreed to make radio broadcasts at the Germans' behest. Jebsen's report proves that while Wodehouse himself may have been passively apolitical, his wife was so anti-Nazi that she was considered a potential spy.

Jebsen believed he was safe. Elements within the Abwehr saw him as 'anti-Nazi and latterly defeatist', but he had his defenders. A colleague in Berlin promised to warn him of any imminent danger: if he received a 'telegram saying "come back immediately" this was a pre-arranged signal which in fact meant "do not come, the Gestapo are after you".' He had also recruited a new bedroom mole within the Lisbon Abwehr station: Baroness Marie von Gronau, the twenty-three-year-old daughter of a pioneer aviator who was the Luftwaffe attaché in Tokyo. Marie was a secretary in the counter-intelligence section, and happily told Jebsen whatever was passing across her boss's desk. In jest, he asked Marie to marry him. She turned him down, but was 'fascinated by his intelligence and wide knowledge'. She may have been equally attracted to the 'seemingly inexhaustible funds at his disposal'. After the war, Marie von Gronau was asked if she had known Jebsen was a British agent. She replied that he had denied it so often she assumed he must be, and recalled how he dropped telltale remarks such as: 'I am His Majesty's Most Loyal Enemy' and 'Friendship goes across borders of nations, regardless of a state of war'.

Marie von Gronau was generous with her favours. When Jebsen arrived in Lisbon, she was already the mistress of the Italian air attaché, and being courted by an SD officer named Volbrecht. One evening Volbrecht told Marie that Jebsen was a '*macaco*', a Portuguese term of abuse meaning 'monkey', and the Baroness passed the insult on to Jebsen. 'Although he had not the slightest idea what a *macaco* was, he did not like the sound of the word and challenged Volbrecht to a duel with pistols.' Volbrecht refused, 'saying his department did not allow duels'. During this period, Jebsen's wife Lore came to Lisbon to see him, a visit that seems to have done nothing to slow down his extra-marital liaisons.

Jebsen's was spiralling into a most volatile frame of mind. Lily Grass, he declared, was still 'infatuated' with him, and passing on useful titbits from the correspondence of her boss, Aloys Schreiber, the head of counter-intelligence: 'Schreiber has written to Berlin that in his opinion Tricycle is absolutely reliable and should be given the biggest and most secret tasks for big money,' she told him. This was reassuring, yet 'Jebsen's nervousness and excitability' was a headache. In late January, Charles de Salis telephoned Jebsen's villa in Estoril to find that he had vanished. A discreet but intensive manhunt was launched. After three days British intelligence was starting to panic, when

Jebsen reappeared, none the worse for his disappearing act save for a hangover: he had been on an almighty binge with his new best friend, Hans Brandes.

Hans Joachim Brandes was one of numerous shady characters loosely attached to the Lisbon Abwehr station. He was twenty-four years old, fair-haired, half-Jewish, Swiss-educated, and so overweight that he had been declared unfit for military service. His father had owned a large machine tool factory in Berlin, and on the outbreak of war Brandes and his brother, principally through bribery, had successfully registered themselves as non-Jewish. Brandes spent money liberally wherever he went, and was 'known to give as much as 30,000 marks to reserve officers whose salary is only some 700 marks monthly, merely to make things easier for himself'. A shareholder in a Berlin armaments firm, he won a contract to supply arms to the Portuguese government.

Arriving in Lisbon in 1943, Brandes set himself up as a trader in platinum, diamonds and shoe leather, and occasional spy. 'He is personally befriended by Canaris who has sent him here to be out of harm's way as he is partly Jewish,' reported Jebsen. 'He is supposed to report through von Karsthoff but he does practically nothing' and seemed to have some sort of 'hold over' the Abwehr station chief, almost certainly financial: 'His bribes go a long way and he is certainly a specialist in that art.' Brandes claimed to be running his own espionage network, including an IRA spy in Ireland, agents in Switzerland and a Frenchman in North Africa named Barinki d'Arnoux. Brandes liked to boast: 'With a great deal of cunning and craftiness I have succeeded to settle down here in Lisbon for the duration of the war.' He shared Jebsen's tastes and, it seemed, his politics. 'He made no secret of the fact that he is not only very anti-Nazi but very pro-British and hoped England would win the war.' Together, they roistered around Lisbon, with secretaries in tow. 'Relations between Artist and Brandes seem to have grown very close,' MI6 reported. Early in January, Brandes told his new friend that he was going to Berlin and would 'try to persuade Canaris to cancel his order against Artist's return to Germany'. Jebsen did not tell Brandes about his work for the British, but he believed his new chum could easily be recruited as another double agent.

In fact, MI6 had been tracking the mysterious Brandes ever since his arrival in Lisbon, and had come to the conclusion that, like Ostro, he was a hoaxer. Kim Philby, the head of the MI6 counter-intelligence Iberian desk, followed the progress of Brandes through Most Secret Sources, and concluded 'the organisation he claims to run is fictitious'. Brandes was perpetrating a 'deliberate fraud on the Abwehr', which made him susceptible to blackmail. 'He is only twenty-four and half-Jewish,' wrote Philby. 'It is certain, therefore, that if he fails to maintain his position he would find himself fairly rapidly on the Eastern Front. He is strongly anti-Nazi and has never made any serious attempt to provide the Abwehr with genuine information. He would have a positive motive for accepting our proposition.'

Brandes knew Jebsen had secret agents in Britain, but he assumed that Jebsen's reports to Berlin, like his own, were what he called 'constructive fantasy'. He even offered to back up anything Jebsen might be sending to Berlin with his own inventions. Jebsen told de Salis he had 'enough confidence in Brandes to reveal to him that he was working for the British', but 'had not done so and would not do so without agreement'. Brandes was a 'slippery opportunist', said Jebsen, but he could be a useful ally: 'If he knew the truth he would probably want to join the game.'

MI6 decided to keep a close eye on Jebsen's new friend; if and when the time seemed ripe, he could be brought into the game. 'I think Brandes might develop into a useful straight agent if he has any guts and strong anti-Nazi convictions,' wrote Frank Foley of MI6. Jebsen was certain Brandes would persuade Admiral Canaris to 'lift the veto for my return which was made for my safety, as the Gestapo does not want anything from me any longer. I myself will be able to leave shortly.'

But before Canaris could do any such thing, he was toppled. Early in February, an Abwehr officer named Erich Vermehren slipped out of the Abwehr station in Istanbul, and defected. He and his wife were smuggled to Britain via Cairo and Gibraltar, and took up residence in a South Kensington flat belonging to Kim Philby's mother. Vermehren's defection was the excuse the enemies of Canaris were waiting for. Hitler was enraged. Canaris had long been suspected of being disloyal (which he was) and of working to undermine Hitler (which he probably was too). He was dismissed, given a meaningless job, and finally placed under house arrest. The Abwehr would soon be taken over by the SD and subsumed into the Reich Main Security Office under the control of Himmler and Kaltenbrunner, and then abolished entirely. Jebsen had been predicting 'the downfall of Canaris' for some time. His ousting brought with it an orgy of chaotic score-settling and internecine feuding: some Abwehr officers demanded to be sent to the front; others were dismissed; those remaining in place did so in an atmosphere of crippling paranoia and uncertainty. 'Further dismissals will probably take place,' Jebsen reported, 'together with a weeding out of unsatisfactory double agents.' The British would continue to refer to 'the Abwehr', although the old organisation was effectively obsolete.

The chaos within German intelligence, and the SD's seizure of power at the expense of the Abwehr, sent a shudder of anxiety through the Double Cross team. The Abwehr officers were the devils they knew. There was now a danger, as Masterman observed, that 'new brooms would sweep away much which we had tried to preserve'.

Jebsen had been at university in Freiburg with Erich Vermehren, and had helped him get a job in the Abwehr. The Vermehren family, from Lübeck, was ardently anti-Nazi. Erich's mother, Petra Vermehren, a distinguished German journalist, had come to Portugal early in the war in order to get out from under the Nazi regime. Jebsen knew her well, and on hearing of Vermehren's defection, he rushed to her home to find Petra packing. She explained that she had been recalled to Germany to explain her son's defection. 'Jebsen tried to persuade her not to go,' telling her 'he was on friendly terms with Lord Rothschild who has asked him to come to England' – a hint that he could help arrange her defection. Petra insisted she was not afraid and caught the next plane to Berlin, knowing that under the Nazi system of collective punishment she was probably doomed. She was arrested at the airport and sent to Sachsenhausen concentration camp. Her husband, son and two daughters were also interned in concentration camps.

Vermehren's defection made Jebsen's own position more vulnerable. His friendship with the family was well known, and he was sure to be tarred by association. Canaris, 'the old fox', was no longer on hand to protect him. The 'younger and more energetic' Georg Hansen was appointed head of counter-intelligence, and set about merging the remnants of the Abwehr into a new unified intelligence service. 'He is not a Nazi,' reported Jebsen, 'but he is determined to prevent Germany's defeat. There is no doubt that Hansen means to reform the Abwehr completely.' This new intelligence service would bear little relation to the dozy, dishonest and partly disloyal organisation Jebsen had joined back in 1939. Many of his supporters had been swept away with the fall of Canaris, replaced by men not at all to Jebsen's liking. 'The new officers have no experience of intelligence work, but they are keener and more active than their predecessors and will probably succeed in tightening up the organisation.' One of these new appointees, in particular, made Jebsen 'a little uneasy'.

Major Wilhelm Kuebart was one of the stiffest new brooms in German intelligence. A professional soldier from East Prussia, he had fought on the Eastern Front before transferring to the Abwehr in July 1943, as Hansen's deputy. Kuebart was twenty-eight, 'wide awake', ruthlessly proficient, and 'the most intelligent man in the Abwehr', Jebsen reported. The young Major swiftly concluded that German intelligence was composed of 'elderly men with little or no idea of military organisation'. The Lisbon office, in particular, was 'discharging its functions most unsatisfactorily'. Kuebart paid a visit to Portugal and was 'shocked at the general immorality'. Half the staff appeared to be sleeping with the other half. At least two of the secretaries were passing information to Jebsen. Von Karsthoff might insist that Jebsen was 'an extremely able man', but Kuebart smelled something 'rather fishy'. On returning to Berlin, he drew up a damning report, recommending that von Karsthoff be 'removed and replaced', and the 'sleeping secretaries' fired. 'This brothel must be shut,' Kuebart declared.

Ludovico von Karsthoff, Popov's indolent, charming, corrupt spymaster, was reprimanded for 'indiscretion and inefficiency' (which was putting it mildly), sacked from his post, and sent to the Eastern Front. Dr Aloys Schreiber was now, in effect, the head of German intelligence in Lisbon.

Schreiber was a puzzle. A forty-four-year-old Bavarian, with an oval face and greying hair, he was a First World War veteran with a doctorate in law from Erlangen University. He had been the personal courier to his close friend Canaris, before being sent to Lisbon to take over from Jebsen's arch-enemy Kammler as head of counter-intelligence, although he spoke not a word of Portuguese. 'His specific duties were obtaining intelligence information concerning enemy armies', gathering information about 'the possibility of Allied invasion, and in particular the time, location and strength of such a proposed landing'. Bookish and serious, Schreiber was openly disdainful of his dissolute colleagues, and had a reputation among the Abwehr roustabouts and layabouts for being 'pedantic and ambitious'. Jebsen was unsure what to make of this clever, sober, anti-social man: 'Schreiber is not a Nazi, but nor particularly anti-Nazi,' he reported.

In fact, Schreiber was not only anti-Nazi, but a conspirator in the spreading plot to topple Hitler. Like some others in the Abwehr, he nursed a quiet but profound hatred of Nazism.

In 1942, on the orders of Hans Oster, the deputy head of the Abwehr and a significant figure in the German resistance, he smuggled a Jewish couple named Weiss and their children to Switzerland, and was arrested 'on suspicion of aiding, abetting and camouflaging the illegal departure' of Jews. He was exonerated after his Abwehr bosses intervened. Before leaving for Portugal, Colonel Georg Hansen, another key conspirator, quizzed him closely about 'his general political attitude'. Schreiber was left in no doubt that the conspirators were sounding him out: 'Something was being planned and he was under the impression that they wished to ascertain exactly who belonged to them in sentiment, so they would know on whom they could count.' They could count on Schreiber. As defeat loomed, a determined band of officers, led by Claus von Stauffenberg, began planning Hitler's assassination in the attempted putsch codenamed 'Valkyrie'. These were not soft-hearted liberals, but ruthless military men determined to salvage German honour by destroying Nazism, making peace with the Americans and British, and then turning, with full ferocity, on the Bolshevik menace in the East. A postwar investigation concluded that Schreiber 'belonged to the group of militarists who sponsored the attempt of 20 July 1944' and 'he was sent to Portugal by the 20 July conspirators to ensure having a dependable man in a strategic position who could be called upon'. Schreiber would soon receive the call, with calamitous consequences for the Double Cross plot.

Marie von Gronau, Jebsen's latest 'sleeping secretary', reported that Berlin was demanding 'the names of Abwehr members who are believed to be in touch with the British'. Jebsen relayed this disquieting news to de Salis: 'We must reckon that they will in future pay special attention to us. Even greater care is necessary with regard to meetings.' The danger was reflected in Most Secret Sources. 'Berlin has ordered that a close watch be kept on Artist, presumably on account of the flight of the Vermehrens as he is known to be a friend of theirs,' wrote Tar. 'Artist's friends are not now in Berlin, and his enemies are going to make things unpleasant for him.'

Jebsen was confident: Brandes had been to Berlin, and reported that he had 'defended him strongly'; the secretaries were keeping him fully informed of the correspondence with Berlin; Schreiber did not seem particularly hostile, and the order to keep an eye on him was probably just a routine response to the defection of his friend, Erich Vermehren. 'The clouds are nearly over,' he told de Salis, who reported back to London: 'Artist in extremely good form, owing to fact that suspicions against him have died down due to prompt action by his allies, including Brandes.' Jebsen's confidence rose further with the news that he would soon be reunited with Popov.

Popov landed at the now-familiar Lisbon airport on 26 February, bearing with him another large slice of Operation Fortitude, including photographs of Admiralty documents, notes on aircraft types, information on rationing and a doctored parliamentary speech. Within Popov's cache, as Jebsen had advised, lay a wealth of smaller details which, when put together, would reveal a mighty army assembling in the southeast. Popov had been told to take Jebsen aside as soon as discreetly possible, and 'exert his influence over Artist to prevent the latter from getting nervous or excited and doing foolish things or taking any avoidable risks'. If Jebsen raised the idea of bringing Brandes into the plot, he should be urged to 'take no steps whatever to bring this about, although we would welcome suggestions as to how it might be possible to recruit Brandes'. Above all, Jebsen should be encouraged to find out whether the deception was working, by obtaining 'up-to-date details of the German knowledge of the British Order of Battle'.

Popov's reception was very different from the sort of welcome laid on by von Karsthoff. This time he would be debriefed by Aloys Schreiber, a man who, Jebsen warned, 'had a very great experience of interrogating prisoners'.

Schreiber asked Jebsen to sit in on the debriefing, which was
as intense and penetrating as von Karsthoff's had been cheery
and perfunctory. For two days and nights, pausing only for
beer and sandwiches, Schreiber grilled Popov. Jebsen chipped
in from time to time with his own sharp questions. Popov
later reported that his friend had 'assisted him cleverly during
his interrogation while deliberately appearing to be rather
hostile, with the result that Schreiber is satisfied there is no
collaboration between Artist and Tricycle'. Popov put on a
dazzling performance. Indeed, as he later told Wilson, 'he was
sure he was definitely on top and, as he modestly put it, being the
younger man he stood the strain better than Schreiber'. The
German station chief seemed utterly convinced by Popov's
report, and immediately dictated a telegram to Berlin stating
that he was 'an excellent agent and he had no suspicions'.
Marie von Gronau passed the note on to Jebsen, who gave it
to de Salis, who sent it on to London, where the news was
passed to Churchill: 'His first interview with his spymasters
passed off in a most satisfactory manner.' Popov's confidence
was validated when Bletchley Park decoded a message to
the German High Command, noting that Agent Ivan had
furnished 'particularly valuable information about the British
formations in Great Britain. The report confirmed our own
overall operational picture.'

    After the debriefing, Popov and Jebsen hit the town, hard.
Jebsen was 'in funds, having managed to wangle authority to
transfer some gold he has put by in Paris', and had bought
himself a Rolls-Royce, which he could not drive. Jebsen
did not seem unduly anxious for his own safety, and spoke
of maintaining 'long-term contact with the British secret
services' and wanting 'to be regarded by them as a reliable
agent even after the war'. Popov was confident his own high
standing in Berlin would protect his friend. They were joined
in their carousing by Hans Brandes, Jebsen's new friend.
Brandes seemed wary of Popov. Jebsen later suggested why:

'He is afraid that he [Popov] will report the date and place of the invasion and thus prolong the war.' It was an odd thing to say. Brandes often made overtly anti-Nazi remarks, as if fishing for a reaction. De Salis reported: 'Although convinced that Brandes is not trying to trap him, Artist always reacts to such suggestions as a good German should.'

Ian Wilson flew out to Lisbon and met Popov and Jebsen at the safe house. Jebsen was ambitious to do more for the cause. 'He is keen to go to Germany as he wanted to do something big for us,' Wilson reported. 'He could arrange to be sent to Germany for a visit under a false name if we really desired it.' Wilson thought it safer for Jebsen to remain in Lisbon, particularly after he casually referred to 'Kühlenthal's controlled agents in UK', and the need for these to back up whatever Popov reported. Here was proof positive that Jebsen knew the Garbo network, or 'the Spaniards', as he called them, were bogus. Brandes had 'brought word back from Berlin on how the British spies were seen in Berlin', which suggested that Popov was now even more valued than Pujol. 'Ivan [Popov] is now considered to be by far the best connection and the Spaniards, as regards quality, are following a long way behind,' Brandes reported. 'The confidence in him has grown very much.' Such comparisons were of limited value since, as Jebsen observed, it was 'common for members of the Abwehr to run down each others' agents'.

Still, Brandes was being remarkably helpful, and Jebsen again urged his recruitment: 'He is certain that Brandes would collaborate with us.'

Jebsen did not realise, and MI5 did not tell him, that Brandes was an even more slippery opportunist than he knew. Brandes had his own wireless transmitter. With this he was sending messages to Berlin, reporting on Jebsen – who he was meeting, where he was going, and what he was saying. These transmissions, decoded at Bletchley Park, revealed yet another layer of deception: the man Jebsen considered his close friend, to whom he was prepared to entrust his life by inducting him into his terrifying secret, was betraying him behind his back.

'Brandes is playing a game of his own,' reported Ian Wilson, a note of fear creeping for the first time into his words. 'Brandes is clearly telling tales.'

'Am I Not Always Careful?'

Brutus, Bronx, Treasure, Tricycle and Garbo would never meet. Yet individually, and together, as spring advanced and the Allied armies prepared for the biggest amphibious assault in history, they spun a tapestry of lies so thick and wide it would envelop the entire German intelligence system. In April 1944, anxiety was still high, and expectations low: Tommy Harris declared that the effort would be worthwhile if the deception caused just '*one* division to hesitate *48 hours* before proceeding to oppose our landing in the Cherbourg peninsula'. As the real army mustered in the southwest to attack Normandy, the double agents deployed their fake army in the southeast and the north. At first Pujol and Harris had merely sprinkled untruths among the chicken-feed, but now they began to 'increase the percentage of false in the mixture until the entire substance of our reports would be based on the false or notional', a creeping barrage of deception.

Popov's latest report to Lisbon had established the names and locations of units within the fictional invasion force; knowing that the Germans would now be paying attention, the double agents started to move these south and east. Most Secret Sources showed that Garbo's reports, five or six a day, were being relayed to Berlin, promptly and almost verbatim, along with his analysis of their meaning. The hoax was being injected straight into the central nervous system of the Third Reich.

The deceivers wondered if they were being too subtle. Would the Germans pick up the hints and reach the right conclusions? As a test, Tar Robertson called in a 'military expert who had no previous dealings with B1A', sat him down with forty boxes of paper – the entire double-agent traffic from March 1943 to April 1944 – and asked him to interpret the lot. The poor man ploughed through the files every day for two weeks, and then offered his conclusions as to what the Germans must be thinking:

1. Agents have been at pains to make no definite forecast.
2. Strong likelihood of attack in the Mediterranean at same time.
3. An attack in Norway, possibly of a diversionary nature, prior to the main attack.
4. The initial landings will be made against Belgium and the Pas de Calais.

The assessment fitted with the deception almost perfectly.

A German intelligence report of 4 April stated that the Fourth Army was assembling in Scotland, and cited a 'credible Abwehr source'. This source was Roman Czerniawski, whose reputation expanded with every message: 'He is very well regarded and up till now has produced much accurate information,' Oscar Reile noted. Hugh Astor hit on a way to bind Brutus even more firmly to the Germans, while reinforcing the lie that a fictional American-led army was assembling in Kent: 'If Brutus were posted notionally to FUSAG just before D-Day, he would be in an excellent position to report on the Order of Battle and operational intentions of FUSAG.' When the time was ripe, Czerniawski would announce that, 'on account of his intimate knowledge of France and French military procedure', he had been ordered to join a special unit 'set up under FUSAG with the object of recruiting Poles who worked in the German-occupied territory which was likely to be overrun in the near future'. Since many Poles worked in the coalfields east of Calais, this would in itself bolster the idea that the US Army Group was poised to attack the Calais area. Installed at the heart of the fictional army, the little Pole would be perfectly placed to report exactly what was happening or, more accurately, what was not happening.

While Brutus focused on military matters, Bronx fed her handlers 'the opinions of those whose names and pictures appeared in the column of fashionable newspapers', a peculiar admixture of the weighty and the irrelevant. Beneath the fluff, she pointed unmistakably to forces assembling to attack the Pas de Calais: Lord Kimberley told her an armoured division had moved from Yorkshire to Brighton; one Major Bulteel suggested 'Montgomery's HQ may be near Canterbury'; a friend in the Army petroleum department visited Dover and Folkestone and told her of 'large invasion stores'; another, George Mitchell, resident in Kent, informed her 'roads to beaches widened and concrete barriers removed', suggesting a mass military deployment towards the coast. She helped to focus attention on Scandinavia, relaying a conversation with Commander Sir Guy Domville, who 'believes Denmark place for invasion. S. Norway may be occupied.' Her reports were calculated to maintain German uncertainty about the date: 'Invasion seems imminent,' she reported on 25 April. 'Many US troops leaving west coast for S. E. Command.' A few days later, she corrected herself: 'Prime Minister's conference indicates invasion not imminent. Montgomery still training invasion force.'

As Emile Kliemann had instructed, Lily Sergeyev headed to Bristol to stay with her relatives, and toured the south coast by bicycle, while never leaving London. 'I make imaginary visits to places which I did not know existed, and from which I bring back rich harvests of information,' she wrote in her diary. 'In this world of fiction, I spend my time in trains, clubs, messes, canteens. I transmit a hodgepodge of descriptions of badges, vehicles, tanks, planes and airfields, garnished with conversations overheard, from which the Germans cannot fail to derive the correct conclusions.' Like many spies, caught up in the make-believe, she began to wonder who she really was. 'For three years I have been acting a part . . . If I survive the war, will I be able to readapt? Will I be able to become *normal* again?'

Mary was pleased with Lily's compliant attitude, and her apparent recovery from the death of Babs: 'She is working hard on her transmissions,' she told Tar. Inside, Lily was still seething, and her resentment was redoubled by some ill-advised penny-pinching on the part of MI5. She was told to make her own way to Hampstead by Tube: 'I don't think it would break the War Office to take me there by car,' she grumbled. She was moved out of Rugby Mansions and into a smaller flat at 39 Hill Street, where she had to pay rent, albeit reduced. A stern note from John Marriott instructed her: 'The furniture, fittings and books will be maintained in the condition that they are now in and expenses for cleaning etc. will be paid promptly. I shall expect you to carry out this undertaking.' It was the wrong tone to use to an agent who had just risked her life. As Lily pointed out, Kliemann was eating out of her hand – 'the German intelligence service seems entirely satisfied with the information I supply. From time to time there are congratulations in their messages.' The British, on the other hand, were charging her rent, and telling her to keep the carpet clean.

MI5 refused to reimburse Lily for her lost suitcase, while O'Shagar, the MI6 officer who had promised to look after Babs when she left Gibraltar, had also failed to send on the case's contents: Lily demanded their return, but her possessions were irretrievably lost in the fog of war. The suitcase had contained a jade necklace, a chamois leather pillow, two dozen handkerchiefs in a red leather case and, oddly, 'three shoes (not pairs) valued at £12'. Lily reckoned the total value was £128 2s 6d, but said she would settle for £50. MI5 declined to pay her a penny.

'I think we ought NOT to pay up,' declared Marriott, and listed the reasons why: 'She has no legal claim. She has behaved in an unreasonable fashion in the past and may therefore do so again. She is trying to bully us.' John Masterman agreed: 'We owe nothing.' Mary Sherer was appalled:

> Treasure is not a money grubber. In view of what she has accomplished and what we hope to get out of her case, I urge you very strongly to reconsider your decision. I have had a difficult time with Treasure on more than one occasion in the past and it will not make things any easier if she has a private grudge against the department and British authorities on the whole because of their apparently niggardly behaviour towards her for the sake of £50.

But the bosses were adamant. John Masterman did not like women in general, and Lily in particular, considering her 'exceptionally temperamental and troublesome'.

A few days later, as she and Mary were preparing a wireless message, Lily remarked darkly: 'It is very difficult not to take advantage of one's strength when one is the strongest.' Mary assumed she was referring to the parsimony of MI5 with its 'meticulous accounts'. Most likely, she was alluding to her own secret strength: the knowledge that a couple of undetected dashes in a mass of Morse could bring the entire Double Cross system crashing down.

Dusko Popov arrived back in Britain on 13 April, with a spring in his step, a fresh batch of questionnaires and a wad of cash. His last days in Lisbon had been spent wrangling over money, the sort of negotiation at which Popov excelled. He told Aloys Schreiber he wanted a staggering $150,000 as an advance payment on future information about Allied invasion plans, and declared that 'any further activities on his part would depend on the receipt of the stipulated sum'. When this was relayed to Berlin, the demand was flatly refused. Popov was offered just 1,500 Swiss francs a month. He threatened to resign. This gave

Wilhelm Kuebart, the officer who had ousted von Karsthoff, an 'uncomfortable feeling' about Popov, 'as it seemed to him highly improbable that an agent who was really independent and acting for himself could afford to threaten the Abwehr in this manner'. Even MI5 considered Popov's demands 'outrageous', and his threat to quit an unauthorised gamble. In the end, Popov was given $14,000, with the promise of more to come. Before leaving, he had been interviewed again by Schreiber, who told him to find out the date and target of the invasion, which attacks would be real, and which merely diversions. If the landings started, he should 'stay in London and give up-to-date news on what was happening'. Schreiber also asked him to report on bomb damage when the V1s started landing, but Popov refused, saying they could 'send some lower-grade agent round to look for holes in London'.

Popov and Jebsen spent a last night together at the casino in Estoril. At dawn, they shook hands and parted, but as Popov was walking away, Jebsen called him back: 'I just wanted to have a good look at you,' he said. 'It's going to be a while. I feel we are going in different directions.' Then he walked away.

Back in London, Popov was ebullient, convinced the Germans had 'complete faith in him'. Schreiber had no idea he was playing a double game. The Germans were paying good money. Johnny was safe. 'Tricycle is now considered to be the Abwehr's best agent in the UK,' MI6 reported.

The B1A case officers pored over Popov's latest offerings from the other side, which included a long questionnaire largely composed of wishful thinking: 'What are Churchill's prospects of remaining at the helm? How is his health? Does he by any chance already think of retiring, and if so, when?' To which the answers were: 'good', 'good', 'no' and 'never'. Popov's briefcase contained no fewer than five typed reports from Jebsen, on aircraft production, industrial output, military reserves and the restructuring of German intelligence: he noted the rise of SS officer Walter Schellenberg, 'personally agreeable and quite ruthless', who would eventually take over as intelligence supremo.

Popov was 'not unduly worried' for Jebsen's safety, since the Gestapo had apparently rescinded an order to have him arrested if he returned to Germany. Even so, Tar insisted 'it was much safer that he should remain in Lisbon rather than return to Germany, where he might find himself in an awkward position, under which his nerves would give way'. Before leaving Lisbon, Popov learned from Marie von Gronau that the SD was 'sending a representative to interrogate Artist at the end of April or beginning of May in Lisbon, in order to clear up certain financial matters', but this was no cause for concern. 'These allegations have nothing to do with activities on behalf of the British, but relate to questionable financial transactions. He is satisfied that he can easily clear himself. The intended interrogation is likely to be a formality, so that the file against Jebsen can be closed.' Popov was convinced his friend was finally 'free from danger'.

MI5 knew otherwise.

On 11 February, Hans Brandes, using the codename 'Ballhorn', sent a message to Berlin, reporting that Jebsen was asking suspicious questions, and 'trying to find out about Ostro'. The message was intercepted and decoded at Bletchley Park. Under British instructions, Jebsen was investigating the fake agent Paul Fidrmuc, whom MI5 had considered eliminating a few months earlier. Another intercepted message referred to 'oral reports made by Ballhorn', indicating that Brandes had been snitching during his trip to Berlin. The next day brought further evidence of his duplicity, when Brandes reported that through the secretaries, Jebsen 'learns everything' that happened in the German intelligence station. Schreiber fired off his own message to Berlin: 'As cannot continue to work in such circumstances, it is urgently requested that Grass and Von Gronau be immediately recalled, giving routine reduction of staff as justification in order not to give Johnny prior warning.'

What was Brandes up to? Why was he dripping poison into his superiors' ears about a man supposed to be his friend? Brandes 'might be playing some deep game for his own interests', thought Wilson, 'possibly with the ultimate intention of blackmailing Artist, or ourselves. He is far from stupid and quite unscrupulous, as are so many spoilt children of rich German industrialists.' Brandes had recently been ordered to send his agents 'to France for instruction'. But Brandes had no agents. He had made them all up, and he was now trying to find a way of 'worming, or bribing, his way out of this dilemma'. Ratting on Jebsen would divert attention. 'It may well be that in order to prevent his being discovered he is trying to build himself up with the Abwehr by unmasking Artist.' Ambitious and avaricious, Brandes knew how much money was being passed to Popov, and what Jebsen and von Karsthoff had made on the side. A postwar investigation revealed that Brandes was 'very jealous of the fact that Artist was in touch with Tricycle, the best German secret intelligence man in England. Brandes wanted to get rid of him so that he might get the credit for Tricycle's work.'

The evidence of Brandes's treachery presented MI5 with an appalling dilemma. If Jebsen was warned that his friend was betraying him, he would immediately wonder how MI5 had come by that information, and perhaps conclude that the British must be intercepting German wireless messages. At all costs, Most Secret Sources must be protected. After an intense debate, it was agreed that MI6 would pass on a general warning to Jebsen, hinting that Brandes should not be trusted because some of what he had told Jebsen had turned out to be inaccurate. A telegram was sent to Charles de Salis in Lisbon: 'Strong impression that Brandes is playing a game of his own and may be trying to provoke Artist into confidences which he might use for his own interests. Instruct Artist not to expose himself in any way to Brandes, even if this restricts his acquisition of information on our behalf.' De Salis was not told that MI5's 'impressions' came from Most Secret Sources. Wilson meanwhile sounded out Popov on how well Jebsen might hold up under interrogation, should he be arrested. Popov replied that he had 'absolutely no doubts whatsoever that Artist would never betray Tricycle or confess his own work for the British under any normal form of interrogation [but he] doubts his powers to withstand any physical violence'.

Jebsen had been 'hasty in assuming that the clouds have quite rolled away'. A storm was gathering with terrifying speed. On 16 April, Schreiber informed Jebsen that they had both been ordered to travel to Biarritz, in the South of France, to meet the paymaster of the reformed German intelligence service and discuss Popov's demands for money. Sensing a trap, Jebsen refused to go, claiming that this would blow 'his cover' as an independent businessman, since travelling to France required official German approval. Schreiber insisted the telegram from Berlin 'should be looked upon as an order', and refusal to obey 'would be considered desertion'. Jebsen dug in his heels. Schreiber reported this back to Berlin, and headed off to Biarritz alone. Jebsen, deeply alarmed, told Brandes what had happened; Brandes immediately sent a telegram to Berlin:

> On the 17th Johnny told me he had been ordered to a conference in Biarritz on the subject of Ivan. Johnny said he saw a clear trap in this and was certain that his immediate arrest was intended in Biarritz. Johnny added that if in the next few days any further signs of mistrust existing towards him on the part of Berlin are to be observed he intends to draw his own conclusions and will inform Ivan in good time.

Further signs of mistrust were not long in coming. The next day the office secretaries, Lily Grass and Marie von Gronau, were ordered to return to Berlin within twenty-four hours. This was 'a routine reduction of staff', Schreiber claimed, since 'all

secretaries who have been here more than two years are to leave
on the principle that they have had a long period of work in
a pleasant place and should therefore be moved to somewhere
less pleasant'. But Jebsen knew his moles within the system were
being weeded out. The women were instructed not to speak
to him before they left; both ignored the order. Jebsen even
escorted Marie to the airport. As they parted, he said something
that made her even more convinced that he must be a British
agent. 'Three days after the end of hostilities, a British pilot
will report to a restaurant in Flensburg, Schleswig-Holstein, the
Grossadel Bylond, and if you are present he will pick you up
and bring you to England.' Marie promised to be there.

Jebsen met Charles de Salis at the safe house. He was deeply
agitated, smoking furiously with trembling fingers. The MI6 man
passed on the veiled warning about Brandes, but Jebsen seemed
preoccupied with the forced departure of the secretaries. 'Artist
does not consider this a very good sign,' de Salis reported. 'He feels
very bitter. He rails against the pig-headed administration which
has ordered this.' The order to go to Biarritz with Schreiber had
been a 'test' of his loyalty and obedience: 'Further traps of this
nature will be laid,' he predicted. Despite the precariousness of
his own position, Jebsen had some important new intelligence
to report: the latest strategic assessment by the German General
Staff, as presented to a conference of generals in France. This
predicted a 'large-scale invasion attempt' across the Channel
and in southern France, revealed doubts as to 'whether Norway
could be defended successfully', and concluded that a precise
assessment of American troops in the UK would be 'decisive'.
The Germans appeared to be concentrating on exactly the right
areas. Before she was ordered home, Lily Grass had passed on
some good news. 'Tricycle's reports have made a tremendous
impression in Berlin and the General Staff are considering
modifying their plans in consequence. The last report had already
been classified as being "as good as sure", which is an almost
unparalleled evaluation.' By the end of the meeting, Jebsen had

regained some of his composure. 'Artist is confident that Brandes will keep him warned of future traps, and hopes that in this way the "tests" may be negotiated successfully. If this can be done, Tricycle's position as the Ace Abwehr agent in the UK will be assured and all thenceforward should be comparatively easy.'

Before they parted, de Salis told Jebsen to be careful.

'Am I not always careful?' said Jebsen, with a pale smile.

The warning about Brandes had not registered. Or perhaps Jebsen chose to ignore it. He was a firm believer in friendship. Later the same day, he showed a document to Brandes, who was on the radio to Berlin within hours. 'A telegram which has just arrived from England was shown to me by Johnny at his house. It was signed by his friend Baronet Anthony Rothschild. The contents read as follows "Don't worry, our business shall be finished very soon".'

This was, of course, part of Jebsen's elaborate tale about a rich member of the Rothschild family (now downgraded from peer to baronet) who was helping him get a refugee visa to Britain. He probably showed it to Brandes, knowing he might soon have to disappear. There was no such person as Sir Anthony Rothschild. But Brandes did not know this, and to his mind the 'telegram conveyed a hidden meaning, that the time was nearly due for Artist to come over to the British with such information as he had been able to gather'. Brandes told Berlin that Jebsen was again showing 'noticeable curiosity about Ostro'.

Robertson brought together Masterman, Marriott and Wilson for a crisis meeting. The intercepts revealed that 'while Artist considered Brandes to be entirely his friend, Brandes was reporting unfavourably on Artist'. On the other hand, Most Secret Sources indicated that the Gestapo was no longer on his trail, and although the authorities wanted to interview him, they were concerned 'solely with financial matters'. If Jebsen was asked why he was so interested in Ostro, he could 'take a bold line' and insist that it was his 'desire to expose Ostro if he could find proof that Ostro was a fraud'. (Which, as MI5 well knew, he was.)

Wilson summed up the situation, while admitting this was 'too complicated to enable one to make any very confident appreciation of the position':

Brandes is clearly telling tales about Artist but there is no indication, at least so far, that Brandes is trying to suggest Artist is working for the British. I am personally satisfied that the telegram [summoning Artist to Biarritz] was not a trap, but Artist is apt to get into a state of nerves where he quite genuinely imagines traps which do not exist. He may not have seen as clearly as we have that the Gestapo seems now to be convinced that he is best left in Lisbon, and he may quite honestly fear that the Gestapo are behind the attempt to get him into occupied territory where they will arrest him. No immediate action can be taken by us. There is a risk that, despite our warning, Artist may continue to place some confidence in Brandes, but we cannot strengthen our warning without danger to our sources.

They agreed to do nothing. The protection of Most Secret Sources was paramount. 'I see no reason to be unduly nervous,' said Wilson, with a confidence he certainly did not feel.

Jebsen, meanwhile, decided to brazen it out with his bosses, and conduct his own 'test'. He told Schreiber he had received a message from Popov, stating he would 'brook no further delay over money'. To Jebsen's surprise, Schreiber was most accommodating. He agreed to cable Berlin immediately, and came back with the answer that he had 'received immediate instructions to hand over all available funds to Artist'. He then presented Jebsen with $75,000 in cash. This, he said, was only a down payment. Jebsen was ecstatic.

'Artist considers this proof all is well and that general staff will repeat will act on strength of Tricycle's reports,' Charles de Salis reported back to London. 'He now believes the investigation is over and Abwehr are satisfied both he and Tricycle are sound.

Tricycle's position as an ace agent is assured.' The crisis was over. Schreiber could not have been more friendly, and told him that Berlin had cabled 'at the last minute' to say that Jebsen was not needed at the Biarritz meeting after all. There was even talk of bringing back his lover Marie von Gronau. Jebsen wrote a triumphant letter to Popov:

You will know by reports coming from Cobb [de Salis's cover name] about the tests the Abwehr tried to carry out. I am quite happy that it is over now and I congratulate you on being my beloved Führer's best agent without any doubt, because, after having hesitated for some time, the Abwehr have decided the money should be transferred to you as arranged. I got 75,000 dollars, of which I will send 50,000 today. We might settle accounts later, but my share I am keeping here because I might be in need of some money to bribe heaven knows whom. Please give my best greetings to Ian, Frank and the Bentons. Be a good boy, and try to behave . . . Yours always, Johnny.

Relief flooded through B1A. The Tricycle network was safe, and with it, the rest of the Double Cross deception. This called for a celebratory dinner with Popov as guest of honour, to be held at the Hyde Park Hotel on 26 April. A report was sent to Churchill:

The agent Tricycle has now returned from visiting his masters in Lisbon. He has once more succeeded in persuading them of his complete reliability and has extracted from them a large sum of dollars as an advance against his future services. He has received an interesting questionnaire. They appear to have the highest respect for him.

The day before the dinner, Jebsen met de Salis again and 'confirmed that everything was fine'. Schreiber had congratulated him on his handling of Popov, and told him he was to receive a medal, a War Merit Cross (*Kriegsverdienstkreuz*, or KVK) 1st Class without swords, a civilian medal usually awarded for bravery behind the lines. Now that he was no longer under suspicion, Jebsen said he planned to go to Berlin, where he would gather more information for British intelligence. 'From Artist's point of view the outcome is a complete triumph,' de Salis reported. 'To crown it all, Artist has been awarded the KVK 1st Class, an honour shared by no one in Lisbon. Schreiber in particular is envious.'

Jebsen dictated a letter to Mabel Harbottle (now fully in his confidence) telling Popov the good news:

> A proof of the fact that Schreiber did not tell me stories [i.e. lie] is that I got another decoration, and this time the KVK First Class. First Class probably was given because you double-crossed them first class! I feel a little bit ashamed of getting the decoration for the work you and Ian did. I made up my mind to give it to Ian. Unfortunately I cannot get the Germans to put his name on the certificate, but I shall give him the decoration itself. If, as I hope, he collects curiosities, he might find a place for it in his collection. After all, he is an exceptional man and has the exceptional honour of getting a decoration with a swastika on it.

Schreiber had promised more money:

> Knowing your mentality, I am sure you are much more interested in this than in the really funny story of my decoration.
>
> Brandes is no longer your friend because he is terribly afraid you might betray the circumstances and date of the invasion and not only prolong the war but endanger his position as only 50% Aryan which must be more and more difficult. It might come out in the end that he is going to

hang instead of the Nazi leaders if the war goes on for a very long time. Last time I forgot to send my best greetings to Frano [de Bona, Agent Freak]. This was because at the time I didn't remember that he should know that I know what after all we all know. I sometimes forget to whom I have to cover what, and what I have to cover to whom. I think this letter is too long already. Besides, I have to think of the poor lady who has to type it and probably has something better to do than to amuse you. [Mabel Harbottle wrote in the margin with what, for her, was very nearly coquetry: *'The lady herself is of course delighted at the thought of helping to keep you amused.'*]

He ended with a flourish:

I hope you will give my love to all you can give it to without spoiling your, my, or anybody else's cover. To you I can give my love anyhow, yours, as always, Johnny.

The letter was typical Jebsen: funny, insouciant, mercenary, and more worried about the fate of Hans Brandes than his own. De Salis reported that Jebsen had been 'in a very good mood and the difference between this and the last meeting, when he was obviously worried, was very noticeable.' Jebsen agreed to return to the safe house on 5 May, one month and one day before D-Day.

Amid all the excitement and relief, no one spotted a message, sent the day before Popov's dinner, from Aloys Schreiber to Georg Hansen, the new head of German counter-intelligence: 'The carrying out of the threatened plan is imminent. Request your permission to prevent this plan even if it should become necessary to use extreme measures.' Hansen gave his permission.

The dinner at the Hyde Park Hotel was most convivial. The key players in the Tricycle case were all there, in evening attire: Guy Liddell, Tar Robertson, John Masterman, John Marriott and Ian Wilson, who had just steered the network through such rocky waters. MI6 was represented by Frank Foley. MI5's Director General, Sir David Petrie, raised a toast to Agent Tricycle. Popov was 'full of praise for Wilson for whom he clearly has the greatest respect', Liddell noted in his diary. 'I think he realises that if Wilson had not been at his side coaching him, he could never have achieved the position which he has now reached. He told me also that Wilson had made a very good impression on Artist.' In a rare departure from intelligence protocol, as a mark of trust in Popov, 'all those present used their own names'.

They did however, keep one secret from Popov: 'It was unknown to Tricycle that the cigars smoked at dinner were kindly provided by Dr Emile Kliemann of the Paris Abwehr station.'

Operation Dora

On the afternoon of 29 April, Aloys Schreiber telephoned Johnny Jebsen and asked him to come to the offices on Rua Buenos Aires, as he wanted to discuss the award of his War Merit Cross. Jebsen had a friend staying with him in Estoril, Heinz Paul Moldenhauer, a young Abwehr officer from the Cologne branch. Schreiber suggested that Jebsen bring Moldenhauer along, as he would like to discuss some intelligence matters with him.

Jebsen and Moldenhauer arrived at the office at dusk. The place was deserted. In Schreiber's outer office sat two men Jebsen knew only vaguely, a signals officer named Bliel and Karl Meier, a burly civilian car mechanic. Schreiber welcomed Jebsen and Moldenhauer warmly, and after chatting for a few minutes, invited Jebsen to step into the inner office alone. Once Jebsen was seated and the door closed, Schreiber calmly explained that he had orders to take him 'to Berlin by force, since he would not go of his own free will'. Jebsen made a bolt for the door, but Schreiber was faster, and fitter. He punched Jebsen once, and knocked him cold. When Jebsen came to, he found himself tied to a chair, along with Moldenhauer, who had been overpowered by Meier in the adjoining room.

Schreiber told his captives what would happen next: 'They would be knocked out and while unconscious placed in two large trunks, in which they would be shipped by car the same evening over the Portuguese-Spanish and Spanish-French borders to Biarritz. To guard against all possible surprises at the borders, he had decided to drug them by injections.' Schreiber asked them to surrender without a struggle. Jebsen seemed to realise that the time to fight would come later. 'Both of them submitted to the injections.'

At around 2 a.m., a Studebaker sedan with diplomatic plates and two large trunks in the boot arrived at Badajoz, the border crossing into Spain. In the rear seat sat Schreiber. Meier knew 'border conditions and officials personally', and the car was waved through. They drove north, stopping only for 'a few rests in the open'. From Madrid, Schreiber sent a telegram to Hansen: 'Mission has been carried out as far as Madrid'. At midnight the following evening, the party crossed into France. In Biarritz, Jebsen and Moldenhauer, still heavily drugged, were removed from the trunks and handed over to an intelligence officer named Fuchs. Schreiber sent another cable: 'Luggage handed over Biarritz to be sent on to Berlin. Undertaking was successful and everything all right.'

The following day Hans Brandes in Lisbon received a message of congratulations from Georg Hansen: 'Many thanks for reports and special recommendation'.

Plans for the kidnapping of Johnny Jebsen had been laid two weeks earlier. The message from Brandes, warning that Jebsen might be about to defect, had 'provoked considerable excitement' in Berlin. 'Jebsen's desertion had to be prevented at all costs,' Hansen told Kuebart, who was instructed 'to see personally that Jebsen reached German-occupied territory or at any rate to thwart any attempt on his part to reach Allied territory'. Kuebart briefed Schreiber, telling him that 'Berlin had proof that Jebsen had been working for both sides for some time and was now prepared to go over to the Allies' while also 'seeking to take financial advantage of the Abwehr'. Stopping this defection was 'of extreme importance to the war effort'.

Schreiber had tried to object, pointing out that this was surely 'a police matter', but Kuebart was insistent. The operation should be conducted in strict secrecy: neither the counter-espionage section in Lisbon, nor the Gestapo, nor the Portuguese police 'were to know anything about the affair'. The Abwehr and the SD, the Nazi party intelligence service, were not yet fully merged, and this was strictly a matter for the Abwehr: 'Once Jebsen was in Berlin, he would have to answer only to the military authorities and under no circumstance to the SD.' Still dubious, Schreiber cabled Berlin asking Hansen to 'accept full responsibility, in case the abduction caused difficulties with the Portuguese'. Hansen replied 'specifically charging Schreiber with the task' and telling him to hurry up: how Jebsen was bagged and delivered to Berlin was 'left entirely up to Schreiber'.

The Nazis had a taste for attaching female codenames to the most secret operations. Their espionage campaign against Britain was 'Lena'; the plan to seize the Canary Islands was 'Isabella'. The kidnapping of Jebsen was codenamed 'Operation Dora'.

Jebsen was suspected of being a double agent and probably a crook, but the real reason for the urgency and secrecy of Operation Dora had little to do with either his spying or his dodgy dealings. Hansen, Kuebart and many other intelligence officers were now actively plotting to kill Hitler. Jebsen, if he absconded, would derail those plans.

Hansen was deeply implicated in the anti-Nazi conspiracy that would culminate in the 20 July plot to assassinate the Führer. His home at Rangsdorf was used as a meeting place for the conspirators. Like many of the plotters, Hansen's loathing for Hitler was coupled with a deeply conservative patriotism, the urgent desire to save Germany before Hitler destroyed the Fatherland utterly. He wanted to remove Hitler and then launch a concerted assault on the Soviets, even if that meant Germany ended up with the 'status of a British dominion'. Kuebart shared his views, believing Hansen was 'the man to put things right'. The previous March, Hansen had begun to 'instruct Kuebart in the details of his machinations against the German regime'. By May, a plot was in place: Hansen told Kuebart he had 'arranged for someone to place some British-manufactured explosives in an aircraft in which Hitler was to fly'. Once Hitler was dead, the anti-Nazi resistance would rise up and overthrow the regime. But Jebsen was in the way.

Himmler's SD was itching for an opportunity to purge the remaining Canaris loyalists and anti-Nazi elements within German intelligence – men like Hansen, Kuebart and Schreiber. If Jebsen defected, Hansen feared, then the blame would be pinned on what remained of the Abwehr, as yet more proof of treachery: Hitler's henchmen would 'pounce on the Abwehr as they had done after the Vermehren incident', Hansen told Kuebart, which would 'put an end to schemes he was already concocting for the liquidation of Hitler and Himmler and the ultimate overthrow of the Nazi party'. A postwar investigation into the power struggle within German intelligence concluded that Operation Dora was a pre-emptive strike aimed at shielding the conspirators from their Nazi enemies. 'The Vermehren case had been used by Himmler and Schellenberg as a lever for gaining control of the Abwehr. Hansen and Kuebart were particularly concerned to prevent another desertion.'

Jebsen was kidnapped to preserve the plot to kill Hitler, a plot in which Jebsen would have been delighted to participate.

Schreiber had lulled Jebsen into thinking he was safe: the cash, the medal, the soothing words were all aimed at ensuring Jebsen did not flee before Schreiber was ready. The unexpected appearance of Heinz Moldenhauer at Jebsen's house complicated matters. Moldenhauer was the half-Jewish son of a former German minister and 'one of a number of anti-Nazis who have avoided active participation in the war by undertaking service with the Abwehr which they make no effort to carry out conscientiously'. He was regarded with suspicion in Berlin. Schreiber assumed that he must also be planning to defect, and decided to abduct him too. 'If innocent, Moldenhauer would have no trouble clearing himself with the military authorities in Berlin.' But Moldenhauer was not planning to defect: he was simply in the worst place at the worst possible time.

On 27 April, the day after the party for Popov, Hansen authorised the payment of 25,000 escudos to Schreiber 'in order to ensure the execution of Operation Dora'. Schreiber bought a sleeping drug from a Lisbon chemist, a syringe, rope and two trunks 'large enough for a grown person, fitted with adequately large openings for ventilation'. Four days later, Jebsen, dazed, battered and terrified, was lying on the floor of a cell in the Gestapo prison in Berlin.

Jebsen's disappearance sent a bolt of pure horror through the Double Cross team. The dreadful news arrived in a single line from Lisbon: 'Artist has disappeared since the afternoon of 29.4 and investigations have been instituted.' Most Secret Sources offered no clues to explain the mystery. 'This has clearly been done in great secrecy,' wrote Wilson. The first the SD in Lisbon knew of it was a message stating that Jebsen had been 'taken to France by the Abwehr as he was acknowledged as being unreliable'.

But what did 'unreliable' mean? The stakes went far beyond the fate of one man. If Jebsen's captors considered him untrustworthy, they might well suspect Popov, his best friend and agent, and if Popov was identified as a double agent that would inevitably cast suspicion on the other controlled agents in the UK. But worse than that, Jebsen knew the entire Garbo network was fiction, feeding false information in huge quantity back to Berlin. He had told Wilson he believed all the German spies in Britain were frauds. If Jebsen revealed this to his captors, the Germans would re-examine all the information received from their agents and look for the patterns of disinformation; they would quickly work out that the spies were directing them to defend the Pas de Calais and Norway. Operation Fortitude would be blown, with incalculable consequences. The invasion

was just one month away, and the immense machinery of
Operation Overlord was already in motion. Popov had told Ian
Wilson he was 'afraid that Jebsen would break down if physical
pressure were applied'. His abduction could spell disaster.

Wilson frantically combed Most Secret Sources for evidence
of what might have happened to Jebsen: 'A number of messages
on MSS have become available,' he reported, 'but none of them
seem very conclusive.' Two days after Jebsen's disappearance,
Popov's brother in Yugoslavia was still at large; if Dusko was
under suspicion, they would surely have pulled in Ivo. Wilson
tried to sound a positive note:

> Artist's present troubles arise primarily from the reports
> against him made by Brandes. The general tenor of the
> intercepts seems to be that the Abwehr are afraid that Artist
> was intending to go over to the British or to cause the
> Tricycle messages to be intercepted rather than that Artist is
> already a traitor to Germany or that Tricycle is a controlled
> agent. If they do not yet suspect the latter there is a good
> chance that Artist will not be subjected to pressure which
> will break him.

There was no sign that the Germans suspected Popov.
Indeed, the capture of Jebsen may have been ordered in part
because it was feared that if he defected to the Allies, this would
compromise a spy that Hansen considered 'the one agent of
real value in the UK'. Here was yet more black irony. Jebsen,
it seems, had been abducted not because the Germans suspected
Popov was a double agent, but because they didn't.

If Jebsen remained out of the hands of the Gestapo and the SD,
there was just a chance that the self-interest of those involved
might protect him. 'All the parties involved have their weak
spots. Brandes will fear a counter-investigation. Schreiber will
not willingly admit that Tricycle has been fooling them. Hansen
will not willingly reach a conclusion that will undermine the

whole Abwehr.' But these were fragile hopes, and Wilson knew it: 'The next few days will provide evidence to show clearly whether he is merely to be interrogated on relatively minor charges and kept in preventive custody, or forced to disclose the true position of Tricycle and possibly other controlled agents.' If Jebsen was made to talk, then instead of pulling off a great deception coup, the Double Cross team would have set the scene for a bloodbath on the beaches of Normandy.

At a crisis meeting on 9 May, John Masterman laid out the grim situation:

> The cover plan has been to a considerable extent built up on the reports of XX agents. The fact that Artist, who is fully cognizant of the Tricycle network and has some knowledge of the other cases, has fallen under suspicion and been removed to Berlin therefore threatens the whole cover plan. We cannot tell exactly why Artist has fallen under suspicion – we only know that he is regarded as 'unreliable'. His 'unreliability' may be connected with his financial operations, his intrigues, or his unwise inquisitiveness about the undertakings of Brandes and Ostro, and not with his dealings with Tricycle at all. There is no proof that treason on the part of Artist is part of the charge. But obviously under interrogation at Berlin, he may reveal what he knows. We must act on the assumption that the Tricycle case may be blown. In these circumstances, what should be done?
>
> We should leave the door open to continue our present policy in the hope that the Berlin investigation may be confined to Artist's personal delinquencies and leave Tricycle untouched. With good fortune we should get information through secret sources telling us how the inquiry proceeds. It may be that Tricycle will be confirmed in his position of trust and that we can operate him as before. The case of the other agents is more difficult. Clearly they must not change their style in any way, but should they, or should

they not, continue to implement Fortitude? The danger of
their doing so is that if all or most of them are blown as
a result of Artist's revelations, their traffic will be 'read in
reverse' and interpreted accordingly.

Masterman laid out the options:

1. They should for the time being continue to operate
   without change, though specific indication of the false
   objective should be avoided.
2. Attempt by diversity of messages to create confusion
   in the enemy's mind even though we have to abandon
   the hope of getting a complete cover plan over to the
   enemy.
3. If we come to the conclusion that practically all the
   agents are in fact blown we could take the extreme
   step of abandoning all efforts at deception and deny all
   information to the enemy by closing down all agents.

Shutting down the Double Cross system would nullify more
than four years of hard work and extreme risk, but it would leave
the enemy 'deprived of all information from agents at a time
when he needs it most and would have to prepare himself in the
dark to meet any eventuality'. Masterman's recommendation
was to continue the deception but 'if, and only if, the blowing
of Tricycle and Garbo is certain, we close down *all* agents
shortly before D-Day'.

Within B1A, Jebsen's capture sparked a blazing row, the
worst so far. Tommy Harris was particularly enraged. He
had warned that Jebsen was a liability, and now the delicate
structure of deception he had created with Juan Pujol was
liable to be smashed to pieces. 'The confidence which has
been deposited in Artist during the last few months has left
him in little doubt that Kühlenthal's network in this country
is controlled by us. Developments in the Artist case have, to

say the least, very seriously compromised the Garbo channel for passing operational deception.' Harris did not believe that Most Secret Sources would give sufficient warning of disaster. The intercepts, after all, had failed to alert MI5 before Jebsen was snatched – 'the same night that our confidence in him was at its height'. Garbo could be blown 'without our getting any warning on MSS that he has been denounced by Artist'. The Tricycle network should be shut down, said Harris, immediately and permanently. It took Guy Liddell to point out that this would amount to Jebsen's death sentence, for it would prove to his captors that both he and Popov had been in league with the British: 'Packing up Tricycle will finish Artist,' he observed.

If the double agents were exposed, would the Germans be able 'to deduce the cover plan and the real plan from the previous traffic'? Could the Germans extract, in less than a month, the essence of Operation Fortitude from the reams of misinformation they had received? Masterman thought it would require a 'lengthy and exhaustive study [to] sift the truth from the falsehood', but Harris disagreed: 'I maintain that the enemy could, within twenty-four hours, analyse the entire B1A traffic for the [last] two months and they would be able to draw the conclusions that the cover plan threat is against the Pas de Calais, and we wish the enemy to believe that the assault will be two-pronged. Such a discovery by the enemy would be catastrophic.'

> In the hands of the Gestapo inquisitors, Jebsen might reveal the true state of affairs and so compromise the entire network of controlled agents in this country. From now onwards the Germans might, at any moment, tumble to the fact that all their spies in England were under Allied control. They would then conclude that the messages they were receiving were the opposite of the truth. There could only be two reasonable objectives for the cross-Channel assault, namely the Pas de Calais and Normandy. If the Germans perceived we were trying to induce them to believe that we were

coming to the Pas de Calais, the true objective would thus
be automatically disclosed.

As the dispute raged, Tar Robertson found himself under
attack from MI6. Charles de Salis had lost not only a valued
agent, but a friend. The MI6 officer had been instructed only to
warn Jebsen that Brandes was an unreliable informant; he was
not told that Brandes was informing on Jebsen, and had warned
Berlin that he was about to flee. When de Salis discovered that
he had been given a doctored version of events, he hit the roof,
and accused MI5 of throwing Jebsen to the wolves.

'Why lead *me* up the garden path? The obvious way of putting
this over to Artist was to attribute the information to one of
23700's sources [a reference to MI6 informants].' Jebsen's
'respect for 23700 penetration of the German services was
profound', de Salis argued, and if told that the warnings came
from a British spy, he 'would have been really on his guard, and
would no doubt have been suspicious enough not to fall into the
German trap'. de Salis accused MI5 of giving him misleading
information, of which the acute danger to Jebsen was 'the most
flagrant and tragic example'. If he had been allowed to warn
Jebsen properly, de Salis railed, then the kidnapping could have
been thwarted. 'If I cannot be trusted to act a little comedy as
simple as this, I should not be here at all.'

Tar struggled to defend himself.

No one can have greater concern than I do over the
affairs of Artist, but a direct warning could not be given to
Artist. We had no indication that there was any imminent
danger of an attempt to kidnap Artist. The most careful
consideration was given to whether we should inform
Artist that Brandes was reporting on him, and it was
accepted by all the numerous officers here that we could
not run the risk to the source [Most Secret Sources] that
would be involved in warning Artist. All we could do was

warn Artist against putting confidence in Brandes. At my suggestion the warning was based on the suspicion we had of the accuracy of Brandes' reports. Operation Dora was not known to us until after the event had taken place. There was a message the day before, not mentioning Artist by name which, had we at the time had sufficient knowledge to link it with Artist, would have indicated that he was in danger of some sort. But because of the source, we could not have taken the risk of giving him any additional warning. I have naturally given a great deal of thought to this matter and I am satisfied that we went as far as we possibly could in protecting Artist.

Tar was blustering. His excuses were thin, as he was well aware. He knew there was a world of difference between the suggestion that Brandes was unreliable, and a tip-off that he was actively betraying Jebsen. He knew that a warning, carefully couched, would not necessarily have alerted Jebsen to Most Secret Sources. He knew that he and his team, paranoid about protecting the Allies' most valuable secret, had failed to appreciate the mortal danger to Jebsen, and as a consequence he was in prison, probably undergoing torture, and possibly already dead. Tar was a good and honourable man, and in his heart he must have known that Jebsen had trusted the British completely, and they had let him down. This was the worst moment of his war; perhaps, the worst moment of his life.

Dread throbbed through the building at 58 St James's Street. 'Anthony Blunt told me Tommy Harris was extremely worried about the Artist situation,' Liddell wrote. 'The whole situation is rather worrying. Tricycle has been told that all is not well with Artist who has disappeared. This news obviously caused Tricycle considerable worry as it obviously showed it was possible that Artist had been kidnapped.' MI5 could not reveal Most Secret Sources evidence of his abduction, but Popov soon reached the independent realisation that his friend had, 'by trick or by force, been taken back to Germany'. Another Abwehr defector, Hans Ruser, who knew Jebsen well, was asked whether his former colleague would be able to withstand interrogation. 'Jebsen was a mine of information and had always talked too much,' he said. 'Under third degree pressure, he would tell the Germans everything.'

As the crisis erupted, Winston Churchill was kept, if not exactly in the dark, then certainly in the shade. Blunt's report was a masterpiece of deliberate understatement:

> There has been an unfortunate development in the case of Tricycle, the true purport and consequences of which have not yet been determined. It was learnt from Most Secret Sources that Artist, his spymaster, was lured with great secrecy into France and there dispatched to Berlin. The reasons for this action are for the moment obscure, but it is certain that the Tricycle case is passing through a most critical phase and must be handled with the greatest care in view of Overlord.

'Unfortunate', 'rather worrying', 'most critical': these were delicate British euphemisms for what one officer described as 'near-panic'. MI5 had once worried Churchill might go 'off the deep end' if he knew too much about espionage matters. It can only be imagined how far off the deep end he would have plunged had he learned not only that the Double Cross system was in danger of unravelling, but that the invasion itself was in jeopardy.

Popov had already sent the Germans copious deceptive material relating to Fortitude. But could he continue to do so, given that Jebsen might expose him at any moment? If he suddenly ceased to send good information, or altered the thrust of the deception, the Germans would smell a rat. One option was to shut him down, but as Liddell pointed out this 'would undoubtedly put Artist completely in the cart and seriously jeopardise Tricycle's

brother'. By sheer good fortune an opportunity presented itself
to suspend the Tricycle network without further endangering
Jebsen. Earlier in May, a message was intercepted revealing that
German intelligence knew Frano de Bona, Agent Freak, was
suspected by some of his fellow Yugoslavs of spying for Germany.
If de Bona was under suspicion, he would naturally be brought
in for questioning. 'This gives us an opportunity of closing down
Tricycle's transmitter, at any rate temporarily,' wrote Liddell. 'If
we see from the traffic that Artist is once more on a good wicket
we can go on the air again.' On 18 May, de Bona sent a message
to Lisbon saying he was going off the air, which was followed
by a letter from Popov, in secret ink, reporting that 'certain
inquiries were in progress against Freak and for that reason they
had temporarily hidden the wireless set'.

The other double agents would continue building Operation
Fortitude to its climax. Henceforth, Brutus, Garbo, Bronx and
Treasure would only hint that the Pas de Calais was the target,
but not state this as bald fact in case Jebsen revealed the deception.
Once the troops had landed, the spies would point specifically
to Calais as the target of a second, even bigger assault, by the
fictional FUSAG: 'After D-Day we can go absolutely all out.'
At the same time, Most Secret Sources would be dissected daily
for any indication that Jebsen had confessed, either willingly or
under duress. If it became clear he had told all, B1A would shut
down Double Cross, and hope the Germans would not have
time to work out Operation Fortitude. The race was on: to put
as much of the deception in place as possible before D-Day, and
pray that Jebsen did not crack too soon.

The deception – and perhaps the success or failure of the
invasion itself – now depended on the fortitude of Johnny
Jebsen, a strange and dishonest spy with unhealthy habits, who
might, even now, be languishing in a Nazi torture cell.

Masterman was pessimistic: 'Under interrogation it was to
be presumed that much, if not all, of the history of his activities
would come to light, and in that case many of our best cases

were doomed. The whole deception through Double Cross was in danger.' Every hour mattered. The longer Jebsen held out, the less time the Germans would have to unravel the deception.

All the Double Cross team knew was that Jebsen had been bound for Berlin. 'We do not know how quickly the interrogation of Artist will be started,' Wilson remarked miserably. 'I hope the RAF have made the train journey from Biarritz to Berlin a lengthy matter.'

Guest of the Gestapo

The double-crossers needed to get inside Hitler's head, and for their purposes the most direct access to the mind of the Führer was via Lieutenant Colonel Alexis von Roenne, the head of Fremde Heere West, or FHW, the intelligence branch of the High Command of the German army. The FHW gathered information from all branches of German intelligence – aerial reconnaissance, wireless intercepts, POW interrogations, captured documents and spy reports – and tried to make sense of it. Every letter from Bronx, every transmission by Treasure and Brutus, every report from Tricycle, ended up, eventually, with this 'erudite, imaginative, level-headed' intelligence expert, whose monumental task it was to explain what, in military terms, it all amounted to.

Every day von Roenne's intelligence branch, a secret hive inside a concrete bunker at Zossen, south of Berlin, produced a three-page situation report with an update on enemy military activity. The intelligence unit also compiled a more detailed picture of the Order of Battle every fortnight, and an occasional long-range forecast of Allied intentions. These were distributed to the relevant intelligence agencies, the High Command, and commanders in the field: in the case of France, Field Marshal Gerd von Rundstedt, Supreme Commander of the German armies in the West. Von Roenne, an aristocrat with refined manners, pious beliefs and a sinuously clever mind, was aided

by the head of the English section, Major Roger Michael, who
could not have been more different from his boss. Half-English
and half-German, Michael was a bald, back-slapping, heavy-
drinking hearty who had played rugby for Germany. He had
a 'jolly, easy, happy disposition', but 'a quick understanding of
essentials'. He was also credited with insight into the British
mentality, having spent much of his youth in Britain. He was
Gisela Ashley's opposite number.

Hitler had complete faith in von Roenne. As Anton
Staubwasser, Rommel's intelligence chief, put it, 'the opinions
held by Hitler and OKW about the invasion were based
principally on the information supplied by FHW and did not
deviate from that department's ideas in essentials'. If von Roenne
and his analysts could be fooled into thinking that another army,
far larger than the real D-Day force, was assembling on Britain's
coast, then Hitler himself would probably fall for the deception.
What Hitler did not know, and never knew, was that Alexis von
Roenne and Roger Michael were running their own deception
operation.

From 1943 onwards, von Roenne overestimated the strength
of Allied forces in Britain consistently, massively and quite
deliberately. Once an enemy army unit had been identified and
logged by the analysts, it was never removed from what von
Roenne called the *Feinbild*, his picture of the enemy. More than
that, by the spring of 1944 he was intentionally embellishing
the picture. In January 1944, Michael told von Roenne that the
troop estimates they sent to the High Command were being
deliberately reduced by the SD (which took every opportunity
to undermine the experts in military intelligence) before
being passed to Hitler. Michael reckoned the numbers were
being halved. So he made a suggestion that was logical, daring
and extremely dangerous. Why not double the figures? Then
something close to the right number would be achieved. That,
at least, was how he rationalised the plan to von Roenne, who
went along with it, knowing that inflating these vital numbers

might cost him his life. Every single sighting of an Allied unit was chalked up as genuine, no matter how feeble the evidence; if only part of a troop was spotted, it was assumed the entire force was present, even when other parts of the unit were spotted elsewhere. Every anomaly was quietly wished away. Gradually at first, and then faster and faster, the numerical gap between the forces that were really poised to invade France and the statistics being relayed to Hitler grew ever wider. At the beginning of 1944, FHW estimated there were fifty-five divisions in Britain, when there were really only thirty-seven. By mid-May, von Roenne calculated that seventy-seven enemy divisions were in place. And by D-Day he had magnified the forty-four divisions in Britain to a remarkable eighty-nine, more than enough men under arms to launch diversionary attacks on Normandy and Norway, and a main assault on the Pas de Calais.

Quite why von Roenne exaggerated the Allied Order of Battle so extravagantly remains a matter of debate and conjecture. He may simply have been covering his back, knowing that if he underestimated enemy strength he would be in serious trouble. Perhaps, like many purveyors of official statistics, he moulded his numbers to fit what his audience wanted to hear. Perhaps his act of rebellion was just another skirmish in the bitter internecine battle within German military intelligence.

What is certain is that von Roenne was bitterly opposed to the Nazi regime, and actively plotting to oust Hitler, whom he detested. He had already played an important part in Operation Mincemeat in 1943 by giving the firm stamp of approval to documents he had every reason to distrust. Some historians believe von Roenne was deliberately sabotaging the German war effort from within. His precise motives may never be known, because Hitler, when he discovered von Roenne's disloyalty, had him murdered. Roger Michael's purpose was possibly more straightforward. After the war, unlike most officers of the German General Staff, Michael was quickly released. He was said to have been seen in Heidelberg, wearing an American army uniform and claiming to be part of the US Counter Intelligence Corps. He then vanished, having apparently defected to the Soviet Union. He was never seen again. The cheery, rugby-playing, half-English Major Michael may have been a spy, for Britain, America or the Soviets, and conceivably all three.

Piece by piece, the double agents dropped the jigsaw into the hands of FHW, where they were slotted together in the ever-expanding projections of von Roenne. Czerniawski reported the 4th US Armoured Division in Bury St Edmunds; one of Garbo's Welsh Aryans saw the 6th Armoured Division in Ipswich, while another spotted the 28th Infantry Division in Kent. Pujol himself reported troops of the 83rd Infantry Division gathering in a Dover car park. Lily sent a wireless message confirming that the First US Army was serving under Montgomery, to reinforce the idea that US troops could serve under British command, and vice versa. Bronx was vaguer, but the very insouciance with which she relayed her information lent it greater force: 'To Newmarket for the races. Expected invasion has produced political unity. Many US troops in East Anglia.' On 18 May, as planned, Czerniawski told his handlers that he had joined FUSAG itself. Henceforth he would be able to relay the fake Order of Battle from within the fake army. The loss of the Tricycle network, wrote Masterman, meant that 'a heavier burden had to be carried by Brutus'. He lifted it with ease.

Pujol told Kühlenthal he had obtained a job in the Ministry of Information, and now had access to propaganda documents intended to 'hide the facts in order to trick us' that would offer new insight into the Allies' real intentions. Wulf Schmidt, Agent Tate, was the longest serving double agent of all, but B1A had doubts about using him, largely because his handlers communicated with Berlin by telephone and there was therefore no way to check his status through Most Secret Sources. Even so, it was decided to move him, in German minds, from a farm in Hertfordshire to another in Kent, where he could observe the deployment of the fictional FUSAG at first hand. 'Have found first-class lodgings with elderly couple in Wye,' he told his handler. 'So far as I can see, ideal for radio purposes.'

Von Roenne was too busy adding weight to his already bloated Order of Battle to wonder why three key agents had suddenly, and almost simultaneously, moved into positions where they had access to the highest-grade information. Perhaps, through his monocle, he turned a blind eye. At the expeditionary force headquarters, Fleetwood-Hesketh and Harmer moved their fake units to where they wanted them to be in German minds; the double agents passed them on, bit by bit, to the Germans; and von Roenne and Michael reassembled the map, and passed it up the military chain to Hitler.

The pins on the board at the intelligence office in Zossen were massing in the right places, but MI5 remained fretfully aware that if Jebsen cracked and Double Cross was revealed, von Roenne's projections, built up from the spies' reports, would show exactly where the Allied armies were *not* assembling. Guy Liddell was certain that once the Gestapo went to work on Jebsen, he would eventually crack 'under duress'.

Ian Wilson scanned the intercepts with dread. If Jebsen's friends and associates were rounded up, if his Abwehr colleagues were interrogated, if Popov's brother was arrested, then that would prove the game was up. The moment Jebsen revealed that the double agents were all part of a grand sham, the evidence would crackle like lightning across Most Secret Sources. Incompetence was a crime under Hitler's rule, and guilt came by association: Kühlenthal, Kliemann, Reile, Bleil and von Karsthoff would all find themselves hauled in to explain how they had been hoodwinked for so long. Everyone Jebsen knew would be considered suspect, and probably arrested: wife, lovers, friends, even Mabel Harbottle. The bloody retribution would start immediately, and be reflected in the intercepts. Here was cold consolation: if Double Cross was rumbled, at least they would know it.

At first, Most Secret Sources were mute, save for some baffled enquiries from German officials in Lisbon who were not privy to Operation Dora, wondering where Jebsen had gone. But within a week of the kidnapping, it became clear that an interrogation must be under way, as a flurry of messages were intercepted relating to Jebsen's financial activities. Berlin asked Madrid to 'report whether 2.7 million Moroccan francs which Johnny is alleged to have remitted to Tangier have been received'. This was followed by an even more cryptic message from Schreiber to Berlin: 'French money Dora can be received to the full amount through Dora friends here. Furthermore we may also count on receiving shortly through Dora friends here the original material about Dora which was asked for by his fat friend.' Dora was a reference to the kidnapping, and 'his fat friend' was probably Hans Brandes; but the only thing to be deduced with any certainty was that Jebsen's finances were being probed, and large sums of money were involved. Berlin was also trying to trace the cash handed to Jebsen for Popov.

After two weeks, Ian Wilson reported that there was still 'no evidence to prove conclusively what effect the return of Artist to Germany has had'. Encouragingly, there was not yet a general round-up of Jebsen's contacts. Freak's control station in Germany was still sending messages on the agreed frequency; if the Germans were trying to get in touch with Popov then they must still trust him, which might indicate that Jebsen had not betrayed the network. Unless, of course, that was just what the Germans wanted the British to think. Wilson allowed himself a glimmer of hope. The references in Most Secret Sources, he wrote, 'are consistent with the theory that Artist was taken to Germany so that his financial dealings could be probed and for fear that at some future date he might come over to the Allies. If he has confessed, one would have expected that some of the Abwehr officials closely connected to Artist and Tricycle would have ceased to carry out their normal functions' – like breathing.

Wilson began to wonder if, by some miracle, Jebsen could yet be rescued. Hans Brandes had betrayed him; perhaps he might now be bribed, beguiled, bullied or blackmailed into saving him, or at least providing information on what had become of him. Might now be the moment to revive Kim Philby's idea of recruiting this horrible man to British intelligence?

> If Brandes could be persuaded to play with us, he could as well as informing us of the position of Artist, give us a lot of information about what is going on in the inner circles of the Abwehr, and particularly the political struggle which seems to have resulted in the Abwehr coming under the control of Himmler. I do not regard Brandes as being in the least bit reliable. There is plenty of evidence that Brandes is unprincipled [but] if the proposition was put to him that he should re-insure himself with the British he might accept it. If he reported the approach to the Germans we would know that fact from MSS.

John Masterman stamped hard on this idea. Brandes was a snake, and if he told Berlin that British intelligence was sniffing around, this would reinforce suspicion that Jebsen was a British spy and plunge him into even hotter water. 'I do not agree with the proposal to approach Brandes,' he wrote on Wilson's memo, underlining the word 'not' three times. But Wilson was not going to give up on Jebsen. 'I feel a strong personal sense of responsibility in this matter,' he wrote. Wilson liked and trusted Jebsen; he had encouraged him to stick to his mission, and he had lost him. He would make it his own mission to find him.

Popov waited anxiously for news. Frano de Bona, no longer transmitting to Germany, was also at a loose end. They distracted themselves in the usual way. When MI5 found out that women of the Auxiliary Territorial Service were 'being introduced to the Clock House for immoral purposes and that there might be security interest involved', Wilson told them sharply to 'stop drawing attention to themselves in this manner'. Unable to play an active part in the deception, Popov fired off letters to Churchill, offering to intercede in Yugoslavia between the forces of Mihailović and Tito's communists. He was told that while Churchill 'had a paternal interest in his wellbeing', he did not want him meddling in politics. He should stay calm, stay put and stand ready in case there should be news of Jebsen: 'This was not the time for hasty or violent action . . . The only course for the time being was to take no action and await results.'

On 19 May, Bletchley Park deciphered a personal message from Georg Hansen to Aloys Schreiber in Lisbon: 'I wish to convey special appreciation and thanks for carrying out Operation Dora.' Schreiber replied that 'a written report on Dora matters was following by air'.

Then, just two weeks before D–Day, the references to 'Johnny', 'Dora' and all the missing money abruptly ceased. Ian Wilson wondered if the sudden silence was ominous: 'It seems to me not unlikely that Artist may have been shot, or may have committed suicide shortly after his arrest.' Yet he tried to look on the bright side: 'There is still no indication that Artist has made any confession.'

Wilson's flicker of hope would have been swiftly extinguished had he known where Jebsen was at that moment.

Jebsen and Moldenhauer had arrived in Berlin by train, under guard, on 1 May. From there they were driven to the military prison at Wünsdorf, near Zossen, and lodged in separate cells, while Georg Hansen made 'arrangements for their interrogation by legal experts'. The SD, however, had already got wind of Jebsen's abduction, and demanded that Hansen put 'the captive at the disposal of Kaltenbrunner as soon as possible'. A full investigation into another potential defector was exactly what Hansen hoped to avoid. He refused to surrender the prisoners, and instructed Kuebart to tell the SD that 'as Jebsen was a soldier he regarded it as a matter within the exclusive jurisdiction of the Abwehr'.

For several days, Kuebart 'did his best to place difficulties in the way of Jebsen being handed over'. The dispute even reached the desk of Field Marshal Wilhelm Keitel, head of the OKW. Finally a 'brusque ultimatum' arrived from SS Obergruppenführer Heinrich Müller, demanding that Jebsen be handed over to the Gestapo at once. Among the murderous sycophants surrounding Hitler, Müller stood out for his brutality: the head of the secret state police, he was a principal architect of 'the final solution', directed the SS murder squads that followed the German army into the Soviet Union, and personally presented Himmler with evidence of Canaris's links to the anti-Nazi resistance. He loathed anyone with an education – 'One really ought to drive all the intellectuals into a coal mine and then blow it up,' he declared – and he was not a man who took anything but yes for an answer. The demand to surrender Jebsen had already 'produced a great deal of ill-feeling in the Abwehr', according to Kuebart, but there was no point in arguing with 'Gestapo' Müller. Jebsen was taken into police custody by one Sturmbannführer Schmitz, an aide to Schellenberg, who accused Jebsen of 'having betrayed the work of the SS to the Abwehr', and consigned him to a cell in the notorious Gestapo prison on Prinz Albrecht Strasse to await interrogation.

Jebsen had often hinted to his British handlers that he was involved in shady business deals with high officials. Indeed, he had told Marie von Gronau he had 'so much information on the SD they would not dare investigate him'. But his financial chicanery, it seems, went far beyond the forgery scam that had first put him on the wrong side of the Gestapo. Jebsen had been using diplomatic bags to smuggle money from one occupied country to another, and 'engaging in large-scale manipulations of currency and gold' with the connivance of high-ranking officers, who got a cut of the profits but had since 'got into difficulties because it became apparent they had more money to spend than could be justified by their apparent incomes'. In addition, some senior SS and

Gestapo figures had used Jebsen as an unofficial banker: 'Certain sizeable sums of money [have] been given to Jebsen, who deposited the sums in such a way as to render the sums inaccessible.' He was also back in the forgery business: 'Some SS officials had been printing foreign currency and he had exchanged it for gold value. He was now suspected of having made too much profit for himself and the SS wanted to remove him for knowing too much.' To cap it all, he was accused of 'improperly converting SD monies for his own use'. Jebsen was nothing if not bold in his financial corruptions: he had contrived to diddle senior officers in each of the three most brutal elements of the Third Reich – the Gestapo, the SS and the SD – and they were out for his blood.

MI5 was right to believe that Jebsen was being investigated for his financial dealings, but wrong to assume that this was the only, or even the main reason he had been kidnapped. Müller was in no doubt that Jebsen was a British spy. Schellenberg confirmed in a postwar interview that Jebsen had been 'accused of working for Britain'. According to Eduard Waetjen, an Abwehr officer with links to American intelligence, Jebsen had been tipping off members of the anti-Nazi resistance when they were about to be arrested. 'Because of good connections he helped many people who had difficulties with the Nazi organisation,' Waetjen testified. 'By his warning, many people were saved.' Kuebart's postwar testimony also confirms that Jebsen was suspected of conspiring with the British and planning to defect. The extent of that guilt was, as yet, undetermined, but Müller and his thugs intended to find out.

The two officers in charge of Jebsen's case were SS Standartenführer Eugen Steimle, and Obergeheimrat Quitting. They went to work on Jebsen at once.

The Gestapo prison at 8 Prinz Albrecht Strasse, a neo-classical former Museum of Decorative Arts, consisted of thirty-nine basement solitary cells, and one communal cell. Torture was conducted in specially equipped rooms in the upper floors.

The term *Verschärfte Vernehmung*, or 'sharpened interrogation', was coined by Müller himself in 1937 to describe the torture techniques used on 'Communists, Marxists ... saboteurs, terrorists, members of the resistance movement, asocial persons, Polish or Soviet persons who refuse to work'. By 1944, the extraction of confessions had been refined to a vicious art. Müller's Gestapo torturers were masters of the electrode and rubber nightstick, the genital vice, the soldering iron and the ice-cold bath, in which prisoners were thrust to the point of drowning. Captured members of the French resistance were told to try to resist torture for at least twenty-four hours; the Gestapo boasted that in forty-eight hours they could squeeze any man or woman dry.

Gestapo interrogation records were destroyed before the end of the war. The only evidence of what happened to Jebsen comes from a handful of witnesses, postwar interviews and the testimony of other prisoners. Karl Weigand, an Abwehr officer in Madrid, was summoned to Berlin to discuss the interrogation of Jebsen and returned, according to colleagues, 'in a highly nervous condition and mentioned something about the unpleasantness of having one's fingernails torn off'. Hjalmar Schacht, once Hitler's trusted economist who was arrested on suspicion of resistance activities, briefly occupied the cell next to Jebsen. According to Popov, Schacht 'caught a glimpse of Johnny once as he was being brought back from an interrogation. His shirt was drenched with blood. As the guards were about to lock him in his cell, Johnny turned to them, haughty as ever, saying "I trust I shall be provided with a clean shirt".' A former Abwehr colleague who visited Jebsen in prison (itself a brave act) described Jebsen as looking like a 'typical concentration camp victim'. Jebsen was never a physically robust man, with his varicose veins and rattling smoker's cough, but after the attentions of the Gestapo he was barely recognisable: 'His flesh and muscle had melted away, and his head looked enormous, sitting on top of his wasted neck and shoulders.'

Torture usually extracts a confession in the end. But it does not always work quickly, and it doesn't work on everyone, and sometimes it extorts information that is wrong. 'Violence is taboo,' wrote Robin 'Tin-eye' Stephens, who ran Britain's wartime interrogation centre in London. 'Not only does it produce answers to please, but it lowers the standard of information.' A person in terror and pain will often tell their torturers what they imagine they want to hear, just to stop the agony, just for a while.

Johnny Jebsen knew much that Steimle and Quitting wanted to hear – for a start, the details of his various business operations. Merely offering up the names of officers implicated in his financial dealings would have provided Müller with useful ammunition and bought, perhaps, some respite. He could have confessed to everything he had told MI6 about Hitler's secret weapon, the workings of German intelligence and even his suggestion that the wife of P. G. Wodehouse would make a good spy. The Gestapo, the SS and the SD would have been more than interested. He could have revealed that Popov was a double agent, and that every German spy in Britain was either turned or invented, by admitting that he had identified them all to the British, and they were still functioning. He could have told them enough to scupper the looming invasion, and change the course of the war. But by 20 May, with less than three weeks to go until D-Day, he had told them nothing at all.

Bronx Gets Toothache

As D–Day approached, MI5 told Winston Churchill that Jebsen seemed to be holding out – 'there is still no indication that Artist has made any confession, or that the Abwehr have come to realise the true position', wrote Guy Liddell. In further evidence that the deception remained on track, the Germans continued to shower the double agents with praise, encouragement and even medals. When Agent Tate 'transmitted his 1,000th message', the Prime Minister was informed, 'he took the opportunity of referring to this fact and expressing his loyal devotion to the Führer. A cordial reply has been received, and it is hoped that this will be followed up by the further advancement of Tate in the order of the Iron Cross, of which he already holds the first and second class.'

The case officers were now competing for German decorations. Eddie Chapman, Agent Zigzag, had been awarded the Iron Cross; Agent Tate might get as many as three; Jebsen had promised Wilson his War Merit Cross. Hugh Astor believed Brutus deserved a decoration, and began actively lobbying for a Nazi gong. He suggested that Chopin, Brutus's fictional wireless operator, send a message to Oscar Reile recommending that 'Agent Hubert' be awarded a medal, since this would 'remind the Germans Brutus is running great risks and working under great difficulties solely for ideological motives'. Astor drafted a message, in what he hoped was the style of a 'not very intelligent old man':

Colonel, please forgive me for troubling you with a personal matter . . . Hubert would never forgive me if he got to learn about it. He has made great personal and financial sacrifices in the interests of our work. He frequently works until the early hours of the morning preparing lengthy reports. He has mentioned casually to me the daring exploits which he has carried out in order to obtain the information and I am sure that his honour would be more than satisfied if you could recommend him for some decoration.

Wireless intercepts showed that the Germans thought Lily Sergeyev's wireless was 'functioning flawlessly'; her messages were being conveyed, word for word, to the intelligence analysts at Zossen. By comparing her original message with its coded repetition on the German intelligence network, the cryptanalysts at Bletchley Park could break that day's code almost immediately: 'The messages of Treasure and Brutus are being so consistently relayed verbatim on the German w/t [wireless] network that, with the assistance of this "crib", there has been a very considerable saving of time and manpower in deciphering Most Secret Sources.' For the first time, a note of excited pride crept into the report to Churchill. The Double Cross agents, he was told, 'have, at a critical moment, acquired a value which it is scarcely possible to overestimate'.

But just as this upbeat assessment was handed to Churchill, fresh disaster loomed in the shape of a small, dead dog.

On 17 May, Mary Sherer took Lily Sergeyev to see *Gone with the Wind* in the West End. Lily's kidneys ached, and she was running a temperature. She had convinced herself, once again, that she was dying. Mary decided she needed a treat. Both women wept copiously during the film, and emerged red-eyed and in high spirits. 'I always cry in the cinema,' said Mary. They linked arms as they walked home. In her diary, Lily wrote: 'Mary crying at the cinema! Is she human, after all, this Mary with whom I've been working for seven months, trying to discover some signs that she is a living being and not an automaton.'

Perhaps it was this newfound amity, or perhaps her premonition of impending death prompted the revelation, or perhaps, frankly, she didn't give a damn. But the next morning, as they were preparing another wireless message, Lily leaned over with a conspiratorial air and observed that if she should die, Mary should not try to work the transmitter without her.

Mary, suddenly alert, asked her what, exactly, she meant by that remark. Lily, realising she had revealed too much, was defensive, and dug herself in deeper.

'I didn't mean to warn you; I'm not concerned about what happens to your people. I don't owe them anything. I trusted them. You know the result! But I have told you now. You are warned.'

With a flush of horror, Mary understood that this was not a warning but a thinly veiled threat. Lily must have been given a control signal after all – otherwise why should they not run the transmitter without her? Indeed, she might already have alerted Kliemann that she was being run as a double agent. Mary was appalled, and suddenly very worried.

'The landing is very near, and thousands of lives depend on our ability to deceive the Germans . . .'

'Why do you suppose I have told you all this?' asked Lily.

Mary knew the answer. 'You were very fond of Babs.'

She demanded that Lily describe her control signal, and reveal whether she had used it. Lily refused, on both counts. 'You can go through all my transmissions with a mathematical genius, but you won't find it.'

'You realise I must warn Colonel Robertson,' Mary said. She immediately sent a message to the head of B1A that was short, precise, and deeply alarming.

Sergeyev made a statement to the effect that when she visited Lisbon she fixed up a control signal with Kliemann which she had not told us about on her return. She had meant, on her return, to get the W/T working well and then blow the case. She confessed that her motive was revenge for the death of her dog for which she considered we were responsible. On return from Lisbon she had changed her mind about blowing the case. She refused to divulge what the signal was.

Tar Robertson was not merely displeased, he was scorchingly furious. Lily was holding Operation Fortitude to ransom over a dog. She might have alerted the enemy already, but as she refused to divulge the signal there was no way of checking. Kliemann's messages of congratulation might be bluff. And if the Germans had realised Lily was passing over deceptive material, they would compare the thrust of her messages with information from the other agents, spot the similarities, and find out the truth. Robertson faced a dreadful choice: if he shut down Treasure's wireless and she had not warned Kliemann she was controlled, it would immediately arouse German suspicions while depriving Bletchley Park of its useful 'crib' at a time when breaking the codes quickly was vital. But keeping the channel open would be a dangerous gamble, since he had only Lily's word (whatever that was now worth) that she had genuinely changed her mind about wrecking the deception. But however fickle she might be, Treasure was too enmeshed in the deception to be extracted now. Mary wrote: 'In spite of Sergeyev's confession, she should carry on operating her W/T herself. However the nature of her traffic would have to be altered and anything of a deceptive nature would now be out of the question.'

An emergency plan was drawn up. 'We see no particular object in having a showdown with her at this moment,' wrote Liddell; the showdown would come later. Lily would be kept under surveillance. Her past and future transmissions would be closely monitored for any evidence of the control signal. Her telephone would be tapped. A radio technician would stand by, ready to take over and mimic her radio 'fist' at the first sign she had alerted Kliemann. And then, as soon as D-Day was over, Lily would be admonished, fired and quite possibly arrested. She had deceived her case officers, conspired with the enemy, and perhaps tipped off Kliemann, putting countless lives in jeopardy for reasons of personal pique and in retaliation for a dog-killing that may, or may not, have taken place.

The Double Cross team, so confident in its report to Churchill, was plunged back into a state of roiling insecurity. On top of the continuing uncertainty over Jebsen's fate, now came the gnawing fear that Lily was lying, and Kliemann – tardy, inept Kliemann – might be stringing them along. Since Lily was working her own radio, she might yet be able to scupper the operation. 'Treasure is in a position to blow her case to the Germans at any time she wished to do so,' wrote Liddell. 'She is a very temperamental person. Although her statement may not be true, it shows she is unreliable.' The Tricycle network had already been shut down as a means of deception, and now Treasure had been taken out of the equation too. That left Garbo, Brutus and Bronx.

On 27 May 1944, Antonio Manuel de Almeida, director and general manager of the Banco Espirito Santo in Lisbon, received a telegram, in French, from one of the bank's London clients. It read: '*Envoyez vite cinquante livres. J'ai besoin pour mon dentiste*': 'Send £50 quickly, I need it for my dentist'.

Señor Almeida knew that this particular client was always short of money; he knew, too, that any message relating to her doctor or dentist was intended for the Germans: he immediately passed the telegram to the German intelligence station on Rua Buenos Aires. From Lisbon the message passed to Hauptmann Schluetter in Cologne, then to Berlin, and from Berlin to Zossen, where Elvira de la Fuente Chaudoir's telegram would be interpreted not as a dental emergency, but as a warning: 'I have definite news that a landing is to be made in the Bay of Biscay in one week.'

On the day she sent the telegram to Lisbon, Elvira wrote a letter in secret ink which would arrive in Lisbon after D-Day, *ex post facto* evidence that her tip-off had been genuine. It was one of Bronx's finest confections.

> After a cocktail party I stayed on at the Four Hundred Club with Captain David Ormsby-Gore. After having a good deal to drink, he told me that I should hear some startling news on the wireless the next day, as there was to be an airborne attack on the U-boat base at Bordeaux, preliminary to the invasion. Yesterday he came to see me, very much upset, and asked me to swear not to repeat anything as he had been drunk and now the attack had been postponed by a month, and if I repeated the conversation I would endanger thousands of lives. I am convinced that he spoke the truth and have, therefore, decided to send you a telegram to warn you of the raid.

David Ormsby-Gore was a figure of profound respectability. Son of a baron, grandson of a marquis, and great-grandson of a prime minister, he was an officer in the Royal Artillery serving in a secret reconnaissance unit with airborne troops and special forces. After the war, he became an MP, Ambassador to the US and a peer. He was a pallbearer at Robert Kennedy's funeral. He supplied John F. Kennedy with Cuban cigars, brought in by diplomatic bag. Elvira had never clapped eyes on him. He was not a heavy drinker, and would never have been so imprudent as to discuss an imminent invasion with someone like Elvira. He was press-ganged into the fiction; he had no choice in the matter. David Ormsby-Gore died in 1985, a pillar of the British establishment, wholly unaware that he had taken part, unwittingly, in tipping off the Germans to an invasion that never was.

★

On the day Elvira sent her telegram to Lisbon, Major Ignacio Molina Pérez, Spanish liaison officer and spy for the Germans, was looking out of a window of Government House, Gibraltar, into the courtyard below, when he saw a large car draw up, out of which hopped an instantly recognisable figure, 'wearing battledress and famous beret'. He was greeted by the Governor, Lieutenant General Sir Ralph 'Rusty' Eastwood. With the window open, Molina could hear every word.

'Hello, Monty, glad to see you,' said Sir Ralph.

'Hello, Rusty, how are you?' said Lieutenant Clifton James, until recently a star turn on the Leicester variety stage.

Molina had been invited to Government House to discuss routine business with the Colonial Secretary, who had stepped into the next room, the better to allow Molina a free view of the courtyard. 'His interest in happening on this significant scene was too great to hide,' reported the Colonial Secretary who, when quizzed by Molina about what Montgomery was doing in Gibraltar 'with well-feigned embarrassment, was forced to confess that the commander-in-chief was on his way to Algiers'.

James was suffering an attack of stage fright, but he 'played his difficult part with expert skill', MI5 recorded. He had breakfast with the Governor, who congratulated him on his performance, and told him: 'You *are* Monty. I've known him for years.' Then, with perfect stage management, 'His Excellency was handing "General Montgomery" into his car', at the very moment Molina emerged from the building.

The spy sped away in his own car, and was observed making 'an urgent trunk call' in the Spanish town of La Linea. 'The material reached Berlin in twenty minutes,' MI5 estimated. Molina even embellished his own role, telling one of his confidants (who happened to be a spy working for the British) that he had shaken hands with Montgomery himself. 'The Governor introduced me to him. He seems *muy simpatico*.' This informant (who rejoiced in the codename 'Pants') reported that Molina was 'very satisfied with himself'. The next day, Bletchley

Park intercepted a message from Madrid to Berlin which read: 'General Montgomery arrived Gibraltar. Discussions held with Governor and French General.' The British had a double agent working in Algiers airport codenamed 'Gaol', a former wireless operator for the Free French. Gaol informed Berlin of Monty's arrival in Algiers, and his reception by General Maitland 'Jumbo' Wilson, the Supreme Allied Commander in the Mediterranean. German reviews of the performance, as revealed in Most Secret Sources, were uniformly positive, and a subsequent report by von Roenne concluded that the presence of Monty in North Africa 'might point towards additional operations in South of France in addition to the main invasion'. Liddell wondered if the masquerade had been performed 'a little too early', but German intelligence seemed satisfied that Monty was still in North Africa on 28 May. And if he was there, then he could hardly be organising a massive assault across the Channel. The plot 'had gone through from start to finish without a hitch, and we knew that the main feature of its story had reached the Germans', MI5 reported.

Clifton James found playing the part of Monty extremely stressful. He was taken to a safe house in Cairo where he remained, with a copious supply of whisky, until the Normandy landings were under way. Like all method actors, he struggled to get out of character: 'He was under terrible pressure and strain,' said the wife of an intelligence officer detailed to look after him as he decompressed following the performance of his life. 'Coming out of that part was very difficult for him.'

On the sunny afternoon of 27 May, Adolf Hitler had tea with one of his favourite guests in the Berghof, his chalet in the Bavarian Alps above Berchtesgaden. General Baron Hiroshi Oshima, Japan's Ambassador to the German Reich, was a regular visitor to Hitler's private retreat, and the Führer's closest foreign confidant. A deep-dyed fascist and fawning Hitler devotee, Oshima had first met Hitler in 1935, when he was Japanese military attaché in Berlin. No one worked harder than the Japanese Ambassador to cement the alliance between Germany and Japan. The American journalist William L. Shirer called him 'more Nazi than the Nazis'. He spoke German fluently, and shared Hitler's views on Jews, the iniquity of the Soviet Union and the need to kill the survivors of U-boat attacks. If Hitler had been able to make friends with a racially inferior being, then he might have counted Oshima as a friend. A professional soldier with formidable powers of recall, after each cosy and informal chat with the Führer, Oshima compiled a detailed update on Hitler's military thinking and planning, which was encrypted and sent by wireless, with German approval, to the Japanese Foreign Office. These reports were read with avid interest in Tokyo; and Washington, and London.

American cryptanalysts had broken the Japanese wireless code in 1940. Using a duplicate of the cipher machine used by Japanese Foreign Office officials, the Allies were able to read the enemy's sensitive diplomatic cables as soon as they were sent. Indeed, the messages were sometimes read by the Allies *before* they were read in Tokyo, since wireless traffic from Germany to Japan was often held up in transmission. This was the Japanese equivalent of Most Secret Sources, codenamed 'Magic', an almost miraculous insight into Japan's secrets. Oshima supplied the most interesting reading of all: some seventy-five of the Ambassador's reports were picked up in 1941, a hundred in 1942, 400 in 1943, and no less than 600 in 1944. His commentaries were like having a bug in Hitler's headquarters, only more efficient, since the Japanese Ambassador was a military expert with a crisp prose style, who boiled down his conversations with Hitler to the essentials – so Allied intelligence analysts did not have to.

Oshima furnished copious information on U-boats, mobile forces, military production, technological developments, the effects of Allied bombing and the state of the German economy. In November 1943, he was taken on a four-day tour of German fortifications on the Channel coast of France. His resulting twenty-page report described the location, strength and weaponry of every German division, the dimensions of anti-tank ditches and the layout of machine-gun emplacements. If the invaders landed there, he predicted, 'lateral shell fire from the neighbouring posts and the appearance of mobile forces would annihilate them'. Allied intelligence could not have produced a better picture of the enemy's defences had they been invited on the tour themselves. As early as December 1943, Oshima reported that his friend, Joachim von Ribbentrop, Hitler's Foreign Minister, expected an invasion in Belgium or across the Dover Straits. In January 1944, he informed Tokyo that Hitler was speculating that the Allies might attack Bordeaux – giving hope to Operation Ironside. General George Marshall, the US Army Chief of Staff, paid tribute to Oshima's contribution to the Allied war effort: 'Our main basis of information regarding Hitler's intentions in Europe was obtained from Baron Oshima's messages from Berlin.' If Baron von Roenne was the best way of planting an idea in Hitler's head, then Baron Oshima was the most reliable way of finding out if it had lodged there.

Hitler was ludicrously proud of his hideously kitsch, self-furnished chalet at Berghof, purchased with the profits from *Mein Kampf*. 'This place is mine,' he told *Homes and Gardens* magazine in 1938. 'I built it with money that I earned.' The Führer welcomed the Japanese Ambassador into an entrance hall 'filled with a curious display of cactus plants in majolica pots'. Together, they strolled down a path to the Tea House in the woods. On the way, Hitler remarked that the Japanese government ought to publicly hang every US pilot captured during air raids on Japan. 'Our attitude cannot be ruled by any humane feelings,' he believed, a view with which Oshima heartily concurred. This was the kind of brutal small-talk they enjoyed. Tea was served by members of the SS acting as waiters. The two allies sat on the wooden terrace, under a large colourful parasol, overlooking the Berchtesgaden valley.

'What is your feeling about the Second Front?' Oshima asked.

'I believe that sooner or later an invasion of Europe will be attempted,' mused the Führer. 'I understand that the enemy has already assembled about eighty divisions in the British Isles. Of that force, a mere eight divisions are composed of first-class fighting men with experience in actual warfare.'

'Does Your Excellency believe that those Anglo-American forces are fully prepared to invade?'

'Yes.'

'I wonder what ideas you have as to how the Second Front will be carried out.'

'Well, judging from relatively clear portents, I think that diversionary actions will take place in a number of places – against Norway, Denmark, the southern part of Western France, and the French Mediterranean. After that – when they have established bridgeheads in Normandy and Brittany, and have sized up their prospects – they will then come forward with an all-out Second Front across the Straits of Dover. We ourselves would like nothing better than to strike one great blow as soon as possible. But that will not be feasible if the enemy does what I anticipate; their men will be dispersed. In that event we intend to finish off the enemy's troops at several bridgeheads. The number of German troops in the west still amounts to about sixty divisions.' Oshima scurried back to Berlin to write up his notebook.

When Oshima's report of his teatime conversation with Hitler duly arrived in Britain on 1 June, relief flooded through Allied intelligence. In almost every respect, Hitler's assessment mirrored what the framers of Operation Fortitude had hoped for. 'It gave the first definite assurance that the Germans greatly overestimated our strength,' wrote Roger Fleetwood-Hesketh. Hitler believed the major assault would come in the Pas de Calais, with precursor attacks in Norway and southwestern France; he believed von Roenne's wildly inflated estimates of Allied troop strength; he had faith in the 'clear portents' being fed to Germany by the double agents; he expected a number of attacks at different points, whereas the Allies were even now preparing, in Hitler's own words, 'one great blow', at Normandy. Some were uneasy that Hitler had, correctly, predicted an attack on Normandy, but he had made clear that he believed this would be nothing more than a diversionary assault, a prelude to the main invasion across the Straits of Dover.

Hitler told Oshima he thought an attack would come 'sooner or later'. With five days until D-Day, the attack would come far sooner than he imagined.

24

Garbo's Warning

The Allied armies streamed down the country lanes of southern England, like water running through numberless rivulets and channels towards the coast, gathering and spreading into a wide estuary of men, weapons, tanks and ships. 'The south coast was just unimaginable,' recalled Private Fred Perkins of the Royal Berkshire Regiment. 'It was just one vast marshalling yard of men and materiel all the way along.' Sergeant Joe Stephens of the Royal Artillery was waiting on the parade ground at Hawick camp when Montgomery arrived for a last, sinew-stiffening visit. Monty climbed onto the bonnet of his jeep. 'Gather round me, men,' he said. 'We're going to Europe; the Germans know we're going to Europe, but they don't know when and where, and this will be the deciding factor. I wish you good luck.' Then he drove away.

Major Peter Martin led his men past ripening fields towards the coast, wondering at the 'unreal feeling' of marching to war through this gentle bucolic landscape. 'Everything was totally normal and the countryside was gorgeous, and in a few days' time one would be going into an absolute charnel house.'

Within a week, 7,000 warships and landing craft, 11,000 planes and nearly 160,000 men would be hurled at the Atlantic Wall, the largest amphibious invasion ever attempted, and the first and naval phase of Operation Overlord, codenamed Neptune. German defences would be pummelled by air and naval bombardment; one British airborne division would try to secure the eastern flank, while American forces would land to the west by parachute and glider; shortly after dawn, six Allied infantry divisions – three American, two British and one Canadian – would storm onto five selected Normandy beaches.

Eisenhower called it the 'great crusade', but in his pocket he carried a scribbled note, the basis of what he would say if D-Day did not succeed, and his forces 'failed to gain a satisfactory foothold'. In the General's mind, victory was anything but certain. 'The troops, the air and the navy did all that bravery and devotion to duty could do,' he wrote, in dread anticipation. 'If any blame is found attached to the attempt it is mine alone.' Before turning in for the night on 5 June, Churchill, haunted by memories of slaughter on the beaches of Gallipoli in the First World War, told his wife Clementine: 'Do you realise that when you wake up in the morning, 20,000 men may have been killed?'

As a real army along the southern edge of England prepared for battle, another deployment, even larger, but wholly bogus, was under way in two quite unremarkable, pebble-dashed semi-detached houses in the London suburbs. With Treasure and Tricycle *hors de combat*, it fell to Brutus and Garbo to ram home the Fortitude deception in the hours before D-Day. Mr and Mrs Roman Czerniawski had recently moved into 61 Richmond Park Road, Barnes: from here, Agent Brutus 'drew all the loose threads together'. Through his invented wireless operator Chopin, Brutus laid out the Order of Battle for the fake army FUSAG, with its HQ in Wentworth, under the command of George Patton. In three long reports, packed with details supposedly gathered from within the army's operations room at Staines, and tours of Kent and East Anglia, he was able to present the Germans with, as Fleetwood-Hesketh put it, 'the entire chain of command of the shadow army group in southeast England'. Patton's army, he warned, gave 'the impression of being ready to take part in active operations in the near future'.

While Brutus sketched out the contours of the fake army, on the other side of London, at 35 Crespigny Road, Garbo added the shading and colours. From Scotland came reports of major naval exercises in Loch Fyne, soldiers seen wearing Arctic uniforms, and troops assembling in east coast ports, preparing for an assault on Norway. Garbo reported that his sub-agent in Exeter, one of the Welsh Aryans, had been arrested for lacking the correct documentation in a prohibited zone, a convenient explanation for the lack of intelligence from the southwest. Backing up Bronx's warning of an assault on Bordeaux, Garbo's agent in Liverpool spotted American forces 'destined for an attack on the South Atlantic French coast in cooperation with another army which will come direct from America'. Pujol himself described troops assembling in East Sussex. The Germans were so convinced of Garbo's accuracy that on at least one occasion his report was simply tacked, unedited, onto the German situation analysis. But in case the enemy was unable to reconstruct this 'imaginary Order of Battle' without help, Garbo, the 'self-trained military reporter', offered his own conclusions, leading the enemy by the hand to the wrong place: 'I conclude that the Harwich–Ipswich area has become an important operational base for future operations,' he advised, while news from the north 'indicates the possibility of an imminent attack against Norway'. No one asked him for his opinion, he merely proffered it, and the Germans grabbed it.

As the reports poured in from Britain, von Roenne faithfully drew and redrew his map: 'The main enemy concentration is showing itself ever more clearly to be in the south and southeast of the island,' the German analysts noted on 15 May. Then, two weeks later: 'Further transfer of formations to the south and southeast of the British Isles again emphasises that the main point of enemy concentrations is in this area.' By 2 June, the two-army scheme laid out by Brutus was as good as gospel: 'According to a reliable Abwehr message of 2nd June, the forces at present in the south of England are organised into two army groups (twenty-one English and First American).' The German spymasters asked for details about the 21st Army Group under Montgomery, the real army, but entirely failed to sense danger in the way their agents seemed so much keener to report what was happening farther east.

There is often one much-praised player on a team who fails to perform on the big day. Wulf Schmidt, Agent Tate, the veteran slogger who had clocked up more than 1,000 messages, was not playing at anything like the expected level. He fed the enemy a 'sustained diet of high-grade deceptive intelligence', but none of it was being swallowed. The bogus units and their locations identified by Brutus and Garbo reappeared dependably in the German military summaries, but for some reason Tate scored a duck. 'By the date of the invasion, not one of the messages which we had sent through him had found a place in the OKW intelligence summary,' wrote Fleetwood-Hesketh.

Even more worrying than the reluctance to accept Tate's deceptions was the danger that they might believe the fabrications of another informant, which just happened to be correct. Paul Fidrmuc, Agent Ostro, had been inventing reports for the Abwehr since 1940, based on gossip and guesswork. MI5 had long feared that Ostro might hit the truth with his scattergun inventions and, since he was evidently trusted by Berlin, draw the enemy towards the landing site by accident. Sure enough, in early June, Bletchley decoded a message in which Ostro reported that one of his non-existent informants, a colonel on Montgomery's staff, had identified Normandy as the *Schwerpunkt*. 'Ostro, in a long message, though entirely inaccurate, has hit on the target area,' Liddell wrote in his diary for 5 June. With just twenty-four hours to go, there was nothing to do but hope that one lucky, accurate falsehood would not be enough to outweigh the great mass of misleading untruths that had already been dumped on the enemy.

★

Shortly before midnight on the eve of D-Day, in deep blackout, a peculiar little procession entered the house at 35 Crespigny Road in Hendon. Leading the way was Juan Pujol, followed by Tar Robertson, Tommy Harris and Roger Fleetwood-Hesketh. Bringing up the rear was Sergeant Charles Haines, the former bank clerk who operated Garbo's wireless. All wore civilian clothes. Earlier in the evening, they had enjoyed dinner at Harris's home in Mayfair, lubricated with a magnum of Château Ausone 1934 from his excellent cellar. Refreshed, eager and extremely tense, this oddly assorted group was about to commit what was, on the surface, an act of astounding treachery, by tipping off the Germans to the time and place of the D-Day landings.

Harris had argued strenuously that in order to maintain Garbo's standing with the Germans, Pujol must be allowed to send advance warning of the invasion – not so soon as to make any military difference, but sufficiently early that when the Allies duly landed in Normandy, Pujol would be able to say he had told them so. This was not vanity. The follow-up phase of Fortitude – maintaining the threat to the Pas de Calais to prevent the Germans redeploying forces to Normandy – was as important as the first, and sustaining German belief in Garbo's infallibility was crucial. After some hesitation, Eisenhower had agreed that the Double Cross team could alert the Germans no more than three and a half hours before the first troops landed at 6.30 a.m. The delay in transmission from Madrid to Berlin was about three hours, so by the time the German High Command got the message, the invasion should be under way. Pujol had told Kühlenthal he was expecting important news from Scotland, and asked him to ensure that the wireless operator in Spain was waiting to receive a message at 3.00 a.m.

Number 35 Crespigny Road was and is a perfectly nondescript house on a quiet street in an unremarkable corner of London. It looked like every other house in the road and a million other houses across Britain which was, of course, why MI5 chose it.

If any building could claim to be a master of disguise, it was this one. But if the house seemed innocuous, unlikely to play any part whatever in winning the war, then so did Juan Pujol. He was now all but bald, and wore large glasses, which made him seem less like the fighting bantam he had resembled on first arriving in England, and more like a tiny, intensely focused owl. He appeared to be exactly what his neighbours in Crespigny Road thought he was: a shy, polite foreign gentleman who did something dull at the BBC.

Just before 3.00 a.m., with Allied paratroopers already in action in France, the five men gathered around the wireless in the upstairs bedroom, and Haines prepared to send the message. The story, as befitted the occasion, was a dramatic one, although buried, as usual, in Pujol's nomadic circumlocutions. Fred, the Gibraltarian waiter, had linked up with two American deserters from Hiltingbury Camp, and gone AWOL in order to bring Garbo the news that the invasion had started.

> He has told me that three days ago cold rations and vomit bags had been distributed to troops of the 3rd Canadian Division and that the division had now left the camp, its place now taken by Americans. There were rumours that the 3rd Canadian Division had now embarked. The situation of this agent is very compromising because his absence must have been noted due to the many hours which have elapsed since he left the camp. In order to protect the service [i.e. the network] I have taken a decision to put him into hiding.

If the Canadian troops had not returned, that could only mean they had set sail for France; and since Hiltingbury is just eight miles from Southampton, and Southampton is opposite Cherbourg, then the logical target must be Normandy. The Germans would read the clues instantly.

At 2.59 a.m., Tar told Haines: 'All right Sergeant, let them have it!' Haines keyed in the call sign. The only response was a crackle of static. 'I don't get it,' said Haines. 'Normally Fritzy answers right away.' He repeated the call after fifteen minutes. Again there was no reply. The radio operator had either left his post, or fallen asleep. Haines kept calling. Harris observed: 'The trouble is, life in Madrid really only begins at midnight. Kühlenthal's operator is probably at Chiquotes having a *copita* with his friends.' Robertson and Fleetwood-Hesketh eventually made their excuses and went home to bed, like guests peeling off from a dud party. The message was strengthened, adding information that would have breached security a few hours earlier, to make the warning more stark and enhance Garbo's standing further. Finally, at 8 a.m., the Madrid wireless operator either woke up or came into work, and the message was picked up and acknowledged. By which time the Canadian Third Division was no longer gathering up its vomit bags and preparing to embark, but under heavy fire from the German 716th Division on Normandy's Juno beach.

So far from being an anticlimax, Garbo's carefully timed non-warning had achieved its purpose. He had passed over what must be seen, in German eyes, as the most important intelligence tip-off of the war, and they had missed it. Like the Madrid radio operator, the Germans had been caught napping.

On the afternoon of 4 June, Lieutenant Commander George Honour gingerly manoeuvred his midget submarine into its reconnaissance position, a quarter of a mile off the beach codenamed Sword; the most easterly of the landing beaches where, in just thirty-six hours, the British 3rd Infantry Division was due to attack. He raised the periscope and peered towards the shore. 'We saw a lorry-load of Germans arrive. They started playing beach ball and swimming and at the back of my mind I thought, "I hope there are no Olympic swimmers and they don't swim out and find us." There were the Germans having a Sunday afternoon recreation and little did they know what was sitting and waiting for them.'

The invasion of Normandy came as a stunning surprise to the

senior German commanders who were not only unprepared, but positively relaxed. Rommel, in charge of improving the Channel defences, was 500 miles away at home in Ulm, celebrating his wife's birthday. Hans von Salmuth of the Fifteenth Army, defending the Calais area, was on a hunting expedition. The intelligence chief Colonel Georg Hansen was taking the waters at Baden Baden. Divisional commanders in Seventh Army's area had left for a war-gaming exercise in Rennes, designed to simulate an Allied landing. The German navy, having reported that an invasion was 'improbable' owing to the poor weather, cancelled patrols in the Channel, and the troops in their dugouts and bunkers were told to get some rest. Von Roenne's situation report for 6 June did not even mention Britain, and focused almost exclusively on the Mediterranean.

The day before D-Day, Rundstedt, with 1.5 million men of the Wehrmacht under his command, sent out a reassuring situation report: 'That the invasion is actually imminent does not seem to be indicated as yet.' Even his convoluted grammar suggests a man who thought he had time on his hands. The defenders manning the great Atlantic Wall were assured of its impregnability – convinced that the enemy would be repulsed – and thoroughly disinclined to get agitated. When a private in the German Seventh Army Intelligence Corps informed the duty officer that the front line was reporting an attack, he was told 'Don't make a big production of it. Remember Dieppe' – a reference to the failed Allied raid of 1942.

Colonel Oscar Reile, Brutus's wily case officer in Paris, had become an expert in interpreting hidden messages to the French resistance contained in apparently meaningless phrases broadcast in French by the BBC. On 5 June, German intelligence picked up fourteen such messages and concluded that the invasion was imminent. The Seventh Army, in Normandy, ignored the warning; the Fifteenth Army, at Calais, raised its state of alert, but von Salmuth remained catatonically calm: 'I'm too old a bunny to get excited about this,' he said.

Hitler had stayed up late on 5 June, discussing films with Eva Braun and Goebbels. Since the Normandy attack was assumed to be a diversion, it was not thought necessary to wake Hitler and tell him it had started. On D-Day he slept in until 10 o'clock. When finally told the invasion had begun, he was cheerful, convinced the attack would be repelled with ease.

The Double Cross team could not (and did not) claim sole credit for wrong-footing the Germans on 6 June. The bombing campaign in northeast France had steadily increased, until every bomb that landed on Normandy was matched by two dropped on the Pas de Calais; twice as many radar stations were attacked outside the invasion zone as in it. Far behind the lines, paratroopers set off flares and fireworks, and blasted out recordings of small-arms fire to draw German troops away from the landing beaches, while an airborne army of dummy parachutists compounded the confusion. As the real army ploughed through the waves towards Normandy, two more fake convoys were scientifically simulated heading for the Seine and Boulogne, by dropping a blizzard of tin foil from planes, codenamed 'Window', which would show up on German radar as two huge flotillas approaching the French coast.

The Germans might have been taken by surprise, but they were far from defenceless. The coastline bristled with field and coastal batteries, mortars, machine guns and snipers; barbed wire, wooden stakes, mines, anti-tank 'hedgehogs' made from welded steel girders; concrete pyramid-shaped 'dragon's teeth' to slow down and channel tanks into 'killing zones', and more than a million upright stakes in the fields beyond, known as 'Rommel's Asparagus', to impede airborne landings. From bunkers, machine-gun nests, trenches and gun emplacements, the German defenders poured fire onto the attackers. At Omaha beach, the first men to land faced an 'inhuman wall of fire'. More than 2,400 were killed or wounded. At Juno, the Canadians suffered 50 per cent casualties in the first hour. Beyond Sword beach, where German forces had played Sunday beach ball a few hours earlier, the Gestapo began reprisals: at the city prison in Caen, more than seventy members of the French Resistance were marched into the courtyard and shot.

News of the landings was brought back to Britain by Gustav, an RAF homing pigeon released by the Reuters war correspondent Montague Taylor. 'His name might sound suspiciously foreign,' said the bird's trainer, Frederick Jackson of Cosham in Hampshire, 'but he was as English as they come.' Montague reported: 'The invasion army has thought of everything, including carrier pigeons to carry the big news home if all else fails. A wing commander arrived here only a few hours before I embarked on my landing ship and presented me with a basket of four pigeons, complete with food and message-carrying equipment.' At 8.30 a.m., Montague released Gustav. Flying through 30 mph headwinds, dense cloud and sporadic enemy fire, the pigeon completed the journey to his home loft in Thorney Island, near Portsmouth, in just five hours, sixteen minutes – a D-Day record. Sergeant Harry Halsey removed the message strapped to his leg, and relayed it to London: 'We are just 20 miles or so off the beaches. First assault troops landed 0750. Steaming steadily in formation. Lightnings, Typhoons, Fortresses crossing since 0545. No enemy aircraft seen.'

D-Day was the reason for the Double Cross system, the grand finale to which every preceding deception was a foretaste. The men who fought that day have become lasting symbols of courage and skill. But while they battled their way up the bloody dunes, an unseen force fought alongside them, from many miles away, not with guns, bullets and bombs, but with subterfuge and stealth, to whittle away German strength and confidence, to confuse, surprise and mislead, and shield the invaders with lies. By the end of the first day of the invasion, the Allies had suffered at least 10,000 casualties, and 2,500 dead. But 156,000 men had landed in France from the sea and 23,000 from the air, thrusting a spearpoint into occupied France.

What those numbers might have been without the Fortitude deception, and what measure of that deception was attributable to the double agents is, of course, impossible to judge.

But this is certain: if the Double Cross deception had backfired, if Johnny Jebsen had cracked, if Lily Sergeyev had inserted her control signal, if the great defensive net of lies had unravelled and the Germans had been ready and waiting in Normandy, reinforced and alert, then the invasion would have failed, and D-Day would have ended in a massacre.

Second Innings

The 6th of June was the longest day. It had been assumed that for the double agents, it might also be the last, once the Germans realised they had fallen victim to an elaborate hoax. They did not, and the Double Cross team now had a second innings to play: to foster the illusion that another, even larger invasion, would soon strike the Pas de Calais – and maintain that sham as long as possible. The spies would surely soon be exposed, but every hour that the fiction held, every hour that the Fifteenth Army awaited the fake invasion, could make a critical difference in blood spilled and territory won. The planners hoped the twin threats to Norway and Calais might be maintained for as much as ten days. Eisenhower would have settled for less. He knew that if even a part of the mighty German army in the north moved its guns to the fragile Normandy bridgehead, the invasion could still fail: 'Just keep the Fifteenth Army out of my hair for the first two days,' he told the deception planners. 'That's all I ask.'

The Double Cross agents plunged back into the shadow battle, following up the D-Day invasion with a volley of apologies from the spies who had failed to give prior warning, and a blast of recrimination from the only one who had.

Brutus's excuse was that he had been busy finding out about the other army poised to cross the Straits of Dover: 'Unfortunately, by remaining without contact with 21 Army Group and through awaiting a state of alert at FUSAG, I was not able to give you details of the first landings.' Tate was also contrite, pointing out that more troops seemed to be arriving in Kent. As soon as the Normandy invasion was publicly announced, Bronx sent a letter in secret ink, knowing it would not arrive for many weeks, insisting that her prediction of an attack on Bordeaux had been sent in good faith. 'Distraught by the news of invasion and convinced of the genuineness of the information given by Captain Ormsby-Gore. Dined with him last night but he did not respond to my teasing on the subject of his indiscretion, merely reminding me that I had promised never to speak of it again. Can only suppose there has been a change of plan or else that this attack, also, will take place.'

Garbo, by contrast, took a verbal flame-thrower to his German handler for failing to pick up the warning message sent before the invasion began:

> This makes me question your seriousness and your sense of responsibility. I therefore demand a clarification immediately as to what has occurred. I am very disgusted in this struggle for life or death. I cannot accept excuses or negligence. Were it not for my ideals and my faith I would abandon this work. I write these messages to send this very night though my tiredness and exhaustion, due to the excessive work I have had, has completely broken me.

Kühlenthal squirmed. He blamed the weather. He blamed Garbo's wireless operator, and his own. He blamed anyone but himself, and offered a flood of grovelling flattery.

> I wish to stress in the clearest terms that your work over the last few weeks has made it possible for our command to be completely forewarned and prepared. Thus I reiterate to you, as responsible chief of the service, and to all your collaborators, our total recognition of your perfect and cherished work and I beg of you to continue with us in the

supreme and decisive hours of the struggle for the future of Europe.

Churchill made what he doubtless thought was a helpful contribution, by lying to the House of Commons and announcing that the assault on Normandy was 'the first of a series of landings'. The only problem was that Garbo had already reported to Madrid, from his notional perch within the Ministry of Information, that officials had been specifically ordered *not* to allude to further attacks in order to preserve the element of surprise, and here was the Prime Minister doing just that, in the most public way. Pujol scrambled to explain that Churchill's failure to follow the directive had caused consternation, and an investigation was under way. In the end, the Prime Minister's gaffe probably did more good than harm.

So far the double agents had dropped hints of an impending invasion of the Pas de Calais; now they could 'go all out', and baldly state that FUSAG was preparing to 'attack across the Channel at any moment'. If the deception before D-Day was composed of subtle hints and nudges, the second phase was spoon-fed to the Germans, with a spade. 'Fortitude requires a threat to the Pas de Calais to be continued indefinitely,' wrote Astor, 'to contain the maximum number of troops during the next few critical days.' Brutus immediately sent a message to Reile depicting the Normandy invasion as merely a starter before the main course. 'It is clear that the landing was made only by units of the 21st Army Group,' he radioed on the evening of D-Day. 'FUSAG, as I reported, was ready for an attack which is capable of being released at any moment, but it is now evident that it will be an independent action.' The agents reported American troops pouring into southeast England, radio traffic was increased, and sabotage in the Calais area was intensified, all pointing to a second army in an 'advanced state of preparedness for offensive action'.

Garbo was also categorical. 'I never like to give my opinion unless I have strong reasons to justify my assurances,' he told

Kühlenthal. (This was hardly true, since he gave his opinions all the time, on everything.) In the longest message to date, sent from Crespigny Road in the early hours of 9 June, he and Harris laid out exactly what the German High Command ought to think.

> After personal consultation on 8th June with my agents . . . I am of the opinion, in view of the strong troop concentrations in S.E. and E England which are not taking part in the present operations, that these operations [in Normandy] are a diversionary manoeuvre designed to draw off enemy reserves in order then to make a decisive attack in another place. It may probably take place in the Pas de Calais area, particularly since in such an attack the proximity of the air bases will facilitate the operation by providing continued strong air support . . . The constant aerial bombardment which the area of the Pas de Calais has suffered and the strategic disposition of these forces give reason to suspect an attack in that region of France which at the same time offers the shortest route for the final objective of their illusions, which is to say Berlin.

Garbo listed every unit, genuine and invented, in the south of England, and calculated the Allies must be 'left with some fifty divisions with which to attempt a second blow'. He concluded with what sounded like an order.

> I trust you will submit urgently all these reports and studies to our High Command since moments may be decisive in these times and before taking a false step, through lack of knowledge of the necessary facts, they should have in their possession all the present information which I transmit with my opinion which is based on the belief that the whole of the present attack is set as a trap for the enemy to make us move all our reserves in a hurried strategical disposition which we would later regret.

If the receivers of this vast scree had paused to reflect, they might have registered how unlikely it was that a wireless would have been able to operate for more than two hours without detection. But they did not. Garbo's report, boiled down to readable form, hurtled up the chain of command, gaining traction as it went: from Madrid it passed to Berlin, and then on to Berchtesgaden. There it was read by Freidrich-Adolf Krummacher, the head of the High Command intelligence branch, who underlined the sentence describing the Normandy landing as 'diversionary', and passed it on to General Alfred Jodl, head of the OKW operations staff, who underlined 'S.E. and E England'. Then it was handed to Hitler.

The Führer's response may be deduced from the resulting intelligence assessment, which embraced Garbo's conclusions with the sort of blind enthusiasm ideologues usually display on being told what they already believe.

> The report is credible. The reports received in the last week from the Arabel undertaking have been confirmed almost without exception and are to be described as exceptionally valuable. The main line of investigation in future is to be the enemy group of forces in south-eastern and eastern England.

Elvira lent a hand with a letter in secret ink reporting: 'Only part of Allied force in Normandy operation, bulk remains here at present.' The very artlessness and apparent naivety of her letters made them, in a different way, as powerful as Czerniawski's military reportage and Pujol's detailed analysis. Two weeks after D-Day, she was still hinting at a looming second invasion, worrying about her overdraft, and wondering what to spread on her toast. 'Lord Stanley of Alderney says bad weather hinders ships leaving south coast ports,' she wrote. 'Fruit spoiled by frosts, jam to be sent from America. Still no money.'

As planned, as soon as Overlord was under way, Treasure, once the darling of the Double Cross team, was unceremoniously fired. Lily Sergeyev had taken extraordinary risks on behalf of British intelligence, and played a crucial part, not just in the deception, but in winning Kliemann's trust to the extent that her wireless traffic, relayed verbatim, had 'absolutely saved the bacon of GC and CS [the Government Code and Cipher School at Bletchley] during June'. But she had allowed her feelings to intrude into a business that had little time for such things; she had loved her dog too much, and in withholding information and seeking revenge for its death, she had broken the most fundamental rules of intelligence. And she was still refusing to reveal her control signal.

Three days after D-Day, Tar came to the Hill Street flat to sack her in person, accompanied by Mary Sherer. He was wearing his Glengarry cap and the trousers of the Seaforth Highlanders. He sat in the armchair. Mary took up a position by the window.

'I have some hard things to say. I'll come straight to the point.'

'Go ahead,' she said, with mock insouciance.

Tar did not easily rise to anger, but when he did, he flushed scarlet. Gripping the arms of the chair, Robertson leaned forward: 'Mary has told me that when you were in Lisbon you arranged a security check. We have accordingly decided that you are no longer trustworthy. It is quite impossible for me to place any confidence in someone who behaves in this manner. You will not transmit any more. We'll do that ourselves. We have already started to work without you.'

Lily smiled. Tar turned a deeper shade of red.

'The situation is as follows: you cease to work for us; we shall continue to pay you £5 a week for your maintenance; as soon as possible I shall organise your return to Paris. You must leave this flat. You have a fortnight to clear out.'

Lily still said nothing. Tar was beginning to boil.

'If I have any cause to think that you are in any way acting contrary to the interests of the Allied cause, I will at once take severe action and either put you in prison or hand you over to the French authorities, who would no doubt deal with you pretty severely.'

Lily noticed a darning hole in the left knee of his tartan trousers. Tar was unshaven, and looked tired and a little shabby, she thought.

Tar waited for a response: 'What do you have to say?'

'Your first allegation is correct,' said Lily. 'And you can keep your money.'

'You will take the money whether you like it or not. You can do what you like with it after that. I suppose that you don't want to give us the security check?'

Lily shrugged. 'You said a while ago I couldn't be trusted,' she muttered. 'If I gave you the sign, how would you know it is not exactly the opposite of what you wanted?'

Tar had had enough of the game. 'I didn't say we would believe you.'

Without another word, he left, followed by Mary Sherer. As soon as she heard the front door close, Lily burst into tears, of self-pity, perhaps, but also of regret. This had been, as she later put it, the 'big scene from Act Three'. She had planned to end the drama in her own way, either as a heroine for the Allies or by blowing the whole operation in retaliation for the death of Babs. Instead, she was being sent away with a meagre pay-off, and a dressing down from a man with a red face and a hole in his trousers.

In a last attempt to get Lily to divulge the control signal, Tar sent Gisela Ashley to see her. They had always got on well, and Gisela was a dab hand at extracting information.

'Why did you do it?' she asked.

'I refuse to be beaten by them, by your damned intelligence service.'

Gisela Ashley put her arm around Lily. 'Ducky, that's just pride.'

In a rare moment of self-knowledge, Lily wrote in her diary: 'I have destroyed my own work, or at any rate rendered it useless.'

★

Double Cross was built on sideways thinking. But as Operation Fortitude stretched beyond D–Day, the thinking went from lateral to outlandish. Intoxicated by their success, Hugh Astor and Roman Czerniawski came up with an idea that was ingenious, daring, and quite mad: what if they could entice the Germans into sending an assassination squad to kill General Eisenhower and his senior officers at the fake headquarters of the fake army?

The plan was simple: Brutus would send an urgent radio message to Reile 'inviting the Germans to make an airborne raid on the notional FUSAG Headquarters at Wentworth'. The message would read: 'General Eisenhower and a few other eminent persons are holding a conference, at the end of which Eisenhower is to address all officers. This represents an ideal and unprecedented opportunity for capturing or destroying some of the most eminent personages on which the success of the invasion depends.' Wentworth, Brutus would point out, is 'surrounded by golf courses suitable for airborne landings'. Czerniawski himself would 'flash a torch to indicate the exact landing point, and direct the raiders to the mess where the exalted persons will be holding their post prandial celebrations'. Immediately on landing, the German paratroopers would be ambushed and taken prisoner. 'Arrangements will have to be made to give the raiders a suitable reception and to ensure none of them escape.' Czerniawski would need an excuse for why the assassination plot had failed. 'On the following day Brutus will himself transmit a furious message explaining that although he was vigorously flashing his lantern, the airborne troops landed several fields away, where they were naturally rounded up by the Home Guard.' The plot, Astor argued, would reinforce German belief in the invented army in the southeast: 'If the Germans refuse to play, no harm will have been done, as the threat to the Pas de Calais will have been continued and Brutus will again have shown himself to be a man of courage and resource.' The Germans surely could not resist this 'appetising dish'.

Tar Robertson rejected the idea out of hand, pointing out that there were easier ways to catch German attention than inciting heavily armed Nazi assassins to run around the golf courses of the Home Counties in the middle of the night, looking for American generals to kill.

Some elements of the grand deception were more effective than others. Flight Lieutenant Richard Walker had spent months preparing his pigeon double-cross scheme. He recruited hundreds of second-rate homing pigeons, equipped them with faked German leg rings, and dropped them over occupied Europe, in the expectation that they would destroy the German pigeon service from within.

Walker's grand deception was a damp squab: there is no evidence that it had any effect whatever. The Germans never detected the double-agent pigeons in their midst. Indeed, when the Wehrmacht officer in command of the pigeon service was interrogated after the war, and asked whether his lofts might have been infiltrated by Allied pigeons, he responded that such a thing was impossible since the impostors would have been spotted immediately: no one, he said, could attach a fake leg ring to a pigeon without soldering it. This, of course, was precisely what Walker had managed to do. The plot failed because of its excessive ingenuity. The double-agent pigeons, too feeble to fly home, simply blended in with the local pigeon populations, and like so many ex-combatants, made new lives for themselves, their wartime heroics unsuspected and, until now, unsung.

The charade of Monty's double may also have had only a limited effect on German thinking. The *mise-en-scène* in Gibraltar was certainly reported back to Berlin, but as MI5 candidly admitted, 'what they deduced from it, and how far it had any effect upon their plans, unfortunately we have never been able to find out'. The ruse may have concentrated German attention on a possible landing in the South of France, but the meeting between the fake General Montgomery and the real General Wilson at Algiers does not appear to have been reported to von

Rundstedt, or to have affected German defence of the Channel. The most that can be said of Operation Copperhead is that it compounded German confusion, and provided considerable entertainment for its organisers. It also put paid to Molina Pérez, whose career as a Nazi spy came to an abrupt end. Armed with hard evidence of his espionage activities, the British declared the Spanish officer *persona non grata*, and permanently excluded him from Gibraltar, much to his baffled annoyance.

Elvira's telegram warning of the imminent attack on the Bay of Biscay undoubtedly reached German intelligence, although the invasion was graded, at most, a 'small calibre' operation. Even so, it was considered real enough that when German reconnaissance spotted Allied convoys near Brest it was assumed these must be heading for the Biscay area for a 'diversionary attack'. Allied military planners had anticipated that within a week of D-Day, two Panzer divisions would be sent from southwest France to Normandy. In fact, only one, the 17th SS Panzergrenadier Division, headed north to join the counter-attack, and even that did not move immediately: it finally reached Normandy and engaged in combat on 11 June. The 11th Panzer Division remained in position, defending southwest France from an attack that never came. John Masterman was sure that this was attributable to Elvira: 'When the invasion took place, the Panzer division *was* kept in the Bordeaux area and not pushed north at once towards Cherbourg.' Astor agreed: 'Their movement of a Panzer division to the Bordeaux area may to some extent be attributed to Bronx's telegram', ensuring those troops remained 'impotent near Bordeaux while the battle raged in Normandy'.

Elvira's follow-up letter, suggesting that the Biscay invasion might yet happen, further muddied the waters. As late as July, General Jodl told Admiral Abe, the Japanese naval attaché in Berlin, that a second series of invasions was expected: 'We are prepared for landings in the vicinity of Bordeaux.' Agent Bronx and Operation Ironside may not have fully convinced the Germans that an attack on southwest France was imminent, or even likely, but it undoubtedly added to German confusion. And the credit for that uncertainty goes, in large part, to a frivolous party girl who lied about meeting a drunken officer in a club, and told her spymasters of a conversation that never took place.

The stated, limited aim of Fortitude North had been to 'contain some first quality divisions' in Scandinavia by a threatened assault on Norway. In this, it succeeded, though perhaps less dramatically than hoped. The Germans certainly believed in the fictional Fourth Army under General Thorne, but they seem to have assumed that it was not big enough, or sufficiently backed by air cover, to do more than mount a diversionary attack. In early May, the Germans had described an attack on Norway as a 'strong possibility', and action against Denmark as a 'certainty'. The seventeen German divisions across Scandinavia were put on full alert. The Germans certainly feared an attack, albeit not on a large scale. The deception may not have persuaded Hitler to do anything he was not already disposed to do; but it undoubtedly encouraged him to continue doing something he was already doing, and the Allies needed him to continue doing. At no point did Hitler redeploy the 250,000 troops in Norway to the real zone of destiny, in northern France.

If some subsidiary elements of Operation Fortitude were of debatable effectiveness, the main thrust of the deception was an undisputed, unalloyed, world-changing triumph. As the Battle of Normandy raged, the Germans held fast to the illusion, so carefully planted and now so meticulously sustained, that a great American army under Patton was preparing to pounce and the German forces in the Pas de Calais must remain in place to repel it.

On D-Day itself, von Roenne insisted that 'another landing would come in the Fifteenth Army area and no troops would be withdrawn from there'. Rommel agreed, arguing that the forces in the north should not be weakened. Nonetheless, the Fifteenth Army reserves were mobilised and on 9 June, the mighty 1st

Panzer division, 25,000-strong, was ordered to head south from the Pas de Calais to join the counter-attack against the Allied bridgehead. But then came Garbo's explicit warning that the Normandy invasion was a ruse, specifically designed to draw off troops from Calais before the main assault. The order to the 1st Panzers was countermanded. The division would remain in place for another, crucial week. Several factors were at work in that decision, but Field Marshal Keitel later stated he was '99 per cent certain' that the warning from Garbo 'provided the reason for the change of plan'.

A week after D-Day, only one German division had moved from the Pas de Calais to Normandy. German belief in the phantom army was unshakeable. On 23 June, Oshima reported to Tokyo that 'twenty-three divisions commanded by General Patton are being held in readiness to make new landings. This is one reason why Germany has avoided pouring a great number of men into the Normandy area.' Physical proof of success came when the British forces in Italy captured a map, drawn up by German intelligence on 15 June, which showed exactly where the enemy believed the second Allied army was waiting in southeast England to cross the Channel. 'It was almost identical with Plan Fortitude,' wrote Liddell.

A month after D-Day, no fewer than twenty-two German divisions were still held back in the Fifteenth Army sector. 'Patton's army group,' Jodl reported, 'is being made ready in London and in southern England for the next landing.' The ever-helpful Oshima confirmed that the Germans still expected that 'Patton's forces will land in the neighbourhood of Dieppe'. Hitler had 'reposed an almost mystic confidence in Garbo', MI5 later concluded, and even in late July he 'still could not rid his mind of the belief that a second landing was intended'. But von Roenne was now starting to have doubts, or pretending to. After warning for weeks that another, even larger attack was coming, he began to hedge his bets, suggesting that FUSAG 'has not been given the decisive role' after all. Perhaps, like all experts, he was just adopting new certainties as events unfolded. But perhaps von Roenne had never been fooled by the chimera of Patton's army, which he had done so much to reinforce. By 27 July he was singing a new tune: 'A second major landing on the Channel Coast no longer seems to be so probable in view of the situation in Normandy.' Seven weeks after the first landings, four divisions were finally released from the Fifteenth Army to head south, far too late. As Eisenhower put it, 'every additional soldier who then came into the Normandy area was then caught up in the catastrophe of defeat'. The bridgehead, so vulnerable in the first days and weeks, was firmly established. The war was not won, but the end was in sight.

Looking back, the most clear-sighted German officer knew that the failure to counter-attack in Normandy had cost them the battle, and perhaps the war. Shortly before he was forced to kill himself, Rommel conceded that it had been a 'decisive mistake to leave the German troops in the Pas de Calais'. But so far from realising they had been fooled, the Germans assumed that Allied plans had changed. On 30 August, Garbo reported that the planned attack on the Pas de Calais had been cancelled, and the Germans believed him, as they had believed him from the start. Only later did the truth dawn. 'All this Patton business wasn't a trick, was it?' Professor Percy Schramm, the keeper of the OKW War Diary, asked his interrogators. 'Were all those divisions sent to southeast England simply to hold our forces in the Pas de Calais?' But others clung to the deception long after the war was over. Jodl was interrogated in 1946, still congratulating himself on being fooled:

We knew that you had one Army Group in the south of England and one in the southeast. We know now that the South-Eastern Army Group was not in fact launched against the Channel coast, but its continued presence in the southeast of England constituted a threat which it was not possible for us to ignore. We therefore did not feel justified in authorising any large-scale release of Fifteenth

Army formations for use in Normandy until a considerable
time after the invasion had started. Had our picture of your
dispositions in the UK been less complete and had we not
been aware of the presence of the First US Army Group in
the southeast of England we might have dispatched more of
the Fifteenth Army to Normandy earlier, which might have
had very serious results for yourselves.

On the Allied side, there was no doubt that the Germans had
been induced into making what Major General Kenneth Strong,
Eisenhower's intelligence chief, called an 'unparalleled blunder'.
If the huge German army in the north had been deployed to
Normandy at once, instead of waiting for a second invasion,
then the Allies would have faced an even bloodier fight, with
every possibility of defeat. Those additional forces 'might well
have tipped the scales against us', wrote Eisenhower: 'I cannot
overemphasise the importance of maintaining as long as humanly
possible the Allied threat to the Pas de Calais area, which has
already paid enormous dividends and, with care, will continue
to do so.' Montgomery concurred: 'The deception measures,'
he wrote, 'played a vital part in our successes in Normandy.' The
Double Cross report for Churchill was a fully justified hymn of
self-congratulation.

It seems from all indications that the Germans have accepted
the stories which we have told them about an impending
attack on the Pas de Calais. It seems pretty clear that the
congratulatory messages, especially to Garbo, to some extent
reflect the general military appreciation of the German High
Command. It is known for a fact that the Germans intended
at one time to move certain Divisions from the Pas de Calais
area to Normandy but, in view of the possibility of a threat
to the Pas de Calais area these troops were either stopped on
their way to Normandy and recalled, or it was decided that
they should not be moved at all.

John Masterman knew, as Churchill did not, just how close the deception had come to disaster: 'We were not very far from failure just before the period of our greatest success,' he later wrote. But the team had put on a superb all-round performance in what his colleague in American intelligence, Norman Holmes Pearson, called 'the greatest Test Match of the century'. After the war, British intelligence combed through captured records and established exactly which elements in German military thinking could be traced directly to agents' reports: only eleven of Tate's messages registered with the German analysts; Garbo's network clocked up an impressive eighty-six, but it was Brutus who made the highest score, with no fewer than ninety-one messages reflected in the German intelligence summaries, just nine short of his century.

The post-match analysis was, and remains, universally admiring. Thaddeus Holt, author of the most comprehensive account of wartime deception, has called Operation Fortitude 'the most successful strategic deception of all time'. Even Kim Philby, that master of deceit, called it 'one of the most creative intelligence operations of all time'.

But the most important tribute to the deception's success came from the Germans themselves. On 29 July, nearly two months after D-Day, Kühlenthal sent a wireless message to Garbo:

> With great happiness and satisfaction I am able to advise you today that the Führer has awarded the Iron Cross to you for your extraordinary merits, a decoration which, without exception, is granted only to front-line combatants. For that reason we all send you our most sincere and cordial congratulations.

In reply, Garbo professed to be so overcome with pride and emotion that he was lost for words. Then the words came tumbling out in a great, frothing torrent.

I cannot at this moment, when emotion overcomes me, express in words my gratitude for the decoration conceded by our Führer, to whom humbly and with every respect I express my gratitude for the high distinction which he has bestowed on me, for which I feel myself unworthy as I have never done more than what I have considered to be the fulfilment of my duty. Furthermore, I must state that this prize has been won not only by me but also by the other comrades, who, through their advice and directives, have made possible my work here, and so the congratulations are mutual. My desire is to fight with great ardour to be worthy of this medal which has only been conceded to those heroes, my companions in honour, who fight on the battlefront.

You can almost hear Pujol and Harris sniggering with glee in the background. But Garbo was right to see the award as a collective honour. He had not mounted the deception alone. His 'comrades' included the agents he had invented, the other agents and their own inventions, and behind them the men and women who built the system, the case officers, spymasters and inspired dissemblers who imagined the Double Cross project, and the far-sighted planners who, amazingly, let them get on with it. Those who fought on the battlefront of D-Day never knew that a Polish patriot, a Peruvian gambling-girl, a French dog-lover, a Serbian playboy and a Spanish chicken farmer, together and in deepest secrecy, had lied them to victory.

Agent Garbo accepted the Iron Cross on behalf of them all.

Aftermath

In German eyes, Agent Brutus had proved himself 'the noblest Roman'. In the wake of D-Day, having failed to predict the real invasion and pumped his handlers full of lies about the false one, he could do no wrong. Most Secret Sources showed that his reports were being 'studied not only by the operational sections, but by the most prominent persons in Berlin, including Hitler and Goering'. German intelligence regarded him as an oracle, a sage: 'We shall presently reach a stage where high-level questions on military matters are addressed personally to Brutus,' Astor crowed. In July 1944, a flying bomb landed in Barnes in southwest London, blowing out the windows of 61 Richmond Park Road, and leaving Monique Czerniawski with serious facial injuries. MI5's bean-counters agreed to pay the £50 needed for plastic surgery, noting that Czerniawski had 'worked valiantly for us over a long period of time without receiving any remuneration'.

In his assumed role as a secret international statesman, Czerniawski bombarded the Germans with unsolicited and unhelpful advice. 'Nobody here believes any more in a German victory,' he told them. 'As a Pole, can I suggest that neither is it in our interest nor in yours [that] the Russians be allowed to occupy Central Europe . . . I believe this is a good psychological moment for attempting to reach an agreement with the Anglo-Saxons, and I am inclined to think they may accept your military propositions.' The reply came back from Reile: 'Once again I thank you with all my heart for your excellent work. I have passed on all your political propositions, especially concerning your country, recommending them to accept them.' Still hungry for an Iron Cross, Astor longed to deploy Czerniawski on one final deception, and suggested parachuting him into France ahead of the retreating German forces. Once there, he would contact German intelligence and explain that he had been sent by the British 'to recruit and organise an intelligence service behind the lines' – and offer to work for Germany, again. He would then be 'in a position to receive the Germans' deception plans which might reveal their real intentions'. No other spy had made so many journeys back and forth between loyalty and betrayal: first as an agent in occupied Paris; then a double agent for the Germans; then a triple agent, working for the Allies once more; he now offered to go back to France, as a quadruple agent, while in reality a quintuple agent, still working for Britain.

By the terms of the deal with the Germans, Czerni-awski's family and former colleagues in the Interal-lié network would not be harmed if he played his part. When Paris was liber-ated, so were the hostages. Before leaving, the Germans left a final token of their faith. Beside the road out of Paris, Reile dug a hole, in which he buried a new radio transmitter and 50,000 French francs, in the expectation that if the

Roman Czerniawski (*right*) and Hugo Bleicher, the German intelligence officer who captured him, reunited in Paris in 1972.

indefatigable Agent Hubert arrived with the advancing Allied troops, he would wish to keep in touch – an act which hardly squares with Reile's later claim that he knew Czerniawski was a double agent. 'On Nationale 3 between Paris and Meaux there is a milestone which, according to the inscription upon it, is 2.3 km from Claye and 12.4 km from Meaux. The equipment is concealed 5 metres from this stone in a ditch under a mark on the grass, buried 10 cm deep.' The German retreat was too swift to put the Quintuple Cross plan into operation, and Czerniawski's parting gift from his German spymaster was forgotten. In the 1960s, Route Nationale 3 was widened, covering over the hiding place. Every day, thousands of motorists on the road from Paris to the German border pass over this buried memento to Agent Brutus.

After the war, Roman Czerniawski settled in Britain. Though he thought a 'Polish government set up by Moscow is a degree better than having no Polish government at all', he could never return to his homeland with a communist regime in power. He was secretly appointed OBE for his wartime role. He became a printer, settled in West London, amicably divorced Monique, remarried, divorced, married again. He adored cats, and in old age he liked to sit in his front room, watching James Bond films, with his cats. The cat population in the Czerniawski household eventually reached thirty-two. He never lost his heavy Polish accent, or his whole-souled Polish patriotism, and he intrigued to the end, spending his final years secretly working for the Solidarity movement. He died in 1985, aged seventy-five.

Mathilde Carré, once Czerniawski's partner in the Interallié network, was extradited to France in January 1949 after six years in British prisons, and charged with treason. The trial of 'The Cat' was a sensation. She sat wordless throughout, with a 'withdrawn air of detachment', as thirty-three witnesses came forward to denounce her for sleeping with the enemy. The prosecution summed up with an entry from her own diary from the night she first made love to Hugo Bleicher: 'What I wanted most was a good meal, a man, and, once more, Mozart's *Requiem*'. Mathilde was sentenced to death, later commuted to hard labour for life. In Rennes prison she suffered cat-filled 'nightmares which turned into hallucinations'.

She was finally released in 1954. A few months later she was approached by Bleicher, who had served time in prison and was now running a tobacconist in Württemberg. He asked her to write a book with him, a 'harmless literary collaboration', he called it. She had done enough collaborating with Bleicher, and wrote her own book, *I Was The Cat*, insisting that her crimes had been 'committed to achieve a noble, patriotic ideal'. Few believed her. She died in 1970, a recluse. Mathilde Carré was either treacherous, or just desperately unlucky. Like Czerniawski, she claimed she had only worked for the Germans in order to betray them. As her lawyer argued, 'at certain moments in the life of a spy, the double-cross is all part of the game'. Czerniawski felt a residual sympathy for his fellow spy, forced by war to make impossible choices in circumstances not of her making. Years later, he was still troubled by her fate. 'I don't know how I would have behaved,' he wrote. 'Do you?'

A month after D-Day, Lily Sergeyev divulged her last secret. Mary Sherer had turned up with a cake, and invited Lily to come for a walk. She was still fishing for the control sign, and as they walked down Piccadilly she asked Lily, for the last time, to reveal the arrangement she had made with Kliemann. She asked her not as an MI5 case officer, but as a friend. It was the nearest these two diametrically different women – one melodramatically French and the other so stolidly English – had come to intimacy.

Lily suddenly turned to her former case officer: 'OK, you win.'

On a piece of paper, she sketched out the system of dashes agreed with Kliemann to indicate when she was operating her wireless under British control.

'Is that all?'

Lily nodded.

Mary raced back to the office, pulled out the file for Agent Treasure, and extracted the wireless traffic, every message sent by Lily since her return from Lisbon. Sometimes Lily had put a dash in the original, sometimes in the repeated message, and sometimes in neither. But never in both. There was no double-dash. Lily had never gone through with her threat. MI5 had been sent into a completely needless tailspin by the fear that their D–Day plan had been scuppered by a hysterical woman in mourning for her dog. But by putting her British handlers through the mill, Lily felt she had evened up the score. 'I will be able to close my notebooks and forget,' she wrote in her diary. 'One forgets quickly. Maybe it's for the best.' Babs was avenged.

When peace came, Lily was soon reunited with her parents in Paris. 'My joy has no end,' she wrote. She then took a job with the US occupation forces in Germany, helping to administer vaccinations under the command of Major Bart Collings, a bluff former parachutist from the Midwest, who was most attentive to her. 'I've lost my solitary state,' she wrote. 'I'm no longer alone.' Her health improved and, for the first time in her life, she was completely happy. But Lily had not quite finished tormenting MI5.

In March 1946, Billy Luke warned Tar Robertson that Lily was planning to write a book about her wartime experiences: 'You may find your name appearing in a first-class spy thriller.'

Tar was aghast. 'I don't honestly think there is anything we can do with this wretched woman,' he told Gisela Ashley. 'She will always be a source of trouble to us, no matter what restrictions we put on her, short of imprisonment for life. I don't know if there is anything you can say which might appeal to her better nature, if she has one.'

He need not have worried. The book would not appear for another twenty years. Lily was simply doing what she had done before: driving the strait-laced British into a lather with a threat she would not carry out.

In 1947, Bart Collings and Lily Sergeyev married, and moved to Michigan. Theirs was a happy marriage, though childless, and tragically brief. Lily's illness returned, this time with a vengeance. She died of kidney failure in 1950. Determined, petulant and spirited, she had played a double-edged role in the Double Cross story; a mainstay of the deception, she had also planned to destroy it. The good folk of St Mary's Avenue, Detroit, had no inkling that Mrs Collings, the excitable Frenchwoman with many dogs who lived at number 17542, was really Agent Treasure, a spy of the highest value, whose life, in her own words, had been one of 'unbelievable reality'.

Juan Pujol maintained the façade, and the Germans loved him to the end: 'We have in your personality, your character, your valour, all those virtues that become a gentleman.' As the Third Reich disintegrated in a welter of blood and fury, Garbo exhorted his handlers to keep the Nazi faith. 'The noble struggle will be revived,' he told Kühlenthal. 'I only regret not being at your side.' The last act of the drama was the dismantling of a network that had never existed. Even the Welsh fascists were becoming disillusioned, Pujol reported: 'They cannot hope for anything from us.' Garbo's final wireless message was a wordy eulogy to the martyred Hitler: 'His deeds and the story of his sacrifice to save the world from the danger of anarchy which threatens us will last forever in the hearts of all men of goodwill,' he waffled. 'I am certain that the day will arrive in the not too distant future when the noble struggle will be revived.' On 8 May 1945, the Catalan watched the crowds celebrating in central London, and allowed himself a flush of private pride.

After the war, MI5 wondered whether to continue his espionage career, by 'selling' him to the Soviets; if recruited by Moscow, he might be able to deceive the KGB as he had once foxed the Abwehr. But Garbo knew when to leave the stage. He had extracted an estimated $350,000 from the Germans, and

Juan Pujol, MBE, outside Buckingham Palace, 1985

an Iron Cross. The British gave him £15,000, and an MBE. He divorced Aracelli, and settled in Venezuela. A lifelong lover of language and literature, he became a Spanish teacher for Shell Oil and opened a bookshop. At his urging, Tommy Harris spread a rumour that Pujol had died of malaria in Angola. Garbo slipped quietly and completely out of the limelight, settling in Zulia, on the shores of Lake Maracaibo. 'No one knew about my past. Nobody knew what I had done.' In 1984, he briefly emerged from the shadows, when the writer Nigel West found him and persuaded him to return to London for a formal recognition of his wartime achievements at Buckingham Palace. He then

disappeared back to Venezuela. He died in 1988, and is buried in
Choroní, by the sea. 'My main pride and satisfaction,' he wrote,
'has been the knowledge that I contributed to the reduction of
casualties among the tens of thousands of servicemen fighting to
hold the Normandy beachheads. Many, many more would have
perished had our plan failed.' Pujol was a warrior who fought to
save lives, not to take them, using words as his only weapons.

Elvira de la Fuente Chaudoir, the sexually venturesome,
boredom-prone gambler with the elegant fingernails, had proved
her worth: as the Third Reich collapsed, she was deployed to find
out which elements in the German hierarchy might sue for peace.
'Bronx is the most suitable of all B1A cases for a political role,'
wrote Astor. 'They will take the initiative in putting out definite
peace feelers through Bronx.' Elvira wrote a letter on 15 August
1944, offering her continued services to Germany, at a price.

> It is quite evident that you have lost the war [and] I am
> extremely worried that the advancing Allied armies may
> come into possession of my dossier which would provide
> evidence of my espionage activities. Will you please give
> me an assurance that all incriminating evidence will be
> destroyed? I am prepared to go on working, even after the
> war if you wish, provided that you continue to pay me . . .

The response was as keen as ever: 'Good work. Write quickly
and often.'

Elvira was instructed to go to Madrid, make contact with
German intelligence, and 'learn as much as possible about
German ideas on peace terms but not in any way attempt to act
as intermediary between the two powers'. The idea that Elvira
could conceivably have acted as an international go-between
would once have been regarded as ludicrous: the good-time girl
had come a long way.

Elvira flew to Madrid on 19 December 1944. 'I believe that
she will make a good job of it,' Astor wrote. 'She is likely to

be closely questioned about her telegram threatening Bordeaux. Bronx has never met Ormsby-Gore but I have attempted to give her a description of him and believe that she is now able to give a colourful account of the incident.' Before leaving she told Astor that 'if any mishap should befall her I should notify her friend Miss Monica Sheriffe'. With that, she set off, 'in cheerful heart'. But by now the German intelligence organisation in Madrid, once a byword for ruthless efficiency, had all but disintegrated. Elvira could not find a single German spy.

Back in London, she dispatched a furious letter of complaint to the Germans: 'Absolutely livid about the uselessness of the journey which was expensive and disagreeable. You let me down. I only made the journey because I was expecting a handsome bonus.' She received an abject apology, and a request to send word if she learned of another Allied invasion in Scandinavia or northern Germany. The suggested code was almost identical to the one she had used before D-Day. This time, the demand for £50 for her dentist would indicate Denmark, whereas a request for £100 would mean 'parachuting to the west of Berlin and landing in the German Bay'.

Here was fresh evidence that the earlier ruse had worked. 'It is difficult to believe that the Germans would have used this same code again,' Masterman observed, 'if they had been dissatisfied with its use by Bronx in May 1944.'

The Germans 'eagerly await her news and will probably believe any information she puts over', said Astor, and as the end drew near, she passed on news intended 'to lower the German will

Elvira Chaudoir, 1995

to resist', and encourage capitulation. 'Guerrillas will be treated without mercy,' she reported, citing her friends in the government. Agent Bronx was helping to shape post-war Germany. The debt-driven spy recruited as a gamble and picked up in a French casino had paid huge dividends. MI5 was delighted: 'Her long-term possibilities should not be overlooked.'

There would be no long-term career. The declaration of peace brought a simultaneous declaration from Elvira that she was retiring from espionage. She received a parting gift of £197. 'Words of gratitude and appreciation were freely expressed on both sides.' She moved to a small village in the South of France, having inherited the remains of her father's guano fortune. For the next half a century, she ran a gift shop in Beaulieu-sur-Mer on the Côte d'Azur. She avoided casinos, but ran short of money nonetheless. In 1995, Hugh Astor informed Stella Rimington, then Director General of MI5, that the former Agent Bronx was broke. In December 1995, Elvira received a cheque for £5,000, as 'a way of making the point that her wartime service is still remembered and appreciated'. Elvira died the following month at the age of eighty-five. To some, her later life may have seemed dull, but Elvira was never bored again. Of her role in the war, she remarked: 'I recall the adventure as the most wonderful and intense period of my life.'

With the coming of peace, Dusko Popov, the playboy spy, got married, became British, and was awarded a medal, marks of respectability that did nothing whatever to change his habits. 'I am getting fed up with my married friends criticising my immoral life,' he told Billy Luke, his first case officer, adding that his fiancée was a 'young and pretty French girl (just your type)'. He married Janine on 6 March 1946, in Megèves, France. Popov's bride was just eighteen, but 'apparently entering into this matrimonial adventure with her eyes open', MI5 noted sardonically. His application for citizenship was swiftly approved: 'I will try to do my best to be worthy of

my new country,' he told Tar Robertson. 'I am still at your
disposal whenever you think I might be useful.' A year later,
they met at the bar of the Ritz, where Tar handed Popov a
leather box containing an OBE, in recognition of his role 'in
deceiving the enemy prior to the Normandy invasion'. Tar
apologised for the unorthodox presentation ceremony, but the
setting could hardly have been more appropriate: an espionage
relationship that had started at the Savoy was brought to a
close at the Ritz.

The British secret services were still trying to disentangle
Popov's finances long after the war ended. 'We are making
arrangements as regards the receipts for his furniture,' wrote
Kim Philby in 1948, with infinite weariness. Popov's businesses
prospered, though never conventionally: one week Tarlair Ltd
was trading cholera serum to the Egyptian government, the next
Popov was importing Peugeot cars, selling rubber hosepipes to
the French and setting up a German textile industry. 'His activities have freewheeled far outside any MI5 commitment,' observed
Ian Wilson, who started acting as Popov's solicitor as soon as he
ceased to be his case officer. Popov purchased a castle overlooking

Nice. His marriage did not
last. In 1961, he met a blonde
eighteen-year-old Swedish
student named Jill Jonsson,
and married her the following
year. They moved into the
former summer palace of the
Bishop of Grasse. His finances
remained opaque, his tastes
extravagant, and his mysterious glamour undimmed.

Only in 1974, when the
truth about Britain's wartime
deceptions began to emerge,
did Popov reveal that he had

Dusko Popov, 1974

been Agent Tricycle. His book *Spy/Counterspy* was vigorously
written, entertaining, and partly invented. James Bond was
all the rage, and the book contained scenes straight from the
007 playbook – gorgeous women appearing naked in his hotel
bedroom, punch-ups with evil Nazis, the staking of thousands
of dollars on the turn of a card. Popov was a conscientious spy
who told his British case officers everything; none of these
episodes appears in the MI5 files. Popov's true story reads like
fiction, but like most spies, he could not resist making it up.
In the 1970s Popov and his brother Ivo, the former Agent
Dreadnought, opened a rejuvenation clinic in the Bahamas,
an appropriate last venture for a man who continued to live
life like a twenty-five-year-old. He died in 1981, at the age of
sixty-nine.

Most of the B1A team drifted back into civilian life. In 1948,
Tar Robertson retired to Worcestershire to look after sheep,
farming his flock as gently and diligently as he had tended
the Double Cross agents. John Masterman, soon 'Sir John,
OBE', became Provost of Worcester College, Oxford, then
Vice-Chancellor of that university. He played cricket, wrote
detective novels, sat on various worthy boards, and scandalised
some of his former colleagues in 1971 by publishing his account
of the Double Cross system in defiance of the Official Secrets
Act. Hugh Astor became Middle East Correspondent of *The
Times*, and covered the birth of an independent Israel, before
joining the newspaper's board in 1956. Billy Luke resumed his
business career, and in 1958 became Master of the Worshipful
Company of Makers of Playing Cards of the City of London.
Christopher Harmer returned to practising law. In memory of
his favourite double agent, the Harmers would occasionally
go to the Hyde Park Hotel bar and drink a cocktail made
from rum, orange juice and vermouth, called a Bronx. Mary
Sherer met Phyllis McKenzie, who had worked for British
intelligence in New York during the war, and the two women
became inseparable. They lived together for the rest of their

lives, 'perfect foils for each other'. Within MI5 they were assumed to be lesbians or, rather, Lesbians. Together they moved to Rome, and opened the Lion Bookshop on Via del Babuino near the Spanish Steps. 'Mary was a very fast runner and would think nothing of pursuing the rather numerous petty thieves that abounded in Rome during and after the war. She loved a challenge.' This formidable pair of English ladies, known as 'the Lionesses', spent their days surrounded by books and a large posse of dogs: Pekinese, French bulldogs and pugs, 'all of which Mary doted on'.

Flight Lieutenant Walker spent the rest of his days happily breeding pigeons. Gustav, the pigeon who brought back the first news of D-Day, was awarded the Dickin Medal, the animal equivalent of the Victoria Cross, to 'signalise its performance on D-Day', but died soon after the war when his breeder trod on him while mucking out his loft.

Tommy Harris settled in Spain after the war, where he painted, and gave memorable parties at which he told outrageous spy stories which few believed. He was killed in 1964 at the age of fifty-four after his car spun off a road in Majorca and crashed into a tree. Some saw the accident as sinister.

Guy Liddell remained in MI5, a continued fount of good humour and good sense. 'There is no doubt that the Russians are far better in the matter of espionage than any other country in the world,' he wrote prophetically in 1945. 'They will be a great source of trouble to us when the war is over.' When the Cambridge spies were finally exposed, Liddell would be caught up in the scandal, and even, unfairly, suspected of being a double agent himself.

Anthony Blunt left MI5 as soon as the war ended, and resumed his career as an academic. He was knighted, courted, feted and went on to become Professor of the History of Art at the University of London, Director of the Courtauld Institute of Art, and Surveyor of the Queen's Pictures. When he was finally outed as a spy in 1979 and publicly disgraced, he became a semi-recluse, taking refuge in 'whisky and concentrated work'. In a posthumously published memoir, Blunt wrote that spying for the Soviets had been 'the biggest mistake of my life'. Yet soon after his exposure as a double agent, he bumped into Tar Robertson, and told the former boss of B1A: 'It has given me great pleasure to have been able to pass the names of every MI5 officer to the Russians.'

Other players in the Double Cross team faded into obscurity. Wulf Schmidt, Agent Tate, became Harry Williamson, a British citizen, a photographer on the *Watford Observer*, a breeder of tropical fish and a 'respected judge at cage bird exhibitions around the country'. Paul Fidrmuc, Agent Ostro, invented spy reports for the Germans until the end of the war, and then vanished. He achieved immortality eleven years later when Graham Greene, who had seen reports on both Garbo and Ostro as a young MI6 officer, combined them as the inspiration for Wormold in *Our Man in Havana*, the spymaster with the imaginary network. Clifton James published a book in 1954 entitled *I Was Monty's Double*: he acted the part of himself in the film adaptation, and of Monty.

Emile Kliemann, Lily's case officer, was arrested by American troops in Louveciennes on 20 August 1944. He might easily have escaped with the rest of the German intelligence officers, but he was running late. The preceding weeks had been most unsettling for Kliemann: suspected of involvement in the July Plot (wrongly, he was far too idle for conspiracy), his flat had been searched by the Gestapo and he had then come under machine-gun fire from the Free French forces as he tried to flee the city. He surrendered with alacrity, and was imprisoned in Fresnes, where Czerniawski had once been held. Yvonne Delidaise and her brother Richard were arrested the same day.

Kliemann's American interrogators found him 'somewhat shifty; responds well to flattery; talking as much to save his own skin and that of his fiancée as anything else'. Quizzed about his intelligence work, Kliemann grew crafty, explaining that he had run a top-level woman agent in Britain codenamed 'Tramp', and was 'very proud and gratified at the results achieved'. Kliemann then played what he thought was his trump card, and suggested that Treasure should be run, with his help, as a double agent, entirely unaware that she had been one from the start. 'He has no idea,' wrote Liddell, 'that he himself is the sucker.'

Kliemann was released in May 1945. He returned to Austria, and his wife, taking with him memories of Yvonne, and a pigskin wallet from Dunhill's of London, inscribed to 'Octave . . . a souvenir from London'. In the 1960s, an over-excited newspaper article on German spies described Kliemann as having a 'sharp and ruthless brain'. The clipping was inserted into his MI5 file, with an eloquent, one-word comment alongside that description: 'Kliemann?!'

More than 5,000 people were arrested in the orgy of violence and score-settling that followed the July plot of 1944. A few days before the attempt to assassinate Hitler, Georg Hansen told his deputy, Wilhelm Kuebart, to stand by to 'arrest various Nazis on the day of the attempt'. The day after the bomb planted by Claus von Stauffenberg failed to kill the Führer, they were both arrested. Heinrich Müller, the Gestapo chief, orchestrated the bloody reprisals against anyone considered defeatist, disloyal or ideologically suspect. Hansen and Kuebart were soon joined in Lehrterstrasse prison by Alexis von Roenne, the anti-Nazi intelligence expert. Kuebart was interrogated as to why he had 'made difficulties' over surrendering Johnny Jebsen. His answers were dismissed as a 'tissue of lies'. Brought before the Volksgerichtshof, the People's Court, the prisoners were accused of conspiring with a 'small clique of cowardly officers to murder the Führer, to overthrow the National Socialist regime and conclude an unworthy peace pact with the enemy'.

Hansen was executed by hanging on 8 September 1944 at Plötzensee jail, Berlin. Von Roenne was executed next, without ever explaining whether his falsification of the Allied Order of Battle had been a deliberate act of sabotage. Canaris, the former Abwehr chief, was kept alive by Himmler as a possible pawn for use in negotiating with the British; but finally he, too, was killed in Flossenbürg concentration camp in April 1945, along with his deputy Hans Oster, two weeks before the camp was liberated. Kuebart, surprisingly, survived. He had already written farewell letters, after his lawyer said 'he considered the case already lost from the intrinsic gravity of the charge', when he learned he had been acquitted for lack of evidence. He was dishonourably discharged from the German army, and spent the remainder of the war working on a farm.

'Gestapo' Müller was last seen in the Führerbunker the day before Hitler's suicide. 'Defend Berlin to the last man, the last bullet,' he ordered, and then disobeyed himself by vanishing. His fate remains a mystery. Documents discovered in 2001 appeared to indicate that he was still in American custody at the end of 1945. Over the years, Müller was variously 'sighted' in East Germany, Czechoslovakia, Switzerland, Brazil, Argentina, Paraguay, Cairo, Damascus, Moscow, Washington DC and New Hampshire.

Aloys Schreiber, Jebsen's kidnapper, went back to teaching the law. Ludovico von Karsthoff (or Kremer von Auenrode, to restore his real name), the pleasure-loving Lisbon Abwehr chief, fell into the hands of the Soviets, and is believed to have been executed. Oscar Reile returned to Germany and wrote no fewer than three academic works on the theory and practice of intelligence, in one of which he claimed, not quite credibly, that he had always suspected that Roman Czerniawski was a double agent. The spy-catcher Hugo Bleicher wrote a substantially misleading autobiography, *Colonel Henri's Story*, and died in 1982. Karl-Erich Kühlenthal became a wealthy and respected clothing retailer in Koblenz. He died in 1975, unaware of how thoroughly he had been duped.

Hans Brandes, the betrayer of Johnny Jebsen, was arrested

in Portugal, and held in a civilian internment camp in the American-occupied zone in Germany. He convinced his captors that he was 'a poor, half-Jewish businessman and as a result was cleared, used as a trustee and eventually released'. MI5 was enraged to find Brandes had slipped through the net, describing his interrogation as 'pure whitewash' and his release as a 'grave miscarriage of justice'. Tar Robertson launched a manhunt: 'Brandes was mixed up with the kidnapping of Johnny. It would be a good idea to lay hands on him.' But as time passed, the memory of his perfidy faded. By 1954, he was back in the family firm, as managing director of Fritz Werner Machine Tools. On 15 April 1971, Hans Brandes was found in his car on a dirt road in Schäftlarn, near Munich, dead from poisoning.

Johnny Jebsen was dragged into the Oranienberg sector of Sachsenhausen concentration camp in July 1944, a month after D-Day. Skeletally thin, he could hardly walk and 'his hair had fallen out in patches'. The camp, thirty miles north of Berlin, was a place of unimaginable horror. More than 30,000 political prisoners, homosexuals, gypsies and Jews died there during the course of the war from exhaustion, disease, malnutrition, execution, or under brutal medical experimentation.

Petra Vermehren, the journalist arrested after her son defected in Istanbul, was interned at Sachsenhausen and learned of Jebsen's arrival through the camp barber. She found out which cell he was in, and threw stones at the window 'until she attracted his attention'. Jebsen was overjoyed to see his old friend. In a whisper, 'he told her that the Gestapo had abducted him because he had divulged information to the British'. He had been arrested on a charge of high treason, he said, but because he had refused to talk, he was now under investigation for *Devisen Verbrechen*, the foreign currency crime of exchanging forged British £5 notes. Jebsen did not know it, but in Sachsenhausen, Himmler had employed a team of 140 imprisoned Jewish photographers, lithographers and photoengravers to churn out forged British and American currency. His 'crime' had been started in this prison camp, by the very people accusing him.

For the next two months, Jebsen lay on his bunk, his ribs too badly broken to stand. Completely cut off from the outside world, he was unaware that in Frankfurt, his wife Lore was expecting his child. Slowly, despite the starvation rations and freezing cold, his strength started to return, and with it, hope. Jebsen began to imagine ways to escape. A number of British prisoners were held at Sachsenhausen, including Lieutenant Commander Mike Cumberlege, a piratical Royal Navy officer with a gold earring, and Lieutenant Colonel John Churchill, widely known as 'Mad Jack', a commando who fought armed with a claymore, longbow and bagpipes. Cumberlege had been captured in 1943 while attempting to blow up the Corinth canal. Churchill had led an ill-fated commando attack on the German-held island of Brač in Yugoslavia in 1944: surrounded with six of his men, he played *Will Ye No Come Back Again* on the bagpipes until a mortar shell landed, killing everyone but him, and he was captured. These were men, as the writer Saki put it, 'who wolves have sniffed at'. Jebsen, a man who would have run a mile from a wolf, struck up an unlikely friendship with them both.

In September 1944, Jack Churchill crawled through an abandoned drain under the camp wire, and set off on foot for the Baltic coast. He was recaptured, transferred to a camp in the Tyrol under SS guard, and then set free by a German army captain after the SS moved out. He walked ninety-three miles into Italy, and linked up with an American armoured unit. When Churchill finally got back to Britain, he produced a letter written by Mike Cumberlege to his wife. The letter contained a message, in code, which read: 'JOHNNY JEBSEN HUN HELD HIGH TREASON CAN D REPEAT D POPOFF HELP URGENT FO KNOW OF JJ ALL CHARGES AGAINST

US ARE BASELESS.' The Foreign Office had never heard of Johnny Jebsen, and to make matters worse, as the message was passed around, his name was garbled. 'I can make little of this. We appear to have no record of any Johnny Jebsen or Debsen,' wrote one official.

In February 1945, a Gestapo escort arrived from Berlin with orders to collect Jebsen and Heinz Moldenhauer. Petra Vermehren saw the two men leave under guard. On 12 April, Moldenhauer was returned to the camp alone. He told Vermehren that he was surprised not to find Jebsen back in Sachsenhausen already. The Red Army was now closing in. A week later, the SS ordered 33,000 inmates to begin the forced march northeast. Moldenhauer was among the thousands killed on the way. Mike Cumberlege had already been transferred to Flossenbürg camp, where he was executed, five days before it was liberated. Petra Vermehren was one of 1,400 women still in Sachsenhausen when the camp was liberated on 30 April. She returned to Hamburg, and resumed her writing career.

Johnny Jebsen had vanished. Ian Wilson, Artist's one-time case officer, set out to find him. Wilson was a man of deep, if well-hidden, feelings and granite loyalty. It was, he said, 'my personal wish to help those who helped us', and none had been more helpful than Jebsen. 'I do feel that it is up to this office to use all possible diligence in finding out exactly what happened.'

Wilson owed Jebsen a debt and, with the single-mindedness that was his trademark, he meant to discharge it. Recalling that Jebsen had spoken about meeting Marie von Gronau in a café in Flensburg three days after the end of the war, in May 1945 he wrote to the British intelligence officer in that part of Germany, and asked him to be ready in case Jebsen turned up.

My old friend Johnny Jebsen stated long ago that when the Allies defeated Germany he would hope to have made his way to Flensburg in Schleswig Holstein. It is just possible that he may have been able to get himself to SH, in which case I have little doubt that he will get in touch with British intelligence. Should he come to your notice it might be as well to have him sent to this country, purely for his own cover and protection. He knows my own name which will serve as a password. I hope he has got the KVK [War Merit Cross] First Class which he said he was going to give me.

Jebsen did not appear. Recalling the 'assurance we gave Johnny that if anything happened to him we would look after the welfare of his wife', Wilson went looking for Lore Jebsen, who had by now given birth to their son. With the help of Popov, he found her in the Russian sector of Berlin, arranged for her to move to the British zone, helped her get a job back on the stage, lobbied MI5 to request the German government for a state pension, and found a lawyer to untangle Jebsen's financial affairs. 'She will be able to live in comfort,' he wrote. John Marriott could not understand why his colleague was going to such lengths: 'We have no financial and very little moral responsibility for Mrs Jebsen,' he wrote. 'Wilson is, as you know, obstinate, pertinacious and kind-hearted and he feels a great sense of responsibility.' He shared that responsibility with Popov, who, heartsick at the disappearance of his friend, had launched his own hunt for Jebsen and those who had abducted him. He travelled to Switzerland and Germany, interviewing anyone who might know of his fate.

Wilson and Popov tracked down Jebsen's business associates, his lovers and his secretary Mabel Harbottle. 'None of these people had any definite information about what had happened to Artist.' One of Jebsen's business partners, a Yugoslavian named Glusevic, said the Gestapo had quizzed him about Jebsen, and formed the impression they 'had not extracted full information about anything from Artist'. Wilson went hunting for the German officers, notably chief investigator Obergeheimrat Quitting, 'who would be most likely to know of Artist's ultimate fate'. Popov was keen for vengeance: 'If you have luck and find the man, keep him alive until I come.' Quitting never resurfaced.

The NKVD, it seemed, was also on the trail of Jebsen. Soviet intelligence officers had interrogated Popov's family in Yugoslavia before the war's end, and seemed to 'know everything about Jebsen, including his visits to Lisbon'. Wilson wondered 'how the NKVD could be aware of Jebsen's movements?' – the answer of course was Anthony Blunt.

Wilson refused to lose hope. 'We do not know whether or not Artist is still alive, but if he is, he may yet prove to be a valuable agent.' He went back to work at McKenna & Co. Solicitors, but continued the search. Others came to the conclusion that Jebsen must be dead. Tar Robertson had shared Wilson's determination to find out 'what actually happened to him in the end, as Johnny did some extremely good work on our behalf', but reluctantly decided he must have been transferred to Mauthausen concentration camp, 'which was the normal place for internees to be sent who were to be killed'. Popov eventually came to believe that his friend had been 'shot while trying to escape'. On 17 February 1950, a court in Berlin formally pronounced Johnny Jebsen dead.

Wilson was not convinced, and nor was Lore. 'She refuses to believe he is dead,' wrote Wilson. Petra Vermehren, 'the last person to see him alive', was also 'emphatic that he did not die' in Sachsenhausen. A rumour persisted that Jebsen 'was liberated by the Russians only to be rearrested and consigned to some camp in Russia'. That might explain the interest of the Soviet NKVD. A strange report from MI6, citing an American source in Lisbon, reported that 'Johnny Jebson [sic] has left for England.' In a postwar interrogation, Walter Schellenberg, the Nazi intelligence chief, stated categorically: 'Jebsen has not been killed.'

The mystery lingered, but Wilson's investigations had proved one thing beyond doubt: Jebsen had 'kept the faith'; he had never revealed anything to his captors about the Double Cross plot, either before D-Day, or after it. 'There is nothing to indicate that whatever may have happened to him he was forced to disclose facts which we wanted kept secret.' Jebsen had taken his secret with him to the grave, or wherever else he had vanished to.

Perhaps Jebsen was caught up in the last murderous spasms of the Nazi regime, as Tar believed, killed and tossed into some unmarked mass grave, like so many others. Or perhaps he made good his escape. In the chaos and confusion of those final days, it was easy to disappear. Heinrich Müller vanished, as did Quitting and other Nazis. So did Juan Pujol and Paul Fidrmuc, Agents Garbo and Ostro. Roger Michael, von Roenne's assistant who may have spied for all sides, or none, reached the end of the war, and then evaporated. Johnny Jebsen had the ingenuity, the means and the motive to disappear. His funds had seemed, to his colleagues, 'inexhaustible', and he was an acknowledged expert in bribery. He had many debts to call in, many an underworld contact to shield him, and any number of places he could hide. He had bank accounts in Paris, London, Berlin, San Francisco, Dubrovnik and Shanghai. He had every reason not to stay in Germany to discuss his questionable business activities with the authorities, and every motive to want to start afresh, somewhere else, as someone else. Ian Wilson died in 1978, still wondering what had happened to his lost spy.

The Double Cross double agents spied for adventure and gain, out of patriotism, greed and personal conviction. They made an eccentric, infuriating, courageous and astonishingly successful team. And the most important of them has disappeared from history, just as he vanished from the world, at the age of twenty-seven: Johnny Jebsen, former international playboy turned 'businessman'; a man of cynicism, humour, deep intellect and frailty; the chain-smoking Anglophile who took up spying in order not to fight. He was unable to resist worldly temptations, but he resisted his Gestapo torturers to the end. Like many ordinary, flawed people, he did not know his own courage, until war revealed it. Jebsen might easily have turned history in a disastrous direction to save his own skin, and he chose not to. Agent Artist was not a conventional D-Day hero, but he was a hero nonetheless.

Johnny Jebsen

Notes

Citations
Citations marked KV refer to the Security Service files, CAB to Cabinet Office files and FO to Foreign Office files at the National Archives (TNA), Kew.

Epigraphs
vii 'Tangle within tangle': Winston Churchill, *Thoughts and Adventures* (London, 1991), p. 55.

vii 'The enemy must not': Sun Tzu, *The Art of War*, Chapter VII.

Preface
2 'It may well be the': Field Marshal Lord Alanbrooke, *War Diaries* 1939–1945, (London 2001), p. 554.

3 'In wartime, the truth': 4th Eureka meeting, 30 November 1943, quoted in Thaddeus Holt, *The Deceivers: Allied Military Deception in the Second World War* (London, 2004), p. 505.

3 'This is what we call': ibid.

3 'utterly impossible to disguise': J. C. Masterman, *The Double Cross System in the War 1939–1945* (London, 1972), p. 150.

3 It is here that the': Fuhrer Directive No. 51, 3 November 1943, cited in Joshua Levine, *Operation Fortitude: The Story of the Spy Operation that Saved D-Day* (London, 2011), p. 199.

Chapter 1: Raw Recruits
7 'We both had some intellectual': Dusko Popov, *Spy/Counterspy* (New York, 1974), p. 5.

7 'He smiles freely, showing': KV 2/846.

7 'A well-flattened': ibid.

8 'loose, sensual mouth': ibid.

8 'His coldness, aloofness': Popov, *Spy/Counterspy*, p. 6.

8 'He had much warmth too': ibid.

8 'deliberately stir up situations': ibid.

8 'not thinking my looks would be': ibid., p. 7.

9 'Some of my love of my country': ibid.

9 'like a young Anthony Eden': ibid.

9 'pro-Nazi student intelligentsia': ibid.

9 'Under that mask of a snob': ibid.

9 'Need to meet you urgently': ibid., p. 2.

10 'two girls from the chorus': ibid., p. 16.

10 'sharp intelligence, cynicism': ibid., p. 14.

10 'ordered his whiskies double, neat': ibid.

10 'because it saved him from': KV 2/845.

10 'a wangle by Canaris': KV 2/856.

10 'time travelling throughout Europe': KV 2/859.

10 'Hitler is the undisputed master': Popov, *Spy/Counterspy*, p. 23.

11 'Would you dine with a friend': ibid.
11 'No country can resist': ibid., p. 24.
11 'We have many agents': ibid.
11 'General. Political': ibid.
11 'a little idea of my own': ibid.
11 'our sole source of information': KV 2/72.
12 'His loyalty is entirely to his own': ibid.
12 'a man who lives and thinks': ibid.
12 'based on the highest ideals': Roman Garby-Czerniawski, *The Big Network* (London, 1961), p. 14.
13 'Every signpost': ibid., p. 21.
13 'vision': ibid., p. 22.
13 'small cells of resistance': ibid.
13 'She was small': ibid., p. 43.
13 'Thin and muscular': Lily Mathilde Carré, *I Was the Cat* (London, 1959), p. 69.
.14 'in an appalling French': ibid., p. 68.
14 'under the eyes of an enormous': ibid., p. 66.
14 'Instead of throwing myself': ibid., p. 67.
14 'Every time he spoke': ibid., p. 70.
14 'A great bond of friendship': ibid., p. 69.
14 'he could count on her': Garby-Czerniawski, *The Big Network*, p. 47.
15 'you walk so quietly': ibid., p. 49.
15 'And I can scratch': ibid.
15 'It will be inter-Allied': ibid., p. 56.
15 'who had received a': Carré, *I Was the Cat*, p. 86.
15 'In her black fur coat': Garby-Czerniawski, *The Big Network*, p. 79.
15 'To defeat the enemy': ibid., p. 124.
16 'a tall, thin Pole': Carré, *I Was the Cat*, p. 81.
16 '*Remplacez le couvercle*': Garby-Czerniawski, *The Big Network*, p. 77.
16 'Big Network composed': ibid., p. 83.
17 'packed in such a way': ibid., p. 125.
17 'RE: GOERING TRAIN': ibid., p. 144.
17 'a typical little provincial': Carré, *I Was the Cat*, p. 98.
17 'no question of any jealousy': Garby-Czerniawski, *The Big Network*, p. 120.
17 'strange woman, idealistic': ibid., p. 58.
17 '*C'est la vie*': ibid., p. 180.
17 'You've kept us all busy': ibid., p. 188.
17 'the head of some business': ibid., p. 187.
17 'We are perfect partners': ibid., p. 194.
17 'I was petrified by the': ibid., p. 205.
18 'Subconsciously I felt': ibid.
18 'exceedingly dull': KV 2/2098.
18 'she had nothing in common': ibid.
19 'an utter shit, corrupt': Cited in Anthony Read & David Fisher, *Colonel Z: The Secret Life of a Master of Spies* (London, 1985), p. 361.
20 'I realised he must have': Nigel West, 'High Society Spy', *Mail on Sunday*, 7 May 1995.
20 'Attractive in appearance': KV 2/2098.
20 'tastes appear to be in the direction': ibid.
20 'hilarious parties': ibid.
20 'rowdy behaviour, singing': ibid.
20 'favours the companionship': ibid.

21 'apparently innocuous letters': West, 'High Society Spy'.
21 'Between the lines': ibid.
21 'She is very intelligent': KV 2/2098.
21 'she was being taught': ibid.
21 'she must abstain from': ibid.
22 'I must do something': Nigel West and Juan Pujol García, *Operation Garbo* (London, 2011), p. 48.
22 'a psychopath': ibid.
22 'I wanted to work for them': ibid., p. 49.
22 'My plans were fairly': ibid., p. 49.
22 'extremely busy': ibid.
22 'I was fascinated by the origin': ibid., p. 29.
22 'The pen is mightier': ibid.
22 'rant away as befitted': ibid., p. 50.
23 'He should be careful': Mark Seaman, Introduction to Tomás Harris, *Garbo: The Spy Who Saved D-Day* (London, 2004), p. 50.
24 'There are men here': ibid., p. 58.
25 'did not particularly like Germans': Lily Sergueiev, *Secret Service Rendered: An Agent in the Espionage Duel Preceding the Invasion of France* (London, 1968), p. 10.
26 'promised to obtain for her': José António Barreiros, *Nathalie Sergueiew: Uma Agente Dupla em Lisboa* (Lisbon, 2006), p. 34.
26 'let the French down badly': KV 2/464.
27 'It might be quite easy': Barreiros, *Nathalie Sergueiew*, p. 56.
27 'I am interested': Sergueiev, *Secret Service Rendered*, p. 32.
27 '*Why* do you want to work': ibid., p. 33.
27 'Major, you are an intelligent': ibid.
27 'I will make contact': ibid.
27 'Babs lifts up his shaggy': ibid., p. 15.
27 'I take Babs on my knees': ibid., p. 56.

Chapter 2: A Bit of an Enigma
28 'to get an easy living': KV 2/853.
28 'an awful crook': KV 2/859.
28 'Be a good thing for you': Dusko Popov, *Spy/Counterspy* (New York, 1974), p. 21.
28 'Continue your conversation': ibid., p. 29.
29 'insignificant letter in': KV 2/845.
29 'a young girl, about twenty-two': ibid.
29 'Your spymaster will be Major': Popov, *Spy/Counterspy*, p. 45.
29 'Who were Churchill's enemies': ibid., p. 31.
29 'We are now both': KV 2/845.
30 'strongly pro-British': ibid.
30 'British at heart': ibid.
30 'a bit of an enigma': ibid.
30 'What is Canaris like': ibid., p. 18.
30 'A sensitive man': ibid.
31 'There was a curious ambiguity': ibid., p. 45.
31 'blackish hair on his hands': KV 2/847.
31 'I have been instructed to': Popov, *Spy/Counterspy*, p. 47.
31 'He was tall and dark': KV 2/847.
32 'Popov, hello': Popov, *Spy/Counterspy*, p. 53.
32 'Let's get acquainted': ibid.

32 'many agents in England': Popov, *Spy/Counterspy*, p. 24.
32 'excellent': ibid.
33 Fifth Column Neurosis': KV 4/186, Diaries of Guy Liddell, 15 March 1940.
33 'the gentlemen who are': FO, TNA INF 1/264-8.
34 'junk': Liddell Diaries, 30 March 1941.
34 'a high proportion': KV 4/8, Robin 'Tin-eye' Stephens, Report on the Operations of Camp 020.
35 'You have forfeited your life': Cited in Emily Wilson, 'The War in the Dark: The Security Service and the Abwehr 1940–1944', PhD Thesis (Cambridge, 2003), p. 63.
36 'an almost suicidal appetite': Alistair Robertson, correspondence with the author.
36 'a perfect officer type': Thaddeus Holt, *The Deceivers: Allied Military Deception in the Second World War* (London, 2004), p. 131.
36 'friendly eyes and an assertive': Miranda Carter, *Anthony Blunt: His Lives* (London, 2001), p. 284.
36 'less than promising': Alastair Robertson, correspondence with the author.
36 'immensely personable': Christopher Harmer, address at Memorial Service for Tar Robertson, 17 October 1994.
36 'with a charm that could melt': ibid.
36 'unmistakable twinkle': Peter Stormonth Darling, address at Memorial Service for Tar Robertson.
36 'delightful chuckle': ibid.
36 'by and large pretty stupid': Christopher Andrew, *Secret Service: The Making of the British Intelligence Community* (London, 1985), p. 645.
36 'real genius': Hugh Trevor-Roper, cited in Wilson, 'The War in the Dark', p. 67.
37 'shifty look': KV 2/448.
37 'stupid little man': Joshua Levine, *Operation Fortitude: The Story of the Spy Operation that Saved D-Day* (London, 2011), p. 45.
37 'work on logical lines': ibid.
37 'saved us from absolute': Christopher Andrew, *The Defence of the Realm: The Authorised History of MI5* (London, 2009), p. 249.
38 'fanatical Nazi': Robin 'Tin-eye' Stephens, *Camp 020: MI5 and the Nazi Spies*, introduction by Oliver Hoare (London, 2000), p. 138.
39 'he had helped the man': KV 2/60.
39 'The double agent is a tricky': J. C. Masterman, *The Double Cross System in the War 1939–1945* (London, 1972), p. 52.
39 'blow our whole show': Andrew, *Defence of the Realm*, p. 258.
39 'they will be liquidated': ibid.
40 'I have a strong feeling': KV 2/845.
40 'absolutely obsessed with': ibid.
40 'It will be necessary': ibid.
40 'Skoot left an exceedingly': ibid.
41 'was obviously pleased': ibid.
41 'He enjoyed himself thoroughly': ibid.
41 'both viewing things': ibid.
41 'I much enjoyed': ibid.
42 'definitely members of the party': ibid.
42 'I found him a most charming': ibid.
42 'Giraffe's case died chiefly': Masterman, *The Double Cross System*, p. 55.
43 'The Club': Wilson, 'The War in the Dark', p. 138.
43 'Running a team of double': Masterman, *The Double Cross System*, p. 91.

43 'a thoroughly well-trained': ibid.
43 'required a good deal': ibid.
43 'initiated into the mysteries': See Oliver Locker-Lampson, 'Adolf Hitler As I Know Him', *Daily Mirror*, 30 September 1930.
43 'withdrawal of the use': ibid.
43 'bigger and harder ball': ibid.
43 'ready to take the field': Masterman, *The Double Cross System*, p. 91.
44 'The prime difficulty': ibid.
44 'We have in him a new agent': KV 2/845.

Chapter 3: Roman and the Cat

45 'I wonder if anybody': Roman Garby-Czerniawski, *The Big Network* (London, 1961), p. 218.
45 'a complete picture': ibid., p. 10.
45 'Many Happy Returns': ibid., p. 233.
45 'AGAINST THE GERMANS': ibid.
46 'overworked and was obviously': ibid.
46 'Why did you ask': ibid., p. 238.
46 'I must be tired': ibid., p. 237.
46 'The light was switched': ibid., p. 240.
46 'intelligent face': ibid., p. 142.
46 'If only someone': ibid., p. 245.
46 'It was a great gamble': Lily Mathilde Carré, *I Was the Cat* (London, 1960), p. 104.
46 'an ordinary denunciation': KV 2/72.
47 'wide boy': Carré, *I Was the Cat*, p. 90.
47 'I was like an animal': ibid., p. 107.
47 'You have committed enough': ibid.
47 'If you double-cross': ibid.
47 'Great Britain makes': ibid.
47 'inhumanely': ibid. p. 116.
47 'not only with handcuffs': ibid.
47 'the greatest act of cowardice': ibid., p. 115.
47 'purely animal': ibid.
47 'winning Bleicher's confidence': ibid., p. 126.
47 'You must behave': ibid., p. 112.
48 'You see how easy it is': ibid.
48 a strangely haunted': ibid., p. 110.
48 'one by one': ibid., p. 117.
48 'A few men proved': KV 2/72.
48 'We have decided': Carré, *I Was the Cat*, p. 119.
48 'I had felt the icy': ibid., p. 115.
49 'started to laugh contentedly': Garby-Czerniawski, *The Big Network*, p. 243.
49 'treated severely': KV 2/72.
49 'the completeness': ibid.
49 'intelligent and quick-witted': ibid.
49 'always boasting': ibid.
49 'Also a man of great': ibid.
49 'terrified eyes': Garby-Czerniawski, *The Big Network*, p. 242.
49 'given everything away': KV 2/72.
49 'the Germans felt': ibid.
49 'might exploit this': ibid.
50 'It is possible she': ibid.

50 'When working in this': ibid.
50 'by force': ibid.
50 'a firing squad did': ibid.
50 'If the German nation': ibid.
50 'thick grey hair': ibid.
51 'manicured': ibid.
51 'We do not deny': ibid.
51 'You have tied': ibid.
51 'By joining us': ibid.
51 'Whatever collaboration Poland': ibid.
51 'excellent knowledge': ibid.
51 'raise the Polish nation': ibid.
51 'war of nerves': ibid.
51 'as though I had really': ibid.
51 'In my opinion': ibid.
52 'The Germans were': ibid.
52 'be working for the': ibid.
52 'he would never under': ibid.
52 'The future of Poland': ibid.
52 'I am prepared': ibid.
52 'preparations for': ibid.
52 'do for Germany': ibid.
52 'I will group around': ibid.
52 'the moment that': ibid.
52 'That the agents': ibid.
52 'an extremely odd': Oscar Reile, *Geheime West Front* (Munich, 1962), p. 214.
52 'in unusually polite': KV 2/72.
53 'highly appreciative': ibid.
53 'I told them': ibid.
53 'Your companions': ibid.
53 'You know yourself': ibid.
53 'If I work for you': ibid.
53 'Should I fail': ibid.
53 'I knew that the fate': ibid.
53 'like an intelligent boxer': ibid.
54 'enable him to go': ibid.
54 'The prison would': ibid.
54 'The English knew': Reile, *Geheime West Front*, p. 214.
54 'If the enemy attempted': ibid.
54 'fantastic': ibid.

Chapter 4: Coat Trailing
55 'cosmopolitan cover': Nigel West, 'High Society Spy', *Mail on Sunday*, 7 May 1995.
55 'small class of': KV 2/2098.
55 'People who get all': ibid.
55 'altogether more agreeable': West, 'High Society Spy'.
55 'I felt I was doing': ibid.
56 'obviously rolling': KV 2/2098.
56 'very tall' : ibid.
56 'The German seemed': ibid.
56 'He was young': ibid.

56 'I'll introduce you': ibid.
56 'He is a secret agent': ibid.
56 'been recruited personally': ibid.
56 'one of the most expensive': ibid.
56 'graceful walk': ibid.
56 'obviously a gentleman': ibid.
56 'inferiority complex': ibid.
56 'spotted as a German': ibid.
56 'seemed to want': ibid.
56 'he laughed': ibid.
57 'pleasant fellow': ibid.
57 'enjoyed everything': ibid.
57 'The war was very silly': ibid.
57 'Why are you going' to 'How?': ibid.
57 'After the war': ibid.
57 'rather vague': ibid.
57 'You will have': ibid.
58 'to start with': ibid.
58 'marvellous trick': ibid.
58 'We just want facts': ibid.
58 'This is infinitely': ibid.
58 'He looked around': ibid.
58 'The Germans are': ibid.
58 'I always act on': ibid.
58 'I felt rather sorry': ibid.
59 'You must never': ibid.
59 'I have no desire': ibid.
59 'a nice girl but without': KV 2/464.
59 'pretty but rather fat': ibid.
59 'looked a little like': Lily Sergueiev, *Secret Service Rendered: An Agent in the Espionage Duel Preceding the Invasion of France* (London, 1968), p. 24.
60 'ordinary writing paper': KV 2/464.
60 'This has been dragging': Sergueiev, *Secret Service Rendered*, p. 53.
60 'I am sick of it': ibid.
60 'You shall not continue': ibid.
60 'It is the first time': ibid.
61 'serve the Allied': ibid., p. 53.
61 'He could recognise you': ibid.
61 'I have confidence': ibid., p. 53.
61 'I wave a handkerchief': ibid., p. 73.

Chapter 5: The Club

62 'scrofulous Nazi': Joshua Levine, *Operation Fortitude: The Story of the Spy Operation that Saved D-Day* (London, 2011), p. 125.
62 'manifestly unemployable': Robin 'Tin-eye' Stephens, *Camp 020: MI5 and the Nazi Spies*, introduction by Oliver Hoare (London, 2000), p. 156.
62 'He died at': ibid.
63 'newfound loyalty': Levine, *Operation Fortitude*, p. 88.
63 'a pearl among agents': J. C. Masterman, *The Double Cross System in the War 1939–1945* (London, 1972), p. 53.
64 'I cannot help regarding': KV 2/845.
64 'not very impressed': ibid.
64 'blind confidence': ibid.

64 'You'll soon want': Dusko Popov, *Spy/Counterspy* (New York, 1974), p. 95.

64 'expected much from': KV 2/845.

64 'London is rather': ibid.

65 'hinted that a little': ibid.

65 'suggestions as to possible': ibid.

65 'a woman purely': ibid.

65 'I won't be able': ibid.

66 'Complexion depends': ibid.

66 'typical Scottish scenery': ibid.

66 'filled with jovial': ibid.

66 'There was a law': Popov, *Spy/Counterspy*, p. 66.

66 'he made no effort': KV 2/845.

66 'He did not think it would': ibid.

66 'especially if he could': ibid.

66 'It may be desirable': ibid.

66 'He is quite definitely': ibid.

67 'Clever, versatile and firm': ibid.

67 'He is fond of the society': ibid.

67 'Skoot is an ingenious': ibid.

67 'he hates them all': ibid.

68 'link with people': ibid.

68 'in a position': ibid.

68 'They propose to buy': KV 2/860.

68 'the answers we had': KV 2/845.

68 'slight moral scruples': ibid.

68 'The strictest moral': ibid.

68 'that the work': ibid.

68 'It would be difficult': ibid.

68 'somewhat tired': ibid.

68 'an expensive evening': ibid.

68 'a small automatic': ibid.

68 'We could do nothing': ibid.

68 'a slightly rolling': ibid.

69 'A case officer should': Masterman, *The Double Cross System*, p. 70.

69 'command the best talent': Emily Wilson, 'The War in the Dark: The Security Service and the Abwehr 1940–1944', PhD Thesis (Cambridge, 2003), p. 96.

70 'The running and control': Masterman, *The Double Cross System*, p. 15.

70 'the whole-time service': ibid.

70 'the collector of facts': Peggy Harmer, cited in Emily Wilson, 'The War in the Dark', p. 127.

71 'overgrown schoolboys': Christopher Harmer to Hugh Astor, 28 October 1992, Collection of Robert Astor.

71 'casual agent': Christopher Andrew, *The Defence of the Realm: The Authorised History of MI5* (London, 2009), p. 242.

71 'real understanding': KV 2/1067.

72 'Thank God for Tar': Christopher Harmer to Hugh Astor, 28 October 1992, Collection of Robert Astor.

72 'born leader': J. C. Masterman, *On the Chariot Wheel: An Autobiography* (Oxford, 1975), p. 219.

72 'gifted with independent': ibid.

72 'In this game one never': KV 4/70.

72 'in an obviously': Masterman, *The Double Cross System,* p. 101.
73 'since he always does': Miranda Carter, *Anthony Blunt: His Lives* (London, 2001), p. 273.
73 'that's what Tiggers': ibid.
73 'He was a very nice': Andrew, *Defence of the Realm*, p. 270.
74 'I couldn't stick the man': Carter, *Blunt*, p. 284.
74 'Tony is a thorough': Andrew, *Defence of the Realm*, p. 272.
74 'He tries to fulfil': ibid.

Chapter 6: Garbo Takes the Stage
76 'Who was this Arabel': Nigel West with Juan Pujol García, *Operation Garbo,* (London, 2011), p. 88.
77 'drunken orgies': Christopher Andrew, *The Defence of the Realm: The Authorised History of MI5* (London, 2009), p. 254.
77 '87 shillings and 10 pence': Tomás Harris, *Garbo: The Spy Who Saved D-Day* (London, 2004), p. 59.
77 'very wild messages': Joshua Levine, *Operation Fortitude: The Story of the Spy Operation that Saved D-Day* (London, 2011), p.160.
78 'I do not see why': Guy Liddell, *The Guy Liddell Diaries, 1939–1945*, ed. Nigel West (London, 2005), 26 March 1942.
78 'The whole thing': ibid.
78 'a miracle that he': Harris, *Garbo: The Spy Who Saved D-Day*, p. 77.
78 'inexhaustibly fertile': ibid., p. 34.
79 'With fierce black': Sefton Delmer, *The Counterfeit Spy* (London, 1973), p. 73.
79 'He played his game': J. C. Masterman, *The Double Cross System in the War 1939–1945* (London, 1972), p. 118.
80 'mysterious business deals': KV 2/845.
80 'We are going': ibid.
80 'In time of war': KV 2/848.
80 'The Germans may': KV 2/847.
80 'His latest girlfriend': ibid.
80 'Missing you terribly': KV 2/846.
81 'degenerating in prison': KV 2/848.
81 'which makes for much': KV 2/847.
81 'I wonder whether': ibid.
81 'submitting to her': KV 2/1067.
81 'We are the Double': ibid.
81 'After all, any decent spy': ibid.
81 'He is by temperament': KV 2/848.
82 'some sort of decoration': KV 2/847.
82 'I do not like': ibid.
82 'I am still satisfied': KV 2/845.
82 'extremely pleased': KV 2/847.
82 'like whores on': Dusko Popov, *Spy/Counterspy* (New York, 1974), p. 109.
83 'in this business': KV 2/847.
83 'I am not cruel enough': ibid.
84 'If there is anyone': ibid.
84 'I would be willing': ibid.
84 'They are like cat': ibid.
84 'Whenever I go to': ibid.
84 'advised it was': KV 2/856.
85 'If this is Upper Silesia': Robert McCrum, *Wodehouse: A Life* (London 2004), p. 198.

86 'to take revenge': KV 2/856.
86 'I know too much': KV 2/847.
86 'If you are caught': KV 2/859.
86 'He is very pro-British': KV 2/847.
86 'placed in honourable': ibid.
87 'I am not at all sure': ibid.
87 'not as confident as': KV 2/848.
87 'virile telegraphese': Masterman, *The Double Cross System*, p. 17.
87 'I am beginning': Levine, *Operation Fortitude*, p. 126.
87 'I shit on Germany': ibid.
89 'He was in a complete': KV 2/848.
89 'I said enough to': ibid.
89 'Heartiest congratulations': Levine, *Operation Fortitude*, p. 138.
89 'On no account': ibid.
89 'The actual cash': Masterman, *The Double Cross System,* p. 16.

Chapter 7: Popov Goes Shopping
90 'Popov is a clever': KV 2/846.
90 'For the moment' Dusko Popov, *Spy/Counterspy* (New York, 1974), p. 112.
90 'we shall probably': ibid.
91 'greatest spy round-up': Russell Miller, *Codename Tricycle* (London, 2005), p. 94.
91 'His first innings': KV 2/849.
91 'It is a great pity': ibid.
91 'Hoover obviously only': Ewen Montagu, *Beyond Top Secret Ultra* (London, 1977), p. 89.
92 'The mistake we made': Joshua Levine, *Operation Fortitude: The Story of the Spy Operation that Saved D-Day* (London, 2011), p. 146.
92 'No one ever dreamed': ibid.
92 'The questionnaire indicated': J. C. Masterman, *The Double Cross System in the War 1939–1945* (London, 1972), p. 82.
93 'embarrass the bureau': ibid.
93 'gold-digger': Miller, *Codename Tricycle*, p. 98.
94 'His financial behaviour': KV 2/850.
94 'I cannot distinguish': ibid.
94 'Tricycle should have': KV 2/849.
94 'so that he should': ibid.
94 'found him depressed': Montagu, *Beyond Top Secret Ultra*, p. 92.
94 'Hoover's management of': ibid.
94 'that there were people': ibid.
94 'Berlin suspected Tricycle': KV 2/860.
94 'a larger sum in dollars': KV 2/850.
95 'I cannot continue': ibid.
95 'Tricycle suspects the evil': ibid.
95 'to maintain him': KV 2/849.
95 'Popov has been totally': Miller, *Codename Tricycle*, p. 132.
95 'I need not repeat': KV 2/850.
95 'He could end his': ibid.
96 'entertaining, social life': ibid.
96 'razor-keen mind': author's interview with Wilson's daughter, Fiona Agassiz, 18 May 2011.
96 'Quiet and introverted': ibid.
96 'failed to produce any': ibid.

96 'how he had': ibid.
96 'a very pro-British': ibid.
96 'extremely objectionable': ibid.
96 'The FBI have lost': ibid.
97 'to prevent any further': ibid.
97 'It is a very outspoken': ibid.
97 'Tricycle himself showed': ibid.
97 'His chances were nothing': Montagu, *Beyond Top Secret Ultra*, p. 92.
97 'an enormous number': KV 2/850.
97 'the greatest instance': Montagu, *Beyond Top Secret Ultra*, p. 92.
97 'Will telephone office': KV 2/849.
98 'stiff in manner': KV 2/850.
98 'as if he learned': ibid.
98 'some suspicion': ibid.
98 'very good . . . excellent . . . terribly bad': ibid.
98 'Now you know what': ibid.
98 'You send me there': Popov, *Spy/Counterspy*, p. 184.
98 'We did all we could': KV 2/851.
99 'embezzled': KV 2/850.
99 'Berlin are stupid': KV 2/851.
99 'might make a scene': KV 2/850.
99 'Kammler begged': ibid.
99 'severe': ibid.
99 'double work': ibid.
99 'Lisbon seem to have': ibid.
100 'Berlin wants information': ibid.
100 'we are not so': ibid.
100 'What about invasion': ibid.
100 'so that I can satisfy': ibid.
100 'voluble and rather confused': ibid.
100 'a great deal of vague': ibid.
100 'He is entirely friendly': ibid.
101 'extraordinary casualness': ibid.
101 'It is quite probable': ibid.
101 'both by making': ibid.
101 'I was cheated by Johnny': ibid.
101 'very anti-Nazi': ibid.
101 'Johnny would give': ibid.
101 'Any suspicion against': ibid.
101 'ability to impose': ibid.
101 'not in any way': ibid.
101 'Von Karsthoff has defended': ibid.
101 'We may be able': ibid.

Chapter 8: The Great Game

102 'in enormous quantities': KV 2/72.
103 'realised that any': ibid.
103 'a mere formality': ibid.
103 'starting to work': ibid.
103 'Long Live Hitler': ibid.
103 'super-spy': ibid.
103 'great daring and initiative': ibid.
103 'He is a natural leader': ibid.

103 'amazing': ibid.
103 'everyone was prepared': ibid.
103 'there was something': ibid.
104 'tiny, vivacious': Roman Garby-Czerniawski, *The Big Network* (London, 1961), p. 126.
104 'The plan was that': Lily Mathilde Carré, *I Was the Cat* (London, 1960), pp. 137–8.
104 'a couple of pairs': ibid., p. 143.
104 'Anglo-Saxon hypocrisy': ibid., p. 157.
105 'Her guilt is the greater': KV 2/72.
105 'but there is no excuse': ibid.
105 'the bombshell': ibid.
105 'The Germans are entering': ibid.
105 'the wireless crystals': ibid.
105 'carrying out a carefully': ibid.
105 'During the whole': ibid.
106 'I shall discuss personally': ibid.
106 'The story of my escape': ibid.
106 'I am convinced': ibid.
106 'demanded a revolver': ibid.
106 'certain of the degree': ibid.
106 'sinister individual': ibid.
107 'There are considerable': ibid.
107 'His loyalty is entirely': ibid.
107 'a loyal and fervent': ibid.
108 'As his condition': ibid.
108 'He finds that so': ibid.
108 'I do not think': ibid.
108 'There is no evidence': ibid.
108 'rendered very great': ibid.
109 'The Germans would': ibid.
109 'we are never going': ibid.
109 'the Germans have really': ibid.
109 'knowing pretty well': ibid.
109 'We are not yet': ibid.
109 'hell-bent on chopping': Christopher Harmer to Hugh Astor, 28 October 1992, Collection of Robert Astor.
109 'intrigued behind my back': ibid.
109 'one of the rudest': ibid.
109 'I loved the old boy': ibid.
109 'throw the case away': KV 2/72.
109 'under close supervision': ibid.
110 'non-job': ibid.
110 'The Germans lost': ibid.
110 'Roman Czerniawski had': Joshua Levine, *Operation Fortitude: The Story of the Spy Operation that Saved D-Day* (London, 2011), p. 175.

Chapter 9: The Flock
111 'one of the most': Nigel West, 'High Society Spy', *Mail on Sunday*, 7 May 1995.
111 'beautifully varnished nails': ibid.
111 'She was really': ibid.
111 'carried out to the': KV 2/2098.
111 'Mr Palmer': ibid.

111 'made a good impression': ibid.
111 'It is by no means': ibid.
112 'Lesbian tendencies': ibid.
112 'she would appear': ibid.
112 'disclosed no possible': ibid.
112 'We have not': ibid.
112 'We ought *not*': ibid.
112 'She is a rather': ibid.
112 'I think this woman': ibid.
112 'typical member of the': ibid.
113 'She replied that she had': ibid.
113 'impressed on her': ibid.
113 'I chose the name': West, 'High Society Spy', 7 May 1995.
113 'It was one': ibid.
113 'It was a very': ibid.
114 'remarkable talent': Tomás Harris, *Garbo: The Spy Who Saved D-Day* (London, 2004), p. 77.
114 'entire existence remained': ibid.
114 'absolute loyalty': ibid., p. 78.
114 'thoroughly undesirable': ibid., p. 318.
115 'to swamp the': ibid., p. 69.
115 'I do not wish to end': ibid., p. 95.
115 'in as much confusing': ibid., p. 69.
115 'The greater the work': ibid., p. 71.
115 'the fanatical loyalty': ibid., p. 78.
115 'temperamental genius': ibid., p. 70.
115 'expressions of high satisfaction': ibid.
115 'Why have I been made': ibid., p. 90.
115 'I want you to know': ibid.
116 'who seldom or never': Michael Howard, *Strategic Deception in the Second World War* (London, 1995), p. 12.
116 'the possible uses': T. A. Robertson to Major H. Petaval, 24 June 1943, CAB 154/35 (TNA).
117 'Years of breeding': KV 4/10.
117 'magical': ibid.
117 'Out of a hundred': ibid.
117 'Himmler, who has': ibid.
117 'any lofts where': ibid.
117 'to accustom as many': ibid.
118 'It was positively': Emily Wilson, 'The War in the Dark: The Security Service and the Abwehr 1940–1944', PhD Thesis (Cambridge, 2003), p. 169.
118 'accent': KV 4/10.
118 'they are easier to work': ibid.
118 'Both birds are now': ibid.
119 'The falconry unit proved': ibid.
119 'If all the fanciers': ibid.
119 'covered an area': ibid.
119 'Had they done': ibid.

Chapter 10: True Agent, False Agent, Double Agent
120 'the idea there might': J. C. Masterman, *The Double Cross System in the War 1939–1945* (London, 1972), p. 59.

120 'reasonably certain': Michael Howard, *Strategic Deception in the Second World War* (London, 1995), p. 20.
121 'powerful weapon': KV 4/70.
121 'The only network': ibid.
121 'fill the German files': Ewen Montagu, *Beyond Top Secret Ultra* (London, 1977), p. 102.
122 'It was always': Masterman, *The Double Cross System*, p. 72.
122 'The enemy is': Emily Wilson, 'The War in the Dark: The Security Service and the Abwehr 1940–1944', PhD Thesis (Cambridge, 2003), p. 174.
122 'if one pearl': ibid.
122 'It is always impossible': KV 3/7.
122 'the Nazis are very': KV 2/1067.
122 'carefully and cleverly': ibid.
122 'The very few really': Masterman, *The Double Cross System*, p. 152.
122 'glittering possibility': ibid.
123 'the most highly polished': Thaddeus Holt, *The Deceivers: Allied Military Deception in the Second World War* (London, 2004), p. 185.
123 'prepare deception': ibid., p. 189.
123 'any matter calculated to': ibid.
123 'We had an instrument': Masterman, *The Double Cross System*, p. 108.
124 'lingering malady': ibid., p. 119.
124 'I fulfil my duty': Tomás Harris, *Garbo: The Spy Who Saved D-Day* (London, 2004), p. 103.
124 'Your last reports': ibid., p. 104.
125 'The success was not': Masterman, *The Double Cross System*, p. 111.
125 'the team was distinctly': ibid., p. 126.
125 'If the agents': ibid., p. 72.
125 'an older, wiser': Christopher Harmer to Hugh Astor, 28 October 1992, Collection of Robert Astor.
125 'guaranteed to argue': ibid.
125 'come down with': ibid.
126 'without any training': ibid.
126 'What may appeal to': KV 2/1067.
126 'The case officer': Masterman, *The Double Cross System*, p. 22.
126 'He had to see': ibid.
127 'most careful psychological': ibid., p. 23.
127 'We were playing': ibid., p. 14.
127 'Gonorrhoea expert': KV 2/850.
127 'This might be a heavily': ibid.
127 'only a well-kept record': Masterman, *The Double Cross System*, p. 28.
127 'a truly formidable size': ibid., p. 68.
128 'the messages of any one': ibid.
128 'Tangle within tangle': Winston Churchill, *Thoughts and Adventures* (London, 1991), p. 55.
128 'could not claim': KV 4/70.
129 'on seeing some': Guy Liddell, *The Guy Liddell Diaries, 1939–1945*, ed. Nigel West (London, 2005), 10 March 1943.
129 'In all, 126 spies': KV 4/83.
129 'Deeply interesting': ibid.
129 'seen more detailed': Christopher Andrew, *The Defence of the Realm: The Authorised History of MI5* (London, 2009), p. 292.
129 'Why don't you': KV 4/83.
130 'very competent': Masterman, *The Double Cross System*, p. 123.

130   'no evidence of any': KV 2/2098.
130   'She plays bridge': ibid.
130   'She is not engaged': ibid.
130   'completely meaningless': ibid.
130   'This text is so': ibid.
130   'Last week I saw': ibid.
130   'Her friends are to': ibid.
131   'We took great care': Nigel West, 'High Society Spy', *Mail on Sunday*, 7 May 1995.
131   'I hope you won't': KV 2/2098.
131   'As she is woman': ibid.
131   'satisfactory regularity': ibid.
131   'minus several hundred': ibid.
131   'somebody on their': ibid.
131   'It was hoped that': ibid.
131   'ignored this suggestion': ibid.
132   'Tank production retarded': KV 2/3639.
132   'Money must be sent': KV 2/2098.
132   'a glowing account': Masterman, *The Double Cross System*, p. 9.
132   'the British had': Nigel West, 'High Society Spy'.
132   'we can in some': Masterman, *The Double Cross System*, p. 9.
132   'He has apparently': KV 2/2098.
132   'We have no knowledge': ibid.
132   'a member of the international': ibid.
133   'Bronx is believed': ibid.
133   'The evidence suggests': ibid.
133   'They had studied': Masterman, *The Double Cross System*, p. 145.
133   'sparingly': KV 2/72.
133   'allowed to lead': ibid.
134   'exceedingly good': ibid.
134   'lengthy report on the': ibid.
134   'telegraph French': ibid.
134   'Brutus is very easy': ibid.
134   'Several of my old': ibid.
134   'if I have your': ibid.
134   'Every now and then': Joshua Levine, *Operation Fortitude: The Story of the Spy Operation that Saved D-Day* (London, 2011), p. 31.
135   'Almost certainly Brutus': KV 2/72.
135   'a little anxious about': ibid.
135   'might warn the': ibid.
135   'evidence that he is': ibid.
135   'no qualification to suggest': ibid.
135   'very valuable wireless agent': ibid.
135   'As confidence grew': Masterman, *The Double Cross System*, p. 146.
135   'threw his weight about': KV 2/72.
135   'at loggerheads with': ibid.
135   'he is a vain and conceited': ibid.
135   'infernal nuisance': ibid.
135   'He spends his whole': ibid.
136   'embroiled in Polish': ibid.
136   'extreme anti-Bolshevism': ibid.
136   'sensed that he was hurt': ibid.
136   'In Defence of our': ibid.

136 'The Soviets committed': ibid.
136 'The Polish Air Force': ibid.
137 'the gravest military': ibid.
137 'little tin-pot hero': ibid.
137 'threatened the extinction': Masterman, *The Double Cross System*, p. 146.
137 'any patriotic Pole': KV 2/72.
137 'meddling in affairs': ibid.
137 'it was the duty': ibid.
137 'which demonstrate a desire': ibid.
137 'I foresee my arrest': ibid.
137 '20th June arrested': ibid.
137 'whether the Germans': ibid.
138 'indiscipline and offensiveness': ibid.
138 'for the harm he': ibid.

Chapter 11: Cockade
139 'perhaps the highest-grade': Guy Liddell, *The Guy Liddell Diaries, 1939–1945,* ed. Nigel West (London, 2005),, 5 June 1943.
139 'The one-man band': J. C. Masterman, *The Double Cross System in the War 1939–1945* (London, 1972), p. 146.
139 'Garbo himself works on': KV 4/83.
140 'hysterical, spoilt and selfish': Tomás Harris, *Garbo: The Spy Who Saved D-Day,* (London, 2004), pp. 327–34.
140 'for a week': ibid.
140 'unbalanced': ibid.
140 'I am telling you': ibid.
140 'a woman of Mrs G's': ibid.
141 'read her the Riot Act': Liddell, *Diaries,* 22 June 1943.
141 'outburst of jealousy': Harris, *Garbo: The Spy Who Saved D-Day,* pp. 327–34.
141 'ruin the whole undertaking': ibid.
141 'give the whole': ibid.
141 'hysterical outburst': ibid.
141 'her husband had': ibid.
141 'ninety per cent': ibid.
141 'She pleaded that': ibid.
141 'considerable comfort': Russell Miller, *Codename Tricycle: The True Story of the Second World War's Most Extraordinary Double Agent* (London, 2005), p. 163.
141 'Please try': KV 2/853.
142 'undoubtedly be an easier': KV 2/854.
142 'Your writing is wonderful': KV 2/853.
142 'He gets particularly obscure': ibid.
142 'humour and spirit': Dusko Popov, *Spy/Counterspy* (New York, 1974), p. 193.
142 'Everyone, the Germans included': ibid., p. 223.
142 'realised that Germany': KV 2/851.
142 'Johnny has never': ibid.
142 'full details of the': ibid.
142 'Johnny is always': ibid.
142 'amoral, opportunist': ibid.
143 'to arrange for Johnny': ibid.
143 'The Germans regard': KV 2/853.
143 'We must seek to take': KV 2/854.

143 'the shabbiest and coldest': KV 2/851.
143 'My heart is in very': ibid.
143 'The chocolates': ibid.
143 'We have done our best': ibid.
144 'Tricycle has the Balkan': ibid.
144 'The one thing that': KV 2/853.
144 'his desire to do': KV 2/851.
144 'certainly no intention': ibid.
144 'he was ready to': KV 2/853.
144 'white silk shirts': KV 2/846.
144 'Tricycle is continuing': KV 2/853.
144 'Every Double Cross': Masterman, *The Double Cross System*, p. 24.
145 'invasion questions are no': KV 2/854.
145 'he ought to be': ibid.
146 'in his best mood': KV 2/853.
146 'He should be back': ibid.
146 'taken his girlfriends to': KV 2/854.
146 'active as a supply': ibid.
146 'hospital arrangements': KV 2/3639.
146 'France to be attacked': ibid.
147 'in the hope that': ibid.
147 'I gather some': CAB 154/35.
147 'But some fall into': ibid.
147 'It occurs to me': ibid.
147 'the questionnaire carried': ibid.
147 'The mere fact of': ibid.
148 'It was an inspiring': Thaddeus Holt, *The Deceivers: Allied Military Deception in the Second World War* (London, 2004), p. 488.
148 'a German coast-artillery': ibid.
148 'disappointing in the': ibid.
148 'It appears the operation': ibid., p. 489.
148 'Your activity and': Harris, *Garbo: The Spy Who Saved D-Day,* p. 147.
148 'These reports': ibid.
149 'There can be no doubt': KV2/42.
149 'looked forward to the day': Masterman, *The Double Cross System*, p. 130.
149 'the actual uses that Pigeons': CAB 154/35.

Chapter 12: Discovered Treasure
150 'sly fox': Kenneth Benton, 'The ISOS Years: Madrid 1941–3', *Journal of Contemporary History*, vol. 30, no. 3 (July 1995), pp. 359–410.
151 'rather attractive' to 'first and foremost': ibid.
151 'doubtful': ibid.
151 'I should be very': KV 2/464.
151 'She has respectable': ibid.
151 'pro-German': ibid.
151 'a White Russian': ibid.
151 'perfectly sure that': ibid.
151 'something of an adventuress': ibid.
152 'often at other people's': Memoir of Mary Sherer, unpublished, by Prue Evill, 18 July 2011.
152 'Mary was someone': ibid.
152 'She appears to be': KV 2/464.
152 'had a great deal of character': Kenneth Benton, 'The ISOS Years'.

152 'full of menace': Lily Sergueiev, *Secret Service Rendered: An Agent in the Espionage Duel Preceding the Invasion of France* (London, 1968), p. 80.
152 'I have got very': ibid., p. 91.
153 'The heat in Madrid': KV 2/466.
153 'We know a certain': Kenneth Benton, 'The ISOS Years'.
153 'Babs licks his face': Lily Sergueiev, *Secret Service Rendered*, p. 92.
153 'I look at them': ibid.
153 'It will be quite something': ibid., p. 98.
154 'thoughtfully at the space' to 'Major Kliemann, I don't care': ibid., pp. 100–105.
155 'appears to be extremely': KV 2/464.
155 'pathologically jealous': ibid.
155 'the object of Kliemann's': Kenneth Benton, 'The ISOS Years'.
155 'Whatever the truth may': Sergueiev, *Secret Service Rendered*, p. 107.
155 'purely fictitious but reassuring': KV 2/464.
155 'who was under great': ibid.
155 'What view is taken': ibid.
156 'the personification': Sergueiev, *Secret Service Rendered*, p. 10.
156 'if any harm came': KV 2/464.
156 'Naturally, should she': ibid.
156 'help and sympathy': ibid.
156 'a cheery wave': Sergueiev, *Secret Service Rendered*, p. 109.
156 'He has gone': ibid.
157 'I was getting to know': Benton, 'The ISOS Years'.
157 'Mr Benton': Sergueiev, *Secret Service Rendered*, p. 87.
157 'That's exactly it': ibid.
157 'I'll see what I can do': ibid.
157 'If my work is important' to 'You shall not': ibid., p. 88.
158 'it was going to be': Benton, 'The ISOS Years'.
158 'Get her to Gibraltar': ibid.
158 'My Gibraltar colleagues': ibid.
158 'suspicious looks': ibid.
158 'I picked up Babs': Sergueiev, *Secret Service Rendered*, p. 110.
159 'From now on': ibid.
159 'Mr Benton's promise': ibid.
159 'see to that too': ibid.
159 'Why don't you' to 'You have my word': ibid.
159 'a rich dowry': Sergueiev, *Secret Service Rendered*, p. 10.
159 'feeling of guilt': Benton, 'The ISOS Years'.
160 'After all': ibid.

Chapter 13: The Walk-in
161 'First of all a very': KV 2/859.
161 'make it clear that': ibid.
161 'absolutely sure': ibid.
161 'The way he talks': ibid.
161 'that idiot Hitler': ibid.
161 'funny smile in': ibid.
162 'some new invention': KV 2/854.
162 'with the same effect': ibid.
162 'for the first time': KV 2/859.
162 'Tricycle has just returned': KV 4/83.
163 'I consider this plan': Russell Miller, *Codename Tricycle: The True Story of the Second World War's Most Extraordinary Double Agent* (London, 2005), p. 182.

164 'His main mission': KV 4/83.
165 'used as a bedroom' to 'No, I shook them off': Kenneth Benton, 'The ISOS Years: Madrid 1941–3', *Journal of Contemporary History*, vol. 30, no. 3 (July 1995), pp. 359–410.
166 'their special fields': ibid.
166 'There is hardly': KV 2/855.
166 'During an air raid': ibid.
166 'which would spread' : Benton, 'The ISOS Years'.
166 'I'm giving you': ibid.
166 'I shall take poison': KV 2/859.
167 'piece of extreme': ibid.
167 'He was an interesting': Benton, 'The ISOS Years'.
167 'He had a great': ibid.
167 'visible shudder': ibid.
167 'trained hijack team': ibid.
167 'It is in your interest' to 'He's a prolific agent': ibid.
168 'Artist is telling you': ibid.
168 'I was very sorry': ibid.
168 'You won't have to': Lily Sergueiev, *Secret Service Rendered: An Agent in the Espionage Duel Preceding the Invasion of France* (London, 1968), p. 112.
168 'should be dealt': KV 2/465.
168 'particularly anxious': ibid.
168 'fat, with big ears': ibid.
168 'rather ill-advised': ibid.
169 'on the edge of a chair': Sergueiev, *Secret Service Rendered*, p. 119.
169 'through slightly slanted': ibid.
169 'You can be extremely': ibid., p. 123.
169 'So you are here': ibid., p. 124.
170 'We look on you': ibid., p. 125.
170 'I want you': ibid.
170 'That only leaves': ibid.
171 'I am not': ibid.
171 'rather a far cry': KV 2/464.
171 'A French citizen': KV 4/83.
171 'to be informed when': KV 2/464.
171 'very strong conviction': Benton, 'The ISOS Years'.
171 'Poor girl': Geoffrey Elliott, *Gentleman Spymaster* (London, 2011), p. 246.
171 'clean and impersonal': Sergueiev, *Secret Service Rendered*, p. 124.
171 'bleak and gloomy': ibid.
171 'plain-fronted house': ibid.
172 'What strikes me': ibid., p. 126.
172 'I still cannot quite': ibid., p. 129.

Chapter 14: A Time for Fortitude
173 'haggard with sleeplessness': Thaddeus Holt, *The Deceivers: Allied Military Deception in the Second World War* (London, 2004), p. 505.
175 'one of the best claret': ibid., p. 478.
175 'charming and witty': ibid.
175 'most tidy and meticulous': Christopher Harmer to Hugh Astor, 28 October 1992, Collection of Robert Astor.
175 'essentially a scorer': ibid.
175 'impossible and insufferable': ibid.
175 'rewrote the thing entirely': Holt, *The Deceivers*, p. 536.

176 'We had always': J. C. Masterman, *The Double Cross System in the War 1939–1945* (London, 1972), p. 149.

176 'the German General': Joshua Levine, *Operation Fortitude: The Story of the Spy Operation that Saved D-Day* (London, 2011), p. 196.

176 'An agent who turned': Masterman, *The Double Cross System*, p. 151.

177 'I have managed': Miranda Carter, *Anthony Blunt: His Lives* (London, 2001), p. 286.

177 'Our task is to understand': ibid.

178 'all the data': ibid.

178 'far more powerful': Masterman, *The Double Cross System*, p. 148.

179 'These bats should': John Crossland, 'MI5 planned to threaten Hitler with A-bomb', *Sunday Times*, 1 December 2002.

179 'It sounds like a': ibid.

179 'our pigeon expert': CAB 154/35.

179 'began to wonder': ibid.

179 'double-cross pigeon racket': KV 4/10.

180 'Pigeon Contamination Plan': ibid.

180 'A stray or lost pigeon': ibid.

180 'throw them off': ibid.

180 'perfectly invisible joint': ibid.

181 'when aircraft were': ibid.

182 'a tall, pleasant-looking': Holt, *The Deceivers*, p. 442.

182 'audition at the': ibid.

183 'an extremely selfish': ibid., p. 456.

183 'Although he might': ibid.

184 'regarded in Berlin': KV 2/856.

184 'If liquidation means': KV 2/197.

184 'We should try': ibid.

185 'try to discredit Ostro': KV 4/66.

Chapter 15: Enriching the Chicken-feed

186 'less than beautiful': Nigel West with Juan Pujol García, *Operation Garbo* (London, 2011), p. 122.

186 'delightfully indiscreet': ibid.

186 'I would never': Tomás Harris, *The Spy Who Saved D-Day* (London, 2004), p. 290.

186 'jocular and fairly talkative': West and Pujol, *Operation Garbo*, p. 124.

187 'There is no concentration': ibid., p. 130.

188 'more military in character': KV 2/2098.

188 'radio controlled rockets': ibid.

188 'big magnetic': ibid.

188 'showed German faith': ibid.

188 'Great invasion problem': KV 2/3639.

188 'hundreds of American': ibid.

188 'Good work. Good reward': ibid.

188 'The principal': ibid.

188 'Of the cases I have': KV 2/2098.

189 'a lot of perhaps interesting': ibid.

189 'Bronx assures me': ibid.

189 'She was a British': ibid.

189 'It is absolutely': ibid.

189 'to twist our tails': ibid.

189 'She has no right': ibid.

190 'absolutely certain of': ibid.
190 'the general manager': ibid.
190 'in view of the': ibid.
190 'If it is desired to send': ibid.
191 'would appear too professional': ibid.
191 'Anxious to hush': KV 2/72.
191 'declined to give': ibid.
191 'most unorthodox proposal': ibid.
191 'Ah, but you must': ibid.
192 'her personal loyalty': ibid.
192 'peculiar circumstances': ibid.
192 'We can never guarantee': ibid.
192 'Of all the agents': ibid.
192 'dynamic and industrious': ibid.
192 'an excellent agent': ibid.
192 'become sufficiently': ibid.
193 'an enemy radio-operator': Oscar Reile, *Geheime West Front* (Munich, 1962), p. 214.
193 'a probability bordering': ibid.
193 'Not the least of my': ibid.
193 'suggested, half-jokingly': KV 2/72.
193 'send a personal message': ibid.
193 'an excellent idea': ibid.
193 'I like the suggestion': ibid.
193 'Colonel! I conceive': ibid.
194 'The Germans appear': ibid.
194 'the Germans expressed': ibid.
194 'The Brutus case could': ibid.
194 'a complete waste': ibid.
194 'We have caught your man': ibid.
195 'the opportunities': ibid.
195 'Brutus is getting questions': ibid.
195 'even better wireless': ibid.
195 'The objectives': ibid.
195 'The risks involved': ibid.
195 'The information doesn't': Lily Sergueiev, *Secret Service Rendered: An Agent in the Espionage Duel Preceding the Invasion of France* (London, 1968), p. 134.
196 'lonely countryside': ibid.
196 'For the last few months': ibid., p. 125.
196 'I don't try to': ibid., p. 135.
196 'I want to love': ibid., p. 147.
196 'There is something': ibid.
197 'very unreasonable': KV 2/465.
197 'Treasure is very': ibid.
197 'I do not quite know': ibid.
197 'her *internal* troubles': ibid.
197 'seized with a fit': Sergueiev, *Secret Service Rendered*, p. 131.
197 'You cannot be ill': ibid.
197 'Mary, it's obvious' to 'My brain is empty': ibid., pp. 135–6.
198 'Treasure is behaving': KV 2/465.
198 'It seems I won't live' to 'I don't want to die': Sergueiev, *Secret Service Rendered*, pp. 140–41.
199 'Information very interesting': KV 2/465.

199 'Why should he have': Sergueiev, *Secret Service Rendered*, p. 143.
200 'Treasure could be': KV 2/465.
200 'There is something': Sergueiev, *Secret Service Rendered*, p. 143.
200 'If we let him': KV 2/465.
200 'I believe': ibid.
200 'first-hand information': ibid.
200 'You've made Kliemann': Sergueiev, *Secret Service Rendered*, p. 151.
200 'My poor Darling': ibid., p. 146.
201 'Everything is indifferent': ibid.
201 'Report from Mary Sherer': KV 2/465.
201 'in good spirits': ibid.
202 'I can change my': Sergueiev, *Secret Service Rendered*, p. 97.

Chapter 16: Artist Paints a Picture
203 'both in quantity': KV 2/855.
203 'violently against machinations': ibid.
203 'intention of throwing': ibid.
203 'malicious': ibid.
203 'the cover under': ibid.
204 'if, as he says': KV 2/859.
204 'He was convinced': ibid.
204 'unconditionally': ibid.
204 'The fact that Johann': Guy Liddell, *The Guy Liddell Diaries, 1939–1945*, ed. Nigel West (London, 2005), 2 September 1943.
204 'A difficult situation': KV 4/83.
205 'If Artist is energetic': KV 2/855.
206 'I agree with his': ibid.
206 'interrogate him at leisure': ibid.
207 'I find myself in complete': ibid.
207 'less danger of Gestapo': Kenneth Benton, 'The ISOS Years', *Journal of Contemporary History*, vol. 30, no. 3 (July 1995), pp. 359–410.
207 'under the wing': ibid.
207 'a modest aesthete': obituary of Charles de Salis, *The Times*, 26 March 2007.
207 'an amusing raconteur': ibid.
207 'Artist is determined': KV 2/855.
208 'a very efficient': Tomás Harris, *Garbo: The Spy Who Saved D-Day* (London, 2004), p. 69.
208 'the characteristics of': KV 2/3568.
208 'set the example': ibid.
208 'were leading a rather': ibid.
208 'All had enormous': ibid.
209 'post-war job': KV 2/855.
209 'a debt of gratitude': ibid.
209 'influential friends': ibid.
209 'a discontented German': ibid.
209 'for some months': ibid.
209 'there is a whole file': ibid.
209 'the powerful backing': ibid.
209 '*was diese Juden*': ibid.
210 'Lord Rothschild has made': ibid.
210 'ingenious, but not': ibid.
210 'It might appear': ibid.

210 'After he returns': KV 2/854.
211 'in time to participate': ibid.
211 'To make him feel': KV 2/855.
211 'any action that': ibid.
211 'should anything happen': ibid.
212 'If through information': ibid.
212 'I made it clear': ibid.
212 'The Abwehr generally': KV 2/856.
212 'Himmler is the most': ibid.
212 'a living dictionary': ibid.
213 'The Baroness is very': KV 2/855.
213 'of going to a country': ibid.
213 'spun a yarn to': ibid.
213 'She immediately promised': ibid.
213 'experimental station': ibid.
213 'lazy': ibid.
213 'never disclosed to anyone': KV 2/856.
213 'full details of most': KV 2/855.
214 'He has given us': KV 2/856.
214 'He left us in no doubt': ibid.
214 'confuse Artist's state': ibid.
214 'relatively unimportant work': ibid.
214 'Artist left me with': ibid.
214 'controlled or non-existent': ibid.
214 'considerably improved': ibid.
214 'that the Gestapo': KV 2/855.
214 'kidnapping in Portugal': ibid.
214 'They have a poison': ibid.
215 'Jebsen has been': ibid.
215 'We have formed': ibid.
215 'highly complex': KV 2/856.
215 'Never let a pal down': P. G. Wodehouse, *The Code of the Woosters* (London, 1938), p. 24.
215 'He at no time spoke': KV 2/856.
215 'Artist says that': KV 2/855.
215 'Looks ten years': KV 2/861.
216 'No doubt Artist': KV 2/859.
216 'I am convinced': ibid.
216 'I hope our collaboration': ibid.
216 'The extent of Artist's': KV 2/856.
216 'Obviously if Artist': KV 2/855.
216 'I do not think': KV 2/856.
216 'Artist's zeal and ability': KV 4/83.
217 'worth his pay': KV 2/856.
217 'really valuable': ibid.
217 'good and had been': ibid.
217 'the best man': ibid.
217 'This may well have': ibid.
218 'if his work was': ibid.
218 'short of a detailed': Dusko Popov, *Spy/Counterspy* (New York, 1974), p. 185.
218 'Some batsmen are nervous': P. G. Wodehouse, 'Now, Talking About Cricket', Essay in *Tales of St Austin's: A Selection of the Early Works of P. G. Wodehouse* (London, 2008) p. 143.

218 'I shall spend': KV 2/856.
218 'dilemma': KV 2/855.
219 'helping a friend': ibid.

Chapter 17: Monty's Double
220 'a physical handicap': KV 2/3123.
221 'fell victim to a road': ibid.
221 'From then onwards': ibid.
221 'Supposing he were': ibid.
221 'bad from head': ibid.
222 'Molina has been': ibid.
222 'One of the most': ibid.
222 'Monty is rather flattered': Guy Liddell, *The Guy Liddell Diaries, 1939–1945*, ed. Nigel West (London, 2005), 6 May 1944.
223 'I ought to shoot': Olivier Wieviorka, *Normandy: The landings to the liberation of Paris*, (London, 2008), p. 79.
223 'There's no such': Stanley Hirshon, *General Patton: A Soldier's Life* (New York, 2002), p. 203.
223 'that's the best': Thaddeus Holt, *The Deceivers: Allied Military Deception in the Second World War* (London, 2004), p. 541.
223 'a goddam natural': Joshua Levine, *Operation Fortitude: The Story of the Spy Operation that Saved D-Day* (London, 2011), p. 229.
223 'see you in the': ibid.
223 'I am thoroughly': ibid., p. 231.
223 'it is the evident destiny': ibid.
224 'strange mental attitude': ibid., p. 221.
224 'As time went on': ibid.
224 'zone of destiny': Henrik O. Lunde, *Hitler's Pre-Emptive War: The Battle for Norway, 1940* (London, 2010), p. 550.
226 '98 per cent': KV 4/70.
227 'It has been suggested': KV 2/856.
227 'No ban': ibid.
227 'passed fit': J. C. Masterman, *The Double Cross System in the War 1939–1945* (London, 1972), p. 153.
228 'once confined to': ibid., p. 154.
228 'it was not impossible': ibid., p. 155.
228 'In short, the German turncoat': ibid., p. 157.
228 'gnawing anxiety': ibid., p. 132.
228 'The whole existence': ibid., p. 153.
228 'I can't believe': Holt, *The Deceivers*, p. 538.

Chapter 18: The Double Dash
229 'You cannot baldly': J. C. Masterman, *The Double Cross System in the War 1939–1945* (London, 1972), p. 114.
229 'He had a good reason': Roger Hesketh, *Fortitude: The D-Day Deception Campaign* (London, 1999), p. 126.
230 'Your latest wires': ibid.
230 'to increase the efficiency': KV 2/72.
230 'Urgently require': ibid.
230 'Many thanks for your hard': ibid.
230 'whether the lack': ibid.
230 'I have complete': ibid.
231 'He is a man who': ibid.

231 'amplification of your network': Nigel West with Juan Pujol García, *Operation Garbo* (London, 2011), p. 137.
231 'giving the best results': ibid., p. 138.
231 'would not happen' : ibid.
231 'until an assault force': ibid.
231 'I am surprised to hear': ibid.
232 'An extensive programme': KV 2/863.
232 'a lot of work': ibid.
232 'His stock is very high': KV 2/856.
232 'mass of detailed': ibid.
232 'the landing in Western Europe': ibid.
232 'the best in the whole': ibid.
232 'Their chief hope': ibid.
232 'It is quite possible': ibid.
232 'containing a wealth': KV 2/857.
233 'very important': KV 2/2098.
233 'Important. Invasion details': KV 2/3639.
234 'She is independent': KV 2/2098.
234 'a good-time girl': ibid.
234 'In order to achieve': ibid.
234 'indicate to the Germans': ibid.
234 'providing a get-out': ibid.
234 'ludicrous': ibid.
234 'I told her I consider': ibid.
234 'Sometimes Louisa': Lily Sergueiev, *Secret Service Rendered: An Agent in the Espionage Duel Preceding the Invasion of France* (London, 1968), p. 196.
234 'a polite little laugh': ibid., p. 207.
235 'Robertson and his gang': ibid., p. 159.
235 'If Kliemann questions' to 'I am absolutely': ibid., p. 180.
235 'a slim, fair youngster': ibid., p. 157.
235 'Berlin were very pleased': KV 2/464.
235 'get the sack': ibid.
235 'Kliemann is a saboteur': Sergueiev, *Secret Service Rendered*, p. 164.
236 'very excited': ibid., p. 170.
236 'Our friend is here!': ibid.
236 'He looks much': ibid., p. 175
236 'My stock has gone': ibid., p. 173
236 'lazy and impertinent': ibid.
236 'shabby': KV 2/464.
236 'Here are the two': Sergueiev, *Secret Service Rendered*, p. 175.
237 'Berlin was very': KV 2/465.
237 'It is a very worrying': ibid.
237 'The situation is quite': Sergueiev, *Secret Service Rendered*, p. 180.
237 'What about a': ibid., p. 178.
237 'What a good idea': ibid.
238 'at midday tomorrow' to 'Now listen to me': ibid., pp. 179–182.
238 'everything seen in': ibid.
238 'Information obtained': ibid.
238 'I want the transmissions': ibid.
239 'These are the instructions': ibid.
239 'What is our hold': ibid., p. 183.
239 'My parents are still': ibid.
239 'I would like to': ibid., p. 182.

239 'planned to hide': ibid.
240 'this was a wise': ibid.
240 'We must take': ibid., p. 187.
240 'If she was discovered': ibid.
240 'silly': ibid.
240 'the British would': ibid.
240 'At the beginning': ibid.
240 'That's excellent': ibid., p. 188.
240 'Strich zwischen': ibid.
241 'Even if it meant': ibid., p. 173.
241 'I would rather go': ibid.
241 'Five months ago': ibid., p. 188.
241 'He must be daft': ibid., p. 192.
242 'So here you are' : ibid., p. 193.
242 'indistinguishable from' KV 2/465.
242 'I have nothing': ibid.
242 'What would he do': Sergueiev, Secret Service Rendered, p. 190.
242 'I am absolutely sure': ibid.
242 'Treasure gave a': KV 2/465.
242 'no suggestion for': KV 2/464.
242 'She states she': ibid.
243 'Arrived Safely': Sergueiev, Secret Service Rendered, p. 197.
243 'Every time I know': ibid., p. 200.

Chapter 19: Jebsen's New Friend

244 'even an account': KV 2/856.
244 'no authority from C': ibid.
244 'seriously and earnestly': KV 2/855.
244 'This proposal sounds': ibid.
245 'P. G. Wodehouse and his': KV 2/856.
245 'anti-Nazi and': ibid.
245 'telegram saying': ibid.
246 'fascinated by his intelligence': KV 2/861.
246 'seemingly inexhaustible': ibid.
246 'I am His Majesty's': ibid.
246 'Friendship goes': ibid.
246 'macaco': KV 2/856.
246 'Although he had': ibid.
246 'saying his department': ibid.
246 'infatuated': ibid.
246 'Schreiber has written': KV 2/855.
246 'Jebsen's nervousness': KV 2/856.
247 'known to give as': KV 2/3295.
247 'He is personally': ibid.
247 'He is supposed to': ibid.
247 'hold over': KV 2/856.
247 'His bribes go a long': KV 2/858.
247 'With a great deal': KV 2/856.
247 'He made no secret': ibid.
247 'Relations between Artist': ibid.
248 'try to persuade Canaris': ibid.
248 'the organisation he': KV 2/3295.
248 'deliberate fraud': ibid.

248 'He is only twenty-four': ibid.
248 'constructive fantasy': ibid.
248 'enough confidence in': KV 2/856.
248 'had not done': ibid.
248 'slippery opportunist': KV 2/857.
248 'If he knew the': KV 2/856.
248 'I think Brandes': KV 2/3295.
248 'lift the veto': KV 2/856.
249 'the downfall of': ibid.
249 'Further dismissals': KV 2/855.
249 'new brooms would': J. C. Masterman, *The Double Cross System in the War 1939–1945* (London, 1972), p. 156.
250 'Jebsen tried to': KV 2/861.
250 'he was on friendly': ibid.
250 'the old fox': KV 2/857.
250 'younger and more': KV 2/855.
250 'He is not a Nazi': ibid.
250 'The new officers': ibid.
250 'a little uneasy': ibid.
250 'wide awake': ibid.
250 'the most intelligent': ibid.
251 'elderly men with': KV 2/410.
251 'discharging its functions': ibid.
251 'shocked at the': ibid.
251 'an extremely able': ibid.
251 'rather fishy': KV 2/855.
251 'removed and': KV 2/410.
251 'sleeping secretaries': KV 2/857.
251 'This brothel must': ibid.
251 'indiscretion and inefficiency': ibid.
251 'His specific duties': KV 2/3568.
251 'the possibility of Allied': ibid.
251 'pedantic and ambitious': ibid.
251 'Schreiber is not a': KV 2/856.
252 'on suspicion of aiding': KV 2/3568.
252 'his general political': ibid.
252 'Something was being': ibid.
252 'belonged to the group': ibid.
252 'he was sent to Portugal': ibid.
252 'the names of Abwehr': KV 2/856.
252 'We must reckon': ibid.
252 'Berlin has ordered': ibid.
252 'Artist's friends': ibid.
253 'defended him strongly': KV 2/857.
253 'The clouds are': ibid.
253 'Artist in extremely': ibid.
253 'exert his influence': ibid.
253 'take no steps': ibid.
253 'up-to-date details': ibid.
253 'had a very great': ibid.
254 'assisted him cleverly': ibid.
254 'he was sure': ibid.
254 'an excellent agent': KV 2/72.

254 'His first interview': KV 4/83.
254 'particularly valuable': Roger Hesketh, *Fortitude: The D-Day Deception Campaign* (London, 1999), p. 112.
254 'in funds': KV 2/857.
254 'long-term contact': KV 2/856.
254 'to be regarded': ibid.
255 'He is afraid that': KV 2/858.
255 'Although convinced that': ibid.
255 'He is keen to': KV 2/857.
255 'Kühlenthal's controlled': ibid.
255 'the Spaniards': ibid.
255 'brought word back': ibid.
255 'Ivan [Popov] is now': ibid.
255 'The confidence in': ibid.
255 'common for members': ibid.
255 'He is certain that': ibid.
256 'Brandes is playing': ibid.
256 'Brandes is clearly': ibid.

Chapter 20: 'Am I Not Always Careful?'

257 '*one* division to hesitate': Tomás Harris, *Garbo: The Spy Who Saved D-Day* (London, 2004), p. 183.
257 'increase the percentage': ibid., p. 176.
258 'military expert': KV 2/858.
258 'credible Abwehr source': Roger Hesketh, *Fortitude: The D-Day Deception Campaign* (London, 1999), p. 95.
258 'He is very well regarded': KV 2/72.
258 'If Brutus were posted': ibid.
258 'on account of his': KV 2/72.
258 'set up under FUSAG': Hesketh, *Fortitude,* p. 126.
259 'the opinions of': KV 2/3639.
259 'Montgomery's HQ may': ibid.
259 'large invasion stores': ibid.
259 'roads to beaches': ibid.
259 'believes Denmark place': ibid.
259 'Invasion seems imminent': ibid.
259 'Many US troops': ibid.
259 'Prime Minister's': ibid.
259 'I make imaginary visits': Lily Sergueiev, *Secret Service Rendered: An Agent in the Espionage Duel Preceding the Invasion of France* (London, 1968), p. 204.
259 'In this world of': ibid.
260 'For three years I': ibid., p. 153.
260 'She is working hard': KV 2/465.
260 'I don't think it would': Sergueiev, *Secret Service Rendered,* p. 201.
260 'The furniture, fittings': KV 2/465.
260 'the German intelligence': Sergueiev, *Secret Service Rendered,* p. 206.
260 'three shoes (not pairs)': KV 2/465.
260 'I think we ought': ibid.
261 'We owe nothing': ibid.
261 'Treasure is not a money': ibid.
261 'exceptionally temperamental': J. C. Masterman, *The Double Cross System in the War 1939–1945* (London, 1972), p. 174.
261 'It is very difficult not': Sergueiev, *Secret Service Rendered,* p. 201.

261   'meticulous accounts': ibid., p. 196.
261   'any further activities': KV 2/861.
262   'uncomfortable feeling': KV 2/860.
262   'as it seemed': ibid.
262   'outrageous': KV 2/857.
262   'stay in London': ibid.
262   'send some lower-grade': ibid.
262   'I just wanted': Dusko Popov, *Spy/Counterspy* (New York, 1974), p. 245.
262   'Tricycle is now': KV 2/857.
262   'What are Churchill's': ibid.
262   'personally agreeable': KV 2/856.
263   'not unduly worried': KV 2/857.
263   'it was much': ibid.
263   'sending a representative': ibid.
263   'These allegations have nothing': ibid.
263   'free from danger': ibid.
263   'trying to find out about': KV 2/860.
263   'learns everything': ibid.
263   'As cannot continue': ibid.
264   'might be playing': KV 2/857.
264   'possibly with the': ibid.
264   'to France for': KV 2/858.
264   'worming, or bribing': ibid.
264   'It may well be that': ibid.
264   'very jealous of the': KV 2/860.
264   'Strong impression that': KV 2/857.
265   'absolutely no doubts': ibid.
265   'hasty in assuming': KV 2/858.
265   'his cover': ibid.
265   'should be looked': KV 2/857.
265   'would be considered': ibid.
265   'On the 17th Johnny': ibid.
265   'a routine reduction': ibid.
265   'all secretaries': KV 2/858.
266   'Three days after': KV 2/861.
266   'Artist does not': KV 2/857.
266   'He feels very': ibid.
266   'Further traps of this': ibid.
266   'large-scale invasion': ibid.
266   'whether Norway': ibid.
266   'decisive': ibid.
266   'Tricycle's reports have': ibid.
267   'Artist is confident': ibid.
267   'Am I not always': obituary of Charles de Salis, *The Times*, 26 March 2007.
267   'A telegram which has': KV 2/858.
267   'telegram conveyed': ibid.
267   'while Artist considered': ibid.
267   'solely with financial': KV 2/859.
267   'take a bold line': KV 2/857.
267   'desire to expose': ibid.
268   'too complicated': ibid.
268   'Brandes is clearly': ibid.
268   'I see no reason': ibid.

268 'brook no further': KV 2/858.
268 'received immediate': ibid.
268 'Artist considers this': ibid.
268 'He now believes': ibid.
269 'You will know': KV 2/857.
269 'The agent Tricycle': KV 4/83.
269 'confirmed that everything': KV 2/858.
270 'From Artist's point': ibid.
270 'To crown it all': ibid.
270 'A proof of the fact': ibid.
270 'Knowing your mentality': ibid.
271 'I hope you will': ibid.
271 'in a very good': ibid.
271 'The carrying out of': KV 2/3568.
272 'full of praise': Guy Liddell, *The Guy Liddell Diaries, 1939–1945*, ed. Nigel West (London, 2005), 26 April 1944.
272 'I think he realises': ibid.
272 'all those present': ibid.
272 'It was unknown': ibid.

Chapter 21: Operation Dora
273 'to Berlin by force': KV 2/3568.
273 'They would be knocked': ibid.
274 'Both of them': ibid.
274 'border conditions': ibid.
274 'a few rests': ibid.
274 'Mission has been': ibid.
274 'Luggage handed': ibid.
274 'Many thanks for': KV 2/858.
274 'provoked considerable': KV 2/410.
274 'Jebsen's desertion': ibid.
274 'to see personally': KV 2/3568.
274 'Berlin had proof': KV 2/861.
274 'seeking to take': ibid.
275 'a police matter': KV 2/3568.
275 'were to know anything': ibid.
275 'Once Jebsen was': ibid.
275 'accept full responsibility': ibid.
275 'specifically charging': KV 2/861.
275 'left entirely up to': KV 2/3568.
275 'status of a British dominion': KV 2/410.
275 'the man to put': ibid.
275 'instruct Kuebart in': ibid.
276 'arranged for someone': ibid.
276 'pounce on the Abwehr': ibid.
276 'put an end to': ibid.
276 'The Vermehren case': KV 2/860.
276 'one of a number': KV 2/859.
276 'If innocent': KV 2/861.
277 'in order to ensure': KV 2/3568.
277 'large enough for a': ibid.
277 'Artist has disappeared': KV 2/860.
277 'This has clearly been': KV 2/858.

277 'taken to France': ibid.
278 'afraid that Jebsen': KV 2/857.
278 'A number of messages': KV 2/858.
278 'Artist's present troubles': ibid.
278 'the one agent of real': KV 2/857.
278 'All the parties involved': KV 2/858.
279 'The next few days': ibid.
279 'The cover plan has': ibid.
280 'deprived of all': ibid.
280 'if, and only if': ibid.
280 'The confidence which': ibid.
281 'the same night': ibid.
281 'without our getting': ibid.
281 'Packing up Tricycle': Guy Liddell, *The Guy Liddell Diaries, 1939–1945*, ed. Nigel West (London, 2005), 10 May 1944.
281 'to deduce the cover plan': KV 2/858.
281 'lengthy and exhaustive': ibid.
281 'I maintain that the': ibid.
281 'In the hands': Roger Hesketh, *Fortitude: The D-Day Deception Campaign* (London, 1999), p. 111.
282 'Why lead *me* up': KV 2/859.
282 'respect for 23700': ibid.
282 'would have been': ibid.
282 'the most flagrant': ibid.
282 'If I cannot': ibid.
282 'No one can have': ibid.
283 'Anthony Blunt told me': Guy Liddell, *Diaries*, 10 May 1944.
283 'by trick or by': KV 2/858.
284 'Jebsen was a mine': KV 2/859.
284 'There has been': KV4/83.
284 'near-panic': Sefton Delmer, *The Counterfeit Spy* (London, 1973), p. 160.
284 'would undoubtedly put': Guy Liddell, *Diaries*, 10 May 1944.
285 'This gives us': ibid., 18 May 1944.
285 'certain inquiries': ibid.
285 'After D-Day we': Thaddeus Holt, *The Deceivers: Allied Military Deception in the Second World War* (London, 2004), p. 565.
285 'Under interrogation': J. C. Masterman, *The Double Cross System in the War 1939–1945* (London, 1972), p. 159.
286 'We do not know': KV 2/858.

Chapter 22: Guest of the Gestapo
287 'erudite, imaginative': David Kahn, *Hitler's Spies: German Military Intelligence in World War II* (New York, 1978), p. 424.
288 'jolly, easy, happy': ibid. See also Anthony Cave Brown, *Bodyguard of Lies*, vol. 1 (London, 1976), p. 497.
288 'the opinions held': ibid., p. 496.
290 'To Newmarket for': KV 2/3639.
290 'a heavier burden' J. C. Masterman, *The Double Cross System in the War 1939–1945* (London, 1972), p. 159.
290 'hide the facts': Nigel West with Juan Pujol García, *Operation Garbo* (London, 2011), p. 151.
291 'Have found first-class': Roger Hesketh, *Fortitude: The D-Day Deception Campaign* (London, 1999), p. 121.

291 'under duress': Guy Liddell, *The Guy Liddell Diaries, 1939–1945*, ed. Nigel West (London, 2005), 15 May 1944.

292 'report whether': KV 2/859.

292 'French money Dora': ibid.

292 'no evidence to prove': ibid.

292 'are consistent with': ibid.

293 'If Brandes could': ibid.

293 'I do not agree': ibid.

293 'I feel a strong': KV 2/860.

293 'being introduced to': KV 2/858.

293 'stop drawing attention': ibid.

294 'had a paternal interest': KV 2/859.

294 'This was not the': ibid.

294 'I wish to convey': KV 2/860.

294 'a written report': KV 2/859.

294 'It seems to me': ibid.

294 'There is still': ibid.

294 'arrangements for their': KV 2/860.

294 'the captive at the': KV 2/858.

294 'as Jebsen was a soldier': KV 2/860.

295 'did his best to': ibid.

295 'brusque ultimatum': KV 2/861.

295 'One really ought': Christopher Hudson, 'Architects of Genocide', *Daily Mail*, 19 January 2002.

295 'produced a great': KV 2/860.

295 'having betrayed': KV 2/861.

295 'engaging in large-scale': KV 2/859.

295 'got into difficulties': ibid.

296 'Certain sizeable': ibid.

296 'Some SS officials': ibid.

296 'improperly converting SD': ibid.

296 'accused of working for Britain': KV 2/860.

296 'Because of good': ibid.

297 'Communists, Marxists': Rebecca Wittmann, *Beyond Justice: The Auschwitz Trial* (Harvard, 2005), p. 120.

297 'in a highly nervous': KV 2/860.

297 'caught a glimpse of': Dusko Popov, *Spy/Counterspy* (New York, 1974), p. 261.

297 'typical concentration': ibid.

297 'His flesh and muscle': ibid.

298 'Violence is taboo': https://www.mi5.gov.uk/output/bad-nenndorf.html

Chapter 23: Bronx Gets Toothache

299 'there is still no': KV 4/83.

299 'transmitted his 1,000th': ibid.

299 'remind the Germans': KV 2/72.

299 'not very intelligent': ibid.

300 'Colonel, please forgive': ibid.

300 'functioning flawlessly': KV 2/464.

300 'The messages of Treasure': KV 4/83.

300 'have, at a critical moment': ibid.

300 'I always cry in': Lily Sergueiev, *Secret Service Rendered: An Agent in the Espionage Duel Preceding the Invasion of France* (London, 1968), p. 207.

300 'Mary crying at the': ibid.
301 'I didn't mean to': ibid., p. 205.
301 'The landing is very' to 'You realise I': ibid.
301 'Sergeyev made a': KV 2/466.
302 'In spite of Sergeyev's': ibid.
302 'We see no particular': Guy Liddell, *The Guy Liddell Diaries, 1939–1945*, ed. Nigel West (London, 2005), 28 May 1944.
303 'Treasure is in a position': KV 2/466.
303 '*Envoyez vite*': KV 2/2098.
304 'After a cocktail party': ibid.
305 'wearing battledress': ibid.
305 'Hello, Monty': KV 2/3123.
305 'Hello, Rusty': ibid.
305 'His interest in happening': ibid.
305 'with well-feigned': ibid.
305 'played his difficult': ibid.
305 'You *are* Monty': ibid.
305 'His Excellency was': ibid.
305 'The material reached': ibid.
305 'The Governor introduced': ibid.
305 'very satisfied with': ibid.
306 'General Montgomery': ibid.
306 'might point towards': ibid.
306 'a little too early': Liddell, *Diaries*, 28 May 1944.
306 'had gone through': KV 2/3123.
306 'He was under': Thaddeus Holt, *The Deceivers: Allied Military Deception in the Second World War* (London, 2004), p. 562.
306 'Coming out of that': ibid.
307 'more Nazi than': Reinhard R. Doerries, Gerhard L. Weinberg, *Hitler's Intelligence Chief: Walter Schellenberg* (New York, 2009), p. 99.
308 'lateral shell fire': Charles Fenyvesi, 'Japan's Unwitting D-Day Spy', *Washington Post*, 26 May 1998.
308 'Our main basis': ibid.
308 'This place is mine': Ignatius Phayre, 'Hitler's Mountain Home', *Homes & Gardens*, November 1938.
308 'filled with a curious': ibid.
308 'Our attitude cannot': *Trial of German Major War Criminals*, vol. 3, p. 387.
309 'What is your feeling' to 'Well, judging': Holt, *The Deceivers*, p. 566.
309 'It gave the first': Roger Hesketh, *Fortitude: The D-Day Deception Campaign* (London, 1999), p. 194.

Chapter 24: Garbo's Warning
311 'The south coast': Roderick Bailey, *Forgotten Voices of D-Day* (London, 2010), p. 38.
311 'Gather round me': ibid., p. 48.
311 'unreal feeling': ibid., p. 66.
311 'Everything was totally': ibid.
312 'great crusade': http://www.eisenhowermemorial.org/legacyreport/military-legacy.htm
312 'failed to gain a': ibid.
312 'The troops': ibid.
312 'Do you realise': Tony Hall, Bernard C. Nalty, *D-Day: The Strategy, The Men, The Equipment* (London, 2002), p. 8.

312 'drew all the loose': Roger Hesketh, *Fortitude: The D-Day Deception Campaign* (London, 1999), p. 176.
312 'the entire chain': ibid.
312 'the impression of being': Thaddeus Holt, *The Deceivers: Allied Military Deception in the Second World War* (London, 2004), p. 550.
313 'destined for an attack': Hesketh, *Fortitude*, p. 190.
313 'imaginary Order of Battle': ibid.
313 'self-trained military reporter': Tomás Harris, *Garbo: The Spy Who Saved D-Day* (London, 2004), p. 189.
313 'I conclude that the': ibid., p. 188.
313 'indicates the possibility': ibid.
313 'The main enemy': ibid.
313 'Further transfer': ibid.
313 'According to a': Harris, *Garbo: The Spy Who Saved D-Day*, p. 188.
314 'sustained diet of high-grade': Hesketh, *Fortitude*, p. 187.
314 'By the date of the': ibid.
314 'Ostro, in a long message': Guy Liddell, *The Guy Liddell Diaries, 1939–1945*, ed. Nigel West (London, 2005), 5 June 1944.
316 'He has told me': Juan Pujol and Nigel West, *Operation Garbo* (London, 2011), p. 154.
316 'All right Sergeant': Sefton Delmer, *The Counterfeit Spy* (London, 1973), p. 176.
316 'I don't get it': ibid., p. 177.
317 'The trouble is': ibid.
317 'We saw a lorry-load': Bailey, *Forgotten Voices of D-Day*, p. 192.
318 'improbable': David Kahn, *Hitler's Spies: German Military Intelligence in World War II* (New York, 1978), p. 512.
318 'That the invasion': Holt, *The Deceivers*, p. 579.
318 'Don't make a big': ibid.
318 'I'm too old a bunny': Kahn, *Hitler's Spies*, p. 513.
319 'inhuman wall of fire': Bailey, *Forgotten Voices of D-Day*, p. 269.
320 'His name might': KV 4/10.
320 'The invasion army': Montague Taylor, 'Carrier Pigeons Ready', *Belfast Telegraph*, 6 June 1944.
320 'We are just 20': ibid.

Chapter 25: Second Innings
322 'Just keep the Fifteenth': Thaddeus Holt, *The Deceivers: Allied Military Deception in the Second World War* (London, 2004), p. 579.
322 'Unfortunately, by remaining': Roger Hesketh, *Fortitude: The D-Day Deception Campaign* (London, 1999), p. 148.
323 'Distraught by the': KV 2/3639.
323 'This makes me question': Nigel West with Juan Pujol García, *Operation Garbo* (London, 2011), p. 161.
323 'I wish to stress in': ibid., p. 162.
324 'the first of a series': Christopher Andrew, *The Defence of the Realm: The Authorised History of MI5* (London, 2009), p. 305.
324 'attack across the Channel': Hesketh, *Fortitude*, p. 199.
324 'Fortitude requires a threat': KV 2/72.
324 'It is clear that': Hesketh, *Fortitude*, p. 199.
324 'advanced state of': ibid.
324 'I never like': Tomás Harris, *Garbo: The Spy Who Saved D-Day* (London, 2004), p. 188.
325 'After personal consultation': West with Pujol, *Operation Garbo*, p. 166.

325   'left with some': ibid.

325   'I trust you will': ibid.

326   'The report is credible': ibid., p. 167.

326   'Only part of Allied': KV 2/3639.

326   'Lord Stanley of Alderney': ibid.

326   'Fruit spoiled by frosts': ibid.

327   'absolutely saved the': KV 2/72.

327   'I have some hard' to 'I didn't say we': Lily Sergueiev, *Secret Service Rendered: An Agent in the Espionage Duel Preceding the Invasion of France* (London, 1968), pp. 209–11.

328   'big scene from': ibid., p. 209.

328   'Why did you': ibid., p. 212.

328   'I refuse to be': ibid.

328   'Ducky, that's': ibid., p. 213.

328   'I have destroyed': ibid., p. 212.

329   'inviting the Germans' to 'appetising dish': KV 2/72.

330   'what they deduced': KV 2/3123.

331   'small calibre': Holt, *The Deceivers*, p. 561.

331   'diversionary attack': ibid.

331   'When the invasion': J. C. Masterman, *The Double Cross System in the War 1939–1945* (London, 1972), p. 167.

331   'Their movement of': KV 2/72.

331   'impotent near Bordeaux': personal account of Elvira Chaudoir, collection of Robert Astor.

331   'We are prepared': KV 4/247.

332   'contain some': Joshua Levine, *Operation Fortitude: The Story of the Spy Operation that Saved D-Day* (London, 2011), p. 224.

332   'another landing': Holt, *The Deceivers*, p. 582.

333   '99 per cent': Levine, *Operation Fortitude*, p. 285.

333   'provided the reason': ibid.

333   'twenty-three divisions': Thaddeus Holt, *The Deceivers*, p. 581.

333   'It was almost': Guy Liddell, *The Guy Liddell Diaries, 1939–1945*, ed. Nigel West (London, 2005), 30 June 1944.

333   'Patton's army group': Holt, *The Deceivers*, p. 582.

333   'Patton's forces will': ibid.

333   'reposed an almost': KV 4/247.

333   'still could not': ibid.

333   'has not been given': Holt, *The Deceivers*, p. 589.

334   'A second major landing': ibid.

334   'every additional': Terry Crowdy, *Deceiving Hitler: Double Cross and Deception in World War II* (London, 2008), p. 272.

334   'decisive mistake': Holt, *The Deceivers*, p. 589.

334   'All this Patton': Levine, *Operation Fortitude*, p. 295.

334   'Were all those divisions': ibid.

334   'We knew that you': KV 4/247.

335   'unparalleled blunder': Crowdy, *Deceiving Hitler*, p. 272.

335   'might well have': Andrew, *Defence of the Realm*, p. 309.

335   'I cannot overemphasise': ibid.

335   'The deception measures': ibid.

335   'It seems from': KV4/83.

336   'We were not very': Masterman, *The Double Cross System*, p. 148.

336   'the greatest Test': Norman Holmes Pearson, introduction to Masterman, *The Double Cross System*.

336 'the most successful': Holt, *The Deceivers*, p. 590.
336 'one of the most': Kim Philby, *My Silent War* (London, 1968), p. 17.
336 'With great happiness': West with Pujol, *Operation Garbo*, p. 183.
337 'I cannot at this moment': ibid., p. 184.

Aftermath
338 'studied not only by': KV 2/72.
338 'We shall presently': ibid.
338 'worked valiantly for': ibid.
338 'Nobody here believes': ibid.
339 'Once again I thank': ibid.
339 'to recruit and organise': ibid.
340 'On Nationale 3': ibid.
340 'Polish government set up': ibid.
340 'withdrawn air of': Lily Mathilde Carré, *I Was the Cat* (London, 1960), p. 10.
341 'What I wanted most': ibid., p. 132.
341 'nightmares with': ibid., p. 202.
341 'harmless literary': ibid., p. 219.
341 'committed to achieve': ibid., p. 175.
341 'I don't know how': Roman Garby-Czerniawski, *The Big Network* (London, 1961), p. 246.
341 'OK, you win': Lily Sergueiev, *Secret Service Rendered: An Agent in the Espionage Duel Preceding the Invasion of France* (London, 1968), p. 214.
342 'Is that all': ibid.
342 'I will be able': ibid., p. 223.
342 'My joy has no': KV 2/465.
342 'I've lost my solitary': ibid.
342 'You may find': ibid.
342 'I don't honestly': ibid.
342 'She will always': ibid.
343 'unbelievable reality': Sergueiev, *Secret Service Rendered*, p. 7.
343 'We have in your personality': Nigel West with Juan Pujol García, *Operation Garbo* (London, 2011), p. 200.
343 'The noble struggle': ibid., p. 207.
343 'They cannot hope': ibid., p. 204.
343 'His deeds and': ibid., p. 206.
343 'I am certain': ibid.
343 'selling': Emily Wilson, 'The War in the Dark: The Security Service and the Abwehr 1940–1944', PhD Thesis (Cambridge, 2003), p. 227.
344 'No one knew': West with Pujol, *Operation Garbo*, p. 216.
345 'My main pride': ibid., p. 217.
345 'Bronx is the': KV 2/2098.
345 'They will take': ibid.
345 'It is quite evident': ibid.
345 'Good work': ibid.
345 'learn as much': ibid.
345 'I believe that': ibid.
346 'if any mishap': ibid.
346 'in cheerful heart': ibid.
346 'Absolutely livid': ibid.
346 'parachuting to the': ibid.
346 'It is difficult to': J. C. Masterman, *The Double Cross System in the War 1939–1945* (London, 1972), p. 167.

346 'eagerly await': KV 2/2098.

346 'to lower the German' : ibid.

347 'Guerrillas will': ibid.

347 'Her long-term': ibid.

347 'Words of gratitude': ibid.

347 'a way of making': Stella Rimington to Hugh Astor, 6 November 1995, Collection of Robert Astor.

347 'I recall the adventure': Nigel West, 'High Society Spy', *Mail on Sunday*, 7 May 1995.

347 'I am getting fed up': KV 2/861.

347 'young and pretty': ibid.

347 'apparently entering': ibid.

347 'I will try to do': ibid.

348 'in deceiving the': ibid.

348 'We are making': ibid.

348 'His activities have': ibid.

350 'perfect foils for': Memoir of Mary Sherer by Prue Evill, 18 July 2011.

350 'Mary was a very': ibid.

350 'the Lionesses': ibid.

350 'all of which': ibid.

350 'signalise its performance': KV 4/10.

350 'There is no doubt': Emily Wilson, 'The War in the Dark', p. 228.

350 'They will be a great': ibid.

351 'whisky and concentrated': 'Anthony Blunt: Confessions of a spy who passed secrets to Russia during the war', *Daily Telegraph*, 28 May 2010.

351 'the biggest mistake': ibid.

351 'It has given me': Chapman Pincher, *Too Secret Too Long* (London, 1984), p. 351.

351 'respected judge': obituary of Wulf Schmidt, *Daily Mail*, 28 October 1992.

351 'somewhat shifty': KV 2/278.

352 'very proud and': ibid.

352 'He has no idea': Guy Liddell, *The Guy Liddell Diaries, 1939–1945*, ed. Nigel West (London, 2005), 22 October 1944.

352 'sharp and ruthless': KV 2/278.

352 'arrest various Nazis': KV 2/410.

352 'made difficulties': ibid.

352 'tissue of lies': ibid.

352 'small clique of': ibid.

353 'he considered the': ibid.

353 'Defend Berlin to': 'US may have used Gestapo chief as cold war warrior', *Sunday Times*, 8 April 2001.

354 'a poor, half-Jewish': KV 2/3295.

354 'pure whitewash': ibid.

354 'grave miscarriage': ibid.

354 'Brandes was mixed': ibid.

354 'his hair had': Dusko Popov, *Spy/Counterspy* (New York, 1974), p. 261.

354 'until she attracted': KV 2/861.

354 'he told her that': ibid.

355 'who wolves have': Saki, *The Unbearable Bassington* (first published 1912; London, 2008), p. 108.

355 'JOHNNY JEBSEN HUN': Communications from Lt Cdr Cumberlege, Code 92 File 10046 FO 371/48935.

356 'I can make': ibid.

356   'my personal wish': KV 2/860.
356   'I do feel that': KV 2/861.
356   'My old friend Johnny': KV 2/860.
357   'assurance we gave': ibid.
357   'She will be able': KV 2/861.
357   'We have no financial': KV 2/862.
357   'None of these people': KV 2/859.
357   'had not extracted': ibid.
357   'who would be': KV 2/860.
357   'If you have luck': ibid.
358   'know everything about': ibid.
358   'how the NKVD could': ibid.
358   'We do not know whether': ibid.
358   'what actually happened': KV 2/861.
358   'which was the normal': ibid.
358   'shot while trying': Popov, *Spy/Counterspy*, p. 263.
358   'She refuses to': KV 2/861.
358   'the last person': ibid.
358   'emphatic that he did': ibid.
358   'was liberated by': Sefton Delmer, *The Counterfeit Spy* (London, 1973),
          p. 162.
358   'Johnny Jebson': KV 2/860.
358   'Jebsen has not': ibid.
358   'kept the faith': Delmer, *The Counterfeit Spy*, p. 164.

Select Bibliography

Archives
British Library Newspaper Archive, Colindale
Bundesarchiv–Militärarchiv, Freiburg
Churchill Archives Centre, Churchill College, Cambridge
IWM Archives, Imperial War Museum, London
National Archives, Kew
National Archives, Washington DC

Published Sources
Andrew, Christopher, *Secret Service: The Making of the British Intelligence Community* (London, 1985)
————— *The Defence of the Realm: The Authorised History of MI5* (London, 2009)
Bailey, Roderick, *Forgotten Voices of D-Day* (London, 2010)
Barbier, Mary Kathryn, *D-Day Deception: Operation Fortitude and the Normandy Invasion* (Mechanicsburg, PA, 2009)
Barreiros, José António, *Nathalie Sergueiew: Uma Agente Dupla em Lisboa* (Lisbon, 2006)
Beesley, Patrick, *Very Special Admiral: The Life of Admiral J. H. Godfrey* (London, 1980)
Beevor, Antony, *D-Day* (London, 2009)
Bennett, Gill, *Churchill's Man of Mystery: Desmond Morton and the World of Intelligence* (London, 2007)
Bennett, Ralph, *Behind the Battle: Intelligence in the War with Germany 1939–45* (London, 1999)

——————*Ultra and Mediterranean Strategy 1941–1945* (London, 1989)

Benton, Kenneth, 'The ISOS Years: Madrid 1941–3', *Journal of Contemporary History*, vol. 30, no. 3 (July 1995)

Bower, Tom, *The Perfect English Spy: Sir Dick White and the Secret War, 1935–1990* (London, 1995)

Bristow, Desmond, with Bill Bristow, *A Game of Moles: The Deceptions of an MI6 Officer* (London, 1993)

Carré, Lily Mathilde, *I Was the Cat* (London, 1960)

Carter, Miranda, *Anthony Blunt: His Lives* (London, 2001)

Cave Brown, Anthony, *Bodyguard of Lies*, vol. 1 (London, 1975)

Crowdy, Terry, *Deceiving Hitler: Double Cross and Deception in World War II* (London, 2008)

Curry, J., *The Security Service 1908–1945: The Official History* (London, 1999)

Delmer, Sefton, *The Counterfeit Spy* (London, 1973)

Elliott, Geoffrey, *Gentleman Spymaster* (London, 2011)

Farago, Ladislas, *The Game of the Foxes: The Untold Story of German Espionage in the US and Great Britain During World War Two* (New York and London, 1972)

Fest, Joachim, *Plotting Hitler's Death: The German Resistance to Hitler 1933–1945* (London, 1996)

Foot, M. R. D., *SOE: The Special Operations Executive 1940–1946* (London, 1999)

Garby-Czerniawski, Roman, *The Big Network* (London, 1961)

Gilbert, Martin, *Winston S. Churchill, Vol. 6: Finest Hour, 1939–1941* (London, 1983)

Harris, Tomás, *Garbo: The Spy Who Saved D-Day*, introduction by Mark Seaman (London, 2004)

Hastings, Max, *Finest Years: Churchill as Warlord 1940–45* (London, 2009)

——————*Overlord: D-Day and the Battle for Normandy, 1944* (London, 1984)

Hennessy, Thomas, and Claire Thomas, *Spooks: The Unofficial History of MI5* (Stroud, 2010)

Hesketh, Roger, *Fortitude: The D-Day Deception Campaign* (London, 1999)

Hinsley, F. H., *British Intelligence in the Second World War: Its Influence on Strategy and Operations*, vol. 1 (London, 1979)

Hinsley, F. H., and C. A. G. Simkins, *British Intelligence in the Second World War: Security and Counter-Intelligence,* vol. 4 (London, 1990)

Holmes, Richard, *Churchill's Bunker: The Secret Headquarters at the Heart of Britain's Victory* (London, 2009)

Holt, Thaddeus, *The Deceivers: Allied Military Deception in the Second World War* (London, 2004)

Howard, Michael, *British Intelligence in the Second World War, vol. 5: Strategic Deception* (London 1990)

——————— *Grand Strategy* (London, 1972)

Jeffery, Keith, *MI6: The History of the Secret Intelligence Service 1909–1949* (London, 2010)

Johnson, David Alan, *Betrayal: The True Story of J. Edgar Hoover and the Nazi Saboteurs Captured During WWII* (New York, 2007)

———————*Righteous Deception: German Officers against Hitler* (Westport, Connecticut, 2001)

Kahn, David, *Hitler's Spies: German Military Intelligence in World War II* (New York, 1978)

Knightley, Philip, *The Second Oldest Profession* (London, 1986)

Levine, Joshua, *Operation Fortitude: The Story of the Spy Operation that Saved D-Day* (London, 2011)

Liddell, Guy, *The Guy Liddell Diaries, 1939–1945,* vols 1 & 2, ed. Nigel West (London, 2005)

McLachlan, Donald, *Room 39: Naval Intelligence in Action 1939–45* (London, 1968)

Masterman, J. C., *On the Chariot Wheel: An Autobiography* (Oxford, 1975)

———————*The Double Cross System in the War 1939–1945* (London, 1972)

Miller, Russell, *Codename Tricycle: The True Story of the Second World War's Most Extraordinary Double Agent* (London, 2005)

Moen, Jan, *John Moe: Double Agent* (London, 1986)

Montagu, Ewen, *Beyond Top Secret Ultra* (London, 1977)

Mure, David, *Practise to Deceive* (London, 1997)

Paine, Lauran, *The Abwehr: German Military Intelligence in World War II* (London, 1984)

Philby, Kim, *My Silent War: The Autobiography of a Spy* (London, 1968)

Popov, Dusko, *Spy/Counterspy* (New York, 1974)

Rankin, Nicholas, *Churchill's Wizards: The British Genius for Deception 1914–1945* (London 2008)

Reile, Oscar, *Geheime West Front* (Munich, 1962)

Rose, Kenneth, *Elusive Rothschild: The Life of Victor, Third Baron* (London, 2003)

Sebag-Montefiore, Hugh, *Enigma: The Battle for the Code* (London, 2000)

Sergueiev, Lily, *Secret Service Rendered: An Agent in the Espionage Duel Preceding the Invasion of France* (London, 1968)

Smith, Michael, *Foley: The Spy Who Saved 10,000 Jews* (London, 1999)

Stafford, David, *Churchill and the Secret Service* (London, 1997)

—————*Roosevelt and Churchill: Men of Secrets* (London, 1999)

—————*Ten Days to D-Day* (London, 2004)

Stephens, Robin 'Tin-eye', *Camp 020: MI5 and the Nazi Spies*, introduction by Oliver Hoare (London, 2000)

Waller, John H., *The Unseen War in Europe: Espionage and Conspiracy in the Second World War* (New York and London, 1996)

West, Nigel, *At Her Majesty's Secret Service: The Chiefs of Britain's Intelligence Agency, MI6* (London, 2006)

—————*Mask: MI5's Penetration of the Communist Party of Great Britain* (London, 2005)

—————*MI5: British Security Service Operations 1909–45* (London, 1981)

—————*Venona: The Greatest Secret of the Cold War* (London, 1999)

West, Nigel, and Oleg Tsarev, eds, *Triplex: Secrets from the Cambridge Five* (Yale, 2009)

West, Nigel, with Juan Pujol García, *Operation Garbo* (London, 2011)

Wilson, Emily Jane, 'The War in the Dark: The Security Service and the Abwehr 1940–1944', PhD Thesis (Cambridge, 2003)

Winterbotham, F. W., *The Ultra Secret* (London, 1974)

Acknowledgements

Once again, I am deeply indebted to scores of people who have helped me to write this book by generously providing guidance, hospitality, gentle mockery, food and fellowship, as well as access to documents, photographs, recorded interviews and memories. I am particularly grateful to the families of the agents and their case officers, German as well as British, who provided me with so much valuable material: Fiona Agassiz, Robert Astor, Marcus Cumberlege, Gerry Czerniawski, Prue Evill, Jeremy Harmer, the late Peggy Harmer, Anita Harris, Caroline Holbrook, Alfred Lange, Karl Ludwig Lange, David McEvoy, Belinda McEvoy, Marco Popov, Misha Popov and Alastair Robertson. I have benefited greatly from the expertise of a number of brilliant historians and writers, including Christopher Andrew, Michael Foot, Peter Martland, Russell Miller, Nigel West and Paul Winter. My thanks to Jo Carlill for her superb picture research, Ben Blackmore for long hours of research at Kew, Mary Teviot for her genealogical sleuthing, Manuel Aicher for research work in Germany, José António Barreiros in Lisbon, and Begoña Pérez for her help with translations from the Portuguese. I am also grateful for the advice, help and encouragement of Hugh Alexander, David A. Barrett, Paul Bellsham, Roger Boyes, Martin Davidson, Sally George, Phil Reed, Stephen Walker, Matthew Whiteman, and all my friends and colleagues at *The Times*. I owe a particular debt to Terry Charman, Robert Hands and Mark Seaman for reading the manuscript and saving me from some excruciating howlers. The remaining errors are all my own work. To those who prefer not to be named, I am deeply grateful for all your help.

It is a pleasure and a privilege to be published by Bloomsbury; my thanks go to Anna Simpson and Katie Johnson for their unfailing efficiency and patience, and to Michael Fishwick, loyal editor and dear friend. My agent, Ed Victor, has been a rock of support throughout my writing career. My children have kept me sane through another book with their support and good humour; and to Kate, as ever, all my love.

Index

Page numbers in **bold** refer to illustrations.

A SPY AMONG
FRIENDS

In memory of Rick Beeston

'The Friends *n.* General slang for members of an intelligence service; specifically British slang for members of the Secret Intelligence Service, or MI6.'

'If I had to choose between betraying my country and betraying my friends, I hope I should have the guts to betray my country. Such a choice may scandalise the modern reader, and he may stretch out his patriotic hand to the telephone at once and ring up the police. It would not have shocked Dante, though. Dante places Brutus and Cassius in the lowest circle of Hell because they had chosen to betray their friend Julius Caesar rather than their country Rome.'

E. M. Forster, 1938

Contents

Preface

There is a voluminous literature on Kim Philby, including the invaluable pioneering work of writers such as Patrick Seale, Phillip Knightley, Tom Bower, Anthony Cave Brown and Genrikh Borovik. But to many readers, Philby remains opaque, like the Cold War itself, often alluded to but little understood. Moreover, in recent years the release of much previously classified material, along with authorised histories of MI5 and MI6, have shed new light on both that conflict, and Philby's place within it.

This is not another biography of Kim Philby. Rather, it is an attempt to describe a particular sort of friendship that played an important role in history, told in the form of a narrative. It is less about politics, ideology and accountability than personality, character, and a very British relationship that has never been explored before. Since the MI6, CIA and KGB files remain closed, much source material is secondary: the evidence of third parties, often expressed in retrospect. Spies are particularly skilled at misremembering the past, and the protagonists in this story are all guilty, to some extent, of distorting their own histories. Many of the 'facts' about the Philby case are still hotly disputed, and theories, conspiratorial and otherwise, abound. Some of the more contentious issues are discussed in the endnotes. Much that has been written about Philby derives from memory, or speculation, without documentary support; some is coloured by propaganda, and some is pure fantasy. Until and unless the official files are released in their entirety, a degree of mystery will always be attached to these events. For the narrative historian, this creates particular challenges. Presented with conflicting accounts, different viewpoints and divergent recollections, I have had to make judgements about the credibility of different sources, and choose which of the many strands of evidence seem to run closest to reality. Others will doubtless disagree with my choices. This is not an exact science: but what follows is as close to a true story as I can make it.

This book does not purport to be the last word on Kim Philby. Instead, it seeks to tell his story in a different way, through the prism of personal friendship, and perhaps arrive at a new understanding of the most remarkable spy of modern times.

Introduction

Beirut, January 1963

Two middle-aged spies are sitting in an apartment in the Christian Quarter, sipping tea and lying courteously to one another, as evening approaches. They are English; so English that the habit of politeness that binds them together and keeps them apart, never falters for a moment. The sounds of the street waft up through the open window, car horns and horses' hooves mingling with the chink of china and the murmured voices. A microphone, cunningly concealed beneath the sofa, picks up the conversation, and passes it along a wire, through a small hole in the wainscoting and into the next room, where a third man sits hunched over a turning tape-recorder, straining to make out the words through Bakelite headphones.

The two men are old friends. They have known each other for nearly thirty years. But they are bitter foes now, combatants on opposing sides of a brutal conflict.

Kim Philby and Nicholas Elliott learned the spy trade together during the Second World War. When that war was over, they rose together through the ranks of British intelligence, sharing every secret. They belonged to the same clubs, drank in the same bars, wore the same well-tailored clothes, and married women of their own 'tribe'. But all that time, Philby had one secret he never shared: he was covertly working for Moscow, taking everything he was told by Elliott, and passing it on to his Soviet spymasters.

Elliott has come to Beirut to extract a confession. He has wired up the apartment, and set watchers on the doors and street. He wants to know how many have died through Philby's betrayal of their friendship. He wants to know when he became a fool. He needs to know the truth, or at least some of it. And once he knows, Philby can flee to Moscow, or return to Britain, or start anew as a triple agent, or drink himself to death in a Beirut bar. It is, Elliott tells himself, all the same to him.

Philby knows the game, for he has played it brilliantly for three decades. But he does not know how much Elliott knows. Perhaps the friendship will save him, as it has saved him before. Both men tell some truth, laced with deception, and lie with the force of honest conviction. Layer upon layer, back and forth.

As night falls, the strange and lethal duel continues, between two men bonded by class, club and education but divided by ideology; two men of almost identical tastes and upbringing, but conflicting loyalties; the most intimate of enemies. To an eavesdropper, their conversation appears exquisitely genteel, an ancient English ritual played out in a foreign land; in reality it is an unsparing, bare-knuckle fight, the death throes of a bloodied friendship.

Apprentice Spy

One moment Nicholas Elliott was at Ascot racecourse, watching the favourite, Quashed, come romping home at 7–2, and the next, rather to his own surprise, he was a spy. The date was 15 June 1939, three months before the outbreak of the deadliest conflict in history. He was twenty-two.

It happened over a glass of champagne. John Nicholas Rede Elliott's father, Sir Claude Aurelius Elliott, OBE, was headmaster of Eton, England's grandest public school, a noted mountaineer, and a central pillar of the British establishment. Sir Claude knew everybody who was anybody, and nobody who wasn't somebody, and among the many important men he knew was Sir Robert Vansittart, chief diplomatic adviser to His Majesty's Government, who had close links to the Secret Intelligence Service (SIS), better known as MI6, the agency responsible for intelligence-gathering abroad. Nicholas Elliott arranged to meet 'Van' at Ascot and, over drinks, mentioned that he thought he might like to join the intelligence service.

Sir Robert Vansittart smiled and replied: 'I am relieved you have asked me for something so easy.'

'So that,' Elliott wrote, many years later, 'was that.'

The Old Boy recruitment network had worked perfectly.

Nicholas Elliott was not obviously cut out to be a spy. His academic record was undistinguished. He knew little about the complexities of international politics, let alone the dextrous and dangerous game being played by MI6 in the run-up to war. Indeed, he knew nothing whatsoever about espionage, but he thought spying sounded exciting, and important, and exclusive. Elliott was self-confident as only a well-bred, well-heeled young Etonian, newly graduated from Cambridge, with all the right social connections, can be. He was born to rule (though he would never have expressed that belief so indelicately) and membership of the most selective club in Britain seemed like a good place to start doing so.

The Elliotts were the backbone of empire; for generations, they had furnished the military officers, senior clerics, lawyers and colonial administrators who ensured that Britain continued to rule the waves, and much of the globe in between. One of Elliott's grandfathers had been the Lieutenant Governor of Bengal; the other, a senior judge. Like many powerful English families, the Elliotts were also notable for their eccentricity. Nicholas's Great-Uncle Edgar famously took a bet with another Indian Army officer that he could smoke his height in cheroots every day for three months, and smoked himself to death in two. Great-Aunt Blanche was said to have been 'crossed in love' at the age of twenty-six and thereafter took to her bed, where she remained for the next fifty years. Aunt Nancy firmly believed that Catholics were not fit to own pets since they did not believe animals had souls. The family also displayed a profound, but frequently fatal, fascination with mountain climbing. Nicholas's uncle, the Reverend Julius Elliott, fell off the Matterhorn in 1869, shortly after meeting Gustave Flaubert, who declared him 'the epitome of the English gentleman'. Eccentricity is one of those English traits that looks like frailty but masks a concealed strength; individuality disguised as oddity.

Towering over Nicholas's childhood was his father Claude, a man of immovable Victorian principles and ferocious prejudices. Claude loathed music, which gave him indigestion, despised all forms of heating as 'effete', and believed that 'when dealing with foreigners the best plan was to shout at them in English'. Before becoming headmaster of Eton, Claude Elliott had taught history at Cambridge University, despite an ingrained distrust of academics and an aversion to intellectual conversation. But the long university vacations gave him plenty of

time for mountain climbing. He might have become the most celebrated climber of his generation, but for a broken kneecap injured by
a fall in the Lake District, which prevented him from joining Mallory's
Everest expedition. A dominating figure, physically and psychologically, Claude was nicknamed 'The Emperor' by the boys at Eton.
Nicholas regarded his father with awed reverence; in return, Claude
alternately ignored or teased his only child, believing, like many fathers
of his time and class, that displaying affection would make his son
'soft', and quite possibly homosexual. Nicholas grew up convinced
that 'Claude was highly embarrassed by my very existence'. His
mother avoided all intimate topics of conversation, according to her
only son, including 'God, Disease and Below the Waist'.

The young Elliott was therefore brought up by a succession of
nannies, and then shunted off to Durnford School in Dorset, a place
with a tradition of brutality extreme even by the standards of British
prep schools: every morning the boys were made to plunge naked
into an unheated pool for the pleasure of the headmaster, whose
wife liked to read improving literature out loud in the evenings with
her legs stretched out over two small boys, while a third tickled the
soles of her feet. There was no fresh fruit, no toilets with doors, no
restraint on bullying, and no possibility of escape. Today, such an
institution would be illegal; in 1925 it was considered 'character-
forming'. Elliott left his prep school with the conviction that 'nothing as unpleasant could ever recur', an ingrained contempt for
authority, and a hardy sense of humour.

Eton seemed like a paradise after the 'sheer hell' of Durnford, and
having his father as headmaster posed no particular problem for
Nicholas, since Claude continued to pretend he wasn't there. Highly
intelligent, cheerful and lazy, the young Elliott did just enough work
to get by. 'The increased legibility of his handwriting only serves to
reveal the inadequacy of his ability to spell,' noted one report. He
was elected to his first club, Pop, the Eton institution reserved for the
most popular boys in the school. It was at Eton that Elliott discovered a talent for making friends. In later life he would look back on
this as his most important skill, the foundation of his career.

Basil Fisher was Elliott's first and closest friend. A glamorous figure with an impeccable academic and sporting record, Fisher was captain of the First XI, the chairman of Pop, and son of a bona-fide war hero, Basil senior having been killed by a Turkish sniper at Gaza in 1917. The two friends shared every meal, spent their holidays together, and occasionally slipped into the headmaster's house, when Claude was at dinner, to play billiards. Photographs from the time show them arm in arm, beaming happily. Perhaps there was a sexual element to their relationship, but probably not. Hitherto, Elliott had loved only his nanny, 'Ducky Bit' (her real name is lost to history). He worshipped Basil Fisher.

In the autumn of 1935, the two friends went up to Cambridge. Naturally, Elliott went to Trinity, his father's old college. On his first day at the university, he visited the writer and history don Robert Gittings, an acquaintance of his father, to ask a question that had been troubling him: 'How hard should I work, and at what?' Gittings was a shrewd judge of character. As Elliott remembered: 'He strongly advised me to use my three years at Cambridge to enjoy myself in the interval before the next war' – advice which Elliott followed to the letter. He played cricket, punted, drove around Cambridge in a Hillman Minx, and attended and gave some very good parties. He read a lot of spy novels. At weekends he went shooting, or to the races at Newmarket. Throughout the 1930s Cambridge boiled with ideological conflict: Hitler had taken power in 1933; the Spanish Civil War would erupt in the summer of 1936; extreme right and extreme left fought it out in university rooms and on the streets. But the fervid political atmosphere simply passed Elliott by. He was far too busy having fun. He seldom opened a book and emerged after three years with many friends and a third-class degree, a result he considered 'a triumph over the examiners'.

Nicholas Elliott left Cambridge with every social and educational advantage, and absolutely no idea what he wanted to do. But beneath a complacent and conventional exterior, and the 'languid, upper-class manner' lay a more complex personality, an adventurer with a streak of subversion. Claude Elliott's Victorian rigidity had instilled in his son a deep aversion to rules. 'I could never be a good soldier because I am insufficiently amenable to discipline,' he reflected. When told to do something, he tended to 'obey not the order which he had actually been given by a superior, but rather the order which that superior would have given if he had known what he was talking about'. He was tough – the brutality of Durnford had seen to that – but also sensitive, bruised by a lonely childhood. Like many Englishmen, he concealed his shyness behind a defensive barrage of jokes. Another paternal legacy was the conviction that he was physically unattractive; Claude had once told him he was 'plug ugly', and he grew up believing it. Certainly Elliott was not classically handsome, with his gangly frame, thin face and thick-rimmed glasses, but he had poise, a barely concealed air of mischief, and a resolute cheerfulness that women were instantly drawn to. It took him many years to conclude that he 'was no more or less odd to look at than a reasonable proportion of my fellow creatures'. Alongside a natural conservatism, he had inherited the family propensity for eccentricity. He was no snob. He could strike up a conversation with anyone, from any walk of life. He did not believe in God, or Marx, or capitalism; he had faith in King, country, class and club (White's Club, in his case, the gentleman's club in St James's). But above all, he believed in friendship.

In the summer of 1938, Basil Fisher took a job in the City, while Elliott wondered idly what to do with himself. The Old Boys soon solved that. Elliott was playing in a cricket match at Eton that summer when, during the tea interval, he was approached by Sir Nevile Bland, a senior diplomat and a family friend, who tactfully observed that Elliott's father was concerned by his son's 'inability to get down to a solid job of work'. (Sir Claude preferred to speak to his son through emissaries.) Sir Nevile explained that he had recently been appointed Britain's Minister at The Hague, in the Netherlands. Would Nicholas like to accompany him as honorary attaché? Elliott said he would like that very much, despite having no idea what an honorary attaché might actually do. 'There was no serious vetting procedure,' Elliott later wrote. 'Nevile simply told the Foreign Office that I was all right because he knew me and had been at Eton with my father.'

Before leaving, Elliott underwent a course in code-training at the Foreign Office. His instructor was one Captain John King, a veteran cipher clerk who was also, as it happened, a Soviet spy. King had been passing Foreign Office telegrams to Moscow since 1934. Elliott's first tutor in secrecy was a double agent.

Elliott arrived at The Hague, in his Hillman Minx in the middle of November 1938, and reported to the legation. After dinner, Sir Nevile offered him a warning: 'in the diplomatic service it is a sackable offence to sleep with the wife of a colleague' – and some advice: 'I suggest you should do as I do and not light your cigar until you have started your third glass of port.' Elliott's duties were hardly onerous: a little light bag-carrying for the minister, some coding and decoding in the wireless room, and attending formal dinners.

Elliott had been in the Netherlands only four months when he got his first taste of clandestine work and an 'opportunity to see the German war machine at first hand'. One evening, over dinner, he fell into conversation with a young naval officer named Glyn Hearson, the assistant naval attaché at the embassy in Berlin. Commander Hearson confided that he was on a special mission to spy on the port of Hamburg, where the Germans were believed to be developing midget submarines. After a few more glasses, Hearson asked Elliott if he would care to join him. Elliott thought this a splendid idea. Sir Nevile gave his approval.

Two days later, at three in the morning, Elliott and Hearson broke into Hamburg port by climbing over the wall. 'We discreetly poked our noses all over the place for about an hour,' taking photographs, before 'returning to safety and a stiff drink'. Elliott had no diplomatic cover and no training, and Hearson had no authority to recruit him for the mission. Had they been caught, they might have been shot as spies; at the very least, the news that the son of the Eton headmaster had been caught snooping around a German naval dockyard in the middle of the night would have set off a diplomatic firestorm. It was, Elliott happily admitted, 'a singularly foolhardy exploit'. But it had been most enjoyable, and highly successful. They drove on to Berlin in high spirits.

The twentieth of April 1939 was Hitler's fiftieth birthday, a national holiday in Nazi Germany, and the occasion for the largest military parade in the history of the Third Reich. Organised by propaganda minister Josef Goebbels, the festivities marked a high point of the Hitler cult, a lavish display of synchronised sycophancy. A torchlight parade and cavalcade of fifty white limousines, led by the Führer, was followed by a fantastic five-hour exhibition of military muscle, involving 50,000 German troops, hundreds of tanks and 162 warplanes. The ambassadors of Britain, France and the United States did not attend, having been withdrawn after Hitler's march on Czechoslovakia, but some twenty-three other countries sent representatives to wish Hitler a happy birthday. 'The Führer is feted like no other mortal has ever been,' gushed Goebbels in his diary.

Elliott watched the celebrations, with a mixture of awe and horror, from a sixth-floor apartment in the Charlottenburger Chaussee belonging to General Nöel Mason-MacFarlane, the British military attaché in Berlin. 'Mason-Mac' was a whiskery old warhorse, a decorated veteran of the trenches and Mesopotamia. He could not hide his disgust. From the balcony of the apartment there was a clear view of Hitler on his saluting podium. Under his breath, the general remarked to Elliott that the Führer was well within rifle range: 'I am tempted to take advantage of this,' he muttered, adding that he could 'pick the bastard off from here as easy as winking'. Elliott 'strongly urged him to take a pot shot'. Mason-MacFarlane thought better of the idea, though he later made a formal request to be allowed to assassinate Hitler from his balcony. Sadly for the world, the offer was turned down.

Elliott returned to The Hague with two new-minted convictions: that Hitler must be stopped at all costs, and that the best way of contributing to that end would be to become a spy. 'My mind was easily made up.' A day at Ascot, a glass of fizz with Sir Robert Vansittart and a meeting with an important person in Whitehall did the rest. Elliott returned to The Hague still officially an honorary attaché, but in reality, with Sir Nevile Bland's blessing, a new recruit to MI6. Outwardly, his diplomatic life continued as before; secretly, he began his novitiate in the strange religion of British intelligence.

Sir Robert Vansittart, the Foreign Office mandarin who smoothed Elliott's way into MI6, ran what was, in effect, a private intelligence agency, outside the official orbit of government but with close links to both MI6 and MI5, the Security Service. Vansittart was a fierce opponent of appeasement, convinced that Germany would start another war 'just as soon as it feels strong enough'. His network of spies gathered copious intelligence on Nazi intentions, with which he tried (and failed) to persuade Prime Minister Neville Chamberlain of the looming confrontation. One of his earliest and most colourful informants was Jona von Ustinov, a German journalist and fierce secret opponent of Nazism. Ustinov was universally known as 'Klop' – Russian slang for bedbug – a nickname that derived from his rotund appearance, of which he was, oddly, intensely proud. Ustinov's father was a Russian-born army officer; his mother was half-Ethiopian and half-Jewish; his son, born in 1921, was Peter Ustinov, the great comic actor and writer. Klop Ustinov had served in the German army during the First World War, winning an Iron Cross, before taking up a post with the German Press Agency in London. He lost his job in 1935 when the German authorities, suspicious of his exotically mixed heritage, demanded proof of his Aryanism. That same year he was recruited as a British agent, codenamed 'U35'. Ustinov was fat and monocled, with a deceptively bumbling demeanour. He was 'the best and most ingenious operator I had the honour to work with', later declared his case officer, Dick White, who would go on to head both MI5 and MI6.

Elliott's first job for MI6 was to help Ustinov run one of the most important and least known pre-war spies. Wolfgang Gans Edler zu Putlitz was the press attaché at the German embassy in London, a luxury-loving aristocrat and a flamboyant homosexual. Ustinov recruited Putlitz and began to extract what was described as 'price-less intelligence, possibly the most important human-source intelligence Britain received in the prewar period', on German foreign policy and military plans. Putlitz and Ustinov shared Vansittart's conviction that the policy of appeasement had to be reversed: 'I was really helping to damage the Nazi cause,' Putlitz believed. When

Putlitz was posted to the German embassy at The Hague in 1938, Klop Ustinov had discreetly followed him, posing as the European correspondent of an Indian newspaper. With Ustinov as go-between, Putlitz continued to supply reams of intelligence, though he was frustrated by Britain's apparent unwillingness to confront Hitler. 'The English are hopeless,' he complained. 'It is no use trying to help them to withstand the Nazi methods which they so obviously fail to understand.' He began to feel he was 'sacrificing himself for no purpose'.

In The Hague, Klop Ustinov and Nicholas Elliott established an instant rapport, and would remain friends for life. 'Klop was a man of wide talents,' wrote Elliott, '*bon viveur*, wit, raconteur, mimic, linguist – endowed with a vast range of knowledge, both serious and ribald'. Ustinov put Elliott to work, boosting the spirits of the increasingly gloomy and anxious Wolfgang Putlitz.

Putlitz was a 'complicated man', Elliott wrote, torn between his patriotism and his moral instincts. 'His motivation was solely idealistic and he went through acute mental torture at the knowledge that the information he gave away could cost German lives.' One evening in August, Elliott took Putlitz to dinner at the Royale Hotel. Over dessert, he remarked that he was thinking of taking a holiday in Germany: 'Is Hitler going to start the war before we get back at the end of the first week of September?' he asked, half in jest. Putlitz did not smile: 'On present plans the attack on Poland starts on 26 August but it may be postponed for a week, so if I were you, I'd cancel the trip.' Elliott swiftly reported this 'startling statement' to Klop, who passed it on to London. Elliott called off his holiday. On 1 September, just as Putlitz had predicted, German tanks rolled into Poland from the north, south and west. Two days later, Britain was at war with Germany.

Not long afterwards, the German ambassador to The Hague showed Wolfgang Putlitz a list of German agents in the Netherlands; the list was identical to one which Putlitz had recently handed over to Klop Ustinov and Nicholas Elliott. Clearly, there must be a German spy within the MI6 station, but no one for a moment suspected Folkert van Koutrik, an affable Dutchman working as assistant to the station chief, Major Richard Stevens. Van Koutrik had 'always displayed perfectly genuine faithfulness', according to his colleagues. Secretly he was working for the Abwehr, German military intelligence, and 'by the autumn of 1939, the Germans had a pretty clear picture of the whole SIS operation in Holland'. Van Koutrik had obtained the list of German spies Putlitz had passed to MI6, and passed it back to German intelligence.

Putlitz knew 'it could only be a matter of time before he was discovered and dealt with'. He immediately requested asylum in Britain, but insisted he would not leave without his valet, Willy Schneider, who was also his lover. Putlitz was whisked to London on 15 September, and lodged in a safe house.

The loss of such a valuable agent was bad enough, but worse was to follow.

On 9 November, the head of station, Major Stevens, Elliott's new boss, set off for Venlo, a town on the Dutch border with Germany, in the expectation that he would shortly bring the war to a speedy and glorious conclusion. He was accompanied by a colleague, Sigismund Payne Best, a veteran military intelligence officer. Elliott liked Stevens, considering him a 'brilliant linguist and excellent raconteur'. Best, on the other hand, he regarded as 'an ostentatious ass, blown up with self-importance'.

Some months earlier, Stevens and Best had secretly made contact with a group of disaffected German officers plotting to oust Hitler in a military coup. At a meeting arranged by Dr Franz Fischer, a German political refugee, the leader of the group, one Hauptmann Schämmel, explained that elements within the German High Command, appalled by the losses suffered during the invasion of Poland, intended to 'overthrow the present regime and establish a military dictatorship'. The Prime Minister was informed of the anti-Hitler conspiracy, and Stevens was encouraged to pursue negotiations with the coup plotters. 'I have a hunch that the war will be over by the spring,' wrote Chamberlain. Stevens and Best, accompanied by a Dutch intelligence officer, headed to Venlo in high spirits convinced they were about to link up with 'the big man himself', the German general who would lead the coup. In fact, 'Schämmel' was Walter Schellenberg of the Sicherheitsdienst (SD), the Nazi Party intelligence agency, an intelligent and ruthless master spy who would eventually take over German intelligence, and Dr Fischer was in Gestapo pay. The meeting was a trap, personally ordered by SS Reichsführer Heinrich Himmler.

Shortly before 11 a.m., they arrived at the rendezvous point, Café Backus, on the Dutch side of the frontier, a few yards from the border post. 'No one was in sight except a German customs officer,' wrote Stevens, 'and a little girl who was playing ball with a big dog in the middle of the road.' Schellenberg, standing on the café veranda, beckoned them over by waving his hat. That was the signal. As they climbed out of their car, the British officers were immediately surrounded by SS commandos in plain clothes, firing machine guns in the air. The Dutch officer drew his revolver and was shot down.

'The next moment,' recalled Best, 'there were two fellows in front of each of us, one holding a pistol to our heads and the other putting handcuffs on. Then the Germans shouted at us "March!", and prodding us in the back with their pistols and calling "Hup! Hup! Hup!", they rushed us along toward the German frontier.' The commandos bundled the captives into waiting cars, dragging the dying Dutch officer with them.

'At one stroke,' wrote Elliott, 'all British intelligence operations in Holland were compromised.' Worse still, Stevens had been carrying in his pocket, idiotically, a list of intelligence sources in Western Europe. MI6 scrambled to extract its network of agents before the Germans pounced.

The Venlo incident was an unmitigated catastrophe. Since the Dutch were clearly involved, and had lost an officer, Hitler could claim that Holland had violated its own neutrality, providing an excuse for the invasion of Holland that would follow just a few months later. The episode left the British with an ingrained suspicion of German army officers claiming to be anti-Nazi, even when, in the final stages of the war, such approaches were genuine. Stevens and Best were imprisoned for the rest of the war. By December, through information derived from the British captives and the double agent van Koutrik, the Germans were 'able to construct detailed and largely accurate charts of [MI6's] agent networks', as well as the structure of MI6 itself. It was the first and most successful German Double Cross operation of the war. Oddly, it was also one of the last.

Looking back on the Venlo incident, Elliott blamed the 'intense ambition' of Stevens, who had scented the 'possibility of winning the war off his own bat, and this completely clouded his operational judgment'. Instead of maintaining the fiction of a resistance cell inside German High Command, Schellenberg sent a crowing message: 'In the long run conversations with conceited and stupid people become boring. We are cutting off communications. Your friends the German opposition send you hearty greetings.' It was signed 'The German Secret Police'.

In his first six months as a spy, Elliott had learned a salutary lesson in the forgery and fraud that is the currency of espionage. His boss was now in a German prison, having fallen for an elaborate deception; a valuable spy had fled to London, betrayed by a double agent; the entire intelligence network in Holland had been fatally compromised. Even the innocuous Captain John King, the cipher clerk who had taught Elliott coding, was now in prison, serving a ten-year sentence for spying, after a Soviet defector revealed that he had been 'selling everything to Moscow' for cash.

So far from being repelled by the duplicity around him, Elliott felt ever more drawn to the game of skulduggery and double cross. The Venlo debacle had been 'as disastrous as it was shameful', Elliott concluded, but he also found it fascinating, an object lesson in how highly intelligent people could be duped if persuaded to believe what they most wanted to believe. He was learning quickly. He even made up a ditty in celebration:

> *Oh what a tangled web we weave*
> *When first we practise to deceive.*
> *But when you've practised quite a bit*
> *You really get quite good at it.*

At three on the morning of 9 May 1940, Elliott was awoken by the arrival of an emergency telegram from London. He extracted the code books from the ambassador's safe, sat down at the embassy dining table, and began to decode the message: 'Information has been received that the Germans intend to attack along the entire Western Front ...' The next day, Germany invaded France and Holland. 'It soon became apparent,' wrote Elliott, 'that the Dutch, bravely though they fought, would not last out for long.'

The British prepared to flee. Elliott and his MI6 colleagues made a swift bonfire of compromising files in the embassy courtyard. Another officer seized most of Amsterdam's industrial diamond stocks and smuggled them to Britain. The Dutch Queen sailed to safety on a Royal Navy destroyer, along with her Cabinet, her secret service, and her gold. Elliott's principal task, he found, was to evacuate the terrified dancers of the Vic-Wells touring ballet company, which he did by loading them onto a dredger commandeered at Ijmuiden. On 13 May, a British destroyer, HMS *Mohawk*, anchored off the Hook of Holland, waiting to carry the last British stragglers to safety. As he raced in a convoy towards the coast, Elliott watched as flames from burning Rotterdam lit up the horizon. He was one of the last to climb aboard. The following day, the Dutch surrendered. As the young MI6 officer alighted in Britain, he was greeted by the words: 'We're in the final now.'

★

Elliott had expected to find a nation in crisis but he was struck by the 'normality and calmness' of London. From that moment, he wrote, it 'never occurred to me for one moment that we might lose the war'. Within days he was commissioned into the Intelligence Corps, and then, to his astonishment, he found himself behind bars.

Wormwood Scrubs, the Victorian prison in West London, had been adopted as the wartime headquarters of the security service, MI5, and was now expanding rapidly to cope with the threat of German espionage. The fall of France and the Netherlands was attributed, in part, to Nazi fifth columnists, enemy spies working from within to aid the German advance. The threat of a German invasion set off an intense hunt for spies in Britain, and MI5 was swamped by reports of suspicious activity. 'England was gripped by spy fever,' wrote Elliott, who was seconded to MI5 to 'give evidence of what I had seen at first hand of Fifth Column activity in Holland'. The fifth column threat never materialised, for the simple reason that it did not exist – Hitler had not intended to go to war with Britain, and little effort had been made to prepare the ground for a German invasion.

The Abwehr soon set about making up the deficit. Over the next few months, so-called 'invasion spies' poured into Britain, by boat, parachute, and submarine; ill-trained and underequipped, they were swiftly duly rounded up. Some were imprisoned, and a handful executed, but a number were recruited as double agents, to feed false information back to their German handlers. This was the embryo of the great Double Cross system, the network of double agents whose importance would steadily expand as the war progressed. Under interrogation, many of these spies provided information of vital interest to the Secret Intelligence Service. Elliott was appointed liaison officer between the sister services, and based in Wormwood Scrubs. It was a bizarre place to work: malodorous and dingy. Most of the inmates had been evacuated but a handful remained, including an Old Etonian contemporary of Elliott's, Victor Hervey, the future 6th Marquess of Bristol, a notorious playboy who had been jailed in 1939 for robbing a Mayfair jeweller's. Elliott worked from a soundproofed jail cell, with no handle on the inside; if his last visitor of the day accidentally turned the outside handle on leaving, he was locked in until morning.

Elliott loved his new life, in prison by day and at liberty at night, in a city under siege and threatened with invasion. He moved into a flat in Cambridge Square, Bayswater, belonging to the grandmother of another friend from Eton, Richard Brooman-White, who was also in MI6. Basil Fisher was now a fighter pilot with 111 Squadron, flying Hurricanes out of Croydon. Whenever Fisher was on leave, the three friends would gather, usually at White's. The Blitz hammered down, and Elliott was elated by the 'feeling of camarade-rie' as he sat with his friends in the smoky, mahogany-panelled luxury of London's oldest and most exclusive gentleman's club. 'My only moment of real danger was when drinking a pink gin in the bar of the club. A bomb fell on the building next door, upsetting my gin and knocking me flat. I got another pink gin with the compli-ments of the barman.' Elliott was enjoying his war. Then, three months after returning to London, he discovered what war is about.

On 15 August, 111 Hurricane Squadron was scrambled to inter-cept a formation of Luftwaffe Messerschmitts that had crossed the Channel at Dungeness. In the ferocious, sky-sprawling dogfight that followed, one of the fiercest engagements in the Battle of Britain, seven of the German fighter-bombers were shot down. Basil Fisher's plane was seen peeling away with smoke and flames streaming from the fuselage. He managed to bail out over the village of Sidlesham in West Sussex, with his parachute on fire. The cables burned through, and Elliott's friend tumbled to earth. The pilotless Hurricane crashed into a barn. The body of Flying Officer Basil Fisher was found in Sidlesham pond. He was buried in the churchyard of the Berkshire village where he had been born.

Elliott was quietly but utterly distraught. Like many upper-class Englishmen, he seldom spoke about his feelings, but in its taut, agonised understatement, his private epitaph for Basil Fisher said more than any number of emotive words. The mask of flippancy slipped. 'Basil Fisher was killed in action. I felt this very deeply. He had been virtually a brother to me. This was the first time I had been hit by tragedy.'

Elliott was still dazed by grief when, just a few weeks later, he met another new recruit to the secret world, a product of Westminster School, a fellow graduate of Trinity College, Cambridge, and a man who would define the rest of his life: Harold Adrian Russell Philby, better known as Kim.

Section V

The word most consistently used to describe Kim Philby was 'charm', that intoxicating, beguiling, and occasionally lethal English quality. Philby could inspire and convey affection with such ease that few ever noticed they were being charmed. Male and female, old and young, rich and poor, Kim enveloped them all. He looked out at the world with alert, gentle blue eyes from under an unruly fore-lock. His manners were exceptional: he was always the first to offer you a drink, to ask after your sick mother, and remember your children's names. He loved to laugh, and he loved to drink, and to listen, with deep sincerity and rapt curiosity. 'He was the sort of man who won worshippers,' said one contemporary. 'You didn't just like him, admire him, agree with him; you worshipped him.' A stutter, which came and went, added to his appeal, betraying an attractive glimmer of fragility. People waited on his words, for what his friend, the novelist Graham Greene, called his 'halting stammered witticisms'.

Kim Philby cut a dashing figure in wartime London. As *The Times* correspondent in the Spanish Civil War, reporting from the rebel Nationalist side, he had narrowly cheated death in late 1937 when a Republican shell landed near the car he was sitting in eating choco-lates and drinking brandy, killing all the other three fellow war correspondents. Philby escaped with a minor head wound and a reputation for 'great pluck'. General Franco himself had pinned a medal, the Red Cross of Military Merit, on the young war reporter.

Philby had been one of only fifteen newspaper correspondents selected to join the British Expeditionary Force sent to France on the outbreak of the Second World War. From the continent, he wrote wry, distinctive despatches for *The Times* as he waited with the troops for the fighting to start: 'Many express disappointment at the slow tempo of the overture to Armageddon. They expected danger, and they have found damp,' he wrote. Philby continued reporting as the Germans advanced, and quit Amiens with the Panzers already rumbling into the city. He took a ship for England with such haste that he was forced to leave behind his luggage. His expenses claim for lost items became a Fleet Street legend: 'Camel-hair overcoat (two years' wear), fifteen guineas; Dunhill pipe (two years old, and all the better for it), one pound ten shillings.' It is a measure of his reputation that *The Times* compensated its star correspondent for the loss of an old pipe. Philby was a fine journalist, but his ambitions lay elsewhere. He wanted to join MI6, but like every would-be spy he faced a conundrum: how do you join an organisation to which you cannot apply, because it does not formally exist?

In the end, Philby's entry into the secret services turned out to be as straightforward as that of Elliott, and by much the same informal route: he simply 'dropped a few hints here and there' among influential acquaintances, and waited for an invitation to join the club. The first indication that his signals had been picked up came on the train back to London after the retreat from France, when he found himself in a first-class compartment with a *Sunday Express* journalist named Hester Harriet Marsden-Smedley. Marsden-Smedley was thirty-eight years old, a veteran of foreign wars, and as tough as teak. She had come under enemy fire on the Luxembourg border, and witnessed the German surge across the Siegfried Line. She knew people in the secret services, and was said to do a little spying on the side. Inevitably, she too was charmed by Philby. She did not beat about the bush.

'A person like you has to be a fool to join the Army,' she said. 'You're capable of doing a lot more to defeat Hitler.'

Philby knew exactly what she was alluding to, and stammered that he 'didn't have any contacts in that world'.

'We'll figure something out,' said Hester.

Back in London, Philby was summoned to the office of the Foreign Editor of *The Times*, to be told that a Captain Leslie Sheridan of the 'War Department' had called, asking if Philby was available for 'war work' of an unspecified nature. Sheridan, the former night editor of the *Daily Mirror*, ran a section of MI6 known as 'D/Q', responsible for black propaganda and disseminating rumours.

Two days later, Philby sat down to tea at St Ermin's Hotel off St James's Park, just a few hundred yards from MI6 headquarters at 54 Broadway, with another formidable woman: Sarah Algeria Marjorie Maxse, chief of staff for MI6's Section D (the 'D' stood for 'Destruction') which specialised in covert paramilitary operations. Miss Marjorie Maxse was chief organisation officer for the Conservative Party, a role that apparently equipped her to identify people who would be good at spreading propaganda and blowing things up. Philby found her 'intensely likeable'. She clearly liked him too, for two days later they met again, this time with Guy Burgess, a friend and Cambridge contemporary of Philby's, who was already in MI6. 'I began to show off, name-dropping shamelessly,' wrote Philby. 'It turned out I was wasting my time, since a decision had already been taken.' MI5 had conducted a routine background check, and found 'nothing recorded against' him: young Philby was clean. Valentine Vivian, the deputy head of MI6, who had known Philby's father when they were both colonial officials in India, was prepared to vouch personally for the new recruit, giving what may be the quintessential definition of Britain's Old Boy network: 'I was asked about him, and said I knew his people.'

Philby resigned from *The Times*, and duly reported to a building near MI6 headquarters, where he was installed in an office with a blank sheaf of paper, a pencil and a telephone. He did nothing for two weeks, except read the papers and enjoy long, liquid lunches with Burgess. Philby was beginning to wonder if he had really joined MI6 or some strange, inactive offshoot, when he was assigned to Brickendonbury Hall, a secret school for spies deep in Hertfordshire where an oddball collection of émigré Czechs, Belgians, Norwegians,

Dutchmen and Spaniards were being trained for covert operations. This unit would eventually be absorbed into the Special Operations Executive, SOE, the organisation created, in Winston Churchill's words, to 'set Europe ablaze' by operating behind enemy lines. In its early days, the only thing the agents seemed likely to ignite was Brickendonbury Hall and the surrounding countryside. The resident explosives expert mounted a demonstration for visiting Czech intelligence officers, but set fire to a wood and nearly immolated the entire delegation. Philby was soon transferred to SOE itself, and then to another training school at Beaulieu in Hampshire, specialising in demolition, wireless communication and subversion. Philby gave lectures on propaganda for which, having been a journalist, he was considered suitably trained. He was champing at the bit, eager to join the real wartime intelligence battle. 'I escaped to London whenever I could,' he wrote. It was during one of these getaways that he encountered Nicholas Elliott.

★

Elliott could never recall exactly where their first meeting took place. Was it the bar in the heart of the MI6 building on Broadway, the most secret drinking hole in the world? Or perhaps it was at White's, Elliott's club. Or the Athenaeum, which was Philby's. Perhaps Philby's future wife, Aileen, a distant cousin of Elliott's, brought them together. It was inevitable that they would meet eventually, for they were creatures of the same world, thrown together in important clandestine work, and remarkably alike, in both background and temperament. Claude Elliott and Philby's father St John, a noted Arab scholar, explorer and writer, had been contemporaries and friends at Trinity College, and both sons had obediently followed in their academic footsteps – Philby, four years older, left Cambridge the year Elliott arrived. Both lived under the shadow of imposing but distant fathers, whose approval they longed for and never quite won. Both were children of the Empire: Kim Philby was born in the Punjab where his father was a colonial administrator; his mother was the daughter of a British official in the Rawalpindi Public Works

Department. Elliott's father had been born in Simla. Both had been brought up largely by nannies, and both were unmistakably moulded by their schooling: Elliott wore his Old Etonian tie with pride; Philby cherished his Westminster School scarf. And both concealed a certain shyness, Philby behind his impenetrable charm and fluctuating stammer, and Elliott with a barrage of jokes.

They struck up a friendship at once. 'In those days,' wrote Elliott, 'friendships were formed more quickly than in peacetime, particularly amongst those involved in confidential work.' While Elliott helped to intercept enemy spies sent to Britain, Philby was preparing Allied saboteurs for insertion into occupied Europe. They found they had much to talk and joke about, within the snug confines of absolute secrecy.

The void in Elliott's life left by the death of Basil Fisher was filled by Philby. 'He had an ability to inspire loyalty and affection,' wrote Elliott. 'He was one of those people who were instinctively liked but more rarely understood. For his friends he sought out the unconventional and the unusual. He did not bore and he did not pontificate.' Before the war, Philby had joined the Anglo-German Fellowship, an organisation with pro-Nazi leanings, but now, like Elliott, he was committed to battling 'the inherent evil of Nazism'. The two friends 'very rarely discussed politics', and spent more time debating 'the English batting averages and watching the cricket from the Mound Stand at Lord's' – home to the Marylebone Cricket Club, the central citadel of cricket, of which Elliott was a member. Philby seemed to share Elliott's firm but simple British loyalties, uncomplicated by ideology. 'Indeed,' wrote Elliott, 'he did not strike me as a political animal.' Philby was only twenty-eight when they met, but to Elliott he seemed older, matured by his experience of war zones, confident, competent and agreeably louche.

MI6 enjoyed a reputation as the world's most redoubtable intelligence agency, but in 1940 it was in a state of flux, rapidly reorganising under the pressure of war. Philby seemed to bring a new air of professionalism to the job. He was plainly ambitious, but hid his drive, as English manners required, behind a 'pose of amiable, disengaged worldliness'.

Hugh Trevor-Roper was another new recruit to wartime intelligence. One of the cleverest, and rudest, men in England, Trevor-Roper (later the historian Lord Dacre) had hardly a good word for any of his colleagues ('by and large pretty stupid, some of them very stupid'). But Philby was different: 'An exceptional person: exceptional by his virtues, for he seemed intelligent, sophisticated, even real.' He appeared to know exactly where he was going. When Philby spoke about intelligence matters, Elliott thought he displayed impressive 'clarity of mind', but he was neither drily academic nor rule-bound: 'He was much more a man of practice than of theory.' Philby even dressed distinctively, eschewing both the Whitehall stiff collar with pinstripe and the military uniform to which, as a former war correspondent, he was entitled. Instead, he wore a tweed jacket with patches at the elbows, suede shoes and a cravat, and sometimes a coat of green fabric lined with bright red fox fur, a gift from his father who had received it from an Arab prince. This eye-catching outfit was topped off with a Homburg, and a smart, ebony-handled umbrella. Malcolm Muggeridge, another writer recruited to wartime intelligence, noted Philby's unique sartorial swagger: 'The old Secret Service professionals were given to spats and monocles long after they passed out of fashion,' but the new intake of officers could be seen 'slouching about in sweaters and grey flannel trousers, drinking in bars and cafés and low dives ... boasting of their underworld acquaintances and liaisons. Philby may be taken as a prototype and was indeed, in the eyes of many of them, a model to be copied.' Elliott began to dress like Philby. He even bought the same expensive umbrella from James Smith & Sons of Oxford Street, an umbrella that befitted an establishment man of the world, but one with panache.

Through Philby, Elliott was introduced to a fraternity of ambitious, clever, hard-drinking intelligence officers, the 'Young Turks' of MI5 and MI6. This informal – almost entirely male – group often gathered, in off-duty hours, at the home of Tomás Harris, a wealthy, half-Spanish art dealer who worked in MI5, where he would play a central role in the great Double Cross deception as the case officer for double agent 'Garbo', Juan Garcia Pujol. Harris and his wife Hilda were generous hosts, and their Chelsea home, with its large wine cellar, became an open-house salon for spies. 'You'd drop in to see who was around,' Philby remembered. Here, in an 'atmosphere of *haute cuisine* and *grand vin*', might be found Philby's friend Guy Burgess, extravagant in his homosexuality, frequently drunk, faintly malodorous and always supremely entertaining. Here too came their friend Anthony Blunt, a Cambridge art scholar now ensconced at the heart of MI5. Other regulars included Victor, Lord Rothschild, the aristocratic chief of counter-sabotage at MI5, and Guy Liddell, MI5's head of counter-intelligence whose diaries from the period offer an extraordinary glimpse into this private dining and drinking club within the secret world. From MI6 came Tim Milne, who had been at Westminster with Philby (and was the nephew of Winnie-the-Pooh creator A. A. Milne), Richard Brooman-White, now head of MI6's Iberian operations, and, of course, Nicholas Elliott. Hilda Harris served up sumptuous Spanish meals. Liddell, who had once contemplated a professional career as a musician, would sometimes pick up his cello. Burgess, usually accompanied by his latest rent boy, added scandalous unpredictability. And among them moved Philby, with his aura of smiling charm, holding forth on intelligence matters, provoking arguments ('out of fun rather than malice', Elliott insisted), and dispensing Harris's fine wine in torrential quantities.

Even by the heavy-drinking standards of wartime, the spies were spectacular boozers. Alcohol helped to blunt the stress of clandestine war, serving as both a lubricant and a bond, and the gentlemen's clubs were able to obtain supplies for their members far beyond the reach of ordinary rationed folk. Dennis Wheatley, the novelist, who worked in the deception section of British intelligence, described a typical lunch with fellow officers: 'To start with we always had two or three Pimm's at a table in the bar, then a so-called "short-one" well-laced with absinthe ... There would be smoked salmon or potted shrimps, then a Dover sole, jugged hare, salmon or game, and a Welsh rarebit to wind up with. Good red or white wine washed this down, and we ended with port or Kümmel.' After this blowout, Wheatley tended to sneak off to bed 'for an hour to sleep it off', before returning to work.

No one served (or consumed) alcohol with quite the same *joie de vivre* and determination as Kim Philby. 'He was a formidable drinker,' Elliott wrote, and held to the arcane theory that 'serious drinkers should never take exercise or make sudden or violent movements' since this would provoke a 'violent headache'. Philby sucked down the drink, and poured it into others, as if on a mission.

Elliott was flattered to find himself in such company, and relaxed. Englishmen are naturally reticent. Englishmen of Elliott's class and character even more so. Members of the secret services were forbidden to tell their friends, wives, parents or children what they did, yet many were drawn to this closed clique, bound by shared secrets others must never know. In the civilian world, Elliott never breathed a word about his job. But inside the secular monastery that is MI6, and particularly at Harris's raucous soirées, he was among people he could trust utterly, and speak to openly in a way that was impossible outside. 'It was an organisation in which a large proportion of one's colleagues, male and female, were personal friends,' wrote Elliott. 'A sort of convivial camaraderie prevailed, rather like a club, in which we all called each other by our first names, and saw a lot of one another outside the office.'

The friendship between Philby and Elliott was not just one of shared interests and professional identity, but something deeper. Nick Elliott was friendly to all, but emotionally committed to few. The bond with Philby was unlike any other in his life. 'They spoke the same language,' Elliott's son Mark recalls. 'Kim was as close a friend as my father ever had.' Elliott never openly expressed, or demonstrated, this affection. Like so much of importance in the masculine culture of the time, it was left unsaid. Elliott hero-worshipped Philby, but he also loved him, with a powerful male adoration that was unrequited, unsexual and unstated.

Their relationship grew still closer when both were plucked from the outer reaches of British intelligence, and placed at the very centre, in Section V of MI6, the division devoted to counter-intelligence. MI5 was responsible for maintaining security, including the combating of enemy espionage, within the UK and British Empire. MI6 was responsible for gathering intelligence and running agents abroad. Within MI6, Section V played a specific and vital role: collecting information on enemy intelligence in foreign parts, by means of spies and defectors, and furnishing MI5 with advance warning of espionage threats to Britain. A vital link between Britain's secret services, Section V's task was to 'negate, confuse, deceive, subvert, monitor or control the clandestine intelligence collection operations and agents of foreign governments or agencies'. Before the war, the section had devoted most of its energies to monitoring the spread of international communism and battling Soviet espionage; but as war progressed, it came to focus almost exclusively on the intelligence operations of the Axis powers. The Iberian Peninsula was a particular concern. Neutral Spain and Portugal stood on the frontline of the espionage war. Many of the German intelligence operations directed at Britain were launched from these two countries, and in 1941, MI6 began beefing up the Iberian operation. One evening Tommy Harris told Philby that the bosses were looking for someone 'with a knowledge of Spain to take charge of the expanded sub-section'. Philby immediately expressed an interest; Harris spoke to Richard Brooman-White, Elliott's friend, the chief of MI6's Iberian operations; Brooman-White spoke to the head of MI6. 'The Old Boy network began to operate,' as Philby put it, and within days he was summoned to see the head of Section V.

Major Felix Cowgill was the model of the old-style intelligence officer: a former officer in the Indian police, he was rigid, combative, paranoid and quite dim. Trevor-Roper dismissed him as a 'purblind, disastrous megalomaniac', and Philby, privately, was equally scathing. 'As an intelligence officer, he was inhibited by lack of imagination, inattention to detail and sheer ignorance of the world.' Cowgill was 'suspicious and bristling' towards anyone outside his section, blindly loyal to those within it, and no match for the Philby charm.

Philby never formally applied for the job, and Cowgill never formally offered it, but after one long, bibulous evening, Philby emerged as the new head of Section V's Iberian department, a job which, as Philby happily noted, entailed wider responsibilities as well as 'personal contacts with the rest of SIS and MI5'. Before Philby took up the post, however, Valentine Vivian – known as 'Vee-Vee' – the deputy head of MI6, decided to have another chat with Philby's father. Hillary St John Bridger Philby was a figure of considerable notoriety. As adviser to Ibn Saud, the first monarch of Saudi Arabia, he had played (and would continue to play) a key role in the oleaginous politics of that region. He had converted to Islam, taking the name Sheikh Abdullah, spoke Arabic fluently, and would eventually marry, as his second wife, a slave girl from Baluchistan presented to him by the Saudi King. He remained, however, quintessentially English in his tastes, and wildly unpredictable in his opinions. The elder Philby's opposition to the war had seen him arrested and briefly imprisoned, an episode that did no harm to his own social standing, or his son's career prospects. Over lunch at the club, Colonel Vivian asked St John Philby about his son's politics.

'He was a bit of a communist at Cambridge, wasn't he?'

'Oh that was all schoolboy nonsense,' St John Philby airily replied. 'He's a reformed character now.'

Nicholas Elliott, meanwhile, was making a parallel career move. In the summer of 1941, he was also transferred to Section V, with responsibility for the Netherlands. Henceforth Philby would be fighting German espionage in the Iberian Peninsula, and Elliott would be doing the same in Nazi-occupied Holland, from the next-door office. Each would be paid a salary, in cash, of £600 a year and neither, in accordance with longstanding secret services rules, would pay any tax. Philby and Elliott were now fighting shoulder to shoulder in the 'active pursuit and liquidation of the enemy intelligence services'.

★

Section V was not housed in London with the rest of MI6, but head-quartered in Glenalmond, a large Victorian house in King Harry Lane, St Albans, some twenty miles north of the capital, codenamed 'War Station XB'. Kim Philby and Aileen rented a cottage on the outskirts of the town.

Philby had been introduced to his future wife, on the day war was declared, by Flora Solomon, a friend from Cambridge. The daughter of a Jewish–Russian gold tycoon, Solomon was another exotic bloom in the colourful hothouse of Philby's circle: as a young woman she had had an affair with Alexander Kerensky, the Russian Prime Minister deposed by Lenin in the October Revolution, before going on to marry a British First World War general. In 1939, she was hired to improve working conditions by Marks and Spencer, and here she met and befriended Aileen Furse, a store detective in the shop's Marble Arch branch. 'Aileen belonged to that class, now out of fashion, called "county",' wrote Solomon. 'She was typically English, slim and attractive, fiercely patriotic.' Working undercover, in her twinset and raincoat, she was virtually invisible when discreetly policing the aisles of Marks and Spencer. Aileen tended to disappear in a crowd, hanging back, watchful and careful. Her father had been killed in the First World War, when she was just four years old, and her upbringing in the Home Counties had been strictly conventional, boring and quite lonely. Secretly, she was 'subject to depressions'. Aileen Furse and Kim Philby met over drinks at Solomon's Mayfair home. Philby began talking about his experiences as a correspondent in Spain. 'He found an avid listener in Aileen,' wrote Solomon, and 'the next I knew they were sharing a flat.'

Their union, it seemed to Elliott, was an ideal one, founded on a shared love of good company. Elliott liked Aileen almost as much as he liked Philby, an affection that deepened after he developed diabetes and she gently nursed him back to health. 'She was highly intelligent,' wrote Elliott, 'very human, full of courage and had a pleasant sense of humour.' Indeed, Aileen was just the sort of wife he hoped for himself: loyal, discreet, patriotic, and willing to laugh at his jokes. The Philbys' first child, a daughter, was born in 1941; a son followed the next year, and another the year after that. Philby was a doting father, Elliot noted approvingly, bursting with 'parental pride'.

The Philby home became a gathering place for the young intelligence officers of Section V, an out-of-town version of the Harris salon in London, where the doors, and various bottles, were always open. Graham Greene, then one of Philby's deputies, recalled the 'long Sunday lunches in St Albans when the whole subsection relaxed under his leadership for a few hours of heavy drinking'. Philby was adored by his colleagues, who recalled his 'small loyalties', his generosity of spirit, and his distaste for petty office politics. 'He had something about him – an aura of lovable authority like some romantic platoon commander – which made people want to appear at their best in front of him. Even his senior officers recognised his abilities and deferred to him.'

Section V was a tight-knit little community, just a dozen officers and their deputies, and a similar number of support staff. Officers and secretaries were on Christian-name terms, and some were on more intimate terms than that. Philby's 'merry band' included his old school friend Tim Milne, a jovial eccentric named Trevor Wilson, who had formerly been 'a purchaser of skunk excrement in Abyssinia for the French perfume company Molyneux', and Jack Ivens, a fruit exporter who spoke fluent Spanish. The local townsfolk were led to believe that the educated young men and women in the big house were a team of archaeologists from the British Museum, excavating the ruins of Verulamium, the Roman name for St Albans. Mrs Rennit, the cook, served solid English fare, and fish and chips on Fridays. At weekends, they played cricket on the pitch behind Glenalmond, before repairing to the King Harry pub next door.

Colonel Cowgill was the boss, but Philby was the animating spirit of the group: 'The sense of dedication and purpose to whatever he was doing gleamed through and inspired men to follow him.' Elliott was not alone in his adulation. 'No one could have been a better chief than Kim Philby,' wrote Graham Greene. 'He worked harder than anyone else and never gave the impression of labour. He was always relaxed, completely unflappable.' In even the most casual bureaucracies there is room for jockeying, but Philby was the epitome of loyalty. 'If one made an error of judgment he was sure to minimise it and cover it up, without criticism.' Desmond Bristow, a new Spanish-speaking recruit, arrived at Glenalmond in September 1941, and was welcomed by Philby, 'a gentle-looking man with smiling eyes and an air of confidence. My first impression was of a man of quiet intellectual charm ... he had a spiritual tranquillity about him.' The 'cosiness' of Section V distinguished it from other, more reserved parts of MI6. The team kept few secrets from one another, official or otherwise. 'It was not difficult to find out what colleagues were doing,' wrote Philby. 'What was known to one would be known to all.'

The admiration of his subordinates was echoed by the approbation of Philby's superiors. Felix Cowgill called him 'a good cricket umpire'. There could be no higher praise. Here was a man who played by the most honourable rules. But some saw a flicker of something else in Philby, something harder and deeper, a 'calculating ambition', a ruthless 'single-mindedness'. Like Elliott, he used humour to deflect inquiry. 'There was something mysterious about him,' wrote Trevor-Roper. 'He never engaged you in serious conversation – it was always irony.'

As head of the Iberian section, Philby faced a formidable challenge. Although Spain and Portugal were officially neutral non-combatants in the war, in reality both countries tolerated, and even actively encouraged, German espionage on a grand scale. Wilhelm Leissner, the Abwehr chief in Spain, presided over a well-funded, sprawling intelligence network made up of more than 200 officers (more than half the German diplomatic presence) with some 1,500 agents deployed around the country. Leissner's principal target was Britain: recruiting and despatching spies to the UK, bugging the British embassy, bribing Spanish officials and sabotaging British shipping. Portugal was another hotbed of espionage, although Abwehr operations were less efficient under the command of a dissolute German aristocrat named Ludovico von Karsthoff. The Abwehr poured spies and cash into Spain and Portugal, but in his duel with Leissner and Karsthoff Philby had one overwhelming advantage: Bletchley Park, the top-secret decoding station where intercepted German wireless messages were decrypted, furnishing a priceless insight into Nazi intelligence. 'It was not long before we had a very full picture of the Abwehr in the Peninsula,' wrote Philby. That information would soon be put 'to good use in disrupting, or at least seriously embarrassing, the enemy on his own chosen ground'.

Nicholas Elliott's task of attacking German intelligence in the Netherlands, his former stamping ground, was a different proposition, and even harder. The Abwehr in Nazi-occupied Holland was highly effective, recruiting, training and despatching a stream of spies to Britain. By contrast, infiltrating agents into Holland was exceptionally difficult. The few networks that had survived the Venlo incident were riddled with Nazi informers.

In a plot that smacks of James Bond (and has all the hallmarks of an Elliott ruse) a Dutch agent named Peter Tazelaar was put ashore near the seafront casino at Scheveningen, wearing full evening dress covered with a rubber suit to keep him dry. Once ashore, Tazelaar peeled off his outer suit and began to 'mingle with the crowd on the front' in his dinner jacket, which had been sprinkled with brandy to reinforce the 'party-goer's image'. Formally dressed and alcoholically perfumed, Tazelaar successfully made it past the German guards, and picked up a radio previously dropped by parachute. The echo of 007 may not be coincidental: among the young blades of British intelligence at this time was a young officer in the Naval Intelligence Department named Ian Fleming, the future author of the James Bond books. Ian Fleming and Nicholas Elliott had both experienced the trauma of being educated at Durnford School; they became close friends.

Peter Tazelaar was one of the few to make it back to Britain. Of the fifteen agents sent into Holland between June 1940 and December 1941, only four survived, thanks to the brutal efficiency of Major Hermann Giskes, the head of Abwehr counter-intelligence in Holland, Elliott's opposite number. In August 1941, Giskes intercepted a team of Dutch SOE agents shipped into Holland by fast torpedo boat and forced them, under threat of execution, to send

encrypted wireless messages back to Britain, luring more spies across
the water. Some fifty-five Dutch agents were subsequently captured
and dozens executed, in a Double Cross operation codenamed
Englandspiel ('The England Game'), before two managed to escape
and alert the British to the fact that they were being hoaxed. Winding
up the operation, Giskes sent a final, mocking wireless message: 'This
is the last time you are trying to make business in Netherlands without our assistance Stop we think this rather unfair in view our long
and successful co-operation as your sole agents Stop but never mind
whenever you will come to pay a visit to the Continent you may be
assured that you will be received with the same care and result as all
those who you sent us before Stop so long.' The episode was, in
Philby's words, 'an operational disaster', but almost equally alarming
was the discovery that German intelligence in Holland had managed
to slip at least one spy into Britain undetected.

In the spring of 1941, the body of a Dutchman was found in an air
raid shelter in Cambridge. His name, unimprovably, was Engelbertus
Fukken. In his pockets and suitcase were found a Dutch passport, a
forged identity card, and one shilling and sixpence. He had parachuted into Buckinghamshire five months earlier, passed himself off
as a refugee and shot himself in the head when he ran out of money.
No Nazi spy had managed to remain at large for so long, and there
was no trace of him in the Bletchley Park intercepts, which raised, for
Elliott, the worrying possibility that there might be others at large.

Under Cowgill's relaxed regime, the officers of Section V could
visit London 'virtually at will'. Philby and Elliott seized every opportunity to do so, in order to cultivate 'contacts with other SIS sections,
with MI5 and with other government departments', while also visiting their clubs and, in the summer, watching the cricket together at
Lord's. Both volunteered for 'fire-watching nights', once or twice a
month, at MI6 headquarters, monitoring the telegrams that came in
overnight from around the world, which offered a fascinating insight
into British intelligence operations. Within the secret brethren,
Elliott and Philby were the closest of siblings, revelling in the shared
risks, hard work and ribaldry.

One morning in 1941, Kim Philby caught the train to London, taking with him, as usual, a 'bulging briefcase and a long visiting list'. He also carried a detailed description of the workings of Section V, its personnel, aims, operations, failures and successes, written out in 'longhand, in neat, tiny writing'. After completing his round of meetings at MI5 and MI6, Philby did not head to the bar beneath MI6, nor to his club; nor to the Harris home for an evening of drinking and secret-sharing. Instead he descended into the St James's Park Underground station. He let the first train leave without boarding. Then he waited until every other passenger had boarded the next train, before slipping on just as the doors closed. Two stops later, he alighted and caught a train in the opposite direction. Then he hopped on a moving bus. Finally certain that he was not being followed ('dry-cleaned', in spy jargon), Philby made his way to a park, where a stocky, fair-haired man was waiting for him on a bench. They shook hands; Philby handed over the contents of his briefcase, and then headed to King's Cross to catch the train home to St Albans.

Had Nick Elliott examined the report about Section V written by his best friend, he would have been amazed, and then mortified. One passage read: 'MR NICHOLAS ELLIOTT. 24, 5ft 9in. Brown hair, prominent lips, black glasses, ugly and rather pig-like to look at. Good brain, good sense of humour. Likes a drink but was recently very ill and now, as a consequence, drinks little. He is in charge of Holland . . .'

Elliott would have been still more astonished to discover that the man hurrying away into the night with the bundle of papers was an officer of the NKVD, Stalin's intelligence agency, and that his friend Kim Philby was an experienced Soviet spy of eight years' standing, codenamed 'Sonny'.

3

Otto and Sonny

Philby's father nicknamed his son Kim after the eponymous hero in the popular Rudyard Kipling novel. Brought up by an Indian nanny, Philby's first language was a sort of nursery Punjabi; like Kipling's Kim, he was a white child who could pass for an Indian. The name stuck forever, but its aptness would not emerge for years. The fictional Kim has two distinct personalities; he is a two-sided man.

> Something I owe to the soil that grew
> More to the life that fed,
> But most to Allah Who gave me two
> Separate sides to my head.

The soil that grew Kim Philby had produced a conventional upper-class, public school-educated Englishman; the life that fed him had created something entirely different, and it was a life that his dear friend Nicholas Elliott knew nothing about. He did not know that Philby had become a Soviet agent in the very year that Elliott had gone up to Cambridge; he did not know that Philby's idyllic marriage was a fraud, and that his friend was really married to an Austrian communist spy; he did not know that Philby had joined MI6, not as an eager patriot like himself, but rather, in Philby's own words, as a 'penetration agent working in the Soviet interest'. And he did not know that during the convivial Sunday lunches in St Albans, the boozy evenings at the Harris home, the drinks in the basement of MI6 and the bar at White's, Philby was hard at work, absorbing his friends' secrets as fast as the gin, and then passing them all to Moscow.

The seeds of Philby's double life lay in his childhood, his father, his upbringing and the intense ideological conversion that shaped him in early adulthood. Philby maintained that his dual existence emerged from an unwavering belief in a set of political principles that he discovered at the age of eighteen, and never abandoned: what Philby's enemies described as betrayal, he saw as loyalty. But there was more to Philby than mere ideology. Like many late-Empire products of the establishment, he had an inborn faith in his ability, and right, to change and rule the world. This he shared with Elliott, though their views of how the world should be run could not have been more opposed. Both were imperialists, but for rival empires. Beneath Philby's golden charm lay a thick substratum of conceit; the charmer invites you into his world, though never too far, and only on his terms. The English love their secrets, the knowledge that they know a little more than the man standing next to them; when that man is also a secret-keeper, its redoubles what Trevor-Roper called 'the exquisite relish of ruthless, treacherous, private power'. Philby tasted the powerful drug of deception as a youth, and remained addicted to infidelity for the rest of his life.

Kim was his father's pet, and project. Like Claude Elliott, St John Philby was ambitious for his son, but showed him little affection. He moulded him for Westminster and Cambridge, and was proud when his son achieved those goals; but mostly he was absent, charging around the Arab world courting controversy, and searching for celebrity. 'My ambition is fame, whatever that may mean,' he said. St John Philby was a notable scholar, linguist and ornithologist, and he did achieve fame of a sort, but might have found more lasting appreciation had he not been so profoundly irritating, wilful and arrogant. He was a man who regarded his opinions, however briefly adopted, as revealed truth: he never backed down, or listened, or compromised. He was equally swift to give and take offence, and ferociously critical of everyone except himself. He alternately neglected and hectored his wife Dora. He was snobbish, and in many ways conventional, but also instinctively contrarian, forever bucking the system and then complaining furiously when the system failed to reward him. Kim idolised him, and loathed him.

At school, the young Philby was 'constantly aware of his father's long shadow'. Alongside his fine academic record, and general popularity, the boy showed a small streak of mendacity, prompting some parental disquiet: 'He should always be careful to be truthful whatever the consequences,' observed his father. Kim arrived at Cambridge at the age of seventeen on a history scholarship, having inherited both his father's intellectual self-confidence, and his determination to swim against the tide.

The violent ideological currents sweeping Cambridge in the 1930s had created a vortex which quickly swept up Philby and many other clever, angry, alienated young men. He made friends on the political left, and some on the extreme left. Fascism was on the march in Europe, and only communism, it seemed to many, could oppose it. Late at night, over copious drinks, in panelled rooms, students argued, debated, tried on one ideological outfit or another, and, in a small handful of cases, embraced violent revolution. The most significant, and certainly the most colourful, of Philby's radical new friends was Guy Francis de Moncy Burgess, amoral, witty, supremely dangerous and loud in his advocacy of communism. Another was Donald Maclean, a clever young linguist destined for the Foreign Office.

Philby joined the Cambridge University Socialist Society. He canvassed on behalf of the Labour Party. But there was no 'sudden conversion', no revolutionary epiphany when the religion of communism seized his soul. Instead, the student Philby moved slowly leftwards, and then faster after visiting Berlin in 1933 and witnessing at first hand, like Elliott, the brutality of Nazism during an anti-Jewish rally. Unlike many of his friends, Philby never joined the Communist Party. His beliefs were radical, but simple: the rich had exploited the poor for too long; the only bulwark against fascism was Soviet communism, 'the inner fortress of the world movement'; capitalism was doomed and crumbling; the British establishment was poisoned by Nazi leanings. 'I left the university,' he wrote, 'with the conviction that my life must be devoted to communism.' Yet he wore his convictions so lightly they were all but invisible. With the £14 he was awarded for his degree, he bought the collected works of Karl Marx. But there is no evidence he ever studied them in depth, or even read them. Though politics would dictate his life, he was not greatly interested in political theory. As Elliott later observed, 'I can hardly see him as a lecturer in dialectical materialism.'

Before leaving Cambridge, Philby sought out his supervisor, the Marxist economist Maurice Dobb, and asked him how best he might 'devote his life to the communist cause'. It was a measure of how deeply Marxism had penetrated the university that Philby felt no danger in asking such a loaded question, and Dobb had no qualms in answering it. Dobb directed him to Louis Gibarti, a Paris agent of the Comintern, the international communist organisation, who in turn furnished an introduction to the Austrian communist underground. It was that easy: the radical left had its own Old Boy network.

In the autumn of 1933, Philby travelled to Vienna, ostensibly to improve his German before applying to join the Foreign Office – in reality to witness, and if possible take part in, the battle between left and right then under way in the Austrian capital. Engelbert Dollfuss, Austria's extreme right-wing dictator, had already suspended the constitution and outlawed strikes and demonstrations in his efforts to suppress the socialist movement. A full-scale conflict was imminent, and the situation, as Philby put it, was 'at a crisis point'. Philby made his way to the address provided by Gibarti, and introduced himself to its occupants, Israel and Gisella Kohlman, and their daughter Alice – with whom he promptly fell in love. Alice, known as Litzi, was twenty-three, dark-haired, Jewish, vivacious, direct to the point of bluntness, and newly divorced, having married at eighteen. When Philby met Litzi, he was still a virgin and a political naif; she swiftly attended to both deficiencies. Litzi was a fully committed revolutionary and, according to one contemporary, a 'tremendous little sexpot'.

Litzi was active in the Viennese communist underground, and in contact with Soviet intelligence. She had spent two weeks in prison for subversive activities. Philby was instantly besotted. They made love in the snow. ('Actually quite warm, once you get used to it,' he recalled to a later girlfriend.) Philby had been in Austria for only a few weeks, when Dollfuss moved to crush the Leftists, arresting socialist leaders, banning trades unions and catapulting Austria into a brief but vicious civil war. Philby and Litzi plunged into the fray on behalf of the Revolutionary Socialists, the short-lived alliance of socialists and communists, passing messages, drafting leaflets, and helping to smuggle wanted men and women out of the country. The left was crushed in four days; 1,500 people were arrested, and the socialist leaders were executed. Litzi was on the wanted list, and the police were closing in, but Philby's British passport would offer her protection: on 24 February 1934, he married Litzi in Vienna Town Hall. This was more than just a marriage made in Marxism; as Mrs Philby she could flee with her new husband to the safety of Britain. Litzi, or 'Lizzy' as he called her, may be the only woman to whom Philby remained both ideologically and sexually faithful. 'Even though the basis of our relationship was political to some extent, I truly loved her and she loved me.'

A few weeks later, the newlyweds arrived in London, where they lodged with Philby's mother. Conventional Dora Philby, desperate to keep up appearances despite a perennial shortage of money, was not best pleased to find her son married to a foreign communist. She regarded his politics as another passing adolescent phase, like acne. 'I do hope Kim gets a job to get him off this bloody communism,' Mrs Philby wrote to her husband in Saudi Arabia. 'He's not quite extreme yet, but may become so.' St John was unconcerned by his son's radicalism. 'Excess can always be toned down afterwards,' he declared.

Just a few weeks after his return from Vienna, Philby sat on a bench in Regent's Park, waiting to meet a 'man of decisive importance' who, Litzi had promised, would change his life. When Philby had asked her who he was, and what made him so important, she clammed up.

Out of the June sunshine appeared a short, stout man in his early thirties with curly fair hair and intelligent eyes. He spoke English with a strong East European accent, and introduced himself as 'Otto'.

Philby never forgot their first conversation. Otto spoke about art and music, his love of Paris and his dislike of London. This, Philby reflected, was a 'man of considerable cultural background'. Philby was entranced: 'He was a marvellous man. Simply marvellous. I felt that immediately. The first thing you noticed about him were his eyes. He looked at you as if nothing more important in life than you and talking to you existed at that moment.' That was a quality many found in Philby too. Gradually, their conversation drifted towards politics, and then the works of Marx and Lenin, which Otto seemed to know by heart. Philby, in turn, described his political experiences in Cambridge, his activities in Vienna, and his wish to join the Communist Party. They spoke in euphemisms, with Otto hinting that he could put 'important and interesting work' in Philby's direction. As with most espionage relationships, this one began not with politics, but with friendship. 'I trusted him from the start,' wrote Philby. 'It was an amazing conversation.' They agreed to meet again.

Otto's real name, which Philby would not learn for decades, was Arnold Deutsch. He was the chief recruiter for Soviet intelligence in Britain, the principal architect of what would later become known as the Cambridge Spy Ring. Born of Czech Jewish parents, Arnold and his family had moved to Austria when he was a child. Prodigiously clever, he emerged from Vienna University after just five years with a doctorate in chemistry, a fervent commitment to communism, and a passionate interest in sex. His first career was as publisher and publicist for the German sexologist Wilhelm Reich – the 'prophet of the better orgasm' who sought to bring sexual enlightenment to the prudish Viennese as part of the 'sex-pol' (sexual politics) movement, which equated sexual repression with fascist authoritarianism. Reich developed the radical, though slightly implausible, theory that 'a poor man's sexual performance led him to fascism'. While promoting Reich's idea that better sex makes better revolutionaries, Deutsch was also secretly working for Soviet intelligence, having undergone a training course in Moscow. The Gestapo arrested Deutsch briefly in 1933; the anti-pornography section of the Vienna police were also on his trail, on account of his sex-pol activities. A year later, he arrived in Britain, to begin a postgraduate degree in Phonetics and Psychology at University College London, while working as a spy-recruiter. Deutsch had relatives in the UK, notably his wealthy cousin Oscar, the founder of the Odeon cinema chain, which was said to stand for 'Oscar Deutsch Entertains Our Nation'. One Deutsch was doing well out of British capitalism; the other was hellbent on destroying it.

Deutsch was an 'illegal', espionage parlance for a spy operating without diplomatic status. His mission was to recruit radical students at the best universities (using his academic work as cover), who might later rise to positions of power and influence. Deutsch was on the hunt for long-term, deep-cover, ideological spies who could blend invisibly into the British establishment – for Soviet intelligence was playing a long game, laying down seed corn that could be harvested many years hence, or left dormant for ever. It was a simple, brilliant, durable strategy of the sort that only a state committed to permanent world revolution could have initiated. It would prove staggeringly successful.

Philby's introduction to Deutsch appears to have been arranged by Edith Tudor-Hart, an Austrian communist friend of Litzi's. Born Edith Suschitzky, the daughter of a wealthy Viennese publisher, Edith married an English doctor and fellow communist named Alexander Tudor-Hart, and moved to England in 1930, where she worked as a photographer and part-time talent-scout for the NKVD, under the remarkably unimaginative codename 'Edith'. She had been under MI5 surveillance since 1931 but not, fatefully, on the day she led Philby to meet Deutsch in Regent's Park.

Philby was just the sort of recruit Deutsch was looking for. He was ambitious, well connected and devoted to the cause, but unobtrusively: unlike others, Philby had never made his radical views obvious. He sought a career in diplomacy, journalism or the civil service, all excellent perches for a spy. Deutsch was also under the impression that St John Philby was an agent of British intelligence, with access to important secret material.

At their second meeting, Deutsch asked Philby if he was willing to act as an undercover agent for the communist cause. Philby did not hesitate: 'One does not look twice at an offer of enrolment in an elite force,' he wrote. That was a most telling remark: the attraction of this new role lay in its exclusivity. In some ways, Philby's story is that of a man in pursuit of ever more exclusive clubs. In a brilliant lecture written in 1944, C. S. Lewis described the fatal British obsession with the 'inner ring', the belief that somewhere, just beyond reach, is an exclusive group holding real power and influence, which a certain sort of Englishman constantly aspires to find and join. Westminster School and Cambridge University are elite clubs; MI6 is an even more exclusive fellowship; working secretly for the NKVD within MI6 placed Philby in a club of one, the most elite member of a secret inner ring. 'Of all the passions,' wrote Lewis, 'the passion for the Inner Ring is most skilful in making a man who is not yet a very bad man do very bad things.'

'My future looked romantic,' Philby wrote. Deutsch laid out a vision of that future: Philby and Litzi must break off all communist contacts; rather than join the party, he should establish a new political image as a right-winger, even a Nazi-sympathiser. He must become, to all outward appearances, a conventional member of the very class he was committed to opposing. 'By background, education, appearance and manners you are an intellectual, a bourgeois. You have a marvellous career ahead of you. A bourgeois career,' Deutsch told him. 'The anti-fascist movement needs people who can enter into the bourgeoisie.' Hidden inside the establishment, Philby could aid the revolution in a 'real and palpable way'. Deutsch began to instruct Philby on the rudiments of tradecraft: how to arrange a meeting; where to leave messages; how to detect if his telephone was bugged; how to spot a tail, and how to lose one. He presented Philby with a new Minox subminiature camera, and taught him how to copy documents. Philby memorised Deutsch's lessons 'like poetry'. His double life had begun.

Deutsch gave Philby the affectionate codename 'Sonny' (Söhnchen in German), and reported his catch to the London *rezident*, the regional control officer of the NKVD (the predecessor organisation to the KGB), who passed on the news to Moscow Centre, the Soviet intelligence headquarters: 'We have recruited the son of an Anglo agent, advisor to Ibn-Saud, Philby.' Moscow was impressed: 'What are his prospects for a diplomatic career? Are they realistic? Will he choose his own path or will his father "suggest" he meet someone and discuss it? That would be good.' Deutsch instructed his new protégé to draw up a list of acquaintances and contemporaries, from Oxford as well as Cambridge, who might also be recruited to the cause. He told him to discreetly explore whatever documents St John Philby kept in his office at home, and to photograph 'the most interesting'.

Asking Philby to spy on his own father was surely a test of his commitment, and Philby passed it easily. He did what was asked of him without hesitation. Deutsch reported that his new recruit 'refers to his parents, who are well-to-do bourgeois, and his entire social milieu with unfeigned contempt and hatred'. Philby was doubtless putting on a display of class-warrior zeal for Deutsch, for he was spellbound by his spymaster, 'his marvellous education, his humanity, his fidelity to building a new society'. They met often, always in 'the remoter open spaces in London', and once in Paris. Deutsch flattered and inspired his young ward. When Philby's relationship with Litzi began to falter, the older man dispensed marital advice. ('His wife was his first lover in his life,' Deutsch reported to Moscow, keen, as ever, to establish a link between sex and socialist zeal. 'When difficulties arose in their relationship, they would confide in me and both followed my advice.')

Philby was bonded, ideologically and emotionally, to his charismatic Soviet controller. 'I sometimes felt we had been friends since childhood,' he wrote. 'I was certain that my life and myself interested him not so much professionally as on a human level.' The fatal conceit of most spies is to believe they are loved, in a relationship between equals, and not merely manipulated. Deutsch made a careful study of Philby's psychology, the flashes of insecurity beneath the debonair exterior, the unpredictable stammer, his veiled resentment of a domineering father. Deutsch reported to the Centre that Philby had potential but needed 'constant encouragement': 'Söhnchen comes from a peculiar family. His father is considered at present to be the most distinguished expert on the Arab world ... he is an ambitious tyrant and wanted to make a great man out of his son.' Deutsch noted his acolyte's intellectual curiosity, his fluctuating moods, his old world manners, and his resolve: 'It's amazing that such a young man is so widely and deeply knowledgeable ... He is so serious he forgets that he is only twenty-five.'

Deutsch urged Philby to get a job in journalism – 'Once you're inside, you'll look around and then decide which way to go' – and he reassured Moscow that Philby's family contacts would ensure swift promotion. 'He has many friends from the best homes.' Philby soon obtained a job as a sub-editor at the *World Review of Reviews*, a literary and political monthly, before moving on to the *Anglo-German Trade Gazette*, a magazine devoted to improving economic relations between Britain and Germany which was partly financed by the Nazi government. Completing this lurch from extreme left (secretly) to extreme right (publicly), he joined the Anglo-German Fellowship, a society formed in 1935 to foster closer understanding with Germany. A sump for the forces of appeasement and Nazi admiration, the fellowship included politicians, aristocrats and business leaders, some naive or gullible, others rampantly fascist. With views diametrically opposed to his own, such people offered Philby ideal political camouflage, as well as information, eagerly received in Moscow, about links between the Nazis and their British sympathisers. Philby travelled regularly to Berlin on behalf of the fellowship, and even met the German foreign minister, von Ribbentrop. He later claimed to have found playing the part of a keen young fascist 'profoundly repulsive' because 'in the eyes of my friends, even conservative ones, but honest conservatives, I looked pro-Nazi'. Former friends from the left were aghast at his apparent conversion, and some shunned him. Deutsch commiserated, telling Philby he knew 'how difficult it is to leave old friends'.

Litzi and Philby's commitment to communism proved more durable than their commitment to each other; they separated, without rancour, and she moved to Paris. To Moscow's surprise, Philby found nothing of intelligence value among his father's papers. The NKVD was convinced that someone as well connected as St John Philby, who travelled widely and freely, must be a spy. 'It seems unlikely that his father ... would not be a close and intimate collaborator with the Intelligence Service.' Not for the last time, Moscow elevated its erroneous expectations into fact. Meanwhile Philby dutifully handed over a list of potential recruits among his left-wing Cambridge friends, including Donald Maclean and Guy Burgess.

★

Maclean, still a committed communist, was by now in the Foreign Office. Philby invited him to dinner, and hinted that there was important clandestine work to be done on behalf of the party. 'The people I could introduce you to are very serious.' Philby instructed Maclean to carry a book with a bright yellow cover into a particular café on a given day. 'Otto' was waiting for him, and duly signed up this 'very serious and aloof' young man with 'good connections'. Codenamed 'Orphan', Maclean, too, began to shed his radical past. 'Sonny has high praise for Orphan,' Deutsch reported to Moscow. Burgess seemed a more dubious prospect: 'Very smart ... but a bit superficial and could let slip in some circumstances.'

Characteristically, Burgess sensed he was being denied admission to a most enjoyable and risky party, and brazenly barged his way in. One night he confronted Maclean: 'Do you think that I believe for even one jot that you have stopped being a communist? You're simply up to something.' A little reluctantly, Deutsch added Burgess to his roster. Burgess duly announced, with maximum fanfare, that he had swapped Marx for Mussolini, and was now a devotee of Italian fascism. It was Burgess who subsequently introduced Deutsch to yet another recruit, Anthony Blunt, already an art historian of note. Slowly, discreetly, with paternal diligence and Philby's help, Deutsch added one link after another to the Cambridge spy chain.

While Deutsch handled recruitment, much of the day-to-day management of the spies was carried out by another 'illegal', Theodore Stephanovich Maly, a Hungarian former monk who, as an army chaplain during the First World War, had been taken prisoner in the Carpathians and witnessed such appalling horrors that he emerged a revolutionary: 'I lost my faith in God and when the revolution broke out I joined the Bolsheviks. I became a communist and have always remained one.' After training as an agent-runner, he arrived in London in 1932, under the alias Paul Hardt. For a spy, Maly was conspicuous, standing six feet four inches tall, with a 'shiny grey complexion', and gold fillings in his front teeth. But he was a most subtle controller, who shared Deutsch's admiration for Philby, describing him as 'an inspirational figure, a true comrade and idealist'. The feeling was reciprocated; in Philby's mind the bewitching personalities of his handlers were indistinguishable from their political allure: 'Both of them were intelligent and experienced professionals, as well as genuinely very good people.'

Philby's work for the *Anglo-German Trade Gazette* came to an abrupt end in 1936 when the Nazis withdrew financial support. But by then, Moscow Centre had other plans for him. Civil war had erupted in Spain between the Republican forces and the fascist-backed Nationalist rebels under General Franco. Philby was instructed to spy on the Nationalists, using freelance journalism as a cover, and report back on troop movements, communications, morale, and the military support being provided to Franco's forces by Germany and Italy. Moscow would pay for his passage. Philby 'handles our money very carefully', Deutsch told his bosses. In Spain, Philby quickly ingratiated himself with Franco's press officers, and began sending well-informed articles to British newspapers, notably *The Times*. On a return trip to Britain, he persuaded Britain's most influential paper to appoint him special correspondent in Spain: 'We have great difficulty getting any information at all from the Franco side,' Ralph Deakin, *The Times*'s foreign editor, told Philby.

Meanwhile Philby assiduously gathered intelligence for his Soviet spymasters, on 'unit strengths and locations, gun calibres, tank performance' and other military information. This he sent in code to 'Mademoiselle Dupont' in Paris (to an address which he later learned was the Soviet embassy itself). He began an affair with Frances

Doble, Lady Lindsay-Hogg, an aristocratic former actress ten years his senior, a supporter of Franco and 'a royalist of the most right-wing kind' who gave him access to Franco's inner circle. 'I would be lying if I said I started the affair only for the sake of my work,' he later observed. Philby was untroubled about making love to some-one whose opinions he despised.

Philby's controller in Paris, a Latvian named Ozolin-Haskins, was full of praise: 'He works with great willingness [and] always knows what might be of interest to us. He never asks for money. He lives modestly.' Nor did Philby neglect his role as a recruiter for the cause. During a return trip to London, he lunched with Flora Solomon, the Marks and Spencer executive who would later introduce him to Aileen. Despite her inherited wealth, and marriage to a general-turned-stockbroker, Flora Solomon was firmly on the left. According to one MI5 officer, she had 'obviously been in the thick of things in mid-1930s, part inspiration, part fellow accomplice, and part courier'. During the conversation, Philby remarked, in an intense undertone, that he was 'doing a very dangerous job for peace and that he needed help. Would she help him in his task? It would be a great thing if she would join the cause.' He did not specify what his 'important work for peace' entailed, but insisted 'You should be doing it too, Flora.' Solomon, surprised at what was unmistakably an invitation to take on covert and dangerous work for communism, turned down the offer but told Philby 'he could always come to her if he was desper-ate'. She would not forget that strange exchange.

In Moscow a still more radical plan was being hatched for Agent Sonny. Philby had already been asked to report on General Franco's security arrangements. Now Moscow Centre wondered whether he might be able to get close enough to the *Caudillo* to kill him, and deliver a devastating blow to the Nazi-backed Nationalists. The officer with the unenviable task of passing on this idea was Theodore Maly, who knew that it was virtually impossible to achieve and, even if possible, suicidal. Maly discussed the proposal with Philby, but then sent a message to the Centre quashing the idea, fully aware that in doing so he was inviting Moscow's mortal displeasure. 'Even if he

had been able to get close to Franco . . . then he, despite his willingness, would not be able to do what is expected of him. For all his
loyalty and willingness to sacrifice himself, he does not have the
physical courage and other qualities necessary.' The plan was quietly
dropped, but it was another mark of Philby's growing status in Soviet
eyes: in just four years he had gone from a raw recruit to a potential
assassin. *The Times* was also impressed with his performance: 'They
are very pleased with Kim, they have the highest opinion of him,'
the diarist Harold Nicolson told Guy Burgess. 'He has made a name
for himself very quickly.' That reputation expanded hugely when,
the day before his twenty-sixth birthday, New Year's Eve 1937, Philby
narrowly avoided being killed by a Republican shell (of Russian
manufacture) while covering the battle of Teruel. The award of a
medal from Franco himself convinced the Nationalists that Philby
was, as one Spanish officer put it, 'a decent chap'.

In the summer of 1939, with Franco victorious in Spain, Philby
returned to London to a warm reception from his colleagues at *The
Times.* There was no equivalent welcome from his Soviet spy friends,
for the simple reason that they were all dead, or had disappeared,
swept away by Stalin's Terror. In the wild, murderous paranoia of the
Purges, anyone with foreign links was suspected of disloyalty, and the
outposts of Soviet intelligence came under particular suspicion.
Theodore Maly was among the first to be recalled to Moscow, an
obvious suspect on account of his religious background: 'I know that
as a former priest I haven't got a chance. But I've decided to go there
so that nobody can say "That priest might have been a real spy after
all".' Maly was tortured in the cells of the Lubiyanka, headquarters
of the secret police, until he eventually confessed to being a German
spy, and was then shot in the head.

The fate of Arnold Deutsch has never been fully explained. Philby
would later claim he had died when a ship taking him to America,
the *Donbass*, was torpedoed by a U-boat, thus making him a victim
of Hitler's aggression rather than Stalin's. The KGB history reports
he died en route to South America, but another KGB report claims
he was heading to New York. It seems just as probable that

bright-eyed 'Otto', founder-recruiter of the Cambridge spy chain, shared Maly's fate. As a foreign-born, Jewish intellectual who had spent years abroad, he was a likely candidate for purging.

The task of running the Cambridge spies was taken over by one Grigori Grafpen, until he too was arrested and sent to the Gulag. Philby's controller in Paris, Ozolin-Haskins, was shot in Moscow in 1937. His successor, Boris Shapak, lasted two more years before he too was ordered home to be killed. A few defected before they could be seized, further fuelling Stalin's paranoia, but most submitted to the inevitable. As Maly put it: 'If they don't kill me there, they will kill me here. Better to die there.' One by one, Philby's handlers were declared enemies of the people. Philby knew they were nothing of the sort. He had revered them for their 'infinite patience' and 'intelligent understanding', their 'painstaking advice, admonition and encouragement'. But in later life, he expressed little sadness over the murder of these 'marvellous men', and offered no criticism of the tyranny that killed them. Only the politics mattered.

By 1939, however, politics was becoming extremely complicated. In August the foreign ministers of the Soviet Union and Germany signed a non-aggression pact. Philby had become a Soviet agent in order to fight fascism; under the Molotov–Ribbentrop pact, communism and fascism were now effectively in alliance. For the first and only time in his life, Philby seems to have experienced an ideological wobble: 'What's going to happen to the single-front struggle against fascism now?' he asked his new Soviet controller. The relationship cooled markedly. Philby complained that he was not receiving sufficient political instruction. The replacement case officer did not know him, and may not have trusted him. For a time contact was broken off, for reasons that still remain obscure.

That same year, the head of MI5 blandly declared that Soviet 'activity in England is non-existent, in terms of both intelligence and political subversion'. He could not have been more wrong, for the Soviet network in Britain was not only far more substantial than anything Germany could muster, but also developing new tactics, and encouraging its spies to seek positions within British intelligence

itself, where they would have access to secrets of the greatest importance. Anthony Blunt would soon join MI5. Burgess had talked his
way into MI6, known as 'The Hotel' in Soviet spy code, and helped
to haul in Philby after him. 'I had been told in pressing terms by my
Soviet friends that my first priority must be the British secret service,' Philby wrote. Obediently, he began putting out feelers.

The coolness between Philby and his Soviet handlers was short-
lived. In the spring of 1940, *The Times* sent its star correspondent to
France to join the British Expeditionary Force as the paper's accred-
ited war correspondent. Philby had already memorised elaborate
instructions for contacting Soviet intelligence in Paris. He should
stand near the Thomas Cook office in Place de la Madeleine with a
copy of the *Daily Mail*; the Soviet contact would be carrying a copy
of the same newspaper. Philby would ask him: 'Where is the Café
Henri round here?' The man would reply: 'It's near the Place de la
République.' Having performed this mini-drama, Philby passed on
information he had gathered in the course of his reporting, about
British military strength and weaponry, as well as French forces
behind the Maginot Line – information of great interest to Moscow,
and of even greater interest to Berlin. But whatever qualms he may
have felt about the Nazi–Soviet pact seem to have evaporated.
Returning to London after the retreat, he hastened to contact
Maclean, saying he had brought back 'extraordinarily valuable materials' which he wanted to pass to 'the appropriate hands'. Philby's
loyalties were unchanged, his determination undimmed, and his
hints about wanting to join the secret services already bearing fruit,
in the shape of Hester Marsden-Smedley.

This, then, was the man who met and befriended Elliott in 1940,
a two-sided man who used one side to disguise the other. Nick
Elliott loved and admired Philby, the upper-crust, Cambridge-
educated *bon viveur*; the charming, happily married, conservative
clubman; the battle-scarred war correspondent now playing a vital
part in the thrilling world of espionage. Elliott had no inkling of the
other Philby, the veteran communist spy, and it would be many more
years before he finally met him.

Boo, Boo, Baby, I'm a Spy

Sir Stewart Menzies, the head of MI6, was very nearly a caricature of what a spy chief ought to be: aristocratic, wily and enigmatic. Some said he was the illegitimate son of Edward VII, a rumour almost certainly untrue that he did nothing to gainsay. Like all chiefs of MI6, he was known as 'C', a tradition begun by the initial of the earliest chief, (Mansfield) Cumming. Menzies was a member of White's Club, rode to hounds, mixed with royalty, never missed a day at Ascot, drank a great deal, and kept his secrets buttoned up behind a small, fierce moustache. He preferred women to men, and horses to both. He was impenetrably polite, and entirely ruthless: enemy spies, foxes and office rivals could expect no quarter. Nicholas Elliott revered 'The Chief' for what he called his 'true sense of values' – which was his way of saying that Menzies, an Old Etonian and a friend of his father, shared his own view of the world. Outwardly, Kim Philby was equally admiring of Menzies; privately he considered him a prime specimen of the doomed ruling-class elite. 'His intellectual equipment was unimpressive,' Philby later wrote, 'his knowledge of the world, and views about it, were just what one would expect from a fairly cloistered son of the upper levels of the British establishment.' C was ripe for manipulation.

Like many small, sealed, self-replicating communities, MI6 was riven with internecine feuding. Its senior officers loathed each other, and intrigued ferociously. Claude Dansey, the assistant chief, was described by Hugh Trevor-Roper as 'an utter shit, corrupt, incompetent, but with a certain low cunning'. Valentine Vivian, 'Vee-Vee', who had eased Philby's entry into the secret world, was an old-style veteran of colonial policing, a stickler for form and protocol who, as the son of a mere portrait painter, lived in a state of permanent social anxiety. He reacted to the smallest slight, real or perceived, with fury. 'Vivian was long past his best if, indeed, he had ever had one,' observed Philby. 'He had a reedy figure, carefully dressed crinkles in his hair, and wet eyes.' Dansey hated Vivian, and Vivian hated Dansey; Philby's boss Felix Cowgill feuded with both, and was detested in turn. Philby cultivated, flattered and despised them all, while nurturing his relationships with other branches of intelligence, most notably MI5. The security service was the main customer for his counter-intelligence gatherings, but more than that, it was responsible for counter-espionage within Britain: if Philby ever came under suspicion, then MI5 would come hunting. It was, therefore, an important place to make friends. Philby's closest contact within MI5 was Guy Liddell, the refined, cello-playing head of counter-intelligence and a regular at the Harris spy salon. A rumpled, genial figure, Liddell looked more like a country banker than a spymaster. 'He would murmur his thoughts as if groping his way towards the facts of a case, his face creased in a comfortable, innocent smile,' wrote Philby. 'But behind the façade of laziness, his subtle and reflective mind played over a storehouse of photographic memories.' Philby admired Liddell's professionalism, and feared it.

Secrets are the currency of intelligence work, and among professional spies a little calculated indiscretion raises the exchange rate. Philby took to passing on titbits to selected colleagues, off the record, and they would respond in kind. As Philby put it: 'The rewards of such unorthodoxy were often generous.' A secret shared was a friend made, and friendship, or its simulacrum, was the best way to extract more secrets. Philby became a familiar and popular figure in the corridors of both MI5 and MI6, always happy to exchange pleasantries, gossip or confidences, always ready for a drink after work, and then another. Philby's Soviet handler reported smugly that Agent Sonny was probably 'the only man in The Hotel without any enemies'.

Menzies saw Philby and Elliott as his protégés, his 'golden lads' representing a new generation of intelligence officers, far removed from the whiskery ex-policemen and military leftovers who had dominated pre-war MI6. They were keen, ambitious and well educated (but not intellectuals – C had little time for those). They belonged to the right clubs, and spoke with the right accents. It soon became apparent that both young men were being groomed for promotion by Menzies, who fought off every attempt to lure them away. When the Foreign Office inquired whether Philby might be seconded to the diplomatic service, C rejected the request with a tart note: 'You know as well as I do the valuable work which Philby is doing for me . . . the essential nature of Philby's contribution to the war effort compels his present employers regretfully to refuse to let him go.' Similarly, the King's private secretary, Tommy Lascelles, sent a note to Guy Liddell telling him that Elliott was being considered for employment as a secretary to the monarch, and asking for his opinion. Liddell replied that he had got to know Elliott 'in the hurly-burly of the Scrubs' and found him 'a pleasant personality highly recommended by Nevile Bland'. He might make a fine courtier. Menzies, whose mother was a lady-in-waiting to Queen Mary, quashed that idea too. He wanted his lads in the inner circle, and Philby and Elliott, for rather different reasons, were only too happy to remain there.

★

The work of Section V, battling German espionage around the world, was fascinating, complicated, and frequently frustrating. 'For every lead that produced results,' wrote Philby, 'a dozen lured us tortuously into dead ends.' Elliott found the 'monstrous' volume of paperwork – an essential part of intelligence – particularly tedious, and tried to emulate Philby's brisk memo-writing style, 'a model of economy and lucidity'. The officers of Section V might complain about the hours, but they formed a tight-knit group, with their own bonding rituals and routine: Sunday lunch at the Philbys', cricket at weekends, drinks at the King Harry, a club dinner in London from time to time, and occasional weekends at Eton. 'I had the advantage of being able to invite these friends to spend a night from time to time with my parents, who were fortunate enough to have some old retainers to help cope with a very large house,' wrote Elliott.

Philby seemed to be working twice as hard as anyone else, which was unsurprising, since he was working for two masters or, more precisely, appearing to serve one, for the benefit of the other. As Philby's influence on British intelligence grew, so did his importance to the Soviets. Moscow Centre sent a message to its London *rezident*, describing Sonny as 'an interesting and promising agent' and ordering that he be put to greater use. Philby responded with devoted diligence. On night duty in Broadway, he combed incoming telegrams for anything of interest to the NKVD; messages between London and the military mission in Moscow were 'especially valuable'. He described everyone in Section V with waspish precision. Elliott was not the only colleague who would have been shocked to discover Philby's secret opinion: his boss Felix Cowgill had 'few social graces'; his school friend Tim Milne was 'inclined towards inertia'; Trevor Wilson, the former skunk-dung collector, had a 'weakness [for] women', and young Desmond Bristow was 'the weak link ... owing to immaturity and inferior brain'.

Every evening, Philby took home a 'fat briefcase', and sat in his study laboriously copying out files, while Aileen cooked dinner and looked after the children. He even reported on Aileen, like some commissar assessing the ideological weakness of his nearest kin: 'Her political views are Socialistic, but like the majority of the wealthy middle class, she has an almost ineradicable tendency towards a definite form of philistinism (petite bourgeoisie) namely: she believes in upbringing, the British navy, personal freedom, democracy, the constitutional system, honour etc ... I am certain that I can cure her of these confusions, although of course I haven't yet attempted to do so; I hope that the revolutionary situation will give her the necessary shake-up and cause a correct revolutionary response.' Marriage, family, friendships: all were subservient to the demands of revolutionary orthodoxy.

Philby did whatever his Soviet controllers asked, although he found it 'difficult, exhausting and often very ordinary, even boring work that required enormous patience, will power and control'. It was also nerve-racking. Philby suffered 'twinges of panic', his controller reported, which was hardly surprising, since he was playing an astonishingly precarious game. If just one Soviet intelligence officer switched sides and identified him to the British secret service, he was doomed. One had very nearly done so.

In 1937, a Soviet intelligence officer named Walter Krivitsky had defected to the West, bringing with him a dowry of top-level intelligence, including the identities of no fewer than seventy Soviet intelligence personnel working abroad. Krivitsky's defection had led to the arrest and trial of John King, Elliott's former coding instructor. But much of his information was contradictory and fragmentary. In 1940 he was debriefed by the MI5 officer Jane Archer, in St Ermin's Hotel, where Philby had been recruited to MI6. The interview did not start well when Krivitsky (alias 'Mr Thomas') was offered a saccharin tablet for his tea (sugar was rationed). He immediately assumed this was a poisoned pill and that he was being murdered by the British secret service, albeit rather obviously, and very politely. Once that moment of social embarrassment had passed, Krivitsky opened up and revealed an important new nugget of information: during the Spanish Civil War, Soviet intelligence had sent an agent to kill General Franco. Krivitsky could not provide a name, or any other specifics, but described the would-be assassin as 'a young Englishman, a journalist of good family, an idealist and fanatical anti-Nazi'. MI5 launched an investigation, but there had been several well-born journalists in Spain in the 1930s, and the inquiry fizzled out. No one thought to connect the tip with Philby. The clue would rattle around British intelligence for years, before assuming vast significance many years later.

Philby was slaving for the Soviet cause, risking his life and prepared to report on whatever interested Moscow, including his father, his wife and his best friend. Yet Moscow was not happy. The Cambridge spies – Guy Burgess in MI6, Donald Maclean in the Foreign Office,

Anthony Blunt in MI5, John Cairncross in Bletchley Park and Kim Philby in Section V – were producing top-level intelligence. But their very productivity posed a conundrum. In the insanely distrustful world of Soviet espionage, the quality, quantity and consistency of this information rendered it suspect. A misgiving began to take root in Moscow that British intelligence must be mounting an elaborate, multi-layered deception through Philby and his friends; they must all be double agents. Moreover, Philby's story failed to meet firmly held Soviet preconceptions: MI6 was supposed to be impregnable, yet Philby had practically sauntered into the organisation; he had been a left-winger at university, yet supposedly rigorous background checks had failed to pick this up; he had been asked to find evidence that his own father was a spy, and had failed to do so.

Was Philby a plant? Was he shielding his father? Was he, too, an enemy of the people, masquerading as a friend? To find out, a test was set. The information provided by Philby was all very well, but what interested Moscow most was the identity of British spies within the Soviet Union; who had MI6 recruited in the USSR, what were their names, and what Soviet secrets had they revealed? If Philby exposed these spies, then he was reliable and loyal; but if not, then Moscow would draw its own conclusions. Philby politely pointed out that his role in MI6 was catching enemy spies, not agent-running, which was the responsibility of a different section, in a completely different place. But Moscow was adamant: 'We told him he must use whatever plausible and reasonable pretexts in order to get these files.' As his former controller Theodore Maly had discovered to his cost, in the warped logic of Stalinism, refusing to do something just because it was impossible was a sign of disloyalty. Philby obediently set to work.

The Central Registry was the memory and reference library of MI6, housed at Prae Wood in St Albans, next door to Section V headquarters. The registry source books collated the personal files of all current British secret agents, and every agent who had spied for Britain since the creation of MI6 in 1909, including names, codenames, aliases, character, performance and pay, a running tally of MI6 spies across the world. Presiding over this fabulously important and dangerous trove of secrets was Captain William Woodfield, the chief registrar, a puce-faced former policeman whose drinking habits were extreme even by MI6 standards. In a description for his Soviet controller, Philby described Woodfield with typical concision: 'About 58, 5 feet 6 inches, slight build, dark hair, bald on top, wears glasses, long narrow face, formerly attached for some years to Special Branch.' Woodfield liked dirty jokes and pink gin: Philby made a point of seeking him out at the King Harry pub, and supplying him with copious quantities of both. Soon they were the best of drinking buddies, and when Philby asked to see the source books for Spain and Portugal, Woodfield signed them out without question. The Iberian Peninsula was Philby's sphere of work, and he had every reason to be interested in the MI6 agents in the region. Next, Philby requested the source books for the Soviet Union. Again Woodfield obliged, never pausing to wonder why his amiable new pub-chum was digging into an area so far removed from his allotted patch.

Philby duly sent a report to Moscow. It described Britain's spies in the Soviet Union with typical bluntness: 'There aren't any.' The station chief of MI6 in Moscow had not recruited a single major spy in the Soviet Union, Philby reported, and had only a few minor informants, mostly Poles. The USSR, moreover, was 'tenth on the list of countries to which agents are to be sent'. The files showed there was no British spy network in Soviet Russia, no MI6 espionage campaign, and 'no Soviet citizens whatsoever who worked as secret agents either in Moscow or anywhere else on Soviet territory'. The report was received with incredulity; Moscow's paranoia, and sense of self-importance, combined to provoke a reaction of furious disbelief. The Soviet Union was a world power and MI6 was the most feared intelligence organisation in the world; it therefore stood to reason that Britain *must* be spying on the USSR. If Philby said otherwise, then he *must* be lying. That Britain could conceivably relegate the mighty Soviet state to number ten on its espionage target list was an 'obvious absurdity' (and frankly quite wounding). An outraged Soviet intelligence officer took a red pen, and scrawled

two large and angry question marks over the report. Philby's asser-
tion was 'highly suspicious'; his failure to corroborate expectations
was 'dubious'; henceforth he must be 'tested and retested'. In truth,
British intelligence was overwhelmingly focused on the Nazi threat,
and since Moscow had become an ally the Foreign Office had
imposed strict restrictions on covert activities inside the Soviet
Union. But when Anthony Blunt confirmed that MI6 had no secret
agents in the USSR, he too fell under suspicion; Philby and Blunt
must be in league. And so began a bizarre situation in which Philby
told Moscow the truth, and was disbelieved, because the truth
contradicted Moscow's expectations.

Philby's successful and unauthorised foray into the Soviet files was
a remarkable feat of espionage, and a complete waste of time: it not
only deepened Moscow's suspicions, but very nearly ended Philby's
career. One morning, Bill Woodfield, of the beetroot complexion,
sent a polite note asking him to return the Soviet source books;
Philby responded that he had already done so. Woodfield, a sloppy
drunk but a meticulous librarian, said that there was only one Soviet
source book on the shelves, and the registry had no record of the
second volume being returned. Philby was convinced the books had
been sent back to the repository, but nonetheless turned his office
'upside down' in a fruitless search for the missing volume. He met
Woodfield at the King Harry 'to discuss the mystery over a few pink
gins' and discovered to his horror that, under registry rules, C would
have to be informed of the missing records. This was Friday.
Woodfield said he would send a memo on Monday. Nothing to
worry about, said Bill: just paperwork. Philby was now in deep peril.
Menzies might understand, even applaud, his interest in MI6 agents
in Spain and Portugal, but he would surely wonder what on earth
his protégé was doing with material on the Soviet Union, an area
'far outside the normal scope of [his] duties'. At best Philby would
have some tricky explaining to do; at worst, he was sunk.

After a weekend of simmering panic, Monday came, and with it a
last-minute reprieve. Woodfield's secretary, who had been ill with flu
for a few days, returned to work and explained that she had

amalgamated the two source books into one volume to save shelf space. Philby had indeed returned the files. Woodfield offered profuse apologies for the embarrassing mix-up, over 'another flood of pink gin'. Had Woodfield's secretary been slightly more ill, for longer, or had Woodfield been a little less pickled, then Philby's story would have ended then and there. But his luck held: he had escaped a Republican shell in Spain, dodged the clue furnished by the defector Krivitsky, and narrowly avoided exposure for trawling the Soviet files. 'Luck played an enormous role in my life,' he later wrote. 'But you have to know how to use luck.'

★

Nicholas Elliott was becoming restless. Life in St Albans was pleasant enough, but 'cloistered'. Running counter-intelligence operations in occupied Holland involved a great deal of memo-writing for meagre results, and nothing in the way of action. The world of intelligence, he concluded, was divided into 'those who sit at desks at home analysing and evaluating the information as it comes in, and those who go out into the highways and byways of the world in order to get hold of it'. Philby was of the former sort, a gifted analyst and collator of facts, but Elliott belonged to the latter type, and he was 'anxious to get away to another theatre of war'. He longed to travel, partly in reaction to his father's acute distrust of 'abroad'. ('All foreigners are bloody unless they climb mountains,' Claude insisted, 'and Germans are bloody even if they do.') Elliott hungered for risk. With Philby's support, he began lobbying for a more active role in the field, preferably somewhere dangerous. In the spring of 1942, Elliott was summoned to Cowgill's office and told he would soon be heading to Cairo, and from there to Istanbul as Section V's representative in Turkey. At the age of twenty-six, Nicholas Elliott would be running counter-espionage operations in an espionage hothouse, for Turkey was neutral and, like Spain and Portugal, the scene of a fierce, secret war. 'I was delighted,' he wrote. Philby threw a farewell party for him. The next day, 11 May 1942, Acting Lieutenant Elliott climbed, somewhat unsteadily, up the gangplank of a 5,000-ton passenger cargo vessel in Liverpool docks, part of a forty-ship convoy bound for Africa.

Elliott spent the three-week passage to Lagos playing bridge with an SOE officer 'who was being sent out to Angola to blow things up', taking his turn to man the ancient Japanese gun mounted on the stern, and tucking into a 'well-stocked bar'. Although never a drinker in Philby's league, Elliott was a keen tippler – despite his diabetes, which he treated merely by avoiding sugar. Most of his colleagues were entirely unaware that he was diabetic; with typical recklessness Elliott was not about to let his health stand in the way of a good time. When the ship put in at Freetown, he was greeted on the quayside by Graham Greene, who was now the somewhat disgruntled MI6 representative in Sierra Leone – a good place to gather material for fiction, but an intelligence backwater. Greene took one look at Elliott and proclaimed him 'the tattiest army officer I had ever seen'. Over a drink, Greene explained that his principal concern was 'the shortage of contraceptives in Sierra Leone', a problem Elliott 'managed to alleviate through the generosity of some of our passengers'. Elliott assumed these were for Greene's personal use: in fact, the future novelist had set up a 'roving brothel' to entice secrets out of 'two lonely Germans suspected of spying on British shipping', and his brothel workers were demanding protection from venereal disease.

In Lagos, Elliott transferred to a Dakota transport plane, and five days later he reached Cairo, after hopscotching across Africa via Kano, Fort Lamy, El Fasher and Khartoum. On reporting to Intelligence Headquarters, Elliott was informed that his first job was to take a lorry-load of confidential files to Jerusalem for safekeeping, before travelling on to Beirut. He would then catch the fabled Taurus Express to Turkey.

The elderly train puffed slowly up the Taurus Mountains and then ambled gently across the Anatolian plateau to Ankara, and on to Istanbul, never exceeding thirty miles an hour and stopping frequently for no discernible reason. The food in the restaurant car was excellent, and Elliott found the journey a 'delight', made still more pleasant still by the company of his new secretary, a young Englishwoman named Elizabeth Holberton.

Elliott was rather struck by Miss Holberton. She had spent the early part of the war in the Motorised Transport Corps, driving Jeeps in the desert, before becoming a secretary at General Headquarters (GHQ) in Cairo. She was quick-witted, resourceful, beautiful in a demure sort of way, a devoted Catholic and quite posh. Her father was a former managing director of the Bombay Burmah Trading Company and her mother descended from a long line of Irish judges. They got on famously. When the train ran out of supplies of water, the conductor brought Elizabeth a bottle of Turkish Cointreau in which to brush her teeth. She declared the experience refreshing. Elliott liked that.

Ankara was the diplomatic capital of Turkey, but the major powers kept embassies in Istanbul, on the cusp between Europe and Asia; this was where the serious spying was done. Britain's ambassador to Turkey was Sir Hughe Montgomery Knatchbull-Hugessen, a diplomat of the old school who spent much of his time on the ambassadorial yacht and was, perhaps inevitably, an Old Etonian friend of Elliott's father. Hugessen adopted an attitude of 'pained tolerance' towards the activities of British intelligence in Turkey. Formally a junior diplomat, Elliott joined a swiftly expanding, multi-layered British intelligence force under the overall command of Lieutenant Colonel Harold Gibson, a veteran MI6 professional of 'great ability and energy'. 'Gibbie' oversaw a vast system of intelligence-gathering and agent-running, extending from Turkey into Romania, Bulgaria, Greece, Yugoslavia and Hungary. As the representative of Section V, Elliott's task was to undermine enemy intelligence operations, principally those of the Abwehr. Gibson gave Elliott a fairly free rein to explore and attack espionage targets in Turkey, and there were plenty to choose from.

Istanbul was 'one of the great espionage entrepôts of the war', in the words of MI6's official historian. The city was just forty miles from Nazi-occupied Bulgaria; it was Germany's gateway to the Middle East, and an access point for the Allies into occupied Europe.

The Turks feared the Germans, distrusted the Soviets, and felt little love for either the British or the Americans. But the authorities were prepared to tolerate espionage by foreign powers, so long as this did not impinge on Turkish sovereignty, and the spies did not get caught. By 1942, some seventeen different intelligence organisations had converged on Istanbul, to mix and mingle, bribe, seduce and betray, and with them came a vast and motley host of agents and double agents, smugglers, blackmailers, arms dealers, drug-runners, refugees, deserters, black-marketeers, pimps, forgers, hookers and spivs. Rumours and secrets, some of them true, whirled around the bars and back alleys. Everyone spied on everyone else; the Turkish secret police, the Emniyet, spied on all. Some Turkish officials were prepared to cooperate on intelligence sharing, if the price was right, but every so often, if the spying became too brazen or insufficiently remunerative, the Emniyet would stage an arrest. The spy battle was intense, and oddly intimate. The head of the Abwehr was on nodding terms with his opposite numbers in MI6 and Soviet intelligence. 'Everyone was well informed as to the identity of everyone else,' wrote Elliott. When one or other of the intelligence chiefs entered the ballroom of the Park Hotel, the band would strike up the song 'Boo, Boo, Baby, I'm a Spy':

> *I'm involved in a dangerous game,*
> *Every other day I change my name,*
> *The face is different but the body's the same,*
> *Boo, boo, baby, I'm a spy!*
> *You have heard of Mata Hari,*
> *We did business cash and carry,*
> *Poppa caught us and we had to marry,*
> *Boo, boo, baby, I'm a spy!*
> *Now, as a lad, I'm not so bad,*
> *In fact, I'm a darn good lover,*
> *But look my sweet, let's be discreet,*
> *And do this under cover.*
> *I'm so cocky I could swagger,*

The things I know would make you stagger,
I'm ten percent cloak and ninety percent dagger,
Boo, boo, baby, I'm a spy!

But the dagger beneath the cloak was razor sharp. Just two months before Elliott's arrival, a Macedonian student had attempted to assassinate the German ambassador Franz von Papen, but the bomb exploded prematurely, blowing up the assassin and only injuring the German diplomat. Moscow blamed the Gestapo; the Germans blamed the Allies; von Papen suspected the British. The plot was almost certainly the work of the Soviet NKVD. A year earlier, a German suitcase bomb planted in the lobby at the Pera Palace Hotel had killed a member of the British consular staff, and badly injured the vice consul, Chantry Page. Espionage in Istanbul, as the MI6 station chief Harold Gibson observed, was 'not a kid glove affair'.

Elliott was immediately seduced by Istanbul's sleazy glamour. He moved into an office in the embassy 'crammed from top to bottom with intelligence operatives engaged in various aspects of skulduggery', and a garden surprisingly full of copulating tortoises, and plunged into the espionage fray. On his first evening he was swept up by Major Bernard O'Leary, an enormous multilingual former cavalry officer, 'extremely erudite, but irredeemably idle', who was responsible for liaison with Turkish intelligence. O'Leary announced they were going to Taksim's, the spy centre of Istanbul, a cross between a restaurant, a nightclub, a cabaret and a casino. 'Its clientele,' wrote Elliott, 'combined the representatives – mainly engaged in espionage – of all the Axis and Allied powers.' Taksim's was run by a charming White Russian who accepted bribes from everyone, without favouritism, and endeavoured to place rival spies at adjacent tables to facilitate eavesdropping. The waitresses were said to be former Czarist duchesses. Nothing at Taksim's was quite as it seemed. One night Elliott was admiring the club's resident belly-dancer, a stunning woman with 'white-coloured skin and jet black hair', when she fell off the stage, twisted an ankle and swore loudly in a thick Yorkshire accent: she was from Bradford. When not at Taksim's,

Elliott might be found at Ellie's Bar, a favourite watering-hole of British military personnel that served 'a ferocious dry Martini with the kick of a horse'. Ellie was buxom, blonde and thought to be Romanian. She 'spoke excellent English, and purported to fear and hate the Germans'. In fact, Elliott discovered, she was in German pay, employed by the Abwehr to get British officers as drunk as possible in the hope that they would eventually divulge valuable information.

Elliott set about making friends with the sort of people who would have made his father shudder. In later years, he wrote that 'the capacity for friendship is a particularly important characteristic' in an intelligence officer. 'A large amount of intelligence work in the field is all about the establishment of personal relationships; of gaining other people's confidence and on some occasions persuading people to do something against their better judgement.' He befriended the Russian maître d' at Taksim's, and the waiters at Ellie's Bar; he went drinking with a former Czarist guards officer called Roman Sudakov, who was plugged into Russian intelligence and agreed to work for MI6; he got to know the porters at the embassies, the consular officials and the clerks at the telegraph office. He made contacts among the press corps, and Lars the fisherman who plied the Bosphorus and did a little smuggling and information-gathering to supplement the catch. He made a particular point of befriending the conductors on the wagon-lits of the Taurus Express, who were much in demand as couriers for the intelligence organisations, since the railway was the only reliable way of getting from Turkey to the Middle East. The conductors would supply information about who was travelling where, report gossip, smuggle documents and even, for an additional consideration, steal travel papers. They were for sale to the highest bidder, but to none exclusively: 'One particularly remarkable man at one stage was working for both the Abwehr and the SD [Sicherheitsdienst] (each unknown to the other); for the Italians, and for the Japanese; as well as for the British.'

At the other end of Istanbul society, Elliott mixed with high-ranking officials, military officers, diplomats and religious leaders.

The papal legate, Monsignor Angelo Giuseppe Roncalli, who would later become Pope John XXIII, proved to be a fund of good intelligence, and a vigorous anti-fascist. Like so many in wartime Istanbul, Roncalli was playing a double game, dining with von Papen and taking his wife's confession, while using his office to smuggle Jewish refugees out of occupied Europe. A few months after they became friends, Elliott discovered that Roncalli's assistant, one Monsignor Rici, 'a most unattractive little man', was a spy, 'operating a clandestine wireless set on behalf of the Italian military intelligence'. Elliott tipped off the Turkish secret police and had Rici arrested. When he informed Roncalli, with some embarrassment, that his assistant was likely to be spending a considerable period breaking rocks in an Anatolian penal colony, the future Pope merely shrugged, leaving Elliott with the strong impression that he 'was not altogether displeased'.

After just a few months in Istanbul, Elliott concluded there were 'more people involved in various forms of skulduggery per head of population than any other city in the world'. And he had identified a good proportion of them: German intelligence officers, Italian agents, Polish, Czech and Yugoslavian informers, Free French and Jewish Agency spies, and officers of the NKVD and the GRU (Soviet military intelligence). 'All were kept under close observation by the Turks, who ran their own informers.'

Elliott's energetic counter-intelligence activities met with approval in London. Sir Stewart Menzies had always had what Philby called a 'schoolboyish' attitude to counter-espionage: 'Bars, beards and blondes.' Elliott was experiencing plenty of all three, and his stock rose still higher when one of his informants on the Taurus Express handed over a bomb, saying he had been given the device by the Japanese military attaché, Colonel Tateishi, with instructions to detonate it on the line between Aleppo and Tripoli. Elliott gingerly handed the package over to the counter-sabotage section in Istanbul, and paid his informant a large bonus; the informant told Colonel Tateishi the bomb had failed to detonate, and demanded another bonus. Everyone was happy.

Elliott relished his new posting. Even a nasty bout of foot and mouth disease picked up on his travels could not blunt his happiness. And he was falling in love. Elizabeth Holberton was proving to be more than just an excellent secretary. Her Catholicism and his cordial aversion to all religion did nothing to hinder a blossoming relationship. They went everywhere together, and drank quantities of Egyptian Bordeaux, which Elliott declared 'the worst claret I have ever drunk'. Shy beneath his bonhomie, it took Elliott months to summon up the courage to say what was on his mind. A cocktail made for spies finally did the trick: 'After three of Ellie's volcanic Martinis we decided to get married.' Marriages between officers and their secretaries were something of a tradition in MI6, where secrecy bred a special sort of intimacy. Even C was conducting a long-running affair with his secretary.

Elliott dashed off a letter to Sir Edgar Holberton saying that he planned to marry his daughter and 'hoping he didn't mind'. Even if Sir Edgar had minded, it would have made no difference, for Elliott had no intention of waiting for a reply. Roman Sudakov, his best man, threw a stag party for him at the Park Hotel – an event made even more auspicious by the presence at the next table of von Papen, the German ambassador, and his military attaché. After the ceremony on 10 April 1943, performed by Monsignor Roncalli in the papal legate's private chapel, the newlyweds moved into a flat with a view over the Golden Horn – accompanied by a tiny Russian cook named Yaroslav, who made vodka in the bath and began teaching Elliott to speak Russian.

Philby was delighted by Elliott's success, his growing reputation and the news of his marriage. Nicholas Elliott was a rising star in the service, and a valued friend, and no one understood the value of friendship better than Kim Philby.

Three Young Spies

Philby's life in the English suburbs seemed drab in comparison to Elliott's colourful experiences on the frontline of the espionage battle. St Albans was a long way from Istanbul. In Philby's opinion, it was too far from anywhere, including London, where the important intelligence decisions were being made, and the most valuable secrets might be found. Early in 1943, Felix Cowgill announced that Section V would be moving to new premises on Ryder Street, in the heart of St James's. Philby was elated, since the new office would be just 'two minutes from MI5 and 15 from Broadway', the MI6 headquarters. He would now be closer to his club, closer to the gossipy parties hosted by Tommy Harris, and closer to his Soviet handlers. Ryder Street was also the ideal vantage point from which to assess, befriend and manipulate an important new force in the wartime intelligence battle.

The attack on Pearl Harbor catapulted America into the war, and brought into being the Office of Strategic Services, a new and well-funded intelligence service presided over by the extrovert, hard-driving lawyer William 'Wild Bill' Donovan. The OSS would eventually evolve into the CIA, the most powerful intelligence service in the world, but in 1942 America was still new to the game of wartime intelligence, long on resources and energy, but short on expertise. The first OSS officers began arriving in London, keen to learn, late in 1942, and occupied offices in Ryder Street. Malcolm Muggeridge compared them to innocent young maidens, about to be deflowered in 'the frowsty old intelligence brothel' that was MI6. Philby was unimpressed with the first American arrivals, 'a notably bewildered group'. Even their leader Norman Holmes Pearson, a Yale academic, was scathing about his own team, describing them as 'a bunch of amateur bums'. Novices they may have been, but they were also frightfully keen, in a way the hardened veterans of MI6 found rather quaint. 'They lost no opportunity of telling us that they had come to school,' wrote Philby, who, as a respected three-year veteran of the service, was about to become one of their most influential instructors, briefing the Americans on the work of MI6's counter-espionage section, the structure of the British secret services and decoding operations at Bletchley Park. Philby dismissed these eager Americans as a 'pain in the neck', but there was one who stood out from the rest: a tall, intense, cadaverously thin young man, who wrote poetry, cultivated tropical plants, and studied the minutiae of espionage with the dedication of a true obsessive. His name was James Jesus Angleton and he would rise, in time, to become one of the most powerful and controversial spies in history. Angleton was the product of a romantic and unlikely marriage between Hugh Angleton, a soldier turned cash-register salesman, and Carmen Mercedes Moreno, an uneducated, fiery and exceptionally beautiful woman from Nogales, Arizona, with a mixture of Mexican and Apache blood. The two had met in 1916, when Hugh Angleton was serving as a cavalry officer under General Pershing during the campaign against the Mexican rebel Pancho Villa. James Angleton was born in 1917 in Boise, Idaho, and given the middle name Jesus by his Catholic mother – he hated it, but with his ascetic looks and oddly spiritual air, the name fitted him. The boy was fourteen when his father moved to Italy to run, and then own, the Milan branch of the National Cash Register Company. The young Angleton was sent to England for his education, first at a prep school in Buckinghamshire, and then at Malvern College, a British public school firmly in the Victorian tradition. He became a Boy Scout, a prefect, and joined the Officer Training Corps. These were, in Angleton's words, his 'formative years': he left Malvern with courteous manners, a sense of fair play, an air of cultivated eccentricity and a faint English accent that never left him. The boy from Idaho was already 'more English than the English', a disguise he would wear, along with his Savile Row suits, for the rest of his life. He enrolled at Yale in 1937 to study English literature, but spent most of his time listening to jazz, chasing girls and running a literary magazine, *Furioso*, which published the work of such notable poets as Ezra Pound and e.e.cummings, both of whom became his friends. An insomniac night-owl, Angleton developed a reputation as a fierce anti-communist and an aesthete: he wrote romantic verse, most of it execrable, and was nicknamed The Poet. His classmates found him enigmatic, 'a mysterious person, with dark mysterious looks'. Soon after Pearl Harbor, he enlisted in the US Army, and through his former English professor, Norman Pearson, was offered work in London in the newly formed OSS. Before heading to England, he married a twenty-one-year-old heiress to a Minnesota lumber fortune. It was a slightly odd thing to do, but then much of what Jim Angleton did was unexpected. 'What a miracle of momentous complexity is The Poet,' wrote e.e.cummings to a mutual friend.

Angleton was attached to X-2, the OSS counter-intelligence section and the direct counterpart of MI6's Section V. X-2 would eventually expand to take up the entire second floor of the Ryder Street building, while Section V occupied the floor above. Philby was drafted in to lecture the newcomers on the 'arts and crafts' of counter-espionage, penetrating enemy intelligence organisations, and the running of double agents. As one American officer observed, 'I do remember being very impressed. He really knew what he was doing.'

Philby took a shine to the twenty-four-year-old American, and later wrote that Angleton 'earned my respect by openly rejecting the Anglomania' of so many of the new American arrivals. Angleton did not need to be Anglophile since he was, in many ways, so very English already. The extent of the friendship between Philby and Angleton at this point is hard to gauge since Angleton's allies later tried to downplay it, just as his enemies tended to exaggerate it.

According to Angleton's biographer, 'Philby may have felt he had a mentoring relationship with Angleton; Angleton may have shared that feeling.' The two men became patron and protégé, the expert and the prodigy. 'Philby was one of Angleton's instructors, his prime tutor in counter-intelligence; Angleton came to look up to him as an elder-brother figure.' Philby enjoyed having acolytes, and Angleton may have filled a gap left by Nicholas Elliott's absence. The new arrivals and the old hands got to know one another over drinks, lots of them. 'Our European friends were formidable consumers of alcoholic beverages, with apparently little effect,' recalled one OSS officer. Angleton could drink with a Philby-like determination, but then he did everything with an intensity that others found impressive, and slightly odd. He moved a cot-bed into his Ryder Street office, and seemed to spend most of the night studying the esoteric secrets of counter-espionage with devout fervour, 'as if they contained the secret of the Trinity'. He mixed with writers and poets, including William Empson and T. S. Eliot, and occasionally inserted a poem into his reports. Empson noted his 'restless appetite for organising things'. Colleagues in OSS found him 'extremely brilliant, but a little strange ... full of impossible, colossal ideas'. Angleton was a little like one of the rare orchids he would later cultivate with such dedication: an exotic hybrid, a Mexican-Apache-Midwestern English-sounding poet-spy, rare and remarkable, alluring to some, but faintly sinister to those who prefer simpler flora. The bosses recognised that Angleton, for all his peculiarities, had found a vocation, and after six months he was promoted to the rank of second lieutenant and made chief of the Italian desk of X-2, controlling counter-intelligence operations in the country where he had spent much of his youth. His rapid ascent was due, in part, to Philby's tutelage and patronage, and Angleton would later cite him as an inspiration. 'Once I met Philby, the world of intelligence that had once interested me consumed me,' he said. 'He had taken on the Nazis and Fascists head-on and penetrated their operations in Spain and Germany. His sophistication and experience appealed to us ... Kim taught me a great deal.'

With his mixture of charm and competence, Philby's stature within Allied intelligence continued to grow, along with his responsibilities. Late in 1942, Cowgill asked him to take over counter-intelligence operations in North Africa, an area of key importance with the impending Allied invasion of French Morocco and Algeria. The region had previously been the responsibility of Captain Felix Russi, a former soldier from Gibraltar whom Philby described to his Soviet handlers as 'an almost total moron'. Philby was happy to colo-nise his region. 'We had achieved a fair stranglehold on the Abwehr in Spain and Portugal,' he wrote, and 'there was no reason why I should not shoulder additional responsibilities.' A few months later, his brief expanded yet again, to include counter-espionage in Italy (the region James Angleton would soon cover, in parallel, for OSS). Soon after the move to London, Cowgill asked Philby to act as his deputy 'in all intelligence matters' while he paid a three-week visit to the US on MI6 business. Philby reflected, with wry false modesty, that he was 'beginning to make a career in the secret service'. Promotion, however, was only a means to an end. 'I regarded my SIS appointments purely in the light of cover jobs, to be carried out sufficiently well to ensure my attaining positions in which my serv-ice to the Soviet Union would be most effective.'

Even the most ideologically driven people usually need to test their convictions; to have others understand them, support them or challenge them. Philby never shared his beliefs; he never discussed politics, even with his fellow Soviet spies; after his early ideological discussions with Arnold Deutsch, the subject of communism was seldom raised with his Soviet handlers. He had persuaded himself of the rectitude of his course back in 1934, and after that the subject was closed. He retained and sustained his certainties in perfect isolation.

One of the richer ironies of Philby's position is that while he could do no wrong in British eyes, in Moscow he continued to be viewed with mistrust. The main source of Soviet suspicion was a plump, blonde, highly intelligent, politically doctrinaire and fabu-lously paranoid NKVD analyst named Elena Modrzhinskaya, the head of the British department at Moscow Centre. Like many who lived through Stalin's Purges, fear, propaganda and obedience had left a deep residue of mistrust in the soul of Modrzhinskaya, one of the very few women in a senior position within Soviet intelligence. She suspected a gigantic plot: she simply could not credit the 'incomprehensible' risks the Cambridge spies claimed they were taking on behalf of the Soviets; it was surely impossible that men with communist pasts could enter the British secret service so easily, and rise so fast; the British were known to be foisting an elaborate deception on the Nazis, and it stood to reason that they must be attempting to do the same thing to Moscow. In short, she simply could not, and would not, believe that Philby was what he proclaimed himself to be: 'A straight penetration agent working in the Soviet interest.' Philby was a plant, an imposter, a double-crosser: 'He is lying to us in a most insolent manner.' Anatoly Gorsky, the new *rezident* in London, was instructed to find out exactly what disinformation was being spread by Philby and the other British double agents. In time, the Centre would even despatch undercover agents to trail them, and collect incriminating evidence. The surveillance team spoke no English and got repeatedly lost, a problem they ascribed to brilliant spycraft on the part of Philby and the others, rather than their own inability to read a map. The Soviets set out to find evidence that did not exist, and when they failed to find it assumed this must be proof of how well that evidence had been hidden. In the end, Philby's very Englishness rendered him suspect. As Yuri Modin, the Soviet officer who would take over the Cambridge spy network, observed: 'He was so completely, psychologically and physically, the British intelligence officer that I could never quite accept that he was one of us, a Marxist in the clandestine service of the Soviet Union.'

Modrzhinskaya's suspicions of disloyalty did not outwardly alter the way Philby was handled by his Soviet controllers. Gorsky was ordered to maintain contact with the British spies 'in such a manner as to reinforce their conviction that we trust them completely'. Here, then, was a truly bizarre situation: Philby was telling Moscow the truth, but was disbelieved, and allowed to go on thinking he was believed; he was deceiving the British in order to aid the Soviets, who suspected a deception, and were in turn deceiving him. Moscow's faith in Philby seemed to ebb and flow; sometimes he was considered suspect, and sometimes genuine, and sometimes both simultaneously.

Britain and the USSR had been allies ever since Hitler's attack on the Soviet Union in the summer of 1941. Philby could argue that, by passing on information to Moscow, he was simply helping an ally and supporting the 'single-front struggle against fascism'. His colleagues in MI6 and OSS would not have seen matters that way. Some high-grade intelligence was already passing between London and Moscow, but in restricted form, for both sides continued to view one another with deep suspicion. Philby was passing on secrets that his bosses in MI6 would never have dreamed of sharing with Stalin: deception operations, the identities of agents and officers, and a detailed (and damning) picture of the very structure of the secret service itself. There was also the danger – never confirmed or disproved – that German spies had penetrated Soviet intelligence, and information supplied by the Cambridge network was passing back to Berlin. If that possibility crossed Philby's mind, it does not seem to have worried him. His loyalty was to Moscow; what Moscow did with the information he provided was not his concern. He knew he was committing treason by spying for a foreign power, and the implications of doing so. If caught, he would almost certainly be prosecuted under the Treachery Act of 1940, which carried the death penalty.

Death was part of the game. Philby had accepted the liquidation of his much-loved Soviet handlers with the acquiescence of a true believer. More than a dozen spies intercepted through the Bletchley Park decrypts had ended their lives on the gallows or in front of a firing squad. British intelligence was not above 'bumping off' enemy spies, to use the cheery euphemism favoured by MI6. Philby would later claim that he had done his 'modest bit towards helping to win the war', by killing large numbers of Germans. He saw himself as a combatant, albeit one who fought from behind a desk, with all the risks that war involves. But as the war headed to its climax, Philby's espionage career was about to enter a new and much more lethal phase, in which he would help to destroy not Nazi spies, but ordinary men and women whose only crime was to oppose the political creed he had espoused. Philby would soon kill for the communist cause and Nicholas Elliott, unwittingly, would help him.

★

Elliott's principal adversary in the Istanbul spy battle was a tall, bald, bespectacled, urbane and probably homosexual lawyer named Paul Leverkühn. Plucked from his comfortable legal practice in Lübeck to be the Abwehr chief in Turkey, Leverkühn was an unlikely spymaster. He had studied law at Edinburgh University, and worked in New York and Washington. 'Moody and nervous', he disliked Turkey and, like many Abwehr officers, had little time for the brutality and vulgarity of Nazism. He looked more like an academic than a spy. But he was a first-class espionage operative and, as Elliott was discovering, a worthy enemy with a formidable spy network, employing German expatriates and Turkish informants, as well as Russian thugs, Persian hitmen, Arab informants and even an Egyptian prince. 'The city is riddled with their agents,' warned an OSS report. Germany had broken Turkey's diplomatic codes early in the war. Leverkühn's spies, tipsters and honey traps could be found wherever secrets might be gleaned. Hildegard Reilly, the attractive German widow of an American officer, haunted Taksim's, where she 'specialised in making Britons and Americans more talkative'. Wilhelmina Vargasy, a blonde, blue-eyed Hungarian, prowled Ellie's bar, and was said to have seduced no less than six Allied soldiers. Leverkühn ran agents into the Middle East, gathering information on Allied military forces in Palestine, Jordan, Egypt and Iraq, and infiltrated spies into the Soviet Union to foment revolution against Moscow – just as the CIA and MI6 would seek to do after the war.

Elliott's work frequently took him to Ankara where he stayed in the ambassador's residence as a guest of the Knatchbull-Hugessens. On these occasions, the obliging British ambassador even lent Elliott his personal valet, an Albanian named Elyesa Bazna, to help him dress for dinner. 'I remembered him vividly,' wrote Elliott, a 'small roundish man with a high forehead, thick black hair and a large drooping moustache'. Before joining the domestic staff of the British embassy, Bazna had been a low-level criminal, a servant in the Yugoslav embassy, and valet to a German diplomatic official, who had caught him reading his letters, and fired him. Bazna was also a spy for the Germans.

Sir Hughe Knatchbull-Hugessen had developed the unsafe habit of bringing official papers home to the ambassador's residence in his dispatch box, and reading them in bed before turning in for the night. Elliott liked the ambassador, but later conceded that he should have been 'instantly dismissed' for this flagrant breach of security. Bazna identified the nature of his boss's bedtime reading, and spotted a money-making opportunity. In October 1943 (at about the time that Elliott first encountered Bazna laying out his dinner jacket) the Albanian valet made contact with German intelligence and offered to hand over photographs of the documents in exchange for cash, lots of it. Over the next two months, Bazna made some ten deliveries of documents and was paid a fortune in cash, which he carefully stashed away, unaware that the Germans had taken the precaution of paying him in forged notes. Since he spoke almost no English, Bazna was ignorant of precisely what secrets he was spilling, but he knew what the word 'Secret' meant: reports on British diplomatic efforts to bring Turkey into the war against the Germans, infiltration of Allied personnel into Turkey, and US military aid to the USSR. The Albanian spy – codenamed 'Cicero' by the Germans – even furnished accounts of decisions taken by Churchill, Roosevelt and Stalin at the Tehran conference, and the codename of the impending D-Day invasion: 'Overlord'. The impact of these revelations was limited by German scepticism: having been badly misled by the deception plans covering the Sicily invasion (most famously 'Operation Mincemeat', in which a dead body carrying false papers was put ashore in Spain) there were some in the German High Command who suspected that Cicero might be another fiendish

British ruse to mislead them at a crucial juncture in the war. The Bletchley Park intercepts, and a spy in the German Foreign Office, eventually alerted the British to the leakage at the British embassy in Ankara. Suspicion swiftly focused on Bazna who, sensing the danger, shut down his espionage operations. He survived the war, and later tried to sue the West German government when he discovered that he had been paid in worthless notes. He gave singing lessons, sold used cars and ended his life working as a doorman at one of Istanbul's seedier hotels. The Cicero affair was an embarrassing debacle, and further evidence of Germany's proficient spy network in Turkey. British propaganda later tried to claim that Bazna had been a double agent, but Elliott was under no illusions. 'The information obtained by Cicero was completely genuine,' he wrote, and 'the plain truth is that the Cicero case was probably the most serious diplomatic security leak in British history.'

British intelligence fought back, reinforced in 1943 by the arrival of the OSS. The head of Turkish operations for American intelligence was Lanning 'Packy' Macfarland, an extrovert Chicago banker with a taste for trouble and a spy's wardrobe, including a trench coat and slouch hat: 'If he had not been a spy, dressed like that he would have had to become one,' remarked a fellow officer. Aided by British intelligence, Macfarland began setting up his own agent network, starting with a Czech businessman named Alfred Schwartz, code-named 'Dogwood', who claimed to have access to anti-Nazi resistance groups inside Germany, Austria and Hungary. Elliott liked Macfarland, despite his 'penchant for involving himself in unfortunate escapades', and established an effective working relationship with the Americans. Together, they successfully introduced a Turkish informant into one of Leverkühn's sabotage cells. 'The names of the Azerbaijanis, Persians and Caucasians who work for German intelligence are now known,' reported OSS officer Cedric Seager, 'where they congregate of an evening, where they work and what they look like.'

Iraq was a particular focus of Abwehr interest. In 1941, British forces had invaded the country, fearing that a pro-Axis government

in Baghdad might cut off oil supplies. Elliott discovered that
Leverkühn was attempting to foment anti-British rebellion among
Iraq's Kurdish tribes, while encouraging and financing the revolutionary underground. Three German agents were parachuted into
Iraq, and intercepted soon after they landed. Next, Elliott planted a
double agent within the revolutionary cell, codenamed 'Zulu'. On 3
September 1943, Leverkühn picked up Zulu in his Mercedes at a
pre-arranged rendezvous in Istanbul. As they drove around the city,
Leverkühn delivered a propaganda lecture, insisting that 'the Arab
cause depended on German victory', before instructing the agent
on how to identify British military units in Iraq and handing over a
radio code along with $2,000 in cash. The British authorities in
Baghdad duly rounded up the entire revolutionary ring.

The duel between Nicholas Elliott and Paul Leverkühn was ferocious and unrelenting, but it was also oddly gentlemanly. If Elliott
spotted his rival dining in Taksim's, he would always send over a
bottle with his compliments. Each side wanted the other to know
who was on top, and sometimes made the point in ways that were
deeply silly. When Leverkühn discovered that Britain's secret wireless code for Germany was '1200', he immediately informed his
colleagues: henceforth, whenever Elliott or another British intelligence officer walked into an Istanbul bar where German officers
were drinking, they faced a humiliating chorus of 'Twelve-land,
Twelve-land, über alles'. The tit-for-tat battle raged, without a clear
winner. But as 1943 drew to a close, Elliott pulled off a feat of espionage so remarkable that it rocked the Third Reich, tipped Hitler
into a towering rage, crippled the Abwehr and sent Elliott's stock
soaring at MI6. The first hint that such a spectacular coup might be
in the offing came from Kim Philby.

The German Defector

In the spring of 1943, Kim Philby learned that a young German named Erich Vermehren had turned up in Lisbon, where his mother was working as a journalist, and made a tentative approach to British intelligence. The Vermehrens were a prominent family of Lübeck lawyers with known anti-Nazi leanings, and Erich Vermehren hinted that he was thinking of defecting to the British. This first contact went no further. Vermehren had little of intelligence value to offer, his wife was still in Berlin, and he soon returned there. But the approach was intriguing, and Philby filed it away for future use.

Erich Vermehren was one of those rare people whose conscience expands and strengthens under stress. In body he was fragile, the result of a gunshot injury suffered as a youth; but his soul was made of some tensile, almost impossibly resilient, material that never broke or even bent in its certainty. Patriotic and pious, Vermehren was convinced of his own moral rectitude. In 1938, at the age of nineteen, he won a Rhodes scholarship to Oxford, but was prevented from taking it up because his repeated refusal to join the Hitler Youth had rendered him, in Nazi eyes, 'unfit to represent German youth'. Hitler himself is said to have ordered that his name be struck off the list of scholars. Unfit to serve in the army on account of his injury, he worked in a prisoner of war camp. In 1939 he converted to Catholicism and married the aristocratic Countess Elisabeth von Plettenburg, a devout Catholic thirteen years his senior whose loathing for Nazism was as staunch as his own. Elisabeth had come to

Gestapo attention before the war for distributing religious tracts critical of the pagan Nazis. The Plettenburgs were deeply implicated in the anti-Nazi resistance, as were the Vermehrens. Adam von Trott zu Solz, a German foreign office official who would become a key player in the plot to oust Hitler, was Vermehren's cousin. The marriage of Erich and Elisabeth thus brought together two wings of the secret anti-Nazi resistance – which was, in part, a family affair. In this small band of German resisters, religious and moral outrage fused with politics. These were not liberals: they were deeply conservative, often wealthy, fiercely anti-communist, old-fashioned German families, fearful that Hitler was leading Germany into a calamity that would usher in rule by the godless Bolsheviks. The plotters dreamed of ousting Hitler, making peace with Britain and the US, and then defeating the Red menace from the East, to create a new German state that was democratic, anti-communist and Christian. Erich and Elisabeth Vermehren decided, along with a handful of like-minded conspirators, that Hitler must be destroyed, before he destroyed Germany.

In late 1943, with the help of von Trott, Erich Vermehren was assigned to the Abwehr, given two weeks' training in the use of wireless codes and secret inks, and then deployed to Istanbul as personal assistant to Paul Leverkühn, a friend and legal colleague of his father from Lübeck. Officially, wives were not allowed to accompany their husbands on diplomatic postings, to discourage any possibility of defection. Elisabeth, already a marked woman, remained in Berlin, in effect held hostage. Vermehren arrived in Istanbul in early December, and began work at the Abwehr office under Leverkühn. Two weeks later, he again made contact with British intelligence; Harold Gibson of MI6 passed his name on to Section V; Kim Philby's Iberian section flagged up his earlier approach in Lisbon; the Vermehren file was forwarded to Elliott in Istanbul, and the wheels began to turn.

On 27 December 1943, at seven in the evening, Erich Vermehren made his way to an address in the İstiklal Caddesi, the main street of Pera. A servant with a strong Russian accent answered the door to the apartment, showed the young German into the sitting room, and handed him, unbidden, a large Scotch. A few moments later, a lanky, bespectacled man emerged from behind a sliding door, and stuck out his hand with a friendly grin. 'Erich Vermehren?' he said. 'Why, I believe you were coming up to Oxford.' Nicholas Elliott had done his homework.

Vermehren vividly recalled that moment, and Elliott's unmistakable, reassuring Englishness. 'I had a sense of tremendous relief. I felt almost as if my feet rested already on English soil.'

The two men talked while Elizabeth Elliott served dinner, and they continued talking through the night. Vermehren explained that he was anxious to strike a blow against Hitler, but agonised at the thought that he might be betraying his country. He insisted he could not leave without his wife, who would certainly be arrested and probably killed if he defected. Elliott detected 'signs of instability' in the young man: he coaxed and cajoled him; he summoned Elizabeth to stress the moral responsibility incumbent on Vermehren through his Catholic faith; he explained that it would take some time to arrange the false paperwork, but when the moment was right he would spirit the Vermehrens out of Turkey, and bring them safely to Britain. Vermehren's defection, Elliott promised, would strike a devastating blow to Nazism. When the German still hesitated, Elliott's voice took on a harder edge. Vermehren was in too deep to back out now. As dawn broke over Istanbul, Vermehren rose to his feet, and shook Elliott's hand. He would do what Elliott, and God, required of him.

In his report to MI6, Elliott described Vermehren as 'a highly strung, cultivated, self-confident, extremely clever, logical-minded, slightly precious young German of good family', who was 'intensely anti-Nazi on religious grounds'. Elliott was 'fully convinced' of Vermehren's sincerity.

Vermehren flew back to Berlin and told his wife to prepare for the moment they had long discussed. Von Trott had arranged a job for her at the German embassy in Istanbul, where her cousin, Franz von Papen, was the German ambassador. This might provide some

protection if the Gestapo demanded to know how husband and wife
had travelled abroad together in violation of the rules. Elisabeth
divided her bank accounts among her siblings, and the Vermehrens
set off by rail for Istanbul. But as the train trundled through Bulgaria
they learned, to their horror, that the man occupying the wagon-lit
compartment next door was a Gestapo officer. They were already
under surveillance. Sure enough, at the Bulgarian border, Elisabeth
was arrested and taken to the German embassy in Sofia. Erich had
no choice but to continue on to Istanbul alone. After a wait of two
weeks, again with the help of Adam von Trott, Elisabeth wangled her
way onto a courier plane to Istanbul, and was finally reunited with
her husband. Leverkühn knew Frau Vermehren was on the Gestapo
blacklist, and he was distinctly alarmed to find her turning up, unannounced, in his city; he instructed Vermehren to write a memo to
Berlin explaining exactly how, and why, his wife had come to
Istanbul.

The Vermehrens had to move fast, and so did Elliott. Under the
pretence of familiarising himself with the office paperwork,
Vermehren began extracting what seemed to be the most important
Abwehr files, including an organogram of 'the complete Abwehr
setup in Istanbul' and a 'quantity of detailed information' about
Abwehr operations in the Near and Middle East. These were photographed by Elliott, and then returned to the Abwehr office by
Vermehren. Leverkühn gave his new assistant full access to the files,
and Vermehren was soon passing on huge quantities of information
every night. But time was running out. On 25 January, one of Elliott's
informants in the Turkish police tipped him off that they knew
Vermehren was in contact with the British; Leverkühn had his own
police spies, and 'it would not be long, therefore, before the Germans
got wind' of what was afoot.

Two days later, Erich and Elisabeth Vermehren attended a cocktail
party at the Spanish embassy. As the couple left the building, they
were seized by two men and bundled into a waiting car. The scene
was stage-managed by Elliott to make it appear that they had been
kidnapped, in order to buy time and perhaps limit reprisals against

their families. The Vermehrens were driven southeast to the coast near Smyrna, transferred to a fast motor launch, which then accelerated into the Mediterranean darkness. Twenty-four hours later they were in Cairo, still wearing their party clothes.

Paul Leverkühn reacted to the Vermehrens' disappearance with bafflement, followed by anger, and then sheer, paralysing panic. The Abwehr chief, MI6 reported happily, was in 'a hell of a flap'. Von Papen cut short a skiing holiday in the Bursa Mountains to take personal command of the crisis, and demanded that the Turkish police track down the fugitives. The Turks politely agreed to help, and did nothing at all. Leverkühn was ordered back to Berlin. As the Germans scoured Istanbul, Ernst Kaltenbrunner, Hitler's brutal security chief, gave orders that the Istanbul Abwehr be thoroughly investigated and purged, since more enemy spies must be lurking there. He was right. Several of Luverkühn's colleagues now also decided to bolt. Karl Alois Kleczkowski, a forty-three-year-old journalist who had worked as a German propagandist and rumour-collector for the Abwehr, went into hiding in a safe house on the city's outskirts. Wilhelm Hamburger, the heir to an Austrian paper fortune, was one of Leverkühn's most trusted deputies. Posing as a flax buyer, he had spent much of the war gathering intelligence on the Middle East, while seldom leaving his table at the Park Hotel. He was also in touch with the Allied intelligence services. On 7 February he was woken by two German officers and told he was under arrest. Hamburger asked if he could call his most important Turkish agent 'lest his disappearance provoke controversy'.

Bizarrely, he was allowed to do so: Hamburger dialled a pre-arranged number, got through to his OSS contact, and uttered the following words: 'I am going to Berlin for a week and will be back. *Tell it to the Marines.*' (Slang for nonsense.) Half an hour later, with Hamburger still packing and stalling, a car pulled up outside his house. Hamburger raced out of the front door before his captors could stop him, jumped in the back seat, and was driven at high speed to the British consulate, where 'he was given breakfast and a new identity'. The two defectors followed the Vermehrens' secret

escape route to Egypt. Packy Macfarland of OSS sent a jubilant
message to Washington, reporting that Cairo was in danger of being
'swamped by an invasion of evaders and turncoats'. Kaltenbrunner
conveyed the bad news to Hitler:Vermehren's defection had 'gravely
prejudiced the activities not only of the Abwehr-Istanbul but of our
other military agencies in Turkey. The entire work of the Abwehr
station has been exposed and its continuation seems impracticable.'

Having spirited no fewer than four defectors out of Istanbul,
Elliott followed them to Britain. He travelled by train to Lebanon,
and then on by air via Cairo, Algiers and Casablanca, before finally
arriving at Newquay, Cornwall, after an 'exceedingly tedious and
uncomfortable' journey lasting more than a week.

Kim Philby, ever helpful, had offered the use of his mother's
Kensington flat as a place to house the Vermehrens on their arrival in
London. The defection was so secret that not even MI5 knew they
were in the country. Elliott went straight to Dora Philby's flat in
Drayton Gardens, South Kensington, where he was greeted by a
beaming Philby, and reunited with the Vermehrens. Over the next
fortnight, Philby and Elliott put the couple through a friendly, detailed
and rigorous debriefing. Vermehren had worked for the Abwehr for
only a few months, yet the information he had to impart was
supremely valuable: the structure of German intelligence, its operations in the Middle East, the identities of its officers and agents;
Elisabeth Vermehren furnished chapter and verse on the Catholic
underground resistance in Germany. The Vermehrens' piety made
them quite irritating. Whereas most spies are compelled by a variety
of motives, including adventure, idealism and avarice, and can thus be
manipulated, the Vermehrens served only God, which made them
unpredictable and occasionally uncooperative. 'They are so God-awful
conscientious you never know what they're going to do next,' Elliott
complained to Philby in exasperation, after sitting through another of
Vermehren's religious homilies.Vermehren was codenamed 'Precious',
because that is what he was, in more ways than one.

During a break in the debriefing process, Elliott at last had an
opportunity to meet his parents-in-law, which might have been a

confusing experience for someone less familiar with the eccentricities of the British upper class. Sir Edgar Holberton turned out to be
convivial, pompous and distinctly odd. Years in the tropics had left
him with a peculiar verbal habit: every so often, and quite without
warning, he would say something entirely inappropriate. Elliott met
Sir Edgar for lunch at his club. The older man launched into an
exceptionally boring disquisition on the Chilean economy, and then
suddenly observed, without breaking stride: 'I don't mind telling
you, my boy, that I too kept a Burmese girl in Rangoon. Didn't cost
me a penny more than £20 a month.' Conversation with Sir Edgar,
Elliott reflected, was an 'obstacle race with frequent jumps'.

Some of the material extracted from the Vermehrens was deemed
of sufficient value to be passed on to Britain's allies. Moscow was
informed that Vermehren had revealed that certain Turkish officials
were passing information to the Abwehr. The Soviets protested
loudly over this violation of Turkish neutrality, and Turkey immediately ceased all 'German-Turkish intelligence exchanges regarding
the USSR'. But many of the defectors' revelations, notably those
relating to the anti-communist resistance organisation in Germany,
were considered far too sensitive to be shared with the Soviet Union.
More than a year later, Moscow was still complaining that it had not
seen a full account of Vermehren's debriefing.

The news of Vermehren's defection was carefully leaked. The
Associated Press reported: 'The twenty-four-year-old attaché and
his wife declared that they had deserted the Germans because they
were disgusted with Nazi brutality. He is said to possess detailed
information of the greatest value.' MI5 was annoyed to discover that
the defection was being exclusively handled by MI6. 'If an enemy
alien is to be brought here solely for the purposes of his being
pumped for information he should, I think, be under our control,'
wrote Guy Liddell. This was pure professional jealousy. In securing
Vermehren's defection, MI6 trumpeted that Elliott had struck an
'outstanding blow' against the enemy: the information he brought
was useful enough in terms of intelligence, but the symbolic impact
of his defection on Germany was quite shattering.

Hitler is said to have 'exploded' when told of Vermehren's defection. For some time, he had suspected (rightly) that Admiral
Wilhelm Canaris and many of his fellow Abwehr officers were less
than fully loyal to the Nazi project, and secretly conspiring with the
enemy. Here was proof. Hitler also believed (wrongly) that
Vermehren had taken the Abwehr's secret code books with him.
Anyone who had aided, or even merely known the Vermehrens,
was now under suspicion. Vermehren's father, mother, sisters and
brother were all rounded up and imprisoned in concentration
camps. Hitler summoned Canaris for a ferocious dressing down,
and told him the Abwehr was falling apart. With more bravery than
tact, Canaris replied that this was 'hardly surprising given that
Germany was losing the war'. Two weeks later Hitler abolished the
Abwehr, and created a new, over-arching intelligence service under
Himmler's Sicherheitsdienst. Canaris was shuffled into a meaningless job, placed under effective house arrest and finally, following
the failure of the July Plot in 1944, executed. The Abwehr might
have been corrupt, inefficient and partly disloyal, but it was, at least,
a functioning worldwide intelligence service. The defections set off
a chain reaction that destroyed it utterly, just three months before
D-Day. In the words of the historian Michael Howard, German
intelligence was 'thrown into a state of confusion just at the moment
when its efficient functioning was vital to the survival of the Third
Reich'.

★

Nicholas Elliott was now the darling of MI6. An internal assessment
concluded that he had handled the case with 'consummate skill and
sympathy, but with just the necessary touch of firmness'. Some of
the glory rubbed off on Philby, who had helped orchestrate the
defections from afar, and then debriefed the Vermehrens in his
mother's flat. The operation, it seemed, had ended in complete
triumph. Elliott would 'dine out' on this success for a very long time,
but the wining and dining began immediately, in celebration of
Elliott's 'dazzling coup'.

It was through Philby that Elliott met the gaunt but convivial young American, James Jesus Angleton. The three intelligence officers became firm friends, and spent a good deal of time in each other's company, from which Elliott emerged 'formidably impressed both by Jim's intellect and his personality, as well as by his enjoyment and capacity for food and drink'. Angleton had taken to wearing a Homburg, like Philby, and he peered out from underneath it through heavy-lidded eyes. 'Beneath the rather sinister mystique was a very likeable man,' Elliott recorded, 'with a formidable personality and breadth of vision.' Angleton and Elliott had much in common: fierce ambition, daunting fathers and, of course, a shared admiration for Kim Philby.

Before heading back to Istanbul, Elliott was summoned to MI6 headquarters by the head of security, a former soldier newly appointed to oversee vetting and secrecy procedures within the diplomatic service and MI6. This was an issue that had never been raised before with Elliott, who was almost pathologically discreet. 'At that time, secrets were secrets,' he wrote. But he now wondered if he had let his guard down in some way, or spilled some information to the wrong person. He need not have worried. The ensuing conversation, which he wrote down afterwards, said a great deal about the organisation of which Elliott was now a most valued part:

Security officer: 'Sit down, I'd like to have a frank talk with you.'
Nicholas Elliott: 'As you wish colonel.'
Officer: 'Does your wife know what you do?'
Elliott: 'Yes.'
Officer: 'How did that come about?'
Elliott: 'She was my secretary for two years and I think the penny must have dropped.'
Officer: 'Quite so. What about your mother?'
Elliott: 'She thinks I'm in something called SIS, which she believes stands for the Secret Intelligence Service.'
Officer: 'Good God! How did she come to know that?'
Elliott: 'A member of the War Cabinet told her at a cocktail party.'

Officer: 'Then what about your father?'
Elliott: 'He thinks I'm a spy.'
Officer: 'Why should he think you're a spy?'
Elliott: 'Because the Chief told him in the bar at White's.'

And that, once again, was that.

Elliott and Philby existed within the inner circle of Britain's ruling class, where mutual trust was so absolute and unquestioned that there was no need for elaborate security precautions. They were all part of the same family. 'For centuries the Office had operated on trust,' said George Carey Foster, the Foreign Office security officer. 'In that family atmosphere they couldn't conceive that there was a wrong 'un among them.' Elliott trusted his wife to keep a secret; Elliott's employer trusted his father to keep a secret; and Elliott trusted his friend Philby to keep his secrets, never suspecting that those secrets were now being put to murderous use.

The information passed on by the Vermehrens included a detailed description 'of all their contacts in the Catholic underground in Germany, and the role they could play in a post-war democratic and Christian Germany'. This was intelligence of the greatest value, since it listed the names, addresses and occupations of all those who, like the Vermehrens, opposed Hitler but wished to prevent a communist takeover of their country – the 'leading Catholic activists who could be instrumental in the post-war period in helping the Allies establish an anti-communist government in Germany'. For obvious reasons, with the Red Army poised to march into Germany from the East, MI6 did not pass this list on to Moscow.

But Philby did.

After the war, Allied officers went in search of the anti-communist activists identified by the Vermehrens, people who 'could have formed the backbone of a Conservative Christian post-war German political leadership'. They found none of them: 'All had been deported or liquidated.' The final months of the war were bloody and chaotic: Nazi loyalists killed some 5,000 people in the wake of the July Plot, including many in the Catholic resistance. It was not until years later that MI5 worked out what had really happened: Philby had passed the list to his Soviet controller, who had passed it to Moscow Centre, which had sent in the killers with a readymade shopping-list of influential ideological opponents to be eliminated as Stalin's armies advanced. 'Because Moscow had decided to eliminate all non-communist opposition in Germany,' writes Phillip Knightley, 'these Catholics had been shot.'

No one knows how many died as a consequence of Philby's actions, because MI5 and MI6 have never released Vermehren's list. In his diary, Liddell of MI5 noted reports that Soviet forces were liquidating opposition in East Germany in the 'drive against the Catholic Church, which the Russians recognise as the most powerful international force in opposition to communism'. Years later, Philby observed: 'I was responsible for the deaths of a considerable number of Germans.' It was assumed he was referring to Nazis, but among his victims were also an unknown number of German anti-Nazis, who perished because they did not share Philby's politics. Any lingering doubts Moscow may have had about Philby seem to have evaporated at this moment.

The Vermehrens believed they were alerting the Allies to the men and women who might save Germany from communism; unwittingly, they were handing them over to Moscow. Through Philby's betrayal, Elliott's greatest triumph was a secret, sordid tragedy.

The Soviet Defector

D-Day was approaching, the Allies were advancing and Kim Philby, Nick Elliott and their OSS colleague Jim Angleton, like so many others who had come of age in war, began to wonder what they would do with their lives when it was over. Each was determined to remain in the intelligence game, and make a career of it; each had found success in the arcane art of espionage, and all three were destined for rapid promotion, two through merit, and one by an office putsch.

As the Nazi threat receded, the fear of Soviet espionage revived. Before the war, MI5 and MI6 had expended considerable energy, resources and anxiety on combating the communist menace, both inside and outside Britain. But the overwhelming challenge of the war with Germany, and the alliance with Stalin, had diverted attention from Moscow's covert activities. By 1944 the Soviet espionage threat was coming back into sharp focus. 'We've been penetrated by the communists,' Sir Stewart Menzies told Angleton, 'and they're on the inside, but we don't know exactly how.' Waking up to the threat of communism from within, the chiefs of British intelligence were increasingly aware that new weapons, and a restructured service, would be needed to take on 'the next enemy', the Soviet Union. The battle lines of the Cold War were being drawn.

In March 1944, Philby suggested to C that the time had come to resume the fight against communist spies by establishing a new section, Section IX, for the 'professional handling of any cases coming to our notice involving Communists or people concerned in Soviet espionage'. C was enthusiastic, and so was the Foreign Office 'provided you do not do anything in the USSR itself (despite Soviet espionage in this country)'. An MI5 officer, Jack Curry, was initially placed in charge, but the obvious person to run the new division in the long term was the experienced head of Section V, Felix Cowgill. Philby later claimed that Moscow ordered him to elbow aside Cowgill, a task he did not relish. 'I must do everything, but *everything*, to ensure that I become head of Section IX,' Philby wrote. 'Cowgill must go.' It seems more likely that Philby suggested the setting up of Section IX with the firm intention of taking it over, and Cowgill was in the way.

The removal of Cowgill was carried out with surgical detachment, and no remorse. Philby carefully stoked the antagonism between Cowgill and his senior colleagues, brittle Valentine Vivian and venomous Claude Dansey; he whispered darkly to those in authority of the sour relations between Cowgill and MI5; and he manoeuvred himself into a position as prime candidate to take over Section IX in Cowgill's stead. Finally, in September 1944, Philby was summoned to C's office, received with 'great warmth', and told that he would be running the new Soviet section. Philby accepted with pleasure, but not before planting a small and suitably deferential suggestion in C's mind. Since Cowgill's dealings with MI5 had been so bad, might it be sensible to ensure the sister service had no objection to his own appointment? Philby was not remotely fearful that MI5, where he had many friends, would actually challenge his promotion. He merely wanted to be sure that MI5's fingerprints were all over this decision; that way, if the Security Service should ever investigate how he had come to be in such a powerful position, he could point out that they had helped to put him there. Menzies swiftly became convinced that 'the idea was his own'. When Cowgill discovered he had been passed over for the top job, he resigned in fury, as Philby knew he would.

Section IX was originally envisaged as a counter-intelligence unit, to attack Moscow's espionage efforts abroad, but it would soon expand to include running intelligence operations *against* the Soviet bloc, as well as monitoring and secretly attacking communist movements in Europe. Philby, the veteran Soviet spy, was now in charge of Britain's anti-Soviet intelligence operations, in a position to inform Moscow not only of what Britain was doing to counter Soviet espionage, but also of Britain's own espionage efforts against Moscow. The fox was not merely guarding the hen house, but building it, running it, assessing its strengths and frailties, and planning its future construction. As a contemporary later observed, 'At one stroke he got rid of a staunch anti-communist and ensured that the whole post-war effort to counter communist espionage would become known in the Kremlin. The history of espionage offers few, if any, comparable masterstrokes.'

The reaction in Moscow was, naturally, ecstatic. 'The new appointment is hard to over-estimate,' the British section of the NKVD reported, noting that Philby was 'moving up in his institution, he is respected and valued'. Soviet suspicion of Philby had already waned, and now dispersed altogether, in part because Elena Modrzhinskaya, the doyenne of conspiracy theory, had retired with the rank of colonel to give lectures on the evils of cosmopolitanism at the Soviet Institute of Philosophy. Notwithstanding her suspicions, Philby and the other Cambridge spies had been loyal throughout the war, and astonishingly productive. Philby had reported on the 'Manhattan' atomic bomb programme, the plans for D-Day, Britain's Polish policy, OSS operations in Italy (thanks to Angleton), MI6 activities in Istanbul (thanks to Elliott), and much more, all perfectly truthfully. In the course of the war an estimated 10,000 documents, political, economic and military, were sent to Moscow from the London office of the NKVD. Modrzhinskaya stands as a symbol of Stalinism at its oddest: she was consistently ideologically correct, while being utterly, hilariously wrong.

Philby's latest Soviet case officer was Boris Krötenschield, a young workaholic codenamed 'Max' – a 'jovial, kindly man' who spoke an antique, courtly English that made him sound like a tweedy country squire. Krötenschield was closer, in mentality and character, to the men who had recruited Philby back in 1934, 'a splendid professional and a wonderful person' to whom he could 'unburden' his thoughts and feelings. Some of his former hero-worship was returning. The Centre showered him with praise and presents. 'I must thank you once again for the marvellous gift,' Philby wrote in December 1944. 'The prospects that have opened before me in connection with my recent change at work inspire me to optimistic thoughts.' Philby's new job in MI6 was coincidentally reflected in a change of spy name: agent 'Sonny' was now agent 'Stanley'.

*

In Istanbul, Elliott remained oblivious to the way Philby had ousted their old boss. He knew only that his friend had landed an important new job as head of MI6's powerful Soviet counter-espionage section, and Elliott was rising through the ranks in tandem. After a few months back in Turkey, Elliott was summoned to London and told by C that he had been appointed MI6 station chief in neutral Switzerland, a crucial intelligence battleground during the war that would acquire even greater importance as the Cold War grew hotter.

After a long and difficult journey across newly liberated, war-wrecked France, Elliott crossed the Swiss frontier in early April 1945, and checked into Geneva's Hotel Beau-Rivage as night was falling. 'After the gloom of London and France it was an extraordinary contrast to be shown up to a clean bedroom with a view across the lake and to relax in a hot bath with a whisky and soda.' After Turkey, Switzerland seemed disconcertingly civilised, tidy and regulated, an almost artificial world. Here were no dodgy nightclubs where spies swapped secrets with belly-dancers, no bomb-throwing assassins or corrupt officials ready to sell truth and lies for the same inflated price. Elliott was nettled to hear the Swiss complain of their wartime privations, when the war seemed to have swept around and over Switzerland.

But beneath a placid, neutral surface, the place was riddled with spies. Swiss efforts to discourage espionage during the war failed utterly: Allied, Axis and freelance agents had converged on the country, as a base from which to launch intelligence operations into enemy territory. The Soviets had run at least two, linked spy networks based in Switzerland, the Rote Kapelle (Red Orchestra) and the Lucy Ring, extracting top-secret information from Nazi Germany and funnelling it to Moscow. In 1943, an anti-Nazi German diplomat named Fritz Kolbe had turned up in Berne and offered his services to the Allies: first to the British embassy, which turned him away, and then to the OSS station chief Allen Dulles (who would go on to become director of the CIA). Kolbe became, in Dulles's words, 'not only our best source on Germany but undoubtedly one of the best secret agents any intelligence service has ever had'. He smuggled more than 2,600 secret Nazi documents into Switzerland, including German plans before D-Day and designs for Hitler's secret weapons, the V1 and V2 rockets. As Hitler's regime crumbled, Switzerland became a magnet for defectors, resisters and rats leaving the sinking Nazi ship, all clutching their secrets. During the war, the Soviets ran their own networks, and the British and Americans ran theirs, in wary cooperation. But with the coming of peace, Soviet and Western intelligence forces would turn on each other.

In Berne, Elliott rented a flat on the Dufourstrasse, not far from the British embassy, in which he installed his family, which now included a baby daughter, Claudia. (Elliott had insisted that the baby be born on English soil; had she arrived on her due date, VE Day, 8 May 1945, she would have been christened Victoria Montgomeriana, in patriotic tribute to the British general. Luckily for her, she arrived late.) The baby was the responsibility of 'Nanny Sizer', the widow of a sergeant-major, who had enormous feet, drank gin from a bottle labelled 'Holy Water' and doubled up as Elliott's informal bodyguard. Officially, Elliott was second secretary at the British embassy and passport control officer; in reality, at the age of thirty, he was Britain's chief spy in another espionage breeding ground. In the summer of 1945, after only a few months in post, he was invited to meet Ernest Bevin, the new Foreign Secretary. One of Britain's earliest Cold Warriors, Bevin remarked over lunch: 'Communists and communism are vile. It is the duty of all members of the service to stamp upon them at every possible opportunity.' Elliott never forgot those words, for they mirrored the philosophy he would take into his new role.

★

While Elliott settled in to Switzerland, James Angleton took up residence in neighbouring Italy. In November 1944, the young OSS officer was appointed head of 'Unit Z' in Rome, a joint US–UK counter-intelligence force reporting to Kim Philby in London. A few months later, at the age of twenty-seven, he was made chief of X-2 (Counter-espionage) for the whole of Italy, with responsibility for mopping up remaining fascist networks and combating the growing threat of Soviet espionage. With an energy bordering on mania, Angleton set about building a counter-espionage operation of extraordinary breadth and depth. It was said that during the final months of the war he captured 'over one thousand enemy intelligence agents' in Italy. Philby kept Angleton supplied with the all-important Bletchley Park decrypts. The American was 'heavily dependent on Philby for the continuation of his professional success'.

Angleton chatted up priests and prostitutes, ran agents and double agents, and tracked looted Nazi treasures. An 'enigmatic wraith' in sharp English tailoring, he 'haunted the streets of Rome, infiltrating political parties, hiring agents, and drinking with officers of the Italian Secret Service'. At night he was to be found among his files, noting, recording, tracking, plotting, and wreathed in cigarette smoke. 'You would sit on a sofa across from the desk and he would peer at you through this valley of papers,' a colleague observed. His fevered approach to his work may have reflected a poetic, if misplaced conviction that he, like Keats, was destined to die of consumption in Rome. He smiled often, but seldom with his eyes. He never seemed to sleep.

Over the coming years, as Soviet intelligence penetrated deeper into Western Europe, James Angleton and Nicholas Elliott worked ever more closely with Philby, the coordinator of Britain's anti-Soviet operations. Yet the separate sides of Philby's head created a peculiar paradox: if all his anti-Soviet operations failed, he would soon be out of a job; but if they succeeded too well, he risked inflicting real damage on his adopted cause. He needed to recruit good people to Section IX, but not too good, for these might actually penetrate Soviet intelligence, and discover that the most effective Soviet spy in Britain was their own boss. Jane Archer, the officer who had interrogated Krivitsky back in 1940, joined the section soon after Philby himself. He considered her 'perhaps the ablest professional intelligence officer ever employed by MI5', and a serious threat. 'Jane would have made a very bad enemy,' he reflected.

As the war ended, a handful of Soviet officials with access to secret information began to contemplate defection, tempted by the attractions of life in the West. Philby was disdainful of such deserters. 'Was it freedom they sought, or the fleshpots?' In a way, he, too, was a defector, but he was remaining in place (though enjoying the fleshpots himself). 'Not one of them volunteered to stay in position and risk his neck for "freedom",' he later wrote. 'One and all, they cut and ran for safety.' But Philby was haunted by the fear that a Soviet turncoat would eventually emerge with the knowledge to expose him. Here was another conundrum: the better he spied, the greater his repute within Soviet intelligence, and the higher the likelihood of eventual betrayal by a defector.

In September 1945, Igor Gouzenko, a twenty-six-year-old cipher clerk at the Soviet embassy in Ottawa, turned up at a Canadian newspaper office with more than a hundred secret documents stuffed inside his shirt. Gouzenko's defection would be seen, with hindsight, as the opening shot of the Cold War. This trove was the very news Philby had been dreading, for it seemed entirely possible that Gouzenko knew his identity. He immediately contacted Boris Krötenschield. 'Stanley was a bit agitated,' Krötenschield reported to Moscow with dry understatement. 'I tried to calm him down. Stanley said that in connection with this he may have information of extreme urgency to pass to us.' For the first time, as he waited anxiously for the results of Gouzenko's debriefing, Philby may have contemplated defection to the Soviet Union. The defector exposed a major spy network in Canada, and revealed that the Soviets had obtained information about the atomic bomb project from a spy working at the Anglo-Canadian nuclear research laboratory in Montreal. But Gouzenko worked for the GRU, Soviet military intelligence, not the NKVD; he knew little about Soviet espionage in Britain, and almost nothing of the Cambridge spies. Philby began to relax. This defector, it seemed, did not know his name. But the next one did.

★

In late August 1944, Chantry Hamilton Page, the vice consul in Istanbul, received a calling card for Konstantin Dmitrievich Volkov, a Soviet consular official, accompanied by an unsigned letter requesting, in very poor English, an urgent appointment. Page discussed this odd communication with the consul, and concluded that it must be a 'prank': someone was taking Volkov's name in vain. Page was still suffering from injuries he had sustained in the bomb attack on the Pera Palace Hotel, and he was prone to memory lapses. He failed to answer the letter, then lost it, and finally forgot about it. A few days later, on 4 September, Volkov appeared at the consulate in person, accompanied by his wife Zoya, and demanded an audience with Page. The Russian couple were ushered into the vice consul's office. Mrs Volkov was in a 'deplorably nervous state', and Volkov himself was 'less than rock steady'. Belatedly realising that this visit might presage something important, Page summoned John Leigh Reed, first secretary at the embassy and a fluent Russian speaker, to translate. Over the next hour, Volkov laid out a proposal that promised, at a stroke, to alter the balance of power in international espionage.

Volkov explained that his official position at the consulate was cover for his real job, as deputy chief of Soviet intelligence in Turkey. Before coming to Istanbul, he explained, he had worked for some years on the British desk at Moscow Centre. He and Zoya now wished to defect to the West. His motivation was partly personal, a desire to get even after a blazing row with the Russian ambassador. The information he offered was priceless: a complete list of Soviet agent networks in Britain and Turkey, the location of the NKVD headquarters in Moscow and details of its burglar alarm system, guard schedules, training and finance, wax impressions of keys to the files, and information on Soviet interception of British communications. Nine days later Volkov was back, now with a letter laying out a deal.

The Russian had 'obviously been preparing his defection for a long time', for his terms were precise: he would furnish the names of 314 Soviet agents in Turkey, and a further 250 in Britain; copies of certain documents handed over by Soviet spies in Britain were now in a suitcase in an empty apartment in Moscow. Once a deal was agreed, and Volkov and his wife were safely in the West, he would reveal the address, and MI6 could collect the papers. In exchange for this haul, Volkov demanded £50,000 (equivalent to about £1.6 million today), and political asylum in Britain under a new identity. 'I consider this sum as a minimum considering the importance of the material given to you, as a result of which all my relatives living in the territory of the USSR are doomed.' The Russian provided just enough detail to prove that his information was genuine: among the Soviet spies in important positions in Britain, he revealed, were seven in the British intelligence services or the Foreign Office. 'I know, for instance, that one of these agents is fulfilling the functions of head of a section of the British counter-espionage service in London.'

Volkov insisted on several more conditions. On no account should the British allude to him in wireless messages, since the Soviets had broken the British codes and were reading everything sent through official channels; the Russians also had a spy inside the British embassy, so any paperwork relating to his offer should be closely guarded, and handwritten. All further communications would be through Chantry Page, who could contact him on routine consular business without raising suspicions among his Soviet colleagues. If he did not hear from Page within twenty-one days, he would assume the deal was off, and take his information elsewhere. Volkov's nervousness was entirely understandable. As a veteran NKVD officer he knew exactly what Moscow Centre would do, and how quickly, if it got wind of his disloyalty.

The new British ambassador to Turkey, Sir Maurice Peterson, was allergic to spies. His predecessor, Knatchbull-Hugessen, had come horribly unstuck through the spy Cicero. Peterson wanted nothing to do with such people, and his reaction to Volkov's approach was to shovel the whole thing, as fast as possible, onto MI6: 'No one's going to turn my embassy into a nest of spies . . . do it through London.' Even the MI6 station chief in Istanbul, Cyril Machray, was kept in the dark. John Reed wrote up a report, by hand, and put it in the diplomatic bag. It landed on the desk of Sir Stewart Menzies ten days later. C immediately summoned his head of Soviet counter-espionage, Kim Philby, and handed him the report. Here was another potential intelligence coup, a trove of information that might, like the Vermehren defection two years earlier, change the game completely.

Philby read the memo with mounting, if hidden, horror: Volkov's allusion to the Soviet spy running a counter-intelligence section in London could only refer to himself. Even if Volkov did not know his identity he had promised to hand over 'copies of the material provided' to Moscow, which would soon be traced back to him. The spies Volkov threatened to uncover in the Foreign Office must be Guy Burgess, now working in the news department, and Donald Maclean, first secretary at the British embassy in Washington. This lone defector had enough information to break up the entire Cambridge spy chain, expose the inner workings of Soviet intelligence, and destroy Philby himself. Struggling to compose his features, Philby stalled, telling C the Volkov approach was 'something of the greatest importance'. He would ponder the memo overnight, he said, and report back in the morning.

'That evening I worked late,' Philby wrote many years later. 'The situation seemed to call for urgent action of an extra-curricular nature.' The insouciant tone is misleading: Philby was close to panic. He arranged a hasty meeting with Krötenschield, and told him what had happened. Max tried to calm him, in language that sounds like one Englishman discussing a cricket match with another: 'Don't worry, old man. We've seen a lot worse. The score will be settled in our favour.' Philby should prevaricate, said Krötenschield, and try to control the situation. That evening, British radio interceptors picked up (but failed to attach any significance to) a sudden surge in coded radio messages passing from London to Moscow, followed by another increase in traffic between Moscow and Istanbul.

The next morning, Philby was back in C's office, full of enthusiasm, since any hint of reluctance would look deeply suspicious if matters came to the crunch. 'Someone fully briefed should be sent out to take charge of the case on the spot,' he said, with the task of 'meeting Volkov, bedding him down with his wife in one of our safe houses in Istanbul, and spiriting him away, with or without the connivance of the Turks, to British-occupied Egypt'. C agreed. In fact, he had met just the man for the job at White's Club the night before: Brigadier Sir Douglas Roberts, head of Security Intelligence (Middle East) – SIME – based in Cairo, who happened to be in London on leave. Roberts was an experienced intelligence officer and a veteran anti-Bolshevik. Born in Odessa to an English father and Russian mother, he spoke Volkov's language fluently. Indeed he was the only Russian-speaking intelligence officer in either the Middle East or London, which says much about MI6's state of preparation for the Cold War. Roberts would be able to smuggle Volkov out of Istanbul with ease, and Philby knew it. All he could do was hope that his 'work the night before would bear fruit before Roberts got his teeth into the case'.

Once again, Philby's uncanny good fortune intervened. Brigadier Roberts was a brave man, a veteran of the First World War, but he had one fear: flying. Indeed, so extreme was his aviophobia that his job description explicitly excused him from having to fly anywhere. When asked to head to Istanbul at once and take over the Volkov case, he barked: 'Don't you read my contract? I don't fly.'

The obvious replacement for Roberts was Nicholas Elliott. From Berne he could reach Istanbul, his old stamping ground, in a matter of hours. He had done a fine job of extracting Vermehren two years

Harold Adrian Russell 'Kim' Philby at the age of eighteen: the secret Cambridge communist.

Philby as a boy of
about eight years old.

The young Philby: 'He was
the sort of man who won
worshippers.'

St John Philby, noted Arab
scholar, explorer, writer, trouble-
maker and demanding father.

Basil Fisher (*left*) and Nicholas Elliott: their close friendship came to a tragic end when Fisher was shot down in the Battle of Britain.

Elliott, the Eton schoolboy, born to rule, who hid his shyness behind a barrage of jokes.

Claude Elliott, father of Nicholas, celebrated mountaineer and provost of Eton, accompanies a young Queen Elizabeth II on a tour of the school.

The Cambridge spies

Donald Maclean (*right*): a talented linguist destined for the Foreign Office.

Anthony Blunt (*below, left of picture*) with Cambridge friends: a brilliant art historian and a Soviet spy.

Guy Burgess (*above*): witty, flamboyant, highly intelligent and pure trouble.

Great Court, Trinity College, Cambridge: the unlikely crucible of communist revolution.

Alice 'Litzi' Kohlman, Philby's first love and first wife, an activist in the Viennese communist underground.

Edith Tudor-Hart, an Austrian photographer married to an Englishman, arranged Philby's rendezvous with the Soviet intelligence service.

Street violence erupts in Vienna in 1933, as the extreme right-wing government goes to war with the left.

Nicholas Elliott, as a new recruit to MI6. 'A convivial camaraderie prevailed, rather like a club.'

James Jesus Angleton, an apprentice intelligence officer in wartime London. An American from Idaho, he was 'more English than the English' and an honorary member of the club.

Philby (*second from left*), *The Times* war correspondent, at a lunch with Lord Gort (*to Philby's left*), commander of the British Expeditionary Force in France, 1939.

Arnold Deutsch, alias 'Otto', Philby's charismatic recruiter and spy-master.

Theodore Maly, Philby's NKVD controller, later murdered in Stalin's purges.

Yuri Modin, the subtle and ingenious handler of the Cambridge spy network.

Klop Ustinov, Russian-born German journalist, secret agent for Britain and father of the actor Peter Ustinov.

Alexander Foote, British-born radio operator for the Soviet spy network 'Rote Kapelle'.

Igor Gouzenko, masked, awaiting interviews with the press after his defection in 1945.

Dick White, a former schoolmaster, was the chief of MI5 counter-intelligence in 1951.

Felix Cowgill, chief of Section V, the MI6 counter-intelligence unit based in St Albans.

Victor Rothschild, MI5 head of counter-sabotage and friend of Kim Philby.

C: Sir Stewart Menzies, the wartime head of MI6.

Guy Liddell: MI5 head of counter-intelligence and diarist.

Valentine Vivian, known as Vee-Vee, the Deputy Chief of MI6 who vouched for Philby: 'I knew his people.'

Hester Harriet Marsden-Smedley, the *Sunday Express* war correspondent who steered Philby into MI6.

Sarah Algeria Marjorie Maxse, organisation officer for the Conservative Party and recruiter for MI6. Philby found her 'intensely likeable'.

Elizabeth Holberton, Nicholas
Elliott's MI6 secretary, confidante
and finally wife.

The Elliotts on their
wedding day, outside
the Park Hotel, Istanbul,
10 April 1943.

Erich and Elisabeth
Vermehren. The
Vermehrens' defection,
organised by Elliott,
plunged the German
intelligence service
into crisis.

Kim Philby (*left*) was appointed the MI6 station chief in Washington in September 1949. *Above*, the RMS *Caronia*, the luxury Cunard liner nicknamed the 'Green Goddess' on which he sailed to New York. 'Philby was a great charmer. He came to us with an enormous reputation,' said one CIA colleague.

Guy Burgess, Philby's problematic lodger: frequently drunk, faintly malodorous and always supremely entertaining.

James Angleton, poet, orchid-
enthusiast, CIA chief of counter-
intelligence and America's most
powerful mole-hunter.

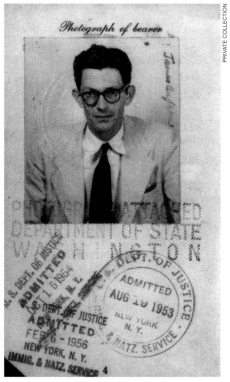

Bill Harvey of CIA counter-intelligence,
the former FBI agent and Philby's most
dangerous opponent in the US.

Harvey's Oyster Salon, the smart
Washington restaurant where Philby
and Angleton lunched together:
'Philby picked him clean.'

Enver Hoxha, Albania's hardline communist ruler.

David de Crespigny Smiley, an aristocratic British Army officer with a legendary taste for derring-do, seen here with Yemeni resistance fighters.

The *Stormie Seas*, a forty-three-ton schooner disguised as a pleasure boat, carrying enough munitions to start a small war.

En route to the Albanian coast for the start of 'Operation Valuable', one of the most catastrophic secret operations of the Cold War.

The 'pixies' prepare for action: three of the four men in this photograph were killed within hours of landing on the Karaburun peninsula.

WANTED

Donald D. Maclean

Date of birth: 25 May 1913

Home: Beacon Shaw Tatsfield, Kent. England

PP Nr. Br. C 36575, Issued in Rome, 20 July 1949

Discription:

6'3", normal built, short hair, brushed back, part on left side, slight stoop, thin tight lips, long thin legs, sloppy dressed, chain smoker, heavy drinker.

WANTED

Guy Francis Be Money Burgess

Date of birth: 6 April 1911

Home: Unknown

PP.Nr. 1674591, Issued in London, 20 July 1950

Discription:

5'9", slender built, dark complexions, dark curly hair, tinged with gray, chubby face, clean shaven, slightly Pidgeon toed.

Call in case apprehended:
Vohenstrauss 112
Munich Civ. 481688
Munich Military 7401
Herford 2297
Herford 2172

"Maybe using forged pass-ports"

Two typically irreverent cartoons drawn by Guy Burgess in Moscow: Lenin with a chip on his shoulder and a ferocious Stalin declaring: 'I'm very human!'

earlier, and had excellent contacts in Turkey. He even appears to have met Volkov at some point during his stint in Istanbul. But Elliott, precisely because of his suitability, was the last person Philby wanted to handle the case. For once, instead of delicately planting an idea on the boss and waiting for him to believe he had coined it, Philby directly intervened, and suggested that C send him to Turkey to extract Volkov in person. Menzies agreed, 'with obvious relief' at this bureaucratic problem solved. Philby now gave the impression of busily making preparations, while dragging his feet as slowly as possible. He first underwent a crash course in wireless coding, to ensure he could bypass the penetrated embassy systems, and then dawdled for three more days. When his plane finally took off for Cairo, it was diverted to Tunis, causing further delay. He was still en route when the Turkish consulate in Moscow issued visas for two Soviet 'diplomatic couriers' travelling to Istanbul.

Philby finally arrived in Turkey on 26 September 1945, twenty-two days after Volkov's initial contact. The city was looking particularly beautiful in the late summer sun, but Philby grimly reflected that if he failed to prevent Volkov's defection, 'this might be the last memorable summer I was destined to enjoy'. When Reed asked him why MI6 had not sent someone sooner, Philby lied blandly: 'Sorry, old man, it would have interfered with leave arrangements.' Reed later found himself pondering the 'inexplicable delays and evasions of Philby's visit', but at the time the Foreign Office man held his tongue. 'I thought he was just irresponsible and incompetent.'

The following Monday, with Philby standing over him, Chantry Page picked up the telephone, dialled the number of the Soviet consulate, and asked the operator for Konstantin Volkov. Instead, he was put through to the consul general. Page phoned again. This time, after a lengthy pause, the telephone was answered by someone who claimed to be Volkov but who spoke good English, which Volkov did not. 'It wasn't Volkov,' said Page. 'I know Volkov's voice perfectly well. I've spoken to him dozens of times.' The third call got no further than the telephone operator.

'She said he was out,' complained Page. 'A minute ago, she put me on to him.' Page's face was 'a study in puzzlement'. Silently, Philby rejoiced. The next day, Page called the Soviet consulate again. 'I asked for Volkov, and the girl said "Volkov's in Moscow". Then there was a sort of scuffle and slam, and the line went dead.' Finally, Page marched over to the Soviet consulate in person, and returned enraged. 'It's no bloody good. I can't get any sense out of that madhouse. Nobody's ever heard of Volkov.' Philby was privately triumphant. 'The case was dead.' And so, by this point, was Volkov.

The two 'diplomatic couriers', hitmen despatched by Moscow Centre, had worked with crisp efficiency. A few hours earlier, two figures, bandaged from head to foot, were seen being loaded onto a Soviet transport aircraft, 'on stretchers and heavily sedated'. In Moscow, Volkov was taken to the torture cells of the Lubyanka where, under 'brutal interrogation', he confessed that he had intended to reveal the identities of hundreds of Soviet agents. Volkov and his terrified wife, Zoya, were then executed.

Philby later reflected that the episode had been 'a very narrow squeak', the closest he had yet come to disaster. As for Volkov, Philby dismissed the Russian as a 'nasty piece of work' who 'deserved what he got'.

Konstantin Volkov left no traces: no photograph, no file in the Russian archives, no evidence about whether his motives were mercenary, personal or ideological. Neither his family, nor that of his wife, have ever emerged from the darkness of Stalin's state. He had been right to assume that his relatives were doomed. Volkov was not merely liquidated, he was expunged.

Philby sent a coded message to Menzies, explaining that Volkov had vanished and requesting permission to wind up the case. In a subsequent report, he proffered several plausible explanations for Volkov's disappearance: perhaps he had changed his mind about defecting, or had got drunk and talked too much. If the Soviets bugged the consulate telephones, they might have discovered the truth that way. At no point did he even hint at the possibility of a tip-off from the British side. Menzies, comfortable with Philby's explanations, concluded it was 'extremely unlikely' that 'indiscretion in the British embassy in Istanbul was the cause. The more probable explanation is that Volkov betrayed himself . . . It is quite possible that his quarrels [with the Soviet ambassador] led to him being watched, and that either he or his wife, or both, made some mistake.'

On his way home, Philby stopped off in Rome to visit James Angleton. The strain of the Volkov scare had rattled him, and he proceeded to get extremely drunk. American intelligence knew of the failed defection, and Philby's desire to see Angleton may have been partly to 'test the waters', and find out how the story was playing in Washington. Angleton listened attentively to Philby's account, and 'expressed sympathy that so promising a case had been lost'. But the American seemed more preoccupied with his own concerns: he was worried about 'the effect his work was having on his marriage' since he had not seen his wife, Cicely, for over a year and 'felt guilty about it'. Philby was sympathetic. 'He helped me to think it through,' Angleton said. After three days of bibulous secret-sharing and mutual support, Angleton poured Philby onto a plane, 'worse for wear of the considerable amount of alcohol he had consumed'.

Settling into his new job, Philby's life developed a pattern of duality, in which he consistently undermined his own work, but never aroused suspicion. He made elaborate plans to combat Soviet intelligence, and then immediately betrayed them to Soviet intelligence; he urged ever greater efforts to combat the communist threat, and personified that threat; his own section worked smoothly, yet nothing quite succeeded. Information from the defector Igor Gouzenko had enabled MI5 to identify Alan Nunn May, another secret communist recruited at Cambridge, as a Soviet mole working on nuclear research in Canada. May's method of contacting his Soviet controller was to stand outside the British Museum carrying a copy of *The Times*. A trap was set, but neither May nor his handler turned up. Philby had tipped off Moscow, just as he almost certainly 'warned the Centre about other agents identified by Gouzenko who were under British and American surveillance'.

Philby worked closely alongside the other panjandrums of the secret elite of the powerful Joint Intelligence Committee; in formal meetings and private parties, he mixed with the cream of the secret services, people intensely secretive outside this charmed circle, and so indiscreet inside it. Philby's Section IX gathered information to discredit Soviet dignitaries, it laboured to stimulate defections, glean secrets from former Soviet prisoners of war, and eavesdropped on diplomats and spies. Philby approved every move in the game, and then told Krötenschield, who told the Centre. From his contacts in MI5 and MI6, from Elliott and Angleton, Menzies and Liddell, from every corner of the intelligence machine, Philby extracted secrets to bolster the revolution and stymie the West, and passed on everything, 'without reserve', to Moscow.

During the war, the Bletchley Park decoders had enabled Britain to discover what German intelligence was doing. Philby's espionage went one better: he could tell his Soviet handlers what Britain's spymasters were intending to do, before they did it; he could tell Moscow what London was *thinking*. 'Stanley informed me of a plan to bug simultaneously all the telephone conversations of all staff in Soviet institution [the embassy] in England,' reported Krötenschield. Thanks to Philby, the Russians were not one step ahead, but two. And they were grateful: 'Stanley is an exceptionally valuable source ... His eleven years of flawless work with us is irrefutable proof of his sincerity ... Our goal is to protect him from discovery.'

Spies love to receive medals they can never wear in public, secret rewards for secret acts. In 1945, Elliott was awarded the US Legion of Merit, although with typical modesty he joked that he had probably been given the medal for rescuing Packy Macfarland, his OSS counterpart in Turkey, drunk, from an Istanbul bar. Early the following year, a grateful Britain appointed Kim Philby to the Order of the British Empire for his wartime work. A few months previously in Moscow, Philby had been secretly recommended for the Soviet Order of the Red Banner in recognition of his 'conscientious work for over ten years'. By the end of 1946, Philby had achieved something no other spy could boast: the award of three separate medals from nationalist Spain, the communist Soviet Union, and Britain.

Kim Philby, OBE, was increasingly seen by his colleagues in British intelligence as a man marked out for great things: the consummate intelligence professional, the captivating star of the service who had worsted the Germans at the intelligence game and was now leading the fight against Soviet espionage. Stewart Menzies had served throughout the war as Britain's spy chief, but eventually C would have to pass on the torch. 'I looked around,' wrote waspish Hugh Trevor-Roper, 'at the part-time stockbrokers and retired Indian policemen, the agreeable epicureans from the bars of White's and Boodle's, the jolly, conventional ex-Navy officers and the robust adventurers from the bucket shop; and then I looked at Philby . . . he alone was real. I was convinced that he was destined to head the service.'

Rising Stars

With the coming of peace, the denizens of the secret world emerged onto a new political landscape fraught with uncertainty, and ripe with opportunity. James Angleton, anti-communist to the core, was elated at the prospect of doing battle with the Soviet spy machine. 'I believed we were in the dawn of a new millennium,' he later recalled. Nicholas Elliott moved easily from loathing Nazism to hating communism; both threatened the British way of life he cherished, and both were therefore evil. In Elliott's mind, the threat from Russia represented a stark choice: 'The continuation of a civilization mainly fit to live in, or Armageddon.' For Kim Philby, too, the political frontiers shifted, though his convictions altered not at all. For most of the war, he had spied on behalf of Britain's ally; now he was spying for Britain's sworn enemy, and from within the very heart of the British intelligence machine.

Elliott plunged into his role as Britain's spy chief in spy-saturated Switzerland with the enthusiasm of a schoolboy – which, in many ways, he remained. He was now a husband, a father (a son, Mark, would arrive in 1947) and a career intelligence officer, an MI6 professional with weighty responsibilities, yet there was still something boyish about him, an engaging combination of worldliness and naivety, as he waded cheerily through the moral and ethical quicksand of espionage. He found the challenge of intelligence-gathering not merely enjoyable, but frequently absurd. 'I'm in it for the belly-laughs,' he said. He knew his tendency to see the funny side in the worst situations was 'a form of defence mechanism', a way of holding back reality with jokes, the dirtier the better. Elliott's character was a distinctly English combination of the staid and the unconventional, conservatism and oddity: he was popular with colleagues, for he was unfailingly courteous, and never raised his voice. 'Verbal abuse is not the right course of action,' he once reflected. 'Except perhaps in dealing with Germans.' Elliott could not abide bureaucracy, administration or rules. His knack for intelligence-gathering relied on personal contact, risk, hunch, and what he called 'the British tradition of somehow muddling through despite the odds'. Jocular, old-fashioned and eccentric, Elliott struck some as a posh bumbler. It was a useful disguise.

As he had in Istanbul, Elliott gathered around him a collection of more or less motley characters, agents, informers and tipsters; he cultivated new friends, and imported old ones. 'One of the joys of living in Switzerland in the immediate post-war period was to be able to have friends out to stay from deprived England and feed them up.' The spare bedroom in Dufourstrasse became temporary home to a succession of British and American spies criss-crossing Europe. Richard Brooman-White, Elliott's chum who had eased Philby into Section V, came to stay in 1946, and was very nearly immolated when a waitress in Elliott's favourite restaurant attempted to flambé an omelette at the table by pouring brandy onto a heated pan, causing a violent explosion that set fire to the hair of a Swedish diner. Elliott extinguished her with three glasses of white wine. Philby made a point of stopping off in Switzerland during his regular tours of Europe, for working holidays with Elliott involving copious drink, Swiss cuisine and spy gossip. Another frequent visitor was Peter Lunn, one of Elliott's 'oldest and closest friends' from Eton. Slight, blue-eyed and with a pronounced lisp, Lunn had joined MI6 at the same time as Elliott in 1939, but on the whole he preferred skiing to spying. The Lunns were 'British skiing aristocracy': Peter's grandfather was a former missionary who spent a lifetime preaching the joys of skiing, and founded the ski travel company that still bears his name; his father successfully campaigned to have downhill skiing recognised as an Olympic sport, and Peter himself captained the British ski team at the 1936 Winter Olympics. Under Lunn's instruction, Elliott took to the sport with a typical combination of enthusiasm and recklessness. Where his father had climbed mountains slowly, Elliott discovered the thrill of sliding down them as fast as possible. Most weekends he could be found on the slopes of Wengen or St Moritz. Elliott's life in Berne was rendered still more pleasurable by the arrival of Klop Ustinov, his old friend and mentor from The Hague. After successfully extracting the spy Wolfgang zu Putlitz from the clutches of the Gestapo, the part-Jewish, part-Ethiopian Russian with the upper-class English accent had spent a fascinating war working for British intelligence, most recently in Germany where, in the uniform of a British colonel, he had proved to be 'the ideal person to be entrusted with the interrogation of Nazi suspects'. In 1946, Ustinov was sent to Berne to work with Elliott on 'attempting to piece together a picture of the post-war Soviet intelligence networks in Europe'. Elliott was delighted to be reunited with this spherical, jovial man, whose eye permanently twinkled with merriment behind his monocle. Klop believed that life was a 'superficial existence', an attitude of mind which fused perfectly with Elliott's frivolity and taste for danger. The Elliott–Ustinov partnership proved extraordinarily effective, but rather fattening: a fine chef, Klop tended to turn up unexpectedly, carrying *rognons de veau à la liégoise* inside a leather top-hat case.

Elliott and Ustinov focused first on the remnants of the wartime Soviet spy system in Switzerland, notably the network codenamed the Rote Kapelle, which at its height had run some 117 agents, including forty-eight inside Germany, producing high-grade intelligence. One of the most important members of the network was British, a young communist named Alexander Foote. Born in Derbyshire, Foote had served in the RAF before deserting to join the British Battalion of the International Brigades during the Spanish Civil War. Shortly before the Second World War he was recruited by Soviet military intelligence and sent to Switzerland as a radio operator for the fledgling Rote Kapelle. In January 1945, Foote moved to Moscow, convinced his interrogators of his continued loyalty, and was redeployed to the Soviet sector of post-war Berlin under the pseudonym 'Major Grantov'. There, in July 1947, he defected to the British. Foote produced a detailed picture of Soviet intelligence methods, offering a 'unique opportunity to study the methodology of a Soviet network', from which Elliott and Ustinov were able to draw up a 'blueprint for communist activities during the Cold War'. Foote's debriefing contained some deeply worrying elements, most notably the revelation that Moscow had many long-term, deeply embedded spies in Britain, some of whom had been recruited long before the war. Elliott and Ustinov concluded that most of these spies were 'lifelong communist activists', but not necessarily with any overt connection to the party.

★

James Angleton had come to see the task of combating Soviet espionage as 'not so much an ideology, as a way of life'. In the last years of war and the first years of peace, Angleton's agents pervaded every corner of Italy, the civil service, armed forces, intelligence services and political parties, including the Soviet-backed Italian Communist Party. Like Elliott, Angleton cultivated a brand of high eccentricity: he gave his agents botanical codenames, such as Fig, Rose or Tomato, and sported a fur cape with a high collar, which made him look 'like a British actor emulating a thirties spy'. Behind his back, colleagues called him 'the cadaver' and wondered at his strangeness. 'The guy was just in another world,' said one. But he was good. By 1946, he had successfully penetrated no fewer than seven foreign intelligence services, and had a roster of more than fifty active informants – most of them quite dodgy, and some of them entirely so. Among the most glamorous, and least trustworthy, was Princess Maria Pignatelli, the widow of an Italian marquis with links to Mussolini who had offered her services to the OSS as an informant on what remained of Italian fascism. Angleton discovered, however, that she had previously been in contact with the German intelligence service; he was never sure how far he could trust the spy he knew, with only limited affection,

as 'Princess Pig'. Even more dubious was Virgilio Scattolini, a corpulent Italian journalist who wrote bestselling, semi-pornographic
novels, including one entitled, rather unenticingly, *Amazons in the
Bidet*. This sideline did not prevent him from obtaining a job on the
Vatican newspaper. In 1944, he offered to supply the OSS in Rome
with Vatican diplomatic documents and cable traffic, including
copies of reports from the papal nuncio in Tokyo, who was in direct
contact with senior Japanese officials. Angleton paid Scattolini a
princely retainer of $500 a month. His reports were sent straight to
Roosevelt, and were considered so secret that only the President or
Secretary of State could authorise access to them. Angleton, however,
began to have doubts when it emerged that Scattolini was hawking
similar material to other intelligence organisations, including MI6.
The crunch came when Scattolini reported a conversation between
the Japanese envoy to the Holy See and his American counterpart,
which the State Department discovered had never taken place.
Scattolini was making it up, and he continued to do so, even after he
was sacked by Angleton. In 1948 he was imprisoned for fabricating
two entire volumes purporting to be the 'Secret Documents of
Vatican Diplomacy'.

   The Scattolini episode was deeply embarrassing, the first blemish
on Angleton's career. It also ingrained his natural propensity for
extreme suspicion. His time in Britain, observing the successful
Double Cross operation against the Germans, had taught Angleton
'how vulnerable even the most supposedly secure counter-
intelligence service is to clandestine penetration'. On reflection, he
wondered whether Scattolini might have been a Soviet double
agent, deployed to plant damaging disinformation. The duplicity of
spies like Princess Pig and Virgilio Scattolini seemed to reinforce
Angleton's distrust of all but a few intimates; he became increasingly
obsessed with double agents and 'the Byzantine possibilities open to
the counter-intelligence practitioner'. On Angleton's visits to Berne,
Elliott noted his American friend's deepening mistrust, his compul-
sive compilation of secret files, his adherence to secrecy as a sort of
religion. Every day, Angleton scoured his Rome office for bugs,

'crawling around on his hands and knees', convinced the Soviets were attempting to listen in on his conversations, just as he was eavesdropping on theirs. 'His real love was unravelling the web of deception, penetration and general intrigue woven by the KGB,' wrote Elliott. 'Above all, he loved secrecy, perhaps even secrecy for its own sake.'

Angleton's only real intimacy was with other spies, and he later remarked on the way friendship, secrecy and professional comrade-ship seemed to merge during his years in Rome. 'We were ... damned good friends,' he later said. 'I feel that's the only way you can keep a service going.' There was rivalry between the American and British services in many parts of the world, but Angleton and Elliott kept few secrets from one another, and fewer still from Kim Philby.

During one of Philby's visits to Rome, Angleton described one of his proudest achievements: a bugging device planted in the offices of Palmiro Togliatti, the veteran leader of the Italian Communist Party. Togliatti had spent the war in the Soviet Union, making radio broad-casts urging Italian communists to resist the Nazis, before returning to Italy after the fall of Mussolini to serve in a democratic govern-ment of national unity. Togliatti's links with Moscow rendered him deeply suspect in American eyes, and Angleton boasted that he was recording every word spoken in the communist leader's office. A few weeks later, Boris Krötenschield sent a message to Moscow Centre: 'Stanley reported that the counter-intelligence section of the OSS in Italy has set up a microphone in the building where Togliatti works, thanks to which they can monitor all conversations in that building.'

In the autumn of 1946, Philby announced that he was marrying Aileen Furse – news that came as a shock to both Elliott and Angleton, who had always assumed that the mother of Philby's chil-dren was already his wife. Philby had hitherto refused to marry Aileen, despite her entreaties, for the simple reason that he was already married, to a foreign communist. But as he rose within MI6, Philby concluded that this particular skeleton, in a cupboard packed with such things, would have to be revealed. He approached Valentine

Vivian, the man who had so casually waved him into the service in the first place, and explained that, as an impetuous youth, he had married a left-wing Austrian, whom he now planned to divorce in order to make an honest woman of Aileen. The revelation does not seem to have given Vee-Vee a moment's concern.

Philby contacted Litzi, now living in Paris, arranged an uncontested and amicable divorce, and married Aileen a week later, on 25 September, in a civil ceremony at Chelsea registry office. Elliott, occupied with his duties in Switzerland, was unable to attend, but sent an enormous bouquet of flowers and a crate of champagne. The witnesses were Tommy Harris, the MI5 double agent-runner, and Flora Solomon, Philby's friend and Aileen's former employer, who had brought them together in 1939. The wedding party then repaired to the Philby family home in Carlyle Square for a bibulous party that lasted long into the night. Many friends and colleagues from MI6 turned up and drank to a delayed marriage that fitted Philby's faintly bohemian image. One senior MI6 colleague, Jack Easton, who would go on to become deputy director, observed Kim's obvious pride in his growing family, and reflected: 'What a very nice chap Kim must be!' Flora Solomon felt an almost proprietorial pride in the 'happy ending' for the young couple: 'Kim, a happy and devoted father, was making a successful career in the Foreign Office, and Aileen seemed stable and content.' As for Philby's early communism, Solomon reflected, that 'seemed to belong to the misty, juvenile past'.

Philby told Aileen nothing about his MI6 work, let alone his activities on behalf of Soviet intelligence. She knew only that he worked for the Foreign Office. But she, too, was concealing something. For years, unknown to Philby, she had suffered from a psychiatric disorder, later known as Münchausen's syndrome, that manifested itself in episodes of self-harm and bouts of pyromania in order to attract sympathy and attention. As a teenager she had opened an appendix wound and infected it with her own urine, considerably prolonging her recovery. 'Awkward of her gestures and unsure of herself in company,' Aileen's mental health was deteriorating, and the 'accidents' and illnesses were multiplying. Perhaps Aileen's distress reflected the first stirrings of doubt; she may already have begun to wonder whether her husband was really the charming, uxorious, popular, straight-batting bureaucrat that he seemed. He tended to vanish without warning or explanation, sometimes disappearing for twenty-four hours at a time, returning hungover and tight-lipped. Aileen came from a conventional background, of Girl Guides, colonial servants, marital vows and simple patriotism. Flora Solomon considered her 'incapable of disloyalty, either personal or political', but Aileen would not have been human had she not begun to suspect that her husband might be seeing someone else. If she did have her doubts, she told nobody. Mrs Philby, the former undercover detective at M&S, was also good at keeping secrets.

Philby's decision to regularise his domestic arrangements was a sound career move, if he was to become head of MI6. Elliott harboured similar ambitions. But while Elliott had already spent time in the field, in Istanbul and Berne, Philby had so far spent most of his intelligence career behind a desk. Late in 1946, Menzies informed Philby that in order to gain 'all round experience', he would be following in Elliott's footsteps, to Turkey, as MI6 station chief. Section IX was taken over by Douglas Roberts, the veteran officer whose fear of flying had enabled Philby to seize control of the Volkov case. Guy Liddell of MI5 was 'profoundly sorry' to learn that Philby was leaving London, and doubted his successor would be as good. But Philby was happy to be moving on. Istanbul was the 'main southern base for intelligence work against the Soviet Union and socialist countries of the Balkans and central Europe', and his new assignment was a further sign that he was heading for the top. 'Kim gave a large farewell party,' Liddell of MI5 recorded in his diary, 'which consisted mostly of representatives of our office, SIS and the Americans. He is off to Turkey.'

On his way, Philby stopped in Switzerland to see Elliott, who provided him with a detailed briefing on what to expect in Istanbul, and handed over the contents of his contact book. Istanbul's significance as a spy centre was even greater in 1947 than it had been during the war. Tension was mounting between Turkey and the USSR amid fears of a full-scale confrontation between East and West; from Turkey, Western intelligence sought to infiltrate spies and insurgents into the Soviet Union, and vice versa. Before leaving London, Philby had been told that if the opportunity arose, he could set himself up as a 'coat trailer', spy parlance for an agent who seeks to be recruited by the enemy, in order to turn double agent. Philby was 'given permission to play the full double game with the Russians'. Here was an additional layer of protection: if Philby was discovered to be in contact with the Soviets, he had a cast-iron explanation.

Philby landed at the very airport from which, two years earlier, the luckless and insensible Konstantin Volkov had been flown to his death. He rented a villa in Beylerbeyi, on the shores of the Bosphorus, installed his growing family and then, armed with Elliott's introductions, slipped easily into the spy society of Istanbul. He even inherited the services of Elliott's best man, Roman Sudakov, 'a white Russian of boundless charm and appalling energy' in Philby's estimation. The Turkish authorities, when adequately bribed, still allowed foreign intelligence agencies 'a fairly free hand to spy, so long as they didn't spy on Turkey'. Over the next two years, Philby and his five deputies liaised with the Turkish security services, cultivated exiles, trailed for defectors, coordinated British agents and conducted a topographical survey of the Turkish frontier with the Soviet Union – a possible target of invasion in the event of war. But his first priority was to try to infiltrate agents into the USSR along a broad front, into the Caucasus, Ukraine, the Crimea, Georgia, Armenia and Azerbaijan. MI6 believed that Soviet Armenia and Soviet Georgia, in particular, were ripe for subversion. Hundreds of Georgian and Armenian émigrés had fled communism to settle in Beirut, Paris and other Western cities; if the right candidates could be found, trained and then slipped across the borders, these insurrectionists might form the kernel of a counter-revolutionary cell that could 'start weaving a spy network', foment rebellion against the communist government, recruit local allies and eventually roll back the Red tide. That, at least, was the theory. Such infiltrations would loom ever larger in the thinking of MI6 and the CIA in coming years, as the policy of 'roll-back' became intelligence orthodoxy. Philby was an 'energetic enthu-siast' for this policy of war by proxy within the Soviet Union. He found his new assignment fascinating. So did Moscow.

Philby did not make direct contact with Soviet intelligence in Istanbul. Instead, he sent whatever information he gleaned to Guy Burgess, now working at the Foreign Office, who passed it on to the Soviets. With one hand Philby set up infiltration operations, and with the other he unpicked them. Moscow knew exactly what to do with Philby's information: 'We knew in advance about every opera-tion that took place, by air, land or sea, even in the mountainous and inaccessible regions.'

Angleton was also moving on, and up. The Central Intelligence Agency was formally established in September 1947. Three months later, after three years in Rome, Angleton returned to Washington to take up a new role in the Office of Special Operations (OSO), with responsibility for espionage and counter-espionage. Reunited with his long-suffering wife and their young son, Angleton set up home in the Virginia suburbs, and on New Year's Eve he formally applied to join the CIA, the intelligence organisation he would serve, shape and dominate for almost three decades.

The OSO was the intelligence-gathering division within the fledgling CIA, and from here Angleton began to carve out his own empire, working day and night, driving himself, his colleagues and his secretaries with manic determination. He started in a small office, with a single secretary; within a year he had been promoted, rated 'excellent', and awarded a pay rise and a much larger office; two years later he was deploying six secretaries and assistants, and amass-ing a vast registry of files on the British model, which would become 'the very mechanism through which the CIA organised the secret war against the Soviet Union'. As that war expanded, so did Angleton's power. 'He was totally consumed by his work. There was no room for anything else,' said his secretary. At weekends he fished, usually alone, or tended his orchids. Astonishingly, Cicely not only put up with his peculiarities, but loved him for them. 'We rediscovered each other,' she recalled. For all his eccentricities, there was something deeply romantic about the gaunt-faced, half-Mexican, hard-drinking poet-spy who cultivated his secrets, in private, like the rarest blooms.

If the Angletons' marriage was now on firmer ground, that of the Philbys, outwardly so solid, was beginning to come apart. Aileen Philby had become convinced that her husband was having an affair with his secretary, Edith Whitfield, who was young, pretty, and a friend of Guy Burgess, whom Aileen deeply disliked. As he had in London, Philby would sometimes disappear overnight without warning or explanation. On his trips around the country, Edith always accompanied him. Aileen's suspicions, almost certainly justified, tipped her into deeper depression. She became seriously ill. Secretly, she injected herself with urine, causing her body to erupt with boils. Her health became so precarious that after ten months in Istanbul, she had to be hospitalised. While in the clinic she was badly burned, after a fire mysteriously started in her bedroom.

Aileen was back in Beylerbeyi, and seemed to be recovering, when Philby arrived home one evening and announced with a grin: 'I've got sitting in my Jeep outside one of the most disreputable members of the British Foreign Office.' Guy Burgess had arrived, unannounced, for a holiday. He would stay for almost a month. The two old chums and fellow spies painted the town a deep shade of red, with Edith Whitfield in tow. In a single evening at the Moda Yacht Club, they polished off fifty-two brandies. At the end of the evening Burgess could be heard singing, to the tune of Verdi's 'La Donna è Mobile':

> *Little boys are cheap today*
> *Cheaper than yesterday*
> *Small boys are half a crown*
> *Standing up or lying down*

Excluded from the revelries, deeply suspicious, and upset by the presence in her home of this drunken reprobate to whom her husband seemed so deeply attached, Aileen was heading for complete breakdown.

Philby did not seem unduly concerned, or even aware of the impending crisis. He was the same charming, cheerful figure, roué enough to raise the eyebrows of the more strait-laced members of the diplomatic fraternity, but not nearly so wicked as to damage his career prospects in the secret service. In the eyes of MI6, 'He was both efficient and safe.' And besides, he was doing important work, taking the fight to the Reds, even if the results of his efforts to penetrate the Soviet Union were proving less than successful.

A meeting in Switzerland (probably arranged by Elliott), with a Turk representing a number of exiled groups from Georgia and Armenia, secured a verbal agreement that MI6 would be 'willing to back them with training and finance' if the émigrés could furnish suitable counter-revolutionaries. But finding the right people to foment rebellion behind the Iron Curtain was proving tricky: many had been born abroad, or exiled for so long they barely knew their native countries, while others were tainted by association with Nazi efforts to destabilise the USSR during the war. Philby originally envisaged sending half a dozen groups of five or six 'insurrectionists' into Soviet Georgia and Soviet Armenia for several weeks at a time. Finally, among the exiled Georgian community in Paris, just two candidates were selected: 'energetic lads' aged twenty, who were ready to undertake this mission to a homeland neither had ever seen. One was called Rukhadze; the name of the other has never been discovered.

The two young men were trained in London for six weeks and then despatched to Istanbul, to be met by Philby. The operation, codenamed 'Climber', was a 'tip-and-run' exercise, an exploratory foray to assess the possibilities of mounting a rebellion in Georgia: the two agents would establish communication lines with potential anti-communist rebels, and then slip across the border back into Turkey. The young men struck Philby as 'alert and intelligent', convinced they were striking a blow to liberate Georgia from Soviet oppression. One of them, however, perhaps realising he faced certain death if caught, seemed 'notably subdued'. The party travelled to Erzurum in Eastern Turkey, where Philby bustled around briefing the two agents, and issuing them with weapons, radio equipment and a bag of gold coins. 'It was essential I should be seen doing everything possible to ensure the success of the operation,' he later wrote. He had, of course, ensured exactly the opposite. The spot chosen for the infiltration was Posof, in the far northeast of Turkey on the border with Georgia. In the dead of night, the pair were taken to a remote section of the frontier, and slipped into Soviet territory.

Within minutes, a burst of gunfire rang out from the Georgian side. One of the men went down in the first volley. The other, Rukhadze, was spotted in the half-light, 'striding through a sparse wood away from the Turkish frontier'. He did not get far, and was soon in the hands of Soviet intelligence. It is doubtful whether the torturers got much out of him before he died; he had little to reveal. Years later, Philby discussed the fate of the Georgians with the chief of the Georgian KGB: 'The boys weren't bad,' he said. 'Not at all. I knew very well that they would be caught and that a tragic fate awaited them. But on the other hand it was the only way of driving a stake through the plans of future operations.' This ill-conceived, badly planned operation might well have failed anyway; but Philby could not have killed them more certainly if he had executed them himself. Their deaths did not trouble him, now or later. If there was a blot on his happy horizon, it was the increasingly erratic behaviour of his wife.

★

One evening in March 1949, Aileen Philby was found lying beside a country road with a gash in her head. When she regained consciousness, she explained that while taking a walk she had been viciously attacked by a Turkish man, who hit her with a rock. Several potential culprits were rounded up and brought to her hospital bedside 'in chains', but Aileen could not positively identify her assailant. The Turkish police were baffled; so were the doctors when septicaemia set in. Aileen was now extremely unwell. In this moment of crisis, Philby turned to his old friend.

Philby contacted Nicholas Elliott in Berne and told him that Aileen seemed to be 'dying of some mysterious ailment'. Would Elliott find a Swiss doctor who could discover what was wrong with her? Elliott sprang into action. After an intensive trawl, he told Philby he had found just the man: a distinguished Swiss medical professor who had listened to Aileen's symptoms and believed he could cure her. The Philbys immediately flew to Geneva, and travelled on by ambulance to Berne: Aileen was settled into a comfortable clinic, while Philby moved in with the Elliotts. Just days after her arrival, Aileen tried to set her room on fire, and then slashed her arm with a razor blade. The Swiss doctor swiftly established that Aileen's original injury had been self-inflicted, then self-infected. The story of the roadside attack was fictitious. Aileen's doctor in London, Lord Horder, confirmed a history of self-harm dating back to her teenage years, and Aileen was committed to a psychiatric clinic under close observation. Elliott was deeply shocked to discover that this 'charming woman and loving wife and mother suffered, unknown to others, from a grave mental problem'. The Elliotts nursed her with tender solicitude; Nicholas Elliott sat at her bedside, feeding her grapes and jokes. Slowly, Aileen regained her strength, and a measure of mental composure.

Philby was livid, a reaction that struck Elliott as distinctly odd. He had expected Philby to be relieved that his wife had been diagnosed at last. Instead, his friend complained bitterly that Aileen had hoodwinked him, and vowed he would never forgive her. 'It was an intense affront to Philby's pride,' Elliott concluded, that he, an intelligence professional schooled in deception, 'had been tricked for so many years' by his own wife. 'He had to return to Istanbul knowing that all the years he had been living with Aileen, he had himself been deceived.' Elliott would never have criticised Philby, particularly with regard to women. He knew about Philby's extra-marital affairs, and passed no judgement. Indeed, Elliott had his own mistress, a Swedish woman he kept carefully hidden from Elizabeth. A chap's marriage was his own business, and in Nick Elliott's eyes Kim Philby could do no wrong. Still, it seemed strange that his friend should be so angered by a deception that was, in the end, medical rather than moral. From that moment on, Elliott reflected sadly, 'the marriage steadily deteriorated'.

Aileen had been back in Istanbul less than a month when Philby announced that the family was on the move again: he had been offered, and had accepted, one of the most important jobs in British intelligence, as the MI6 chief in Washington DC.

★

The Berlin Blockade had thrown the escalating Cold War tension into sharp relief, and the power balance in the intelligence relationship between Britain and the US was shifting. The time when MI6 could patronise the American amateurs, new to the game of espionage, was long gone, and in Whitehall Britain's spy chiefs wrestled with the novel and uncomfortable sensation that the Americans were now calling the shots, running a new kind of war against the Soviets, and paying the bills for it. For most of the Second World War, the US had been the junior partner on intelligence issues, grateful to follow the British lead. That relationship was now reversing, but the veterans of MI6 were determined to prove that Britain was still a master of the intelligence game, despite mounting evidence of an empire in steep decline. One way to stop the rot was to send a young star to Washington, a decorated wartime intelligence hero with a dazzling record, as living proof that British intelligence was just as vigorous and effective as it had always been.

In the US, Philby would be responsible for maintaining the Anglo-American intelligence relationship, liaising with the CIA and the FBI, and even handling secret communications between the British Prime Minister and the President. MI6 could hardly have offered him a more emphatic vote of confidence. Philby's had been one of three names in the running for this coveted post, and it had been left to the Americans to choose their preferred candidate. According to CIA historian Ray Cline, 'It was James Jesus Angleton who selected Philby's name.'

Aileen was not consulted about the new job. Philby did not even wait for the approval of his Soviet handlers. He accepted this irresistible new posting exactly half an hour after it was offered. 'At one stroke, it would take me right back into the middle of intelligence policy making and it would give me a close-up view of the American intelligence organisations,' he wrote. It also offered 'unlimited possibilities' for fresh espionage on behalf of his Soviet masters.

News of Philby's appointment was greeted with sadness by his colleagues in Istanbul, who had grown used to his combination of conviviality and efficiency. 'Who am I supposed to work with now?' wondered the ambassador, Sir David Kelly. In London, the appointment was seen as a natural progression for a man destined for the top. Elliott was delighted, and if he felt a twinge of envy that his friend seemed to be climbing the ladder faster than he was, he was much too British to show it.

Philby flew back to London in early September to be briefed on his new role. He made a point of looking up old contacts in both MI5 and MI6, and inviting each of them to come and stay with him in Washington. 'I was lunched at many clubs,' he wrote. 'Discussions over coffee and port covered many subjects.' Those very same subjects were also discussed by Philby in a series of meetings, no less cheerful but even more clandestine, in various London parks. Boris Krötenschield was pleased by his agent's new appointment, and deeply impressed by the dedication of this double-sided man: 'One side is open to family and friends and everyone around them,' Krötenschield reported to Moscow Centre. 'The other belongs only to himself and his secret work.'

Much of Philby's time in London was spent discussing Albania. Most citizens of Britain, America and the USSR, if they thought about Albania at all, imagined a wild country on the edge of Europe, a place of almost mythical irrelevance to the rest of the world. But Albania, sandwiched between Yugoslavia, Greece and the Adriatic, was poised to become a key Cold War battlefield. After the war, Albania's King Zog was deposed as the country came under the iron rule of Enver Hoxha, the ruthless and wily leader of the communist partisans, who set about transforming Albania into a Stalinist state. By 1949, Albania presented a tempting target for the anti-communist hawks in British and American intelligence: separated from the Soviet bloc by Yugoslavia (itself split from the USSR), Albania was poor, feudal, sparsely populated and politically volatile. Many exiled Albanian royalists and nationalists were itching to return to their homeland and do battle with the communists. Viewed from London and Washington, through a veil of wishful thinking, Albania appeared ready to shake off communism: trained guerrillas would be slipped into Albania to link up with local rebel groups, eventually sparking civil war and toppling Hoxha. If Albanian communism was success-fully undermined, it was believed, this would set off a 'chain reaction that would roll back the tide of Soviet Imperialism'. The SOE had played an important role in Albania during the war, and it was there-fore agreed that Britain should take the lead in training the Albanian rebels, with the US as an enthusiastic partner. Philby was fully briefed on the plans. The first wave of insurgents would be sent in by boat from Italy in October 1948; the mission was codenamed 'Valuable'.

The Albanian operation was an example of gung-ho wartime thinking wrongly applied to the more nuanced circumstances of the Cold War. But within MI6 it was seen as the opening salvo in a new, covert war. Stalin had backed a communist insurgency in Greece, engineered the communist takeover of Czechoslovakia, and block-aded Berlin. Albania would be the target of a counter-attack, in direct contravention of international law but in keeping with the new mood of aggression. Many greeted the prospect with glee. Richard Brooman-White, Elliott's friend in MI6, even imagined a situation whereby the Albanian campaign could spark 'formal British and American armed intervention'. Philby would be responsible for coordinating Albanian plans with the Americans.

Before leaving for the US, Philby was indoctrinated, with due reverence, into perhaps the most closely guarded secret of the Cold War. Between 1940 and 1948, American cryptanalysts had inter-cepted some 3,000 Soviet intelligence telegrams written in a code that was, theoretically, unbreakable. In 1946, however, due to a single blunder by the Soviets, a team of codebreakers led by the brilliant American cryptanalyst Meredith Gardner began to unpick the messages that had passed between the US and Moscow. What they revealed was staggering: more than 200 Americans had become Soviet agents during the war; Moscow had spies in the Treasury, the State Department, the nuclear Manhattan Project and the OSS. The code-breaking operation, codenamed 'Venona' (a word which, appropriately, has no meaning) was so secret that President Truman himself was not informed of its existence for more than three years; the CIA did not learn about Venona until 1952. But it is a measure of the trust between the British and American intelligence agencies that news of the breakthrough, and its chilling implications, was immediately shared with MI6, because the intercepts also revealed that Soviet spies had penetrated the British government. In particular, the Venona team uncovered evidence of a Soviet agent, code-named 'Homer', who was leaking secrets from within the British embassy in Washington in 1945. The identity of this mole was still a mystery, but it was assumed that, like 'Cicero' in Turkey during the war, 'Homer' was probably an embassy employee, a cleaner perhaps, or a clerk. Philby knew better: Donald Maclean, his Cambridge friend and fellow spy, had been first secretary at the Washington embassy between 1944 and 1948. Maclean was Homer.

The first flicker of a shadow, as yet no more than a mote in the far distance, fell across Philby's long and sunny run of luck.

9

Stormy Seas

Bido Kuka crouched in the hold of the *Stormie Seas*, huddled alongside the other fighters clutching their German Schmeisser submachine guns, as the boat rose and fell queasily in the dark Adriatic swell. Kuka felt patriotic, excited and scared. Mostly, he felt seasick. A pouch filled with gold sovereigns was strapped inside his belt. Taped to the inside of his wristwatch was a single cyanide pill, for use should he fall into the hands of the Albanian secret police, the Sigurimi. In his knapsack he carried a map, medical supplies, hand grenades, enough rations to survive for a week in the mountains, Albanian currency, propaganda leaflets, and photographs of the émigré anti-communist leaders to show to the people and inspire them to rise up against the hated dictator, Enver Hoxha. Through the porthole, the jagged cliffs of Karaburun rose blackly against the moonless night sky, the edge of a country Kuka had not seen for three years. The Englishmen could be heard on deck, whispering muffled orders as the boat drew inshore. They were strange, these Englishmen, huge sun-reddened men, who spoke a barely comprehensible language and laughed when there was nothing funny to laugh at. They had brought along a dog, called Lean-To; one had even brought his wife. They were pretending to be on a boating holiday. The man called 'Lofty' kept his binoculars trained on the cliffs. The one called 'Geoffrey' rehearsed, once more, the procedure for operating the wireless, a bulky contraption powered by a machine that looked like a bicycle without wheels. Kuka and his eight companions smoked in nervy silence. The *Stormie Seas* edged towards the Albanian shore.

Six months earlier Bido Kuka had been recruited for Operation Valuable in a displaced persons camp outside Rome. Kuka was a 'Ballist', a member of the Balli Kombëtar, the Albanian nationalist group who had fought the Nazis during the war, and then the communists after it. With the communist takeover of Albania hundreds of Ballists had been arrested, tortured and killed, and Kuka had fled, with other nationalists, to Italy. Since then he had spent three miserable years in Fraschetti camp, nursing his loathing of communism, rehearsing the Balli Kombëtar motto 'Albania for the Albanians, Death to the Traitors', and plotting his return. When he was approached by a fellow émigré and asked to join a new guerrilla unit for secret anti-communist operations inside Albania, he did not hesitate. As another recruit put it: 'There was no question of refusing. When your life is devoted to your country you are prepared to do anything to help it.' On 14 July 1949, Kuka and a fellow Ballist named Sami Lepenica boarded a military plane in Rome, and flew to the British island of Malta in the Mediterranean. They had no travel documents. A British Army officer, flapping a red handkerchief by way of a recognition signal, marched them past the customs barrier, and into a car. An hour later the bemused Albanians arrived at the gateway to a large castle, surrounded by a moat: Fort Bingemma, a Victorian citadel on the island's southwest corner, selected by British intelligence as the ideal place from which to launch an anti-communist counter-revolution.

Over the next three months, Kuka and some thirty other Albanian recruits underwent intensive training under the watchful (if slightly mad) eye of Lieutenant-Colonel David de Crespigny Smiley, an aristocratic British Army officer with a legendary taste for derring-do. During the war Smiley had fought the Italians in Abyssinia as part of the Somaliland Camel Corps, foiled a German-backed coup to unseat the King of Iraq, fought alongside Siamese guerrillas and liberated 4,000 Allied prisoners ('all absolutely stark naked except for a ball bag'), from the Japanese camp at Ubon. But it was in Albania that he earned his reputation for raw courage: in 1943 he parachuted into northern Greece, and set about blowing up bridges, ambushing German troops, and training guerrillas. He emerged from the war with a deep love of Albania, a loathing for Hoxha and the communists, a Military Cross, and facial scars from a prematurely exploding briefcase. When MI6 needed someone to equip, train and infiltrate anti-communist fighters into Albania, Smiley was the obvious choice. He was imperialist, fearless, romantic and unwary, and in all these respects, he was a neat reflection of Operation Valuable.

The training programme was brief but intensive, and conducted amid rigid secrecy. A series of British instructors, including an eccentric Oxford don, provided instruction in map-reading, unarmed combat, machine-gun marksmanship, and operating a radio with a pedal generator. Since the instructors spoke no Albanian, and the Albanians spoke not a word of English, training was conducted in sign language. This explains why Kuka's conception of his mission was somewhat vague: get into Albania, head for his hometown near the Greek border, sound out the possibilities for armed insurrection, then get out and report back. None of the recruits were officers, and few had any military training. Life in the camps had left some with malnutrition, and all were quite small. The British, with more than a hint of condescension, called them 'the pixies'.

In late September, Bido Kuka and eight other recruits were taken to Otranto on the Italian coast, fifty-five miles across the Adriatic from Albania. Disguised as local fishermen, they were loaded into a fishing vessel, and at a rendezvous point twenty miles off the Albanian coast, they were transferred to the *Stormie Seas*, a forty-three-ton schooner painted to resemble a pleasure boat but containing a mighty ninety-horsepower engine, concealed fuel tanks and enough munitions to start a small war. The *Stormie Seas* was commanded by Sam Barclay and John Leatham, two intrepid former Royal Navy officers who had spent the previous year running supplies from Athens to Salonika for the forces fighting the Greek communist guerrillas. MI6 offered them the sum of £50 to transport the insurgents to the Albanian coast, which Leatham thought was more than generous: 'We were looking only for free adventure and a living.'

Shortly after 9 p.m. on 3 October, 200 yards off the Karaburun peninsula, the heavily armed 'pixies' clambered into two rubber boats and headed towards a cove, rowed by two stout former marines, 'Lofty' Cooling and Derby Allen. The Karaburun was barely inhabited, a wild place of goat tracks and thorny scrub. Having dropped off the men and their equipment, the Englishmen rowed back to the *Stormie Seas*. Looking back at the retreating coast, they saw a light flash suddenly at the cliff top, and then go out again. The nine pixies were already heading up the cliff. The going was slow in the deep darkness. As dawn broke, they split into two parties. Bido Kuka and four others, including his friend Ramis Matuka and his cousin Ahmet, headed south towards his home region, while the remaining four, led by Sami Lepenica, headed north. As they separated, Kuka was struck by a sudden foreboding, the sensation, intense but unfocused, 'that the communists were ready and waiting for them'.

After a day spent hiding in a cave, Kuka and his men set off again at nightfall. In the morning they approached the village of Gjorm, a wartime centre of resistance and home to many Balli Kombëtar sympathisers. As they drew near, a young girl ran towards them shouting: 'Brothers, you're all going to be killed!' Breathlessly, she explained that the other group had already been ambushed by government forces: three of the four had been killed, including Lepenica, and the fourth had vanished. Two days earlier no less a personage than Beqir Balluku, the Albanian army chief of staff, had arrived with hundreds of troops, and the Karaburun ridge was crawling with government forces, scouring every village, track, cave and gully for the 'fascist terrorists'. Local shepherds had been instructed to report anything suspicious, on pain of death. The Albanian guerrillas thanked the girl, gratefully seized the bread and milk she offered, and ran.

★

At the very moment Bido Kuka was scrambling for his life through the Albanian mountains, Kim Philby was steaming towards New York aboard the RMS *Caronia*, the most luxurious ocean liner afloat. His many friends in MI5 and MI6 had given him a 'memorable send-off'. The *Caronia* was barely a year old; a spectacular floating hotel nicknamed the 'Green Goddess' on account of her pale green livery. She was fitted with every modern luxury, including sumptuous Art Deco interiors, an open-air lido and terraced decks. The only class of travel was first. Described as 'a private club afloat', the liner had 400 catering staff for 700 passengers. On arriving in his panelled cabin with private bathroom, Philby had found a crate of champagne awaiting him, a gift from a 'disgustingly rich friend', Victor Rothschild. Philby might have disapproved of Rothschild's riches, but he thoroughly approved of his champagne. The seven-day voyage was made all the more pleasant by the company of the cartoonist Osbert Lancaster, an affable clubland acquaintance of Philby's with a walrus moustache and a terrific thirst. Philby and Lancaster settled into the cocktail bar, and started drinking their way to America. 'I began to feel that I would enjoy my first transatlantic crossing,' wrote Philby.

The *Caronia* docked in New York on 7 October. The FBI sent out a motor launch to meet Philby; like Bido Kuka, he was whisked through customs without any of the usual formalities. That night he stayed in a high-rise hotel overlooking Central Park, before catching the train to Washington DC. Alongside the track the sumac shrubs were still in flower, but autumn was in the air and the leaves were beginning to turn. Philby's first glimpse of the American landscape took his breath away. The fall, he later wrote, is 'one of the few glories of America which Americans have never exaggerated because exaggeration is impossible'.

At Union Station, he was met by Peter Dwyer of MI6, the outgoing station chief, and immediately plunged into a whirlwind of introductions and meetings, with officials of the CIA, FBI, the State Department and the Canadian secret service. All were delighted to shake hands with this urbane Englishman whose impressive reputation preceded him – but none more than James Jesus Angleton, his former protégé, now a powerful figure in the CIA. Angleton had prepared the ground, telling his American colleagues about Philby's wartime work and how much he 'admired him as a "professional"'.

The Anglo-American intelligence relationship was still close in 1949, and no two spies symbolised that intimacy more than Kim Philby and James Angleton.

Angleton remained, in many ways, an Englishman. 'I was brought up in England in my formative years,' he said, many years later, 'and I must confess that I learned, at least I was disciplined to learn, certain features of life, and what I regarded as duty.' Honour, loyalty, hand-made suits, strong drinks, deep leather armchairs in smoky clubs: this was the kind of England that Angleton had come to know, and admire, through Philby and Elliott. There was an element within American intelligence that took a more hard-eyed view of Britain's continuing claims to greatness, a younger generation unmoved by the nostalgic bonds of war, but Angleton was not of that stamp. His time in Ryder Street had left a permanent imprint on him, personally and profes-sionally. Philby had introduced him to the arcane mysteries of the Double Cross system, the strange, endlessly reflecting conundrum of counter-intelligence, and the very British idea that only a few, a select few, can be truly trusted. Philby was Angleton's souvenir of war, a time of duty, unshakeable alliance and dependability. Angleton paraded his English friend around Washington like a trophy.

While Philby was clinking glasses in Washington, on the other side of the world, David Smiley waited, with mounting unease, for the Albanian guerrillas to make contact. Twice a day, morning and evening, the MI6 radio operator stationed in a large mansion on the coast of Corfu tuned in at the agreed time, but a week had passed with no word from the pixies. Finally a hasty message was picked up, sent from the caves above Gjorm where Kuka and his team were in hiding: 'Things have gone wrong . . . three men killed . . . police know everything about us.' The Albanians were terrified: the bulky genera-tor gave out a high-pitched whining sound when pedalled at full speed, the noise bouncing off the hills and threatening to reveal them. They were running out of food, and dared not descend to the village to beg or steal more. Bido Kuka persuaded the others to make a break for it and try to reach his home village of Nivica just twenty-five miles to the south. The route passed though inhospitable terrain and the government forces were doubtless still out in force, but from Nivica it was only thirty-five miles to the Greek border.

A four-day trek, walking at night, skirting patrols and hiding during daylight, brought them to the home Kuka had last seen three years earlier. He was welcomed, but cautiously. When Kuka explained that they were the vanguard of a British-backed force that would overthrow Hoxha, the villagers were sceptical: Why were they so few in number? Where were the British? Where were the guns? Kuka sensed that even here, they faced mortal danger. The group declined offers to spend the night in the village. They retreated instead to the mountains, and agreed to push on for the border as fast as possible, in two groups: Bido Kuka, Ramis Matuka and a third man headed south; his cousin Ahmet and the fifth man took a more direct route. Patrols were everywhere; three times, Kuka's group narrowly avoided capture. They were still a dozen miles from the border, trudging through a narrow ravine, when a voice boomed out of the darkness demanding that they identify themselves or be shot down. 'Who are you?' called Kuka, cocking his machine gun. 'Police,' came the answer. The three men opened fire. The police, dug in above them, returned fire. Ramis Matuka fell dead. Kuka and his last companion, firing wildly, fled into the woods.

Three days later, exhausted and famished, Kuka and his comrade finally reached the Greek border. They were immediately arrested, jailed by the Greek police and interrogated. Kuka stuck to his story that he was 'Enver Zenelli', the name on his forged Albanian identity card. 'We said we were ordinary Albanians fleeing the country.' The Greek border guards were disbelieving, 'and would have shot them for tuppence'. After several weeks, a British officer appeared. Kuka uttered the code phrase agreed back in Malta: 'The sun has risen.' Finally they were free. The survivors were flown to Athens, lodged in a safe house, and debriefed by two British intelligence officers.

By any objective estimate, the first phase of Operation Valuable had been a debacle. Of the nine guerrillas who landed in October, four were dead, one almost certainly captured, one had vanished, the others had barely escaped with their lives, and 'several Albanian civilians had also been arrested and killed', accused of aiding the guerrillas. A second landing group, arriving soon after the first, had fared little better. The Albanian forces were primed and waiting, clearly aware of the incursion, if not of its precise timing and location.

With understatement verging on fantasy, MI6 described the first phase of the operation merely as 'disappointing'. The loss of half the initial force was a setback but not a disaster, and the death toll was 'judged by wartime standards to be acceptable'. Colonel Smiley vowed to press ahead, with fresh incursions, better-trained guerrillas, and greater US involvement. Albania would not be won overnight, and 'it would be wrong to abandon such an important exercise', particularly now that MI6 had one of its highest fliers installed in Washington, ready and more than willing to liaise with the Americans on the next stage of Operation Valuable.

Just a few days after his arrival in Washington, Philby was appointed joint-commander of the Anglo-American Special Policy Committee, responsible for running the Albanian operation with his American opposite number, James McCargar. The Americans would play an increasing role in Operation Valuable (which they codenamed, perhaps more realistically, 'Fiend'), not least by financing it, but Philby 'was the one who made all the operational decisions'.

★

James McCargar was a former journalist from a wealthy Californian family, who had made a name for himself in the post-war period by arranging escape routes out of Hungary for scientists and intellectuals fleeing communism. He smuggled one Romanian woman out in the boot of his car, and then married her. Like many American intelligence officers of the time, McCargar had an exaggerated respect for his British counterparts, and his new colleague came with glowing credentials. 'Philby was a great charmer. He came to us with an enormous reputation,' recalled McCargar. 'One had the feeling one could have confidence in him.' Philby seemed to exemplify the sort of qualities that Americans hoped to see in their British allies: cheerful, resolute, witty and exceedingly generous with the bottle. 'He had charm, warmth and an engaging, self-deprecating humour,' said McCargar. 'He drank a lot, but then so did we all in those days. We floated out of the war on a sea of drink without its having much effect. I considered him a friend.'

Philby loved Washington, and Washington loved him. Doors were flung open, the invitations poured in, and few people needed to meet him more than once before they, too, considered him a friend. Aileen also seemed to find strength in Washington's welcoming atmosphere. The family moved into a large, two-storey house at 4100 Nebraska Avenue, which was soon a riot of children's toys, full ashtrays and empty bottles. In Nicholas Elliott's words, Philby was 'undoubtedly devoted to his children', a trait which further endeared him to his new American friends and colleagues: here was a family man, the quintessential English gentleman, a man one could trust. Within weeks, it seems, Philby had made contact with just about everyone of note in American intelligence. To their faces he was politeness personified; behind their backs, vituperative. There was Johnny Boyd, assistant director of the FBI ('by any objective standard, a dreadful man'); Frank Wisner, head of the Office of Policy Coordination ('balding and self-importantly running to fat'); Bill Harvey of CIA counter-intelligence ('a former FBI man ... sacked for drunkenness'); CIA chief Walter Bedell Smith ('a cold, fishy eye'); deputy CIA head and future chief Allen Dulles ('bumbling'); Bob Lamphere of the FBI ('puddingy') and many more. The house on Nebraska Avenue soon became a gathering place for Washington's intelligence elite. 'He entertained a lot of Americans,' said another CIA officer. 'The wine flowed, and the whisky too.' Aileen played the role of salon hostess, tottering around with trays of drinks, and drinking her fair share. One guest recalled only this of Philby's parties: 'They were long, and very, very wet.'

Philby seemed to invite intimacy. His knowing smile, 'suggestive of complicity in some private joke, conveyed an unspoken understanding of the underlying ironies of our work'. He made a point of dropping in on the offices of American colleagues and counterparts in the late afternoon, knowing that his hosts would sooner or later (and usually sooner) 'suggest drifting out to a friendly bar for a further round of shop talk'. Trading internal information is a particular weakness of the intelligence world; spies cannot explain their work to outsiders, so they seize every opportunity to discuss it with their own kind. 'Intelligence officers talk trade among themselves all the time,' said one CIA officer. 'Philby was privy to a hell of a lot beyond what he should have known.' The CIA and FBI were rivals, sometimes viciously so, with a peculiar social division between the two arms of American intelligence that was echoed by the competition between MI5 and MI6. Philby characterised CIA operatives as upper-class wine-drinkers, while the FBI were earthier beer-drinking types; Philby was happy to drink quantities of both, with either, while trying to 'please one party without offending the other'. Philby's office was in the British embassy, but he was often to be found at the CIA or FBI headquarters, or the Pentagon, where a room was set aside for meetings on the Albanian operation. Few subjects were out of bounds: 'The sky was the limit … he would have known as much as he wanted to find out.'

James Angleton was now chief of Staff A, in command of foreign intelligence operations, and in Philby's estimation 'the driving force' within the intelligence-gathering division of the CIA. A strange mystique clung to Angleton; he used the name 'Lothar Metzl', and invented a cover story that he had been a Viennese café pianist before the war. Behind his house in the suburbs of North Arlington he constructed a heated greenhouse, the better to cultivate his orchids and his aura of knowing eccentricity. In the basement he polished semi-precious stones. He carried a gold fob watch; his suits and accent remained distinctly English. Angleton tended to describe his work in fishing metaphors: 'I got a few nibbles last night,' he would remark obscurely, after an evening trawling the files. In intelligence circles he inspired admiration, gossip and some fear. 'It was the belief within the CIA that Angleton possessed more secrets than anyone else, and grasped their meaning better than anyone else.'

Harvey's, on Connecticut Avenue, was the most famous restaurant in the capital, probably the most expensive, and certainly the most exclusive. Harvey's Ladies' and Gentlemen's Oyster Saloon started serving steamed oysters, broiled lobster and Crab Imperial in 1820, and had continued to do so, in colossal quantities, ever since. In 1863, notwithstanding the Civil War, Harvey's diners were getting through 500 wagonloads of oysters a week. Every US President since Ulysses S. Grant had dined there, and the restaurant enjoyed an unrivalled reputation as the place to be seen for people of power and influence. The black waiters in pressed white uniforms were discreet, the Martinis potent, the napkins stiff as cardboard and the tables spaced far enough apart to ensure privacy for the most secret conversations. Ladies entered by a separate entrance, and were not permitted in the main dining room. Most evenings, FBI director J. Edgar Hoover could be seen at his corner table, eating with Clyde Tolson, his deputy, and possibly his lover. Hoover was said to be addicted to Harvey's oysters; he never paid for his meals.

Angleton and Philby began to lunch regularly at Harvey's restaurant, at first once a week, then three times a fortnight. They spoke on the telephone at least every other day. Their lunches became a sort of ritual, a 'habit' in Philby's words, beginning with bourbon on the rocks and proceeding through lobster and wine and ending in brandy and cigars. Philby was impressed both by Angleton's grasp of intelligence and his appetite for food and drink. 'He demonstrated regularly that overwork was not his only vice,' wrote Philby. 'He was one of the thinnest men I have ever met, and one of the biggest eaters. Lucky Jim!' The two men could be seen, hunched in animated conversation, talking, drinking, laughing and enjoying their shared love of secrecy. Angleton had few close friends, and fewer confidants. Philby had many friends, and had refined the giving and receiving of confidences to an art form. They fitted one another perfectly.

'Our close association was, I am sure, inspired by genuine friendliness,' wrote Philby. 'But we both had ulterior motives ... By cultivating me to the full, he could better keep me under wraps. For my part, I was more than content to string him along. The greater the trust between us overtly, the less he would suspect covert action.

Who gained most from this complex game I cannot say. But I had one big advantage. I knew what he was doing for CIA and he knew what I was doing for SIS. But the real nature of my interest was something he did not know.' Beneath their friendship was an unspoken competition to see who could out-think, and out-drink, the other. Angleton, according to one associate, 'used to pride himself that he could drink Kim under the table and still walk away with useful information. Can you imagine how much information he had to trade in those booze-ups?'

'Our discussions ranged over the whole world,' Philby recalled. They spoke of the various covert operations against the Soviet Union, the anti-communist insurgents being slipped into Albania and other countries behind the Iron Curtain; they discussed the intelligence operations under way in France, Italy and Germany, and resources pouring into anti-communist projects worldwide, including the recruiting of exiles for subversion behind the Iron Curtain. 'Both CIA and SIS were up to their ears in émigré politics,' wrote Philby. Angleton explained how the CIA had taken over the anti-Soviet spy network established by Reinhard Gehlen, the former chief of German intelligence on the Eastern Front who had offered his services to the US after surrendering in 1945. Gehlen's spies and informants included many former Nazis, but the CIA was not choosy about its allies in the new war against communism. By 1948 the CIA was funnelling some $1.5 million (around $14.5 million today) into Gehlen's spy ring. Philby was all ears: 'Many of Harvey's lobsters went to provoke Angleton into defending, with chapter and verse, the past record and current activities of the von Gehlen organisation.' CIA interventions in Greece and Turkey to hold back communism; covert operations in Iran, the Baltics and Guatemala; secret American plans in Chile, Cuba, Angola and Indonesia; blueprints for Allied cooperation in the event of war with the USSR. All this and more was laid before Philby, between friends, as Angleton gorged and gossiped over the starched tablecloths and full glasses at Harvey's. 'During those long, boozy lunches and dinners, Philby must have picked him clean,' a fellow officer later wrote.

But Philby and Angleton were also professionals. After every lunch, Angleton returned to his office, and dictated a long memo to his secretary, Gloria Loomis, reporting in detail his discussions with the obliging MI6 liaison chief. 'Everything was written up,' Loomis later insisted. Philby did likewise, dictating his own memo for MI6 to his secretary Edith Whitfield, who had accompanied him to Washington from Istanbul (much to Aileen's annoyance). Later, at home in Nebraska Avenue, Philby would write up his own notes, for other eyes.

★

Philby liked to portray the Soviet intelligence service as an organisation of unparalleled efficiency. In truth, Moscow Centre was frequently beset by bureaucratic bungling, inertia and incompetence, coupled with periodic blood-letting. Before Philby's arrival, the Soviet spy outpost in Washington had been through a period of 'chaotic' turbulence, with the recall of two successive *rezidents*. Initially, Philby had no direct contact with Soviet intelligence in the US, preferring to send any information via Guy Burgess in London, as he had from Istanbul. Finally, four months after Philby's arrival, Moscow woke up to the realisation that it should take better care of its veteran spy.

On 5 March a young man stepped off the ship *Batory*, newly arrived in New York harbour from Gdynia in Poland. His passport proclaimed him to be an American citizen of Polish origin named Ivan Kovalik; his real name was Valeri Mikhailovich Makayev, a thirty-two-year-old Russian intelligence officer with orders to establish himself under cover in New York and arrange a way for Philby to communicate with Moscow Centre. Makayev swiftly obtained a job teaching musical composition at New York University, and started an affair with a Polish dancer who owned a ballet school in Manhattan. Makayev was a good musician, and one of nature's romantics, but he was a hopeless case officer. His bosses had supplied him with $25,000 for his mission, which he proceeded to spend, mostly on himself and his ballerina. Finally, Makayev got word to

Philby that he had arrived. They met in New York, and Philby's newly arrived case officer handed over a camera for photographing documents. Thereafter, they would rendezvous at different points between New York and Washington, in Baltimore or Philadelphia. After nine months, Makayev had managed to set up two communication channels to Moscow, using a Finnish seaman as a courier and a postal route via an agent in London. The system was slow and cumbersome; Philby was wary of face-to-face meetings, and unimpressed by his new case officer; Makayev was much more interested in ballet than espionage. Philby was producing more valuable intelligence for Moscow than at any time in his life, yet he had never been run more incompetently.

Frank Wisner, the CIA officer in charge of insurgent operations behind the Iron Curtain, was baffled: every bid to undermine communism by secretly fomenting resistance within the USSR and among its satellites seemed to be going spectacularly wrong. But Wisner – or 'The Whiz', as he liked to be known – refused to be downcast, let alone change tack. Despite a disappointing start, the Albanian operation would continue. 'We'll get it right next time,' Wisner promised Philby.

But they did not get it right. Instead, it continued to go wrong, and not just in Albania. Funds, equipment and arms were funnelled to the anti-communist resistance in Poland, which turned out to be nothing more than a front, operated by Soviet intelligence. Anti-communist Lithuanians, Estonians and Armenians were recruited, and then dropped into their homelands by British and American planes; nationalist White Russians were sent in to continue the fight against the Bolsheviks. Almost all mysteriously disappeared. 'We had agents parachuting in, floating in, walking in, boating in,' said one former CIA officer. 'Virtually all these operations were complete failures ... they were all rolled up.' The CIA and MI6 kept one another informed of exactly where and when their respective teams were going in, to avoid overlap and confusion. Philby, as the liaison officer in Washington, was responsible for passing on 'the timing and geographical co-ordinates' from one intelligence agency to another, and then another. Ukraine was considered particularly fertile ground for an insurgency, with an established resistance group active in the Carpathian Mountains. In 1949, the first British-trained team of Ukrainian insurgents was sent in with radio equipment. They were never heard of again. Two more teams followed the next year, and then three more six-man units were parachuted to drop points in Ukraine and inside the Polish border. All vanished. 'I do not know what happened to the parties concerned,' Philby later wrote, with ruthless irony. 'But I can make an informed guess.'

None of the incursions had proved more catastrophic, more spectacularly valueless, than Operation Valuable. Undaunted, the British continued to train the 'pixies' in Malta, while the CIA established a separate training camp for Albanian insurgents, now including teams of parachutists, in a walled villa outside Heidelberg. 'We knew that they would retaliate against our families,' said one recruit, but 'we had high hopes.' At the same time, MI6 prepared to drop thousands of propaganda leaflets over Albania from unmanned hot air balloons: 'The boys in London imagined a rain of pamphlets over Albanian towns with thousands of Albanians picking them out of the air, reading them and then preparing themselves for the liberation.' The first parachutists were flown in by Polish former RAF pilots in late 1950, crossing into Albanian airspace at a height of just 200 feet to avoid radar.

The communist forces were ready and waiting. Two days earlier, hundreds of security police had poured into the area of the drop zone. A policeman was stationed in every village. They even knew the names of the arriving insurgents. Some of the parachutists were killed on landing, others captured. Only a few escaped. The next drop, the following July, was even more disastrous. One group of four parachutists was mown down immediately; another was surrounded, with two killed and two captured; the last group of four fled to a house, and barricaded themselves in. The police set fire to the building, and burned them all to death. British-trained fighters continued to filter into Albania, some by boat and others on foot across the Greek border, only to be intercepted like their predecessors. Meanwhile, across Albania, the Sigurimi began rounding up relatives and friends of the insurgents. A shared surname was enough to invite suspicion. For each guerrilla, as many as forty others were shot or thrown into prison. Two captives were 'tied to the back of a Jeep and dragged through the streets until their bodies were reduced to a bloody pulp'. A handful of the fighters apparently escaped and sent back radio messages, urging the British and Americans to send more forces. Only much later did it emerge that the Sigurimi was running a classic double cross: the messages were sent by captives, forced to reveal their codes and transmitting with guns to their heads. 'Our famous radio game brought about the ignominious failure of the plans of the foreign enemy,' bragged Enver Hoxha. 'The bands of criminals who were dropped in by parachute or infiltrated across the border at our request came like lambs to the slaughter.'

Show trials were later staged with captured survivors – propaganda spectacles at which the tortured, semi-coherent defendants condemned themselves and cursed their capitalist backers, before being sentenced to long prison terms, from which few emerged alive.

In London and Washington, as the operation lurched from failure to calamity, morale slumped, and suspicions rose. 'It was obvious there was a leak somewhere,' said one CIA officer. 'We had several meetings, trying to figure out where the thing was going wrong. We had to ask ourselves how long we were prepared to go on dropping these young men into the bag.' The British privately blamed the Americans, and vice versa. 'Our security was very, very tight,' insisted Colonel Smiley.

In fact, the secrecy surrounding the operation was anything but secure. Soviet intelligence had penetrated not just the Albanian émigré groups in Europe, but every other community of disgruntled exiles. James Angleton learned, through his Italian contacts, that Valuable had been 'well and truly blown' from the start: Italian intelligence had been watching the *Stormie Seas* from the moment she set sail for Albania. Journalists also got wind of the story. Once the first teams of guerrillas had been intercepted, the Albanian authorities were naturally braced for more. The operation was flawed from its inception: Hoxha was more firmly entrenched, and the opposition to him much weaker, than Anglo-American intelligence imagined. The planners had simply believed that 'Albania would fall from the Soviet imperial tree like a ripe plum and other fruit would soon follow'. And they were simply wrong.

Operation Valuable might well have failed without Philby, but not so utterly, nor so bloodily. Looking back, the planners knew whom to blame for the embarrassing and unmitigated failure. 'There is little question that Philby not only informed Moscow of overall British and American planning,' wrote CIA historian Harry Rositzke, 'but provided details on the individual despatch of agent teams before they arrived in Albania.' Yuri Modin, the NKVD controller in London who passed on Philby's messages to Moscow, was also explicit: 'He gave us vital information about the number of men involved, the day and the time of the landing, the weapons they were bringing and their precise programme of action . . . the Soviets duly passed on Philby's information to Albanians who set up ambushes.'

Philby later gloried in what he had done: 'The agents we sent into Albania were armed men intent on murder, sabotage and assassination. They were quite as ready as I was to contemplate bloodshed in the service of a political ideal. They knew the risks they were running. I was serving the interests of the Soviet Union and those interests required that these men were defeated. To the extent that I helped defeat them, even if it caused their deaths, I have no regrets.'

The precise death toll will never be known: somewhere between 100 and 200 Albanian guerrillas perished; if their families and other reprisal victims are taken into account, the figure rises into the thousands. Years later, those who had deployed the doomed Albanian insurgents came to the conclusion that, over the course of two lunch-filled years, James Angleton 'gave Philby over drinks the precise coordinates for every drop zone of the CIA in Albania'.

At the heart of the tragedy lay a close friendship, and a great betrayal. Lunch at Harvey's restaurant came with a hefty bill.

Homer's Odyssey

The annual Thanksgiving party at the Angleton home in 1950 was not a sober affair. Jim and Cicely Angleton invited the entire Philby clan to their Arlington house for a turkey dinner with all the trimmings. The other guests included Wilfred Mann, a physicist in the British embassy's science section. According to some accounts William E. Colby, future head of the CIA, was also present. All four men were deeply involved in the accelerating nuclear arms race, and the espionage attendant on it. The Soviet Union had carried out its first nuclear test a year earlier, thanks in part to Moscow's spies penetrating the West's atomic programme. The Venona intercepts identified one of the Soviet spies at Los Alamos labs as Klaus Fuchs, a German-born nuclear physicist. Philby had alerted Moscow Centre when the trap was closing on Fuchs, but too late to save him: he confessed under questioning and was now serving a fourteen-year prison sentence. A number of other Soviet agents were warned that they too were in danger. Several fled. Two who did not were Julius and Ethel Rosenberg, organisers of a Soviet spy ring in New York. In 1953 they would be executed.

Spies were dying. President Truman was calling for a build-up of weapons to halt the spread of Soviet influence around the globe. There was talk of nuclear war, and the Western intelligence services were locked in increasingly bloody conflict with their Soviet rivals. The opposing sides in that secret war were ranged around Angleton's dinner table, but no hint of discord marred the happy occasion, as

Philby joined his friends in giving bibulous thanks for America's bounty. 'Jim and Kim were very fond of each other,' recalled Cicely Angleton. 'We all liked him.' Philby was only thirty-eight but looked a lot older. There was already something raddled in his handsome features. The eyes remained bright and appealing, but the bags beneath them were growing heavier, and the lunches at Harvey's were taking a toll on his waistline. 'After a year of keeping up with Angleton,' he wrote, 'I took the advice of an elderly lady friend and went on a diet, dropping from thirteen stone to eleven in three months.'

These were heady times in Washington, the young superpower capital suffused with wealth and self-confidence. Philby moved easily among the leaders of this new world order, a warm and reassuring presence among the Cold Warriors. Philby was not a greedy man, but he wanted for nothing. 'If you have a lot of money,' reflected this secret communist at the heart of capitalist power, 'you can organise your life in a rather pleasant way.' Philby's life could not have been organised more pleasantly. He urged Nicholas Elliott to come and visit him. 'The more visitors I had in Washington,' he wrote, 'the more spies I got my finger into.' And Philby wanted a finger in every spy.

On the surface, Philby might appear as serene and affable as ever, but inside a small worm of anxiety was burrowing away. The twinge he had felt on learning that a Soviet spy had been located in the wartime embassy grew markedly more uncomfortable in June 1950, when the Venona decrypts revealed a 'valuable agent network' operating in Britain in 1945, including a 'particularly important' spy codenamed 'Stanley'. The codebreakers were gaining ground every day. Philby decided to pay a visit to the US government decoding centre at Arlington Hall, Virginia. Meredith Gardner, the chief of the Venona project, welcomed Philby to his secret word-laboratory, and later recalled the strange intensity with which the Englishman had observed the decryption teams at work, picking away at the vast spy puzzle. 'Philby was looking on with no doubt rapt attention but he never said a word, never a word.' Philby knew that a single word, correctly identifying 'Stanley' as him, would be enough to sink him.

A joint investigation by the FBI and MI5 had not yet identified the spy codenamed 'Homer'. The investigators seemed convinced that the mole in the British embassy must be a local employee, a janitor or servant, even though the quality of the information 'Homer' had supplied was high grade. After leaving Washington in 1948, Donald Maclean had moved on to Cairo as counsellor and head of chancery at the British embassy. His behaviour had become increasingly bizarre under the strain of his double life, yet no one imagined that this urbane, cultured English diplomat might be a spy for Russia. Maclean was the son of a former Cabinet minister, a product of public school and Cambridge, a member of the Reform Club. And so he was protected from suspicion, in Philby's words, by the 'genuine mental block which stubbornly resisted the belief that respected members of the establishment could do such things'. But that presumption could not shield him for ever. As the investigators dug deeper, Philby kept Moscow informed of their progress. 'Maclean should stay in his post as long as possible,' Moscow Centre told him, while noting that it might be necessary to extract him 'before the net closed in'.

Philby laid out his own safety net, knowing that if the Venona decrypts unmasked Maclean then all his associates would come under suspicion and the trail, eventually, could lead to Philby himself. He discreetly hinted to MI5 that he would like to expand his role in Washington, ostensibly to improve efficiency, in reality to ensure even closer monitoring of the 'Homer' investigation. 'He clearly feels he is not really getting enough scope,' wrote Guy Liddell of MI5. 'I thought I discerned a fly thrown over me in the form of a suggestion that it was really unnecessary for us to have a Washington representative and that he could carry the whole business.' The counter-intelligence chief resisted Philby's veiled offer to represent MI5 as well as MI6, though not out of any suspicion of the real motive behind it. Philby also lobbied C in London to notify him in advance of any decoding breakthrough, to 'give us more time for studying it'; and, if necessary, more time to get away.

Philby's marriage was under severe strain once more. The Philby clan was growing, but while Philby told Nicholas Elliott of his 'parental pride in being the father of five children', the arrival of another baby increased the burden on Aileen, who was again show-ing signs of instability. She was now drinking almost as much as her husband. Their relationship took another body blow when a letter arrived from Guy Burgess, announcing cheerily: 'I have a shock for you. I have just been posted to Washington.' Burgess asked to stay with the Philbys 'for a few days', while he looked for somewhere to live. Aileen was appalled. 'I know him only too well,' she wrote to friends. 'He will never leave our house.'

Burgess was still in the Foreign Office, although how he had managed to retain employment in that staid and respectable organi-sation remains a mystery. In a career not so much chequered as blotched, he had worked in the news department, as assistant to the minister of state in the Foreign Office, and in the Far Eastern section. Throughout that time, he supplied the Russians with every secret document he could lay his hands on, removing them in the evening and returning them in the morning after they had been copied by the Soviets. Burgess was as entertaining as ever, and pure, undiluted trouble: he boasted about his espionage contacts, made no attempt to hide his promiscuous homosexuality, and left a trail of chaos in his wake. He was usually drunk, and frequently insulting, particularly to important people. He failed to pay his bills, picked fights, identified MI6 officers in public places and went on a bender in Gibraltar of such scale that the local MI5 officer could not help being impressed: 'I do not think that even in Gibraltar have I ever seen anyone put away so much hard liquor in so short a time.' On another occasion he got into a fight with a Foreign Office colleague, fell down the marble steps of the Royal Automobile Club and fractured his skull, after which his behaviour grew even more extreme. Burgess was permanently on the point of being sacked. Instead, he was appointed information officer at the British embassy in Washington, a job requiring delicacy and tact for which he was monumentally unsuited. Laughably, Guy Liddell insisted that Burgess 'was not the sort of person who would deliberately pass confidential information to unauthorised persons'. It was hoped that Burgess's 'eccentricities' (code for his homosexuality) might be less conspicuous in the US. But the Foreign Office security chief warned Sir Robert Mackenzie, the security officer at the Washington embassy, that with Burgess in town, he should be prepared for even worse escapades. Mackenzie was heard to mutter: 'What does he mean *worse*? Goats?'

If the prospect of Burgess arriving in Washington worried some officials, it positively horrified Aileen. Philby insisted, however, that his old friend must be made welcome, and could live in the basement of their house. Aileen protested, and a furious row followed, duly reported back, by both parties, to Elliott in Switzerland, who wrote: 'Knowing the trouble that would inevitably ensue – and remembering Burgess's drunken and homosexual orgies when he had stayed with them in Istanbul – Aileen resisted this move, but bowed in the end (and as usual) to Philby's wishes.' Burgess hit the US capital, and the Philby household, like a particularly destructive and volatile meteor. 'The inevitable drunken scenes and disorder ensued,' Elliott wrote, 'and tested the marriage to its limits.'

Philby later depicted his decision to take in Burgess as an act of loyalty. They had been friends for more than twenty years, they had discovered communism together and remained locked in service to Moscow. Burgess was one of the few people to whom Philby could speak openly. He assured the embassy that he would 'keep an eye' on the renegade – a task that was virtually impossible anyway, but perhaps marginally easier with the man living under his roof. Philby had his own motive for welcoming Burgess to Washington. As information officer, Burgess would be able to travel freely without exciting comment; he could therefore act as a courier, taking information to Philby's Soviet controller, Valeri Makayev, in New York. Soon after Burgess's arrival, Philby told him about the hunt for 'Homer', and the increasing risk that Maclean might be exposed and confess all, with potentially calamitous consequences.

Philby had not seen Maclean since the end of the war, but their early friendship would not be hard to prove; Burgess knew Maclean much better, and was also a close friend of Anthony Blunt; the association between Burgess and Philby was evident; Blunt was also in touch with Maclean. If Maclean cracked, MI5 could swiftly establish the links between the spies, and the chain of suspicion would eventually lead to Philby.

Maclean was heading off the rails at fantastic speed. He had tried to persuade his Soviet handler that he no longer wished to be a Soviet spy, apparently unaware that this was not the sort of club one could resign from. Moscow simply ignored the request. In May 1950, the strain became too much for him: he got drunk, smashed up the Cairo flat of two secretaries at the US embassy, ripped up their underwear, and hurled a large mirror off the wall, breaking a large bath in two. He was sent home, placed under the care of a Harley Street psychiatrist, and then, amazingly, after a short period of treatment, promoted to head the American desk at the Foreign Office. Even drunken, unhinged knicker-shredding, it seemed, was no bar to advancement in the British diplomatic service if one was the 'right sort'. But the shortlist of suspects was getting shorter, and Maclean's name was on it. He was plainly on the verge of complete nervous collapse. If MI5 pulled him in for questioning, he was almost certain to crack. With Burgess as his go-between, Philby could now be sure of a 'secure line of communication to Moscow' if and when the crisis erupted.

Once installed in the Philby home, Burgess began to behave entirely in character. He crashed around Washington, dropping names, picking quarrels, downing numberless drinks, and leaving others to pay for them. He wore a filthy old duffel coat, eschewed soap, and loudly declared that Americans were incapable of intellectual thought. Philby introduced Burgess to Angleton as 'the most outstanding historian of his time at Cambridge'. (Anyone familiar with Cambridge historians can attest that Burgess's personal habits did not entirely negate that claim.) He was certainly outstandingly embarrassing. Some days later, Burgess lurched up to Angleton's table at the Occidental Restaurant, sat down without invitation, and demanded a drink of 'the cheapest bourbon'. He was wearing 'a peculiar garb, namely a white British naval jacket which was dirty and stained. He was intoxicated, unshaven, and, by the appearance of his eyes, had not washed since he last slept.' Burgess launched into a description of a mad scheme to import jackets like the one he was wearing to sell 'for fantastic profits' in New York. Then he demanded to be taken for a ride in Angleton's Oldsmobile saloon, and finally asked the CIA officer to lend him some cash. Then he wandered off. There is no evidence Angleton found this behaviour objectionable. He liked British eccentrics, and any friend of Kim Philby was a friend of his.

On 19 January 1951, Philby made a fateful decision: with his wife depressed, his dangerous friend careening around Washington, and his own future uncertain, he decided to throw a dinner party. It was, by almost universal agreement, the dinner party from hell.

Philby invited all his senior contacts in American intelligence: the Angletons, of course, and Robert Lamphere, the FBI mole-hunter, along with the Manns and several others. Also present were Bill Harvey, a former FBI agent now in charge of CIA counter-intelligence, and his highly strung wife Libby. A hard-driving Ohio native, Bill Harvey was intelligent but also 'a bloated alcoholic with the manners of a comically corrupt cop in a Raymond Chandler thriller'. The Harveys had already attended a dinner party chez Philby, which had ended with Bill Harvey slumped insensible at the table.

The evening began, as always, with Martinis served from a pitcher. There was an acrid mood in the air. Cicely Angleton noticed that Bob Lamphere was the only guest not smoking. 'What Freudian impulse causes you not to smoke?' she demanded archly. The drinking continued steadily, and in the case of Libby Harvey, unsteadily. With the meal over (no one could later recall what was said, or eaten), the guests moved on to whisky. At this point Burgess burst in. He was dishevelled, loudly inebriated, and itching for an argument. Libby lurched up to the new arrival, cornered him, and demanded that he draw a cartoon of her. Burgess was a talented sketcher, and his caricatures had become objects of admiration on the Washington dinner-party circuit. Burgess demurred. Libby drunkenly insisted.

Finally, fed up with her badgering, he picked up a pad and pencil, and began to sketch. A few minutes later, with a glinting grin, he handed over the caricature.

Sadly, the finished artwork does not survive, but its broad outlines have been described by witnesses. The woman in the picture was unmistakably Libby Harvey, though her face was 'beastily distorted'. Her face, however, was not the main focus of the cartoon: her dress was hiked up around her waist, her legs spread, and her naked pudenda bared. Libby stared at it, shrieked, and burst into tears. Bill Harvey threw a punch at Burgess. Uproar ensued. The Harveys stormed out.

Burgess found the incident hilarious. Philby did not. 'How could you? How could you?' he demanded, before slumping on the sofa. Aileen retired sobbing to the kitchen. Before drifting home, Angleton and Mann lingered outside 4100 Nebraska Avenue, like two teenagers after a fight, discussing what Angleton termed 'a social disaster'.

Philby later sent the Harveys a 'handsome' apology for Burgess's insulting behaviour.

'Forget it,' said Bill Harvey, charmlessly. But Harvey didn't forget it.

A few weeks later, at Arlington Hall, came the break the decoders had been hoping for, and Philby had been dreading: Meredith Gardner finally decrypted a message dating back to June 1944, indicating that the spy 'Homer' had a pregnant wife who was then staying with her mother in New York. Melinda, Maclean's American-born wife, had been expecting a child in 1944; her wealthy divorced mother lived in Manhattan; therefore Homer must be Donald Maclean.

News of the breakthrough flew to London, and then bounced back to Philby in Washington. He was now the closest to exposure since Volkov had threatened to unmask him in 1945. But time was on his side. There was no evidence, as yet, to connect him directly with Maclean, and the two men had not met for many years. Moreover, instead of arresting Maclean at once, MI5 opted to wait, and watch, in the hope of gathering further evidence. The Venona material was simply too secret to be used in court: by tapping his telephone, bugging his office, intercepting his post and putting him under surveillance, MI5 hoped to catch Maclean in direct contact with his Soviet controller. But the Security Service may also have been suffering from the sort of paralysis that affects organisations when faced with a situation that is deeply embarrassing, potentially ruinous and entirely unprecedented. Maclean, the most senior spy ever detected inside the British government, would remain at liberty for five more weeks.

Philby immediately relayed the bad news to Makayev, and demanded that Maclean be extracted from the UK before he was interrogated and compromised the entire British spy network – and most importantly Philby himself. But with Maclean now under close surveillance, arranging his escape was a delicate task, since any overt contact with the Soviets would trigger his immediate arrest. Maclean must be warned and told to flee by a third party who would not arouse suspicion. The ideal messenger, Philby concluded, was close at hand, in the disreputable and dishevelled shape of Guy Burgess, whose diplomatic career was about to come to an end in a car crash, almost literally. Whether by accident or design, he collected no fewer than three speeding tickets in a single day by hurtling around Virginia in a grey Lincoln convertible, claimed diplomatic immunity on all of them, insulted the officers who stopped him, and provoked a furious official protest from both the State Department and the governor of Virginia. It wasn't quite goats, but for the ambassador it was the last straw. Burgess, in disgrace but wholly unrepentant, was instructed to return to London immediately. Philby would later claim that Burgess's recall had been a carefully engineered ploy; it was probably more a lucky accident, but either way it presented an ideal opportunity to warn Maclean that he must flee to Moscow.

The night before Burgess's departure, the two spies dined in a Chinese restaurant in downtown Washington, selected because it had individual booths with piped music, to stymie any eavesdroppers. They rehearsed the plan: Burgess would make contact with the

Soviets in London, then visit Maclean at his office and, while making innocuous conversation, hand over a sheet of paper setting the time and place for a rendezvous. Burgess had not yet been formally fired, and there would be nothing suspicious in the newly returned information officer from Washington reporting to the head of the American desk. The Soviets would then arrange Maclean's escape. 'Don't you go too,' said Philby, only half-joking, as he dropped Burgess off at Union Station. Burgess, however, was congenitally incapable of doing what he was told.

Burgess arrived back in England on 7 May 1951, and immediately contacted Anthony Blunt, who got a message to Yuri Modin, the Soviet controller of the Cambridge ring. 'There's serious trouble,' Blunt reported. 'Guy Burgess has just arrived back in London. Homer's about to be arrested ... It's only a question of days now, maybe hours ... Donald's now in such a state that I'm convinced he'll break down the moment they arrest him.' Modin informed Moscow, and received an immediate response: 'We agree to your organising Maclean's defection. We will receive him here and provide him with whatever he needs.'

A graduate of the Leningrad Naval Academy, Yuri Modin had, in his own estimation, 'no predisposition to be a spy'. But he was very good at it. He had inherited the Cambridge network at a time when it was falling apart, yet he had handled Burgess's drinking and Maclean's volatility with tact and competence. Spiriting Maclean to Moscow, however, was by far the greatest challenge he had yet faced.

MI5's surveillance unit, A4, was known as 'The Watchers'. In 1951, it numbered about twenty men and three women. Most were former Special Branch police officers, selected for their sharp eyesight, good hearing, and average height ('men who are too short ... are just as conspicuous as tall men', ruled the chief Watcher). They were expected to dress in trilby hats and raincoats, and communicated with each other by hand signals. They stood on street corners, watching, and trying to appear inconspicuous. They looked, in short, exactly like surveillance agents. Since the end of the war, A4 had kept watch on the Soviet intelligence residency in Kensington Palace

Gardens, and the Soviets, in turn, had kept a close watch on them. Modin knew that the Watchers did not work in the evenings or over the weekends. He knew, too, that surveillance of Maclean did not extend beyond London, because MI5 feared that a man hanging around in a trilby might be a giveaway in the countryside. Maclean lived in Tatsfield in rural Kent, and commuted to and from London by train. The Watchers trailed after him during the day but, Modin observed, 'at Victoria, MI5's men saw the train out of the station, and then headed home like good little functionaries. There was no one at Tatsfield to take up the chase.' Modin believed Maclean would be arrested on Monday 28 May. On Friday 25 May, the very day the Foreign Secretary gave formal approval for Maclean's interrogation, the escape plan swung into action.

That evening, which happened to be Maclean's thirty-eighth birthday, Burgess appeared at the Maclean home in Tatsfield with a rented car, packed bags and two round-trip tickets booked in false names for the *Falaise*, a pleasure boat leaving that night for St Malo in France. He had spent the previous day at his club, talking loudly about a road trip he planned to take to Scotland with a new boyfriend. Burgess had dinner with Donald and Melinda Maclean (who was party to the plan), and the two men set off for Southampton in a state of high excitement and unaccustomed sobriety. They arrived just minutes before the midnight sailing, parked the car askew on the dockside, and scrambled up the boat's gangplank. One of the dockworkers shouted that the car door was still open; 'Back on Monday!' Burgess shouted back. He may have thought he was telling the truth.

Before Burgess left Washington, Philby had made him promise he would not flee with Maclean to Moscow. 'Don't go with him when he goes. If you do, that'll be the end of me. Swear that you won't.' Modin, however, had insisted that Burgess must accompany Maclean. Burgess at first objected. He pointed out that he had no desire to defect and found the prospect of life in Moscow perfectly ghastly. But finally he had agreed, apparently on the understanding that he could steer Maclean to Moscow and then return and resume his life just as before. The Soviets had other plans: Burgess and Maclean were travelling on one-way tickets. As Modin wrote: 'The Centre had concluded that we had not one, but two burnt-out agents on our hands. Burgess had lost most of his former value to us ... Even if he retained his job, he could never again feed intelligence to the KGB as he had done before. He was finished.' What the Soviets had failed to take properly into account was the knock-on impact the double defection would have on Kim Philby. Modin later acknowledged that allowing Burgess to leave with Maclean had been an error. In the spy world, nothing is supposed to occur by accident, but in this case, Modin's explanation was probably true: 'It just happened ... intelligence services do silly things sometimes.'

The *Falaise* was popular with wealthy adulterers wanting to take their mistresses on a weekend cross-Channel jaunt. There were no passport controls, and few questions asked. In theory the ship cruised off the coast of France, but unofficially she always put in at St Malo for a few hours of French food and sightseeing. The ship docked at 11.45 the next morning. Burgess and Maclean left their luggage on board, filed down the gangplank with the other passengers, and then slipped away from the crowds. They caught a taxi to the station at Rennes, a train to Paris, and then another train to Berne in Switzerland, where Nicholas Elliott, wholly unaware of the presence of the two fugitives on his patch, was enjoying dinner at the Schweizerhof Hotel.

Elliott considered the hotel restaurant one of the finest in Europe, with particularly good foie gras. 'I have never tasted better,' Elliott insisted, 'even in Strasbourg.' The maître d', Théo, was one of Elliott's paid informants, and always managed to find him a table. Saturday night dinner at the Schweizerhof had become something of an Elliott tradition.

On the evening of 26 May, while Elliott was tucking into his foie gras, a taxi pulled up outside the Soviet embassy, less than a mile away. Elliott would have recognised both passengers. Burgess had been a frequent guest at the Harris parties, and he, Philby and Elliott had often dined together at Pruniers restaurant on Piccadilly. Burgess had once applied for a teaching post at Eton, but was turned down when Claude Elliott discovered how unsuitable he was. 'It seems a pity the Foreign Office did not take the trouble to make a similar inquiry,' Elliott later reflected ruefully. He had also met Maclean on several occasions.

A few hours later, Burgess and Maclean re-emerged from the Soviet embassy carrying fake passports in false names. They then took another train to Zurich, where they boarded a plane bound for Stockholm, with a stopover in Prague. At Prague airport, now safely behind the Iron Curtain, the two men walked out of the arrivals hall and were whisked into a waiting car.

On Monday morning, the Watchers watched in vain as the train from Tatsfield pulled into Victoria Station with no Maclean aboard. A little later, Melinda Maclean called the Foreign Office to report that her husband had left the house on Friday night with a man named 'Roger Styles', and she had not seen him since. The Foreign Office put a call through to MI5. Special Branch reported that a car, hired by Guy Burgess, had been abandoned at Southampton docks. A flush of dawning horror began to spread across the British government.

The Foreign Office sent out an urgent telegram to embassies and MI6 stations throughout Europe, with instructions that Burgess and Maclean be apprehended 'at all costs and by all means'. A Missing Persons poster gave a description of the fugitives. 'Maclean: 6'3", normal build, short hair, brushed back, part on left side, slight stoop, thin tight lips, long thin legs, sloppy dressed, chain smoker, heavy drinker. Burgess: 5'9", slender build, dark complexion, dark curly hair, tinged with grey, chubby face, clean shaven, slightly pigeon-toed'. In Berne, Elliott gave orders to his own Watchers to keep a careful eye on the Soviet embassy. One of his colleagues prepared a 'decanter of poisoned Scotch', just in case the notoriously thirsty fugitives turned up and needed to be immobilised. By that time, Burgess and Maclean were already being toasted in Moscow.

The morning after the discovery of Burgess and Maclean's disappearance, a long, coded telegram arrived at the British embassy in

Washington, marked Top Secret. Geoffrey Paterson, the MI5 representative in Washington, called Kim Philby at home to ask if he could borrow his secretary, Edith Whitfield, to help decipher it. Philby was happy to oblige. A few hours later, he found Paterson in his embassy office, grey-faced.

'Kim,' Paterson half-whispered. 'The bird has flown.'

'What bird?' said Philby, arranging his features to register the appropriate consternation. 'Not Maclean?'

'Yes, but there's worse than that ... *Guy Burgess* has gone with him.'

Philby's alarm was now unfeigned. Burgess had been his houseguest until a few weeks earlier. Philby was one of the few people apprised of the Homer investigation, and in a position to warn Maclean. All three had been at Cambridge together. It was only a matter of time – and probably very little time – before MI5 took an interest in his friendship with Burgess, and started digging into his past. Philby realised, as his Soviet handlers apparently did not, just how seriously Burgess's flight would threaten his own position. He might be placed under surveillance at any moment, sacked, or even arrested. He had to move fast.

An emergency plan was already in place. If MI5 seemed to be closing in, the Soviets would provide money and false papers, and Philby would escape to Moscow via the Caribbean or Mexico. Makayev in New York had been instructed to leave $2,000 and a message at a dead letter drop for precisely this purpose. He failed to do so. Philby never received the money. Makayev was later disciplined for this failure by his superiors in Moscow, who noted his 'lack of discipline' and 'crude manners': it seems likely that he simply spent the money on his ballet dancer.

The British embassy was in secret uproar, as news spread that not one, but two senior Foreign Office officials in Washington had vanished, and were probably Soviet spies. Philby and Paterson together broke the embarrassing news to the FBI. Philby carefully observed the reaction of his FBI friends, including Bob Lamphere, his former dinner party guest, and saw only surprise, tinged with some wry pleasure at the British predicament. So far, Philby himself did not seem to be under suspicion. At lunchtime, Philby told Paterson he was going home for 'a stiff drink', behaviour that anyone who knew him would have considered perfectly normal. Back at Nebraska Avenue, Philby headed not for the drinks cabinet but for the potting shed, where he collected a trowel, and then down to the basement that had, until recently, housed Guy Burgess. There he retrieved from a hiding place the Russian camera, tripod and film given to him by Makayev, sealed the lot in waterproof containers and placed them in the boot of his car. Then he climbed in, gunned the engine, and drove north. Aileen was at home with the children; if she thought it strange that her husband should come home from work early, lock himself in the basement, and then drive away without a word, she did not say so.

Philby had travelled the road to Great Falls many times. Angleton had taken him fishing in the Potomac Valley and there was a faux-English pub called the Old Angler's Inn where they had spent several convivial evenings. The road was little used, and heavily wooded. On a deserted stretch, with woods on one side and the river on the other, Philby parked, extracted the containers and trowel, and headed into the trees. He emerged after a few minutes, casually doing up his fly buttons for the benefit of any passers-by, and drove home. Somewhere in a shallow hole in the woods beside the Potomac lies a cache of Soviet photographic equipment that has lain buried for more than sixty years, a secret memorial to Philby's spycraft.

If Philby was going to make his escape, and join Burgess and Maclean in exile, then now was the moment. But he did not run. He decided to stay and try to bluff it out. Philby later framed this choice (as he interpreted most of his own behaviour) in terms of principle: 'My clear duty was to fight it out.' But the decision was also calculated: the FBI did not yet suspect him, so presumably the same must be true of MI5. No one had identified 'Stanley'. If and when they explored his past, the evidence they might find was mostly circumstantial. His early dabblings with left-wing politics were hardly secret, and he had told Valentine Vivian of his marriage to Litzi. His friendship with Burgess looked bad (back in 1940, Burgess had been instrumental in his recruitment by MI6), but then if they were really both Soviet spies, why would Philby have allowed Burgess to live in his home? 'There is no doubt that Kim Philby is thoroughly disgusted with Burgess's behaviour,' wrote Liddell, after Philby contacted him to express horror at his friend's defection.

The very act of staying put would suggest a clear conscience. True, there were some uncomfortable early clues to his real allegiance: the British spy described by the defector Krivitsky who had worked in Spain as a journalist; Volkov's allusion to a counter-intelligence officer, and the Russian's subsequent disappearance after Philby took over the case. Going back still further, MI6 might recall the Soviet files he had taken out from the registry at St Albans. But for a legal prosecution, MI5 would need harder evidence than this. They might suspect him, interrogate him, urge him to confess, and try to trap him. But they would find it very hard to convict him. And Philby knew it. With a cool head, and the luck that seemed to cling to him, he might yet ride out the coming storm. 'Despite all appearances, I thought my chances were good.'

Philby had one other weapon in his armoury, perhaps the most powerful of all, and that was his capacity for friendship. Philby had powerful friends on both sides of the Atlantic, people who had worked with him and trusted him for many years. These people had witnessed his skill as an intelligence officer, shared secrets with him and drunk his Martinis. To accept Philby's guilt would have been, in a way, to implicate themselves. 'There must be many people in high positions,' Philby reflected, 'who would wish very much to see my innocence established. They would be inclined to give me the benefit of the doubt.'

Philby knew he could rely on his friends to defend him, and two above all: Jim Angleton and Nick Elliott.

Peach

Philby's summons to London arrived in the form of a polite, hand-written note from his immediate superior, Jack Easton, informing him that he would shortly receive a formal telegram inviting him to come home and discuss the disappearance of Burgess and Maclean. Easton was one of the very few senior officers Philby respected, a man with a 'rapier mind', capable of 'deeply subtle twists'. Philby later wondered if the letter was a tipoff, intended to make him flee in order to avoid a scandal. In truth it was probably just a friendly gesture, a reassurance that there was nothing to worry about. Before leaving, Philby made the rounds of his CIA and FBI contacts once more, and again detected no overt suspicion. Angleton seemed as friendly as ever. On 11 June 1951, the evening before Philby's flight, the friends met in a bar.

'How long will you be away?' Angleton inquired.

'About a week,' said Philby nonchalantly.

'Can you do me a favour in London?' asked Angleton, explaining that he needed to send an urgent letter to MI6, but had missed the diplomatic bag that week. Would Philby deliver it by hand? He pushed over an envelope, addressed to the head of counter-intelligence in London. Philby later imagined that this too had been a ruse of some sort, intended to test or trap him. Paranoia was beginning to gnaw. Angleton had no inkling of suspicion: his trusted friend would deliver the letter, and return in a week, when they would have lunch together as usual, at Harvey's. After what Philby called 'a pleasant hour' at the bar, discussing 'matters of mutual concern', Philby boarded the night plane to London. He would never see America, or Jim Angleton, again.

Dark clouds of doubt were swiftly gathering, on both sides of the Atlantic, as Philby knew they would. These would soon blow up into a storm that would knock the 'special relationship' off course and set Britain's secret services at each other's throats. The Americans might appear unruffled, but the disappearing diplomats had provoked a 'major sensation' in Washington. An investigation was now under way focusing on Guy Burgess and, by association, his friend, protector and landlord, Kim Philby. CIA chief Walter Bedell Smith ordered any officers with knowledge of the British pair to relate what they knew of Philby and Burgess as a matter of urgency. The first report to arrive on the CIA chief's desk came from Bill Harvey of counter-intelligence; the second, arriving a few days later, was written by James Angleton. They were markedly different documents.

Harvey's report – 'highly professional, perceptive and accusatory' – was, in effect, a denunciation of Philby. The former FBI agent would later claim to have had his suspicions about Philby long before the Burgess and Maclean defections, and at the FBI he may have had access to the Venona material. Harvey had studied the Englishman's career with meticulous care, and he drew together the strands of evidence with devastating precision over five closely typed pages: he noted Philby's links with Burgess, his part in the Volkov affair, his involvement in the doomed Albanian operations, and his intimate knowledge of the hunt for the spy 'Homer', which had placed him in an ideal position to warn Maclean of his impending arrest. None of these alone amounted to proof of guilt, but taken together, Harvey argued, they pointed to only one conclusion: 'Philby was a Soviet spy.' Philby later described Harvey's condemnation as 'a retrospective exercise in spite', personal revenge for the offence given to his wife at Philby's disastrous dinner party just six months earlier.

The second report stood in stark contrast. Angleton described his various meetings with the drunken Guy Burgess, but he noted that

Philby had seemed embarrassed by his friend's antics, and explained them away by saying that Burgess had 'suffered severe concussion in an accident which had continued to affect him periodically'. Angleton explicitly rejected any suggestion that Philby might have been in league with the defector, and stated his 'conviction' that whatever crimes Burgess might have committed, he had acted 'without reference to Philby'. As one CIA officer put it, 'the bottom line was . . . that you couldn't blame Philby for what this nut Burgess had done'. In Angleton's estimation, Philby was no traitor, but an honest and brilliant man who had been cruelly duped by a friend, who in turn had been rendered mentally unstable by a nasty bump on the head. According to Angleton's biographer, 'he remained convinced that his British friend would be cleared of suspicion', and warned Bedell Smith that if the CIA started levelling unsubstantiated charges of treachery against a senior MI6 officer this would seriously damage Anglo-American relations, since Philby was 'held in high esteem' in London.

In some ways, the two memos echoed the different approaches to intelligence that were developing on opposite sides of the Atlantic. Bill Harvey's reflected a new, American style of investigation, suspicious, quick to judge, and willing to offend. Angleton's was written in the British MI6 tradition, based on friendship and trust in the word of a gentleman.

Harvey read Angleton's memo, so different in tone and import from his own, and scrawled on the bottom, 'What is the rest of this story?' – in effect, accusing his fellow CIA officer of turning a blind eye to the truth. The disagreement between Harvey and Angleton over Philby sparked a feud that would last the rest of their lives. A similarly stark divergence of opinion was emerging within British intelligence.

On the afternoon of 12 June, Kim Philby arrived at MI5 headquarters in Leconfield House, off Curzon Street, feeling exhausted and 'apprehensive', but tensed and primed for the coming duel. The adrenal rush of danger had always stimulated him. Jack Easton insisted on accompanying him to the interview, as a supportive presence. The two MI6 men were greeted by Dick White, the chief of MI5 counter-intelligence, who, over the next few hours, would subject Philby to a grilling, thinly disguised as a friendly chat. Tea was served. A fug of tobacco smoke filled the room. Civilities were exchanged. Dick White (not to be confused with Richard Brooman-White, Elliott's old friend) was a former schoolmaster, the son of a Kentish ironmonger, a frank, even-tempered and honourable man who would go on to head MI5, and then MI6. Philby had known White since the war, and had always got on well with him, while privately disparaging what he considered to be his meagre intellect and vacillating character. 'He did his best to put our talk on a friendly footing,' wrote Philby. The mood in the room was more embarrassed than confrontational. C had reluctantly agreed to allow one of his officers to be interviewed by MI5 on the understanding that Philby was aiding an inquiry, and 'might have views on the case'. White was at pains to point out that Philby was there simply to help shed light on 'this horrible business with Burgess and Maclean'. But, beneath the civilised veneer, cracks were appearing that would soon split one branch of British intelligence from the other.

MI6 was standing by its man. The files contained nothing to incriminate Philby, only accolades of mounting admiration leading up to his appointment in Washington. 'There was no case against him at this time,' recalled Easton. At most, he could be accused of indiscretion, for associating with a degenerate like Guy Burgess. But if that was a crime, many in the Foreign Office and secret services were equally guilty. Philby had not run away, he was happy to help, and he was, importantly, a gentleman, a clubman and a high-flier, which meant he must be innocent. Many of Philby's colleagues in MI6 would cling to that presumption of innocence as an article of faith. To accept otherwise would be to admit that they had all been fooled; it would make the intelligence and diplomatic services look entirely idiotic. MI5, however, had been making inquiries, and already convivial, clubbable Kim Philby was beginning to take on a more sinister shape. The threads of suspicion identified by Bill Harvey in Washington were being pursued with even greater determination in London. In the weeks since the defections, a fat file had been assembled, and it now lay on White's desk, just a few feet away from where Philby sat, sipping tea, smoking his pipe and trying to appear relaxed.

The conflicting attitudes towards Philby between the sister services of British intelligence would expose a cultural fault line that predated this crisis, long outlasted it, and persists today. MI5 and MI6 – the Security Service and the Secret Intelligence Service, broadly equivalent to the FBI and CIA – overlapped in many respects, but were fundamentally dissimilar in outlook. MI5 tended to recruit former police officers and soldiers, men who sometimes spoke with regional accents, and frequently did not know, or care about, the right order to use the cutlery at a formal dinner. They enforced the law and defended the realm, caught spies and prosecuted them. MI6 was more public school and Oxbridge; its accent more *refined*, its tailoring better. Its agents and officers frequently broke the laws of other countries in pursuit of secrets, and did so with a certain swagger. MI6 was White's; MI5 was the Rotary Club. MI6 was upper-middle class (and sometimes aristocratic); MI5 was middle class (and sometimes working class). In the minute gradations of social stratification that meant so much in Britain, MI5 was 'below the salt', a little common, and MI6 was gentlemanly, elitist and old school tie. MI5 were hunters; MI6 were gatherers. Philby's patronising dismissal of Dick White as 'nondescript' precisely reflected MI6's attitude to its sister service: White, as his biographer puts it, was 'pure trade', whereas Philby was 'establishment'. MI5 looked up at MI6 with resentment; MI6 looked down with a small but ill-hidden sneer. The looming battle over Philby was yet another skirmish in Britain's never-ending, hard-fought and entirely ludicrous class war.

White was a decent man, a good administrator and an adept office politician, but he was no interrogator. The evidence against Philby was still, as he put it, 'very sketchy'. He was also facing a spy of polished duplicity, who had hidden himself in broad daylight for nearly two decades. It would take a cleverer man than White to discover him. Philby assumed the room was bugged. His stammer gave the conversation a strange, halting quality: perhaps evidence of nerves, perhaps to buy time and sympathy. White first asked about Maclean: Philby said he remembered him from Cambridge, and knew him by reputation, but had not seen him for years and probably would not even recognise him. Then the focus turned to Burgess, and the tension in the room slid up a notch. Philby insisted it was simply unbelievable that any intelligence service, let alone the Russians, would employ someone so wholly unsuited to espionage, 'an indiscreet, disorganised, drunken, homosexual reprobate'. Philby played his part well, with a careful combination of embarrassment, ingratiation, and self-justification: here was a senior intelligence officer defending himself against the unspoken charge that he had been fooled, and might lose his job through a disastrous friendship. The question of Philby's own loyalty was never mentioned, never even hinted at, but it hung over the conversation like pipe smoke. The meeting broke up with amicable handshakes. Ever helpful, Philby offered to draw up a summary of the conversation, and said he could be contacted at his mother's flat. White hinted that they would probably need to meet again soon.

Both men discussed the conversation with Guy Liddell, who wrote in his diary: 'Kim is extremely worried'. White, for his part, had not found Philby's answers 'wholly convincing'. Liddell had been Philby's friend for twenty years. He knew Guy Burgess well. Anthony Blunt was one of his closest chums. Liddell's diary betrays a man struggling with the realisation that some, and perhaps all, of his closest friends were spies. 'I dined with Anthony Blunt,' he wrote. 'I feel certain that Blunt was never a conscious collaborator with Burgess in any activities that he may have conducted on behalf of the Comintern.' His tone was anything but certain. That Burgess and Maclean might be spies, let alone Philby, was 'hard to believe'. Because he did not want to believe it.

Two days later, Philby was back in White's office, where the atmosphere was now several degrees chillier. In the interim, a letter had arrived from CIA chief Walter Bedell Smith, drafted by Bill Harvey, and with his indictment attached. Aggressive in tone, and addressed to C in person, it stated that under no circumstances would Philby be permitted to return to Washington. The underlying message was blunt: 'Fire Philby or we break off the intelligence relationship.' The relationship was under strain as never before. Noting that confidence in the Foreign Office had been 'severely shaken' by the disappearance of Burgess and Maclean, both of whom were obvious security risks, the US urged the British government to 'clean house regardless of whom may be hurt'. Even more insultingly, Washington suggested that such a security breach would never have happened in the US: 'In the State Department repeated drunkenness, recurrent nervous breakdowns, sexual deviations and other human frailties are considered security hazards and persons showing any one or more of them are summarily dismissed.'

As Angleton had predicted, MI6 did not take kindly to having one of its officers accused of treachery without hard evidence, let alone the suggestion that the Foreign Office was staffed with drunken, mentally unstable sexual deviants. The bosses of MI6 immediately sent a message to Dick White at MI5, stating 'their wholehearted commitment to the protection of their protégé and to the reputation of their service'. White was now facing both a looming confrontation with Philby, and a showdown with MI6 itself. At the same time, the dossier on Philby was growing. Investigations had revealed his left-wing leanings at Cambridge, his marriage to a communist, his subsequent swing to the far right, and the defector Krivitsky's reference to a Soviet spy working as a journalist in Spain during the Civil War. The Volkov case, the wreckage of Operation Valuable, the Homer investigation and the timing of the Burgess and Maclean defections all seemed to indicate, circumstantially if not definitively, that Philby was guilty. 'While all the points against him are capable of another explanation their cumulative effect is certainly impressive,' wrote Liddell. In a mark of the deepening suspicion, Philby was awarded his own codename: Peach. Codenames are supposed to be neutral, but very seldom are. It is tempting to see a hidden meaning in the MI5 codename now attached to Philby, for a peach was a most exotic and enticing fruit in a Britain emaciated by wartime rationing, and ripe for the plucking.

Dick White was as polite as before, but more pointed. He invited Philby to describe once again, but in more detail, exactly when he had met Burgess, what he knew of his politics, and how they had become friends. Philby was told to take his time. 'I'm in no particular hurry,' said White, with a flicker of impatience. A short lie is easy. An extended lie is far harder, as earlier falsehoods overlap, constrain and contradict the lies that follow. Philby admitted that his first wife had been a communist, but insisted that he had 'subsequently converted her' and that 'he himself had never been a communist'. When asked how Maclean might have discovered he was facing arrest, Philby 'denied emphatically that he had ever discussed Maclean with Burgess'.

In the midst of a long, rambling answer, White realised, with perfect certainty, that Philby was lying.

White now switched focus, to 1936, and the first trip to Spain as a correspondent for *The Times*. Philby was quick to correct him: he had initially gone to Spain as a *freelancer*, and only later taken a staff job with the newspaper. White's face grew redder, and his collar tighter. How, then, as an impoverished young man, had Philby found the money to travel to Spain and set himself up as a correspondent? It was, Philby later wrote, a 'nasty little question' because, as White plainly suspected, the order to go to Spain, and the money to do so, had been provided by Soviet intelligence. Philby blustered that he had sold his books and gramophone records to finance the trip. This was White's opportunity to pounce, because just a little more probing would have unpicked that answer: how many books? How many records? Did he sell them for cash? Where were the bank records? Instead, White simply logged Philby's response as another lie. After several more hours, White rose to his feet, indicating that the session was over. This time, they did not shake hands. Philby left the second interview knowing that he was now a prime suspect in White's eyes. He remained convinced that MI5 had little hard evidence, probably not enough to prosecute, and almost certainly not enough to convict him. But there was more than enough to make him intolerable to MI5, and unemployable by MI6. White sent a memo to Stewart

Menzies, laying out the grounds for suspicion against Philby, and suggesting that MI6 take action as a matter of urgency.

Philby was in deep danger. The middle-class hounds of MI5 were baying for his upper-class blood. He was cornered, compromised and running out of ammunition. But he still had allies ready to support him, and one in particular whose loyalty remained as solid and unquestioning as it had ever been.

Nicholas Elliott returned to Britain at the very moment the Philby inquisition was reaching a climax. He now leaped to his friend's defence with ferocity, alacrity and absolute conviction.

The timing of Elliott's recall was probably coincidental. After six successful years as station chief in Switzerland he was due for a promotion, and accepted a new post in London, liaising with the intelligence services of friendly foreign powers. It was a job that required plenty of foreign travel, and fed what Elliott called his 'insatiable appetite for new places and faces'. But it also gave him the opportunity to devote himself to a task closer to home, and closer to his heart: defending Philby against the accusations swirling around Whitehall. Elliott was wholeheartedly, unwaveringly convinced of Philby's innocence. They had joined MI6 together, watched cricket together, dined and drunk together. It was simply inconceivable to Elliott that Philby could be a Soviet spy. The Philby he knew never discussed politics. In more than a decade of close friendship, he had never heard Philby utter a word that might be considered left-wing, let alone communist. Philby might have made a mistake, associating with a man like Burgess; he might have dabbled in radical politics at university; he might even have married a communist, and concealed the fact. But these were errors, not crimes. The rest of the so-called evidence was mere hearsay, gossip of the most vicious sort. The anti-communist campaign led by Senator Joe McCarthy was at its height in the United States, and in Elliott's firm opinion Philby was the victim of a McCarthyite witch-hunt, led by a cabal of lower-class, anti-communist fanatics in MI5.

The Elliotts moved into a house in Wilton Street in Belgravia, just a few minutes from where Philby was lodging in his mother's flat in

Drayton Gardens. Within MI6, Elliott swiftly emerged as Philby's most doughty champion, defending him against all accusers and loudly declaring his innocence. Philby was his friend, his mentor, his ally, and in the world inhabited by Nicholas Elliott, that meant he simply could not be a Soviet spy. This was a friendship Elliott prized above all others; he saw MI5's accusations not just as a test of that bond, but as an assault on the very values of the secret club they had joined in the heat of war. Elliott was standing up for an innocent man, 'guilty only of an unwise friendship'; and in his own mind, he was also defending his tribe, his culture and his class.

But Elliott's resolute defence, and the widespread belief within MI6 that Philby was 'the victim of unsubstantiated conjecture', could not save his job. With both MI5 and the Americans demanding action, Menzies was left with little choice. C summoned his former protégé. Philby knew what was coming. According to some accounts, he may have offered to quit: 'I'm no good to you now ... I think you'd better let me go.' In Philby's version of events, C told him, with 'obvious distress', that he would have to ask for his resignation. His friendship with Burgess, a Soviet spy, had rendered him useless for further work as an MI6 officer. The mere size of his payoff – £4,000, equivalent to more than £32,000 today – was proof that he was leaving with honour, and the support of his service. Philby could 'not possibly be a traitor', Menzies told White. Philby pretended to be sanguine, accepting his role as a scapegoat. But Elliott was furious, and did nothing to hide his belief that a 'dedicated, loyal officer had been treated abominably on the basis of evidence that was no more than paranoid conspiracy theory'.

Philby's glittering career as an MI6 officer was over. He was now unemployed, under suspicion of treason, and under a 'great black cloud' of uncertainty. The family crammed into a rented gatehouse in Heronsgate, deep in the Hertfordshire countryside. Philby spent most of his time in the village pub. He knew he was being watched. Every week or so, a policeman appeared in the village and stood around looking conspicuous. The telephone was bugged, and his mail intercepted, as MI5 gathered evidence and watched to see if he would break cover. The eavesdroppers could find no evidence that he was in contact with the Soviets, but plenty to indicate the continuing support of his colleagues in MI6. Knowing who was listening in, Philby carefully maintained his pose as a man forced out of a job he loved, but without bitterness. 'He said that he had been treated very generously and did not have any recrimination against the old firm.' Elliott tried to cheer him up by joking about the telephone intercepts: 'Personally I would be delighted if MI5 were to bug my own telephone because that would ensure that whenever it went wrong – as from time to time it does – it would be quickly repaired.' Philby may not have found this funny.

Nicholas Elliott called often: his conversations with both Philby and Aileen were carefully logged and transcribed. One of these, intercepted in August, sent a sharp jolt of alarm through MI5, when Aileen was overheard telling Elliott that Philby had gone sailing with a friend, a City businessman with a yacht moored in Chichester on the south coast. 'I suppose he is not doing a "dis"?' Aileen asked Elliott, apparently fearful that her husband might use the boat trip to stage a 'disappearing act', like Burgess and Maclean, and slip over to France. Elliott laughingly reassured her that there was no danger whatever of Philby defecting.

Guy Liddell pondered whether to intercept the sailing party, but concluded that Aileen had only been speaking 'in jest'. In any case, 'it was already too late to stop Philby getting onto the yacht and it seemed equally unjustifiable to issue any warning to the French'. Philby returned home that evening, oblivious to the flap he had caused. But as the evidence mounted, so did MI5's fear that Philby might be planning to make a run for it. In December, the hunters attacked again.

*

The trees were bare beside the road into London, as Philby drove south in answer to another summons from C. The inquiry was entering a new season. 'The case against Philby seems somewhat blacker,' wrote Liddell. As Philby headed towards the office, he imagined that MI5 must have found more evidence, and that the next few hours might be 'sticky'. He was right on both counts. Menzies explained apologetically that a 'judicial inquiry' had now been launched into the disappearance of Burgess and Maclean. Would Philby mind terribly going to MI5 headquarters to answer some more questions? It was an order disguised as an invitation. The Prime Minister, Winston Churchill, had personally approved the decision to bring Philby in for questioning again. Philby's apprehensions were fully realised when he was ushered into a fifth-floor office of Leconfield House, to find a familiar, hefty and distinctly alarming figure awaiting him.

'Hello Buster,' said Philby.

Helenus Patrick Joseph Milmo, universally known as 'Buster', was a barrister of the old school, aggressive, precise, pompous and ruthless. He had not come by his nickname lightly. He liked to flatten his opponents with a barrage of accusation, delivered in a booming baritone with an air of legal omniscience. Philby had witnessed these demolition tactics at first hand during the war when, as MI5's legal adviser, Buster Milmo had joined him in breaking down suspected spies held at Camp 020, the secret interrogation centre in Richmond. After the war, Milmo played a starring role for the prosecution in the Nuremberg trials of Nazi war criminals. He would go on to become a High Court judge. Armed with MI5's dossier, Milmo intended to break Philby and coerce him, by sheer force of argument, into a confession.

Philby sat down and, partly to cover his nerves, took out his pipe and lit it. Milmo instantly told him to put it out, with a sharp reminder that this was a formal judicial inquiry, equivalent to a court of law. This was untrue: the interview had no legal standing, but the exchange set the tone for what followed. Milmo came out with all guns blazing. He accused Philby of spying for the Soviets since the 1930s, sending hundreds to their deaths, betraying Volkov, and tipping off Burgess and Maclean. Philby parried, deflecting and ducking. Milmo then fired his best shot: he revealed that the volume of radio traffic between London and Moscow had jumped dramatically after

Volkov's offer to defect, suggesting a tip-off to Moscow Centre, followed by a similar leap in traffic between Moscow and Istanbul. How did Philby account for this?

Philby shrugged. 'How would I know?'

Milmo moved on to Krivitsky's report of the mysterious Soviet spy sent under journalistic cover to Civil War Spain with a mission to assassinate Franco.

'Who was that young journalist?' Milmo demanded. 'Was it you?'

Philby replied that if the Soviets had really wanted to kill Franco, they would surely have used a professional hitman, not a Cambridge graduate who had never fired a gun. Frustrated, Milmo now overplayed his hand, accusing Philby of handing sensitive papers to Burgess, a charge Philby could refute without even lying.

Milmo next accused Philby of marrying a communist, and smuggling her into Britain. Philby countered that if he had left his Jewish girlfriend in Vienna she would have wound up in a Nazi concentration camp. 'How could I not help her?'

The lawyer was running out of ammunition. At each evasion, Milmo's voice grew louder, his face redder, his manner more bellicose. He banged the table. He snorted in disbelief. He flapped and thrashed.

A stenographer took down every word. In the next room, a posse of senior intelligence officers, including Dick White, Guy Liddell and Stewart Menzies, listened glumly as Milmo grew more enraged, and more ineffectual. 'So far, he has admitted nothing,' Liddell recorded in his diary. 'Milmo is bearing down on him pretty heavily.'

'It all became a shouting match,' said White.

After four hours Milmo was hoarse, Philby was exhausted, and the interrogation had ended in stalemate. Milmo knew Philby was guilty. Philby knew he knew, but he also knew that without a confession, the accusations were legally toothless. 'The interrogation of Philby has been completed without admission,' wrote Liddell that evening, 'although Milmo is firmly of the opinion that he is or has been a Russian agent, and that he was responsible for the leakage about Maclean and Burgess.' Before leaving MI5 headquarters,

Philby was asked to surrender his passport, which he happily did, reflecting that if he needed to flee he would be travelling on false papers provided by his Soviet friends.

'I find myself unable to avoid the conclusion that Philby is and has been for many years a Soviet agent,' Milmo wrote. To White he was even blunter. 'There's no hope of a confession, but he's as guilty as hell.' Reviewing the tapes and the transcript of the Milmo interview, Guy Liddell conceded that Philby, his esteemed former colleague and friend, had failed to behave like a man unjustly accused. 'Philby's attitude throughout was quite extraordinary. He never made any violent protestation of innocence, nor did he make any attempt to prove his case.' But without new, firm evidence, Liddell wrote, Philby 'had all the cards in his hands'. And if Philby was guilty, what of the other friends they shared? What of his good friend Anthony Blunt, who had known both Burgess and Philby? What of Tomás Harris, another former MI5 man, whose home had been the scene of so many well-oiled get-togethers? Fissures of doubt began to creep through the intelligence establishment, as its senior figures eyed one another, and wondered.

Philby described his four-hour grilling to Elliott, angrily insisting that he had been lured into a legal trap. Outraged on his friend's behalf, Elliott complained to Malcolm Cumming, a senior MI5 officer and one of the few Etonians in the Security Service.

> Nicholas Elliott again referred to PEACH's intense anger with MI5 over the Milmo interrogation. He said that PEACH did not in any way object to such an independent interrogation being carried out but he did resent the fact that after his friendly conversations with Dick White, he should be virtually enticed to London under false pretences and then thrown straight into what proved to be a formal inquiry at which even his request to smoke was refused.

As Philby's advocate, Elliott was determined to extract an apology for the way the interrogation had been handled. MI6 was

'counter-attacking', Liddell recorded gloomily, and Elliott was leading the charge.

MI5 was still determined to extract an admission of guilt from
Philby, and now turned to a man who was, in almost every conceiv-
able way, the polar opposite of Buster Milmo. William 'Jim' Skardon,
a former detective inspector in the Metropolitan Police, was
Watcher-in-Chief, head of the surveillance section A4, and by repute
the 'foremost exponent in the country' in the art of interrogation.
Skardon was mild and unassuming in manner; he wore a trilby, a
raincoat, an apologetic expression and a damp moustache. He spoke
in a sibilant, self-effacing whisper, and seldom made eye contact.
Where Milmo relied on intimidation and noise, Skardon wormed
his way into a man's mind by guile and insinuation. He had successfully extracted a confession in January 1950 from Klaus Fuchs, the
atomic spy, winning his confidence during long walks in the country and quiet chats in rural pubs. Skardon uncovered truth by incre-
ments, asking what seemed to be the same questions, subtly varied,
again and again, until his target tripped and became enmeshed in his
own lies. Philby knew a great deal about Skardon, and his reputation.
So when this stooped, unctuous, bland-seeming man knocked on
his door in Heronsgate and asked if he might come in for a cup of
tea, Philby knew he was still in the deepest water.

As both men sucked on their pipes, Skardon seemed to wander,
rather vaguely, from one subject to another, with a 'manner verging
on the exquisite'. Afterwards, Philby thought he had spotted, and
side-stepped, 'two little traps', but wondered anxiously if there had
been others he had failed to detect. 'Nothing could have been more
flattering than the cosy warmth of his interest in my views and
actions.' Skardon reported back to Guy Liddell that his mind
'remained open' on the issue of Philby's guilt. This was the first of
several visits Skardon would pay to Kim Philby over the coming
months, as he probed and prodded, humble, polite, ingenious and
relentless. Then, in January 1952, as abruptly as they had started,
Skardon's interviews ceased, leaving Philby 'hanging', wondering
just how much the detective had detected. 'I would have given a

great deal to have glimpsed his summing up,' he wrote. In fact, Skardon's final report proved that the Philby charm had outlasted Skardon's bogus bonhomie. The interrogator admitted that the hours with Philby had left him with 'a much more favourable impression than I would have expected'. The charges against Philby were 'unproven', Skardon concluded. His passport was returned.

'Investigation will continue and one day final proof of guilt ... may be obtained,' MI5 reported. 'For all practical purposes it should be assumed that Philby was a Soviet spy throughout his service with SIS.' MI6 sharply disagreed: 'We feel that the case against Philby is not proven, and moreover is capable of a less sinister interpretation than is implied by the bare evidence.' And that is how the strange case of Kim Philby remained, for months, and then years, a bubbling unsolved mystery, still entirely unknown to the public, but the source of poisonous discord between the intelligence services. Philby was left in limbo, suspended between the suspicions of his detractors and the loyalty of his friends. Most of the senior officers in MI5 were now convinced that he was guilty, but could not prove it; most of his former colleagues in MI6 remained equally certain of his innocence, but were again unable to find the evidence to exonerate him. There were some in MI5, like Guy Liddell, who clung to the hope that it might all turn out to be a ghastly mistake, and that Philby would eventually be cleared of suspicion; just as there were some in MI6 who harboured doubts about their former colleague, albeit silently, for the sake of the service.

But among those convinced of Philby's guilt was one who knew him better than anyone else, and who was finding it ever harder to remain silent; and that was his wife.

The Robber Barons

When did Aileen Philby, the former store detective, uncover the clues that proved her husband, the Foreign Office high-flier, the doting father, the establishment paragon, was a Soviet spy? Was it when he was summoned home, and lost his job? Or did the appalling realisation come earlier? Did she always suspect there was something fishy about Guy Burgess, her bête noir, who trailed after her husband first to Istanbul, and then Washington? Did the penny drop after Philby locked himself in the basement the day after Burgess's defection, and then drove away with a mysterious bundle and the garden trowel? Or did doubt dawn earlier still, when Philby refused to divorce his first wife, an Austrian communist?

By 1952, Aileen knew that her husband had lied to her, consistently and coldly, from the moment they first met, and throughout their marriage. The knowledge of his duplicity tipped her into a psychological abyss from which she would never fully emerge. She confronted Kim, who denied everything. The ensuing row, far from dissipating her fears, merely confirmed her conviction that he was lying. To others, she began to hint obliquely at her inner turmoil: 'To whom should a wife's allegiance belong?' she asked a friend. 'Her country or her husband?' Questioned by a drunken Tommy Harris at a dinner party, she admitted she was 'suspicious' of her husband, but then backtracked and proclaimed him 'entirely innocent'.

She probably confided in her friend Flora Solomon, who cannot have been wholly surprised since Philby had attempted to recruit her as a Soviet agent back in 1936. Aileen certainly shared her fears with Nicholas Elliott, who blithely laughed off her suspicions. MI5 had assumed that Aileen was joking when she told Elliott that Philby might 'do a "dis"'. She wasn't. She lived in fear that he would defect and join his horrible friend Burgess in Moscow, leaving her with five young children and the perpetual shame of having married a traitor. Each time he left the house, she wondered if he would ever return. She threatened to start legal proceedings to gain custody of the children. She began drinking heavily again. Her grip on reality began to slip.

One day Elliott received a telephone call from Aileen, tearful and slurring.

'Kim's gone.'

'Where?' asked Elliott.

'I think to Russia.'

'How do you know?'

'I got a telegram from Kim.'

At this, even Elliott's granite loyalty wavered for a moment.

'What does the telegram say?' he asked, staggered.

'It says: "Farewell forever. Love to the Children".'

Reeling, Elliott called the duty officer at MI5. An alert was immediately sent out to sea ports and airports, with instructions to intercept Philby if he attempted to leave the country.

Oddly, when asked to produce the telegram, Aileen said she could not, saying it had been read to her over the telephone. Puzzled, Elliott made an inquiry at the Post Office, but could find no trace of a telegram sent to Aileen Philby. Once again, he rang the house in Hertfordshire. It was now late evening. This time, Philby answered. At the sound of his familiar voice, Elliott felt a flood of relief.

'Thank God it's you at last.'

'Who were you expecting it to be?' said Philby.

'I'm glad you're home.'

'Where else would I be at night?'

'The next time I see you I'll tell you where else you could have been tonight,' said Elliott, with a brittle laugh, and rang off.

Aileen had fabricated the entire episode, just as she had invented the story of being attacked in Istanbul, and staged her various maladies and injuries over the years. Elliott was fond and protective of Aileen, but he had become only too familiar with her mental illness. She suffered another series of 'accidents', and drove her car into the front of a shop. Her doctor sent her for psychiatric treatment. Philby told his friends that Aileen was 'insane'. So far from alerting Elliott to the truth, Aileen's behaviour redoubled his sympathy for his beleaguered friend, not only unjustly accused and deprived of his job, but now under attack from a wife who was plainly imagining things. Within MI6, Aileen's suspicions were dismissed as the paranoid ravings of a madwoman.

With five children, one unstable wife and two major drinking habits to support, Philby needed money, but employment was hard to find for a man in his forties, who had ostensibly worked for the Foreign Office, but could not explain why he had left. He toyed with resuming his career in journalism, and submitted a number of articles to newspapers, but could find no permanent position. The telephone intercepts 'disclosed very definitely that Philby was very active in looking for a job', and failing. Finally, Jack Ivens, a 'loyal ex-colleague' from Section V, found him a job in his import-export firm. The salary was a meagre £600 a year. Aileen's mother provided funds for the family to move into a large and ugly Edwardian house in Crowborough, 'the poor man's Surrey' in Graham Greene's words. Philby commuted, miserably, to an office in London, where he filled out paperwork, importing Spanish oranges and exporting castor oil to the US. He did not dare try to re-establish contact with his Soviet controllers. 'Philby was under constant watch,' wrote Yuri Modin. 'Several times our counter-surveillance teams reported the presence of MI5 agents hovering in his vicinity.' He was out in the cold as never before.

Philby had always been a high-functioning, sociable alcoholic. He was fast becoming an ill-functioning one, with a vile temper. MI5, listening in on his telephone line, noted that 'Peach is apt to get blind drunk and behave abominably to his best friends.'

Long-suffering and loyal, Elliott put up with Philby's outbursts. Philby leaned heavily on his old friend. In his strange double world, there was no contradiction here: he genuinely valued Elliott's friendship, needed his support and relied on his advice, while lying to him. Philby did not disguise from Elliott his collapsing marriage but the subject was only ever tackled obliquely. Like most Englishmen of their class, they tended to steer around embarrassing emotional topics.

Elliott lent Philby money when funds ran low, paid his club bills, and took him to watch the cricket at Lord's. He urged Philby to go on the offensive: 'You must fight like hell. If I was accused of spying, I would go to the Prime Minister and complain,' he told him. Philby 'smiled wanly' at this suggestion. 'The whole family went through a bad time,' wrote Elliott, who tried to buoy up his friend by insisting that his exile from MI6 was strictly temporary; Philby would soon be back in the club, and resuming his career where he had left off.

Sir Stewart Menzies was also firm in his support. On 1 April 1952, he took Philby to dinner at the Travellers' Club, and asked him 'whether he wished for any advance of the bonus that was given to him at the time of his resignation'. C later discussed this lunch with Guy Liddell of MI5, who reported:

> C seemed to have reached the conclusion that Kim was innocent. I said that I had come to the conclusion that the only thing to do in cases of this kind, where one knew an individual fairly intimately, was to sink one's personal view and allow those concerned to get on with the job, purely on the basis of ascertainment of facts. Otherwise one was liable to get misled . . . Kim does not, apparently, bear any particular resentment against this department. If he had been in our position he would have reacted in the same way, even down to the question of withholding his passport.

Elliott's conviction that his friend would soon return to the MI6 fold was echoed by Philby's main ally in the US. James Angleton assured a colleague in 1952 that 'Philby would recover from his present predicament and would yet become chief of the British Secret Service.' Philby knew that would never be. Cut off from his Soviet handlers, stuck in an ill-paid job he loathed, expecting MI5 to pounce at any moment, living with a wife who knew his secret, Philby's life was spiralling downwards.

Elliott did what he could to bolster Philby's flagging spirits, dispensing encouragement and support. MI5, combing through the transcripts of Philby's bugged telephone, expressed surprise and irritation at 'the extent to which Peach is still in touch with, and subsidised by, MI6'. Philby's oldest son John was now eleven, and though Philby himself might be committed to destroying the British establishment he was nonetheless anxious to get his sons into a good public school. Eton and Westminster were beyond his budget, but Elliott came up with the solution. He approached his father Claude (now Provost of Eton) who agreed to get John Philby (and later his brother Tommy) into Lord Wandsworth College in Hampshire, 'of which he was governor and which, being heavily endowed, was not too expensive'. The old school tie was still pulling Philby along.

Elliott closely monitored the progress of the Philby case; or rather the lack of it, for the tussle between MI5 and MI6 had settled into acrimonious stalemate. Ronnie Reed, an MI5 officer who had known Philby from the war, noted 'the intense disagreement between our two services on Philby'. In June 1952, Stewart Menzies retired, to be replaced by his deputy, Major General Sir John 'Sinbad' Sinclair, a tall, military traditionalist, set in his ways. (His lunch never varied: one grilled herring and a glass of water.) Sinclair was just as determined as his predecessor to stand by Philby: the new C 'refused to let one of his chaps down'. He did, however, agree that serving MI6 officers should be discouraged from socialising with Philby, a directive which Elliott and others simply ignored. MI5, meanwhile, continued to dig for evidence, convinced that other moles must be lurking inside the establishment, and enraged at the way MI6 had closed ranks. The Watchers listened and observed, waiting for Philby to make a slip.

MI5's telephone intercepts would eventually fill thirty-three volumes: they revealed no espionage on Philby's part, but laid bare the rapidly worsening state of his marriage. He had started an affair with a woman in London, a civil servant, and frequently did not return home for days at a time. When he did, the couple fought bitterly. Philby took to sleeping in a tent in the garden. He told friends that Aileen had denounced him to the Foreign Office, and this had prevented him from getting a decent job. He even claimed she had tried to kill him. Aileen likewise suspected Philby of harbouring murderous designs. Secretly and unethically, her psychiatrist was passing information to MI5. One report noted: 'In [Aileen's] opinion, and that of her psychiatrist, Philby had by a kind of mental cruelty to her "done his best to make her commit suicide".' The same psychiatrist suggested that Philby might be homosexual, despite copious evidence to the contrary. With little money coming in from her estranged husband, Aileen was reduced to working in the kitchen of a grand house on Eaton Square, simply to pay the bills. Nicholas Elliott tried to shore her up, with financial and moral support. Her workplace, he wrote, 'was close enough to our house in Wilton Street to spend her off-duty hours with us'.

After eighteen unhappy months selling castor oil and oranges, Philby found himself jobless again after Jack Ivens's import-export firm went bust. He scratched around, trying to make a living from freelance journalism, but with scant success. He was now virtually dependent on friends and family. His father, living in Saudi Arabia as an adviser to Ibn Saud, sent what money he could spare. Elliott paid the school fees of the Philby children. Tommy Harris arranged for Philby to write a book about the Spanish Civil War for a London publisher with a £600 advance. The book was never written, and the deal appears to have been a ruse by the wealthy Harris to funnel money to his friend without Philby discovering the source.

Philby continued to socialise with his friends in intelligence, but tensely. One evening Guy Liddell went to dinner with Tommy Harris, and discovered that Philby had been invited too. He greeted Philby 'in the normal way', although both knew the situation could hardly have been stranger. MI5 was convinced of Philby's treachery; Harris himself was now under suspicion, his telephone bugged in case some clue emerged during his conversations with Philby. The dinner guests all tried to pretend that the occasion was no different from the many that had preceded it. Philby seemed 'somewhat worried', Liddell wrote in his diary, and left early.

In his darkest moments, Philby considered whether to reactivate his escape plan and defect to Moscow, but there was no way to contact Soviet intelligence without alerting MI5, and he knew it. He was trapped and isolated, aware that he was still just one Soviet defector away from exposure.

★

Vladimir Petrov was a Siberian peasant who, through hard work and docile obedience, had survived Stalin's purges to rise steadily through the ranks of Soviet intelligence. After three decades of service to communism, he was a KGB colonel, and the *rezident* at the Soviet embassy in Canberra. Publicly, Petrov was a time-server; privately, he was a rebel. He had seen his Siberian village destroyed by famine and forced collectivisation. From his work as a cipher clerk, he had learned the full extent of Stalin's crimes. In August 1954, he defected in Australia. His wife Evdokia was picked up by a KGB snatch squad before she could do the same, and then rescued as her captors tried to manhandle her, missing one shoe, aboard a plane in Darwin.

As the highest-ranking defector since the war, Petrov brought a mass of information, on ciphers, agent networks, and the names of some 600 KGB officers working as diplomats around the world. He also furnished the first hard evidence that Burgess and Maclean were indeed in the Soviet Union (hitherto this had been assumed, but unverified), and living in Kuibyshev. Even more explosively, he confirmed that they had been tipped off to escape by another British official, a third man. In Whitehall, Fleet Street and beyond, the identity of this shadowy Third Man became the subject of rumour, innuendo and some highly informed speculation.

Philby heard of Petrov's defection, and waited anxiously for Jim Skardon to reappear on his doorstep, this time with a police posse and arrest warrant. As the weeks passed without a knock on his door, he assumed, rightly, that the defector had not identified him by name. But he was haunted by the 'worry that Petrov had brought in something substantial that I did not know about', which might be used to trip him up if he was interrogated again.

Dick White, Philby's old adversary, was planning precisely such an entrapment, having now taken over as director general of MI5. Guy Liddell had expected to get the post, but his friendships had damaged his reputation beyond repair. MI6 even hinted that Liddell himself might be a gay Soviet spy, pointing out that he 'had parted from his wife, had a faintly homosexual air about him and, during the war, had been a close friend of Burgess, Philby and Blunt'. Bitterly disappointed, Liddell heartily congratulated White on his appointment, and resigned.

White saw the Petrov defection as an opportunity to flush out Philby once and for all, and he urged Anthony Eden, the Foreign Secretary, to put the revelations about a Third Man out in the open. 'It will undermine Philby. It will create uncertainty for Philby. We'll lure him into a new interview and try again to get a confession.' Eden refused, in part because Sir John Sinclair at MI6 insisted White was 'pursuing a vendetta against Philby that was best ignored'. The feud between MI5 and MI6 was as fierce and damaging as ever.

Philby could not know it, but his Soviet masters were observing him, and worried. An assessment drawn up by the KGB British section reported that Agent Stanley was 'desperately short of cash' and drinking heavily. Yuri Modin asked Moscow what to do, pointing out that Philby had 'rendered us immense services [and] might need to be reactivated in the future'. The Centre ordered that Philby be given 'a large sum of money', and a reassurance that the Soviet Union would stand by him. The KGB was not acting out of generosity, or even loyalty, but hard-headed pragmatism: a drunken and destitute spy was a liability, who might confess, or demand to be extricated. A lump of cash would keep him stable, it was hoped, and in place. But the handover (like most of Moscow's directives) was easier ordered than done, since Philby was still under close surveillance. Moreover, Modin was instructed not to make direct personal contact; his mission was to pay Philby, under the noses of MI5, without actually seeing him. The KGB officer had managed to spirit Burgess and Maclean out of England; but getting Philby to stay put would be rather harder.

★

On the evening of 16 June 1954, Professor Anthony Blunt, former MI5 officer, Soviet spy and distinguished art historian, prepared to give a lecture at the Courtauld Institute of Art, of which he was a director. The subject was the Arch of Gallienus, a Roman triumphal arch in danger of demolition to make way for a modern housing project. The audience was composed of eager classicists, art students and learned members of the public who had read about the lecture in *The Times* and wanted to support the worthy cause of protecting Rome's classical heritage. In the front row, facing the lectern, sat a squarely-built, fair-haired young man who had signed the visitors' book in the name Greenglass, and identified himself as Norwegian.

Blunt's long, baggy face wore an expression of scholarly concern as he distributed photographs of the threatened arch, before launching into an attack on the 'villainous Italian authorities' who wanted to do away with it. At the end, everyone clapped, and none more enthusiastically than Greenglass – although he had never been to Italy, knew nothing about classical architecture and could not have cared less if every arch in Rome was bulldozed and covered over in concrete. At the end of the lecture, Professor Blunt was mobbed, as he often was, by a bevy of enthusiastic, upholstered ladies keen to talk about art, who 'vied with one another in showing off their knowledge'. Greenglass hung back on the fringes, and then, rather abruptly, barged through the throng, elbowing one of the professor's admirers in the ribs as he did so, and thrust a postcard of a Renaissance painting into Blunt's hand.

'Excuse me,' asked the rude Norwegian. 'Do you know where I can find this picture?'

Blunt turned the postcard over, while the artistic ladies looked on frostily. On the back was written: 'Tomorrow. 8 p.m. Angel'. The distinctive handwriting, Blunt knew at once, was that of Guy Burgess.

Blunt gave his questioner 'a long stare', and recognised him as Yuri Modin, the Soviet spy handler he had last seen in 1951, just before Burgess and Maclean fled. Then he looked back at the postcard and its message. 'Yes,' he said. 'Yes. Yes.'

The next evening Blunt and Modin met in the Angel pub in Islington off the Caledonian Road, a nondescript drinking hole they had used for clandestine meetings in the past. They spoke first about Blunt's situation – he had been interviewed by MI5, but did not yet seem to be a suspect – before moving on to Philby. Blunt reported that his fellow spy was in poor shape, jobless and penniless, and had already been subjected to a number of hostile interviews by MI5. Modin asked Blunt to pass on some cash to Philby. Reluctantly – for he had long ago forsaken espionage in favour of protecting Roman arches – Blunt agreed.

A few days later, Philby drove from Crowborough to Tonbridge, and bought a ticket for the first train to London. He waited until all the other passengers were aboard and the platform was deserted before boarding. At Vauxhall, he took the Underground to Tottenham Court Road, where he purchased a large coat and hat. For an hour, he wandered around, looking in shop windows to see if he was being followed, then had a drink in a bar, before buying a cinema ticket. He took a seat in the back row. Halfway through the performance, he slipped out. No one seemed to follow him. But for two more hours he walked aimlessly, then hopped on a bus, then jumped off again. By evening, he was in North London: 'I was virtually certain I was clean.'

At dusk, three spies converged on a small square off the Caledonian Road. It appears that Modin, following orders, made no direct contact with Philby that night and spoke only to Blunt as he passed over the package, while Philby kept his distance, ready to run. In Modin's melodramatic recollection, 'the dark silhouette kept pace with us along the tree-lined path; a solid, foursquare figure, shrouded in an overcoat'. Philby returned to Crowborough with £5,000 in cash and a 'refreshed spirit', buoyed by the knowledge that he was back in contact with Soviet intelligence after a four-year hiatus. Modin had also passed on a reassurance, through Blunt, that the defector 'Petrov knew nothing about his career as a Soviet agent'. The handover in the dark London park transformed both Philby's finances and his state of mind. 'I was no longer alone.'

Philby's Soviet friends had rallied to him; his British friends would now do the same. At around the time of the Petrov defection, a group of officers within MI6, led by Nicholas Elliott, launched a concerted campaign to clear his name.

Elliott had by now taken up a new post as head of MI6's London station. Codenamed 'BIN' and based in Londonderry House, Victoria, the London station acted, in effect, like any other MI6 outpost, but on British soil, with a staff of twenty officers running intelligence operations against diplomats, businessmen and spies, recruiting agents in foreign embassies, and monitoring the activities of visiting dignitaries. Elliott's new role enabled him to behave like a spy abroad, but within easy reach of his club.

By 1954, a distinct faction had emerged within MI6, with considerable influence over the chief, Sir John Sinclair: these were the Young Turks of the intelligence service, men like Elliott who had learned the spy game in the heady days of war when, with sufficient grit and imagination, anything had seemed possible. Inside the service, Elliott and his like were known as the 'Robber Barons', swashbuckling types with an acute sense of their own importance and little respect for civilian authority. They believed in covert action, taking risks and, whenever necessary, breaking the rules. Above all, they believed in intelligence as a sort of patriotic religion, a British bulwark against barbarism. George Kennedy Young, a good friend of both Elliott and Philby who would rise to become deputy director of MI6, put into words the creed of this increasingly influential and

ambitious group. 'It is the spy who has been called on to remedy the
situation created by the deficiencies of ministers, diplomats, generals
and priests,' Young insisted, with an arrogance that did not bode well.

> Men's minds are shaped of course by their environments and we
> spies, although we have our professional mystique, do perhaps
> live closer to the realities and hard facts of international relations
> than other practitioners of government. We are relatively free of
> the problems of status, of precedence, departmental attitudes and
> evasions of personal responsibility, which create the official cast
> of mind. We do not have to develop, like Parliamentarians condi-
> tioned by a lifetime, the ability to produce the ready phrase, the
> smart reply and the flashing smile. And so it is not surprising
> these days that the spy finds himself the main guardian of intel-
> lectual integrity.

Men like Young and Elliott saw themselves as Britain's secret guard-
ians, members of a chosen brotherhood unconstrained by normal
conventions. Kim Philby had been a role model for many of the
Robber Barons; his wordly savoir-faire and wartime successes
affirmed their sense of collective identity. They now set out to rescue
him.

On 20 July 1955, 'Sinbad' Sinclair wrote to Dick White, his coun-
terpart in MI5, claiming that Buster Milmo's interrogation of Kim
Philby had been 'biased', and that the former MI6 officer had been
the 'victim of a miscarriage of justice'. In a later memo to Sir Ivone
Kirkpatrick, the Permanent Under-Secretary of State for Foreign
Affairs, 'C' summed up the case for Philby's defence:

> The Milmo Report, which produces no single piece of direct
> evidence to show that Philby was a Soviet agent or that he was
> the 'Third Man', is therefore a case for the prosecution inadmis-
> sible at law and unsuccessful in security intelligence. It is
> constructed of suppositious and circumstantial evidence,
> summing up in a circular argument everything the ingenuity of

a prosecutor could devise against a suspect. It seems likely to remain as a permanently accusing finger pointed at Philby [who] was in fact convicted of nothing by the investigation in 1951 and despite four years of subsequent investigation is still convicted of nothing. It is entirely contrary to the English tradition for a man to have to prove his innocence … in a case where the prosecution has nothing but suspicion to go upon.

The case should be re-examined, he said, and Philby given an opportunity to defend himself. 'Produce the evidence, and there'll be no further dispute,' Sinclair told White. White reluctantly agreed that Philby should be interviewed once more, knowing that the case against him was not much stronger than it had been in 1951. The stage was now set for a final showdown, and Elliott, Philby's 'greatest defender', would be waiting in the wings to stage-manage the drama.

On 18 September, the *People* newspaper broke the story of Vladimir Petrov's defection, with a series of dramatic revelations: Burgess and Maclean had both been recruited as Soviet agents while students at Cambridge; their flight to Moscow, just as Maclean was about to be arrested, had been orchestrated by the Soviet intelligence service; these were not 'missing diplomats', as the government had maintained for so long, but spies on the run. British secrecy laws had been used to hide the truth and shield the government from embarrassment.

Harold Macmillan, the new Foreign Secretary, faced a major crisis: 'We are going to have to say something,' he said gloomily. Five days later, the government issued an eight-page White Paper purporting to explain the Burgess and Maclean affair. It was a peculiar mixture of half-truth and evasion that played down the scandal and made no mention of Kim Philby, whose name was now being widely whispered, and in some cases, shouted. At a dinner party, Aileen Philby rose unsteadily to her feet and upbraided her husband: 'I know you are the Third Man.' Even Philby's wife was denouncing him in public; the press would not be far behind. The White Paper was dismissed as a cover-up.

On the other side of the Atlantic, J. Edgar Hoover was as convinced of Philby's guilt as James Angleton was sure of his innocence, and enraged at Britain's failure to arrest him. The FBI chief decided to bring matters to a head, with a characteristic act of subterfuge. But first, Philby prepared for one last interrogation.

On 7 October, two weeks after the publication of the White Paper, Philby presented himself at an MI6 safe house near Sloane Square, where he was ushered into a room furnished with a patterned sofa and chairs arranged around a small table; on one wall stood an ancient sideboard with a telephone on top. Inside the telephone was a high-quality microphone. An amplifier, placed under the floorboards beneath Philby's chair, fed sound to the microphone, which was then relayed to Leconfield House, MI5 headquarters. Here the conversation would be recorded on acetate gramophone records, and then handed to typists who would transcribe every word.

Philby was nervous. This would be his fourth formal interrogation. Despite Modin's reassurances, he feared Petrov might have armed the investigators with some damning new clue. Philby had told MI6 he 'welcomed the chance to clear his name', but in truth he was tired, and worried. He braced himself for another flaying.

Instead, what he experienced was closer to a fireside chat than an inquisition, an interview utterly different from any that had come before. A committee of inquiry, set up by Macmillan, had formally ruled that this round of questioning should be the responsibility of MI6, not MI5. This would not be an inquisition, in the manner of Buster Milmo, but an internal review of the situation carried out by two of Philby's former colleagues 'who knew him well'. It seems probable that one of them was Nick Elliott.

As the conversation started, and the recording machines began to spin, MI5 officers listened with mounting fury as Philby was given the lightest possible grilling by his friends. 'To call it an interrogation would be a travesty,' one MI5 officer later wrote.

It was an in-house MI6 interview . . . they took him gently over familiar ground. First his communist past, then his MI6 career and his friendship with Guy Burgess. Philby stuttered and stammered and protested his innocence. But listening to the disembodied voices, the lies seemed so clear. Whenever Philby floundered, one or other of his questioners guided him to an acceptable answer. 'Well, I suppose such and such could be an explanation.' Philby would gratefully agree and the interview would move on.

Philby was sent home with a friendly handshake and a not-guilty verdict: 'You may be pleased to know that we have come to a unanimous decision about your innocence'. Philby was jubilant. 'The trail had become stale and muddy,' he wrote. 'The fact that I had made no attempt to escape over a long period was beginning to tell heavily in my favour.' When Dick White read the transcripts, he was 'livid'; the MI5 transcribers formally put on record their 'belief that one of the questioners was prejudiced in Philby's favour, repeatedly helping him find answers to awkward questions and never pressing questions which he failed to answer'. The Robber Barons had launched a highly effective counter-attack. But Philby was not yet safe.

Just over a week later, on Sunday 23 October 1955, the Philby family awoke to find their home surrounded by a pack of journalists in full hue and cry. That morning in New York, the *Sunday News* had run a story naming Philby as the 'Third Man', the 'tipster' who had helped the defectors to flee. This was the work of Hoover, who had leaked Philby's name to a tame journalist, to force the British into launching a full judicial investigation. For more than four years Philby's name had been kept out of the newspapers, despite being common knowledge on Fleet Street. Now the hunt was on. 'The house at Crowborough was besieged,' reported Elliott, who advised Philby to hold off the press as long as possible. If British newspapers repeated what the *Sunday News* had reported, they could be sued for libel. But Philby's name was now in print, and everyone was talking about the Third Man. It took two days more before the dam burst.

The Third Man

Colonel Marcus Lipton MP, the Labour member for Brixton, was a stuffy, old-fashioned trouble-maker, who distrusted government and loathed modern music, which he believed would bring down the monarchy. 'If pop music is going to be used to destroy our established institutions, then it must be destroyed first,' he once declared. He specialised in asking awkward questions. No one ever accused Lipton of being subtle, but he had a firm grip on political procedure, and in particular 'parliamentary privilege', the ancient right of MPs to make statements in Westminster without danger of prosecution.

On Tuesday 25 October, he rose to his feet during Prime Minister's Questions, and dropped a bombshell:

> Has the Prime Minister made up his mind to cover up at all costs the dubious third man activities of Mr Harold Philby who was first secretary at the Washington embassy a little time ago, and is he determined to stifle all discussions on the very great matters which were evaded in the White Paper, which is an insult to the intelligence of the country?

This was raw meat for the press: a feeding frenzy erupted.

That afternoon, on a London Underground train heading home, Kim Philby's eyes idly wandered to the newspaper headline on the front page of the first edition of his neighbour's copy of the *Evening*

Standard: 'MP talks of "Dubious Third Man Activities of Mr Harold Philby".' The newspaper reported Lipton's words verbatim. After more than two decades in hiding, Philby had been flushed into the open.

Back in Crowborough, Philby immediately called Nicholas Elliott.

'My name is in the newspapers. I have to do something.'

Elliott was calm. 'I agree with you. Certainly. But let's think about it for a day, at least. Don't do anything for a day, all right? I'll call you tomorrow.'

Making a statement at this stage would only add fuel to an already raging fire, and 'might prejudice the case'. If Marcus Lipton had new evidence implicating Philby, he would surely have passed it on to the authorities and MI5 would have acted on it. The MP was simply repeating what had already appeared in the American press, under cover of parliamentary privilege. Harold Macmillan, as the minister in charge of the Foreign Office and MI6, would have to make a statement, either supporting Philby, or damning him: since MI5 plainly lacked the evidence to prosecute, there was a good chance Philby might be exonerated. Elliott's advice was to stand firm, say nothing, ride out the storm, and allow his friends in MI6 to go to work on his behalf.

'We've decided that you naturally must respond,' Elliott told him the next day. 'But it should be done only when the parliamentary debates begin. Please bear up for two weeks.'

The Crowborough house presented a bizarre spectacle, with dozens of journalists camped out on the lawn. They followed Philby to the pub at lunchtime, and then trailed him back again, asking questions which he declined, most politely, to answer. The telephone rang incessantly. The *Sunday Express* posted a letter through the front door, offering £100 if Philby would take part in a public debate with Marcus Lipton. Elliott worried about the 'additional stress for Aileen and the children', and helped to spirit them away to stay with a relative. Philby himself took refuge with his mother in her South Kensington flat, where he disconnected the doorbell and stuffed the telephone under a pile of cushions. The press tore off the door knocker in their efforts to gain access. A journalist tried to climb in through the fire escape, terrifying the cook.

The government had promised to make a statement and hold a debate on 7 November. Elliott now set to work ensuring that when Macmillan came to speak, he would say the right thing. The man selected to brief the Foreign Secretary on this tricky issue was none other than Richard Brooman-White, Elliott's friend from Eton and Trinity, who had helped to recruit Philby into MI6 during the war. Brooman-White had left the secret service for a career in politics, and in 1951 was elected Conservative MP for Rutherglen. Philby, Elliott and Brooman-White had been friends since 1939. When Parliament was sitting, Brooman-White lived in the top floor of Elliott's house in Wilton Street; Elizabeth Elliott worked as his secretary; Claudia Elliott was his goddaughter; Elliott and Brooman-White even shared ownership of a racehorse. Brooman-White was the parliamentary voice of the Robber Barons, and Philby's most vigorous defender in the House of Commons. In Philby's words, Elliott, Brooman-White and his other allies remained 'absolutely convinced I had been accused unfairly [and] simply could not imagine their friend could be a communist. They sincerely believed me and supported me.'

The brief Brooman-White drew up for Macmillan purported to be unbiased, but 'leaned heavily in favour of Philby's innocence'. There was no hard evidence, Brooman-White insisted; his former colleague had lost his job simply because of a youthful dalliance with communism and an ill-advised friendship with Guy Burgess. These views chimed with Macmillan's own instincts. An aristocratic Old Etonian, Macmillan regarded intelligence work as faintly dirty, and the row over Philby as an unnecessary spat between MI5 and MI6. He dearly wished to avoid a scandal, let alone a trial. 'Nothing would be worse than a lot of muckraking and innuendo,' Macmillan told the Cabinet, just five days before Lipton launched his attack. The Foreign Secretary simply wanted this embarrassing, unseemly mess to go away.

On 7 November, Macmillan rose in the House of Commons, and made a statement that might have been written by Nicholas Elliott and Richard Brooman-White, and probably was.

> Mr Philby had Communist associates during and after his university days [but] no evidence has been found to show that he was responsible for warning Burgess or Maclean. While in Government service he carried out his duties ably and conscientiously. I have no reason to conclude that Mr Philby has at any time betrayed the interests of this country, or to identify him with the so-called 'third man' if, indeed, there was one.

Richard Brooman-White followed up with a rousing defence of Philby – 'a man whose name has been smeared' – and a ferocious attack on Marcus Lipton as a McCarthyite witch-hunter, too cowardly to repeat his allegations outside the House of Commons and face the legal consequences.

> He [Lipton] is in favour of acting on suspicion, of smearing on suspicion, by directing public suspicion on to an individual against whom nothing at all has been proved. We must leave it to his own conscience to straighten out what that may cost in personal suffering to the wife, children and friends of the person involved. The only thing that has been proved against Mr Philby is that he had Burgess staying with him and he had certain Communist friends. He may not have been very wise in his choice of friends, but what honourable member of this House could say that all his friends were people against whom no shadow of suspicion could ever be cast?

From the Labour benches came grumbling claims of another whitewash. 'Whoever is covering up whom and on what pretext, whether because of the membership of a circle or a club, or because of good fellowship or whatever it may be, they must think again and think quickly,' declared Frank Tomney MP, a tough northerner.

Lipton tried to fight back. 'I will not be gagged by anybody in this House or outside in the performance of my duty,' he blustered. 'Say it outside!' chorused the Tories. Lipton limply responded: 'Even Mr Philby has not asked for it to be repeated outside.' He then sat down, visibly sagging.

Philby now went in for the kill. Elliott had tipped him off that he would be cleared by Macmillan, but mere exoneration was not enough: he needed Lipton to retract his allegations, publicly, humiliatingly and quickly. After a telephone consultation with Elliott, he instructed his mother to inform all callers that he would be holding a press conference in Dora's Drayton Gardens flat the next morning.

*

When Philby opened the door a few minutes before 11 a.m. on 8 November, he was greeted with gratifying proof of his new celebrity. The stairwell was packed with journalists from the world's press. 'Jesus Christ!' he said. 'Do come in.' Philby had prepared carefully. Freshly shaved and neatly barbered, he wore a well-cut pinstriped suit, a sober and authoritative tie, and his most charming smile. The journalists trooped into his mother's sitting room, where they packed themselves around the walls. Camera flashes popped. In a conspicuous (and calculated) act of old world gallantry, Philby asked a journalist sitting in an armchair if he would mind giving up his seat to a lady journalist forced to stand in the doorway. The man leapt to his feet. The television cameras rolled.

What followed was a dramatic tour de force, a display of cool public dishonesty that few politicians or lawyers could match. There was no trace of a stammer, no hint of nerves or embarrassment. Philby looked the world in the eye with a steady gaze, and lied his head off. Footage of Philby's famous press conference is still used as a training tool by MI6, a master class in mendacity.

Philby first read a prepared statement, explaining that he had not spoken out before because, having signed the Official Secrets Act, he could not legally disclose information derived from his position as a government official. 'The efficiency of our security services can only be reduced by publicity given to their organisation, personnel and techniques,' he intoned, sounding exactly like a Whitehall mandarin upholding the ancient rules of British secrecy. Edwin Newman, an American journalist with NBC, was delegated to ask the questions:

If there was a third man, were you in fact the third man?

No, I was not.

Do you think there was one?

No comment.

Mr Philby, you yourself were asked to resign from the Foreign Office a few months after Burgess and Maclean disappeared. The Foreign Secretary said in the past you had communist associations. That is why you were asked to resign?

I was asked to resign because of an imprudent association.

That is your association with Burgess?

Correct.

What about the alleged communist associations? Can you say anything about them?

The last time I spoke to a communist, knowing him to be a communist, was some time in 1934.

That implies that you have spoken to communists unknowingly and not known about it.

Well, I spoke to Burgess last in April or May, 1951.

He gave you no idea that he was a communist at all?

Never.

Would you still regard Burgess, who lived with you for a while in Washington, as a friend of yours? How do you feel about him now?

I consider his action deplorable . . .

And here Philby paused, for just a beat: a man, it seemed, wrestling with his own conflicted feelings, his duty, conscience and personal loyalty, and the pain of betrayal by a dear friend.

. . . on the subject of friendship, I'd prefer to say as little as possible, because it's very complicated.

As for Lipton, Philby invited his accuser to repeat his allegations outside the House of Commons, or else hand over whatever information he had to the proper authorities.

The press conference came to an end. Philby, ever the generous host, served the assembled journalists beer and sherry in his mother's dining room. 'I see you understand the habits of the press very well,' joked an American reporter. The resulting press coverage contained no suggestion that Philby was anything other than an honest, upright government official, brought down by his friendship with a secret communist, and now definitively absolved. The Soviet intelligence officer Yuri Modin watched the press conference on the evening news, and marvelled at Philby's 'breathtaking' performance: 'Kim played his cards with consummate cunning. We concluded, just as he had, that the British government had no serious evidence against him.'

Marcus Lipton had no choice but to retreat in ignominy, formally withdrawing his accusations, which he 'deeply regretted'.

'My evidence was insubstantial,' the MP admitted. 'When it came to a showdown my legal advisers counselled me to retract.' Philby issued a clipped and gracious statement: 'Colonel Lipton has done the right thing. So far as I am concerned, the incident is now closed.'

Philby's triumph was complete. Elliott was 'overjoyed' at Philby's victory and the prospect of bringing him back into the firm. The Robber Barons would now actively 'seek his reemployment by his old service', which in turn raised the prospect, for Philby, of 'further service to the Soviet cause'.

Elliott had rehabilitated his old friend, just as his own career was about to take a most almighty dive.

★

In the dawn light of 19 April 1956, a peculiar figure in a rubber diving suit and flippers waddled sideways down the King's Stairs at Portsmouth Harbour, and clambered into a waiting dinghy. The man was no more than five feet five inches tall. On his head he wore a woolly balaclava with a diving cap on top, and on his back a tank with enough oxygen for a ninety-minute dive. He was a decorated war hero, Britain's most famous frogman, and his name was Commander Lionel 'Buster' Crabb.

In the distance, through the drifting mist, loomed the faint shapes of three Soviet warships, newly arrived in Britain on a goodwill mission and berthed alongside the Southern Railway Jetty. An oarsman rowed the boat out some eighty yards offshore. Crabb adjusted his air tank, picked up a new experimental camera issued by the Admiralty Research Department, and extinguished the last of the cigarettes he had smoked continuously since waking. His task was to swim underneath the Soviet cruiser *Ordzhonikidze*, explore and photograph her keel, propellers and rudder, and then return. It would be a long, cold swim, alone, in extremely cold and dirty water, with almost zero visibility at a depth of about thirty feet. The job might have daunted a much younger and healthier man. For a forty-seven-year-old, unfit, chain-smoking depressive, who had been extremely drunk a few hours earlier, it was close to suicidal.

The mission, codenamed 'Operation Claret', bore all the hallmarks of a Nicholas Elliott escapade: it was daring, imaginative, unconventional and completely unauthorised.

Seven months earlier, Nikita Khrushchev had announced that he would visit Britain for the first time, accompanied by his premier, Nikolai Bulganin. The First Secretary of the Soviet Communist Party would travel aboard the latest Russian cruiser, the *Ordzhonikidze,* escorted by two destroyers. The Soviet leader would then be taken by special train to London, and dine at Number Ten with the Prime Minister, Anthony Eden. The visit was hailed by diplomats as an important thaw in the Cold War. The spies saw other opportunities.

The Soviets were rumoured to have developed a new type of propeller, as well as enhanced underwater sonar technology to evade submarines. With the arms race running at full tilt, MI6 and Naval Intelligence wanted to find out more. There was also an element of tit for tat. British warships had recently docked in Leningrad, and 'frogmen had popped up all over the place', in Elliott's words. Anything the Soviets could do, MI6 could do better, and more secretly.

The intelligence services sprang into action. MI5 set about bugging the Soviet leader's suite at Claridge's Hotel, and installed a listening device in the telephone. The Naval Intelligence Department urged that the investigation of the undersides of the Soviet vessels be undertaken as 'a matter of high intelligence priority'. Elliott, the London station chief for MI6, was charged with exploiting this golden opportunity for espionage. As he put it, with typical ribaldry: 'We wanted a closer look at those Russian ladies' bottoms.' He knew just the man for the job.

Lionel Crabb earned his nickname from the American actor, athlete and pin-up Buster Crabbe, who had played Flash Gordon in the film series and won a gold medal for swimming at the 1932 Olympics. In almost every way, the English Buster Crabb was entirely unlike his namesake, being English, tiny, and a poor swimmer (without flippers, he could barely complete three lengths of a swimming pool). With his long nose, bright eyes and miniature frame, he might have been an aquatic garden gnome. He was, however, spectacularly brave, and supremely resilient. Born to a poor family in South London, he first served in the Merchant Navy and then joined the Royal Navy after the outbreak of war, training as a diver. In 1942 he was dispatched to Gibraltar, to take part in the escalating underwater battle around the Rock, where Italian frogmen, using manned torpedoes and limpet mines, were sinking thousands of tons of Allied shipping. Crabb and his fellow divers set out to stop them, with remarkable success, blowing up enemy divers with depth charges, intercepting torpedoes and peeling mines off the hulls of ships. When war ended, Crabb cleared mines from the ports of Venice and Livorno, and when the militant Zionist group Irgun began attacking British ships with underwater explosives, he was called in to defuse them. The risks were staggering, but Crabb survived and was duly awarded the George Medal for 'undaunted devotion to duty'. He became, briefly, a celebrity. Small boys mobbed him, and he frequently appeared in the newspapers. Long after demobilisation, Crabb continued to do odd, secret or particularly dangerous underwater jobs for the Navy.

Elliott had got to know Crabb during the war, and considered him 'a most engaging man of the highest integrity ... as well as

CLOSING CITY PRICES

SHERRY
GONZALEZ
TIO PEPE
PRODUCE OF SPAIN

Evening Standard

40,863   TUESDAY, OCTOBER 25, 1955   ●● Twopence

ROOTES
CAR HIRE
RING CUNNINGHAM 5141
ABBEY HALL, ABBEY RD., LONDON, N.W.I

EDEN REJECTS INQUIRY INTO MACLEAN CASE

But early debate is promised

General Lopes rides to the Palace

MP TALKS OF 'DUBIOUS THIRD MAN ACTIVITIES OF MR. HAROLD PHILBY'

Sir Anthony Eden refused in the Commons this afternoon to appoint a select committee to investigate the disappearance of Burgess and Maclean and the efficiency of civil service security arrangements in general.

But he said it was desirable to have an early debate on the subject and he would be glad to take part.

Colonel Marcus Lipton (Soc., Brixton) had asked the Prime Minister whether he would appoint a select committee.

"No, sir," replied Sir Anthony Eden.

Colonel Lipton then asked: "Has he made up his mind to cover up at all costs the dubious 'third man' activities of Mr. Harold Philby, who was First Secretary of the Washington Embassy a little while ago, and is he determined to stifle all discussion on the very grave matters he evaded in the wretched White Paper which was an insult to the intelligence of the country?"

Early debate

The Prime Minister said that his answer referred only to the question of a select committee and to this, the reply remained "No."

He went on: "So far as the wider issues raised in the supplementary are concerned, the Government themselves take the view that it is desirable to have a debate and an early debate on this subject.

"I personally, as Prime Minister, would be glad to take part."

Mr. Alfred Robens (Soc., Blyth) asked the Prime Minister whether he had "made any investigation as to the reason why briefs supplied by Foreign Office officials to Ministers answering questions in this House had been so much at variance with the facts of the case?"

Sir Anthony suggested that this might be one of the matters to be raised in the debate.

The Speaker then called the next question.

FOOTNOTE: Mr. Harold Philby lives at Crowborough, Sussex. He joined the Foreign Office after the war with the rank of First Secretary and was posted to Washington.

Mr. Philby, father of five children, is now a free-lance journalist.

Lord Elton asks about Maclean

Earlier in the House of Lords, Lord Elton raised the case of Donald Maclean. He pointed out that a White Paper had now disclosed that Maclean, who had already been guilty of "serious misconduct," had for some time before he disappeared in May, 1951, been under the grave suspicion of being an enemy agent.

He asked the Government to explain statements in reply to a question on October 28, 1953, that Maclean had performed his official duties satisfactorily up to the date of his disappearance and that they knew his background.

◄ Back Page, Col. Five

MISS SHIRLEY HAMPTON
Looking for a ring.

GORDON PIRIE TO MARRY SHIRLEY HAMPTON

Evening Standard Reporter

Gordon Pirie, the 24-year-old British runner, who defeated Zatopek, is to marry 20-year-old Miss Shirley Hampton.

She is also an athlete—the only child of Mr. and Mrs. Harold Hampton, of Crofton Road, Orpington.

Gordon Pirie and Shirley lunched together in London today before making a second attempt to buy an engagement ring. When they tried yesterday they could not find the one they wanted.

Mrs. Hampton said "There will be no special celebration tonight. Gordon has to continue his training. Shirley plans to go to an old girls reunion at her Eltham school."

Said Mrs. Pirie "They became engaged during the weekend."

She did not tell

Miss Hampton works in the accounts department of Shell Tankers, White Kennett Street, City.

A colleague said "she came into the office at the usual time this morning, but left about 10 o'clock. She did not tell us where she was going. She did not mention her engagement."

Shirley was runner-up in the 220 yards in the women's championships this year and was in the British team with Gordon Pirie that competed in Moscow and Prague last month.

CABINET HEARS BUDGET SECRETS

Evening Standard Political Correspondent

The Cabinet met today for a preview of Mr. Butler's supplementary Budget, which he will introduce in the Commons tomorrow.

The Chancellor has now completed his speech. It will last about 75 minutes.

Besides acquainting Ministers with its contents, Mr. Butler briefed them for the socialist attack that will follow.

The Opposition is preparing to censure the Government's economic policy in the strongest terms. The Budget debate on Thursday and Friday will undoubtedly be the toughest that Sir Anthony Eden's administration has yet experienced.

HOUSING SUBSIDIES

Mr. Duncan Sandys, the Minister of Housing, announced in the House of Commons today that he would make a statement later this week on the housing subsidies.

Missing girl found

Sarah Grubb, 16-year-old daughter of the Rev. Geoffrey Watkin Grubb, rector of Cranfield, Beds, who disappeared from her home on Sunday, has been found at Eastbourne, staying with a relative.

The *Evening Standard* headline identifying Philby as the Third Man.

Marcus Lipton MP, defender of parliamentary privilege, enemy of pop music and Philby's primary accuser.

Philby's second wife, Aileen, besieged by the press in October 1955 at the family home in Crowborough.

She made no comment, despite knowing that Philby was guilty.

Aileen would die inside this house, after Philby's departure for Beirut, alcoholic and alone.

James Angleton would later claim that he had long suspected Philby was a spy. The evidence suggests otherwise.

J. Edgar Hoover, the FBI director, was convinced of Philby's treachery and enraged that he had not been prosecuted.

Helenus 'Buster' Milmo, the MI5 barrister who subjected Philby to cross-examination and declared: 'He's as guilty as hell.'

Jim Skardon, former police detective, head of the surveillance section, and MI5's chief interrogator. He set out to break Philby.

Dick White became Director General of MI5 in 1953 and chief of MI6 in 1956. He hunted Philby for over a decade.

Out in the cold: Kim Philby in Moscow. The veteran spy insisted Russia was his 'homeland' while describing himself as 'wholly and irreversibly English', and was never fully trusted by the KGB.

Soviet intelligence officer Anatoly Golitsyn, whose defection rekindled the Philby investigation.

Flora Solomon, Philby's old friend, told MI5 that he had attempted to recruit her for 'dangerous' work in the communist cause in 1935.

George Blake, the Soviet spy within MI6 who was arrested, prosecuted and sentenced to forty-two years in prison.

Philby's disappearance from Beirut, and subsequent reappearance in Moscow, prompted a media frenzy.

The last photograph of Kim Philby together with his father. In 1960,
St John visited his son in Beirut, went to a cocktail party, made a pass at
a member of the embassy staff, and died. The loss of his father plunged
Kim Philby into a deep alcoholic despair.

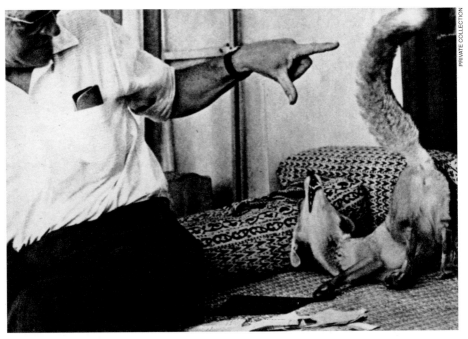

Philby playing with his pet fox, Jackie. The death of this animal left him 'inconsolable'.

Nicholas Elliott in casual pose in
the family's Beirut apartment.

Kim Philby, drunk, at a picnic
in the hills outside Beirut.

A party at the Copelands'. *From left to right*: Eleanor Philby, Kim Philby, Miles Copeland,
Nicholas Elliott, Lorraine Copeland and Elizabeth Elliott. Three spies serving three
intelligence agencies: MI6, the CIA and the KGB.

Kim and Eleanor Philby, his third wife, relax at the luxury bathing hut they shared with the Elliotts on Beirut's Khalde Beach.

Philby relaxes in a mountain pool. These were the 'happiest years', wrote Eleanor.

Prime Minister Anthony Eden gave instructions that no covert operations should take place during the Russian visit. Operation Claret went ahead anyway.

Nikita Khrushchev, First Secretary of the Soviet Communist Party, and his premier, Nikolai Bulganin, are welcomed to Britain.

Commander Lionel 'Buster' Crabb, the most famous frogman in Britain, is mobbed by a group of young admirers.

Buster Crabb prepares for a dive.

The Soviet cruiser *Ordzhonikidze* and curious crowds in Portsmouth harbour.

'On the subject of friendship, I'd prefer to say as little as possible.'

Philby's moment of triumph. His Soviet handler, Yuri Modin, described his performance as 'breathtaking'.

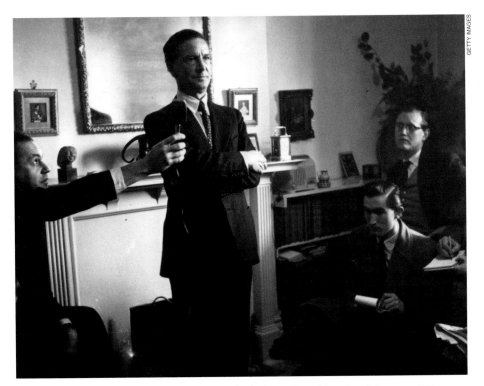

Philby invited the world's press into his mother's flat to hear him clear his name. 'Were you in fact the Third Man?' one journalist asked. Philby answered: 'No, I was not.'

'The last time I spoke to a communist, knowing him to be a communist, was some time in 1934.'

Richard Brooman–White, MP. With Elliott's help, the former MI6 officer drew up a brief for Macmillan, stoutly defending Philby.

Sir John 'Sinbad' Sinclair, head of MI6, accused MI5 of pursuing a vendetta against Philby.

Harold Macmillan, Foreign Secretary in 1955, told the House of Commons there was 'no reason' to suspect Philby of treachery.

James Jesus Angleton never recovered from Philby's betrayal, and launched a mole-hunt that inflicted huge damage on the CIA.

Nicholas Elliott in 1992. He never stopped wondering how a man who had seemed so similar to him in every way could have been so utterly different.

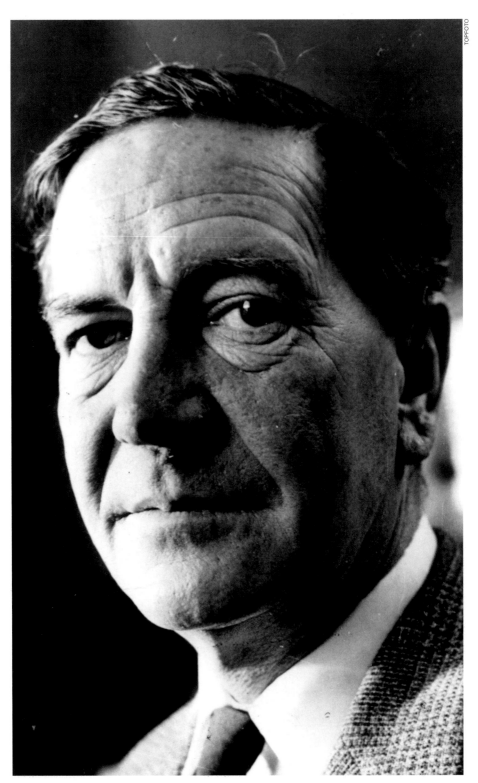

Kim Philby: 'I have always operated on two levels, a personal level and a political one. When the two have come into conflict I have had to put politics first.'

being the best frogman in the country, probably in the world'. He cut a remarkable figure in civilian life, wearing beige tweeds, a monocle and a pork pie hat, and carrying a Spanish swordstick with a silver knob carved into the shape of a crab. But there was another, darker side to this 'kindly bantam cock'. Crabb suffered from deep depressions, and had a weakness for gambling, alcohol and barmaids. When taking a woman out to dinner he liked to dress up in his frog-man outfit; unsurprisingly, this seldom had the desired effect, and his emotional life was a mess. In 1956 he was in the process of getting divorced after a marriage that had lasted only a few months. He worked, variously, as a model, undertaker and art salesman, but like many men who had seen vivid wartime action, he found peace a pallid disappointment. He was also feeling his age. When Elliott contacted him, Buster Crabb was working at Espresso Furnishings in Seymour Place, selling tables to cafés. Crabb accepted the mission without hesi-tation. He wanted, he said, 'to get m' feet wet again, get m' gills back'. Money was not discussed. Instead, Elliott joked that if the investigation of the *Ordzhonikidze* proved successful, Crabb could be assured of 'supplies of whisky for many years'. Others were doubtful that Crabb was up to the task. John Henry, the MI6 technical officer, pointed out that the diver seemed to be 'heading for a heart attack'. But Elliott insisted that 'Crabb was still the most experienced frogman in England, and totally trustworthy . . . He begged to do the job for patriotic as well as personal motives.' Ted Davies, a former sailor who headed MI6's naval liaison unit, was assigned as his case officer.

Operation Claret proceeded with the sort of smoothness that suggested no one in authority was paying adequate attention. Michael Williams, a Foreign Office official recently posted to over-see MI6, was handed a list of possible operations for the Soviet visit. 'The dicey operations [are] at the beginning of the file and the safer ones at the back,' he was told. Williams was distracted by the death of his father that morning. A short while later he handed the file back without comment. MI6 assumed this amounted to Foreign Office approval; Williams assumed someone senior to him must already have given the go-ahead; the Admiralty assumed that MI6 was responsible, since it was carrying out the mission; and MI6 assumed the Admiralty was in the driving seat, since it had asked for the information in the first place. And the Prime Minister assumed that no spies were doing anything, because that was exactly what he had ordered them to do.

Back in September, when the Khrushchev trip was first mooted, Anthony Eden stated categorically: 'These ships are our guests and, however we think others would behave, we should take no action which involves the slightest risk of detection.' Eden shared Macmillan's distaste for spying, and was not about to have the adventurers of MI6 spoiling this moment of delicate international diplomacy. When Elliott was later quizzed about who had signed off on the operation, and in what capacity, his shrugging reply was most revealing. 'We don't have a chain of command. We work like a club.'

A week before the Soviet delegation arrived, Anthony Eden learned that plans were being hatched for underwater surveillance of the *Ordzhonikidze,* and put his foot down even more firmly. 'I am sorry, but we cannot do anything of this kind on this occasion,' he wrote. Elliott would later insist that the 'operation was mounted after receiving a written assurance of the Navy's interest and in the firm belief that government clearance had been given'. He either did not know about the Prime Minister's veto or, more likely, didn't care.

Kim Philby, meanwhile, was in Ireland. Immediately after the triumphant press conference, William Allen, a friend who had been press counsellor at the British embassy in Turkey, offered him a job writing a centenary history of his family firm, David Allen & Sons, a large printing and poster company. Allen was an Old Etonian, and it is possible that Elliott had a hand in arranging what was, in effect, a 'working holiday'. Allen was also a fascist sympathiser, a close friend of Oswald Mosley and as far removed from his guest, politically, as it was possible to be. This did not stop Philby from spending several months living at Allen's expense in the family home in County Waterford, writing a very boring book about printing, ink and paper.

He returned to Britain just as Operation Claret was being uncorked. Philby knew 'Crabbie' well. As head of the Iberian section of Section V, he had been involved in Crabb's wartime exploits off Gibraltar. Elliott would surely have been unable to resist telling Philby that he had brought the great frogman, their old comrade in arms, out of retirement in order to pay an underwater call on the visiting Soviet delegation.

The day before the Soviet mini flotilla was due to arrive, Buster Crabb and Ted Davies took the train to Portsmouth and checked in to the Sally Port Hotel. Davies, somewhat unimaginatively, signed in as 'Smith', but added 'attached Foreign Office'; Crabb signed the hotel register in his own name. He then contacted a friend, Lieutenant George Franklin, the diving instructor from the training ship HMS *Vernon*, who had agreed, unofficially, to help him prepare for the dive and supply additional equipment. The next day Crabb watched through powerful binoculars as the Soviet warships cruised into port. Then he went on a bender. Crabb had many friends in Portsmouth, and they all wanted to buy him a drink. During his prolonged pub crawl, Crabb was heard to boast that he was being paid sixty guineas to go 'down to take a dekko at the Russian bottoms'. The night before the dive, Crabb drank five double whiskies, with a similar number of beer 'chasers'.

The next morning, Franklin helped him into his two-piece Pirelli diving suit, purchased from Heinke of Chichester, handed him his flippers, and adjusted the valves on his air tank. Two uniformed policemen escorted them through the docks, and down the King's Stairs. Franklin rowed the boat, while Crabb sat smoking in the stern. At around 7 a.m., Crabb checked his gear for the last time, and slipped backwards over the gunwale with a gentle splash, leaving behind a trail of bubbles in the murky water. Twenty minutes later, he reappeared, a little breathless, and asked Franklin to attach 'an extra pound of weight'. Then he was gone.

Aboard the *Ordzhonikidze,* the Soviets were waiting.

What happened next has been a matter of conjecture, imaginative guesswork and a great deal of pure fantasy ever since.

In 2007, a seventy-year-old retired Soviet sailor named Eduard Koltsov came forward with this account. Koltsov claimed to have been trained as a combat frogman by the Soviet navy, as part of a team known as the 'Barracudas'. In 1956, he was twenty-two and stationed aboard the *Ordzhonikidze*. On the morning of 19 April he was ordered to dive beneath the ship and patrol for any spying frogmen: at around 8 a.m., on the starboard side of the hull, he spotted a diver carrying what he took to be a limpet mine. At first the swimmer seemed so small that Koltsov thought it was a boy. Swimming up behind him, and believing the ship was in imminent danger, Koltsov says he drew a knife, severed the frogman's air tubes, and then cut his throat. The body then floated to the harbour bottom. Koltsov said he had been awarded a Soviet medal for this action, and even produced the knife with which he claimed to have killed Lionel Crabb.

Koltsov's claim is no more, or less, plausible than the myriad other theories that still cluster around the strange case of Commander Crabb, a story so encrusted with myth that it will never be fully solved. But one part of Koltsov's story has a clear ring of truth: 'A tip-off from a British spy meant that he had been lying in wait.' There now seems little doubt that the Soviet delegation was fully prepared for Crabb's underwater visit. Three Soviet sailors saw the frogman pop up between two of the ships, before diving again. That was the last time Buster Crabb was seen alive.

As the sun came up over Portsmouth harbour with no sign of Crabb, George Franklin came to the appalled realisation that something terrible had happened. He rowed back to the steps, and told Ted Davies that Crabb had vanished. Under normal circumstances, rescue teams would have been sent to scour the harbour at once in the hope of finding the missing frogman alive, but to do so would have alerted the Soviets to what was going on. Davies hurtled back to the Sally Port Hotel, packed up his own belongings and those of Crabb, and rushed back to London. The news of Crabb's disappearance sent a flood of panic through the upper reaches of British intelligence. 'There will be blood all over the floor,' predicted one MI5 officer, before resorting to cricketing metaphor, as Englishmen do in times of stress: 'We'll all be for the pavilion.'

A classic cover-up ensued, as MI5, MI6 and Naval Intelligence conspired to conceal the truth from their political bosses, the visiting Soviet delegation, and the public. An official lie was prepared, stating that Crabb had been 'specially employed in connection with trials of certain underwater apparatus' and had not returned from a test dive in Stokes Bay, about three miles from Portsmouth; he was now missing and 'presumed drowned'. A police officer was despatched to the Sally Port Hotel, where he tore out the incriminating pages from the hotel register. The hotel owner was told it was all hush-hush, and warned to keep his mouth shut. But Dick White of MI5 knew what was coming. 'I'm afraid it rather looks to me as if the lid will come off before too long,' he predicted grimly. Crabb's family and friends were becoming alarmed; the press was sniffing around, and the Soviets were determined to extract maximum diplomatic capital from the situation.

The evening after Crabb's disappearance, Anthony Eden hosted a dinner in London for the Soviet leader, attended by ministers and members of the Royal Family. In the course of the banquet Nikita Khrushchev mentioned the *Ordzhonikidze* and made an apparently jocular reference to 'missing or lost property'. Khrushchev was given to obscure utterances: everyone smiled, and no one had a clue what he was talking about. The next night Rear Admiral V. F. Kotov, the commander of the Soviet ship, attended a formal dinner hosted by the Portsmouth naval authorities. Over coffee he told his British counterpart that three days earlier, sailors aboard the destroyer *Sovershenny*, moored alongside the cruiser, had spotted a diver on the surface. With disingenuous concern, the Soviet admiral noted that the frogman seemed to be 'in trouble' and 'he hoped he was all right'. The British admiral categorically denied that any diving operations had taken place that day.

The carefully timed Soviet inquiry made it impossible to keep the truth from the Prime Minister any longer. When Anthony Eden discovered that his direct orders had been ignored, a covert operation had been launched, a famous frogman was missing and probably dead, and the Soviets knew all about it, he hit the roof. The Prime Minister demanded to know who had authorised the dive, and why its failure had been concealed from him for four days. The press was now in frothing pursuit, Crabb's family wanted answers, and the discovery that the hotel register had been doctored added momentum to what was already a galloping news story. On 5 May, the Soviets weighed in again with a formal diplomatic protest, demanding a full explanation for 'such an unusual occurrence as the carrying out of secret diving operations alongside Soviet warships visiting the British Naval Base at Portsmouth'. The squirming diplomatic reply expressed 'regret about this incident', but continued to insist that Crabb's approach to the destroyers was 'completely unauthorised'. Disgracefully, a draft response drawn up by the Foreign Office, but never issued, tried to blame Crabb for his own death, claiming he had 'paid no attention when recalled by his assistant' and concluding 'it can only be assumed that in a spirit of adventure he was determined on his own initiative to inspect the Russian ships . . . he died while diving on his unauthorised expedition'.

On 9 May, Eden made a statement in the House of Commons, through gritted teeth, in which he refused to provide details of the operation, while making it quite clear that he was not to blame.

It would not be in the public interest to disclose the circumstances in which Commander Crabb is presumed to have met his death. While it is the practice for ministers to accept responsibility, I think it is necessary in the special circumstances of this case to make it clear that what was done was done without the authority or knowledge of Her Majesty's ministers. Appropriate disciplinary steps are being taken.

With unconcealed glee, the Soviet newspaper *Pravda* denounced what it called 'a shameful operation of underwater espionage directed against those who come to the country on a friendly visit'.

Operation Claret was an unmitigated, gale-force cock-up: it embarrassed the government, offered the Soviets an open target, deepened Cold War suspicion, produced no useful intelligence, turned Eden's diplomatic triumph to disaster, provoked renewed infighting between the secret services and led to the death of a certified war hero. A month later, Eden was still fuming, and demanding that heads should roll for this 'misconceived and inept operation'. A twenty-three-page report on the incident, filled with bureaucratic obfuscation, was festooned with the Prime Minister's furious jottings: 'Ridiculous ... Against Orders ... This proves nothing'. The First Lord of the Admiralty offered his resignation. MI5 blamed what one officer called 'a typical piece of MI6 adventurism, ill-conceived and badly executed'. The most prominent victim from the fallout was Sir John 'Sinbad' Sinclair, the head of MI6. Eden ordered that his retirement be swiftly advanced, and by July 1956 he was gone, replaced by Dick White, who was moved from MI5 to take over the sister service. On arrival at MI6 headquarters, White's new deputy, Jack Easton, warned him: 'We're still cloak and dagger. Fisticuffs. Too many swashbuckling green thumbs thinking we're about to fight another second world war.' There is no doubt who he was referring to.

Nicholas Elliott should have been fired, for what one colleague called a 'one man Bay of Pigs'. Astonishingly, he survived; if not unscathed, then at least unsacked, an outcome that would have been highly unlikely in any other organisation. As Elliott had himself demonstrated, this was a club that looked after its members. With typical insouciance, he wrote: 'A storm in a teacup was blown up by ineptitude into a major diplomatic incident which reflected unjustifiable discredit on MI6. The incompetence lay on the shoulders of the politicians, most notably Eden, in the way the matter was handled.' Elliott remained in post as London station chief, flatly denying that he, or anyone else in the intelligence services, was to blame. For the rest of his life, Elliott defended the memory of Buster Crabb, insisting that his friend had perished in the line of duty. 'Crabb was both brave and patriotic,' wrote Elliott. 'Qualities which inspired him to volunteer to do what he did.' Crabb had proven his loyalty and that, in Elliott's world, was all that mattered.

More than a year after Crabb's disappearance, a fisherman spotted a decomposing body floating in the water off Pilsey Island in Chichester Harbour. The head and hands had rotted away completely, but a post mortem concluded, from distinguishing marks on the remains preserved inside the Pirelli diving suit, that the small corpse was that of Lionel Crabb. The coroner's open verdict on the cause of death, and the absence of head and hands, left the way clear for a flood of conspiracy theory that has continued, virtually unabated, ever since: Crabb defected to the USSR; he was shot by a Soviet sniper; he had been captured and brainwashed and was working as a diving instructor for the Soviet navy; he had been deliberately planted on the Soviets as an MI6 double agent. A South African clairvoyant insisted Crabb had been sucked into a secret underwater compartment on the *Ordzhonikidze*, chained up and then dumped at sea. And so on. Eight years later, Marcus Lipton, the indefatigable MP, was still calling for the case to be reopened, without success. The Crabb mystery has never been fully explained, but the diminutive frogman did achieve a sort of immortality. Crabb has been cited as one of the models for James Bond. As an officer in Naval Intelligence, Ian Fleming had known him well, and the Crabb affair inspired the plot of *Thunderball*, in which Bond sets out to investigate the hull of the *Disco Volante*.

Elliott's verdict on Crabb's death still seems the most likely. 'He almost certainly died of respiratory trouble, being a heavy smoker and not in the best of health, or conceivably because some fault had developed in his equipment.' Elliott dismissed out of hand the theory that the Soviets might have killed Crabb, and the idea of betrayal never crossed his mind. But more than half a century later a Russian frogman popped up out of the murk to claim that he had killed Crabb with his own hands, following a tipoff from a British spy.

If the Soviets *were* forewarned of the underwater operation (which now seems probable) and if Crabb *did* die as a result (which seems at least possible), then there was only one person who could have passed on that information.

Kim Philby's heart sank when Nicholas Elliott called him in July, and asked him to 'come down to the firm'. It was barely seven months since Macmillan had cleared him of suspicion. Could it be that MI5 had already found fresh evidence? Had another defector emerged?

'Something unpleasant again?' asked Philby warily.

'Maybe just the opposite,' Elliott replied.

Despite the storm raging around him over the Crabb affair, Elliott had found time to demonstrate his own peculiarly durable brand of loyalty. He had done what he promised to do, and what no one (including Philby) had believed was possible: he had engineered Philby's return to MI6.

Our Man in Beirut

Kim Philby's return to British intelligence displayed the Old Boy network running at its smoothest: a word in an ear, a nod, a drink with one of the chaps at the club, and the machinery kicked in.

Nicholas Elliott made a point of cultivating journalists, and maintained close relations with several highly placed editors. He would host regular dinners at White's to introduce senior journalists to C. Ian Fleming, his friend from wartime Naval Intelligence, had become foreign manager of the Kemsley newspaper group, which included the *Sunday Times*. 'In those days SIS kept in touch with useful persons,' Elliott later recalled. 'And Ian was quite useful: he had important contacts in certain places, and every now and then he got hold of a useful piece of information. I would ask him if I needed someone in the City and, very occasionally, someone out in the field.' Fleming was perfectly willing to oil the wheels of British intelligence. 'Kemsley Press allowed many of their foreign correspondents to cooperate with MI6, and even took on MI6 operatives as foreign correspondents.' Another helpful journalist was David Astor, the editor of the *Observer*. Astor later tried to play down his links with British intelligence, but he and Elliott went back a·long way: a fellow Etonian, Astor had been in The Hague in 1939 'doing secret service stuff' according to his cousin, the actress Joyce Grenfell, at the same time as Elliott.

In the summer of 1956, Elliott asked Astor for a favour: would he take on Philby as a freelance correspondent in Beirut? The newspaper editor was happy to help. With the Suez crisis building, journalists were flocking to the Middle East. Philby had a proven track record, and he had written for the *Observer* before. Through his father, who was now living in the Lebanese capital, he would have access to important people in the region. Astor contacted Donald Tyerman, the editor of the *Economist*, who was also looking for a Beirut stringer, and a deal was struck: the *Observer* and *Economist* would share Philby's services, and pay him £3,000 a year plus travel and expenses. At the same time, Elliott arranged that Philby would resume working for MI6, no longer as an officer, but as an agent, gathering information for British intelligence in one of the world's most sensitive areas. He would be paid a retainer through Godfrey 'Paul' Paulson, chief of the Beirut MI6 station and a close friend of Nick Elliott, who had been at Westminster with Philby. Elliott insisted that Philby was 'being re-engaged for reasons of simple justice', but also because he would be a useful asset, with long experience of the game: 'The country could ill afford to be without Philby's abilities.' Astor later claimed, implausibly, that he had no idea Philby would be working for MI6 while reporting for his newspaper. The grey area between implicit and explicit was Elliott's natural terrain. George Kennedy Young, by now chief of Middle East operations, waved the deal through. 'Nick did all the negotiations,' said Young. 'I simply approved them.'

Philby accepted the double job offer without hesitation. Here was an arrangement that suited everyone: the *Observer* and *Economist* got an experienced reporter with good local contacts; MI6 got a veteran agent in a volatile part of the world, whose cover as a journalist would enable him to travel freely; Elliott got his friend back in the saddle; and Philby got paid, and an opportunity to start a new life in sunny Beirut.

Dick White, the new head of MI6, had led the hunt for the Third Man, but he did not try to prevent the re-hiring of Philby. Indeed, at this stage he may have been unaware of it. After Macmillan's statement, the case against Philby had gone cold and, according to White's biographer, there was 'no appetite for reopening old wounds'.

Though still convinced of Philby's guilt, and 'irritated that Elliott should number himself among Philby's staunchest supporters', White is said to have shown 'no emotion' when the subject of Philby was raised. But it is also possible that Elliott chose not to explain that Philby was back on the payroll. Senior MI6 officers enjoyed considerable latitude, and in the more remote stations they carried on their business with little supervision. Officers in Beirut believed that the new C was 'unaware' of their activities, and would have been 'horrified if he knew'. Some historians have speculated that White sent Philby to Beirut as part of a clever trap to lure him into making contact with Soviet intelligence. More likely, White did not know (and perhaps did not want to know) the full story, and Elliott did not want to tell him. The responsibility for bringing Philby in from the cold was down to one man. As Phillip Knightley writes: 'It was Nicholas Elliott, his old friend, his most ardent defender in SIS who was giving him this chance to work his way back into the club.'

Once again, Elliott and Philby's lives seemed to move in parallel: while Philby headed to the Middle East, Elliott took up a new job as MI6 station chief in Vienna. Usually so ebullient, Elliott could summon little enthusiasm for his new posting. Vienna, he wrote, 'had an ersatz gaiety and smelled of corruption'. The city seemed dowdy and drab, with few opportunities for high-grade espionage. His former school friend Peter Lunn preceded him in the post, and bequeathed him a comfortable apartment overlooking the Belvedere Palace gardens, with room for his growing family. Lunn also left him a bad-tempered Slovene cook called Irene and a red Wolseley (a conspicuous vehicle for a spy since it was the only one of its kind in the city). He went skiing at weekends, enjoyed poking fun at his stodgy Viennese counterparts and set about establishing a network of spies. But he was bored in Austria. 'The climate of Vienna is not conducive to energy,' he wrote.

The Beirut job finally put paid to the Philbys' marriage. 'Haunted by Kim's life of treason' and agonised by the stress of his public acquittal, the discovery that her husband was leaving the country sent Aileen into terminal alcoholic decline. There was never any question that she and the children would accompany him to Beirut; she did not try to stop him, and if she had, it would have made no difference. Her psychiatrist became so alarmed by her disintegration that he had her briefly committed to a mental hospital. With the children at boarding school, Aileen shut herself up in the gloomy house in Crowborough which, according to Flora Solomon, 'she maintained in the hope of a reconciliation with her errant Kim'. Philby told Aileen he would refund her household bills, and left.

★

Beirut was exotic, tense and dangerous, a salmagundi of races, religions and politics, rendered even more febrile by the rising tide of Arab nationalism and Cold War conflict. It was fertile ground for journalism in 1956, and an even better place for espionage. 'Lebanon was the only Arab country without censorship and with good communications,' wrote the newspaper correspondent Richard Beeston, who arrived in the city shortly before Philby. 'So inevitably Beirut became the listening post for the region, with the St Georges [Hotel] and its bar its epicentre – a bazaar for the trading of information between diplomats, politicians, journalists and spies.' Philby landed at Beirut airport in August, and made straight for the bar of the St Georges.

The Beirut beat was a demanding one. Middle Eastern politics were as complex and volatile in 1956 as they are today. But as Philby knew from his years as a correspondent in Civil War Spain, there is no better cover job for a spy than that of journalist, a profession that enables the asking of direct, unsubtle and impertinent questions about the most sensitive subjects, without arousing suspicion. A topic of interest to readers of the *Observer* could, when explored at greater depth, be passed on to British intelligence. Philby began cultivating people – politicians, military officers, diplomats and other journalists – who might prove useful as sources for journalism, or espionage, or both. The line between Philby's two occupations was blurred from the outset. At first he lived in a house rented by his father outside Beirut, where the elder Philby had been exiled after criticising Ibn Saud's successor. When St John Philby returned to Saudi Arabia, Philby took a flat in the Muslim quarter of the city. Richard Beeston met Philby soon after his arrival in the Lebanese capital: 'He was quintessentially English, relaxed and courteous, amusing – and this, combined with a rather painful stammer, made him pretty well irresistible to women. He could charm the birds out of the trees.' But beneath the bonhomie, Beeston sensed Philby's inner solitude. 'He seemed a rather lonely, rumpled figure.' He was not alone for long.

Eleanor Brewer was a forty-two-year-old sometime architect, amateur sculptor and former Red Cross worker from Seattle, married to Sam Pope Brewer, the *New York Times* correspondent in Beirut. She was tall and slim, sweet-natured, and restless. She had met her husband in wartime Istanbul, where he was reporting for the *New York Times* and she was working in the overseas branch of the Office of War Information. Nicholas Elliott had known them both in those years, as another glamorous couple in the Istanbul throng. By 1956 Eleanor was unhappily married and bored. Beeston recalled her as a 'rangy, steady-drinking American, who looked tough and sophisticated. Underneath she was a romantic, and politically naïve.' Like most people who proclaim themselves free spirits, she was fiercely conventional.

Sam Brewer had first encountered Philby while covering the Spanish Civil War, so when the American newspaperman learned that his former colleague had arrived in Beirut, he was eager to extend a welcome. In early September, Brewer left Beirut on an extended reporting trip, and told his wife to keep an eye out for Philby: 'If I should meet Kim I was to introduce him to our friends, and do what I could to help him,' she later recalled. Eleanor's welcome to Philby would prove rather warmer than her husband had intended.

On 12 September 1956, Eleanor Brewer was drinking with some friends at the St Georges, when someone pointed out Kim Philby, sitting at the bar. She sent a message via the waiter, inviting him to join their party.

What touched me first about Kim Philby was his loneliness. A certain old-fashioned reserve set him apart from the easy familiarity of the other journalists. He was then forty-four, of medium height, very lean with a handsome heavily lined face. His eyes were an intense blue ... He had a gift of such intimacy that I found myself talking freely to him. I was very impressed by his beautiful manners. We took him under our wing. He soon became one of our closest friends.

Philby spent Christmas with the Brewers. Sam Brewer enjoyed discussing Middle Eastern politics with Philby; Philby enjoyed sleeping with his wife. The secret lovers met at a little café they called the Shaky Floor, although the shakiness of the floor may have been due to the amount they drank there. They shared picnics in the hills, smoked hubble-bubble pipes in the Arab coffee houses, and exchanged love notes written in gushing teenage prose. 'Kim was a delightful companion,' Eleanor wrote. 'I had never met a kinder, more interesting person in my entire life.' Eleanor was besotted, and blamed her husband for their deteriorating marriage. Sam was only interested in politics, she complained, and criticised her cooking: 'My soufflés were never quite right.' As in his other life, Philby revelled in the subterfuge, the secret messages and surreptitious meetings, the thrill of deception. While conducting his clandestine love affair, Philby discreetly checked for any signs of surveillance. No one was following him.

Philby's journalism from Beirut was solid, if unspectacular. When asked to write on a subject he considered too fluffy – such as Arabian slave girls – he used the pseudonym 'Charles Garner'. Even in journalism, he embraced a double existence. He also began to collect information for his MI6 handlers. He possessed a 'sound knowledge of their requirements'. Much of his early intelligence work in Lebanon involved chatting informally to senior Arab politicians, and then 'telling the British government what they really thought'. MI6 was evidently satisfied: a year after Philby's arrival in Beirut, the visiting head of MI6's Middle East desk took him to lunch at an expensive restaurant overlooking the sea, and told him his status was being confirmed and his retainer increased. 'Anxious to be in their good books,' Philby resolved to work 'as conscientiously as possible' for MI6, while awaiting the inevitable call from the KGB.

Philby's Beirut habits were regular. At midday he would repair to the Normandie Hotel, less conspicuous and cheaper than the St Georges, to down his first drink of the day, vodka with V8, open his post, and read the newspapers. One afternoon, a chunky young man in his thirties, evidently a foreigner, approached Philby at his corner table, and presented him with his card: 'Petukhov, Soviet Trade Mission'.

'I read your articles in the *Observer* and in *The Economist*, Mr Philby,' he said. 'I find them very deep. I sought you out to ask you for the favour of your time for a conversation. I am particularly interested in the prospects for a Common Market of the Arab countries.'

Philby could have put an end to his double life at that moment. He could have explained to Petukhov that he had no interest in discussing Arab economics with him, and so conveyed a message to the KGB that he was no longer in the game. Other agents recruited in the 1930s, including Anthony Blunt, had successfully disengaged from Soviet intelligence. He had a new life, a new lover, and two interesting, compatible and remunerative jobs: with the protection of Nicholas Elliott, he was safe from further investigation by MI5; his reputation as a journalist and Middle East expert was growing. He could have rejected the approach from the KGB with impunity. Instead, he invited Petukhov to tea at his flat.

Philby would later frame his decision as one of ideological purity, consistent with the 'total commitment to the Soviet Union' he had made at the age of twenty-one. He did what he did, in his own estimation, out of pure political conviction, the guiding principle of his life. He looked with disdain on others who had seen the horrors of Stalinism and abandoned ship. 'I stayed the course,' he wrote, 'in the confident faith that the principles of the Revolution would outlive the aberration of individuals.' Philby later claimed that he had experienced moments of doubt, and that his views had been 'influenced and modified, sometimes rudely, by the appalling events of my lifetime'. But there is no evidence that he ever questioned the ideology he had discovered at Cambridge, changed his opinions, or seriously acknowledged the iniquities of practical communism. Philby never shared or discussed his views, either with friend or foe. Instead, he retained and sustained his faith without the need for priests or fellow believers, in perfect isolation. Philby regarded himself as an ideologue and a loyalist; in truth, he was a dogmatist, valuing only one opinion: his own.

But there was more than politics in Philby's eager return to the embrace of the KGB. Philby *enjoyed* deception. Like secrecy, the erotic charge of infidelity can be hard to renounce. Some men like to parade their knowledge. Others revel in the possession of information that they decline to share, and the private sense of superiority that this brings. Philby was a faithless husband, but a kind lover, a good friend, a gentle father and a generous host. He had a talent for tenderness. But he also relished withholding the truth from those he was closest to; there was the Philby they knew, and then there was the Philby only he knew. The alcohol helped maintain the double life. For an alcoholic has already become divorced from his or her real self, hooked on an artificial reality. Philby did not want to give up spying, and he probably could not have stopped if he had wanted to: because he was addicted.

The day after their encounter at the Normandie, Petukhov arrived promptly at Philby's flat at three in the afternoon – it was a dangerous place for a rendezvous, and one that would not be repeated. The ground rules were established. If Philby wanted a meeting, he would stand on his balcony holding a newspaper at a given hour; if he needed to see Petukhov urgently, he would be holding a book. Henceforth, Philby and his new case officer would meet at regular intervals, always after sunset, always in Beirut, always in some discreet corner of the city. The KGB residence in Beirut was 'a hive of activity', according to Yuri Modin, with agents deployed throughout the

Middle East. Philby was told that his first priority was to ascertain 'the intentions of the United States and British governments in the area'. He happily set to work.

In the autumn of 1956, Eleanor Brewer told her husband that she was leaving him. Sam Brewer, who had finally cottoned on to his wife's torrid affair, raised no objection, and Eleanor returned to Seattle with her daughter, telling Philby she would get a 'Mexican Divorce', which was quicker and cheaper than the American variety since the spouse did not need to be present. The only remaining obstacle was Aileen Philby.

*

Since Philby's departure, Aileen had hurtled downhill. She was virtually penniless, deeply unhappy and usually drunk. Philby complained of Aileen's 'idleness', and claimed she spent most of her time at point-to-point races. He refused to send her more cash until she explained what she was spending it on. 'No receipts, no money,' he said. She spent longer and longer periods in psychiatric hospitals. Her old friend Flora Solomon dispatched Stuart Lisbona, of the Marks and Spencer Pensions Department, to keep a 'helpful eye' on 'poor Aileen . . . abandoned by her husband'.

On 12 December 1957, Aileen Philby was discovered dead in the bedroom of the house in Crowborough. Her friends believed she had killed herself, with drink and pills. Her psychiatrist suspected, fantastically, that she 'might have been murdered' by Philby, because she knew too much. The coroner ruled she had died from heart failure, myocardial degeneration, tuberculosis, and a respiratory infection having contracted influenza. Her alcoholism undoubtedly accelerated her death. She was forty-seven.

Elliott was deeply upset when news of Aileen's tragic end reached him in Vienna. She had shown 'considerable strength of character' throughout her suffering, and he would always remember her as she had once been, 'a charming woman, and a loving wife and mother'. But he could not bring himself to blame Philby for her death, which he ascribed to Aileen's 'grave mental problem'. Not so Flora Solomon, who held Philby directly and personally responsible. 'I endeavoured to strike him from my memory,' she wrote. 'This, however, was not to be.'

Richard Beeston and his wife Moyra were Christmas shopping in Beirut's Bab Idriss, when they were spotted by Kim Philby, who rushed across the road: 'I have wonderful news darlings,' he said excitedly. 'I want you to come and celebrate.' Philby dragged the Beestons off to the Normandie, plied them with drink, and then produced a telegram from England informing him of Aileen's death. It was, he said, a 'wonderful escape', as he was now free to marry 'a wonderful American girl'. The Beestons were 'stunned'.

The Furse family took over all the arrangements for her funeral back in England, which Philby did not attend. The five Philby children never knew where their mother was buried.

It took another seven months for Eleanor to obtain her divorce. When it was finalised, she at once sent a telegram to Philby, who cabled back: 'Clever wonderful you fly back happily song in heart life is miraculous greatest love Kim.' The same morning, Philby rushed to the St Georges to find Sam Brewer. Their conversation, as described by Eleanor herself, is one of the classic exchanges between a cuckold and an adulterer:

Philby: 'I've come to tell you that I've had a cable from Eleanor. She has got her divorce and I want you to be the first person to know that I'm going to marry her.'

Brewer: 'That sounds like the best possible solution. What do you make of the situation in Iraq?'

Kim Philby and Eleanor Brewer were married in Holborn registry office in London on 24 January 1959, just over a year after Aileen's death. Nicholas and Elizabeth Elliott returned from Vienna to attend the ceremony, along with other MI6 colleagues, past and present. Elliott had not forgotten Aileen, but he swiftly took Philby's new wife to his heart: 'Eleanor was in many ways not dissimilar to Aileen,' he wrote. 'She had integrity, courage and humour. Like Aileen, she could not be described as intellectual but she was certainly intelligent.' The couple spent their honeymoon in Rome, where Philby wrote: 'We shall take a house in the mountains: she will paint; I will write; peace and stability at last.' Eleanor was his third wife, and the second to know nothing of his true allegiance.

Back in Beirut, the newlyweds moved into a fifth-floor flat on the Rue Kantari, with a large balcony overlooking the mountains and sea which offered a 'ringside view' of the civil war now engulfing Lebanon. 'He would sit in his terrace at night and listen to the guns going off,' Eleanor recalled. The flat was spacious enough to accommodate all their children during the holidays from boarding school. Despite the grim circumstances of Aileen's death and Philby's swift remarriage, his children adored him, and he remained an attentive and caring father.

And so began a period of domestic harmony, unchallenging journalism, and discreet international espionage. There were parties and picnics, and much alcohol. Eleanor described a 'leisurely daily circuit of shopping and gossip', starting at the Normandie ('Kim treated the place like a club') before moving on to the St Georges 'to see what the other journalists were up to'. Philby hinted to his new wife that he was 'connected with British intelligence', but naturally provided no details. He would disappear from time to time. It never occurred to Eleanor to ask where he had been. Compared to her first husband, Philby took a relaxed, even casual, approach to journalism: 'He seemed to write his weekly articles fast and painlessly – often dictating them to me.' Philby's fellow hacks considered him lazy, yet 'compelling a certain respect', in part because he appeared to wear his responsibilities so lightly.

Philby devoted more energy (though not much more) to intelligence-gathering. A fellow journalist noticed that he was often to be seen in the company of 'men whose ostensible jobs as businessmen, bankers, university professors, consultants for foreign companies, and so forth, did not wholly account for their insiders' preoccupation with Arab politics'. Whatever information of value he gleaned was handed over to Paulson of MI6; then Philby passed the same information to Petukhov of the KGB, with whatever additional intelligence might be helpful to the Soviet cause.

On both sides of the Iron Curtain, opinion in intelligence circles was divided over Philby's usefulness. Yuri Modin, still monitoring Agent Stanley, was enthusiastic. 'The information he supplied on British policies in the region proved invaluable to our government in our relations with Arab countries ... I myself read several of his reports, noting with satisfaction that he had not lost his brilliant touch.' Philby's information 'attracted much attention at the top'. Yet some in Moscow complained that Philby was simply peddling re-cycled journalism. 'There was criticism,' Modin noted, 'concerning his tendency to send us hard news wrapped up in beautifully written political evaluations. We did not need this because we had our own people to make evaluations ... the KGB had its own experts here in Moscow and in the capitals, highly trained Arabists all.' This is an old trick of espionage: when spies obtain knowledge but not secrets, they tend to dress up mere information to make it look like intelli-gence; and when they do not have solid information, they fabricate it. Similar grumbling could be heard in parts of Broadway, particu-larly among the Arabists of MI6. 'You could have read it all in the *Economist* last week,' said one London analyst, after looking through Philby's latest submission. 'He's got a lot of it wrong as well. It's invented. He's taking us to the cleaners.' Philby's supporters, notably Elliott and Young, ignored the carping, and circulated Philby's reports as the latest penetrating insights from Our Man in Beirut.

In truth, Philby was going soft, and drinking hard: content to do a little journalism, a little espionage on the side for both sides, but nothing too strenuous. He was coasting, it seemed, towards quiet and comfortable irrelevance as a second-rate journalist, and a minor spy.

Then Nicholas Elliott arrived in Beirut, as the new station chief of MI6, and the wheel of their friendship turned again.

The Fox who Came to Stay

Beirut was another plum posting. The Crabb affair had done Nicholas Elliott's career no lasting damage, and he had performed well during his brief stint in Vienna. Indeed, within MI6 he was still considered a high-flier, the leader of the Robber Barons. It was said that, 'but for his preference for operations, not administration, he might well have been appointed C'. Elliott was pleased to be moving on from Austria. 'I have no wish to be churlish about our time in Vienna,' he wrote (Elliott's politeness even extended to cities), 'nevertheless we were not unhappy' to leave. With the Middle East heating up, Beirut was an important step up the intelligence ladder. The Elliotts travelled by boat from Genoa, and as they pulled into the port, Elliott marvelled at how little Beirut had changed since his last visit in 1942. Elizabeth had been his secretary then, and he had courted her over lunch at the Hotel Lucullus, whose restaurant was famed for its French–Lebanese cuisine. As soon as they landed, Elliott announced, with romantic fanfare, they would be lunching at the Lucullus again. No sooner were they seated, than a beaming Kim Philby appeared and wrapped Elliott in a welcoming hug. 'It was a most agreeable reunion,' recalled Elliott, who pretended that the meeting had been accidental. He was taking over as station chief from Paul Paulson, but Philby was the person he wanted to see on his first day in Beirut. They were joined by Eleanor, an 'excellent bouillabaisse' was served, more bottles were opened, glasses were raised and drained. Elliott happily turned to Philby: 'Fill me in, old boy.'

The Elliotts moved into a flat on the top floor of the Immeuble Tabet on the Rue Verdun, on the border between the Christian and Muslim quarters, not far from the Philbys. The apartment had 'cool, high rooms, wide balconies and marble floors' and was 'perfect in every way'. That evening, as they listened to the muezzin's call wafting over the city, Elliott 'thought nostalgically of the gentle sound of the Mullahs calling the faithful to prayer from the minarets of Istanbul many years before'. He was as happy as he had ever been, and back in his element, in a foreign city seething with espionage possibilities, fighting communist aggression alongside his oldest friend, his most trusted colleague, and the man who would explain to him the mysteries of the Middle East. Once more they would be 'two old friends in Crown service on the frontiers'.

As Eleanor Philby observed, Elliott had hitherto been a 'European specialist and knew little of Arab politics. He came green to the Middle East.' He had much to learn, as he admitted: 'Apart from all the political complexities and the plotting – almost any major financial or political intrigue in the Middle East at that time had its roots in Beirut – you had to get to grips with the Lebanese character. The labyrinths of Lebanese politics were of daunting complexity.' Philby would be his guide, 'his personal adviser'.

The arrival of a new spy chief did not go unnoticed among Beirut's journalists. One left this portrait of Elliott:

> He was a thin, spare man with a reputation as a shrewd operator whose quick humorous glance behind round glasses gave a clue to his sardonic mind. In manner and dress he suggested an Oxbridge don at one of the smarter colleges, but with a touch of worldly ruthlessness not always evident in academic life. Foreigners liked him, appreciating his bonhomie and his fund of risqué stories. He got on particularly well with Americans. The formal, ladylike figure of his wife in the background contributed to the feeling that British intelligence in Beirut was being directed by a gentleman.

Elliott and Philby were once again inseparable, professionally and socially. The pace of Philby's intelligence-gathering, hitherto leisurely, even lackadaisical, suddenly became frenetic, as Elliott 'put Kim to work, setting him targets, sending him on trips, requesting reports which were then combed over in conversation'. During his first four years in Beirut, Philby had ventured outside Lebanon only as far as Syria, and once to visit his father in Saudi Arabia. Now, at Elliott's behest, he scrambled all over the Middle East, ostensibly on newspaper assignments, to Jordan, Iraq, Egypt, Kuwait and Yemen. The hitherto indolent journalist was a reporting whirlwind. But a careful observer might have spotted that his output fell far short of his industriousness; he was visiting many more places and people than he was writing about, at least publicly. In the first nine months of 1960, he filed just six stories for the *Observer*. One editor from the *Economist* paid him a visit, noted how seldom he seemed to write for the magazine, and casually asked him if he found it difficult 'serving two masters'. Philby was momentarily speechless, until he realised she was referring to his newspaper employers, not his espionage.

Philby delivered a torrent of information to Elliott, 'mainly political and personality reporting' and 'reports about political developments in most Arab states'. The two men would huddle together, for long debriefing sessions. 'They used to meet once or twice a week,' wrote Eleanor. 'Vanishing into another room and leaving me to gossip with Elizabeth.' Elliott's support and confidence was demonstrated in other, more practical ways. Towards the end of 1960, Philby returned home late one night, clutching a sheaf of hundred-dollar bills. 'Oh boy,' he said, happily scattering them around the room. 'This is going to make our Christmas!' Eleanor had no doubt the money came from Elliott, an early Christmas present for his best friend and most industrious agent.

Some have claimed that Elliott's energetic deployment of Philby was merely a ruse, to see if 'greater participation in the British intelligence effort' would reveal contact with the Soviets. There is little evidence to support this theory. If Elliott had suspected Philby, he would have put a tail on him, and easily discovered his meetings with

Petukhov. He did not. Dick White's instructions were to 'keep an eye on Philby', but there was no suggestion that he should be investigated, probed or put under surveillance. White seems to have accepted, at least outwardly, that the Philby case was closed. Far from doubting him, Elliott trusted Philby completely, and his determination to employ him to the full reflected only 'Elliott's overt and innocent friendship', and an admiration stretching back twenty years.

Philby, in turn, was buoyed by his return to active intelligence work, and seemed to relish the confidence reposed in him by his old friend. Eleanor noticed the change in her husband's demeanour following Elliott's arrival: 'I had begun to feel that Kim was bored with journalism, and that writing articles for newspapers did not wholly satisfy him. His meetings with [Elliott] were more like *real* work.' What Philby considered his real work, of course, consisted of passing to Soviet intelligence every scrap of information he could gather, both on his travels, and from Elliott. Their relationship was running along the old tracks in more ways than Elliott knew.

Philby's value as a Soviet agent increased in direct proportion to his activities as a British agent, and as Elliott's informant he was privy to important information, including the identities of MI6 contacts in the region, as well as sympathetic Arab politicians and officials on the payroll. Elliott achieved a remarkable coup by being able to 'broker a deal with the director of Mossad [the Israeli intelligence agency] for the exchange of intelligence on the Middle East'. Philby did not know everything that Elliott knew; but from the instructions issued by Elliott, he at least knew what MI6 wanted to know, and that, in the negative world of spying, is almost as valuable. Yuri Modin was pleased with Agent Stanley: 'In all he served us well.'

Elliott and Philby spied, plotted and socialised together, in a family friendship that intensified over time. Eleanor and Elizabeth became as close as their husbands. At weekends the two families shared a bathing cabin named 'Acapulco' on Khalde beach with Colonel Alec Brodie, a much-wounded, one-eyed, pipe-smoking war veteran who was military attaché at the embassy. During school holidays, the Elliott and Philby children mixed happily together. Elliott's teenagers, Mark and

Claudia, both liked Philby, an avuncular, amusing presence. 'He was one of the few adults to take me seriously,' Mark Elliott recalled.

Despite the rising political tension, Beirut was still a happy playground for expatriates and tourists, a place where, in Elliott's words, one could 'ski in the mornings and swim in the afternoons', and enjoy hillside picnics in between. The fun did not stop at nightfall, but extended long into the night, with an endless round of cocktails and dinners. As they had in Switzerland, the Elliotts played host to a stream of visitors. One of the earliest was Ian Fleming, who called unannounced from the airport in November 1960, and invited himself to stay. Fleming was en route to Kuwait, on a lucrative assignment from the Kuwait Oil Company to write about the country. By now a hugely successful writer, Fleming continued his freelance intelligence activities and explained to Elliott that Naval Intelligence was keen to learn more about the defences of the Iraqi port at Basra. Elliott 'promised to look after it'. Elliott asked for a favour in return: a rare fall of rain in Kuwait had brought out a crop of delicious white truffles. Would Fleming send back a box? This was Elliott's style of espionage: a little spying in return for truffles. That evening Fleming announced he was meeting 'an Armenian' in the Place des Canons; Elliott got the distinct impression that the creator of 007 had in fact 'arranged to see a pornographic film in full colour and sound'.

As the months passed, Elliott and Philby socialised together more and more, meeting regularly 'at parties for British diplomats and journalists'. The Elliott family photographs from the summer of 1960 are filled with images of the intermingled Philby and Elliott clans, enjoying Beirut's beachlife and nightlife: Philby is in most pictures, in bathing trunks, T-shirt or suit, smiling, tanned, and frequently, very obviously, drunk.

Philby's behaviour was becoming increasingly outrageous, in ways reminiscent of the antics of Guy Burgess. 'Out of fun rather than malice,' wrote Elliott, he 'would make some remark well calculated to stop the conversation dead in its tracks. Such remarks served to lighten the atmosphere of a dreary party but were often the cause of severe umbrage.' Elliott egged him on, and recalled one particularly spectacular episode of Philby devilry that 'caused a chain reaction of offence unparalleled in my experience'. In social fallout, the Cocktail Party from Hell came close to the Dinner Party from Hell.

> It was at a cocktail party given in our flat by Elizabeth and myself when my parents, then pretty elderly, had come out to stay. We had invited some forty people, including the Philbys and our ambassador, Sir Moore Crosthwaite. There was an unusual pause in the babble of conversation during which Philby was heard to remark to Moore: 'Don't you think Anne [the wife of a member of the embassy staff who was standing next to him] has the finest breasts in Beirut?' Moore was undoubtedly annoyed because he thought that the breasts of the wife of a member of his staff were not an appropriate subject of conversation at a cocktail party. Anne, while doubtless justifiably proud of that part of her anatomy, was annoyed at having it discussed in public and in particular with the ambassador. Her husband was annoyed as he agreed with the ambassador that his wife's breasts were an off-target subject for cocktail party gossip. Jane, the wife of another member of the embassy staff, was annoyed because she thought she had better breasts than Anne. Jane's husband was annoyed possibly because he thought his wife had been slighted. Eleanor Philby was more than just annoyed because she was not particularly well endowed in that respect and comparisons are odious. And, finally, Elizabeth was annoyed because she felt the whole party was getting out of hand. In fact the only person who thought the whole episode was a huge joke was Kim Philby himself.

And Nicholas Elliott, who regaled listeners with it for the rest of his life.

Privately, Elliott worried about Philby's alcoholic intake. He had seen Aileen drink herself into the grave. Philby's mother Dora was drinking a bottle of gin a day by the time of her death in 1957. Elliott feared the effect Philby's boozing might be having on his health, and on his children: 'He had no inhibitions about getting drunk in front of them.' Philby even trained his young son Harry to mix a 'fierce Martini'.

Philby and Elliott both worked assiduously to cultivate Americans, particularly those involved in intelligence, of which Beirut, as a Cold War battleground, was plentifully supplied. Relations between the CIA and MI6 had come under intense strain after the Burgess and Maclean defections and the accusations against Philby, but by 1960, the relationship was back on an even keel. In some quarters of Washington, suspicion of Philby still lingered: at the FBI, J. Edgar Hoover remained convinced of his guilt, as did Bill Harvey. But within the CIA, it was generally agreed that if MI6 considered him trustworthy, and Harold Macmillan had said he was innocent, then Philby must be clean. Angleton had risen to new heights in the CIA. In 1954 he was named chief of the counter-intelligence staff, a position he would retain for the next two decades. As America's premier spy-catcher, he was becoming 'recognised as the dominant counter-intelligence figure in the non-communist world'. More gaunt and aloof than ever, Angleton trusted few, and mistrusted most, inspiring a peculiar mixture of awe and fear among his colleagues. He later claimed to have rumbled Philby, but his actions clearly indicate otherwise. According to one historian, Philby was still in amicable contact with Angleton from time to time, 'and used those opportunities to reassure his American friend of his innocence'. If the CIA had suspected Philby of being a Soviet spy, then Angleton's operatives in Beirut would have been under instructions to avoid him, watch him and, if possible, catch him. Instead, Philby mixed freely among the throngs of American spies.

One of the most flamboyant of these was Wilbur Crane Eveland, a boisterous intelligence veteran from the West Coast, who favoured full morning dress, and arrived in Beirut at around the same time as Philby as a special agent for Allen Dulles, the CIA chief. Working independently of the CIA station, Eveland's role appears to have been that of anti-communist paymaster in the Middle East: he bankrolled CIA efforts to overthrow the Soviet-sponsored government in Syria, provided support to the Saud dynasty in Riyadh, and propped up Lebanon's pro-Western president, Camille Chamoun. 'He travelled regularly to the presidential palace with his briefcase stuffed with Lebanese pounds,' according to Richard Beeston, 'returning late at night to the American embassy to replenish the slush fund.' Eveland had met Philby through the Brewers (Eveland and Eleanor were both from Spokane in Washington state), and they immediately struck up a friendship. He knew Philby had links with British intelligence, and saw him as someone 'whose brain was there to be picked', an attitude that was entirely reciprocated by Philby. Eleanor later told the CIA that Philby had once remarked that 'all he had to do was to have one evening with Bill Eveland in Beirut and before it was over he would know of all his operations'.

Philby established a similarly cosy relationship with Edgar J. Applewhite, the clever, sharp-suited, Yale-educated CIA station chief sent to Lebanon in 1958. Applewhite knew of the earlier suspicions surrounding Philby, but cultivated him nonetheless, at first guardedly, later wholeheartedly. The American concluded Philby was 'much too sophisticated to give his allegiance to such a doctrinaire business as Marxism', and besides, the Anglophile Applewhite 'liked to talk to Philby about Arab problems' and enjoyed the Englishman's erudite company. The American intelligence community was, if anything, even more welcoming to Philby than the British one, for this charming, open-handed Englishman seemed trustworthy, the sort of Englishman who had helped America to win the Second World War and was now helping her to win the Cold War. 'Philby was friendly with all the Yanks in Beirut,' George Young later noted. 'A lot of them babbled. He was pretty good at getting them to talk.'

One American spy talked more than any of the others, and would be drawn into the heart of the Philby-Elliott circle. Miles Copeland Jr was a drawling jazz musician from the Deep South, a wartime spy, former CIA agent and now a public relations executive and espionage fixer. The son of a doctor from Birmingham, Alabama, Copeland had spent his teenage years gambling on the riverboats, before dramatically changing tack and heading to Alabama University to study advanced mathematics. A gifted trumpeter, he played in an otherwise all-black radio band, and ended up in the Glenn Miller Orchestra. Copeland joined the OSS soon after Pearl Harbor, and headed to London with the other young Americans eager to learn the spying game. There he became a close friend of James Angleton (who left him a bequest in his will) and went on to become one of the most effective – and dubious – operatives in the CIA: he helped to organise a coup against Iran's democratically elected Prime Minister in 1953, and tried to steer his friend Colonel Nasser of Egypt away from Moscow. Copeland shared Angleton's views of America's role in the world, believing that the CIA had a right and a duty to steer political and economic events in the Middle East: 'The United States had to face and define its policy in all three sectors that provided the root causes of American interests in the region: the Soviet threat, the birth of Israel, and petroleum.' By 1956 he was living in Beirut, a partner in the industrial consultancy and PR firm Copeland and Eichelberger, no longer officially in the CIA but alert to every aspect of agency activities, with access to the daily cables passing through Applewhite's office. So far from hiding his intelligence links, Copeland paraded them as part of his business pitch.

Copeland had 'known and liked' Philby since 1944 when, along-side Angleton, he had studied the art of counter-espionage under Philby's tutelage in Ryder Street, London. Their friendship was renewed in Beirut, and Copeland would later claim to have known Philby 'better than anyone else, excepting two or three British intel-ligence officers'. Elliott also relished the piratical Copeland, 'a humorous and highly intelligent extrovert [and] a most colourful and entertaining friend'. The three families formed an intense trian-gular bond: Eleanor Philby, Elizabeth Elliott and Lorraine Copeland, Miles's outspoken Scottish wife, studied archaeology in the same class at the American University in Beirut, and went on digs; their husbands plotted and drank together; their children played tennis, swam and went skiing together. The Copelands lived in a large hill-top house (known to the local Lebanese, with blunt precision, as the 'CIA House'), which they filled with their friends and their chil-dren, one of whom, Stewart, would go on to become the drummer in the band The Police. As Beeston recalled, Copeland was the life and soul: 'Generous, outrageous, always fun, he never took himself too seriously and had a thoroughly irreverent approach to the intelligence profession.' He was also, in Elliott's estimation, 'one of the most indiscreet men I have ever met' – which endeared him even more to Elliott and Philby, for different reasons.

Copeland was an incurable gossip and an unstoppable show-off. 'I could trust him with any secret that had no entertainment value,' wrote Elliott. What neither Philby nor Elliott knew was that Copeland was also a paid spy for James Angleton, their friend. As the chief of CIA counter-intelligence, Angleton maintained his own network of informers, and Copeland was one of them, though he appeared nowhere on CIA accounts. Their arrangement was simple: Copeland would forward his (very large) entertainment bills to Angleton for payment; in return, Copeland kept Angleton abreast of what was going on in Beirut.

Many years later, Copeland claimed that Angleton had specifically instructed him to 'keep an eye on Philby' and 'report signs that he might be spying for the Soviets'; he even claimed to have sent a Lebanese security officer to follow Philby but found that the Englishman was 'still practising his old tradecraft [and] invariably shook off his tail'. Like Angleton's later assertions, Copeland's claim to have monitored Philby at Angleton's behest is almost certainly untrue. He was a practised fabulist, given to 'entertaining and colourful invention', in Elliott's words. If he had really put Philby under surveillance, then he would easily have caught him. But he didn't, for the very obvious (and very embarrassing) reason that he did not believe Philby *was* a Soviet spy, and neither did Angleton.

The major players in the Philby story were invariably wise after the event. Spies, even more than most people, invent the past to cover up mistakes. The Philby case has probably attracted more retrospective conspiracy theory than any other in the history of espionage: Dick White of MI6 was running a ruse to trap him; Nicholas Elliott was secretly jousting with him; James Angleton suspected him and set Miles Copeland to spy on him; Philby's fellow journalists (another tribe adept at misremembering the past) later claimed that they had always seen something fishy in his behaviour. Even Eleanor, his wife, would later look back, and claim to have discovered clues to his real identity. No one likes to admit they have been utterly conned. The truth was simpler, as it almost always is: Philby was spying on everyone, and no one was spying on him, because he fooled them all.

Every few weeks, on a Wednesday evening, Philby would stand holding a newspaper on his balcony; later the same night he would slip away to a nondescript backstreet restaurant in the Armenian quarter called Vrej (Armenian for 'revenge'), where Petukhov was waiting.

For Kim Philby, these were days of professional satisfaction and domestic tranquillity. Not since 1949 had his double lives co-existed so comfortably and invisibly: admired and feted by American and British intelligence officials, protected by Elliott and Angleton, paid regularly by the *Observer* and the *Economist*, secretly by MI6 and the KGB. Evenings were spent in a social whirl on the Anglo-American diplomatic circuit. On the rare occasions they stayed in, Philby would cook, and then read German poetry to his wife in 'a melodious voice' without a stutter. The happy household was completed by the addition of an exotic and unlikely pet, after some friends bought a baby fox cub from a Bedouin in the Jordan Valley, and presented it to the Philbys. They called it Jackie, and reared it by hand. The animal slept on the sofa and obeyed commands, like a dog. Jackie also shared Philby's taste for alcohol, 'lapping up' whisky from a saucer. 'She was affectionate and playful, cantering round the top of the parapet of our balcony.' Philby found the animal 'hopelessly endearing', and wrote a sentimental article for *Country Life* entitled 'The Fox Who Came to Stay'.

These were the 'happiest years', wrote Eleanor.

Philby's world of contented marriage and secret duplicity was about to fall apart, with two deaths, one defection and the unmasking of a Soviet spy within British intelligence who had nothing whatever to do with Kim Philby.

A Most Promising Officer

St John Philby, that rebel traditionalist, attended an Orientalists' conference in Moscow in the summer of 1960, then the Lord's cricket test match in London, in which England trounced South Africa, much to his satisfaction. On his way back to Saudi Arabia, he stopped off to visit his son in Beirut. At sixty-five, St John was as cantankerous and complicated as ever. He checked in to the Normandie Hotel, where he was 'treated with the deference due to an Eastern potentate'. Nicholas Elliott threw a lunch party for him, not without trepidation, knowing the elder Philby's capacity for extreme and unprovoked rudeness. 'Elizabeth and I were among the few English people to whom St John Philby was prepared to be civil.' To Elliott's surprise, the lunch was a social and diplomatic success. Humphrey Trevelyan, the British ambassador to Iraq, who was staying with the Elliotts, 'drew the old man out into telling us the story of his relationship with Ibn Saud'. The Philbys, the Copelands and several other friends attended this 'memorable occasion', lubricated by a small river of Lebanese wine.

Elliott described the ensuing events: St John Philby 'left at tea time, had a nap, made a pass at the wife of a member of the embassy staff in a night club, had a heart attack, and died'. The last words of this brilliant and impossible man were: 'God, I'm bored.' He left behind a shelf of scholarly works, two families, a black-throated partridge named after him (*Alectoris philbyi*), and an enduring trail of notoriety.

The relationship between father and son, Elliott reflected, had been 'a mixture of love and hate'. Philby admired and feared his father, whose domination, he felt, had caused his stammer. Back in the 1930s, he had spied on St John, while reporting to Soviet intelligence that his father was 'not completely well in the head'. But they had grown closer in later life, particularly after Kim's move to the Middle East. Philby told Elliott that his father had once advised him: 'If you feel strongly enough about anything you must have the guts to go through with it no matter what anyone might think.' Both Philbys had certainly done that. Kim later wrote that had his father lived to learn the truth about him, he would have been 'thunderstruck, but by no means disapproving'. That verdict is questionable. The elder Philby was a contrarian, a rule-breaker and something of an intellectual thug, but he was no traitor. Even so, he had always supported his son, driven his ambition, and undoubtedly planted the seeds of his sedition.

Kim buried St John Philby with full Islamic rites under his Muslim name, and then disappeared into the bars of Beirut. Elliott noted that Philby 'went out of circulation for days'. Eleanor was more specific: 'He drank himself senseless' and emerged from this ferocious drinking bout a changed man, frailer in both body and spirit. Philby's mother Dora had always doted on him, while his relationship with St John was often tense; yet St John's death affected him far more. 'Kim seemed overwhelmed by his father's death,' wrote Richard Beeston. His moorings began to slip.

★

A few months earlier, the British intelligence community in Beirut had been enlivened by the arrival of a new and glamorous addition to their ranks. At thirty-eight, George Behar had lived several lives already. Born in Rotterdam in 1922, to a Dutch mother and Egyptian-Jewish father, as a teenager he had joined the anti-Nazi resistance in the Netherlands, endured internment, and then fled to London disguised as a monk, where he joined MI6, trained as an interrogator in multiple languages, and changed his name to the more English-sounding George Blake. After the war he was posted to Korea to set up an MI6 intelligence network, but was captured by the advancing North Korean communist forces soon after his arrival, and held in captivity for three years. Finally emerging in 1953, Blake was welcomed back by MI6 as a returning hero and sent to Berlin as a case officer working under Elliott's friend Peter Lunn, tasked with recruiting Soviet intelligence officers as double agents. With his Egyptian blood and gift for languages, Blake was considered ideal material for a Middle East posting, and in 1960 he was enrolled in the Middle Eastern Centre for Arabic Studies, the language school in the hills outside Beirut, run by the Foreign Office. The centre offered intensive, eighteen-month courses in Arabic for diplomats, international businessmen, graduates and intelligence officers. The Lebanese regarded it as a spy school. With his sterling war record and his experience as a prisoner in North Korea, Blake was a minor celebrity in intelligence circles, and when the handsome young MI6 officer arrived in Beirut with his two sons and a pregnant wife, he was eagerly embraced by Anglo-American spy society.

Elliott considered George Blake 'a most promising officer' and a credit to the service, 'a good-looking fellow, tall and with excellent manners and universally popular'. He was stunned, therefore, to receive a message from London in April informing him that Blake was a Soviet spy, who must be tricked into returning to Britain where he would be interrogated, arrested and tried for treason.

Blake had been 'turned' during his North Korean captivity. In detention, he had read the works of Karl Marx and found what he thought was truth. But 'it was the relentless bombing of small Korean villages by enormous American flying fortresses' that triggered his whole-hearted conversion to communism: 'I felt I was on the wrong side.' British snobbery and prejudice may have played a part in his embrace of revolution, for, as a foreign-born Jew, Blake was never fully admitted to the MI6 club. 'He doesn't belong in the service,' sniffed one colleague. Blake considered himself a 'man of no class', but in the long intelligence tradition, he had wanted to marry his secretary, Iris Peake, the upper-crust daughter of an Old Etonian

Conservative MP. The relationship ran aground on the immovable British class system. 'He was in love with her, but could not possibly marry her because of his circumstances,' wrote his wife Gillian, who was also in MI6 (along with her father and sister). She believed the break-up had sharpened his resentment of the British establishment. In Berlin, Blake contacted the KGB, under the guise of recruiting spies within the Soviet service, and began passing over reams of top secret and highly damaging information, including details of numerous covert operations such as the Berlin Tunnel, a plot to eavesdrop on the Soviets from underground. At night he copied out Peter Lunn's index cards, listing and identifying every MI6 spy in Germany. Blake betrayed an estimated 400 agents, sending an untold number to their deaths. Soon after his arrival in Beirut, Blake established contact with Pavel Yefimovich Nedosekin, the KGB head of station, who gave him a telephone number to call in case of an emergency – a moment which was, though neither knew it, imminent.

Early in 1961, a Polish spy with a large moustache and an extravagant ego defected in Berlin. Lieutenant-Colonel Michael Goleniewski had been deputy head of military counter-intelligence and chief of the technical and scientific section of the Polish Intelligence Service. In the 1950s, he passed Polish secrets to the Soviets. Then in 1959, he began anonymously passing Polish and Soviet secrets to the CIA, which passed them on to MI6. Goleniewski was a fantasist (he would later claim to be the Tsarevich Alexei of Russia), but some of his intelligence was first-rate, including the revelation that a Soviet spy codenamed 'Lambda' was operating within British intelligence. And he had proof: copies of three MI6 documents that this spy had handed to his Soviet handlers. MI6 worked out that only ten people, in Warsaw and Berlin, could have had access to all three pieces of paper: one of them was George Blake. By the spring of 1961, MI6 was 'ninety per cent sure' that Blake was 'Lambda'. Dick White sent a cable to Elliott, instructing him that Blake should be lured 'to London immediately, on the pretext of discussing a future posting'. For once, Elliott did not tell his friend Kim Philby what was going on. The trap for George Blake was baited and set for Saturday 25 March.

A direct summons to London would have alerted Blake to the danger. Instead, Elliott contrived a chance meeting. On the morning of the twenty-fifth, Elliott's secretary called on the Blakes and told them that she had a spare ticket to an amateur production of *Charley's Aunt*. Blake's wife was busy looking after a sick child, and the secretary wondered 'whether Blake would like to accompany her'. Blake reluctantly agreed to take a break from his studies and spend a few hours watching British people performing this most English of plays. During the interval, Blake and the secretary repaired to the bar with the other thirsty ex-pats, and found Elliott and Elizabeth. 'In the course of conversation, Elliott drew me aside and said he was glad I happened to be there as this had saved him a trip up the mountain to see me. He had received a letter from Head Office with instructions for me to return to London for a few days' consultation in connection with a new appointment. It suggested that I should travel on Easter Monday so as to be available in London on Tuesday morning.'

The encounter was staged to allay suspicion: an unplanned meeting at a bar, not a directive; a leisurely letter, not an urgent telegram; a suggestion of when he might like to come to London, not an order. Yet Blake was alarmed. He was in the middle of his language course (for which MI6 was paying) and about to sit some important exams. He would be returning to London on holiday in July. What was the urgency? Blake called the emergency number Nedosekin had given him. They met later that evening on a beach near Beirut. Nedosekin said he would consult Moscow Centre: Blake held a valid Syrian visa, and if necessary he could be across the border in a few hours, and then whisked to Moscow. But when they met again the next day, Nedosekin was reassuring: 'Moscow saw no cause for concern. The KGB's enquiries had failed to reveal a leak: Blake should return to London, as requested.'

Before heading to England, Blake paid a last visit to Elliott, to say goodbye and collect some money for his airfare. Elliott was as jovial as ever, but as Blake was leaving, the MI6 station chief asked him whether he would like to be booked into St Ermin's Hotel, on Caxton Street, just a few yards from MI6 headquarters, for the duration of his London visit. (St Ermin's is the spy hotel: it was where Krivitsky was debriefed and Philby was recruited, bristling with intelligence officers, and probably the easiest place in London to keep tabs on a suspected traitor.) Blake politely declined, explaining that he planned to stay with his mother in Radlett, north of London. Elliott pressed the point, insisting it 'would be more convenient to stay at the hotel'. Why was Elliott so insistent he should stay there, rather than with his mother in rural Hertfordshire? 'For a moment a shadow of a doubt passed my mind but it passed away again,' Blake wrote. Elliott was probably just being helpful.

Dick White had seen Philby slip through his fingers in 1951; a decade later, he was not going to make the same mistake with Blake. On arriving in London, Blake was escorted to the MI6 house in Carlton Gardens, ushered into an upstairs room (which was bugged), and told that 'a few matters had cropped up about his time in Berlin that needed to be ironed out'. Elliott had told him he was coming back to discuss a future appointment; there had been no mention of the past. Blake now realised, with grim certainty, what was at hand: 'I was in deep trouble.' On the first day of interrogation, he stonewalled, as a trio of MI6 officers chipped away at his explanations; on the second, as the pressure mounted and he was shown evidence of his own espionage, he began to wobble. 'It wasn't hostile, but it was persistent.' Blake was now in no doubt that MI6 knew he was guilty. On day three, one of the interrogators remarked, in a friendly manner, that Blake must have been tortured by the North Koreans into confessing he was a British intelligence officer, and then blackmailed into working as a communist spy. It was all perfectly understandable.

Then Blake snapped: 'No, nobody tortured me! No, nobody blackmailed me! I myself approached the Soviets and offered my services to them of my own accord.'

Blake's pride could simply not allow him to accept the suggestion that he was spying for anything other than the most lofty ideological motives. Perhaps the same tactic might have flushed out Philby a decade earlier; then again, Blake lacked Philby's innate duality. 'The game was up,' he wrote. Over the ensuing days, his confession tumbled out, in a cathartic affirmation of his own guilt, delivered with some pride. But if Blake imagined that candour would win him clemency, he was mistaken. The British authorities hit him with 'the biggest hammer possible'.

The Blake case was the worst spy scandal since the defection of Burgess and Maclean, and in terms of raw intelligence losses, far more damaging. Blake had exposed scores of agents, though he would always maintain, implausibly, that there was no blood on his hands. He was charged under the Official Secrets Act, remanded in custody at a closed hearing, and incarcerated in Brixton Prison to await trial. A telegram flew around the world, in two sections, to every MI6 station: the first part read: 'The following name is a traitor'; the second, when decoded, spelled out the letters G-E-O-R-G-E-B-L-A-K-E.

The discovery of another spy in MI6 provoked a mixed reaction in the US. For some CIA veterans (including Bill Harvey, Philby's first and most vehement accuser) it was yet more evidence of British incompetence and treachery, but James Angleton was reassuring, telling Dick White: 'It can happen to anyone.'

The news of Blake's arrest and impending trial caused consternation in Beirut's intelligence community; no one was more genuinely shocked and alarmed than Kim Philby. In accordance with established intelligence rules, the KGB had maintained total separation between the Blake and Philby cases. The two spies had never met, and Blake had been recruited quite independently of the Cambridge network. But Blake's capture suggested, rightly, that MI6 must have new sources within Soviet intelligence, and if one mole had been dug out, then Philby might well be next.

Less than a month after confessing, Blake was in the dock at the Old Bailey. The maximum penalty for violation of the Official Secrets Act was fourteen years. The prosecutors, however, brought five separate charges against him, relating to five distinct time periods. The verdict was never in doubt, but the sentence drew gasps from the court. 'Your case is one of the worst that can be envisaged,' the judge declared, and then handed down fourteen-year jail terms for each of the charges; he further ordered that three of the terms should run consecutively – a total of forty-two years' imprisonment. The conviction was front-page news in every newspaper. It was the longest prison sentence ever handed down by a British court. Reporters suggested, fancifully, that Blake had been given a year for every agent he had betrayed and killed. By that arithmetic, he would have been sentenced to some four centuries behind bars.

The news of Blake's harsh sentence left Philby stunned. He had spied for longer than Blake, at a far higher level, and at greater human cost. In the 1950s the government had quailed at the prospect of a public trial for espionage; now the authorities seemed prepared to prosecute, and ruthlessly. If Philby were to be caught, tried and convicted in the same way as Blake, he would never get out of prison. For perhaps the first time, Philby realised the full extent of the peril he was in.

The journalist Richard Beeston visited Philby a few days later, to see what he made of the Blake story.

> I went round to his flat late in the morning to find it in chaos after a party with furniture overturned and bottles and glasses everywhere. Kim was looking terrible, nursing a hangover which made him even more incoherent. 'Never met Blake, never even heard of the chap until I read of his arrest,' Kim told me . . . Kim's appearance had strikingly deteriorated since I had last seen him. And there is little doubt that Blake's arrest and his savage forty-two-year prison sentence precipitated Kim's further decline.

For decades, Philby had drunk heavily, but never uncontrollably; henceforth, he became volatile and unpredictable. As an evening progressed, 'Kim would become insulting, abusive, make lunges at women and not infrequently goose the hostess.' Even Eleanor, a prodigious boozer herself, noticed that her husband was 'not light-hearted about drink any longer'. They argued publicly, and sometimes fought physically: one dinner party ended with the Philbys hurling mantelpiece ornaments at each other, while their appalled hosts looked on. Once a voluble drunk, he now drank himself incoherent, then silent, and finally unconscious. Parties ended with Philby slumped insensible on a sofa, or even under a blanket on the floor while the party continued around him. After sobering up, he would send a charming note of apology, and frequently flowers. 'By the next day he was usually forgiven.'

Philby had always prided himself on maintaining his spycraft no matter how much alcohol he consumed. Now he began to make mistakes. A first rule of espionage is to avoid consistency of behaviour, but friends noticed that Philby was frequently absent on Wednesday nights. One teased him: 'I know all about your Wednesday nights.' Philby looked aghast. Wednesday was his night for meeting Petukhov. He dropped remarks, suggestive of a man in fear. One night at Joe's bar, Moyra Beeston asked Philby, half in jest, if he really was the 'Third Man'. Instead of denying it, or even replying directly, he seized her by the wrist so hard he left a bruise. 'You know Moyra, I always believe that loyalty to your friends is more important than anything else' – a self-revealing remark for a man who had repeatedly betrayed his own friends, in obedience to what he claimed was a higher loyalty. 'What would you do if you knew something awful was going to happen to a friend and only you could do something about it?' he asked her. He was plainly referring to his own decision to tip off Maclean so many years earlier, but also to his current predicament, as he awaited 'something awful'.

In late August 1962, Kim and Eleanor headed to Jordan for a long-planned family holiday. A few days before they were due to come home, Philby announced that he had to return to Beirut at once, offering no explanation for his sudden departure. When Eleanor got back to the flat, she found the lights off, and Philby sitting in the dark on the terrace, sodden with drink and inconsolable with grief.

'What's the matter? What's wrong?'

'Jackie's dead,' said Philby.

The pet fox had fallen from the balcony, dropping five floors to the street below. Eleanor suspected that the Lebanese maid, who had long disapproved of keeping a smelly wild animal in a city flat, had pushed the fox over the parapet.

'Kim seemed to give himself up to grief,' wrote Eleanor, who thought his mourning for the pet, while understandable, 'seemed out of all proportion'. Nicholas Elliott, too, was surprised and worried that Philby seemed 'shattered' by the death of the fox, anguished and tearful: 'Apart from when his father died, this was the only occasion, in all the times I spent with Philby, that I knew him to display visible emotion.' Philby was cracking up, partly through grief, and partly through fear.

★

In Helsinki some seven months earlier, a short, stout Russian wrapped in a fur coat had knocked on the door of Frank Freiberg, the CIA representative in Finland, and announced, in very bad English, that he wanted to defect to the West. Major Anatoly Golitsyn of the KGB had been planning his move for some time. As a senior officer in the KGB's strategic planning department and a fifteen-year veteran of Soviet intelligence, he had accumulated a vast trove of secrets, most of them memorised, or half-memorised, or almost-remembered. For the problem with Golitsyn was that while he knew a great deal about some aspects of Soviet intelligence, he also knew a little about a lot. Much of the information he carried, in his head and in the package of documents he had hidden in the snow before knocking on Freiberg's door, was reliable and accurate; but much was fragmentary, and some was wrong. Golitsyn was whisked to the US, to begin a debriefing process that would continue for many years.

James Angleton was delighted, insisting that Golitsyn was 'the most valuable defector ever to reach the West'. Others considered him unreliable. Some thought he was a fruitcake. In the spring of 1962, the CIA allowed Golitsyn to travel to London to be interviewed by British intelligence. There Golitsyn described how, in Moscow, he had heard tell of a 'very important spy network in the United Kingdom called the Ring of Five', a quintet of British spies who had met at university and over many years had furnished Soviet intelligence with the most valuable information. Although Golitsyn could not identify Philby by name, or even codename, that information alone was enough to revive the long-dormant investigation, and put MI5's mole-hunters firmly back on Philby's trail.

The defection sent shockwaves through the KGB. Some fifty-four KGB stations around the world were instructed to report whatever Golitsyn might know about their operations. Meetings with important KGB agents were suspended, and plans were approved for the assassination, at the earliest opportunity, of Anatoly Golitsyn.

Yuri Modin had left Britain in 1958. But in the summer of 1962, according to CIA records, he travelled to the Middle East, via Pakistan. Not until much later did MI5 investigators work out that Modin's trip coincided with the moment that Philby had suddenly returned early from the family holiday in Jordan, from which point on he had 'exhibited increasing signs of alcoholism and stress'. MI5 concluded that 'Modin had gone to Beirut to alert Philby', and tell him that another, well-informed, defector was spilling secrets. If Modin made contact with Philby in Beirut, the location has never been revealed. He later described the once-irrepressible Agent Stanley as 'a shadow of his former self'. The purpose of his visit was clear: 'To warn Philby not to return to Britain because of the danger of arrest, and to make contingency plans for his escape.' The warning, however, seems to have sent Philby into a tailspin of fear. When Eleanor found Philby sitting in the dark, his tears were not only for his dead fox.

In October 1962, Nicholas Elliott was offered a new post, as the MI6 director for Africa, based in London. It was another major promotion, covering another important Cold War arena. His two years in the Lebanon had been fascinating, fruitful and fun, with plenty of the 'belly laughs' for which Elliott lived. He would be leaving Beirut with regrets, not least over Philby's deteriorated state.

Peter Lunn, his predecessor in Vienna, would replace him as MI6 station chief. Before heading to Beirut to take over from Elliott, Lunn asked Dick White what, if anything, he should do about Kim Philby. White was aware that Philby was back in MI5's sights. 'Of course he's a traitor,' he snapped. 'Just keep an eye on him. Let's wait and see what happens.'

Philby was also waiting, with dread. Bereaved, under threat of exposure, alarmed by the shocking example made of Blake, and now deprived of the companionship and immediate support of the one person who had always defended him, Philby sank ever deeper into the whisky bottle.

The denouement came not by way of new information from a fresh defector, as Philby feared, but through an old friend, recalling a thirty-year-old conversation he had long forgotten.

I Thought it Would Be You

Flora Solomon had lived a life that stretched, rather bizarrely, from the Russian Revolution to the British High Street: after an early affair with a Bolshevik revolutionary and marriage to a British soldier, she had been widowed young, raised her son Peter alone (who by 1961 had founded Amnesty International) and then created the welfare department at Marks and Spencer. A pillar of Anglo-Jewish society, she continued to hold regular salons in her Mayfair home, just as she had in the 1930s. Solomon remained Russian in accent, British in manner, and a committed Zionist in her politics. 'Russian soul, Jewish heart, British passport' was how she described herself. By 1962, her main passion in life was the state of Israel, which she defended and supported, in word, deed and funds, at every opportunity.

It was Flora Solomon's commitment to Israel that brought Kim Philby back into her life. Every week, she read the *Observer*, paying particular attention to coverage of the Middle East, and found herself becoming increasingly irritated by Philby's articles. 'To anyone with eyes to see they were permeated with anti-Israel bias. They accepted the Soviet view of Middle East politics,' she wrote. In the simplistic divisions imposed by the Cold War, while Israel was supported by Washington, Moscow curried favour among the Arab states, and in Solomon's subjective opinion, Philby was churning out Soviet propaganda designed to weaken her beloved Israel. (This was not actually true: Philby was instinctively pro-Arab, but he was far too canny to reveal any overt pro-Soviet bias in his journalism.) During the 1950s she had assumed that the accusations against Philby were merely McCarthyite smears. Now she was not so sure. She remembered his remarks about 'the cause' back in 1935, and the rather clumsy attempt to recruit her. 'The thought occurred to me that Philby had, after all, remained a communist, notwithstanding his clearance by MI5 of possible complicity in the Burgess-Maclean scandal.'

In August 1962, Flora Solomon visited Israel, as she had done many times before, to attend a conference at the Chaim Weizmann Institute, the science research centre in Rehovot founded by Israel's first President and endowed by Baron Sieff, the chairman of Marks and Spencer. At a party in Weizmann's home, she encountered Victor, Lord Rothschild, another patron of the institute. A distinguished scientist himself, Rothschild had headed MI5's sabotage and explosives section during the war and won the George Medal for 'dangerous work in hazardous circumstances'. A regular at the Harris soirées and a Cambridge contemporary of Burgess and Blunt, Rothschild would later be accused, quite unfairly, of being a Soviet spy himself. In fact, though a left-winger in his youth, like Flora Solomon he had no truck with communism, and retained close links with MI5. Rothschild and Solomon had known each other since the 1930s, and their conversation naturally drifted towards their mutual acquaintance, Kim Philby.

'How is it the *Observer* uses a man like Kim? Don't they know he's a communist?' observed Solomon.

Rothschild was startled by the certainty in her voice. Solomon went on to describe how, back in 1935, Philby had told her, with pride, that he was doing a 'very dangerous job for peace', and attempted to enlist her as a communist spy. Rothschild was now listening intently. He had followed the Philby case closely, and knew that despite an array of circumstantial evidence against a man who had once been his friend, no one had come forward to link Philby directly with Soviet intelligence. He began to quiz her about Philby and the wartime circle of friends they had shared. She replied that she had always suspected that Tommy Harris might be a Soviet spy, based on an 'intuitive feeling that Harris was more than just a friend' to Kim Philby.

Flora Solomon later maintained that her motives in exposing Philby were strictly political: he was writing anti-Israeli articles, and she wanted him sacked from the *Observer*. But her reasons were also personal. Solomon had introduced Philby to Aileen back in 1939, and felt partly responsible for the saga that ensued, ending in Aileen's sad and lonely death. Solomon had tried to put the tragedy out of her mind, but she remained furious with Philby for 'the terrible way he treated his women'. The ghost of Aileen Furse was about to exact revenge.

'You must do something,' Flora Solomon told Rothschild, in her imperious way.

'I will think about it,' he told her.

Victor Rothschild was a veteran string-puller. He did more than think. On his return to London, he immediately reported the conversation to MI5, sparking jubilation among the small group of officers still determined to bring Philby to justice. Here, at last, was a 'major breakthrough'. With difficulty, Flora Solomon was persuaded to come to an interview with MI5 officers in Rothschild's flat, which was bugged for the occasion. There she repeated her account of the conversation with Philby from three decades earlier. The investigators found her 'a strange, rather untrustworthy woman', and suspected she had been more deeply implicated in left-wing radicalism than she was admitting. The interview was recorded by MI5 investigator Peter Wright. Writing many years later in his explosive book *Spycatcher*, Wright wondered if she and Philby had been lovers, and whether her belated revelation was motivated by spite: 'She clearly had a grudge against him.'

Flora Solomon was now getting cold feet, alarmed that if she testified against Philby she might invite the attentions of a KGB assassination squad. 'I will never give public evidence,' she told MI5. 'There is too much risk.' The more MI5 pressed her to make a formal legal statement, the more anxious she became: 'It will leak, I know it will leak, and then what will my family do?' She did, however, agree to speak to officers from Mossad, although offended by the implication that she would be more forthcoming with Israeli intelligence officials than British ones.

Solomon's revelation finally provided evidence that Philby had been an active Soviet spy, a recruiter for the communist cause who had deliberately covered up his past and lied repeatedly under interrogation. It was the ammunition that Buster Milmo had lacked, and the evidence of guilt that Philby's supporters had always demanded. 'Why didn't she tell us ten years ago?' said White, when told of Solomon's revelation. She had a ready answer for that question: 'I had not volunteered information as every public statement had pointed to his innocence.' The fault was not hers, she insisted, but theirs: Philby's escape from justice was proof of 'how clubmanship and the old school tie could protect their own'.

That protection was now at an end; MI5 prepared to strike. The officer who had worked on the Philby case since 1951, Arthur Martin, would administer the *coup de grâce*. For more than a decade, Martin had tried to pierce Philby's armour. No one knew the case better. With Solomon's evidence, and the corroborative testimony from Golitsyn, the other elements of suspicion slotted into place. An intense debate now began over how to bring Philby to account, a task that still presented major problems, politically, legally and practically. Even if Solomon could somehow be persuaded to testify, her evidence was hearsay. George Blake had been convicted by his own testimony, but Philby would probably deny everything, as he always had, and without a confession there was no guarantee of a conviction. Any trial would be embarrassing, particularly if it emerged that Philby was still in the pay of MI6; but a trial that failed to secure a conviction would be disastrous. For Harold Macmillan, now Prime Minister, the issue was particularly sensitive: as Foreign Secretary, he had personally cleared Philby; another espionage trial could bring down the Conservative government. Philby might be tricked into returning to England, perhaps by a summons from his editors, and then forced into a confession. But Philby knew very well how Blake had been trapped, and was adjudged 'far too wily' to fall for the same ruse; a summons to London would merely alert him. There were even more radical alternatives: Philby could be abducted from Beirut, or even killed. But given the rising Cold War tension, the murder or kidnapping of a Soviet spy might set off an ugly retaliation, with untold consequences. Besides, since the Crabb affair there had been little appetite for dramatic adventures. Only Philby knew the full extent of his own espionage; alive, he might be persuaded to reveal other Soviet spies lurking inside the British establishment.

'We need to discover what damage he caused,' Dick White told Macmillan. 'A full damage report with all the details of how the Russians had operated and who else was working with Philby is of great importance.' Besides, though he might be a traitor, Philby 'should be treated as a gentleman'. White sketched out a plan of action that would cause least embarrassment, while yielding maximum benefit: Arthur Martin should fly to Beirut as soon as possible, present Philby with the conclusive evidence against him, and then offer him a way out: immunity from prosecution in return for a full confession and complete cooperation. No such deal had been offered to George Blake; but then Blake, a foreigner, was not a gentleman. Macmillan agreed to the plan, but insisted on total secrecy: 'Keep a lid on things,' he instructed Dick White. The Attorney-General and the Under-Secretary at the Foreign Office also approved the plan, though they were careful to commit nothing to paper. MI5 compiled a 'voluminous brief in preparation for the confrontation', which Martin studied as he prepared for the showdown in Beirut: he would break Philby, extract the truth, and destroy him once and for all. The only obstacle to this happy scenario was Nicholas Elliott.

Within days of his return to London, Elliott was summoned to see Dick White, and told, with some relish, that there could no longer be any doubt: Flora Solomon's evidence confirmed that Philby had been a Soviet spy since the early 1930s. He had betrayed his country, his class and his club; he had lied to MI5 and MI6, the CIA and FBI, to his family, friends and colleagues; he had deceived everyone, egregiously, brilliantly, for more than thirty years. But no one had been betrayed more comprehensively than Nicholas Elliott.

Elliott had been just twenty-four, grieving over the death of Basil Fisher, when he was befriended and beguiled by Philby, a man he had then trusted, revered and supported throughout his adult life. Their lives had seemed to run in tandem, through public school, Cambridge and MI6, overlapping professionally, culturally and geographically. From St Albans to Istanbul, Elliott had modelled himself on Philby: his spycraft, his air of worldly irony, his umbrella with the ebony handle. They seldom discussed their fears, or hopes, for theirs was a most English friendship, founded on cricket, alcohol and jokes, based on a shared set of assumptions about the world, and their privileged place in it. They were as close as two heterosexual, upper-class, mid-century Englishmen could be. Elliott's loyalty was of the military type, an unquestioning readiness to stand by a comrade under fire: he had valued this friendship forged in wartime above all else. Now, for the first time, he began to count its cost, to wonder how many people he, James Angleton and others had unwittingly condemned to death. Some of the victims had names: the German anti-communist Catholics identified by the Vermehrens; the Volkovs in Istanbul; the young Georgians slipped across the Turkish border to their deaths; perhaps even Buster Crabb's strange death could be attributed to Philby. Many casualties remain nameless: the multiple agents infiltrated behind the Iron Curtain, and never seen again; the Albanian 'pixies', captured and killed in their hundreds, along with their families; the unknown number of agents exposed in the Middle East. Elliott would never be able to calculate the precise death tally, for who can remember every conversation, every confidence exchanged with a friend stretching back three decades? The weekends at the cricket, the evenings at the club, the nights on the town in Beirut: it had all been a charade, the simulacrum of comradeship, while Philby gathered information for his Soviet masters. Elliott had given away almost every secret he had to Philby; but Philby had never given away his own.

Elliott's emotions on discovering Philby's betrayal can only be surmised, for he preferred not to discuss them. His upper lip remained ramrod stiff. He came from a generation of Englishmen who believed that feelings are a sign of weakness, to be suppressed, ignored or laughed off. A different sort of man might have buckled under the pain, but Elliott was tough, and a dissembler in his own way, for British breeding and schooling produce a very distinctive brand of protective dishonesty. As John le Carré once wrote, the privately educated Englishman 'is the greatest dissembler on earth . . . Nobody will charm you so glibly, disguise his feelings from you better, cover his tracks more skilfully or find it harder to confess to you that he's been a damn fool . . . He can have a Force Twelve nervous break-down while he stands next to you in the bus queue and you may be his best friend but you'll never be the wiser.' Elliott had survived a brutal prep school, the chilliness of his father, the death of his first friend, by pretending that everything was perfectly all right. And he survived Philby's intimate betrayal in exactly the same way. But those who knew him best saw that beneath the ever-languid manner, the armoury of jokes and the insouciant air, from the moment he finally understood and accepted Philby's treachery, Elliott's world changed utterly: inside, he was crushed, humiliated, enraged and saddened. For the rest of his life, he would never cease to wonder how a man to whom he had felt so close, and so similar in every way, had been, underneath, a fraud. Once, he would have died for Philby; now, as he told his son, he would 'happily have killed him'. Philby had made a first-class fool of him and a mockery of their lifelong friendship; he had broken every canon of clubmanship and fraternity, and caused incalculable damage to the service, and the country, that Elliott loved. Elliott needed to know why. He wanted to look Philby in the eye one last time. He wanted to understand.

Elliott demanded to be allowed to confront Philby himself. He had known him more than half his life, and if anyone could extract a confession from the man, it was surely he. The idea appealed to Dick White. Elliott's righteous anger might lend him additional moral weight, and 'there was more chance that Philby could be persuaded to confess by an outraged sympathiser than by a stiff, lower-middle-class MI5 officer'. White calculated that since Elliott had been 'Philby's greatest supporter in 1951, his anger at having been betrayed would suggest that we had more proof than he real-ised'. In the past, White had been nettled by Elliott's support for Philby, but he considered him 'a proficient, clever and determined officer who would stop at nothing if the interests of the Crown required'. It was agreed: Elliott would fly out to Beirut, and nail Philby. The CIA was not informed about the proof of Philby's guilt, or the decision to have Elliott confront him. The Americans could be informed once the case had been resolved. If James Angleton found out what was going on, he would certainly demand some involvement. The decision was made to keep him in the dark. Some wondered whether Elliott would be able to restrain his anger if he was allowed in the same room as the friend who had cheated him so thoroughly, but 'Elliott swore not to exceed his brief, coldly angry though he now was'.

Peter Wright described the reaction inside MI5 to the news that MI6 was sending not the dogged Arthur Martin to confront Philby, but one of their own tribe.

> The few of us inside MI5 privy to this decision were appalled. It was not simply a matter of chauvinism, though, not unnaturally, that played a part. We in MI5 had never doubted Philby's guilt from the beginning, and now at last we had the evidence needed to corner him. Philby's friends in MI6, Elliott chief among them, had continually protested his innocence. Now, when the proof was inescapable, they wanted to keep it in-house. The choice of Elliott rankled strongly.

To strengthen Elliott's hand, Dick White told him that new evidence had been obtained from the defector, Anatoly Golitsyn, although exactly what he revealed remains a matter of conjecture, and some mystery. Golitsyn had not specifically identified Philby as 'Agent Stanley', but White gave Elliott the impression that he had. Was this intentional sleight of hand by White, allowing Elliott to believe that the evidence against Philby was stronger than it really was? Or did Elliott interpret as hard fact something that had only been implied?

Either way, he prepared for his trip to Beirut in the certainty that Philby was bang to rights: 'We'd fully penetrated the KGB, so we had confirmation.' Elliott's instructions were verbal, and only two men knew what they were: Dick White, and Nicholas Elliott himself.

In Beirut, Eleanor Philby watched in despair as her once-charming husband fell apart in a miasma of drink and depression. Philby was 'vertically intoxicated, horizontally intoxicated', and often intoxicated in solitude. 'It was as if our flat was the only place he felt safe.' When he did venture out for social events, he invariably ended up insensible. To her deep embarrassment he had to be bodily carried out of an embassy party. 'He only had to smell a drink to set him off. His depression never seemed to lift,' wrote Eleanor, who 'groped to understand his tension and remoteness'. 'What is the matter?' she asked him repeatedly. 'Why don't you tell me?'

'Oh nothing, nothing,' he would reply.

Looking back, she realised that Philby's desperate drinking, his search for alcoholic oblivion, was the mark of a man living in dread.

Philby's journalism dried to a trickle. Peter Lunn noticed that Philby's hands shook when they met for the first time. Philby insisted that if they should ever encounter each other at a social event, they should pretend to be strangers – a precaution that Lunn considered bizarre and unnecessary. After Elliott's warmth, Eleanor found Lunn a 'very cold fish indeed'.

On New Year's Eve, Philby refused to go to any of the numerous Beirut parties on offer, and instead sat drinking champagne with Eleanor on the balcony of the flat, in gloomy silence. The next day was his fifty-first birthday, and Eleanor had planned a small midday drinks party. By 2.30, the guests had left. The Philbys intended to spend the day quietly at home, but then Miles Copeland appeared: 'He dragged us protesting to an all-day New Year party given by some Americans.' Philby had 'already had a good deal to drink', and became steadily drunker. As night fell, they staggered home to the Rue Kantari. Eleanor was preparing for bed, when she heard a loud crash from the bathroom, a cry of pain, and then another crash. Philby had fallen over, smashed his head on the radiator, lurched to his feet, and fallen again. 'He was bleeding profusely from two great gashes on the crown of his head. The whole bathroom was spattered with blood.' Eleanor wrapped his head in a towel, and rushed frantically to the telephone. Philby, dazed and still drunk, refused to leave the flat. Finally, a Lebanese doctor arrived and declared: 'If we don't get your husband to the hospital I will not be responsible for his life.' Philby was coaxed into the lift and driven to the American University hospital, where he was stitched up and sedated. A doctor took Eleanor aside and told her gravely that with 'one more ounce of alcohol in his blood, he would have been dead'.

Philby insisted on returning home that night. He cut a pathetic figure, in a blood-stained dressing gown, with two livid black eyes and a turban of bandages around his head. 'I was a bloody fool,' he muttered. 'I'm going on the wagon – forever.'

A week later, Nick Elliott broke the journey to Beirut in Athens, where he met Halsey Colchester, the MI6 station chief, and his wife Rozanne, valued friends from Istanbul days. Elliott had already 'prepared himself for a battle of wits he was determined to win', but he needed to unburden himself before heading on to Beirut. 'I've got an awful task,' he told Halsey and Rozanne. 'I've got to beard him.' Like Elliott, the Colchesters had long admired and defended Philby, and they were stunned by the proof of his guilt. 'It was a terrible shock to hear he was this awful spy. He was always so nice, so affable and intelligent.'

Rozanne had known Elliott as a carefree spirit – 'he always laughed about things' – but over dinner in Athens, he was deadly serious, anxious and anguished. Rozanne's account of that night is a picture of a man facing the worst moment of his life.

Nicholas knew he had blood on his hands. He knew Philby so well, and he was horrified by the whole thing. He said he wouldn't mind shooting him. He didn't know what he was going to say, and I remember him coaching himself: 'There's no pretending now. We know who you are.' Nick was usually a very funny man. Like an actor or entertainer, you never felt he was quite real. One never *really* felt one knew him. Nicholas had that English way of not getting too involved, a sort of façade with endless jokes. But that night he was very highly strung. He was dreading it, and it was quite dangerous. He thought he might have been shot by Philby, or the Soviets. 'I hope he doesn't take a pot shot,' he said. He talked obsessively about Philby, about how he had known him so well. He didn't have to go through the ordeal, but he wanted to. It was really quite brave. He wanted to make sure for himself.

Elliott arrived in Beirut on 10 January 1963, and checked into a small, discreet hotel, far from the usual haunts of the spies and journalists. Only Peter Lunn knew he was in the city. Together they prepared the ground for the confrontation. Lunn's secretary had an apartment in the Christian quarter, near the sea. The sitting room was carefully bugged by an MI6 technician with a hidden microphone under the sofa, and a wire running to a tape-recorder in the next-door room. Elliott bought a bottle of brandy. When everything was ready, Lunn telephoned Philby and 'in a casual voice' suggested 'a meeting between himself and Philby to discuss future plans'. He gave no hint that anything was amiss. Since Philby had himself stressed the need for security, Lunn suggested meeting over tea at his secretary's flat, where they could chat in private. Philby had barely left the Rue Kantari since his drunken fall on New Year's Day, but he agreed to meet Lunn at the appointed address the following afternoon. He later told Eleanor: 'The minute that call came through, I knew the balloon was up.'

At four o'clock on 12 January, Philby, his head still swathed in bandages, and a little unsteady on his feet, climbed the stairs and knocked on the apartment door.

When it was opened by Nicholas Elliott, Philby seemed strangely unsurprised. 'I rather thought it would be you,' he said.

Teatime

Philby's reaction to Elliott's unannounced arrival in Beirut was interpreted, in the more paranoia-prone parts of MI5, as evidence that he had been tipped off in advance. It sparked a hunt for another Soviet spy within British intelligence that lasted two decades, and a conspiracy theory that still smoulders today. In reality, when Philby said he was not surprised to find Elliott waiting for him at the flat, he was stating a fact. He had feared exposure for years, and expected it imminently; he knew how Elliott's mind worked, and he knew that if the truth about his spying had finally emerged, then Elliott would want to confront him with it.

The two men shook hands. Elliott inquired about the bandage on Philby's head. Philby explained that he had fallen over after a party. The embassy secretary poured tea, and then discreetly left the apartment. The two men sat down, for all the world as if they were meeting in the club. In the next room, Peter Lunn and a stenographer, both wearing headphones, hunched over a turning tape-recorder.

The full transcript of the ensuing dialogue has never been released by MI5. Indeed, parts of the recording are almost inaudible; Elliott was no technical expert. Shortly before Philby's arrival, he had opened the apartment windows and as a result, much of their dialogue is obscured by the sounds wafting up from the busy Beirut street below. One of the most important conversations in the history of the Cold War takes place to the accompaniment of car horns, grinding engines, Arabic voices and the faint clink of china teacups.

But enough could be heard to reconstruct what followed: a display of brutal English politeness, civilised and lethal.

Elliott asked after Philby's health.

'Perfectly tolerable,' said Philby, adding that he was recovering from a double bout of flu and bronchitis. 'They were both against me.'

Philby asked after Elliott's family. All well, said Elliott. Mark was starting the new term at Eton.

'Wonderful tea,' he said.

A pause.

'Don't tell me you flew all the way here to see me?' said Philby.

Elliott took out his Mont Blanc pen, placed it on the table, and began to roll it back and forth under his palm. It was an act of nervous tension, but also an old interrogation trick, a distraction.

'Sorry for getting right on with it. Kim, I don't have time to postpone this. And we've known each other for ever, so, if you don't mind, I'll get right to the point,' said Elliott, not getting to the point. 'Unfortunately it's not very pleasant.' Another pause. 'I came to tell you that your past has caught up with you.'

Philby immediately counter-attacked. 'Have you all gone mad once again? You want to start all that? After all these years? You've lost your sense of humour. You'll be a laughing stock!'

'No, we haven't lost anything. On the contrary we've found additional information about you. It puts everything in place.'

'What information? And what is there to put in place?'

Elliott stood, walked to the window, and stared down into the street.

'Listen Kim, you know I was on your side all the time from the moment there were suspicions about you. But now there is new information. They've shown it to me. And now even I am convinced, absolutely convinced that you worked for the Soviet intelligence services. You worked for them right up until '49.'

Philby later expressed bafflement as to why Elliott should identify 1949 as the date he stopped spying for the Russians. The answer was simple: 1949 was the year Philby went to Washington; if he admitted to spying while in America then James Angleton, the CIA and the FBI would all want to know what intelligence secrets he had given away, and could well demand his extradition to face charges under US law. The offer of immunity would be meaningless. For the purposes of the deal, Elliott needed Philby to admit spying up to, but no later than, 1949. That way, the problem could be dealt with 'in-house' by MI6, without American involvement.

But Philby was not ready to admit anything.

'Who told you that nonsense? It's totally absurd' – and, appealing to Elliott's sense of fair play – 'You know yourself that it's absurd.'

But Elliott pressed on: 'We have new information that you were indeed working with the Soviet intelligence service ...'

'Do you want me to go into all this again?'

'Kim, the game's up. We know what you did. We've penetrated the KGB, Kim. There's no doubt in my mind any more that you were a KGB agent.'

Decades of friendship were fracturing around them. But still the atmosphere remained calm – though taut – the words polite. More tea was poured. Elliott rolled his pen back and forth. Philby broke the silence.

'Look how stupid this seems. Astonishing! A man is suspected for a long time of mortal sin, they can't prove a thing, they're embarrassed in front of the whole world. They apologise. Then ten years later, some chief is struck by the old idea again. They decide to send an old friend, a wise and decent man, with only one goal, to persuade an innocent man to confess that he's a Russian spy ... Is that why you're here?'

'Kim, if you were in my place, if you knew what I know ...'

'I wouldn't talk to you the way you're talking to me.'

'And how would you talk to me?'

'I would offer you a drink instead of this lousy tea.' It was meant to be a joke, but Elliott did not laugh. And he did not offer him a drink.

'Do you want me to give you my version of your work for the Russians? Do you want me to tell you what you were thinking?'

'Nicholas, are you serious?'

'I am.'

Elliott had spent years believing he knew what was in Philby's mind, only to discover that he had been completely wrong. The speech he now delivered was that of a man struggling to understand the incomprehensible.

I understand you. I've been in love with two women at the same time. I'm certain that you were in the same situation in politics: you loved England and the Soviet Union at the same time. But you've worked for the Soviet Union long enough, you've helped it enough. Now you must help us ... You stopped working for them in 1949. I'm absolutely certain of that. Now it's January 1963. Fourteen years have gone by. In that time your ideas and views have changed. They had to change. I can understand people who worked for the Soviet Union, say, before or during the war. But by 1949, a man of your intellect and spirit had to see that all the rumours about Stalin's monstrous behaviour were not rumours, they were the truth. You decided to break with the USSR.

Philby shrugged, and shook his head. 'You came here to interrogate me. And I keep thinking I'm talking to a friend.'

It was the second time Philby had invoked their friendship. Something snapped: Elliott suddenly exploded.

'You took me in for years. Now I'll get the truth out of you even if I have to drag it out. You had to choose between Marxism and your family, and you chose Marxism. I once looked up to you, Kim. My God, how I despise you now. I hope you've enough decency left to understand why.'

These were the first angry words he had ever spoken to Philby. The pretence of politeness was gone. Neither man moved, or spoke.

Elliott slowly regained his composure, and eventually broke the crackling silence. 'I'm sure we can work something out.'

Elliott laid out the deal. If Philby confessed everything, back in London or, if he preferred, in Beirut, then he would not be prosecuted. But he would need to reveal all: every contact with Soviet intelligence, every other mole in Britain, every secret he had passed to Moscow over a lifetime of spying. 'I can give you my word, and that of Dick White, that you will get full immunity, you will be pardoned, but only if you tell it yourself. We need your collaboration, your help.'

Philby said nothing, and Elliott's voice hardened as he continued. If Kim refused to play ball, if he persisted in denying the truth, he would be left in the cold. His passport would be withdrawn, and his residence permit revoked. He would not even be able to open a bank account. He would never work for another British newspaper, let alone MI6. His children would be removed from their expensive schools. He would live the rest of his life as a penniless pariah, a 'leper' in Elliott's words. The choice was stark: a gentleman's agreement, safety in return for a full confession; or he could stand by his denials, and 'his life would be rendered intolerable'. There was, of course, a third option, so obvious to both men that Elliott had no need to mention it. Philby could cut and run.

Philby was now on his feet, and making for the door. The tea party was over.

'If you cooperate, we will give you immunity from prosecution. Nothing will be published.'

The door was now open.

'You've been a lucky chap so far, Kim. You have exactly twenty-four hours. Be back here at precisely 4 p.m. tomorrow. If you're as intelligent as I think you are, you'll accept.'

Philby's reply, if he made one, was not picked up by the hidden microphone.

'I'm offering you a lifeline, Kim ...'

The door closed behind him.

★

Philby's parting silence was itself an admission. 'He never once asked what the new evidence was.' He was no longer protesting. He would seize the lifeline. 'Kim's broken,' Elliott told Lunn. 'Everything's OK,' and that evening, he dashed off a reassuring telegram to Dick White in London. Inside, however, he was deeply anxious. Would Philby come back? Would he cooperate, clam up, or try to escape? 'The next twenty-four hours were a testing time.'

The next day, on the stroke of four, Philby reappeared at the apartment. He seemed sober and composed.

'OK, here's the scoop,' he said. 'But first you owe me a drink. I haven't had one since my birthday on New Year's Day.'

Elliott poured two large brandies.

Philby then launched into a prepared speech, a peculiar confection of truth, half-truth and lies. He said that he had been recruited into the Soviet secret service by his first wife, Litzi (which was not exactly true), and that he had, in turn, recruited Maclean and Burgess (which was). From his pocket he drew two sheets of paper, on which he had typed a sanitised, incomplete account of his work for Moscow, with few details and fewer names. He admitted he had been recruited by the Soviet intelligence service in 1934, but claimed that he had stopped working for Moscow immediately after the war, having 'seen the error of his ways'. Yes, he had tipped off Maclean in 1951, but merely as an act of loyalty to a friend, not as one active spy protecting another. He listed his early KGB handlers, but made no mention of the Soviet intelligence officers he had dealt with in Istanbul, Washington, London and Beirut.

'Is Nedosekin your contact?' asked Elliott, referring to the KGB station chief who had handled George Blake before his capture and arrest.

'I've got no bloody contact,' lied Philby, with a show of irritation. 'I broke contact with the KGB.'

Elliott knew Philby was withholding. The two-page summary was a 'very bland document' that admitted spying within a narrow timeframe. It was, Elliott knew, a 'limited confession', but it was nonetheless a signed admission of guilt, admissible in a court of law, and a document that transformed the game. Philby had acknowledged being a Soviet spy, and more disclosures would surely follow. By implication he had accepted the deal in principle, and a negotiation was under way: his liberty in exchange for information. MI6 now held a signed confession, however partial. He would never be able to row back from here. Elliott had the upper hand.

But what was Philby up to? The question is hard to answer, because Philby himself never told the whole truth about his own intentions. He would later claim he had been merely playing for time, toying with Elliott, controlling the situation with 'just a little stalling, just a little drinking', while he made his plans. His behaviour suggests otherwise. Philby was in turmoil, trapped, tempted by Elliott's offer, and acutely conscious that his future depended on how he played the game. How much could he get away with concealing? Would MI6 honour the deal? If he said too much, would he end up hanging himself? Was Elliott his friend still, or his nemesis?

Elliott demanded answers. With Philby's confession in hand, he began to increase the pressure. 'Our promise of immunity and pardon depends wholly on whether you give us all the information that you have. First of all we need information on people who worked with Moscow. By the way, we know them.' This was partly bluff, of course, but Philby could not know that. How much did Elliott know? Had Anthony Blunt cracked? Was he deploying the old interrogator's trick, by asking questions to which he already had answers? For two hours they drank and duelled, until the sun was setting and the sound of the muezzin drifted over Beirut. In the language of the sport they both loved, Elliott bowled and Philby batted, padding up, stonewalling, leaving the ball, trying to stay at the crease and knowing that the next delivery could end his long, long innings. Listening to the tape recording many months later, Peter Wright heard Elliott 'trying his manful best to corner a man for whom deception had been a second skin for thirty years'. The game was finely balanced, a brutal fight to the death conducted in tones of perfect English civility played out to a gently drunken tempo. 'By the end, they sounded like two rather tipsy radio announcers, their warm, classical public school accents discussing the greatest treachery of the twentieth century.'

Rising to leave, Philby suggested dinner at his flat that evening. Eleanor knew Elliott was in Beirut, and if he failed to pay a visit she would wonder why. Elliott agreed to come after he had sent another report to Dick White in London. White's response was encouraging; Philby was 'finally broken', and Elliott should continue the interrogation. When Elliott arrived at the Rue Kantari a few hours later, he found Philby passed out on the floor, having consumed an entire bottle of whisky. Not for the first time, Elliott and Eleanor carried him to bed. They chatted for a while afterwards. Elliott did his best to act normally, but Eleanor was no fool. Why, she asked, was he staying in an 'obscure hotel'? Elliott replied that 'he did not want too many people to know he was around'. Eleanor had come to like Elliott, and 'this furtiveness was not characteristic'.

Elliott called the next morning, and invited the Philbys to dinner at Chez Temporel, one of Beirut's most fashionable and expensive restaurants. He would be bringing his former secretary to make up a foursome. The charade of normality would be maintained. Elliott chose a quiet, candlelit corner table. The food was good – steak *au poivre vert* and Syrian truffle salad – the view through the white arches over the sea was enchanting, and the conversation unmemorable. Both Philby and Elliott tried to act 'as if nothing had intervened to destroy an old and treasured friendship'. It was almost like old times. Yet Eleanor was uneasy. Kim was visibly anxious, and Elliott's behaviour was distinctly odd.

His greatest passion was telling naughty stories. He always had one up his sleeve. This was the way he loosened up at parties. But behind the jokes was a keen professional mind. As usual one doubtful joke followed another, but I had a clear feeling the gaiety was false. Something was going on between them that was escaping me ... Here was a man, a very old friend from Kim's past, whom I thought I could confide in. Kim got up to go to the lavatory, and I was on the verge of saying to Elliott: 'Something is worrying Kim terribly. What the hell is going on?'

But before she could do so, Elliott also excused himself, and followed Philby into the restaurant toilets. Over the urinals, Philby handed over a sheaf of typewritten pages, perhaps eight or nine in all, the second instalment of his confession, and much fuller than the first. Philby was producing the goods.

The following day, Philby and Elliott met once more. This time, Elliott brought his own paperwork: a single sheet of paper on which was written a list of names, perhaps a dozen in all. Elliott passed it over. Which of these individuals were Soviet spies? Two of those named were Anthony Blunt and John Cairncross, the Fourth and Fifth Men in the Cambridge network; both had been under investigation ever since the defection of Burgess and Maclean. Another on the list was Tim Milne (Philby's old school friend and the witness at his wedding to Eleanor) who was now an MI6 officer in the Far East. The other names are unknown, but Philby's friend Tomás Harris was surely on the list, along with Guy Liddell, who had left MI5 under a cloud because of his association with Burgess and Blunt.

Elliott was fishing: naming everybody he could think of who might have been in league with Philby, Burgess and Maclean. As Philby later noted, the list included 'several names which alarmed me', and his instinctive response was to mislead, to muddy the waters, to present black as white, or grey. According to Philby: 'Blunt was in the clear but Tim Milne, who had loyally defended him for years, was not.' Milne, of course, was entirely innocent and Blunt, entirely guilty. Elliott pressed him for more names, but Philby 'claimed to know nothing' about any other spies in the UK, and repeatedly insisted he had not been in contact with Soviet intelligence for fourteen years.

The exchange threw Philby's predicament into sharp relief. MI6 would continue to squeeze him until every ounce of information had been extracted. He could never hope to hold them off with a partial confession. Blunt might already have admitted his guilt, in which case Elliott would know Philby's insistence on his innocence was another lie. This time MI6 would not let up. Elliott had told him 'the debriefing would be a long affair', with the clear implication that Philby should expect to be wrung dry, forced into revealing everything he 'knew about the KGB and naming names in Britain'. Whether he returned to London or stayed in Beirut, he would effectively be a prisoner of MI6; if he ever refused to cooperate, or was found to be lying, then the confession he had already signed could be used against him. 'It became clear to me that my immunity could be withdrawn at any time,' he later wrote. Elliott had told Philby that his signed confession 'might stand him in good stead' with the authorities in London; in fact, it gave Elliott the hold he needed. The 'lifeline' offered by Elliott was effectively a noose; the man who had been Philby's protector for so long would now be his jailer. Philby's options were running out, and both of them knew it.

The confrontation had lasted four days. Elliott told Philby that he would be leaving Beirut the next day, and travelling on to the Congo. Peter Lunn would take over the debriefing process in Beirut; London would send more questions; the Americans would want to talk to him; the process of interrogation was only just beginning. Back in London, the mood was jubilant. Dick White was 'effusive in his gratitude' to Elliott, convinced that Philby was playing ball. 'He could have rejected the offer of immunity,' White said. 'But since he has accepted, he'll stay and cooperate.' The head of MI5, Sir Roger Hollis, decided to bring the FBI into the picture and wrote a soothing memo to J. Edgar Hoover:

> In our judgement [Philby's] statement of the association with the RIS [Russian Intelligence Service] is substantially true. It accords with all the available evidence in our possession and we have no evidence pointing to a continuation of his activities on behalf of the RIS after 1946, save in the isolated instance of Maclean. If this is so, it follows that damage to United States interests will have been confined to the period of the Second World War.

The chief FBI officer in London was invited to draw up a list of questions that Lunn should ask Philby when the debriefing resumed.

'What makes you think he will still be there?' the officer asked. 'He will be,' he was told. 'He isn't going anywhere.' The CIA was not informed of developments in the Philby case. There would be plenty of time to fill in James Angleton later. As Elliott prepared to leave Beirut and hand over to Lunn, he reported that Philby was still unpredictable, in a nervous, drunken and depressed state: 'He might, I suppose, commit suicide,' he warned. Elliott no longer cared if his former friend lived or died. That, at least, was the impression he gave.

Kim Philby and Nicholas Elliott shook hands and parted with one last display of their old amity. Ostensibly, they were back on the same side, working together after an unpleasant interlude, and friends once more. Both knew this was untrue.

Elliott's decision to fly to Africa, leaving Philby unguarded in Beirut, was later condemned as a critical mistake, an act of egregious complacency that enabled Philby to pull off one last espionage coup. That is certainly how Philby and his KGB handlers chose to portray the ensuing events. But there is another, very different way to read Elliott's actions. The prospect of prosecuting Philby in Britain was anathema to the intelligence services: another trial, so soon after the Blake fiasco, would be politically damaging and profoundly embarrassing. Blake was foreign and flaky, whereas Philby was an insider and, until very recently, a paid MI6 agent. He had already demonstrated his skill at handling the press. He knew far too much. Elliott was emphatic: 'Nobody wanted him in London'. But keeping him in Beirut indefinitely was almost equally unpalatable. Once Philby was fully interrogated, what would be done with him? He plainly could no longer work for British newspapers, so would MI6 have to continue paying him? The prospect of subsidising a known traitor to prop up the bar of the Normandie Hotel did not appeal.

Elliott later claimed that the idea Philby might defect to the USSR had never occurred to him, or anyone else: 'It just didn't dawn on us.' This defies belief. Burgess and Maclean had both defected; Blake would escape from Wormwood Scrubs prison in 1966 and make his way to Moscow. Elliott must have suspected that Philby would have a back-up escape plan. Moreover, he had deliberately forced him into a corner: Philby knew he now faced sustained interrogation, over a long period, at the hands of Peter Lunn, a man he found 'unsympathetic'. Elliott had made it quite clear that if he failed to cooperate fully, the immunity deal was off and the confession he had already signed would be used against him. Burgess and Maclean had vanished into the Soviet Union, and were barely heard of again. Allowing Philby to join his friends in Moscow – to 'do a fade', in intelligence jargon – might be the tidiest solution all round.

Elliott could not have made it easier for Philby to flee, whether intentionally or otherwise. In defiance of every rule of intelligence, he left Beirut without making any provision for monitoring a man who had just confessed to being a double agent: Philby was not followed or watched; his flat was not placed under surveillance; his phone was not tapped; and MI6's allies in the Lebanese security service were not alerted. He was left to his own devices, and told that Peter Lunn would be in touch in due course. Elliott simply walked away from Beirut, and left the door to Moscow wide open.

That was either monumentally stupid, or exceptionally clever.

The very next evening, on the stroke of six o'clock, Philby stood on the balcony of his flat on Rue Kantari, with a book in his hand.

The Fade

Philby and Petukhov met a few hours later in Vrej, the backstreet Armenian restaurant. It took Philby only a few rushed minutes to explain the situation: MI6 had new and damning information, from Golitsyn, and had offered him immunity in exchange for information. He did not tell his KGB handler that he had already confessed; instead, he allowed Petukhov to believe that he was holding out under questioning (as he had so often before) but would soon face another round of interrogation. Petukhov hurried back to the Soviet embassy and sent a cable to Vassili Dozhdalev, the head of the British desk at Moscow Centre, requesting instructions. Dozhdalev asked whether Philby could withstand another cross-examination. 'Philby does not think he can escape again,' Petukhov told him. Dozhdalev gave the order: Philby should be extracted from Beirut as soon as possible.

'Your time has come,' Petukhov told Philby, at another hurriedly arranged meeting. 'They won't leave you alone now. You have to disappear. There's no other way. There's room for you in Moscow.' This was probably what Philby had hoped to hear, though he had not yet fully made up his mind to flee. Elliott's words, he later hinted, 'had planted doubts in me and made me think about arguments he had used.' He had mentally rehearsed the drama of defection many times, but still he hesitated.

'Arrangements will take some time,' said Petukhov. But when the time came, Philby would have to move swiftly. As before, Petukhov would walk past the Rue Kantari flat at pre-arranged times: 'If you see me carrying a newspaper, that means I have to meet you. If I'm carrying a book, that means everything is prepared for your departure, and you have to get moving.'

Philby waited. A few days later, Peter Lunn called the apartment to ask if he was ready to discuss 'the question that interests us'. Philby said he needed more time. Lunn did not put him under pressure; he did not offer to come to the flat and help to jog Philby's memory. Instead, he announced he was going skiing. Philby learned from a friend at the embassy that a fresh fall of snow in the mountains had created ideal conditions and Lunn, the Olympic skier, would be gone for the next four days. That, at least, is what Philby was told. But Lunn did not go skiing.

On 23 January 1963, Glen Balfour-Paul, the first secretary at the British embassy, and his wife Marnie threw a dinner party. Several journalists were invited, including Clare Hollingworth of the *Guardian* and Kim Philby of the *Observer*. Philby had 'proved a helpful and friendly contact' since Balfour-Paul's arrival in Beirut two years earlier, and the couples had grown close. Eleanor Philby was looking forward to dinner; for the first time in weeks, Philby had agreed to leave the flat for a social occasion. Glen Balfour-Paul was an expert Arabist, and Eleanor wanted to pick his brains about Middle Eastern archaeology, her new hobby. Marnie's cook was making sherry trifle.

Philby spent the morning drinking coffee on the balcony, despite the lashing rain. Beirut was braced for one of the winter storms that batter the city with unpredictable ferocity. A figure carrying a book walked slowly past in the wet street without looking up. In the late afternoon, Philby grabbed his raincoat and scarf, and announced he was going to meet a contact but would be home by six, leaving plenty of time to dress for dinner. He was seen at the bar of the St Georges Hotel, apparently deep in thought. After downing several drinks, Philby asked the barman if he could use the telephone. Eleanor was cooking supper for her daughter Annie and Philby's youngest son Harry, who were staying for the holiday, when the telephone rang. Thirteen-year-old Harry answered it, and shouted to Eleanor in the kitchen: 'Daddy's going to be late. He says he'll meet you at the Balfour-Pauls' at eight.'

Eight o'clock came and went at the Balfour-Pauls' with no sign of Kim Philby. Eleanor apologised for her husband's tardiness, and said she thought he might be sending a story to the *Economist*. By 9.30 what had been a 'cosy gathering' was becoming fractious and hungry. Marnie announced that they should eat anyway. The storm outside was building. When the food was cleared away, fresh drinks were served, and Eleanor, now quite drunk, was becoming worried. 'God, what a horrible night! Perhaps he's been hit by a car, or stumbled into the sea.'

Marnie tried to reassure her: 'Don't be silly, Kim's obviously been held up.' Clare Hollingworth noticed that her host, the diplomat Glen Balfour-Paul, 'had nothing to say about his missing guest', which struck her as strange.

While the Balfour-Pauls' guests were eating trifle, a car with diplomatic plates drove towards the harbour in the sheeting rain. In the back sat Philby, with Pavel Nedosekin alongside him; Petukhov sat in front beside the driver. 'Everything is fine, everything is going the way it should,' said Nedosekin. Philby wondered, with a flicker of malice, just how much trouble Peter Lunn would get into for his ill-timed skiing break. At that moment a Latvian sailor was getting hopelessly drunk, with the generous encouragement of a Soviet intelligence officer, in one of the harbour bars. The car entered the port, drove along the quay and pulled up alongside the *Dolmatova*, a Soviet freighter taking on cargo and bound for Odessa. The Russian captain shook hands with Philby on the gangplank, and led him to a cabin. A bottle of cognac stood on the table. Philby, his minders and the captain raised their glasses and drank. In a few minutes the bottle was empty. Petukhov handed him an identity card in the name of 'Villi Maris', a merchant seaman from Riga. New clothes were laid out on the bed, including warm underwear. It would be cold in Moscow.

Eleanor left the Balfour-Pauls' dinner party before midnight, and returned home through the rain. There was no sign of her husband at the Rue Kantari, and no message. She was now seriously alarmed. Soon after midnight, she telephoned Peter Lunn at home. Lunn's wife Antoinette picked up, and explained that Peter was out. She agreed to pass on a message that he should contact Eleanor as soon as possible. In fact, Lunn was already at the British embassy, attending 'a hastily summoned meeting about Kim'. The speed with which Lunn swung into action that night suggests that he was primed and waiting: perhaps the news of Philby's failure to appear for dinner reached him from Balfour-Paul, but it is also possible that he was tracking Philby's movements by other means. Within minutes, Lunn was on the telephone to Eleanor.

'Would you like me to come round?' he asked.

'I would be most grateful,' she said.

When Lunn duly appeared, Eleanor explained that Philby had left the flat earlier that afternoon, telephoned in the afternoon, and then vanished. Lunn asked if anything was missing, such as clothes, documents or Philby's typewriter, but all was in place, including his British passport. Lunn surely knew that Philby was doing a 'fade', and already on his way to Moscow. The most important Soviet spy in history was on the run. But instead of behaving as one might expect in such a crisis, Lunn was calm; he did not conduct a full search of the flat, alert the Lebanese police, or put a watch on the borders, the ports or the airports. Fearing her husband had suffered some sort of accident, Eleanor wanted to call the hospitals, or search some of his favourite bars, but Lunn was almost nonchalant: 'His advice was to do nothing until morning.' Lunn left the flat at around 2 a.m., and immediately telephoned the British ambassador. Then he wrote a twenty-six-paragraph cable to Dick White in London.

Eleanor spent a sleepless night, waiting and wondering, struggling with the 'terrible fear' that her life had changed for ever. Before dawn, the *Dolmatova* weighed anchor and headed out to sea. The Russian freighter had obviously departed in haste, because some of her cargo was left lying on the quayside. She also left behind a member of her crew, a very drunk Latvian seaman called Villi Maris who would discover, when he finally woke up, that he had lost both his identity card and his ship. Philby stood at the rail of the *Dolmatova*, wrapped up against the cold in his Westminster scarf, and watched the dawn break over the receding bay, knowing that the 'last link with England had been severed forever'.

★

Three years after independence, Congo was in turmoil, a Cold War battleground riven by civil war. It was certainly a logical place for Elliott to be. He always claimed he was in Brazzaville, preparing to cross the Congo River, when he received a coded message informing him of Philby's disappearance, and instructing him to return at once to Beirut. But the speed with which he reappeared in Beirut suggests he may have been somewhere nearer at hand. Elliott concluded at once that 'Philby had vanished into the blue (or rather the red)'. He found Eleanor close to hysteria, fearing that her husband had been abducted, or worse. Within days, she received a mysterious letter, purporting to come from Philby (several more would follow), hinting that he was on a secret journalistic assignment: 'Tell my colleagues I'm on a long tour of the area.' The letter was so peculiar in tone that Eleanor thought it might have been written under duress. Among Beirut's journalists, it was generally assumed that if Philby was not chasing a story, he must be off on a bender, or bedded down somewhere with a mistress. MI6 knew better. The hasty departure of the *Dolmatova* clearly indicated where Philby had gone, and how. The Russian link was confirmed by the discovery of banknotes in Philby's safe with serial numbers matching those recently issued to a Soviet diplomat by a Beirut bank.

Elliott did his best to calm Eleanor, without giving away what he knew. 'There is no question that she was deeply in love with him and had no suspicion that he was a traitor to his country,' Elliott wrote. Philby had disappeared 'in circumstances calculated to do her maximum hurt', but Elliott could not yet bring himself to reveal to Eleanor that Philby was a Soviet spy who had lied to her throughout their marriage, just as he had lied to Aileen throughout his previous marriage, and to Elliott himself throughout their friendship. Yet he hinted at the truth: 'You do realise that your husband was not an ordinary man?' he told her. She would find out just how extraordinary soon enough.

A few weeks later, a scruffy stranger knocked on the door of the apartment in the Rue Kantari, thrust an envelope into Eleanor's hand, and disappeared back down the stairwell. The envelope contained a three-page typewritten letter, signed 'with love from Kim', instructing her to buy a plane ticket for London to throw any watchers off the scent, and then secretly go to the Czech airlines office and buy another ticket for Prague. Then she should go to the alleyway opposite the house, leading to the sea, 'choose a spot high up on the wall, towards the right' and write, in white chalk, the exact date and time of the flight to Prague. Philby instructed her to burn the letter after reading. Eleanor was deeply suspicious, and distraught, 'convinced that Kim had been kidnapped', and that she was being lured into a trap. In fact, Philby's plan to get Eleanor to join him was genuine, if unworkable: the press had by now picked up the story of his mysterious disappearance, her movements were being watched, and the idea that Eleanor could blithely walk onto a plane and fly to Czechoslovakia was ludicrously impractical. After some indecision, she told Elliott about the letter, who instructed her 'on no account to meet any strangers outside the house'. Elliott then crept up the alleyway and chalked a date and flight time on the wall, 'to test the system and cause confusion in the enemy ranks'. It was the first thrust in a peculiar duel across the Iron Curtain.

The news of Philby's defection tore like brushfire through the intelligence communities on both sides of the Atlantic, provoking shock, embarrassment and furious recrimination. Philby's defenders in MI6 were stunned, and his detractors in MI5 enraged that he had been allowed to escape. In the CIA there was baffled dismay at what was seen as yet another British intelligence disaster. Hoover was livid. 'Many people in the secret world aged the night they heard,' wrote one MI5 officer. 'To find that a man like Philby, a man you might like, or drink with, or admire, had betrayed everything; to think of the agents and operations wasted: youth and innocence passed away, and the dark ages began.' Arthur Martin, the officer originally slated to confront Philby in Beirut, was apoplectic: 'We should have sent a team out there and grilled him while we had the chance.' The belief that Philby must have been tipped off by another Soviet spy within British intelligence took root within MI5, prompting a mole-hunt that would continue for years, sowing paranoia and distrust into every corner of the organisation. Even Elliott came under investigation. Arthur Martin was detailed to grill him: 'But after lengthy interrogation Elliott just convinced his interrogator that he was in the clear.'

Desmond Bristow, Philby's protégé back in St Albans who had risen steadily through MI6 ranks, was stunned by the news: 'He had been my boss and in many ways my teacher on the ways of espionage. I could not bring myself to think of him as a Soviet agent. Philby's defection turned into a perennial cloud of doubt hanging over the present, the past, and the future.' Dick White was said to have reacted with 'horror' to the news. 'I never thought he would accept the offer of immunity and then skip the country,' he said. To Elliott he confided: 'What a shame we reopened it all. Just trouble.' White may have been genuinely astounded by events, or he may simply have been playing a part. Philby's defection might be embarrassing, but it had also solved a problem. C's colleagues noted that while he professed surprise at Philby's vanishing act, White, the head of MI6, did not seem unduly 'disappointed'.

To Elliott fell the delicate, and exceedingly unpleasant, task of breaking the news to James Angleton. The FBI knew about the confrontation in Beirut and Philby's confession, but the CIA had been kept entirely in the dark. 'I tried to repair the damage by telephoning Jim Angleton,' Elliott later said, 'but it was too late.' Angleton was publicly incensed, and privately mortified. Like Elliott, he now had to 'face the awful truth and acknowledge that his British friend, hero, and mentor had been a senior KGB agent'. This master spy had been taken in by a spy far more adept than he. The long liquid lunches, the secrets spilled so easily more than a decade earlier, the death and disappearance of so many agents sent to make secret war in the Soviet bloc; it had all been part of a brutal game, which Philby had won, hands down. The impact of that traumatic discovery would have far-reaching consequences for America and the world. In the short term, Angleton set about doctoring the record, putting it about that he had always suspected Philby, had kept him under surveillance, and would have trapped him but for British incompetence – fictions that he would propagate and cling to, obsessively, for the rest of his life. But the truth was in the files. Each of the thirty-six meetings Philby attended at CIA headquarters between 1949 and 1951 had been typed up in a separate memo by Angleton's secretary Gloria Loomis; every one of the discussions at Harvey's restaurant was carefully recorded. Everything that Angleton had ever told Philby, and thus the precise human and political cost of their friendship, was on paper, stored in an archive under the direct control of the chief of CIA counter-intelligence, James Angleton. Years later, the CIA conducted an internal search for these files: every single one has vanished. 'I had them burned,' Angleton told MI5 officer Peter Wright. 'It was all very embarrassing.'

Philby's former friends and colleagues found themselves combing back over the years they had known him, searching for clues. The more candid among them acknowledged they had never suspected him. Others claimed that they had doubted his loyalty since the defection of Burgess and Maclean in 1951. Still others now claimed that they had *always* seen through him, proving that the least trustworthy people are those who claim to have seen it all coming, after it has all come. The most honest admitted that Philby's ruthless charm had seduced them utterly. Glen Balfour-Paul, whose dinner party Philby skipped on the night he vanished, wrote: 'He was an unforgivable traitor to his country, responsible among much else for the assassination by his Soviet associates of many brave men. All I can say is that in the half of him that I knew (the deceitful half, of course) he was a most enjoyable friend.'

Miles Copeland was 'dumbfounded' by Philby's 'unbelievable' defection, concluding: 'He was the best actor in the world' – a reaction that rather undermines his later claim to have kept Philby under surveillance, on Angleton's orders, during the Beirut years. Copeland had been duped like everyone else, and offered a clear-eyed assessment of the damage inflicted by the KGB's most effective spy: 'What Philby provided was feedback about the CIA's reactions. They [the KGB] could accurately determine whether or not reports fed to the CIA were believed or not ... what it comes to, is that when you look at the whole period from 1944 to 1951, the entire Western intelligence effort, which was pretty big, was what you might call minus advantage. We'd have been better off doing nothing.'

In March 1963, under intense pressure from the media, the British government was forced to acknowledge that Philby was missing. Three months later, Edward Heath, the Lord Privy Seal, issued a statement, declaring: 'Since Mr Philby resigned from the Foreign Service in 1951, twelve years ago, he has had no access of any kind to any official information.' That same month, Philby was granted Soviet citizenship. 'Hello, Mr Philby' ran the headline in *Izvestia*, the official Soviet newspaper, accompanied by a sketch of the defector in Pushkin Square. And so began the Great Philby Myth: the super-spy who had bamboozled Britain, divulged her secrets and those of her allies for thirty years, and then escaped to Moscow in a final triumphant *coup de théâtre*, leaving the wrong-footed dupes of MI6 wringing their hands in dismay. That myth, occasionally spruced up by Russian propaganda and eagerly propagated by Philby himself, has held firm ever since.

But there were some to whom the story of Philby's daring night-time getaway did not quite ring true. 'Philby was allowed to escape,' wrote Desmond Bristow. 'Perhaps he was even encouraged. To have brought him back to England and convicted as a traitor would have been even more embarrassing; and when they convicted him, could they really have hanged him?' That view was echoed in Moscow. Yuri Modin, the canny Soviet case officer, wrote: 'To my mind the whole business was politically engineered. The British government had nothing to gain by prosecuting Philby. A major trial, to the inevitable accompaniment of spectacular revelation and scandal, would have shaken the British establishment to its foundations.' Far from being caught out by Philby's defection, 'the secret service had actively encouraged him to slip away', wrote Modin. Many in the intelligence world believed that by leaving the door open to Moscow and then walking away, Elliott had deliberately forced Philby into exile. And they may have been right.

Divining Elliott's precise motives is impossible, because for the next thirty years he carefully obscured and muddied them. To some, he played the role of the sucker, describing Philby's flight as a shock, and claiming that the possibility of defection had never occurred to him. But to others, he gave the opposite impression: that he was entirely unsurprised by Philby's flight, because he had engineered it. In a book written years later under KGB supervision, Philby depicted his defection as the heroic checkmate move of the grandmaster: 'I knew exactly how to handle it,' he wrote. 'How could they have stopped me?' The answer: very easily. Simply posting a Watcher on Rue Kantari would have made it all but impossible for Philby to flee. But no such effort was made. As Modin wrote, 'spiriting Philby out of Lebanon was child's play', because Elliott and MI6 had made it so easy – suspiciously easy, in Modin's mind.

There are two, diametrically opposed interpretations of Philby's flight to Moscow: according to the first, Philby was the virtuoso spy, and Elliott the fool; according to the second, those roles were reversed. Under the first scenario, Philby took the decision, waited until British intelligence was looking the other way, and ran. The ease of his defection, he wrote, was the result of British blundering, 'a mistake, simple stupidity'. This version of events requires the assumption that MI6 was not merely inefficient and naive, but quite astonishingly dim. A second, more plausible story goes like this: Elliott successfully extracted the confession that ensured Philby was now under MI6 control; he made it crystal clear that Philby's continued liberty was dependent on his continued cooperation; then, perhaps with the connivance of Dick White, he stepped away, spread the rumour that Lunn had gone skiing, and allowed Philby to believe the coast was clear, the road to Moscow wide open.

Among those who thought that Elliott, and not Philby, had won the last round, was Kim Philby himself. He left Beirut thinking he had jumped; only later did Philby come to believe that he had been pushed.

★

Kim Philby was welcomed to Moscow by the KGB, given a thorough medical examination, and installed in a flat, luxurious by Soviet standards. A minder was appointed to guard him. He was given a salary of about £200 a month, and a promise that his children would be financially supported back in Britain. The KGB agreed to bring furniture and furnishings from Beirut, including an oak table given to him by Tommy Harris. Two of his favourite pipes were purchased in Jermyn Street, and shipped to Moscow in the diplomatic bag. Guy Burgess and Donald Maclean were both living in Moscow, although they had by now fallen out, partly as a result of an incident during which a drunken Burgess had urinated in the fireplace of the Chinese embassy. The spy's circumstances had changed, but his habits not at all. In the summer of 1963, he died of liver failure, leaving Philby his 4,000-book library. Philby did not see him before he died, though he later claimed that he had been prevented from doing so by his Russian handlers. 'Burgess was a bit of an embarrassment here,' he told the journalist Phillip Knightley. Philby had books, his pipes, furniture and rugs; now he wanted his wife.

In May, four months after Philby's disappearance, Eleanor Philby flew to London. The press was now rampaging all over the story of the defection of the Third Man, and lying in wait for her. A few weeks earlier an 'unmistakably Russian' man had appeared at her door, and declared, 'I'm from Kim. He wants you to join him. I'm here to help.' She refused the offer, reported it to Elliott, and arrived in Britain in a state of utter confusion, still uncertain where her husband was, and not knowing whether to believe the stories about his espionage and defection.

Nicholas Elliott sent a car to pick her up from the airport to escape the press. He found her a doctor to treat a swollen ankle, and then, once she was back on her feet, took her out to lunch. When Eleanor brought up the subject of reuniting with Philby, Elliott was insistent: 'Kim was an active communist agent and [she] should on no account contemplate going to Moscow.' He warned her: 'They probably won't let you out, if you go.' Eleanor was struck, once again, by Elliott's 'surprising tenderness', but was still reluctant to accept that her husband was a Soviet spy. Elliott offered to summon the head of MI6 himself, in order to persuade her. Dick White appeared within the hour, and Elliott installed them together in the sitting room of Wilton Street with coffee and a bottle of brandy. White was courteous, adamant, and only slightly untruthful. 'We have definitely known for the last seven years that Kim has been working for the Russians without pay,' he said. White had suspected Philby for far longer than that, but had discovered clear-cut proof of his guilt less than a year earlier. By the end of the afternoon, Eleanor Philby was in floods of tears, woozy on sedatives and brandy, but finally convinced that her husband was indeed a spy. She had been, in her words, 'the victim of a prolonged and monstrous confidence trick', yet she was still determined to join the conman in Moscow.

In September she received another letter from Kim: 'All I am thinking of now is seeing you.' Elliott did everything he could to dissuade her from going. One day he bought her a ticket to see Alfred Hitchcock's film *The Birds*, in which a community is attacked by avian marauders. 'I don't know what he had in mind, except perhaps to demoralise me,' she later wrote. This was, perhaps, Elliott's way of warning Eleanor that a life that seems calm and secure can swiftly turn to nightmare. She was unmoved, and a few days later found herself in the office of the smiling Soviet consul, who told her to be ready to fly to Moscow in two days, before handing over £500 in cash: 'Buy yourself some very warm clothes.'

When Eleanor announced she was leaving, Elliott mobilised his own wife in a last-ditch attempt to get her to see sense.

'What would *you* do if the man you loved went behind the Iron Curtain?' Eleanor asked Elizabeth, as they drank tea.

The idea of Nicholas Elliott defecting to the USSR was so preposterous that Elizabeth found it hard not to laugh. But as Eleanor wrote later, 'she finally admitted that she would do the same thing I was planning to do'.

Elliott feared that Eleanor might be trapped for ever in Russia, and believed that any attempt to resume her marriage to Philby was doomed. Yet he could not help admiring her bravery, and the 'passionate loyalty and devotion' that the betrayer could still inspire. 'Although I had put the fear of God into her she was determined to return to Moscow and have it out with him. She left the next day.'

Eleanor flew to Moscow on 26 September 1963, and landed at the airport disguised in a turban and dark glasses. Philby and his minder were waiting. 'Eleanor, is that you?' he said.

★

Late one night, a few weeks later, Elliott heard a soft thump as a letter, delivered by hand, dropped into the letter box at 13 Wilton Street. Inside was a typewritten letter, and an empty envelope addressed to Kim Philby at PO Box 509, Central Post Office, Moscow. The letter carried no postmark, date or letterhead, but the handwriting was unmistakable.

Dear Nick,

I wonder if this letter will surprise you. Our last transactions were so strange that I cannot help thinking that perhaps you wanted me to do a fade.

I am more than thankful for your friendly interventions at all times. I would have got in touch with you earlier, but I thought it better to let time do its work on the case.

It is invariably with pleasure that I remember our meetings and talks. They did much to help one get one's bearings in this complicated world! I deeply appreciate, now as ever, our old friendship, and I hope that rumours which have reached me about your having had some trouble on my account, are exaggerated.

It would be bitter to feel that I might have been a source of trouble to you, but I am buoyed up by my confidence that you will have found a way out of any difficulties that may have beset you.

I have often thought that there are a number of questions connected with the whole story that might interest you, and it might be helpful all round if we could get together as in old times and discuss matters of mutual interest. After careful thought, I have come to the conclusion that Helsinki, which you could reach without difficulty, would be a suitable rendezvous – or perhaps Berlin?

I am enclosing an unsealed, addressed envelope. In the event of your agreeing to my proposal, would you post it, enclosing some view of Tower Bridge? On receipt of your letter, I will write again, through the same channel, and make suggestions about the admin. side of the rendezvous.

As you have probably guessed, I am sending this letter by 'safe hand' to your private address for obvious reasons. You will, of course, treat this as a wholly private communication concerning only our two selves. At least, I hope you will see your way to follow my advice in this matter.

Guy's death was a bitter blow. He had been very ill for a long time, and only his ox-like constitution enabled him to live as long as he did. What a pity we shall never be able to gather à trois at Pruniers!

Let me hear from you soon.

Love to Elizabeth (to whom by the way, you had better not disclose the contents of this letter – nor to anyone else of course).

Elliott was astonished. Philby wrote as if his betrayal had been no more than a hiccup in their long friendship. It was as if Vermehren, Volkov, the pixies and the countless others betrayed to their deaths had never existed. Was he trying to lure Elliott into a trap? Or was this an attempt to persuade him to turn double agent, to change his bearings in this 'complicated world'? The sending of a blank post-card of Tower Bridge would convey a message that the KGB could interpret: was this intended to show that Philby was acting without KGB approval, and therefore a hint that he was prepared to be reeled back in, to 'discuss matters of mutual interest'? Elliott's initial reaction was one of outrage. 'It was ridiculous to suppose that I would agree to meet him behind the backs of my boss and my wife.' The old Philby charm, laced with bravado, was there in abundance, with its allusion to their valued friendship, and the hope that he had not damaged his friend's career. Elliott decided that the letter must be 'an incredibly clumsy piece of KGB disinformation, obviously designed to throw doubts on my loyalty'. The next morning he took the letter in to MI6 headquarters, and showed it to Dick White, who was equally intrigued. The strange missive prompted 'many hours of discussion as to what, if anything, should be done about it'. Elliott was in favour of setting up a meeting, 'because first, I was certainly fitter than he was, and secondly because I could choose the rendez-vous'. He was overruled.

The key to Philby's intentions may lie in the first line of the letter. He wanted to know, once and for all, whether Elliott had deliberately cornered him into defecting. Trading once more on their friendship, he hoped to find out if, in the end, he had really won the battle of manipulation, whether he had outmanoeuvred Elliott, or the other way round.

Elliott did not give him that satisfaction, but he did send back a last, unmistakably barbed message, a blunt reference to just one 'tragic episode' among so many, and just one of the many people Philby had destroyed, an epitaph for a friendship brutally betrayed: 'Put some flowers for me on poor Volkov's grave.'

Three Old Spies

Kim Philby did not love Moscow, and Moscow did not love him, though both tried to pretend otherwise. Philby may have believed, back in 1934, that he was joining an 'elite' force, but found he had no KGB rank, and little to do. In Russian eyes, he was an agent, not an officer, and one of little further use. He was welcomed, thanked, debriefed and rewarded; but he was never quite trusted. The ease with which he had escaped from Beirut may have rekindled doubts long dormant in Moscow, the uneasy, queasy suspicion that he might yet be double-crossing the KGB. Yuri Modin found him unreadable: 'He never revealed his true self. Neither the British, nor the women he lived with, nor ourselves ever managed to pierce the armour of mystery that clad him ... in the end I suspect that Philby made a mockery of everyone, particularly ourselves.' A KGB minder accompanied him everywhere, ostensibly as protection against possible British retaliation, but also as guard, and jailer. He remained, in the words of one KGB officer, an 'Englishman to his fingertips', and therefore innately suspect. In Britain, Philby had been too British to be doubted; in Russia, he was too British to be believed.

When Philby's copies of *The Times* arrived in Moscow, usually weeks after publication, he carefully ironed them, and then pored over accounts of cricket matches long since over. He ate thick-cut Oxford marmalade on his toast, sipped imported English tea, and listened to the BBC World Service every evening at seven. When his children visited from the West, they brought Marmite, Worcestershire sauce, and spices for the Indian meals he liked to cook. He wore a tweed jacket in hound's-tooth check, and a woollen tie. He drank Johnnie Walker Red Label whisky, often obliteratingly. He described Russia as his 'homeland', insisting that he had never really 'belonged' to the British ruling class, and could not, therefore, have betrayed it. But more honestly, he admitted that he was 'wholly and irreversibly English'. At times he sounded like a retired civil servant put out to grass (which, in a way, he was) harrumphing at the vulgarity of modern life, protesting against change. The new ways of cricket baffled and enraged him. 'Aluminium bats, white balls, funny clothes ... it is all too confusing for a gentleman of the old school like myself.' In an unconscious echo of Marcus Lipton MP, he grumbled about 'the ghastly din of modern music' and 'hooligans inflamed by bourgeois rock music'.

Other old habits persisted. His marriage to Eleanor staggered on for a time, but it was broken inside. She found Moscow grey, cold and lonely. One day she asked him: 'What is more important in your life, me and the children, or the Communist Party?' Philby's answer was the one he always gave when asked to measure feeling against politics. 'The party, of course.' He not only demanded admiration for his ideological consistency, for having 'stayed the course', but sympathy for what it had cost him. 'If you only knew what hell it is when your political convictions clash with your personal affections,' he wrote in a note to the diplomat Glen Balfour-Paul. On the few occasions he received visitors from the West, he asked hungrily after news of friends. 'Friendship is the most important thing of all,' he declared, as if he had not undermined every one of his own. Lorraine Copeland wrote that it was 'painful to think that during the years we all loved Kim and had him constantly in our homes, he was all the while laughing at us'. Philby bridled at that suggestion. 'I wasn't laughing at them. I have always operated on two levels, a personal level and a political one. When the two have come into conflict I have had to put politics first. The conflict can be very painful. I don't like deceiving people, especially friends, and contrary to what others think, I feel very badly about it.' But not so badly as to stop.

Philby rekindled his friendship with Donald Maclean and his wife Melinda, and the two exiled couples were naturally thrown together. Maclean spoke fluent Russian, and had been given a job analysing British foreign policy. He often worked late. Philby and Melinda started going to the opera, and then on shopping trips together. In 1964, Eleanor returned to the US to renew her passport and see her daughter. In her absence, Kim Philby and Melinda Maclean started an affair. It was a fitting liaison: Philby was secretly sleeping with the wife of an ideological comrade, and cheating on his own wife, repeating once again the strange cycle of friendship and betrayal that defined his world. Eleanor returned, discovered the affair, and announced she was leaving him for good: Philby did not try to stop her. He did, however, present her with his most treasured possession, his old Westminster scarf. 'It had travelled with him – from school days to exile in Moscow,' wrote Elliott. This symbolic loyalty to his old school was, Elliott thought, a 'supreme example of schizophrenia'. At the airport, a KGB officer sent Eleanor on her way with a bunch of tulips.

Like Aileen before her, Eleanor did not long survive their final break-up. She wrote a poignant, pained memoir, and died three years after returning to the US. 'He betrayed many people, me included,' she wrote. 'Kim had the guts, or the weakness, to stand by a decision he made thirty years ago, whatever the cost to those who loved him most.' Eleanor spent the remainder of her life wondering who she had really married, and concluded: 'No one can ever really know another human being.'

★

James Jesus Angleton's personality was transformed by the realisation that he had never really known Kim Philby. His faith in his fellow men had never been strong, but he had believed in the British notion that the inner ring could always be trusted; after Philby's defection a profound and poisonous paranoia seemed to seize him. 'The emotional wreckage of that close friendship made him distrust everybody and coloured his life from that point on.' He became convinced that a vast, overarching conspiracy must be taking place under his nose, orchestrated by Philby, from Moscow. 'Jim just continued to think that Philby was a key actor in the KGB grand plan,' one CIA contemporary said of Angleton. 'To him, Philby was never just a drunken, burned-out ex-spy. He was a leader of the orchestra.' In Angleton's warped logic, if Philby had fooled him, then there must be many other KGB spies in positions of influence in the West. 'Never again would he permit himself to be so badly duped. He would trust no one.'

Convinced that the CIA was riddled with Soviet spies, Angleton set about rooting them out, detecting layer after layer of deception surrounding him. He suspected that a host of world leaders were under KGB control, including British Prime Minister Harold Wilson, Olof Palme of Sweden and German Chancellor Willy Brandt. He drew up more than 10,000 case files on suspect individuals, anti-war protesters and internal dissidents, often gathering information by illegal means. The damage he inflicted on the CIA reached such levels that some even accused him of being a Soviet mole himself, destroying the organisation from within by creating a climate of debilitating suspicion. Uncompromising and obsessive, more than a decade after Philby's vanishing act Angleton was still ascribing every fresh sign of treachery to the man he had once idolised. 'This is all Kim's work,' he would mutter.

Nicholas Elliott watched and wondered as Angleton descended into his wilderness of mirrors. They remained friends, from a distance, but the warmth had gone. The Philby betrayal seemed to metastasise in Angleton's mind. 'He had trusted him and confided in him far beyond any routine relationship between the colleagues of two friendly countries,' wrote Elliott. 'The knowledge that he, Jim, the top expert in the world on Soviet espionage, had been totally deceived, had a cataclysmic effect on his personality. Jim henceforward found it difficult to trust anybody, to make two and two add up to four.' Elliott believed his old friend was being devoured by distrust: 'Over-suspicion can sometimes have more tragic results than over-credulity. His tragedy was that he was so often deceived by his own ingenuity, and the consequences were often disastrous.'

James Angleton was forced out of the CIA in 1974, when the extent of his illegal mole-hunting was revealed. He retired with his orchids, his fishing rods and his secrets, a man of deep and enduring mystery, and a brilliant fool. In retirement, he spent much of his time in the Army and Navy Club, a place strongly redolent of an old-fashioned London gentleman's club. He continued to insist that he had suspected Kim Philby from the start, but his weeding from CIA files of every reference to his relationship with Philby was proof enough of the falsity of that claim. Philby haunted the CIA. 'I don't know that the damage he did can ever be actually calculated,' wrote Richard Helms, the CIA chief appointed in 1966. One CIA historian assessed the cost by means of italics: 'at least twenty-five major, *but* major operations, were destroyed.'

In 1987, Angleton attended a luncheon with former CIA officers at the Officers' Club in Fort Myer outside Washington. He was sixty-nine, but looked a decade older, his body racked by cancer that had started in the lungs. His colleagues urged him to 'come clean in the Philby case'. Angleton gave one of his crippled half-smiles, and said: 'There are some matters that I shall have to take to the grave with me, and Kim is one of them.'

A week later, true to his word, he was dead.

★

Nicholas Elliott's career was hobbled by his association with Philby. Some in MI6 believed he had allowed Philby to flee Beirut out of personal loyalty. Some still do. By the 1960s, the Robber Barons who had come of age in the 1940s were creatures of the past. MI6 was more professional, less buccaneering, and in Elliott's view, a lot less fun. Sir Stewart Menzies and Elliott remained close friends. In 1968, the former C fell off his horse while riding with the Beaufort Hunt, and never recovered. Elliott was the only serving MI6 officer to attend the funeral. By now he was Director of Requirements at MI6, responsible for the quality and relevance of information produced by the intelligence service for other government departments. It was an important job, but bureaucratic, and exactly the sort of role he had always despised. 'To be in administration was, in my view, the last resort.'

Elliott retired in 1968, after almost thirty years as a spy. 'Rather to my surprise I did not miss the confidential knowledge which no longer filtered through my in-tray,' he wrote. He joined the board of Lonrho, the international mining and media company based in Cheapside in the City of London, and led by the maverick business-man Tiny Rowland. Elliott considered Rowland 'a modern Cecil Rhodes', which did not stop him from joining a boardroom coup against him. When this failed, Rowland ousted the rebels, including Elliott, whom he described as 'the Harry Lime of Cheapside'. Elliott was thrilled to be compared to the sinister character played by Orson Welles in Graham Greene's *The Third Man*, and adopted it as his soubriquet. He joined a firm of stockbrokers, but found himself 'incapable of leading that kind of life without relapsing into a slough of depression and boredom' and soon gave it up, to pursue a life of esoteric and eccentric interests.

Elliott bought a share in a racehorse, and never missed a day of Ascot. He watched a great deal of cricket, and built up a fine wine cellar. He became interested in graphology, the pseudo-scientific study of handwriting, and found he had a 'gift for dowsing', the abil-ity to locate underground water, ore and gems. He could be frequently seen marching across the countryside of the Home Counties with his divining rods, and then energetically digging holes. He approached MI6 with a plan to exhume buried Nazi treas-ure from the grounds of a monastery in Rome. He also took up transcendental meditation, which he considered a spiritual 'alterna-tive to involvement in religion'. Klop Ustinov turned up at Wilton Street from time to time, with hot veal kidneys *à la liégeoise*, in a hat box. Elliott's daughter Claudia died tragically young but, as ever, his stiff upper lip precluded public grief. He spent much of his time in clubs, where he was admired as a raconteur of risqué anecdotes, the conversational refuge of the Englishman who does not know quite what to say, or cannot say what he really knows. He was no longer in the inner ring, but he did not yet abandon the secret world.

In the early 1980s, a tall, spare figure in an immaculate three-piece suit could be seen from time to time slipping without fanfare into Number Ten, Downing Street. Nicholas Elliott had become – no one was quite sure how – an unofficial adviser on intelligence matters to Margaret Thatcher. What was discussed during these meetings has never been fully revealed, and Elliott was far too discreet to say, but his political antennae were impeccable: after the break up of the Soviet Union, he correctly predicted the emergence of an authoritarian government in Russia; he foresaw the growth of Islamic fundamentalism, the rise of Iranian aggression, and the growing economic and political clout of China. Thatcher undoubtedly shared his view that post-imperial Britain was 'showing a quite unjustified lack of self-confidence'. The costume of an *éminence grise* fitted him well.

As Elliott aged, the pain of Philby's perfidy ebbed. Unlike Angleton, he would not allow Philby's ghost to torment and destroy him. He came to see the way he had been duped not as a mark of shame, but as a badge of honour. Philby had been able to manipulate Elliott's loyal constancy, his adherence to an old code of behaviour, as a weapon against him, and there was no dishonour in that. Yet he never ceased to wonder how someone who had been raised and educated as he had, someone he had known 'extremely well over an extended period', could have chosen such a radically different path. 'I have naturally given thought to the motivations behind treachery,' he wrote. In later life, he found himself trying to understand 'Philby the man, and make some form of analysis of the personality that evolved.' Whenever he reflected on the lives Philby had wasted, his anger welled up. 'Outwardly he was a kindly man. Inwardly he must have been cold, calculating and cruel – traits which he cleverly concealed from his friends and colleagues. He undoubtedly had a high opinion of himself concealed behind a veil of false modesty and thus a firm streak of egocentricity.' Philby had been a two-sided man, Elliott concluded, and he had only ever seen one, beguiling side, 'a façade, in a schizophrenic personality with a supreme talent for deception'.

Though part of Elliott detested Philby, he also mourned him. He recalled Philby's small kindnesses, the devotion he inspired in others, his enchanting mischief. He imagined him living a 'sad exiled life' in Moscow, with 'dreary people, a spying servant, drab clothes' and felt a twinge of something like sympathy for a man of rare talents, whose life had been 'wasted in a futile cause', who had 'decided to betray his friends, his family, and country for a creed that is now universally discredited'. He missed the spark that had drawn him to Philby on the very first day they met in 1940. 'He had charm to burn,' he wrote, with a reluctant wistfulness. 'He is said to have it still.'

Philby also found his thoughts turning to Elliott in old age, and reached the firm conclusion that he had been manoeuvred into fleeing Beirut: 'The whole thing was staged so as to push me into escaping.' Elliott had been motivated by the 'desire to spare SIS another spy scandal in London', and had unloaded him on Moscow.

As the Cold War raged, Philby was used as a propaganda tool by both sides. The Soviets set out to prove that he was living, in the words of one apologist, a life in Moscow of 'blissful peace'. In 1968, with KGB approval (and editing), he published a memoir, *My Silent War*, a blend of fact and fiction, history and disinformation, which depicted Soviet intelligence as uniformly brilliant, and himself as a hero of ideological constancy. Political voices in the West insisted that the reverse was true, and that Philby, drunken, depressed and disillusioned, was getting his just deserts for a life of betrayal and adherence to a diabolical doctrine. US President Ronald Reagan declared: 'How sleepless must be Kim Philby's nights in Moscow . . . how profoundly he and others like him must be aware that the people they betrayed are going to be victors in the end.' One former MI5 officer even claimed to know what was going through Philby's mind when he did fall asleep: 'He's a totally sad man, dreaming of a cottage in Sussex with roses around the door.'

The truth was somewhere in between. Philby was deeply unhappy during the early years in Soviet Russia, a place Burgess had memorably described as 'like Glasgow on a Saturday night in Victorian times'. The affair with Melinda soon fizzled out; she returned to Maclean, and then left the USSR for good. Philby drank heavily, often alone, and suffered from chronic insomnia. He would later admit that his life became 'burdensome'. At some point he tried to end it, by slashing his wrists. But in 1970, his spirits began to lift when George Blake, his fellow exile, introduced him to Rufina Ivanovna, a Russian woman of Polish extraction twenty years his junior, who would become his fourth wife. The KGB sent them a tea set of English bone china as a wedding present. The lingering suspicion of the Soviet intelligence service cleared, and in 1977, Philby gave a lecture to KGB officers, in which he insisted that the secret agent should admit nothing under interrogation, and on no account provide a confession. 'Any confession involves giving information to the enemy. It is therefore – by definition – wrong.' Some of his audience must have known that Philby had himself confessed to Nicholas Elliott back in 1963. They were much too tactful to point this out.

Philby's last years were quiet, dutiful and domesticated. Rufina tried to wean him off the booze, with only partial success. He did odd jobs for the Soviet state, including the training of KGB recruits and helping to motivate the Soviet hockey team – even though, as Elliott once noted, he was addicted to cricket and 'showed no interest whatsoever in any other sort of sport'. He was awarded the Order of Lenin, which he compared to a knighthood, 'one of the better ones'. In return, he never criticised the system he had supported all his adult life, never acknowledged the true character of the organisation he had served, and never uttered a word of remorse. In the officially approved Soviet style, he maintained that any errors in practical communism lay not with the ideas, but with the people executing them.

Philby died in a Moscow hospital on 11 May 1988. He was given a grand funeral with a KGB honour guard, buried at Kuntsevo cemetery outside Moscow, and lauded for his 'tireless struggle in the cause of peace and a brighter future'. He was commemorated with a Soviet postage stamp. In 2011, the Russian foreign intelligence service put up a plaque with two faces of Kim Philby facing one another in profile, an inadvertently apt monument to a man with two sides to his head.

Elliott hatched a plan for a different sort of memorial. He recommended to MI6 that Philby be awarded the CMG, the order of St Michael and St George, the sixth most prestigious award in the British honours system, awarded to men and women who render extraordinary or important non-military service in a foreign country. Elliott further suggested that he write a signed obituary note to accompany the award, in which he would say only: 'My lips have hitherto been sealed but I can now reveal that Philby was one of the bravest men I have ever known.' The implication would be clear to Moscow: Philby had been acting for Britain all along; he was not a valiant Soviet double agent, but a heroic British triple agent, and Elliott had been his spymaster. The idea that Philby had fooled the KGB would cause 'a tremendous fluttering in the dovecotes of the Lubyanka', Elliott wrote, and inflict the most gratifying posthumous revenge. It would be a splendid tease at Philby's expense, to which he could have no answer. Elliott's proposal was turned down. The new-style MI6 did not do jokes.

As his own end approached, Elliott reflected on a life that had been 'undistinguished, albeit mildly notorious', and tremendous fun.

He had known indignity, misfortune and intimate betrayal, but his fund of natural optimism never ran out. 'I feel I have been extraordinarily lucky,' he wrote. 'I look back on my career with some wonderment.'

Elliott kept a part of Philby with him always. He treasured the old umbrella he had bought so many years ago, in admiring imitation of his closest friend, and his worst enemy. When Elliott died in 1994, he left behind a short memoir, mostly consisting of off-colour stories, with a rueful, self-mocking title: *Never Judge a Man by His Umbrella*.

It was a joke that only two people could have fully appreciated: Nicholas Elliott, and Kim Philby.

Afterword

John le Carré

'God, it would be good to be a fake somebody, rather than a real nobody'
Mike Tyson, world heavyweight boxing champion

Nicholas Elliott of MI6 was the most charming, witty, elegant, courteous, compulsively entertaining spy I ever met. In retrospect, he also remains the most enigmatic. To describe his appearance is, these days, to invite ridicule. He was a *bon viveur* of the old school. I never once saw him in anything but an immaculately cut, dark three-piece suit. He had perfect Etonian manners, and delighted in human relationships.

He was thin as a wand, and seemed always to hover slightly above the ground at a jaunty angle, a quiet smile on his face and one elbow cocked for the Martini glass or cigarette.

His waistcoats curved inwards, never outwards. He looked like a P. G. Wodehouse man-about-town, and spoke like one, with the difference that his conversation was startlingly forthright, knowledgeable, and recklessly disrespectful of authority.

During my service in MI6, Elliott and I had been on nodding terms at most. When I was first interviewed for the Service, he was on the selection board. When I became a new entrant, he was a fifth-floor grandee whose most celebrated espionage coup – the wartime recruitment of a highly placed member of the German Abwehr in Istanbul, smuggling him and his wife to Britain – was held up to trainees as the ultimate example of what a resourceful field officer could achieve.

And he remained that same glamorous, remote figure throughout my service. Flitting elegantly in and out of head office, he would deliver a lecture, attend an operational conference, down a few glasses in the grandees' bar, and be gone.

I resigned from the Service at the age of thirty-three, having made a negligible contribution. Elliott resigned at the age of fifty-three, having been central to pretty well every major operation that the Service had undertaken since the outbreak of the Second World War. Years later, I bumped into him at a party.

After a turbulent spell in the City, Elliott in the most civilised of ways seemed a bit lost. He was also deeply frustrated by our former Service's refusal to let him reveal secrets which in his opinion had long passed their keep-till date. He believed he had a right, even a duty, to speak truth to history. And perhaps that's where he thought I might come in – as some sort of go-between or cut out, as the spies would have it, who would help him get his story into the open where it belonged.

Above all, he wanted to talk to me about his friend, colleague, and nemesis, Kim Philby.

And so it happened, one evening in May 1986 in my house in Hampstead, twenty-three years after he had sat down with Philby in Beirut and listened to his partial confession, that Nicholas Elliott opened his heart to me in what turned out to be the first in a succession of such meetings. Or if not his heart, a version of it.

And it quickly became clear that he wanted to draw me in, to make me marvel, as he himself marvelled; to make me share his awe and frustration at the enormity of what had been done to him; and to feel, if I could, or at least imagine, the outrage and the pain that his refined breeding and good manners – let alone the restrictions of the Official Secrets Act – obliged him to conceal.

Sometimes while he talked I scribbled in a notebook and he made no objection. Looking over my notes a quarter of a century later – twenty-eight pages from one sitting alone, handwritten on fading notepaper, a rusty staple at one corner – I am comforted that there is hardly a crossing out.

Was I contemplating a novel built around the Philby–Elliott relationship? I can't have been. I'd already covered the ground in *Tinker Tailor Soldier Spy*. A piece of live theatre, perhaps? A two-hander, the Nick & Kim Show, spread over twenty years of mutual affection – I dare almost call it love – and devastating, relentless betrayal?

If that was what I secretly had in mind, Elliott would have none of it:

'May we not ever again think about *the play*,' he wrote to me sternly in 1991. And I have tried not to ever since.

Like Philby, Elliott never spoke a word out of turn, however much he drank: except of course to Philby himself. Like Philby, he was a five-star entertainer, always a step ahead of you, bold, raunchy, and funny as hell. Yet I don't believe I ever seriously doubted that what I was hearing from Elliott was the cover story – the self-justification – of an old and outraged spy.

But where Philby's cover story was crafted to deceive his enemies, the purpose of Elliott's was to deceive himself. And as Ben Macintyre points out, over time the cover story began to appear in different and conflicting versions, of which I was treated to one.

In his monologues to me – for such they often were – he made much of his efforts, under Dick White's guidance, to winkle the 'truth' out of Philby in the ten years leading up to the confrontation in Beirut: not the *whole* truth, God forbid! That would have been something that in their worst nightmares both White and Elliott had refused to contemplate.

But the limited truth, the digestible version: namely, in Elliott's jargon, that somewhere back in the war years when it was understandable, Kim had gone a bit squidgy about our gallant Russian ally and given him a bit of this and that; and if he could just get it off his chest, whatever it was he'd given them, we'd all feel a lot better, and he could get on with doing what he did best, which was beating the Russian at his own game.

Alas, Macintyre's researches prove incontrovertibly that no such cat-and-mouse game took place: rather that, as the clouds of suspicion gathered, the two friends went, not face to face, but shoulder to shoulder. Long drunken evenings spent together? Any number of them. Alcohol was so much a part of the culture of MI6 in those days that a non-drinker in the ranks could look like a subversive or worse.

But as to Elliott's claim that he was all the while probing for chinks in Philby's armour: well, Elliott may have believed it – and certainly he was determined that I should believe it too – because, in the world that he and Philby had inhabited together for so long, the man whose cover story is not believed is the man who is operationally dead.

★

'Terrific charmer, with an impulse to shock. I knew Philby terribly well, specially the family. I really cared for them. I never knew a fellow like him for getting pissed. I'd interrogate him, he'd drink Scotch the whole time, I'd literally have to load him into a cab to send him home. Give the driver five quid to cart him upstairs. Took him to a dinner party once. Charmed everyone, then suddenly he started talking about his hostess's tits. Said she had the best breasts in the Service. Totally off-colour. I mean you don't, at a dinner party, start talking about your hostess's tits. But that's how he was. Liked to shock. I knew the father too. I had him to dinner in Beirut the night he died. Fascinating chap. Talked endlessly about his relationship with Ibn Saud. Eleanor, Philby's third wife, adored him. The old boy managed to make a pass at someone's wife, then left. A few hours later he'd died. Last words were 'God I'm bored.'

In the absence of his wife Elizabeth, I had already noted that Elliott consistently referred to Philby by his surname. Only in her presence did Philby become Kim.

★

'My interrogation of Philby lasted a long time. The one in Beirut was the end of a series. We had two sources. One was a pretty good defector. The other was this mother figure. The Office shrink had told me about her. He rang me up, the shrink. He'd been treating Aileen, Philby's second wife, and he said, "She's released me from my Hippocratic Oath. I've got to talk to you." So I went and saw him and he told me Philby was homosexual. Never mind all his philandering, never mind that Aileen, whom I knew pretty well, said Philby liked his sex and was pretty good at it. He was homosexual, all part of a syndrome, and the psychiatrist, on no evidence he knew of, was also convinced he was bad. Working for the Russians. Or something. He couldn't be precise but he was sure of it. He advised me to look for a mother figure. Somewhere there'll be a mother figure, he said. It was this woman Solomon. [Flora Solomon who introduced Philby to Aileen in 1939.] Jewish woman. She was working in Marks and Spencer's, a buyer or something. She was angry with Philby over the Jewish thing. Philby had been working for Colonel Teague, who was Head of Station in Jerusalem, and Teague was anti-Jewish, and she was angry. So she told us some things about him. Five (MI5) were in charge by then, and I passed it all on to Five – get the mother figure, Solomon. Wouldn't listen of course, they're too bureaucratic.'

★

'People were so *naughty* about Philby. Sinclair and Menzies [former Chiefs of MI6] – well, they just wouldn't listen to anything against him.'

★

'So this cable came, saying they had the proof, and I cabled back to White saying I must go and confront him. It had been an on-going thing for so long, and I owed it to the family to get it out of him. Feel? Well, I don't think I'm an emotional sort of chap, much, but I was fond of his women and children, and I always had the feeling that Philby himself would like to get the whole thing off his chest and settle down and follow cricket, which was what he loved. He knew cricket averages backwards and forwards. He could recite cricket till the cows came home. So Dick White said okay. Go. So I flew to Beirut and I saw him and I said to him, if you're as intelligent as I think you are, and for the sake of your family, you'll come clean, because the game is up. Anyway we could never have nailed him in court, he'd have denied it. Between you and me the deal was perfectly simple. He had to make a clean breast of it, which I thought he wanted to do anyway, which was where he fooled me, and he had to give us everything, but *everything* on damage. That was paramount. The damage limitation. After all, I mean one of the things the KGB would have been asking him was, who can we approach independently of you, who's in the Service, who might work for us? He might have suggested people. We had to know all that. Then whatever else he'd given them. We were completely firm on that.'

My notes resort to straight dialogue:

Self: 'So what were your sanctions if he didn't cooperate?'

Elliott: 'What's that, old boy?'

'Your sanctions, Nick, what you could threaten him with in the extreme case. Could you have him sandbagged, for instance, and flown to London?'

'Nobody wanted him in London, old boy.'

'Well, what about the ultimate sanction then – forgive me – could you have him killed, liquidated?'

'My dear chap. One of us.'

'So what *could* you do?'

'I told him, the alternative was a *total* cut-off. There wouldn't be an embassy, a consulate, a legation, in the whole of the Middle East that would have the first bloody thing to do with him. The business community wouldn't touch him, his journalistic career would be dead in the water. He'd have been a leper. His whole life would have been over. It never even crossed my mind he'd go to Moscow. He'd done this one thing in the past, he wanted it out of the way, so he'd got to come clean. After that we'd forget it. What about his family and Eleanor?'

I mention the fate of less favoured traitors who did far less than Philby but spent years in prison for it:

'Ah well, *Vassall* – well he wasn't top league, was he?' [John William Vassall, homosexual son of an Anglican parson and clerk to the naval attaché at the British Embassy in Moscow, was sentenced to eighteen years for spying for the KGB.]

*

'That was the first session and we agreed to meet again at four o'clock and at four o'clock he turned up with a confession, sheets of it, eight or nine closely typed pages of stuff, on the damage, on everything, masses of it. Then he says, you could do me a favour actually. Eleanor knows you're in town. She doesn't know anything about me. But if you don't come round for a drink she'll smell a rat. So I say all right, for Eleanor's sake I'll come round and have a drink with you. But first of all I've got to encode this stuff and cable it to Dick White, which I did. When I got to his place for a drink, he'd passed out. Pissed. Lying on the floor. Eleanor and I had to put him to bed. She took his head, I took his feet. He never said anything when he was pissed. Never spoke a loose word in his life, far as I know. So I told her. I said to her, "You know what this is about, don't you?" She said, "No," so I said, "He's a bloody Russian spy." He'd told me she hadn't rumbled him, and he was right. So I went home to London and left him to Peter Lunn to carry on the interrogation. Dick White had handled the case jolly well, but he hadn't said a word to the Americans. So I had to dash over to Washington and tell them. Poor old Jim Angleton. He'd made such a fuss of Philby when he was head of the Service's station in Washington, and when Angleton found out – when I told him, that is – he sort of went all the other way. I had dinner with him just a few days ago.'

*

'My theory is, you see, that one day the KGB will publish the rest of Philby's autobiography. The first book sort of cut itself dead at 1947. My guess is, they've got another book in their locker. One of the things Philby *has* told them is to polish up their goons. Make 'em dress properly, smell less. Sophisticated. They're a totally different-looking crowd these days. Smart as hell, smooth, first-class chaps. Philby's work, that was, you bet your boots. No, we never thought of killing him. He fooled me though. I thought he wanted to stay where he was.'

*

'You know, looking back though – don't you agree? – at all the things we got up to – all right we had some belly-laughs – my God we had some belly-laughs – we were terribly amateurish, in a way. I mean those lines through the Caucasus, agents going in and out, it was so *amateurish*. Well, he betrayed Volkov, of course, and they killed him. So when Philby wrote to me from Moscow and invited me to go and meet him in Berlin or Helsinki, and not tell Elizabeth or Dick White, I wrote back and told him to put some flowers on Volkov's grave for me. I thought that was rather good.

'I mean, who the *hell* did he think I was, not telling them? The first person I'd tell was Elizabeth, and *immediately* after that, I'd tell Dick White. I'd been out to dinner with Gehlen [Reinhard Gehlen, at that time director of the BND, West Germany's secret service] – did you know Gehlen? – came back late at night, and there was this plain envelope on the doormat with "Nick" written on it. Dropped in by hand. "If you can come, send me a postcard with Nelson's Column on it for Helsinki, Horseguards for Berlin," some damned thing. Who the hell did he think I was? The Albanian operation? Well yes, he probably blew that too. I mean we had some fucking good assets in Russia too in the old days. Don't know what happened to them either. Then he wants to meet me because he's lonely. Well of course he's lonely. He shouldn't have gone. He fooled me. I've written about him. The Sherwood Press. The big publishers all wanted me to write about the interrogation, but I wouldn't. It's more for one's climbing friends, a memoir. You can't write about the Office. Interrogation's an art. You understand that. It went on over a long time. Where was I?'

*

Sometimes Elliott drifted off into reminiscences of other cases that he had been involved in. The most significant was that of Oleg Penkovsky, a GRU colonel who provided the West with vital Soviet defence secrets in the run-up to the Cuba missile crisis. Elliott was infuriated by a book concocted by the CIA as a piece of Cold War propaganda and published under the title of *The Penkovsky Papers*:

'Frightful book. Made out the fellow was some kind of saint or hero. He was nothing of the sort, he'd been passed over and he was pissed off. The Americans turned him down but Shergy [Harold Shergold, controller of MI6's Soviet bloc operations] knew he was all right. Shergy had the nose. We couldn't have been less similar but we got on marvellously. *Les extrêmes se touchent*. I was in charge of Ops, Shergy was my number two. Marvellous field man, very sensitive, almost never wrong. He'd been right about Philby too, from very early. Shergold looked Penkovsky over and thought yes, so we took him on. Very brave thing, in spying, to put your faith in someone. Any fool can go back to his desk and say "I don't altogether trust this chap. On the one hand, on the other hand." It takes a lot of guts to take a flyer and say "I believe in him." That's what Shergy did, and we went along with him. Women. Penkovsky had these whores in Paris, we laid them on, and he complained he couldn't do anything with them: once a night and that was it. We had to send the Office doctor out to Paris to give him a shot in the bum so that he could get it up. You do get some belly-laughs, they were what one lived for sometimes. These marvellous belly-laughs. I mean how could you crack up Penkovsky to be a hero? Mind you, betrayal takes courage. You have to hand it to Philby too. He had courage. Shergy resigned once. He was frightfully temperamental. I came in, found his resignation on my desk. "In view of the fact that Dick White" – he put CSS of course – "has passed information to the Americans without my consent, and has therefore endangered my very sensitive source, I wish to resign as an example to other members of the Service" – something like that. White apologised and Shergy took back his resignation. I had to talk him round though. Wasn't easy. Very

temperamental chap. But a marvellous field man. And he got
Penkovsky dead right. Artist.'

★

Elliott on Sir Claude Dansey, also known as Colonel Z, deputy chief
of MI6 during World War II:

'Utter shit. Stupid too. But tough and rude. Wrote these awful
short minutes to people. Carried on feuds. I mean a real shit. I took
over his networks when I became head of station in Berne after the
war. Well he did have these high level business sources. *They* were
good. He had a knack of getting these businessmen to do things for
him. He was good at that.'

On Sir George Young, vice chief to Sir Dick White during the Cold
War:

'Flawed. Brilliant, coarse, always had to be out on his own. He went
to Hambro's after the Service. I asked them later: how did you make out
with George? Were you up or down? They said they reckoned, about
even. He got them some of the Shah's money, but he made perfectly
awful balls-ups that cost them about as much as he got for them.'

On Professor Hugh Trevor-Roper, historian and wartime member
of SIS:

'Brilliant scholar, all that, but wet and useless. Something perverse
inside him. Laughed my head off when he took a dive on those
Hitler diaries. The whole Service knew they were fake. But Hugh
walked straight in. How *could* Hitler have written them? I wouldn't
have the chap near me in the war. When I was head man in Cyprus
I told my sentry at the door that if a Captain Trevor-Roper showed
up, he should shove his bayonet up his arse. He showed up, the
sentry told him what I'd said. Hugh was puzzled. Belly-laughs. That's
what I liked about the Service. Marvellous belly-laughs.'

On providing a prostitute for a potential SIS asset from the Middle
East:

'St Ermin's Hotel. She wouldn't go. Too near the House of Commons. "My father's an MP." She had to have 4 June off so that she could take her nephew out from Eton. "Well perhaps you'd rather we got someone else?" I said. Didn't hesitate. "All I want to know is, how much?"'

On Graham Greene:

'I met him in Sierra Leone in the war. Greene was waiting for me at the harbour. "Have you brought any French letters?" he yelled at me soon as I came within earshot. He had this fixation about eunuchs. He'd been reading the station code book and found that the Service actually had a code group for eunuch. Must have been from the days when we were running eunuchs in the harems, as agents. He was dying to make a signal with eunuch in it. Then one day he found a way. Head Office wanted him to attend a conference somewhere. Cape Town I think. He had some operation fixed or something. Not an operation, knowing him, he never mounted one. Anyway he signalled back "Like the eunuch I can't come."'

A wartime reminiscence of life in Turkey under diplomatic cover:

'Dinner at the ambassador's. Middle of the war. Ambassadress lets out a yell because I've cut off the nose. "Nose of what?" "The cheese." "The valet *handed* me the bloody cheese," I tell her. "And you cut the nose off it," she says. Hell did they get it from? Middle of the bloody war. Cheddar. And the chap who'd handed it to me was Cicero, the fellow who sold all our secrets to the *Abwehr*. The D-Day landing. The lot. And the Huns didn't believe him. Typical. No faith.'

I am describing to Elliott how, while I was in MI5, Graham Greene's *Our Man in Havana* was published and the Service's legal adviser wanted to prosecute him under the Official Secrets Act for revealing the relationship between a head of station and his head agent.

'Yes, and he jolly nearly got done for it. Would have served him bloody right.'

What for? But I didn't ask.

★

And most memorable of all, perhaps, Elliott recalling a passage, real or imagined, from what he insisted were his early soundings of Philby concerning his Cambridge days:

'They seem to think you're a bit *tarnished* somehow.'

'By?'

'Oh, you know, early passions, membership – '

'Of?'

'Jolly interesting group, actually, by the sounds of it. Exactly what university is for. Lefties all getting together. The Apostles, wasn't it?'

★

In 1987, two years before the Berlin Wall came down, I was visiting Moscow. At a reception given by the Union of Soviet Writers, a part-time journalist with KGB connections named Genrikh Borovik invited me to his house to meet an old friend and admirer of my work. The name of the friend, when I enquired, was Kim Philby. I now have it on pretty good authority that Philby knew he was dying and was hoping I would collaborate with him on another volume of memoirs.

I refused to meet him. Elliott was pleased with me. At least I think he was. But perhaps he secretly hoped I might bring him news of his old friend.

Notes

Citations marked KV refer to the Security Service files, PREM to Prime Minister's Office files and FO to Foreign Office files, all at the National Archives (TNA), Kew.

Epigraphs

   vii 'General slang for members': spymuseum.org/education-programs/spy-resources/language-of-espionage.

   vii 'If I had to choose between': *The Nation*, 16 July 1938.

Chapter 1: Apprentice Spy

   3 'I am relieved': Nicholas Elliott, *Never Judge a Man by his Umbrella* (London, 1992), p. 101.

   3 'So that': ibid.

   4 'crossed in love': ibid., p. 3.

   4 'the epitome of the English': ibid., p. 1.

   4 'effete': ibid., p. 88.

   4 'when dealing with foreigners': ibid., p. 43.

   5 'Claude was highly embarrassed': ibid., p. 13.

   5 'God, Disease and below': ibid., p. 18.

   5 'nothing as unpleasant': ibid., p. 31.

   5 'sheer hell': ibid., p. 21.

   5 'The increased legibility': ibid., p. 34.

   6 'How hard should I work': ibid., p. 80.

   6 'He strongly advised': ibid.

   6 'a triumph over the examiners': ibid., p. 89.

   6 'languid, upper-class manner': Peter Wright, *Spycatcher: The Candid Autobiography of a Senior Intelligence Officer* (London, 1987), p. 174.

   7 'I could never be a': Elliott, *Umbrella*, p. 40.

   7 'obey not the order': ibid.

   7 'plug ugly': ibid., p. 15.

   7 'was no more or less': ibid.

   7 'inability to get down': ibid., p. 91.

7 'There was no serious': Nicholas Elliott, *With My Little Eye: Observations Along the Way* (Norwich, 1993), p. 16.

8 'in the diplomatic service': Elliott, *Umbrella*, p. 93.

8 'opportunity to see': ibid., p. 99.

8 'We discreetly poked': ibid.

8 'a singularly foolhardy': ibid.

9 'The Führer is feted': cited by James Holland, *Daily Mail*, 18 April 2009.

9 'I am tempted': Elliott, *Umbrella*, p. 100.

9 'pick the bastard off': E. Butler, *Mason-Mac: The life of Lieutenant-General Sir Noel Mason-MacFarlane* (London, 1972), p. 75.

9 'strongly urged': Elliott, *Umbrella*, p. 100.

9 'My mind was easily': ibid., p. 101.

10 'just as soon as it feels': Christopher Andrew, *The Defence of the Realm: The Authorised History of MI5* (London, 2009), p. 195.

10 'the best and most ingenious': ibid., p. 196.

10 'priceless intelligence': ibid.

10 'I was really helping': ibid.

11 'The English are hopeless': ibid., p. 204.

11 'sacrificing himself': ibid.

11 'Klop was a man': Elliott, *Umbrella*, p. 149.

11 'complicated man': ibid., p. 102.

11 'His motivation was solely': ibid.

11 'Is Hitler going to start': ibid.

11 'On present plans': ibid.

11 'startling statement': ibid.

12 'always displayed': Andrew, *Defence of the Realm*, p. 246.

12 'by the autumn of 1939': Keith Jeffery, *MI6: The History of the Secret Intelligence Service 1909–1949* (London, 2010), p. 385.

12 'it could only be': Andrew, *Defence of the Realm*, p. 242.

12 'brilliant linguist': Elliott, *Umbrella*, p. 103.

12 'an ostentatious ass': ibid.

12 'overthrow the present regime': p. 382.

12 'I have a hunch': Andrew, *Defence of the Realm*, p. 244.

13 'the big man himself': Jeffery, *MI6*, p. 384.

13 'No one was in sight': ibid.

13 'The next moment': Sigismund Payne Best, *The Venlo Incident* (London, 1950), p. 17.

14 'At one stroke': Elliott, *Umbrella*, p. 103.

14 'able to construct': ibid.

14 'intense ambition': ibid.

14 'possibility of winning': ibid.

14 'In the long run': arcre.com/archive/sis/venlo

14 'selling everything to Moscow': Andrew, *Defence of the Realm*, p. 262.

14 'as disastrous as it was': Elliott, *Umbrella*, p. 103.

14 'Oh what a tangled web': Elliott, *My Little Eye*, p. 11.

15 'Information has been': Elliott, *Umbrella*, p. 106.

15 'It soon became apparent': ibid.

15 'We're in the final': ibid., p. 109.

15 'normality and calmness': ibid.

15 'never occurred to me': ibid.

16 'England was gripped': ibid., p. 111.

16 'give evidence of what': ibid.

17 'feeling of camaraderie': ibid., p. 110.

17 'My only moment': ibid.

17 'Basil Fisher was killed': ibid., p. 111.

Chapter 2: Section V

18 'He was the sort of man': Sir Robert Mackenzie, interview with Phillip Knightley, 1967, quoted in Phillip Knightley, *The Master Spy: The Story of Kim Philby* (London, 1988), p. 119.

18 'halting stammered witticisms': Graham Greene, foreword to Kim Philby, *My Silent War: The Autobiography of a Spy* (London, 1968), p. xx.

18 'great pluck': E. G. de Caux to Ralph Deakin, 14 January 1938, *The Times* Archives.

19 'Many express disappointment': *The Times*, 17 November 1939.

19 'Camel-hair overcoat': expenses claim letter, *The Times* Archives.

19 'dropped a few hints': Philby, *My Silent War*, p. xxviii.

19 'A person like you': Knightley, *The Master Spy*, p. 79.

20 'We'll figure something': ibid.

20 'war work': Philby, *My Silent War*, p. 9.

20 'intensely likeable': ibid.

20 'I began to show off': ibid., p. 10.

20 'nothing recorded against': ibid.

20 'I was asked about him': Patrick Seale and Maureen McConville, *Philby: The Long Road to Moscow* (London, 1973), p. 135.

21 'set Europe ablaze': Hugh Dalton, *The Fateful Years: Memoirs, 1931–1945* (London, 1957), p. 366.

21 'I escaped to London': Philby, *My Silent War*, p. 63.

22 'In those days': Elliott, *Umbrella*, p. 111.

22 'He had an ability': ibid., p. 183.

22 'the inherent evil': ibid., p. 105.

22 'very rarely discussed': ibid., p. 183.

22 'the English batting': ibid.

22 'Indeed he did not strike me': ibid.

23 'pose of amiable': Hugh R. Trevor-Roper, *The Philby Affair: Espionage, Treason, and Secret Services* (London, 1968), p. 42.

23 'by and large pretty stupid': Christopher Andrew, *Secret Service: The Making of the British Intelligence Community* (London, 1985), p. 249.

23   'An exceptional person': ibid.

23   'clarity of mind': Elliott, *Umbrella*, p. 183.

23   'He was much more': ibid.

23   'The old Secret Service': Malcolm Muggeridge, *Chronicles of Wasted Time*, vol. II (London, 1973), p. 136.

23   'slouching about in sweaters': ibid.

24   'You'd drop in to see': Kim Philby, interview with Phillip Knightley, 1988, in Knightley, *The Master Spy*, p. 84.

24   'atmosphere of *haute cuisine*': Philby, *My Silent War*, p. 35.

24   'out of fun rather': Elliott, *Umbrella*, p. 184.

24   'To start with we always': Dennis Wheatley, *The Deception Planners: My Secret War* (London, 1980), p. 30.

25   'for an hour': ibid.

25   'He was a formidable': Elliott, *Umbrella*, p. 183.

25   'serious drinkers should never': ibid.

25   'violent headache': ibid.

25   'It was an organisation': Elliott, *My Little Eye*, p. 22.

25   They spoke the same language': interview with Mark Elliott, 11 November 2013.

26   'negate, confuse, deceive': Leo D. Carl, *The International Dictionary of Intelligence* (McLean Virginia, 1990), p. 83.

26   'with a knowledge of Spain': Philby, *My Silent War*, p. 35.

26   'The Old Boy network': ibid., p. 37.

26   'purblind, disastrous': Trevor-Roper, *The Philby Affair*, p. 37.

26   'As an intelligence officer': Philby, *My Silent War*, p. 46.

26   'suspicious and bristling': ibid.

27   'personal contacts with': ibid., p. 43.

27   'He was a bit of a communist': Seale and McConville, *Philby*, p. 135.

27   'active pursuit and liquidation': Anthony Cave Brown, *Treason in the Blood: H. St John Philby, Kim Philby, and the Spy Case of the Century* (London, 1995), p. 276.

28   'Aileen belonged to that class': Flora Solomon and Barnet Litvinoff, *Baku to Baker Street: The Memoirs of Flora Solomon* (London, 1984), p. 172.

28   'He found an avid listener': ibid.

28   'She was highly intelligent': Elliott, *Umbrella*, p. 182.

29   'parental pride': ibid., p. 187.

29   'long Sunday lunches': Graham Greene, foreword to Philby, *My Silent War*, p. xx.

29   'small loyalties': ibid.

29   'He had something about him': Seale and McConville, *Philby*, p. 133.

29   'merry band': Desmond Bristow with Bill Bristow, *A Game of Moles: The Deceptions of an MI6 Officer* (London, 1993), p. 17.

29   'a purchaser of skunk excrement': ibid., p. 18.

29   'The sense of dedication': Cave Brown, *Treason in the Blood*, p. 276.

29 'No one could have': Graham Greene, foreword to Philby, *My Silent War*, p. xix.

30 'a gentle-looking man': Bristow, *A Game of Moles*, pp. 262–3.

30 'cosiness': Philby, *My Silent War*, p. 63.

30 'It was not difficult': ibid.

30 'a good cricket umpire': Felix Cowgill, interview with Anthony Cave Brown, 1983, in Cave Brown, *Treason in the Blood*, p. 275.

30 'calculating ambition': Knightley, *The Master Spy*, p. 119.

30 'single-mindedness': ibid.

30 'There was something': Hugh Trevor-Roper, interview by Graham Turner, *Daily Telegraph*, 28 January 2003.

31 'It was not long': Philby, *My Silent War*, p. 53.

31 'to good use in disrupting': ibid., p. 55.

31 'mingle with the crowd': Jeffery, *MI6*, p. 387.

31 'party-goer's image': ibid.

32 'This is the last time': Charles Whiting, *Ghost Front: the Ardennes before the Battle of the Bulge* (London, 2002), pp. 203–4.

32 'an operational disaster': Philby, *My Silent War*, p. 52.

32 'virtually at will': ibid., p. 63.

32 'contacts with other SIS': ibid.

32 'fire-watching nights': Graham Greene, foreword to Philby, *My Silent War*, p. xx.

33 'bulging briefcase': Philby, *My Silent War*, p. 63.

33 'longhand, in neat, tiny writing': Sir Robert Mackenzie, interview with Phillip Knightley, 1967, quoted in Knightley, *The Master Spy*, p. 118.

33 'MR NICHOLAS ELLIOTT': Nigel West and Oleg Tsarev, *The Crown Jewels: The British Secrets at the Heart of the KGB Archives* (London, 1998), p. 311.

Chapter 3: Otto and Sonny

34 'Something I owe': Rudyard Kipling, *Kim* (London, 1994), Chapter 8.

34 'penetration agent working': Philby, *My Silent War*, p. xxix.

35 'the exquisite relish': Cave Brown, *Treason in the Blood*, p. 291.

35 'My ambition is fame': Knightley, *The Master Spy*, p. 21.

36 'constantly aware of his father's': Cave Brown, *Treason in the Blood*, p. 133.

36 'He should always': ibid., p. 134.

36 'sudden conversion': Philby, *My Silent War*, p. xxx.

36 'the inner fortress': ibid., p. xxix.

37 'I left the university': ibid., p. xxxi.

37 'I can hardly see him': Elliott, *Umbrella*, p. 183.

37 'devote his life to the': ibid.

37 'at a crisis point': Knightley, *The Master Spy*, p. 40.

37 'tremendous little sexpot': Cave Brown, *Treason in the Blood*, p. 159.

38 'Actually quite warm': Andrew, *The Defence of the Realm*, p. 168.

38 'Even though the basis': Genrikh Borovik, ed. Phillip Knightly, *The Philby Files: The Secret Life of Master Spy Kim Philby* (London, 1994), p. 22.

38 'I do hope Kim gets a job': Cave Brown, *Treason in the Blood*, p. 162.

38 'Excess can always': ibid., p. 137.

38 'man of decisive importance': Andrew, *The Defence of the Realm*, p. 169.

39 'man of considerable': ibid.

39 'He was a marvellous man': Borovik, *The Philby Files*, p. 29.

39 'important and interesting work': ibid., p. 25.

39 'I trusted him': ibid., p. 27.

39 'prophet of the better orgasm': Andrew, *The Defence of the Realm*, p. 170.

39 'a poor man's sexual performance': Cave Brown, *Treason in the Blood*, p. 163.

41 'One does not look twice': Philby, *My Silent War*, p. xxxii.

41 'Of all the passions': C. S. Lewis, *The Inner Ring*, Memorial Lecture at King's College, University of London, in 1944, collected in *Mere Christianity* (London, 2012).

41 'My future looked romantic': Borovik, *The Philby Files*, p. 28.

41 'By background, education': ibid.

41 'The anti-fascist movement': ibid.

41 'real and palpable way': ibid.

41 'like poetry': ibid., p. 33.

42 'We have recruited the son': ibid., p. 39.

42 'What are his prospects': ibid., p. 40.

42 'the most interesting': ibid., p. 52.

42 'refers to his parents': ibid., p. 147.

42 'his marvellous education': ibid., p. 31.

42 'the remoter open spaces': Philby, *My Silent War*, p. xxix.

42 'His wife was his first lover': Borovik, *The Philby Files*, p. 148.

42 'I sometimes felt': ibid., p. 33.

42 'I was certain that my life': ibid., p. 31.

42 'constant encouragement': ibid.

42–3 'Söhnchen comes from': ibid., p. 43.

43 'It's amazing that': ibid., p. 55.

43 'Once you're inside': ibid., p. 56.

43 'He has many friends': ibid., p. 43.

43 'profoundly repulsive': ibid., p. 59.

43 'in the eyes of my friends': ibid.

43 'how difficult it is to leave': ibid.

44 'It seems unlikely that': ibid., pp. 52–3.

44 'The people I could': ibid., p. 46.

44 'very serious and aloof': ibid., p. 44.

44 'Sonny has high praise': ibid.

44 'Very smart': ibid., p. 44.

44 'Do you think that': ibid., p. 48.

45 'I lost my faith': Elisabeth K. Poretsky, *Our Own People: A Memoir of 'Ignace Reiss' and His Friends* (Oxford, 1969), p. 214.
45 'shiny grey complexion': Andrew, *The Defence of the Realm*, p. 180.
45 'an inspirational figure': Cave Brown, *Treason in the Blood*, p. 194.
45 'Both of them were intelligent': Borovik, *The Philby Files*, p. 174.
45 'handles our money': ibid.
45 'We have great difficulty': ibid., p. 88.
45 'unit strengths and locations': Knightley, *The Master Spy*, p. 71.
46 'a royalist of the most': Borovik, *The Philby Files*, p. 111.
46 'I would be lying': ibid., pp. 111–12.
46 'He works with great': ibid., p. 129.
46 'obviously been in the thick': Wright, *Spycatcher*, p. 260.
46 'doing a very dangerous job': ibid., p. 173.
46 'important work for peace': Solomon and Litvinoff, *Baku to Baker Street*, p. 169.
46 'he could always': Wright, *Spycatcher*, p. 173.
46–7 'Even if he had been able': Borovik, *The Philby Files*, p. 89.
47 'They are very pleased': ibid., p. 95.
47 'a decent chap': Knightley, *The Master Spy*, p. 56.
47 'I know that as a former priest': Andrew, *The Defence of the Realm*, p. 183.
48 'infinite patience': Philby, *My Silent War*, p. xxix.
48 'intelligent understanding': ibid.
48 'painstaking advice': ibid.
48 'marvellous men': Borovik, *The Philby Files*, p. 29.
48 'What's going to happen': Knightley, *The Master Spy*, p. 71.
48 'activity in England': Andrew, *The Defence of the Realm*, p. 185.
49 'I had been told in pressing': Philby, *My Silent War*, p. xxviii.
49 'Where is the Café': Borovik, *The Philby Files*, p. 143.
49 'extraordinarily valuable': ibid., p. 151.
49 'the appropriate hands': ibid.

Chapter 4: Boo, Boo, Baby, I'm a Spy

50 'true sense of values': Elliott, *Umbrella*, p. 178.
50 'His intellectual equipment': Philby, *My Silent War*, p. 109.
50 'an utter shit': cited in Anthony Read and David Fisher, *Colonel Z: The Secret Life of a Master of Spies* (London, 1985), p. 361.
51 'Vivian was long past': Philby, *My Silent War*, p. 48.
51 'He would murmur': ibid., p. 69.
51 'But behind the façade': ibid.
51 'The rewards of such unorthodoxy': ibid., p. 70.
51 'the only man in The Hotel': Borovik, *The Philby Files*, p. 205.
52 'golden lads': Cave Brown, *Treason in the Blood*, p. 470.
52 'You know as well as I do': Jeffery, *MI6*, p. 490.
52 'in the hurly-burly': Guy Liddell, *Diaries*, KV4/466.

52 'a pleasant personality': ibid.

52 'For every lead that produced': Philby, *My Silent War*, p. 48.

52 'monstrous': ibid.

52 'a model of economy': Elliott, *Umbrella*, p. 183.

53 'I had the advantage': ibid., p. 110.

53 'an interesting and promising': Borovik, *The Philby Files*, p. 167.

53 'especially valuable': Philby, *My Silent War*, p. 64.

53 'few social graces': West and Tsarev, *The Crown Jewels*, p. 312.

53 'inclined towards inertia': ibid.

53 'weakness [for] women': ibid.

53 'the weak link': ibid., p. 313.

53 'fat briefcase': Philby, *My Silent War*, p. 48.

53 'Her political views': Borovik, *The Philby Files*, p. 208.

54 'difficult, exhausting': ibid., p. 28.

54 'twinges of panic': ibid., p. 203.

54 'a young Englishman': Andrew, *The Defence of the Realm*, p. 267.

55 'We told him he must': Borovik, *The Philby Files*, p. 202.

56 'About 58, 5 feet 6 inches': West and Tsarev, *The Crown Jewels*, p. 298.

56 'There aren't any': Borovik, *The Philby Files*, p. xii.

56 'tenth on the list': ibid., p. 167.

56 'no Soviet citizens': ibid., p. 210.

56 'obvious absurdity': ibid., p. 201.

57 'highly suspicious': ibid., p. 200.

57 'dubious': ibid., p. 196.

57 'tested and retested': ibid., p. 204.

57 'upside down': Philby, *My Silent War*, p. 61.

57 'to discuss the mystery': ibid.

57 'far outside the normal scope': ibid.

58 'another flood': ibid.

58 'Luck played an enormous': ibid., p. 128.

58 'cloistered': ibid., p. 72.

58 'those who sit at desks': Elliott, *My Little Eye*, p. 15.

58 'anxious to get away': Elliott, *Umbrella*, p. 111.

58 'All foreigners are bloody': ibid., p. 16.

58 'I was delighted': ibid., p. 111.

59 'who was being sent': ibid., p. 112.

59 'well-stocked bar': ibid.

59 'the tattiest army officer': ibid., p. 113.

59 'the shortage of contraceptives': ibid.

59 'managed to alleviate': ibid.

59 'roving brothel': Philby, *My Silent War*, p. 78.

59 'two lonely Germans': ibid.

59 'delight': Elliott, *Umbrella*, p. 117.

60 'pained tolerance': Jeffery, *MI6*, p. 418.

60 'great ability and energy': ibid., p. 419.

60 'one of the great espionage': ibid., p. 417.

61 'Everyone was well informed': Elliott, *Umbrella*, p. 122.

61–2 'I'm involved in a dangerous game': Barry Rubin, *Istanbul Intrigues* (New York, 1989), p. xvii.

62 'not a kid glove affair': Jeffery, *MI6*, p. 420.

62 'crammed from top': Elliott, *Umbrella*, p. 120.

62 'extremely erudite': Elliott, *My Little Eye*, p. 73.

62 'Its clientele': Elliott, *Umbrella*, p. 122.

62 'white coloured skin': ibid.

63 'a ferocious dry martini': ibid., p. 123.

63 'spoke excellent English': ibid.

63 'the capacity for friendship': Elliott, *My Little Eye*, p. 15.

63 'A large amount': ibid.

63 'One particularly remarkable man': Elliott, *Umbrella*, p. 117.

64 'a most unattractive': ibid., p. 130.

64 'operating a clandestine': ibid.

64 'was not altogether': ibid.

64 'more people involved': Elliott, *My Little Eye*, p. 50.

64 'All were kept under': ibid., p. 51.

64 'schoolboyish': Philby, *My Silent War*, p. 109.

64 'Bars, beards and blondes': ibid.

65 'the worst claret': Elliott, *Umbrella*, p. 177.

65 'After three of Ellie's': ibid., p. 123.

65 'hoping he didn't mind': ibid., p. 126.

Chapter 5: Three Young Spies

66 'two minutes from MI5': Philby, *My Silent War*, p. 71.

67 'the frowsty old': Malcolm Muggeridge, book review of *A Very Limited Edition*, *Esquire*, May 1966, p. 84.

67 'a notably bewildered': Philby, *My Silent War*, p. 74.

67 'a bunch of amateur bums': ibid., p. 75.

67 'They lost no opportunity': ibid., p. 74.

67 'pain in the neck': ibid., p. 76.

67 'formative years': Tom Mangold, *Cold Warrior: James Jesus Angleton – CIA's Master Spy Hunter* (London, 1991), p. 13.

68 'more English than': ibid., p. 12.

68 'a mysterious person': ibid., p. 13.

68 'What a miracle': Michael Holzman, *James Jesus Angleton, the CIA, and the Craft of Counterintelligence* (Boston, 2008), p. 83.

68 'arts and crafts': Cave Brown, *Treason in the Blood*, p. 298.

68 'I do remember': Holzman, *James Jesus Angleton*, p. 49.

68 'earned my respect': Philby, *My Silent War*, pp. 150–1.

69 'Philby may have felt': Holzman, *James Jesus Angleton*, p. 49.

69   'Philby was one of Angleton's': Knightley, *The Master Spy*, p. 118.
69   'Our European friends': W. Bryher, *The Days of Mars: A Memoir, 1940–1946* (New York, 1972), pp. ix–x.
69   'as if they contained the secret of the Trinity': Cave Brown, *Treason in the Blood*, p. 299.
69   'restless appetite for organizing': William Empson to James Angleton, 19 February 1940, quoted in Holzman, *James Jesus Angleton*, p. 22.
69   'extremely brilliant': ibid., p. 45.
69   'Once I met Philby': Joseph J. Trento, *The Secret History of the CIA* (New York, 2001), p. 37.
70   'an almost total moron': West and Tsarev, *The Crown Jewels*, p. 311.
70   'We had achieved': Philby, *My Silent War*, p. 78.
70   'in all intelligence matters': ibid., p. 80.
70   'beginning to make a career': ibid., p. 79.
70   'I regarded my SIS': ibid., p. xxix.
71   'incomprehensible': Andrew, *Defence of the Realm*, p. 272.
71   'A straight penetration': Philby, *My Silent War*, p. xxix.
71   'He is lying to us': Borovik, *The Philby Files*, p. xiv.
71   'He was so completely': Yuri Modin, *My Five Cambridge Friends: Burgess, Maclean, Philby, Blunt, and Cairncross by Their KGB Controller* (New York, 1995), p. 201.
71   'in such a manner': Borovik, *The Philby Files*, p. 218.
72   'single-front struggle': ibid., p. xi.
72   'modest bit towards': Knightley, *The Master Spy*, p. 128.
73   'Moody and nervous': Vermehren file, TNA KV 2/956.
73   'The city is riddled': Rubin, *Istanbul Intrigues*, p. 224.
73   'specialised in making Britons': ibid.
74   'I remembered him vividly': Elliott, *Umbrella*, p. 135.
74   'small roundish man': ibid.
74   'instantly dismissed': ibid.
75   'The information obtained': ibid., p. 133.
75   'If he had not been a spy': Rubin, *Istanbul Intrigues*, p. 164.
75   'penchant for involving': Elliott, *Umbrella*, p. 120.
75   'The names of the Azerbaijanis': Rubin, *Istanbul Intrigues*, p. 227.
76   'the Arab cause depended': ibid., p. 225.
76   '*Twelve-land, Twelve-land*': ibid., p. 201.

Chapter 6: The German Defector

77   'unfit to represent': Erich Vermehren, obituary by Richard Bassett, *The Independent*, 3 May 2005.
79   'Erich Vermehren?': Richard Bassett, *Hitler's Spy Chief: The Wilhelm Canaris Mystery* (London, 2006), p. 280.
79   'I had a sense': ibid.
79   'signs of instability': Cave Brown, *Treason in the Blood*, p. 315.

79 'a highly strung': Jeffery, *MI6*, p. 504.

79 'intensely anti-Nazi': ibid.

79 'fully convinced': ibid.

80 'the complete Abwehr setup': ibid.

80 'quantity of detailed information': ibid.

80 'it would not be long': ibid.

81 'a hell of flap': ibid., p. 505.

81 'lest his disappearance': Rubin, *Istanbul Intrigues*, p. 232.

81 'he was given breakfast': ibid.

82 'swamped by an invasion': ibid.

82 'gravely prejudiced the activities': ibid., p. 229.

82 'exceedingly tedious': Elliott, *Umbrella*, p. 126.

82 'They are so God-awful conscientious': Philby, *My Silent War*, p. 42.

83 'I don't mind telling you': Elliott, *Umbrella*, p. 127.

83 'obstacle race with frequent jumps': ibid.

83 'German-Turkish intelligence': Rubin, *Istanbul Intrigues*, p. 228.

83 'The twenty-four-year-old attaché': *Associated Press*, 9 February 1945.

83 'If an enemy alien': Liddell, *Diaries*, KV4/466.

83 'outstanding blow': Jeffery, *MI6*, p. 504.

84 'exploded': Cave Brown, *Treason in the Blood*, p. 315.

84 'hardly surprising given': Bassett, *Hitler's Spy Chief*, p. 282.

84 'thrown into a state of confusion': Jeffery, *MI6*, p. 505.

84 'consummate skill and sympathy': ibid.

84 'dine out': interview with David Cornwell, 12 April 2012.

85 'formidably impressed both by': Elliott, *My Little Eye*, p. 81. There is some confusion over where Elliott and Angleton first met. Elliott recalled that Angleton came to stay with him Switzerland in 1946, but it seems more likely, according to his family and other sources, that their first encounter was in London a year earlier, during the period of the Vermehren debriefing.

85 'Beneath the rather sinister': Elliott, *My Little Eye*, p. 81.

85 'At that time, secrets': Elliott, *Umbrella*, p. 62.

85–6 'Sit down, I'd like to have' to 'Because the Chief told him': Elliott, *My Little Eye*, pp. 17–18.

86 'For centuries the Office': Tom Bower, *The Perfect English Spy: Sir Dick White and the Secret War, 1935–1990* (London, 1995), p. 85.

86 'of all their contacts': Bassett, *Hitler's Spy Chief*, p. 23.

86 'leading Catholic activists': Knightley, *The Master Spy*, p. 110.

86 'could have formed the backbone': Cave Brown, *Treason in the Blood*, p. 328.

86 'All had been deported': Bassett, *Hitler's Spy Chief*, p. 23.

87 'Because Moscow had decided': Knightley, *The Master Spy*, p. 110.

87 'drive against the Catholic Church': TNA KV 4/469.

87 'I was responsible for the deaths': Knightley, *The Master Spy*, p. 128.

Chapter 7: The Soviet Defector

88 'We've been penetrated': Bower, *The Perfect English Spy*, p. 66.

88 'the next enemy': Philby, *My Silent War*, p. 92.

88 'professional handling of any cases': Nigel West and Oleg Tsarev (eds), *Triplex: Secrets from the Cambridge Five* (Yale, 2009), p. 115.

89 'provided you do not do anything': Jeffery, *MI6*, p. 566.

89 'I must do everything': Philby, *My Silent War*, p. 94.

89 'Cowgill must go': ibid.

89 'great warmth': ibid., p. 100.

89 'the idea was his own': ibid.

90 'At one stroke': Robert Cecil in Christopher Andrew and D. Dilks (eds), *The Missing Dimension: Governments and Intelligence Communities in the Twentieth Century* (London, 1984), p. 179.

90 'The new appointment': Borovik, *The Philby Files*, p. 236.

90 'jovial, kindly man': ibid., p. 177.

91 'a splendid professional': ibid.

91 'unburden': ibid.

91 'I must thank you': ibid., p. 237.

91 'After the gloom of London': Elliott, *Umbrella*, p. 141.

92 'not only our best source on Germany': Tony Paterson, 'Germany finally honours the "traitor" spy', *Independent*, 25 September 2004.

91 'Communists and communism': Elliott, *My Little Eye*, p. 49.

93 'over one thousand enemy': Ted Morgan, *A Covert Life: Jay Lovestone: Communist, Anti-Communist, and Spymaster* (New York, 1999), p. 257.

93 'heavily dependent on Philby': Cave Brown, *Treason in the Blood*, p. 353.

93 'enigmatic wraith': Holzman, *James Jesus Angleton*, p. 57.

93 'haunted the streets': ibid., p. 59.

93 'You would sit on a sofa': David C. Martin, *Wilderness of Mirrors: Intrigue, Deception, and the Secrets that Destroyed Two of the Cold War's Most Important Agents* (Guilford, CT, 2003), p. 18.

94 'perhaps the ablest': Philby, *My Silent War*, p. 105.

94 'Was it freedom': ibid., p. 108.

94 'Not one of them': ibid.

94 'Stanley was a bit agitated': Borovik, *The Philby Files*, p. 238.

94 'I tried to calm him down': ibid.

95 'prank': Gordon Brook-Shepherd, *The Storm Birds: Soviet Post-War Defectors* (London, 1988), p. 41.

95 'deplorably nervous state': Philby, *My Silent War*, p. 119.

95 'less than rock steady': ibid.

96 'obviously been preparing': ibid., p. 120.

96 'I consider this sum': Jeffery, *MI6*, p. 525.

96 'I know, for instance': Andrew, *Defence of the Realm*, p. 344; Wright, *Spycatcher*, p. 281.

97 'No one's going to turn': Knightley, *The Master Spy*, pp. 135–6.

97 'copies of the material provided': Edward Harrison, *The Young Kim Philby: Soviet Spy and British Intelligence Officer* (Exeter, 2012), p. 177.

97 'something of the greatest importance': Philby, *My Silent War*, p. 121.

97 'That evening I worked late': ibid.

98 'Don't worry, old man': Borovik, *The Philby Files*, p. 178.

98 'Someone fully briefed': Philby, *My Silent War*, p. 121.

98 'meeting Volkov': ibid., p. 120.

98 'work the night before': ibid., p. 122.

98 'Don't you read my contract': Alistair Horne, *But What do you Actually Do? A Literary Vagabondage* (London, 2011), p. 186.

99 'with obvious relief': Philby, *My Silent War*, p. 122.

99 'diplomatic couriers': Andrew, *Defence of the Realm*, p. 344.

99 'this might be the last memorable': Philby, *My Silent War*, p. 118.

99 'Sorry, old man': Knightley, *The Master Spy*, p. 138.

99 'inexplicable delays and evasions': Harrison, *The Young Kim Philby*, p. 178.

99 'I thought he was just irresponsible': ibid.

99 'It wasn't Volkov': Philby, *My Silent War*, p. 126.

100 'She said he was out': ibid.

100 'I asked for Volkov': ibid., p. 127.

100 'It's no bloody good': ibid.

100 'The case was dead': ibid.

100 'on stretchers and heavily sedated': Andrew, *Defence of the Realm*, p. 344.

100 'brutal interrogation': ibid., p. 345.

100 'a very narrow squeak': Philby, *My Silent War*, p. 118.

100 'nasty piece of work': Knightley, *The Master Spy*, p. 138.

100 'deserved what he got': ibid.

101 'extremely unlikely': Jeffery, *MI6*, p. 525.

101 'indiscretion in the British Embassy': ibid.

101 'test the waters': Cave Brown, *Treason in the Blood*, p. 365.

101 'expressed sympathy': Holzman, *James Jesus Angleton*, p. 107.

101 'the effect his work': Trento, *The Secret History of the CIA*, p. 38.

101 'felt guilty about it': ibid.

101 'He helped me to think': ibid.

101 'worse for wear': Cave Brown, *Treason in the Blood*, p. 365.

101 'warned the Centre': Andrew, *Defence of the Realm*, p. 346.

102 'without reserve': ibid.

102 'Stanley informed me': Borovik, *The Philby Files*, p. 242.

102 'Stanley is an exceptionally valuable': ibid., p. 244.

102 'conscientious work for over': ibid., p. 249.

103 'I looked around': Trevor-Roper, *The Philby Affair*, p. 42.

Chapter 8: Rising Stars

104 'I believed we were': Holzman, *James Jesus Angleton*, p. 3.

104 'The continuation of a civilization': Elliott, *My Little Eye*, p. 101.

104   'I'm in it for the belly-laughs': interview with David Cornwell, 12 April 2012.

105   'a form of defence mechanism': Elliott, *My Little Eye*, p. 180.

105   'Verbal abuse is not': ibid., p. 61.

105   'the British tradition': ibid., p. 111.

105   'One of the joys of living': ibid., p. 150.

105   'oldest and closest friends': ibid., p.151.

105   'British skiing aristocracy': Peter Lunn obituary, *Daily Telegraph*, 12 June 2011.

106   'the ideal person': Stephen Dorril, *MI6: Fifty Years of Special Operations* (London, 2001), p. 418.

106   'attempting to piece together': ibid.

106   'superficial existence': ibid., p. 408.

107   'unique opportunity': ibid.

107   'blueprint for communist': ibid., p. 419.

107   'lifelong communist activists': ibid.

107   'not so much an ideology': Holzman, *James Jesus Angleton*, p. 69.

107   'like a British actor': Mangold, *Cold Warrior*, p. 21.

107   'the cadaver': Martin, *Wilderness of Mirrors*, p. 17.

107   'The guy was just': ibid.

108   'Secret Documents of Vatican Diplomacy': *Catholic Herald*, 'Author of "Secret Documents" Sentenced', 30 July 1948.

108   'how vulnerable even': Holzman, *James Jesus Angleton*, p. 50.

108   'the Byzantine possibilities': ibid.

109   'crawling around on his hands': Mangold, *Cold Warrior*, p. 21.

109   'His real love was unravelling': Elliott, *My Little Eye*, p. 81.

109   'We were … damned good friends': Holzman, *James Jesus Angleton*, p. 71.

109   'Stanley reported that': Borovik, *The Philby Files*, p. 241.

110   'What a very nice chap': Cave Brown, *Treason in the Blood*, p. 367.

110   'happy ending': Solomon and Litvinoff, *Baku to Baker Street*, p. 210.

110   'Kim, a happy and devoted father': ibid.

110   'seemed to belong to the misty, juvenile past': ibid., p. 172.

110   'Awkward of her gestures': ibid., p. 169.

111   'incapable of disloyalty': Cave Brown, *Treason in the Blood*, p. 208.

111   'all round experience': Knightley, *The Master Spy*, p. 142.

111   'profoundly sorry': Liddell, *Diaries*, TNA KV 4/468.

111   'main southern base': Philby, *My Silent War*, p. 130.

111   'Kim gave a large farewell party': Liddell, *Diaries*, TNA KV 4/468.

112   'given permission to play': Cave Brown, *Treason in the Blood*, p. 382.

112   'a white Russian': Philby, *My Silent War*, p. 133.

112   'a fairly free hand': ibid.

112   'start weaving a spy network': Borovik, *The Philby Files*, p. 251.

113   'energetic enthusiast': Dorril, *MI6*, p. 210.

113   'We knew in advance': ibid., p. 212.

113   'the very mechanism through': Holzman, *James Jesus Angleton*, p. 91.
113   'He was totally consumed': Mangold, *Cold Warrior*, p. 23.
113–4 'We rediscovered each other': ibid.
114   'I've got sitting in my Jeep': Cave Brown, *Treason in the Blood*, p. 384.
115   'He was both efficient and safe': ibid., p. 380.
115   'willing to back them': Dorril, *MI6*, p. 211.
115   'energetic lads': Borovik, *The Philby Files*, p. 252.
115   'tip-and-run': Philby, *My Silent War*, p. 140.
115   'alert and intelligent': ibid., p. 143.
116   'notably subdued': ibid.
116   'It was essential': ibid.
116   'striding through a sparse wood': ibid.
116   'The boys weren't bad': Borovik, *The Philby Files*, p. 252.
116   'in chains': Elliott, *Umbrella*, p. 185.
117   'dying of some mysterious ailment': ibid., p. 185.
117   'charming woman and loving wife': ibid.
117   'It was an intense affront': ibid.
118   'the marriage steadily deteriorated': ibid.
118   'It was James Jesus Angleton': Cave Brown, *Treason in the Blood*, p. 386.
119   'At one stroke': Philby, *My Silent War*, p. 145.
119   'unlimited possibilities': ibid.
119   'Who am I supposed to work': Borovik, *The Philby Files*, p. 257.
119   'I was lunched at many': *My Silent War*, p. 146.
119   'One side is open': Borovik, *The Philby Files*, p. 261.
120   'chain reaction that would': Nicholas Bethell, *The Great Betrayal: The Untold Story of Kim Philby's Greatest Coup* (London, 1978), p. 41.
120   'formal British and American': ibid., p. 57.

Chapter 9: Stormy Seas
123   'There was no question': Bethell, *The Great Betrayal*, p. 56.
123   'all absolutely stark naked': David de Crespigny Smiley, Interview No. 10340, Imperial War Museum, London, 1988.
124   'We were looking only': Bethell, *The Great Betrayal*, p. 56.
125   'that the communists': ibid., p. 83.
125   'Brothers, you're all going to be killed!': ibid.
125   'fascist terrorists': ibid.
125–6 'memorable send-off': Philby, *My Silent War*, p. 148.
126   'a private club afloat': http://cruiselinehistory.com
126   'disgustingly rich friend': Philby, *My Silent War*, p. 148.
126   'I began to feel that': ibid.
126   'one of the few glories': ibid., p. 149.
126–7 'admired him as a "professional"': Gordon Corera, *MI6: Life and Death in the British Secret Service* (London, 2012), p. 64.
127   'I was brought up in England': Mangold, *Cold Warrior*, p. 13.

127 'Things have gone wrong': Bethell, *The Great Betrayal*, p. 84.

128 'Who are you?': ibid., p. 87.

128 'We said we were': ibid., p. 141.

128 'The sun has risen': ibid., p. 142.

128–9 'several Albanian civilians': ibid., p. 110.

129 'disappointing': ibid., p. 96.

129 'judged by wartime standards to be acceptable': Dorril, *MI6*, p. 389.

129 'it would be wrong to abandon': Bethell, *The Great Betrayal*, p. 97.

129 'was the one who made': Dorril, *MI6*, p. 385.

129 'Philby was a great charmer': Corera, *MI6*, p. 64.

130 'He had charm': James McCargar, writing as Christopher Felix, 'A Second Third Man', *New York Times Book Review*, 26 May 1968.

130 'undoubtedly devoted to his children': Elliott, *Umbrella*, p. 187.

130 'by any objective standard, a dreadful man': Philby, *My Silent War*, p. 162.

130 'a former FBI man … sacked for drunkenness': ibid., p. 152.

130 'a cold, fishy eye': ibid., p. 180.

130 'bumbling': ibid., p. 164.

130 'puddingy': ibid.

130 'He entertained a lot of Americans': Bethell, *The Great Betrayal*, p. 101.

130 'They were long': *The Cost of Treachery*, BBC TV, 30 October 1984.

130 'suggestive of complicity': James McCargar, writing as Christopher Felix, 'A Second Third Man'.

131 'suggest drifting out': Knightley, *The Master Spy*, p. 155.

131 'Intelligence officers talk trade': Cave Brown, *Treason in the Blood*, p. 399.

131 'please one party': Philby, *My Silent War*, p. 150.

131 'The sky was the limit': Bruce Page, David Leitch and Phillip Knightley, *Philby: The Spy Who Betrayed a Generation* (London, 1968), p. 211.

131 'the driving force': ibid.

131 'I got a few nibbles': Holzman, *James Jesus Angleton*, p. 132.

131 'It was the belief': ibid.

132 'habit': Philby, *My Silent War*, p. 151.

132 'He demonstrated regularly': ibid.

132 'Our close association': ibid.

133 'used to pride himself': Mangold, *Cold Warrior*, p. 47.

133 'Our discussions ranged': Philby, *My Silent War*, p. 151.

133 'Both CIA and SIS': ibid., p. 152.

133 'Many of Harvey's lobsters': ibid.

133 'During those long, boozy lunches': Mangold, *Cold Warrior*, pp. 46–7.

134 'Everything was written up': ibid., p. 44.

134 'chaotic': Andrew, *Defence of the Realm*, p. 420.

135 'We'll get it right next time': Corera, *MI6*, p. 67.

135 'We had agents parachuting in': Mangold, *Cold Warrior*, p. 47.

135 'the timing and geographical': Philby, *My Silent War*, p.159.

136 'I do not know what happened': ibid.

136   'We knew that they would': Bethell, *The Great Betrayal*, p. 137.
136   'The boys in London imagined': ibid., p. 146.
137   'tied to the back of a Jeep': ibid., p. 150.
137   'Our famous radio game': Corera, *MI6*, p. 62.
137   'It was obvious there was': Bethell, *The Great Betrayal*, p. 104.
137   'Our security was very': Corera, *MI6*, p. 63.
137   'well and truly blown': Bethell, *The Great Betrayal*, p. 105.
138   'Albania would fall from the Soviet': Nicholas Bethell, 'Profits and Losses of Treachery', *Independent*, 6 September 1994.
138   'There is little question': Bethell, *The Great Betrayal*, p. 212.
138   'He gave us vital information': Modin, *My Five Cambridge Friends*, p. 123.
138   'The agents we sent into Albania': Philby, *My Silent War*, p. 128.
138   'gave Philby over drinks': Corera, *MI6*, p. 65.

Chapter 10: Homer's Odyssey

140   'Jim and Kim were very fond': Mangold, *Cold Warrior*, p. 43.
140   'After a year of keeping up': Philby, *My Silent War*, p. 151.
140   'If you have a lot of money': Borovik, *The Philby Files*, p. 264.
140   'The more visitors I had': Philby, *My Silent War*, p. 146.
140   'valuable agent network': Andrew, *Defence of the Realm*, p. 376.
140   'particularly important': ibid.
140   'Philby was looking on': ibid., p. 378.
141   'genuine mental block': Philby, *My Silent War*, p. 167.
141   'before the net closed in': Andrew, *Defence of the Realm*, p. 423.
141   'He clearly feels': Liddell, *Diaries*, TNA KV 4/472.
141   'give us more time': Andrew, *Defence of the Realm*, p. 379.
142   'parental pride in being': Elliott, *Umbrella*, p. 187.
142   'I have a shock for you': Philby, *My Silent War*, p. 126.
142   'for a few days': Cave Brown, *Treason in the Blood*, p. 416.
142   'I know him only too well': Knightley, *The Master Spy*, p. 165.
142   'I do not think that': Andrew, *Defence of the Realm*, p. 422.
142–3 'was not the sort of person': ibid.
143   'eccentricities': Philby, *My Silent War*, p. 166.
143   'What does he mean *worse*': ibid.
143   'Knowing the trouble': Elliott, *Umbrella*, p. 186.
143   'The inevitable drunken scenes': ibid.
143   'keep an eye': Philby, *My Silent War*, p. 166.
144   'secure line of communication to Moscow': Andrew, *Defence of the Realm*, p. 423.
144   'the most outstanding historian': Cave Brown, *Treason in the Blood*, p. 419.
144   'the cheapest bourbon': Martin, *Wilderness of Mirrors*, p. 53.
145   'a peculiar garb': ibid.
145   'for fantastic profits': ibid.
145   'a bloated alcoholic': Holzman, *James Jesus Angleton*, p. 88.

145   'What Freudian impulse': ibid., p. 121.
146   'beastily distorted': ibid.
146   'How could you?': ibid.
146   'a social disaster': Martin, *Wilderness of Mirrors*, p. 53.
146   'handsome': Philby, *My Silent War*, p. 184.
146   'Forget it': Knightley, *The Master Spy*, p. 168.
148   'Don't you go too': Philby, *My Silent War*, p. 171.
148   'There's serious trouble': Modin, *My Five Cambridge Friends*, p. 200.
148   'Donald's now in such a state': Andrew, *Defence of the Realm*, p. 424.
148   'We agree to your organizing': Modin, *My Five Cambridge Friends*, p. 201.
148   'no predisposition to be a spy': ibid., p. 22.
148   'men who are too short': Andrew, *Defence of the Realm*, p. 335.
149   'at Victoria, MI5's men': Modin, *My Five Cambridge Friends*, p. 207.
149   'Back on Monday!': Cave Brown, *Treason in the Blood*, p. 430.
149   'Don't go with him': Modin, *My Five Cambridge Friends*, p. 204.
150   'The Centre had concluded': ibid.
150   'It just happened': Bower, *The Perfect English Spy*, p. 109.
150   'even in Strasbourg': Elliott, *Umbrella*, p. 156.
151   'It seems a pity the Foreign Office': ibid., p. 46.
151   'at all costs and by all means': Press Association, News Report, 7 July 1951, paimages.co.uk/preview/?urn=2.7587460
151   '6'3', normal build': ibid.
151   'decanter of poisoned Scotch': Cave Brown, *Treason in the Blood*, p. 430.
152   'Kim': Philby, *My Silent War*, p. 172.
152   'lack of discipline': Andrew, *Defence of the Realm*, p. 426.
152   'crude manners': ibid.
153   'a stiff drink': Philby, *My Silent War*, p. 175.
153   'My clear duty was to fight it out': ibid.
154   'There is no doubt': Liddell, *Diaries*, TNA KV 4/473.
154   'who would wish very much': Philby, *My Silent War*, p. 176.

Chapter 11: Peach
155   'rapier mind': Philby, *My Silent War*, p. 113.
155   'deeply subtle twists': ibid.
155   'How long will you be away': Knightley, *The Master Spy*, p. 181.
156   'a pleasant hour': Philby, *My Silent War*, p. 181.
156   'matters of mutual concern': ibid.
156   'major sensation': TNA PREM 8/1524 (no. 1792).
156   'highly professional, perceptive and accusatory': Mangold, *Cold Warrior*, p. 44.
156   'Philby was a Soviet spy': ibid.
156   a retrospective exercise in spite': Philby, *My Silent War*, p. 185.
157   'suffered severe concussion': Martin, *Wilderness of Mirrors*, p. 53.
157   'conviction': Mangold, *Cold Warrior*, p. 45.

157 'without reference to Philby': ibid.

157 'the bottom line was': Martin, *Wilderness of Mirrors*, p. 53.

157 'he remained convinced': Mangold, *Cold Warrior*, p. 45.

157 'held in high esteem': ibid.

157 'What is the rest': Martin, *Wilderness of Mirrors*, p. 57.

157 'apprehensive': Philby, *My Silent War*, p. 182.

158 'He did his best to put': ibid.

158 'might have views on the case': Liddell, *Diaries*, TNA KV 4/473.

158 'this horrible business': Andrew, *Defence of the Realm*, p. 427.

158 'There was no case against': Cave Brown, *Treason in the Blood*, p. 438.

159 'nondescript': Bower, *The Perfect English Spy*, p. 127.

159 'pure trade': ibid., p. 124.

159 'establishment': ibid.

159 'very sketchy': ibid.

160 'an indiscreet, disorganised': ibid., p. 125.

160 'Kim is extremely worried': Liddell, *Diaries*, TNA KV 4/473.

160 'wholly convincing': ibid.

160 'I dined with Anthony Blunt': ibid.

160 'hard to believe': ibid.

161 'Fire Philby or we break off': Burton Hersh, *The Old Boys: The American Elite and the Origins of the CIA* (New York, 1992), p. 321.

161 'severely shaken': TNA PREM 8/1524 (no. 1803).

161 'clean house regardless': ibid.

161 'In the State Department': ibid.

161 'their wholehearted commitment': Bower, *The Perfect English Spy*, p. 126.

161 'While all the points': Liddell, *Diaries*, TNA KV 4/473.

162 'I'm in no particular hurry': Bower, *The Perfect English Spy*, p. 126.

162 'subsequently converted her': Liddell, *Diaries*, TNA KV 4/473.

162 'he himself had never': ibid.

162 'denied emphatically': ibid.

162 'nasty little question': Philby, *My Silent War*, p. 183.

163 'insatiable appetite for new': Elliott, *Umbrella*, p. 173.

164 'guilty only of an unwise friendship': Knightley, *The Master Spy*, p. 183.

164 'the victim of unsubstantiated': Bower, *The Perfect English Spy*, p. 127.

164 'I'm no good to you now': Seale and McConville, *Philby*, p. 217.

164 'obvious distress': Philby, *My Silent War*, p. 184.

164 'not possibly be a traitor': Cave Brown, *Treason in the Blood*, p. 439.

164 'dedicated, loyal officer': Chapman Pincher, *Treachery: Betrayals, Blunders and Cover-Ups: Six Decades of Espionage* (London, 2012), p. 401.

164 'great black cloud': Philby, *My Silent War*, p. 184.

165 'He said that he had been': ibid.

165 'Personally I would be delighted': Elliott, *Umbrella*, p. 176.

165 'I suppose he is not doing': Liddell, *Diaries*, TNA KV 4/473.

165 'in jest': ibid.

165   'it was already too late': ibid.

165   'The case against Philby': ibid.

166   'sticky': Philby, *My Silent War*, p. 185.

166   'judicial inquiry': Andrew, *Defence of the Realm*, p. 427.

166   'Hello Buster': Borovik, *The Philby Files*, p. 297.

167   'How would I know?': Knightley, *The Master Spy*, p. 186.

167   'Who was that young': Borovik, *The Philby Files*, p. 298.

167   'How could I not help her?': ibid.

167   'So far, he has admitted': Liddell, *Diaries*, TNA KV 4/473.

167   'It all became a shouting match': Bower, *The Perfect English Spy*, p. 133.

167   'The interrogation of Philby': Liddell, *Diaries*, TNA KV 4/473.

168   'I find myself unable': Andrew, *Defence of the Realm*, p. 427.

168   'There's no hope': Bower, *The Perfect English Spy*, p. 133.

168   'Philby's attitude throughout': Liddell, *Diaries*, TNA KV 4/473.

168   'had all the cards in his hands': ibid.

168   'Nicholas Elliott again referred': Andrew, *Defence of the Realm*, p. 427.

169   'counter-attacking': Liddell, *Diaries*, TNA KV 4/473.

169   'foremost exponent in the country': Andrew, *Defence of the Realm*, p. 336.

169   'manner verging on the exquisite': Philby, *My Silent War*, p. 187.

169   'two little traps': ibid.

169   'Nothing could have been more': ibid.

169   'remained open': Liddell, *Diaries*, TNA KV 4/473.

169   'hanging': Philby, *My Silent War*, p. 187.

169–70   'I would have given': ibid.

170   'a much more favourable': Andrew, *Defence of the Realm*, p. 427.

170   'unproven': ibid.

170   'Investigation will continue': PREM 11/4457.

170   'We feel that the case': ibid.

Chapter 12: The Robber Barons

171   'To whom should a wife's allegiance': Borovik, *The Philby Files*, p. 311.

171   'suspicious': Liddell, *Diaries*, TNA KV 4/474.

171   'entirely innocent': ibid.

172   'Kim's gone': Borovik, *The Philby Files*, p. 311.

172   'Thank God it's you at last': ibid.

173   'insane': Cave Brown, *Treason in the Blood*, p. 447.

173   'disclosed very definitely': Liddell, *Diaries*, TNA KV 4/473.

173   'loyal ex-colleague': Elliott, *Umbrella*, p. 186.

173   'the poor man's Surrey': Philby, *My Silent War*, p. xx.

173   'Philby was under constant watch': Modin, *My Five Cambridge Friends*, p. 229.

173   'Peach is apt to get blind drunk': Andrew, *Defence of the Realm*, p. 433.

174   'You must fight like hell': Bower, *The Perfect English Spy*, p. 292.

174   'The whole family went through': Elliott, *Umbrella*, p. 186.

174 'whether he wished for': Liddell, *Diaries*, TNA KV 4/474.

174 'C seemed to have reached': ibid.

175 'Philby would recover from': Cave Brown, *Treason in the Blood*, p. 447.

175 'the extent to which Peach': Andrew, *Defence of the Realm*, p. 433.

175 'of which he was governor': Elliott, *Umbrella*, p. 187.

175 'the intense disagreement': Andrew, *Defence of the Realm*, p. 430.

175 'refused to let one of his chaps down': Bower, *The Perfect English Spy*, p. 134.

176 'In [Aileen's] opinion': Andrew, *Defence of the Realm*, p. 433.

176 'was close enough to our house': Elliott, *Umbrella*, p. 186.

176 'in the normal way': Liddell, *Diaries*, TNA KV 4/474.

177 'somewhat worried': ibid.

178 'worry that Petrov had brought': Borovik, *The Philby Files*, p. 312.

178 'had parted from his wife': Andrew, *Defence of the Realm*, p. 430.

178 'It will undermine Philby': Bower, *The Perfect English Spy*, p. 152.

178 'pursuing a vendetta against Philby': ibid., p. 153.

178 desperately short of cash': Modin, *My Five Cambridge Friends*, p. 228.

178 'rendered us immense services': ibid., p. 229.

178 'a large sum of money': ibid.

179 'villainous Italian authorities': ibid., p. 230.

179 'vied with one another': ibid., p. 231.

180 'Excuse me': ibid.

180 'Tomorrow. 8pm. Angel.': ibid.

180 'a long stare': ibid.

180 '"Yes," he said. "Yes. Yes."': ibid.

180 'I was virtually certain': Philby, *My Silent War*, p. 190.

181 'the dark silhouette kept pace': ibid., p. 232.

181 'refreshed spirit': ibid., p. 190.

181 'Petrov knew nothing': Andrew, *Defence of the Realm*, p. 430.

181 'I was no longer alone': Philby, *My Silent War*, p. 190.

182 'It is the spy who has': George Kennedy Young, circular written in 1950s, en.wikipedia.org/wiki/George_Kennedy_Young

182 'Men's minds are shaped': ibid.

182 'biased': Andrew, *Defence of the Realm*, p. 430.

182–3 'The Milmo Report': PREM 11/4457.

183 'victim of a miscarriage of justice': Andrew, *Defence of the Realm*, p. 430.

183 'Produce the evidence': Bower, *The Perfect English Spy*, p. 156.

183 'greatest defender': Corera, *MI6*, p. 72.

183 'We are going to have': Bower, *The Perfect English Spy*, p. 154.

183 'I know you are the Third Man': Andrew, *Defence of the Realm*, p. 433.

184 'welcomed the chance': ibid. p. 430.

184 'who knew him well': Wright, *Spycatcher*, p. 44.

184 'To call it an interrogation': ibid.

185 'You may be pleased': Borovik, *The Philby Files*, p. 315.

185 'The trail had become': Philby, *My Silent War*, p. 192.
185 'livid': Bower, *The Perfect English Spy*, p. 156.
185 'belief that one of the questioners': Andrew, *Defence of the Realm*, p. 430.
185 'tipster': TNA FO 953/2165.
185 'The house at Crowborough': Elliott, *Umbrella*, p. 186.

Chapter 13: The Third Man

186 'If pop music is going to be': cited in Richard Guins and Omayra Zaragoza Cruz, *Popular Culture: A Reader* (London, 2005), p. 368.
186 'Has the Prime Minister': House of Commons debate, 25 October 1955, *Hansard*, Volume 545, cc 28–9.
187 'My name is in the newspapers': Borovik, *The Philby Files*, p. 314.
187 'might prejudice the case': Philby, *My Silent War*, p. 192.
187 'We've decided that you': Borovik, *The Philby Files*, p. 314.
187 'additional stress for Aileen': Elliott, *Umbrella*, p. 186.
188 'absolutely convinced I had': Borovik, *The Philby Files*, p. 322.
188 'leaned heavily in favour': Knightley, *The Master Spy*, p. 195.
188 'Nothing would be worse': Cave Brown, *Treason in the Blood*, p. 454.
189 'Mr Philby had Communist': Harold Macmillan, House of Commons debate, 7 November 1956, *Hansard*, Volume 545, cc 1483.
189 'a man whose name has been smeared': Richard Brooman-White, ibid.
189 'He [Lipton] is in favour of acting': ibid.
189 'Whoever is covering up': Frank Tomney, ibid.
190 'I will not be gagged by anybody': Marcus Lipton, ibid.
190 'Even Mr Philby has not': ibid.
190 'Jesus Christ!': Philby, *My Silent War*, p. 195.
190 'Do come in': Borovik, *The Philby Files*, p. 318.
190–1 'The efficiency of our security services': the press conference can be viewed at youtube.com/watch?v=N2A2g-qRIaU
192 'I see you understand the habits': Borovik, *The Philby Files*, p. 319.
192 'breathtaking': Modin, *My Five Cambridge Friends*, p. 234.
192 'Kim played his cards with': ibid.
192 'deeply regretted': 'Colonel Lipton Withdraws', *The Times*, 11 November 1955.
192 'My evidence was insubstantial': Cave Brown, *Treason in the Blood*, pp. 457–8.
192 'Colonel Lipton has done': Philby, *My Silent War*, p. 197.
192 'overjoyed': Modin, *My Five Cambridge Friends*, p. 234.
192 'seek his reemployment': Bower, *The Perfect English Spy*, p. 158.
192 'further service to the Soviet cause': Philby, *My Silent War*, p. 198.
193 'frogmen had popped up': Elliott, *My Little Eye*, p. 24.
194 'a matter of high intelligence priority': ibid.
194 'We wanted a closer look': ibid.
194 'undaunted devotion to duty': ibid.
194–5 'a most engaging man': ibid.

195 'kindly bantam cock': Rob Hoole, 'The Buster Crabb Enigma', *Warship World*, January 2007.

195 'to get m' feet wet again': Marshall Pugh, *Commander Crabb* (London, 1956), p. 156.

195 'supplies of whisky': Elliott, *My Little Eye*, p. 25.

195 'heading for a heart attack': Wright, *Spycatcher*, p. 74.

195 'Crabb was still the most experienced': Elliott, *My Little Eye*, p. 25.

195 'The dicey operations': Bower, *The Perfect English Spy*, p. 159.

196 'These ships are our guests': Pincher, *Treachery*, p. 417.

196 'We don't have a chain': Bower, *The Perfect English Spy*, p. 160.

196 'I am sorry, but we cannot': Don Hale, *The Final Dive: The Life and Death of Buster Crabb* (London, 2007), p. 172.

196 'operation was mounted': Elliott, *My Little Eye*, p. 24.

196 'working holiday': Cave Brown, *Treason in the Blood*, p. 460.

197 'attached Foreign Office': Bower, *The Perfect English Spy*, p. 160.

197 'down to take a dekko': see BBC, *On This Day*, news.bbc.co.uk/onthisday/hi/dates/stories/may/9/newsid_4741000/4741060.stm

197 'an extra pound of weight': Elliott, *My Little Eye*, p. 24.

198 'A tip-off from a British spy': Corera, *MI6*, p. 78.

198 'There will be blood': Wright, *Spycatcher*, p. 74.

199 'We'll all be for the pavilion': ibid., p. 75.

199 'specially employed in connection': Hale, *The Final Dive*, p. 176.

199 'presumed drowned': ibid.

199 'I'm afraid it rather': Wright, *Spycatcher*, p. 74.

199 'missing or lost property': Hale, *The Final Dive*, p. 172.

199 'in trouble': Elliott, *My Little Eye*, p. 24.

199 'he hoped he was all right': ibid.

200 'such an unusual occurrence': Hale, *The Final Dive*, p. 183.

200 'regret about this incident': ibid., p. 188.

200 'completely unauthorized': ibid.

200 'paid no attention': ibid., p. 183.

200 'it can only be assumed': ibid.

200 'It would not be': ibid., p. 184.

200 'a shameful operation': ibid., p. 191.

201 'misconceived and inept operation': Pincher, *Treachery*, p. 421.

201 'Ridiculous': Francis Elliott, 'Cold War Papers Reveal Lost Diver's Last Minutes', *Independent on Sunday*, 11 June 2006.

201 'a typical piece of MI6 adventurism': Wright, *Spycatcher*, p. 73.

201 'We're still cloak and dagger': Bower, *The Perfect English Spy*, p. 165.

201 'one man Bay of Pigs': ibid., p. 312.

201 'A storm in a teacup': Elliott, *My Little Eye*, p. 25.

201 'Crabb was both brave and patriotic': ibid.

202 'He almost certainly died': ibid.

203 'come down to the firm': Borovik, *The Philby Files*, p. 321.

203 'Something unpleasant again': ibid.

Chapter 14: Our Man in Beirut

204   'In those days SIS kept in touch': Andrew Lycett, *Ian Fleming* (London, 1996), p. 170.

204   'Kemsley Press allowed': ibid., p. 169.

204   'doing secret service stuff': ibid.

205   'being re-engaged for reasons': Seale and McConville, *Philby*, p. 284.

205   'The country could ill afford': Cave Brown, *Treason in the Blood*, p. 470.

205   'I simply approved them': Knightley, *The Master Spy*, p. 199.

205   'no appetite for reopening old wounds': Bower, *The Perfect English Spy*, p. 289.

206   'irritated that Elliott': ibid., p. 292.

206   'no emotion': ibid.

206   'unaware': ibid., p. 235.

206   'horrified if he knew': ibid.

206   'It was Nicholas Elliott': Knightley, *The Master Spy*, p. 206.

206   'had an ersatz gaiety': Elliott, *Umbrella*, p. 157.

206   'The climate of Vienna': ibid.

206   'Haunted by Kim's life of treason': Richard Beeston, *Looking for Trouble: The Life and Times of a Foreign Correspondent* (London, 2006), p. 29.

207   'she maintained in the hope': Solomon and Litvinoff, *Baku to Baker Street*, p. 211.

207   'Lebanon was the only Arab country': Beeston, *Looking for Trouble*, p. 28.

208   'He was quintessentially English': ibid., p. 29.

208   'rangy, steady-drinking American': ibid.

208   'If I should meet Kim': Eleanor Philby, *The Spy I Loved* (London, 1968), p. 28.

209   'What touched me first': ibid.

209   'Kim was a delightful companion': ibid., p. 30.

209   'My soufflés were never': ibid.

209   'sound knowledge of': Philby, *My Silent War*, p. 199.

209   'telling the British government': ibid.

210   'as conscientiously as possible': ibid.

210   'Petukhov, Soviet Trade Mission': Borovik, *The Philby Files*, p. 331.

210   'I read your articles in the *Observer*': ibid.

210   'total commitment': Philby, *My Silent War*, p. xxxi.

210-11   'I stayed the course': ibid.

211   'influenced and modified': ibid.

211   'a hive of activity': Modin, *My Five Cambridge Friends*, p. 234.

212   'the intentions of the United States': Philby, *My Silent War*, p. 199.

212   'idleness': Cave Brown, *Treason in the Blood*, p. 466.

212   'No receipts, no money': ibid.

212   'helpful eye': Solomon and Litvinoff, *Baku to Baker Street*, p. 210.

212   'poor Aileen ...': ibid., p. 211.

212   'might have been murdered': Andrew, *Defence of the Realm*, p. 433.

212 'considerable strength of character': Elliott, *Umbrella*, p. 182.

212 'a charming woman': ibid., p. 185.

212 'grave mental problem': ibid.

213 'This, however, was not to be': Solomon and Litvinoff, *Baku to Baker Street*, p. 211.

213 'I want you to come and celebrate': Beeston, *Looking for Trouble*, p. 29.

213 'wonderful escape': ibid.

213 'a wonderful American girl': ibid.

213 'stunned': ibid.

213 'Clever wonderful you fly back': Eleanor Philby, *The Spy I Loved*, p. 39.

213 'I've come to tell you': ibid.

213 'That sounds like the best': ibid.

213 'Eleanor was in many ways': Elliott, *Umbrella*, p. 187.

214 'We shall take a house': Cave Brown, *Treason in the Blood*, p. 482.

214 'ringside view': Eleanor Philby, *The Spy I Loved*, p. 39.

214 'He would sit in his terrace': ibid.

214 'leisurely daily circuit': ibid., p. 52.

214 'Kim treated the place like a club': ibid., p. 51.

214 'to see what the other journalists': ibid.

214 'connected with British intelligence': ibid., p. 4.

214 'He seemed to write': ibid.

214 'compelling a certain respect': Cave Brown, *Treason in the Blood*, p. 491.

214 'men whose ostensible jobs': Seale and McConville, *Philby*, p. 294.

215 'The information he supplied': Modin, *My Five Cambridge Friends*, p. 234.

215 'attracted much attention': ibid.

215 'There was criticism': Cave Brown, *Treason in the Blood*, p. 480.

215 'You could have read it all': Bower, *The Perfect English Spy*, p. 292.

Chapter 15: The Fox who Came to Stay

216 'but for his preference for operations': Cave Brown, *Treason in the Blood*, p. 470.

216 'I have no wish to be': Elliott, *Umbrella*, p. 162.

216 'It was a most agreeable reunion': Bower, *The Perfect English Spy*, p. 292.

216 'excellent bouillabaisse': Elliott, *Umbrella*, p. 167.

216 'Fill me in, old boy': Eleanor Philby, *The Spy I Loved*, p. 3.

217 'cool, high rooms': Elliott, *Umbrella*, p. 163.

217 'perfect in every way': ibid.

217 'thought nostalgically of the gentle sound': ibid.

217 'two old friends in crown service': Cave Brown, *Treason in the Blood*, p. 492.

217 'European specialist and knew little': Eleanor Philby, *The Spy I Loved*, p. 3.

217 'Apart from all the political complexities': Elliott, *Umbrella*, p. 165.

217 'his personal adviser': Seale and McConville, *Philby*, pp. 295–6.

217 'He was a thin, spare man': ibid., p. 295.

218 'put Kim to work': ibid., p. 296.

218   'serving two masters': interview with former *Economist* correspondent.

218   'mainly political and personality': Cave Brown, *Treason in the Blood*, p. 492.

218   'reports about political developments': Bower, *The Perfect English Spy*, p. 292.

218   'They used to meet once or twice': Eleanor Philby, *The Spy I Loved*, p. 3.

218   'Oh boy': ibid., p. 52.

218   'greater participation in the British': Seale and McConville, *Philby*, p. 298.

219   'keep an eye on Philby': Bower, *The Perfect English Spy*, p. 292.

219   'Elliott's overt and innocent friendship': ibid.

219   'I had begun to feel that Kim': Eleanor Philby, *The Spy I Loved*, p. 3.

219   'broker a deal with the director': Dorril, *MI6*, pp. 670–1.

219   'In all he served us well': Cave Brown, *Treason in the Blood*, p. 480.

220   'He was one of the few adults': interview with Mark Elliott, 17 October 2013.

220   'ski in the mornings': Elliott, *Umbrella*, p. 166.

220   'promised to look after it': Lycett, *Ian Fleming*, p. 376.

220   'an Armenian': ibid.

220   'arranged to see a pornographic film': ibid.

220   'at parties for British diplomats': Bower, *The Perfect English Spy*, p. 292.

220   'Out of fun rather than malice': Elliott, *Umbrella*, p. 184.

221   'caused a chain reaction': ibid.

221   'It was at a cocktail party': ibid.

221–2 'He had no inhibitions': ibid.

222   'fierce martini': ibid., p. 187.

222   'recognised as the dominant': Richard Helms, *A Look Over My Shoulder: A Life in the Central Intelligence Agency* (New York, 2003), p. 275.

222   'and used those opportunities': Trento, *The Secret History of the CIA*, p. 274. No documentary record of these contacts survives, which indicates that either they did not take place, or Angleton destroyed the evidence.

223   'He travelled regularly': Beeston, *Looking for Trouble*, p. 44.

223   'whose brain was there': Cave Brown, *Treason in the Blood*, p. 477.

223   'all he had to do': ibid., p. 478.

223   'much too sophisticated': ibid.

223   'liked to talk to Philby': Borovik, *The Philby Files*, p. 335.

223   'Philby was friendly with all the Yanks': George Young, quoted in *Sunday Times*, 15 May 1988.

224   'The United States had to face': Miles Copeland in George Lenczowski, *American Presidents and the Middle East* (Duke, 1990), p. 6.

224   'known and liked': Cave Brown, *Treason in the Blood*, p. 486.

224   'better than anyone else': Miles Copeland, *Without Cloak or Dagger: The Truth About the New Espionage* (New York, 1974), p. 146.

224   'a humorous and highly intelligent': Elliott, *My Little Eye*, p. 68.

225   'Generous, outrageous, always fun': Beeston, *Looking for Trouble*, p. 106.

225   'one of the most indiscreet men': Elliott, *My Little Eye*, p. 68.

225   'I could trust him with any secret': ibid.

225 'keep an eye on Philby': Copeland, *Without Cloak or Dagger*, p. 212.

225 'report signs that he might': ibid., p. 146.

225 'still practising his old tradecraft': ibid., p. 212.

225 'entertaining and colourful invention': Elliott, *My Little Eye*, p. 69.

226 'a melodious voice': Eleanor Philby, *The Spy I Loved*, p. 53.

226 'lapping up': ibid., p. 5.

226 'She was affectionate': ibid.

226 'hopelessly endearing': ibid.

226 'happiest years': ibid., p. 51.

Chapter 16: A Most Promising Officer

227 'treated with the deference': Eleanor Philby, *The Spy I Loved*, p. 46.

227 'Elizabeth and I were among': Elliott, *Umbrella*, p. 188.

227 'drew the old man out': ibid.

227 'memorable occasion': ibid.

227 'left at tea time': ibid.

227 'God, I'm bored': Cave Brown, *Treason in the Blood*, p. 495.

228 'a mixture of love and hate': Elliott, *Umbrella*, p. 188.

228 'not completely well in the head': Borovik, *The Philby Files*, p. 203.

228 'If you feel strongly enough': Elliott, *Umbrella*, p. 188.

228 'thunderstruck, but by no means disapproving': Philby, *My Silent War*, p. 132.

228 'went out of circulation': ibid.

228 'He drank himself senseless': Eleanor Philby, *The Spy I Loved*, p. 47.

228 'Kim seemed overwhelmed': Beeston, *Looking for Trouble*, p. 33.

229 'a most promising officer': Roger Hermiston, *The Greatest Traitor: The Secret Lives of Agent George Blake* (London, 2013), p. 221.

229 'A good-looking fellow': Cave Brown, *Treason in the Blood*, p. 501.

229 'it was the relentless bombing': Ian Irvine, 'George Blake: I Spy a British Traitor', *Independent*, 1 October 2006.

229 'I felt I was on the wrong side': ibid.

229 'He doesn't belong in the service': Bower, *The Perfect English Spy*, p. 261.

229 'man of no class': Hermiston, *The Greatest Traitor*, p. 56.

230 'He was in love with her': ibid., p. 61.

230 'ninety per cent sure': Bower, *The Perfect English Spy*, p. 263.

230 'to London immediately': Hermiston, *The Greatest Traitor*, p. 221.

231 'whether Blake would like': ibid.

231 'In the course of conversation': ibid., p. 222.

231 'Moscow saw no cause for concern': ibid.

232 'would be more convenient': ibid., p. 223.

232 'For a moment a shadow': ibid.

232 'a few matters had cropped up': ibid., p. 226.

232 'I was in deep trouble': ibid., p. 227.

232 'It wasn't hostile': ibid.

232 'No, nobody tortured me!': ibid., p. 229.

233   'The game was up': ibid.
233   'the biggest hammer possible': Bower, *The Perfect English Spy*, p. 268.
233   'The following name is a traitor': Hermiston, *The Greatest Traitor*, p. 236.
233   'It can happen to anyone': Bower, *The Perfect English Spy*, p. 269.
234   'Your case is one of the worst': Hermiston, *The Greatest Traitor*, p. 250.
234   'I went round to his flat': Beeston, *Looking for Trouble*, pp. 33–4.
234   'Kim would become insulting': ibid., p. 31.
234–5 'not light-hearted about drink': Eleanor Philby, *The Spy I Loved*, p. 5.
235   'By the next day he was usually forgiven': Beeston, *Looking for Trouble*, p. 31.
235   'I know all about your Wednesday nights': Seale and McConville, *Philby*, p. 301.
235   'You know Moyra': Beeston, *Looking for Trouble*, p. 32.
235   'What would you do': ibid.
235   'something awful': ibid.
235–6 'What's the matter?': Eleanor Philby, *The Spy I Loved*, p. 5.
236   'Kim seemed to give himself': ibid., p. 6.
236   'out of all proportion': ibid.
236   'shattered': Elliott, *Umbrella*, p. 187.
236   'Apart from when his father died': ibid.
236   'the most valuable defector': Caroline Rand Herron and Michael Wright, 'A KGB defector who may not be', *New York Times*, 2 February 1986.
237   'very important spy network': Andrew, *Defence of the Realm*, p. 435.
237   'exhibited increasing signs': Wright, *Spycatcher*, p. 193.
237   'Modin had gone to Beirut to alert Philby': ibid.
237   'a shadow of his former self': Modin, *My Five Cambridge Friends*, p. 236.
237   'To warn Philby not to return': Christopher Andrew and Vasili Mitrokhin, *The Sword and the Shield: The Mitrokhin Archive and the Secret History of the KGB* (London, 1999), p. 440.
237   'belly laughs': interview with David Cornwell, 12 April 2012.
238   'Of course he's a traitor': Bower, *The Perfect English Spy*, p. 293.

Chapter 17: I Thought it Would Be You

239   'Russian soul, Jewish heart': Solomon and Litvinoff, *Baku to Baker Street*, p. 229.
239   'To anyone with eyes': ibid., p. 225.
240   'The thought occurred to me': ibid.
240   'dangerous work in hazardous': *London Gazette*, 4 April 1944.
240   'How is it the *Observer* uses': Solomon and Litvinoff, *Baku to Baker Street*, p. 226.
240   'very dangerous job for peace': Wright, *Spycatcher*, p. 173.
241   'intuitive feeling that Harris': Solomon and Litvinoff, *Baku to Baker Street*, p. 226.
241   'the terrible way he treated': Peter Wright, *Spycatcher*, p. 173.
241   'You must do something': Solomon and Litvinoff, *Baku to Baker Street*, p. 226.

241 'I will think about it': ibid.

241 'major breakthrough': Wright, *Spycatcher*, p. 172.

241 'a strange, rather untrustworthy woman': ibid., p. 173.

241 'She clearly had a grudge': ibid.

241 'I will never give public evidence': ibid.

241 'It will leak, I know it will leak': ibid.

242 'Why didn't she tell us': Bower, *The Perfect English Spy*, p. 294.

242 'I had not volunteered information': Solomon and Litvinoff, *Baku to Baker Street*, p. 226.

242 'how clubmanship and the old school tie': ibid., p. 227.

242 'far too wily': Pincher, *Treachery*, p. 473.

243 'We need to discover what damage': Bower, *The Perfect English Spy*, p. 295.

243 'should be treated as a gentleman': ibid.

243 'Keep a lid on things': ibid., p. 294.

243 'voluminous brief in preparation': Wright, *Spycatcher*, p. 173.

243 'is the greatest dissembler': John le Carré, *The Secret Pilgrim* (London, 1990), Part II.

243 'happily have killed him': interview with Mark Elliott, 11 November 2013.

243 'there was more chance that Philby': Bower, *The Perfect English Spy*, p. 296.

243 'Philby's greatest supporter': ibid.

246 'a proficient, clever and determined officer': Cave Brown, *Treason in the Blood*, p. 505.

246 'Elliott swore not to exceed his brief': Andrew Boyle, *The Climate of Treason: Five Who Spied For Russia* (London, 1979), p. 436.

246 'The few of us inside MI5': Wright, *Spycatcher*, p. 174.

247 'We'd fully penetrated the KGB': Bower, *The Perfect English Spy*, p. 296.

247 'vertically intoxicated': Eleanor Philby, *The Spy I Loved*, p. 7.

247 'It was as if our flat': ibid.

247 'He only had to smell a drink': ibid.

247 'What is the matter': ibid., p. 5.

247 'very cold fish indeed': ibid., p. 9.

247 'He dragged us protesting': ibid., p. 8.

247 'already had a good deal': ibid.

248 'He was bleeding profusely': ibid.

248 'If we don't get your husband': ibid.

248 'one more ounce of alcohol': ibid., p. 9.

248 'I was a bloody fool': ibid.

248 'prepared himself for a battle of wits': Boyle, *The Climate of Treason*, p. 436.

248 'I've got an awful task': interview with Rozanne Colchester, 11 June 2013.

248 'It was a terrible shock': ibid.

248 'he always laughed about things': ibid.

248–9 'Nicholas knew he had blood': ibid.

249 'in a casual voice': Bower, *The Perfect English Spy*, p. 297.

249 'a meeting between himself': Pincher, *Treachery*, p. 474.

249 'The minute that call': Eleanor Philby, *The Spy I Loved*, p. 9.

249 'I rather thought it would be you': Bower, *The Perfect English Spy*, p. 297.

Chapter 18: Teatime

251 'Perfectly tolerable …': The dialogue between Kim Philby and Nicholas Elliott is constructed from the following sources: Bower, *The Perfect English Spy*, pp. 297–8; Borovik, *The Philby Files*, pp. 3, 5, 344; Boyle, *The Climate of Treason*, pp. 436–7; and interviews with individuals familiar with the transcript of that conversation.

252 'in-house': Wright, *Spycatcher*, p. 174.

254 'He never once asked': ibid., p. 194.

254 'Everything's OK': Corera, *MI6*, p. 87.

255 'The next twenty-four hours': Bower, *The Perfect English Spy*, p. 299.

255 'Okay, here's the scoop': ibid.

255 'seen the error of his ways': Andrew, *Defence of the Realm*, p. 436.

255 'Is Nedosekin your contact?': Bower, *The Perfect English Spy*, p. 299.

255 'I've got no bloody contact': ibid.

255 'very bland document': Cave Brown, *Treason in the Blood*, p. 507.

255 'limited confession': Andrew, *Defence of the Realm*, p. 436.

256 'just a little stalling': Knightley, *The Master Spy*, p. 217.

256 'Our promise of immunity': Borovik, *The Philby Files*, p. 345.

256 'trying his manful best': Wright, *Spycatcher*, p. 194.

256 'By the end': ibid.

257 'finally broken': Bower, *The Perfect English Spy*, p. 299.

257 'obscure hotel': Eleanor Philby, *The Spy I Loved*, p. 6.

257 'he did not want too many': ibid.

257 'this furtiveness was': ibid.

257 'as if nothing had intervened': Boyle, *The Climate of Treason*, p. 438.

257 'His greatest passion': Eleanor Philby, *The Spy I Loved*, p. 6.

258 'several names which alarmed': Knightley, *The Master Spy*, p. 215.

258 'Blunt was in the clear': Wright, *Spycatcher*, p. 194.

258 'claimed to know nothing': ibid.

258 'the debriefing would be a long affair': Bower, *The Perfect English Spy*, p. 299.

259 'knew about the KGB': ibid.

259 'It became clear to me': Knightley, *The Master Spy*, p. 215.

259 'might stand him in good stead': ibid.

259 'lifeline': Bower, *The Perfect English Spy*, p. 298.

259 'effusive in his gratitude': ibid., p. 300.

259 'He could have rejected': ibid.

259 'In our judgement': Andrew, *Defence of the Realm*, p. 436.

260 'What makes you think': Pincher, *Treachery*, p. 476.

260 'He might, I suppose': Bower, *The Perfect English Spy*, p. 300.

260 'Nobody wanted him in London': interview with David Cornwell, 11 October 2012.

260 'It just didn't dawn on us': Bower, *The Perfect English Spy*, p. 301.
261 'unsympathetic': ibid.

Chapter 19: The Fade

262 'Philby does not think he can escape again': Bower, *The Perfect English Spy*, p. 301.
262 'Your time has come': Borovik, *The Philby Files*, p. 346.
262 'They won't leave you alone': ibid.
262 'had planted doubts in me': ibid., p. 352.
262 'Arrangements will take some time': ibid., p. 347.
263 'If you see me carrying': ibid.
263 'the question that interests': ibid.
263 'proved a helpful and friendly': Glencairn Balfour Paul, *Bagpipes in Babylon: A Lifetime in the Arab World and Beyond* (London, 2006), p. 187.
264 'Daddy's going to be late': Eleanor Philby, *The Spy I Loved*, p. 2.
264 'cosy gathering': ibid., p. 3.
264 'God, what a horrible night': ibid.
264 'Don't be silly': ibid.
264 'had nothing to say': Clare Hollingworth, *Front Line* (London, 1990), p. 191.
264 'Everything is fine': Borovik, *The Philby Files*, p. 349.
265 'a hastily summoned meeting about Kim': Eleanor Philby, *The Spy I Loved*, p. 4.
265 'Would you like me to come': ibid.
265 'His advice was to do nothing': ibid.
265 'terrible fear': ibid.
266 'last link with England': Modin, *My Five Cambridge Friends*, p. 237.
266 'Philby had vanished': Elliott, *My Little Eye*, p. 94.
266 'Tell my colleagues': Eleanor Philby, *The Spy I Loved*, p. 18.
266 'There is no question': Elliott, *Umbrella*, p. 189.
266 'in circumstances calculated': ibid.
267 'You do realise that you': Eleanor Philby, *The Spy I Loved*, p. 18.
267 'choose a spot high up': ibid., p. 19.
267 'convinced that Kim had': ibid., p. 12.
267 'on no account to meet': ibid., p. 21.
267 'to test the system': ibid.
267 'Many people in the secret world': Wright, *Spycatcher*, p. 174.
268 'We should have sent a team': ibid., p. 194.
268 'But after lengthy interrogation': ibid., p. 325.
268 'He had been my boss': Bristow, *A Game of Moles*, p. 229.
268 'horror': ibid.
268 'I never thought he would accept': Bower, *The Perfect English Spy*, p. 304.
268 'What a shame we reopened': ibid.
268 'disappointed': ibid.
268 'I tried to repair the damage': ibid., p. 305.

268 'face the awful truth': Mangold, *Cold Warrior*, p. 45.
269 'I had them burned': ibid., p. 46.
269 'He was an unforgivable traitor': Balfour Paul, *Bagpipes in Babylon*, p. 187.
269 'dumbfounded': Cave Brown, *Treason in the Blood*, p. 487.
269 'unbelievable': ibid., p. 488.
269 'He was the best actor': ibid.
270 'What Philby provided': Holzman, *James Jesus Angleton*, p. 125.
270 'Since Mr Philby resigned': Edward Heath (Lord Privy Seal), House of Commons debate, 1 July 1963, *Hansard*, Volume 680, cc 33–5.
270 'Hello, Mr Philby': Cave Brown, *Treason in the Blood*, p. 527.
270 'Philby was allowed to escape': Bristow, *A Game of Moles*, p. 281.
270 'To my mind the whole business': Modin, *My Five Cambridge Friends*, p. 238.
271 'the secret service had actively': ibid.
271 'I knew exactly how to handle it': Knightley, *The Master Spy*, p. 217.
271 'spiriting Philby out of the Lebanon': Modin, *My Five Cambridge Friends*, p. 236.
271 'a mistake, simple stupidity': Borovik, *The Philby Files*, p. 323.
272 'Burgess was a bit of an embarrassment': Knightley, *The Master Spy*, pp. 222–3.
272 'unmistakably Russian': Eleanor Philby, *The Spy I Loved*, p. 22.
272 'I'm from Kim': ibid.
273 'Kim was an active communist': ibid., p. 56.
273 'surprising tenderness': ibid.
273 'We have definitely known': ibid.
273 'the victim of a prolonged': ibid., p. xiii.
273 'All I am thinking of now': ibid., p. 59.
273 'I don't know what': ibid., p. 64.
273 'Buy yourself some very warm clothes': ibid., p. 66.
273 'What would *you* do': ibid., p. 63.
274 'she finally admitted': ibid.
274 'passionate loyalty and devotion': Elliott, *Umbrella*, p. 182.
274 'Although I had put the fear of God': Elliott, *My Little Eye*, p. 94.
274 'Eleanor, is that you?': Eleanor Philby, *The Spy I Loved*, p. 69.
274–5 'Dear Nick': undated letter from Kim Philby to Nicholas Elliott, Cleveland Cram collection, Georgetown University Library, Washington DC.
276 'It was ridiculous to suppose': Elliott, *My Little Eye*, p. 95.
276 'an incredibly clumsy piece': ibid.
276 'many hours of discussion': ibid.
276 'because first': ibid.
276 'tragic episode': ibid., p. 97.
276 'Put some flowers for me': ibid., p. 98.

Chapter 20: Three Old Spies
277 'elite': Philby, *My Silent War*, p. xxxii.
277 'He never revealed': Modin, *My Five Cambridge Friends*, p. 270.

277 'Englishman to his fingertips': ibid.

278 'homeland': Borovik, *The Philby Files*, p. 373.

278 'belonged': Murray Sayle, 'London–Moscow: The Spies are Jousting', *Sunday Times*, 6 January 1968.

278 'wholly and irreversibly English': Cave Brown, *Treason in the Blood*, p. 527.

278 'Aluminium bats, white balls': Knightley, *The Master Spy*, p. 239.

278 'the ghastly din': ibid., p. 253.

278 'hooligans inflamed': ibid.

278 'What is more important': Eleanor Philby, *The Spy I Loved*, p. 78.

278 'The party, of course': ibid.

278 'stayed the course': Philby, *My Silent War*, p. xxxi.

278 'If you only knew what hell': Balfour Paul, *Bagpipes in Babylon*, p. 186.

278 'Friendship is the most important thing': ibid.

278 'painful to think that during': Cave Brown, *Treason in the Blood*, p. 488.

278 'I wasn't laughing at them': Knightley, *The Master Spy*, p. 254.

279 'It had travelled with him': Elliott, *Umbrella*, p. 189.

279 'supreme example of schizophrenia': ibid.

279 'He betrayed many people': Eleanor Philby, *The Spy I Loved*, p. 175.

279 'No one can ever really know': ibid., p. xiv.

279 'The emotional wreckage': Holzman, *James Jesus Angleton*, p. 206.

280 'Jim just continued to think': Mangold, *Cold Warrior*, p. 48.

280 'Never again would he permit': Martin, *Wilderness of Mirrors*, p. 193.

280 'This is all Kim's work': Holzman, *James Jesus Angleton*, p. 207.

280 'He had trusted him': Elliott, *My Little Eye*, p. 81.

281 'I don't know that the damage': Martin, *Wilderness of Mirrors*, p. 193.

281 'come clean in the Philby case': Cave Brown, *Treason in the Blood*, p. 565.

282 'To be in administration': Elliott, *Umbrella*, p. 179.

282 'Rather to my surprise': ibid., p. 192.

282 'a modern Cecil Rhodes': ibid., p. 191.

282 'the Harry Lime of Cheapside': ibid., p. 192.

282 'incapable of leading that kind of life': ibid., p. 195.

282 'gift for dowsing': ibid.

283 'alternative to involvement': Elliott, *My Little Eye*, p. 65.

283 'showing a quite unjustified lack': ibid., p. 109.

283 'extremely well over an extended period': Elliott, *Umbrella*, p. 182.

283 'I have naturally given thought': ibid.

283 'Outwardly he was a kindly man': ibid., p. 183.

284 'a façade, in a schizophrenic personality': ibid., p. 190.

284 'sad exiled life': ibid., p. 189.

284 'dreary people, a spying servant': ibid.

284 'wasted in a futile cause': Elliott, *My Little Eye*, p. 99.

284 'decided to betray': Elliott, *Umbrella*, p. 190.

284 'He had charm to burn': ibid., p. 189.

284 'The whole thing was staged': Knightley, *The Master Spy*, p. 215.

284 'desire to spare SIS another spy scandal': Borovik, *The Philby Files*, p. 323.

284 'blissful peace': ibid., p. 357.

284 'How sleepless must be Kim Philby's nights': ibid., p. 373.

284 'He's a totally sad man': Knightley, *The Master Spy*, p. 5.

285 'like Glasgow on a Saturday night':Tom Driberg, *Guy Burgess:A Portrait with Background* (London, 1956), p. 100.

285 'burdensome': Knightley, *The Master Spy*, p. 235.

285 'Any confession involves': Rufina Philby, Mikhail Lyubimov and Hayden Peake, *The Private Life of Kim Philby:The Moscow Years* (London, 1999), p. 257.

285 'showed no interest': Elliott, *Umbrella*, p. 185.

285 'one of the better ones': Knightley, *The Master Spy*, p. 257.

285 'tireless struggle in the cause': ibid., p. 260.

286 'My lips have hitherto been sealed': Elliott, *My Little Eye*, p. 95.

286 'a tremendous fluttering': ibid.

286 'undistinguished, albeit mildly notorious': ibid., p. 10.

286 'I feel I have been': ibid.

Bibliography

Archives
British Library Newspaper Archive, Colindale
Bundesarchiv-Militärarchiv, Freiburg
Churchill Archives Centre, Churchill College, Cambridge
IWM Archives, Imperial War Museum, London
National Archives, Kew
National Archives, Washington DC
The Times Archives

Published Sources
Aldrich, Richard J., *GCHQ: The Uncensored Story of Britain's Most Secret Intelligence Agency* (London, 2011)
Andrew, Christopher, *The Defence of the Realm: The Authorised History of MI5* (London, 2009)
————— *Secret Service: The Making of the British Intelligence Community* (London, 1985)
Andrew, Christopher and D. Dilks, eds, *The Missing Dimension: Governments and Intelligence Communities in the Twentieth Century* (London, 1984)
Andrew, Christopher and Oleg Gordievsky, *KGB: The Inside story of its Foreign Operations from Lenin to Gorbachev* (London, 1990)
Andrew, Christopher and Vasili Mitrokhin, *The Sword and the Shield: The Mitrokhin Archive and the Secret History of the KGB* (London, 1999)
————— *The Mitrokhin Archive II: The KGB and the World* (London, 2005)
Balfour Paul, Glencairn, *Bagpipes in Babylon: A Lifetime in the Arab World and Beyond* (London, 2006)
Bassett, Richard, *Hitler's Spy Chief: The Wilhelm Canaris Mystery* (London, 2006)

Beeston, Richard, *Looking for Trouble: The Life and Times of a Foreign Correspondent* (London, 2006)

Bennett, Gill, *Churchill's Man of Mystery: Desmond Morton and the World of Intelligence* (London, 2007)

Bennett, Ralph, *Behind the Battle: Intelligence in the War with Germany 1939–45* (London, 1999)

Best, Sigismund Payne, *The Venlo Incident* (London, 1950)

Bethell, Nicholas, *The Great Betrayal: The Untold Story of Kim Philby's Greatest Coup* (London, 1978)

Borovik, Genrikh, ed. Phillip Knightley, *The Philby Files: The Secret Life of Master Spy Kim Philby* (London, 1994)

Bower, Tom, *The Perfect English Spy: Sir Dick White and the Secret War, 1935–1990* (London, 1995)

Boyle, Andrew, *The Climate of Treason: Five Who Spied For Russia* (London, 1979)

Bristow, Desmond with Bill Bristow, *A Game of Moles: The Deceptions of an MI6 Officer* (London, 1993)

Brook-Shepherd, Gordon, *The Storm Birds: Soviet Post-War Defectors* (London, 1988)

Bryher, W., *The Days of Mars: A Memoir, 1940–1946* (New York, 1972)

Butler, E., *Mason-Mac: The life of Lieutenant-General Sir Noel Mason-MacFarlane* (London, 1972)

Carl, Leo D., *The International Dictionary of Intelligence* (McLean Virginia, 1990)

Carter, Miranda, *Anthony Blunt: His Lives* (London, 2001)

Cave Brown, Anthony, *Bodyguard of Lies*, Vol. I (London, 1975)

——————— *Treason in the Blood: H. St John Philby, Kim Philby, and the Spy Case of the Century* (London, 1995)

Cavendish, Anthony, *Inside Intelligence* (London, 1990)

Copeland, Miles, *The Game of Nations: The Amorality of Power Politics* (New York, 1970)

——————— *The Game Player: Confessions of the CIA's Original Political Operative* (London, 1989)

——————— *Without Cloak or Dagger: The Truth About the New Espionage* (New York, 1974)

Corera, Gordon, *MI6: Life and Death in the British Secret Service* (London, 2012)

Crowdy, Terry, *Deceiving Hitler: Double Cross and Deception in World War II* (London, 2008)

Curry, J., *The Security Service 1908–1945: The Official History* (London, 1999)

Dalton, Hugh, *The Fateful Years: Memoirs, 1931–1945* (London, 1957)

Doerries, Reinhard R., *Hitler's Intelligence Chief: Walter Schellenberg* (New York, 2009)

Dorril, Stephen, *MI6: Fifty Years of Special Operations* (London, 2001)

Driberg, Tom, *Guy Burgess: A Portrait with Background* (London, 1956)

Elliott, Nicholas, *Never Judge a Man by his Umbrella* (London, 1992)

————— *With My Little Eye: Observations Along the Way* (Norwich, 1993)

Foote, Alexander, *Handbook for Spies* (London, 1949)

Gilbert, Martin, *Winston S. Churchill*, Vol. 6: *Finest Hour, 1939–1941* (London, 1983)

Hale, Don, *The Final Dive: The Life and Death of Buster Crabb* (London, 2007)

Hamrick, S.J., *Deceiving the Deceivers: Kim Philby, Donald Maclean, and Guy Burgess* (New Haven, CT, 2004)

Harris, Tomás, *Garbo: the Spy Who Saved D-Day*, introduction by Mark Seaman (London, 2004)

Harrison, Edward, *The Young Kim Philby: Soviet Spy and British Intelligence Officer* (Exeter, 2012)

Hastings, Max, *Finest Years: Churchill as Warlord 1940–45* (London, 2009)

—————*Overlord: D-Day and the Battle for Normandy, 1944* (London, 1984)

Helms, Richard, *A Look Over My Shoulder: A Life in the Central Intelligence Agency* (New York, 2003)

Hermiston, Roger, *The Greatest Traitor: The Secret Lives of Agent George Blake* (London, 2013)

Hersh, Burton, *The Old Boys: The American Elite and the Origins of the CIA* (New York, 1992)

Hollingworth, Clare, *Front Line* (London, 1990)

Holt, Thaddeus, *The Deceivers: Allied Military Deception in the Second World War* (London, 2004)

Holzman, Michael, *James Jesus Angleton, the CIA, and the Craft of Counterintelligence* (Boston, 2008)

Horne, Alistair, *But What do you Actually Do? A Literary Vagabondage* (London, 2011)

Jeffery, Keith, *MI6: The History of the Secret Intelligence Service 1909–1949* (London, 2010)

Kahn, David, *Hitler's Spies: German Military Intelligence in World War II* (New York, 2000)

Knightley, Phillip, *The Master Spy: The Story of Kim Philby* (London, 1988)

————— *The Second Oldest Profession* (London, 1986)

Lenczowski, George, *American Presidents and the Middle East* (Duke, 1990)

Liddell, G., *The Guy Liddell Diaries, 1939–1945*, Vols. I and II, ed. Nigel West (London, 2005)

Lycett, Andrew, *Ian Fleming* (London, 1996)

Mangold, Tom, *Cold Warrior: James Jesus Angleton – CIA's Master Spy Hunter* (London, 1991)

Martin, David C., *Wilderness of Mirrors: Intrigue, Deception, and the Secrets that Destroyed Two of the Cold War's Most Important Agents* (Guilford, CT, 2003)

Modin, Yuri, *My Five Cambridge Friends: Burgess, Maclean, Philby, Blunt, and Cairncross by Their KGB Controller* (New York, 1995)

Morgan, Ted, *A Covert Life: Jay Lovestone: Communist, Anti-Communist, and Spymaster* (New York, 1999)

Muggeridge, Malcolm, *Chronicles of Wasted Time*, Vols. I and II (London, 1973)

Page, Bruce, David Leitch and Phillip Knightley, *Philby: The Spy Who Betrayed a Generation* (London, 1968)

Paine, Lauran, *The Abwehr: German Military Intelligence in World War II* (London, 1984)

Philby, Eleanor, *The Spy I Loved* (London, 1968)

Philby, Kim, *My Silent War: The Autobiography of a Spy* (London, 1968)

Philby, Rufina, Mikhail Lyubimov and Hayden Peake, *The Private Life of Kim Philby: The Moscow Years* (London, 1999)

Pincher, Chapman, *Treachery: Betrayals, Blunders and Cover-Ups: Six Decades of Espionage* (London, 2012)

Poretsky, Elisabeth K., *Our Own People: A Memoir of 'Ignace Reiss' and His Friends* (Oxford, 1969)

Pugh, Marshall, *Commander Crabb* (London, 1956)

Read, Anthony and David Fisher, *Colonel Z: The Secret Life of a Master of Spies* (London, 1985)

———— *Operation Lucy: Most Secret Spy Ring of the Second World War* (London, 1981)

Rose, Kenneth, *Elusive Rothschild: The Life of Victor, Third Baron* (London, 2003)

Rubin, Barry, *Istanbul Intrigues* (New York, 1989)

Seale, Patrick and Maureen McConville, *Philby: The Long Road to Moscow* (London, 1973)

Sisman, Adam, *Hugh Trevor-Roper: The Biography* (London, 2011)

Solomon, Flora and Barnet Litvinoff, *Baku to Baker Street: The Memoirs of Flora Solomon* (London, 1984)

Trento, Joseph J., *The Secret History of the CIA* (New York, 2001)

Trevor-Roper, Hugh R., *The Philby Affair: Espionage, Treason, and Secret Services* (London, 1968)

Weiner, Tim, *Legacy of Ashes: The History of the CIA* (London, 2007)

West, Nigel, *At Her Majesty's Secret Service: The Chiefs of Britain's Intelligence Agency, MI6* (London, 2006)

——————*Mask: MI5's Penetration of the Communist Party of Great Britain* (London, 2005)

——————*MI5: British Security Service Operations 1909–45* (London, 1981)

——————*Venona: The Greatest Secret of the Cold War* (London, 1999)

West, Nigel and Oleg Tsarev, eds, *The Crown Jewels: The British Secrets at the Heart of the KGB Archives* (London, 1998)

——————*Triplex: Secrets from the Cambridge Five* (Yale, 2009)

Wheatley, Dennis, *The Deception Planners: My Secret War* (London, 1980)

Whiting, Charles, *Ghost Front: the Ardennes before the Battle of the Bulge* (London, 2002)

Wright, Peter, *Spycatcher: The Candid Autobiography of a Senior Intelligence Officer* (London, 1987)

Acknowledgements

I am again indebted to many people who have provided guidance, encouragement and hospitality during the writing of this book, as well as access to documents, photographs and their own memories. I am particularly grateful to the families and descendants of people in a story that remains, for many, a painful chapter of the past. This book would have been impossible to write without the generous help of Mark and David Elliott, son and grandson of Nicholas Elliott, who have proved an endless fund of support and practical assistance. I was also privileged to meet Elizabeth Elliott, widow of Nicholas, just a few weeks before her death in 2012. The list that follows is incomplete, since many of those who were most helpful to me have understandably asked, for professional reasons, to remain anonymous: you know who you are, and how grateful I am.

I would particularly like to thank the following: Nathan Adams, Christopher Andrew, Dick Beeston, the late Rick Beeston, Paul Bellsham, Keith Blackmore, Tom Bower, Roger Boyes, Alex Brooman-White, Caroline Brooman-White, Anthony Cavendish, Rozanne Colchester, Gordon Corera, David Cornwell, Jane Cornwell, Leo Darroch, Natasha Fairweather, Frances Gibb, Oleg Gordievsky, Peter Greenhalgh, Barbara Honigmann, William Hood, Alistair Horne, Keith Jeffery, Margy Kinmonth, Jeremy Lewis, Peter Linehan, Robert McCrum, Philip Marsden, Nick Mays, Tommy Norton, John Julius Norwich, Michael Pakenham, Roland Philipps, Harry Chapman Pincher, Gideon Rachman, Felicity Rubinstein,

Jenni Russell, the John Smedley Archives, Xan Smiley, Wolfgang Suschitzky, Anthony Tait, Rupert Walters, Nigel West, Damian Whitworth.

I am indebted to Robert Hands, Peter Martland, Richard Aldrich and Hayden Peake for reading the manuscript and saving me from many embarrassing mistakes: the errors that remain are entirely my own. Once again, Jo Carlill has achieved miracles of picture research; I have enjoyed and profited greatly from working with the BBC: Janice Hadlow, Martin Davidson, Dominic Crossley-Holland, Francis Whateley, Tom McCarthy, Ben Ryder, Louis Caulfield, Adam Scourfield, Dinah Rogers, Gezz Mounter and Jane Chan. My colleagues and friends at *The Times* have provided help and advice. The generous provision of a fellow commonership by St John's College Cambridge enabled me to finish the book in the ideal scholarly surroundings.

It is a pleasure and privilege to be published by Bloomsbury: my thanks to Katie Johnson and Anna Simpson for their unfailing proficiency and patience, and to Michael Fishwick, my dear friend and editor. Ed Victor, as ever, has steered another huge and complicated project into port with the skill of a master-mariner.

My family deserves both praise and sympathy for putting up with yet another consuming spy-project without throwing me out; and to Kate, all my love.

Index